PENGUIN BOOKS

BETTER DAY COMING

Adam Fairclough teaches American history at the University of
East Anglia in England. His books include *To Redeem the Soul
of America; Martin Luther King, Jr.;* and *Race and Democracy,*
which won the Lillian Smith Award.

BETTER DAY COMING

Blacks and Equality

1890–2000

ADAM FAIRCLOUGH

PENGUIN BOOKS

PENGUIN BOOKS
Published by the Penguin Group
Penguin Group (USA) Inc., 375 Hudson Street, New York, New York 10014, U.S.A.
Penguin Group (Canada), 90 Eglinton Avenue East, Suite 700, Toronto, Ontario,
Canada M4P 2Y3 (a division of Pearson Penguin Canada Inc.)
Penguin Books Ltd, 80 Strand, London WC2R 0RL, England
Penguin Ireland, 25 St Stephen's Green, Dublin 2, Ireland
(a division of Penguin Books Ltd)
Penguin Group (Australia), 250 Camberwell Road, Camberwell, Victoria 3124,
Australia (a division of Pearson Australia Group Pty Ltd)
Penguin Books India Pvt Ltd, 11 Community Centre, Panchsheel Park,
New Delhi – 110 017, India
Penguin Group (NZ), 67 Apollo Drive, Rosedale, North Shore 0632, New Zealand
(a division of Pearson New Zealand Ltd)
Penguin Books (South Africa) (Pty) Ltd, 24 Sturdee Avenue,
Rosebank, Johannesburg 2196, South Africa

Penguin Books Ltd, Registered Offices: 80 Strand, London WC2R 0RL, England

First published in the United States of America by Viking Penguin,
a member of Penguin Putnam Inc. 2001
Published in Penguin Books 2002

9 10 8

Copyright © Adam Fairclough, 2001
All rights reserved

THE LIBRARY OF CONGRESS HAS CATALOGED THE HARDCOVER EDITION AS FOLLOWS:
Fairclough, Adam.
Better day coming : Blacks and equality, 1890–2000 / Adam Fairclough.
p.   cm.
Includes bibliographical references.
ISBN 0-670-87592-9 (hc.)
ISBN 978-0-14-200129-5 (pbk.)
1. Afro-Americans—Civil rights—History—20th century.   2. Afro-Americans—Civil rights—
Southern States—History—20th century.   3. Civil rights movements—United States—History—
20th century.   4. Civil rights movements—Southern States—History—20th century.
5. United States—Race relations.   6. Southern States—Race relations.   I. Title.
E185.61 .F167   2001
323.1'196073—dc21   00-051342

Printed in the United States of America
Set in Monotype Bulmer
Designed by Jessica Shatan

To Mary Ellen

ACKNOWLEDGMENTS

I wish to thank my editors at Penguin Putnam: Marion Maneker for suggesting this book, Wendy Wolf for spurring me to finish it, and Michael Millman and Barbara Campo for seeing it through the press. I am grateful, too, for the skillful copyediting of Cathy Dexter. The British Academy enabled me to visit archives in the South, and the National Humanities Center gave me a precious year to read, research, and discuss. I am pleased to acknowledge their generous support for my scholarship. As I have come to expect over a quarter century, librarians and archivists across the South made researching this book a pleasure; I cannot thank them enough. The Research Committee of the School of English and American Studies at the University of East Anglia generously lightened my teaching load during an early stage of the writing, and later provided me with a study leave that facilitated the final revision.

My greatest debts are to the distinguished historians who have inspired me, and whose work, as my endnotes attest, forms the foundation of this book. In no particular order, these scholars include Louis R. Harlan, August Meier, the late Elliott Rudwick, David Levering Lewis, Glenda Elizabeth Gilmore, Leon H. Prather, Linda O. McMurry, Stephen R. Fox, Charles Flint Kellogg, Debra Gray White, John Hope Franklin, James D. Anderson, Patricia L. Sullivan, Gail O'Brien, Winston James, Henry Allen Bullock, David J. Garrow, Gerald Horne, John Dittmer, Charles Payne, Dan Carter, Hugh Pearson, Mark Naison, the late Horace Mann Bond, George Fredrickson, Mary L. Dudziak, John H. Haley, William H. Harris, William H. Chafe, Richard C. Cortner, Virginia L. Denton, Andrew Manis, Mark Tushnet, Harvard Sitkoff, Robert A. Hill and the editorial team of the *Marcus Garvey Papers,* and Clayborne Carson and the assistant editors of the *Martin Luther King Papers.* There are many others, equally important, and I apologize for my failure to mention them all. None of the scholars I cite, however, is responsible in any way for the interpretations I have placed upon their work. The mistakes are all mine.

Most pressing of all debts, and the one that gives me the greatest pleasure to acknowledge, is the one I owe to my wife and fellow historian, Mary Ellen Curtin. I dedicate this book to her, with love.

CONTENTS

Acknowledgments   vi

Preface   xi

1   The Failure of Reconstruction and the Triumph of White Supremacy   1

2   Ida B. Wells and the Campaign Against Lynching   23

3   Booker T. Washington and the Strategy of Accommodation   41

4   The Rise of the NAACP   67

5   The Great War and Racial Equality   87

6   Marcus Garvey and the UNIA   111

7   The Radical Thirties   133

8   Blacks in the Segregated South, 1919–42   161

9   The NAACP's Challenge to White Supremacy, 1935–45   181

10   Two Steps Forward and One Step Back, 1946–55   203

11   The Nonviolent Rebellion, 1955–60   227

12   The Civil Rights Movement, 1960–63   249

13   Birmingham, the Freedom Summer, and Selma   273

14   The Rise and Fall of Black Power   295

15   The Continuing Struggle   323

Notes   337

Index   371

P R E F A C E

This book presents an interpretation of the black struggle for equality in the United States between 1890 and 2000. It concentrates on the South (although not exclusively so) for two main reasons. First, the South was home to the majority of the black population for most of the period 1890–1970, the main focus of this study. Second, the South evolved particular forms of racial domination that set it apart from the rest of the nation, making it the main focus of black campaigns against discrimination and oppression.

Although 1890 to 2000 is a relatively short span of time, these eleven decades comprise a critical period in American history. The collapse of Reconstruction after the Civil War led to the establishment of white supremacy in the Southern states, a system of domination and exploitation that most whites, in the North as well as the South, expected to last indefinitely. In 1900, despite the nation's formal commitment to racial equality as expressed in the Fourteenth and Fifteenth Amendments, racial discrimination remained a basic organizing principle of American society. In the South, racial discrimination, reinforced by racial segregation, became official state policy. In the North, discrimination and segregation also became widely sanctioned customs that amounted to, in effect, semiofficial policy. The federal government practiced racial segregation in the armed services, discriminated against blacks in the civil service, and generally condoned, by its actions if not its words, white supremacy.

Despite suffering massive setbacks, however, black Americans were never reconciled to their subordinate status. They never accepted the notion that white supremacy was a natural, permanent situation. Indeed, the basic argument of this book is that although blacks often differed—and sometimes bitterly so—about the most appropriate tactics in the struggle for equality, they were united in rejecting allegations of racial inferiority and in aspiring to a society where men and women would be judged by merit rather than by race or color.

According to the historian John W. Cell, blacks adopted "three main approaches" to the problem of racial oppression: "accommodation," or submitting to white supremacy with a view to securing improvements inside the system; "militant confrontation," or outright opposition to all forms of racial discrimination; and "separatism," or seeking to create an all-black society or nation either inside the United States or on another continent. Cell's is a useful set of categories, and each of the chapter themes that follow might be broadly classified as accommodation, confrontation, or separatism.[1]

However, the category of "militant confrontation" requires modification. From the establishment of white supremacy in the 1890s until the emergence of the Civil Rights Movement in the 1950s, militant confrontation was not a realistic strategy for black Southerners. Open defiance of whites evoked retaliation that often caused the death of the defier. Lynchings, race riots, private murders, and the killing of blacks by policemen enabled the white population to prevent the black population from engaging in organized, systematic, militant confrontation.

In such unfavorable circumstances, blacks were obliged to oppose white supremacy indirectly. Open opposition often took the form of agitation—speeches, newspaper editorials, "indignation meetings," and so on. However, in the rural areas, where the bulk of the South's black population resided, even agitation remained dangerous. In the cities, where blacks could express themselves more freely, troublesome critics—the antilynching crusader Ida B. Wells, for example—were still sometimes driven out. Nevertheless, agitation, even in a muted form, helped blacks to sustain a vision of equality.

The National Association for the Advancement of Colored People (NAACP), founded in 1909 on a platform of uncompromising opposition to racial discrimination, was also for many years forced to confront the South's racism indirectly. With its Southern branches weak and vulnerable, the NAACP directed its agitation from the relative security of the North. By 1950, when the organization decided to attack the very principle of racial segregation, its tactics had indeed evolved into a form of militant confrontation. Even then, however, this confrontation took place mainly in federal courtrooms.

Only after 1955, when the Civil Rights Movement adopted the tactics of nonviolent direct action and staged its protests in the streets and public places of the South, did opposition to white supremacy become, in the true sense of the term, militant confrontation. I have nevertheless tried to avoid a "heroic" interpretation of the Civil Rights Movement that deems militant confrontation as braver, more audacious, and more worthy than other forms of action. The *apparently* unheroic accommodationism of the period from 1890 to 1940 not only enabled black Southerners to survive and make incremental gains, but also subtly challenged and subverted the principles and foundations of white supremacy. In chapters 3 and 8, in particular, I reappraise accommodationist approaches, stressing the long-term impact of efforts to improve black education and offering a sympathetic interpretation of Booker T. Washington, who is often deemed—mistakenly, I believe—to have betrayed the principle of equality.

In arguing that the accommodationism of Booker T. Washington and his followers laid the groundwork for the militant confrontation of the Civil Rights Movement, I am mindful of John Cell's argument that black strategies were rarely self-contained, mutually exclusive, or entirely consistent. Nor can they be neatly labelled either "conservative" or "radical." Accommodationism, militant confrontation, and separatism, writes Cell, "were not so much distinct schools as they were philosophies in a state of continual tension, interaction, and adaptation. The variations and combinations were virtually endless."

Like all historical formulas, therefore, the accommodation-confrontation-separatism scheme is not perfect; it cannot account for every case. The left-wing organizations that wielded influence in the 1930s and 1940s, for example, do not fit neatly into a single category. The labor unions of the Congress of Industrial Organizations preached interracialism, sometimes challenged racial discrimination, militantly confronted employers, but shrank from directly attacking racial segregation. The Communist Party denounced racism and was militantly interracial within its own ranks, but its shifting tactics moved between, and sometimes combined, separatism, confrontation, and accommodation. Separatist approaches, likewise, cannot be easily categorized. While they often endorsed the goal of racial equality, they also, at times, expressed a racial chauvinism that bordered on racism itself. Moreover, both the United Negro Improvement Association, led by Marcus Garvey, and the Nation of Islam, led by Elijah Muhammad, sought to reach a permanent accommodation with white supremacist groups such as the Ku Klux Klan. In interpreting the black struggle for equality, therefore, I have made no effort to make the story conform to any particular theory. History is too complex, too contingent, and too subject to human passions and foibles to always follow logical paths.

The book is intended for a general reader, including those who may have little or no knowledge about the history of race relations since the American Civil War. Because it is neither a textbook nor a survey, but an interpretation, I have aimed for depth rather than breadth. Each chapter is structured around a single individual, event, or theme while at the same time sketching the larger historical context.

I am well aware that objectivity in the writing of history is more a matter of method than mentality. Despite my efforts at detachment, my views and sympathies will be quite evident to the careful reader. Still, I have tried to be faithful to the evidence, to weigh opposing arguments, and to exercise that most difficult and elusive quality, empathy. Although there is no absolute historical truth, I hope that the following pages ring true.

BETTER
DAY
COMING

Dere's a better day comin', Don't you get weary
Better day a comin', Don't you get weary
Better day a comin', Don't you get weary
Dere's a great camp-meetin' in de Promised Land*

*From a spiritual appearing in *Hampton and Its Students*, by M. F. Armstrong and Helen W. Ludlow (New York: G. P. Putnam's Sons, 1875). Reprinted by Books for Libraries Press (Freeport, N. Y., 1971).

A member of the Ku Klux Klan, North Carolina, circa 1870

North Carolina Museum of History

The Failure of Reconstruction and the Triumph of White Supremacy

EMANCIPATION AND RECONSTRUCTION

In 1865, the population of the United States included 34 million whites and 5 million blacks. Nine-tenths of the black population resided in the South, concentrated in an enormous band of fertile soil that stretched from southern Virginia to eastern Texas. Here, in the "Black Belt," the bulk of the South's four million slaves toiled as the private property of white people, creating wealth for their owners by producing sugar, rice, tobacco, and, most often, cotton. Although whites made up two-thirds of the South's population, blacks were more numerous in the Black Belt, and three states—Louisiana, Mississippi, and South Carolina—contained clear black majorities.

The defeat of the Confederacy in the Civil War, and the passage of the Thirteenth Amendment, ended slavery. Slaves became "freedmen." They could have their marriages recognized in law, form independent families, worship as they saw fit, acquire and hold property, enjoy freedom of movement, and generally live their daily lives free from close white supervision. In one of their first statements of freedom, many blacks left their plantations to seek out friends and family members elsewhere. About a quarter of a million black Southerners had already enjoyed freedom before the Civil War; they had been manumitted by their masters or allowed to purchase their liberty. Although voteless, and subject to all manner of discrimination, these free Negroes had often formed stable families and acquired literacy, skills, and property. After emancipation they formed the backbone of black leadership.

Although the first days of liberation were exhilarating and disorienting, the former slaves were quick to understand that freedom would be empty without land, legal rights, education, and the vote. Meeting in conventions across the South, a black leadership emerged to press the case for full equality. Petitioning the president, Congress, and the white people of the South, these meetings expressed a common sentiment. That of the South Carolina freedmen's convention was typical:

> We simply ask that we be recognized as *men;* that there be no obstructions placed in our way; that the same laws which govern *white men* shall govern *black men;* that we have the right of trial by jury of our *peers;* that schools be established for the education of *colored children* as well as *white; . . .* that no impediments be put in the way of our acquiring homesteads for ourselves and our people; that, in short, we are dealt with as others are—in equity and justice.[1]

The freedmen also asserted their freedom through actions. Expecting the government to provide each family with "forty acres and a mule," they resisted signing labor contracts with their former masters, scornfully rejecting the idea that they should work in gangs, under white supervision, in a system all too reminiscent of slavery. When compelled by necessity to sell their labor to whites, the freedmen shortened their working day, limited their working week, and often insisted that their wives cease laboring in the fields. Across the South, blacks started leaving the white churches and founding their own. From the North, but mostly from the ranks of the ex-slaves, black preachers appeared.[2]

Whites in the North disagreed about what the status of the freedmen ought to be. The Democratic Party had opposed abolition and frankly regarded blacks as racially inferior. The Republican Party had been formed to stop the spread of slavery, and had been forced, under pressure of war, to abolish the institution entirely. But only a minority of Republicans, the "Radicals" led by Congressman Thaddeus Stevens and Senator Charles Sumner, believed that racial equality should be a national commitment. President Lincoln had proposed that the vote be given to educated and literate blacks, as well as to those who had fought in the Union forces. But he had stopped short of compelling individual states to adopt this suggestion. Although most Republicans probably wished to go further than Lincoln on the matter of black suffrage—and to go further in punishing ex-Confederates—they certainly did not envisage enfranchising the freedmen in one fell swoop.

After Lincoln's assassination, however, a peculiar combination of circumstances persuaded the Republican Party to embark upon a program of equal citizenship for the freedmen? For one thing, they were alarmed by the policies of President Andrew Johnson, a former slaveholder from Tennessee, who by a quirk of political fate succeeded Lincoln. Johnson restored self-government to the South with indecent haste, and the North was offended by the election of former Confederate leaders to Congress when the guns of war had barely had time to cool. Furthermore, Johnson was an unabashed racist whose growing sympathy for the Southern whites induced him to break with the Republican Party. Many Northern whites were also appalled by the harsh treatment meted out to the freedmen, especially by the discriminatory laws, passed by Southern state legislatures, known as the Black Codes. Whites accepted the abolition of slavery as the war's decisive verdict, but they resisted the notion that freedmen should enjoy equality of citizenship and live independent of white control. The Black Codes therefore placed freedmen under strict white supervision. They prevented blacks from testifying in court against whites. They limited the areas, especially in towns, in which blacks could buy or rent property, and they required blacks to pay license fees in order to set up businesses. Harsh vagrancy laws tried to compel blacks to work for white employers. "Numerous fines were imposed for seditious speeches, insulting gestures or acts, absence from work, and the possession of firearms," writes historian John Hope Franklin. "There was, of course, no enfranchisement of blacks." The Black Codes expressed the determination of Southern whites to define the freedmen as rural laborers with inferior rights.[3]

The Black Codes convinced the mass of Republicans that the freedmen required some form of federal protection. Bloody race riots that took place in Memphis and New Orleans in 1866, leaving dozens of blacks dead, reinforced that conviction. Equally disturbing were well-attested-to reports of Unionists, including former soldiers now settled in the South, being insulted, harassed, and physically attacked. The Republican Party decided that control of the Reconstruction process had to be wrested from President Johnson, who, they alleged, was conspiring with the ex-Confederates to undermine the Union's victory.

The Republican Party won a decisive victory in the congressional elections of 1866, capturing a two-thirds majority in both House and Senate. When the new Congress convened the following year, the Republicans returned the South to military occupation and began Reconstruction anew. In 1868 they impeached President Johnson and, though they failed to convict him, broke the president's power.

The Republican program of Reconstruction, called "Radical Reconstruction," was a bold experiment in democracy. The Fourteenth Amendment

(1867) struck down the Black Codes by making full citizens of the freedmen and entitling *all* citizens to "equal protection of the law." The Fifteenth Amendment (1870) forbade the denial of the vote to any adult male on the basis of race, color, or previous condition of servitude. In the South, the army compiled a new list of voters, enrolling black men but excluding many former Confederates. The new electorate ratified state constitutions that provided for universal manhood suffrage. Blacks not only voted now, but also held office: they served as sheriffs, judges, city councilmen, county commissioners, legislators, congressmen, and senators. Meanwhile, the Freedmen's Bureau, with the assistance of Northern churches and the aid of blacks themselves, created a rudimentary system of public and private schools for blacks. With education, the ballot, and equality under the law, the freedmen would flourish in a South that had been modernized, democratized, civilized, and completely reintegrated into the Union. So the Republican Party hoped and believed.

Unfortunately for blacks in the South, Radical Reconstruction was grievously flawed. The Republican Party failed to give black families the one thing they most needed in order to prosper in freedom: land. The "forty acres and a mule" that blacks had been led to expect did not materialize—the government even returned to white planters the land it had confiscated, evicting thousands of black families in the process. Though a surprising number of blacks did manage to acquire land—by 1910 about a quarter of the South's black farmers were landowners—most, lacking both land and capital, worked as sharecroppers. They grew cotton for a white landlord in return for a third or a half of the harvest, but rarely made enough money to climb out of debt.[4]

The federal government failed the freedmen in another crucial respect: it declined to ensure their education. The war-crippled, poverty-stricken South was incapable of funding an adequate system of public schools. But Congress closed down the Freedmen's Bureau in 1870, and the federal government withdrew all support for public education, except for small subsidies to "land-grant colleges." Periodic proposals that the federal government should help to fund public schools came to nothing. By leaving public schools under state and local control, the federal government condemned them to underfunding and inequality. Black schools, especially, suffered. In 1890, about half of white school-age children in the South were enrolled in school, compared to 31 percent of black school-age children. The literacy gap was even wider: only 15 percent of whites were unable to write, in contrast to 65 percent of blacks. This abdication of responsibility by the federal government was to bedevil public education, and race relations, for a hundred years.[5]

The worst failure of Reconstruction, however, was the government's inability, and unwillingness, to enforce its own policy of racial equality. Radical Reconstruction may have been radical in conception, but it was weak in execution. By enfranchising blacks and disfranchising many former Confederates, it alienated most white Southerners immediately. Yet instead of using its power to ensure the loyalty and good behavior of the ex-Confederates, the Republican Party quickly readmitted the Southern states into the Union, pardoned most of the disqualified whites, and withdrew all but a skeleton military force from the South.

Even before Radical Reconstruction got under way, many white Southerners attempted to overawe the freedmen by subjecting them to intimidation and violence. With the return of military rule in 1867, the enfranchisement of black men, and the subsequent election of Republican state governments, the level of violence escalated sharply. Most Southern whites rallied to the Democratic Party and fought tooth-and-nail to reestablish white supremacy. Those who supported the Republicans were castigated as "scalawags," threatened, and sometimes murdered. Northern-born Republicans, many of them former Union soldiers, were abused as "carpetbaggers" and received similar treatment.

In states where whites made up a clear majority of voters, the Democratic Party quickly regained power through the ballot box. Where black voters predominated, however, politics became very bloody indeed. White Democrats, sometimes operating through the Ku Klux Klan—a secret society founded in Pulaski, Tennessee, in 1866—threatened and occasionally assassinated white Republicans. Blacks, however, bore the brunt of the violence: countless individuals were beaten or killed; hundreds were slain in riots and massacres. The campaign of terror destabilized and eventually toppled the Republican-controlled state governments. In 1877 the Republican strongholds of South Carolina, Louisiana, and Mississippi collapsed. Radical Reconstruction came to an end.

The Republican Party opposed the wave of terror by deploying troops, forming state militias, suspending the writ of habeas corpus, and prosecuting hundreds of alleged Klansmen under new federal laws. But although the government succeeded in breaking up the Klan, other groups quickly replaced it. The white campaign of violence was too widespread to be contained by 6,000 federal troops, too well-supported to be quashed by a few hard-to-obtain convictions. The use of coercion, moreover, became increasingly unpopular among Northern voters. The national leaders of the Republican Party eventually admitted defeat. Unwilling to police the vast expanses of the South, the government wearied of a policy that had become a political albatross. The violence that accompanied elections in the former Confederacy no longer aroused public opinion; as President U. S. Grant put it, "The whole

public are tired out with these annual autumnal outbreaks in the South."
Shrewdly calculating that it could still capture the White House with North-
ern votes alone, the Republican Party allowed the Democrats to "redeem" the
South.[6]

After regaining state power, the Democratic party tolerated black voting,
and even made some effort to cultivate black support. But the Democrats
were unwilling to share political power with blacks. They never became reconciled to blacks holding office, and looked forward to the day when they
could suppress the black vote entirely. Fearing federal intervention, the
Democrats acted stealthily at first, relying on devious means to whittle away
black political power. They gerrymandered electoral districts, abolished elective posts, and devised complicated procedures for registering to vote. The
replacement of open voting by the secret ballot made voting more difficult for
illiterates, who had an even harder time in South Carolina, where the "Eight
Box Law" of 1882 required a separate ballot box for each contested post. According to historian C. Vann Woodward, outright fraud was common. "The
stuffing of ballot boxes, the use of boxes with false bottoms, the doctoring of
returns, the manipulation of counts, the repeating of votes, and the tampering
of registration books were all highly developed arts."[7]

Many white Southerners, however, particularly the wealthy elite that dominated the Democratic Party, were unhappy with any degree of black political
participation. For one thing, despite all the obstacles placed in front of them,
blacks continued to vote in large numbers, and in several states the Republican Party remained a formidable opposition. The black vote posed a particular threat when disaffected whites abandoned the Democratic Party to form
an independent third party. In that situation, a combination of black Republicans and white independents could form a winning majority, ousting the
Democrats from state power.[8]

In 1890, Mississippi—the state with the largest proportion of blacks—
adopted a new constitution that required electors to "be able to read any section of the Constitution of this State; or he shall be able to understand the
same when read to him, or give a reasonable interpretation thereof." In the
space of two years the number of black voters declined from about 190,000 to
8,000. Although the white electorate also diminished, the net effect of disfranchisement was to banish blacks from the political process. Democrats
elsewhere watched to see if the federal government would challenge Mississippi's new constitution. It did not, and the government's inaction encouraged other states to imitate Mississippi's example.[9]

THE WILMINGTON RIOT AND THE DESTRUCTION OF DEMOCRACY IN THE SOUTH

The formation of the People's Party, or Populists, in 1892 offered a brief hope that biracial democracy might be revived and strengthened. The Populists made earnest appeals for black support, writes Woodward: They "denounced lynch law and the convict lease and called for defense of the Negro's political rights." Above all, the Populists—white farmers who felt betrayed by the conservative policies of the Democratic Party—argued that blacks and whites shared the same economic problems and ought to act together. "The accident of color can make no difference in the interest of farmers, croppers, and laborers," stated Tom Watson, leader of the Populists in Georgia. "You are kept apart that you may be separately fleeced of your earnings." In several states, the Populists made informal arrangements with the Republican Party to form a common front against the Democrats, a policy known as "Fusion."[10]

In North Carolina, where the Populists and Republicans negotiated a fully fledged electoral pact, the so-called "Fusion" ticket triumphed, sweeping the Democrats from power in 1894. The Populist-Republican coalition then changed the state election laws to simplify the act of voting and to ensure that all ballots were counted fairly. This had especial importance for blacks, the voters who were most often cheated by Democratic officials. Thanks to "Fusion," and thanks to fairer elections, more blacks were elected to office in North Carolina than in any other Southern state—one thousand people in all. According to historian Eric Anderson, "North Carolina was the only southern state to tolerate so great a degree of black participation." Unlike Radical Reconstruction, moreover, "Fusion" was not imposed by Yankee bayonets; it was a homegrown experiment in biracial democracy. "[T]he racial political cooperation achieved constituted a daring experiment," judged historian Oliver Orr. "It was . . . the only major such experiment of indigenous origin ever attempted in the South."[11]

It is tempting to believe that the Populist-Republican alliance that governed North Carolina between 1894 and 1898 might have provided a model for the rest of the South. As C. Vann Woodward argued, even after the demise of Reconstruction there were alternatives to the sterile, violent, and undemocratic politics of "white supremacy" as practiced by the Democratic Party. Some variant of Fusion might, perhaps, have worked in virtually every Southern state. If North Carolina's example had spread and taken hold, Fusion could have stemmed the rising tide of lynching, slowed down (perhaps halted) the accelerating onrush of racial segregation laws, improved public education, and narrowed the disparity between black schools and white schools. Fusion might have prevented the South's descent into oligarchy and one-party rule by upholding black voting rights and fostering multiparty competition. Fusion might have made the South a fairer, less violent, more democratic, and more prosperous place.[12]

But Fusion was never given a fair test. The Democrats countered the emerging black–poor white alliance by unfurling the banner of white supremacy, warning that a "great horde of ignorant blacks" would dominate government in the event of a Fusion victory. However, aware that many white voters would resist such threadbare propaganda, the Democrats were also prepared to subvert the electoral process in order to deny their opponents victory. "It is the religious duty of Democrats to rob Populists and Republicans of their votes whenever and wherever the opportunity presents itself," averred one Louisiana newspaper. "The Populists and Republicans are our legitimate political prey. Rob them! You bet!" In Louisiana, Alabama, and Georgia the Democrats resorted to intimidation, violence, and electoral fraud to prevent the Populists from gaining power. By 1896 the People's Party had shot its bolt and, outside North Carolina, quickly faded.[13]

The North Carolina elections of 1898 and the riot that shook Wilmington, the state's biggest city, illustrated how democracy in the South was strangled. North Carolina Democrats organized a quasi-militaristic campaign reminiscent of Reconstruction days, complete with armed and mounted "Red Shirts," to unseat the Fusion government that controlled the state. Seeking to split the Populist-Republican coalition, the Democrats strove to put the fear of God into white voters. Not content with warning of "NEGRO DOMINATION," Democratic newspapers reported an epidemic of rapes, with blacks the attackers and whites the victims. The influential *Raleigh News and Observer*, edited by Josephus Daniels, was one of the worst offenders, printing a stream of headlines that rang the changes on "Estimable Lady Grossly Assaulted by a Black Negro!" Vicious cartoons rammed home the message: one depicted James H. Young, a black politician from Raleigh, lurking in the bedroom of a white woman. The rape scare was, according to historian Glenda Gilmore, a "coldly calculated effort to defame black men."[14]

A few weeks before the state elections, the Democrats seized upon an editorial in the *Wilmington Record*, North Carolina's only black daily newspaper, to intensify their campaign of sexual hysteria. Written by Alexander L. Manly, the piece was entitled "Mrs. Felton's Speech," referring to Rebecca Latimer Felton's virulently racist address to the Georgia Agricultural Society, delivered in 1897 in the incongruously beautiful setting of Tybee Island, a beach resort near Savannah. This outspoken feminist and political independent—she later became America's first woman senator—exhorted the men of

Georgia to defend their womenfolk. Black rapists, "ravenous human beasts," should be lynched "a thousand times a week if necessary."[15]

Alex Manly might have foreseen the consequences of setting pen to paper, for black editors had been run out of town for saying precisely what he wanted to say. In his editorial, Manly wrote:

> [O]ur experience among poor white people in the country teaches us that women of that race are not any more particular in the matter of clandestine meetings with colored men than the white men with colored women. Meetings of this kind go on for some time until the women's infatuation or the man's boldness brings attention to them, and the man is lynched for rape. Every Negro lynched is called "a Big Burly Black Brute," when, in fact, many of those who have thus been dealt with had white men for their fathers, and were not only not "black and burly," but were sufficiently attractive for white girls of culture and refinement to fall in love with them.

Manly was himself the light-skinned descendant of Charles Manly, a slaveholder and sometime governor of North Carolina.

Editor-publisher Josephus Daniels, a ferocious white supremacist, reprinted Manly's "vile and villainous" editorial in his *Raleigh News and Observer*. Newspapers throughout the state then picked up the story. White Carolinians fumed. Senator Ben Tillman, imported from South Carolina to add pep to the Democratic campaign, asked a rally in Fayetteville, "Why didn't you kill that damn nigger editor who wrote that?" Manly's editorial was a boon to the Democrats, keeping the diabolical image of the black rapist in front of the white voters. Charles B. Aycock, the Democratic candidate for governor, made the same emotional appeal everywhere he spoke. "I come to you today on behalf of the goddess of Democracy, the white womanhood of the State, and I appeal to you to come to their relief. Will you come to the rescue? Will you?"

The Democratic leader in Wilmington was a gloomy ex-Confederate colonel named Alfred M. Waddell, who had propelled himself to prominence on the strength of his blood-curdling oratory. Vowing that his party should stop at nothing, he advised what to do if a black man tried to vote come election day: "Kill him, shoot him down in his tracks." If necessary, the Democrats should choke Cape Fear with black corpses. A female cousin wrote Waddell a letter of encouragement: "It is time for the oft-quoted shotgun to play a part, and an active one, in the elections. It has reached the point where blood letting is needed . . . and when the depletion comes let it be thorough!"

The strategy of force worked. The Democratic Party narrowly carried the state and captured a large majority of the elective offices. In Wilmington, the election amounted to an armed insurrection. Bands of "Red Shirts" and "Rough Riders"—the illegal Democratic militia—patrolled the streets and seized the public buildings. The Democrats forced the mayor, the police chief, and the city council to resign, banishing their political opponents from the town. Democrats then terrorized the black community, killing at least fourteen people. The local militia regiment supported the coup, enforcing the expulsion of prominent blacks. When black college president James B. Dudley repaired to the city to protect his family, he "met about a thousand soldiers who were drumming four negroes from the city. They were not the indolent drones or paupers; they represented between thirty and forty thousand dollars worth of property." The *Wilmington Record*'s presses were wrecked and its office burned. Manly fled Wilmington, settled in the North, and passed for white in order to find work. About 1,400 blacks left the city and never came back.[16]

Having defeated their opponents through intimidation and force of arms, North Carolina's Democratic leaders set about annihilating their confused and demoralized opponents. Inspired by the example set by Mississippi, South Carolina, and Louisiana, they aimed for the total disfranchisement of black voters. Within three years they had achieved that goal. The Populists never recovered and the Republican Party—"freed from the stigma of being called the 'Negro Party,'" as Governor Aycock put it—was shattered.[17]

It can be argued, with some merit, that Fusion was a marriage of convenience, inherently unstable, and bound to collapse because of its own contradictions. Blacks remained suspicious of the Populists, who shied away from advocating racial equality. For their part, Populists embraced the Republicans—the party of Lincoln, the Union, and blacks—with great reluctance. Some Populists, frustrated by their failure to attract black voters, and angered by the Democrats' uncanny ability to carry the Black Belt counties, ended up supporting disfranchisement. A few Populists, notably Georgia's Tom Watson, turned upon blacks savagely, giving vent to the most aggressive racism.[18]

It was the Democratic Party, however, that most often stooped to violence and electoral fraud, made the most blatant appeals to racism, and took the decisive steps to destroy universal manhood suffrage. "[T]he proponents of disfranchisement were almost all Democrats," writes the historian J. Morgan Kousser, "whereas, in state after state, the great majority of the Republicans and Populists opposed the [disfranchisement] bills." The wealthy and well-educated whites of the Black Belt, moreover, took the lead in restricting the ballot. As for the Populists' well-attested racism, the important thing to remember is that, as Glenda Gilmore puts it, "Their actions outdistanced their ideology. Left alone to govern in a biracial coalition, they might have changed their ideas to match their actions. . . . They did not get that chance."[19]

THE NORTH FINALLY ABANDONS BLACK SOUTHERNERS

Only an alert, vigorous, and conscientious national government could have guaranteed fair elections in the South. However, the fact that the Republican Party failed to defend its interests in North Carolina—the one Southern state in which Republicans actually wielded power—demonstrated the party's lack of political interest in the South. The state's Republican governor pleaded with the Republican president to dispatch troops to Wilmington to prevent Republican voters from being intimidated and attacked. But William McKinley, although a Union veteran—the last to sit in the White House—declined to intervene. After the collapse of Reconstruction in 1877, the Republican Party made only token gestures toward the principle of racial equality. By 1900 it felt comfortable endorsing white supremacy.

In the late nineteenth century—a period of frantic industrialization and rapid population growth—the problems of blacks in the South seemed increasingly inconsequential to Republican leaders. What really mattered to the Republicans, a Northern-based party, was power at the national level: power to fix tariff rates, to subsidize railroads, to curb labor unions, and to protect business corporations—in short, power to shape and control the emerging industrial order. In this context, what happened in the South, a region of diminishing economic and political significance, was of secondary importance.

By 1900, Republicans—and whites in the North generally—had an additional reason for acquiescing in the disfranchisement of black voters. They had lost faith in the capacity of black people to rise to the level of whites. A dwindling band of true believers, many of them former abolitionists, still insisted that blacks, given half a chance, were just as moral, resourceful, and intelligent as white people. In the harsh industrial world of the 1890s, however, the egalitarian ideals of the abolitionists seemed antiquated. Were all men truly equal? The white Anglo-Saxon Protestants who formed the bedrock of the Republican Party looked askance at the influx of Russians, Eastern Europeans, and Italians. Their democratic faith wavered. If these strange-looking newcomers were, as many believed, inferior white breeds, how could blacks be remotely equal to old-stock Americans?

To the immigrants themselves, desperately scrambling to secure an economic foothold in America, blacks appeared as unwelcome interlopers and competitors. They could not understand the Republican Party's seeming obsession with these people. Like the Irish before them, the "new immigrants" of the 1890s and 1900s quickly assimilated the anti-Negro prejudices of the host society. They would rather blacks remain in the South, firmly excluded from the North's mines, mills, and factories. The owners and employers knew this. So did the Republican bosses, who regarded the votes of these immigrant millions as of far bigger consequence than the votes of Southern blacks. The small black population in the North could vote, but it was increasingly segregated. Black ghettos were forming. More and more public schools were single-race. Labor unions discriminated against blacks and most excluded them completely.

In the last two decades of the nineteenth century, white hostility to people of color flared up again and again. Indians had long been regarded as subhuman savages, and many whites confidently predicted their extinction. In California, white hatred of the Chinese became so virulent that in 1882 Congress banned all further Chinese immigration. A second panic over the "yellow peril" prompted a clamp-down on Japanese immigration in 1907. Race and color was no longer the peculiar obsession of white Southerners; it had become a national preoccupation. Anthropologists constructed elaborate pseudoscientific racial hierarchies, placing "Nordics" at the top and "Negroes" at the bottom. Physicians and social scientists spoke of "race suicide," warning that immigrants from southern and eastern Europe were producing many more children than old-stock Americans. It was in this context that whites in the North became increasingly receptive to the racial arguments of whites in the South.[20]

Southern white leaders made a determined effort to ensure that their own ideas about blacks gained national acceptance. After the demise of Reconstruction, white Southerners launched an ideological offensive aimed at the North. A torrent of books, articles, and pamphlets proclaimed that while chattel slavery had perhaps been wrong, it had rarely been cruel, and rarely even profitable. The masters had regarded their slaves as an extended family, caring for them well, treating them humanely, and training them efficiently. Not only that, the masters had provided moral enlightenment; they had civilized and Christianized their bondsmen, pulling them out of the abject barbarism of their African origins. Emancipation had thus released blacks from the firm but benevolent influence of white people, and since then they had regressed. They no longer worked as hard. They were lapsing into immorality, vice, and crime. "It is the opinion of every man of unbiased mind," stated Dr. Paul Barringer of the University of Virginia, "that the second generation is infinitely worse than the first." Throughout the South, wrote the Virginia-born novelist Thomas Nelson Page, whites "report a general depravity and retrogression of the Negro . . . closely resembling a reversion to barbarism." Many whites professed wonderment that blacks were surviving at all, grimly predicting that, like the Indians, they had no long-term future as a race.[21]

White Southerners also appealed to the Northern yearning for sectional reconciliation. If the North allowed Southern whites to work out their own solution to the "Negro question," there would be no further cause for sectional tension or strife. Disfranchisement, accompanied by legal segregation, would lead to a stable South, one in which blacks accepted their place as servants and laborers. This stable South, on the brink of industrialization, would welcome Northern investment with open arms. Disfranchisement, moreover, would actually benefit the Republican Party in the longer term. It would remove the race issue from Southern election campaigns; white voters would be free to divide into opposing political parties because they no longer need fear "Negro domination." By 1900 few whites dissented from the Southern view that Radical Reconstruction had been a terrible mistake.[22]

America's acquisition of the Philippines, after the Spanish-American War of 1898, gave white Southerners a chance to reinforce the point. When the Republican administration of William McKinley denied self-government to the dark-skinned Filipino people on the grounds that they were a backward race, Senator Ben Tillman smugly noted Northern hypocrisy. "I want to call attention to the remarkable change that has come over the spirit of the dream of the Republicans. . . . Your slogans of the past—brotherhood of man and fatherhood of God—have gone glimmering down through the ages." Southern historian Samuel Chiles Mitchell believed that the "higher developed European races" now had more sympathy for the white South after their contact with "inferior peoples on all the continents and islands." If the Negro was, indeed, a backward, childlike race that needed firm guidance and control, who better to provide that firm hand than the people who knew them best, the Southern whites? "The only development that can come to the negro race must come through the instrumentality of the white race," asserted Senator Oscar Underwood of Alabama. "The negro through his own efforts is incapable of rising above his present condition."[23]

Many white Northerners were disposed to agree, conceding that the principle of racial equality had been flawed, and that blacks had failed to measure up to their expectations. "A perfectly stupid race can never rise to a very high plane," noted President Theodore Roosevelt. Seth Low, former mayor of New York City, reassured a white Southern audience that public schools in Manhattan were also, in fact if not in law, segregated by race. The people of New York "can understand the feeling in the South that . . . the separate education of the races is best for both." As historian David Levering Lewis put it,

most whites shared the view that "African Americans were inferior human beings whose predicament was three parts their own making and two parts the
consequences of misguided philanthropy."[24]

The Supreme Court's pivotal decision in *Plessy* v. *Ferguson* (1896) reflected the emerging national consensus on race. The case was instigated by a
group of Creoles from New Orleans—mixed-race blacks of French cultural
background—who challenged the Louisiana law that required railroad companies to provide separate accommodations for black and white passengers.
But the Court upheld segregation.

Plessy v. *Ferguson* was an unmitigated judicial defeat for black Americans.
Not only did the Supreme Court deny that "enforced separation" discriminated against black people, it also implied that racial segregation was "in the
nature of things." The Fourteenth Amendment did not require "enforced
commingling of the two races." In an argument that reeked of racism, the
Court explained that "if one race be inferior to the other socially, the Constitution of the United States cannot put them upon the same plane." Henry
Brown, who delivered the opinion, hailed from Massachusetts. John M. Harlan, the sole dissenter, was a former slaveholder from Kentucky. Proclaiming
that "Our Constitution is color-blind," Harlan insisted that segregation laws
consigned blacks to a "condition of legal inferiority." The South's separate-
but-equal defense of segregation was a sham: the law in question implied that
"colored citizens are so inferior and degraded that they cannot be allowed to
sit in public coaches occupied by white citizens." By sanctioning such laws,
the Court would only "stimulate aggression, more or less brutal and irritat-
ing," against the rights of black citizens.[25]

Given the Court's endorsement of racial segregation, it was unlikely to resist disfranchisement. The Fifteenth Amendment, however, prohibited denying the vote to adult males on the grounds of "race, color, or previous
condition of servitude." The Court needed an intellectual loophole. Southern
white lawmakers obligingly provided one.

The men who framed the new state constitutions frankly admitted that their
suffrage provisions were designed to eliminate black voters, not white ones.
"Discrimination! Why, that is precisely what we propose," admitted Carter
Glass of Virginia. "Doesn't it let the white man vote," asked E. B. Kruttschnitt
of Louisiana, "and doesn't it stop the negro from voting, and isn't that what we
came here for?" The Fifteenth Amendment, however, did not ban discrimination on grounds *other than* race, gender being the most obvious. Hence the
South's new qualifications for voting—literacy tests, residency requirements,
property qualifications, poll taxes, and tests of how well a prospective voter
"understood" the Constitution—never mentioned race. As they did not discriminate "on their face," the Supreme Court accepted them.[26]

THE CONSOLIDATION OF WHITE SUPREMACY

By 1910 blacks had been purged from the voting rolls throughout the former Confederacy. But the predicted emergence of a healthy two-party system failed to happen. The Democrats—as they had shrewdly calculated—were left ruling the roost. The Republican Party simply collapsed after its electoral base, the black vote, was wiped out. The party survived in name only, its main function being the distribution of federal patronage jobs when Republicans controlled the White House. A dwindling band of party faithful, bitterly divided by race, fought over the shrivelled corpse.

The Populist Party disintegrated completely. Tragically, some Populists had endorsed disfranchisement in the hope that it would eliminate the race issue— the Democrats' main drawing card—and make Southern elections more honest. However, the new registration laws were administered by Democratic officials and—despite assurances to the contrary—a good number of whites fell foul of them. The establishment of a virtual one-party state further depressed voting levels: why pay an annual poll tax merely to select the Democratic candidate? Only a minority of whites regularly voted. "[T]he electorate was tiny," writes historian J. Morgan Kousser, "and party competition almost nonexistent."[27]

Rather than suppressing the race issue and encouraging healthy debate about other political questions, disfranchisement had the opposite effect. Lack of party competition led to a confused politics of factionalism and personality. Moreover, because white supremacy was the only issue that bound the Democrats together, it remained a perennial campaign topic. A new breed of white politicians, known collectively as the "demagogues," specialized in abusing and vilifying blacks. Whether men like Ben Tillman of South Carolina and James K. Vardaman of Mississippi were any more racist than the older patricians whom they displaced has been disputed. However, the demagogue was not inhibited by the presence of a large black vote, and he cynically appealed to the worst instincts of the white electorate. As historian Edward Ayers notes, "He would almost always find it profitable to play to the fear and anger toward black people that festered among so many white Southerners."[28]

Disfranchisement not only secured white supremacy within the South but also strengthened it within the nation. With the Southern black vote eliminated, the Republican Party had neither the means nor the incentive to challenge Democratic hegemony in the former Confederacy. Moreover, disfranchisement magnified the national influence of the white oligarchy that dominated Southern politics. In South Carolina, for example, it took only 4,600 votes to elect a congressman, compared to 40,000 votes to elect a congressman in New York. In addition, the South's one-party system enhanced the political longevity of Southern congressmen, endowing them with seniority and influence. In the Senate especially, long-serving Southerners controlled key committees and, by carefully exploiting complex procedural rules, could block any legislation they opposed. It was an unwritten rule of national politics—which held good until 1948—that no Democratic candidate could be elected to the presidency without carrying the "Solid South."[29]

As blacks lost political ground, racial segregation became more extensive, more rigid, and more harshly enforced. While the issues surrounding the origins of racial segregation are complex, few historians now subscribe to C. Vann Woodward's view that segregation was largely a product of the 1890s and 1900s. Separate facilities for blacks were already the practice in schools, hospitals, orphanages, prisons, asylums, and poorhouses. Theaters already confined blacks to the gallery, and blacks were usually separated at racetracks, fairgrounds, and amusement parks. Most bars, restaurants, and hotels already excluded blacks. It was also the case, as the historian Howard Rabinowitz pointed out, that racial segregation was often an improvement over complete exclusion: better to have segregated schools than none at all; better to have separate seating at athletic events than to be barred from them. Finally, racial segregation sometimes represented a voluntary act on the part of black Southerners. This was especially true in the social sphere, where blacks formed their own churches, societies, and clubs.

In the 1870s and 1880s, however, there was a fluidity and uncertainty about race relations in the South. Segregation was largely a matter of custom rather than law, and custom varied from place to place. After about 1890, however, two important changes took place. First, segregation was extended to public transportation—trains and streetcars—in a form that blacks bitterly resented. The patent inferiority of the colored "Jim Crow" railway carriage, and the humiliating symbolism of being seated at the rear of the streetcar, angered blacks of all classes. Second, states and cities began passing laws and regulations that codified segregation in an increasingly complex and pervasive way. The extent to which segregation, or "Jim Crow," laws reflected an intensification of racism is much debated. It was once believed that segregation laws were passed to appease the poor whites, the alleged fountainhead of antiblack prejudice. But many historians now attribute the spread of legalized segregation to white modernizers and progressives—men and women who saw themselves as racial moderates—not to the extreme Negrophobes like Tillman and Vardaman. "An emerging southern middle-class . . . created the culture of segregation," argues Elizabeth Grace Hale, not the poor whites. This middle class viewed segregation as a rational solution to the problem of racial conflict, especially in the South's growing cities.

Still, the plethora of segregation laws marked the birth of a new social order. Even if the laws made little difference to the degree of actual racial separation, they represented an important change in white attitudes. The "color line," which had previously been indistinct—states had even lacked legal definitions of black and white—became the basic organizing principle of the New South. In both their enactment and execution, segregation laws reflected white supremacy. They were not a neutral, "separate but equal," compromise between the races: they were imposed upon unwilling blacks by a powerful white majority. Without the growing influence of the extreme racists, moreover, who continually referred to blacks as savages and brutes, legalized segregation could not have gained acceptance as the "moderate" solution to the South's race problem. Segregation became a matter of faith among white Southerners, uniting them across lines of class and smoothing political differences. Few dissented from the view that segregation, like disfranchisement and the prohibition of interracial marriage, represented a racial "settlement" that should never be disturbed.[30]

A CONFUSION OF STRATEGIES

By 1900 the South's black population was more powerless than at any other time since the death of slavery. The rapidity and thoroughness with which white Southerners destroyed the Reconstruction order and replaced it with white supremacy left many blacks stunned, confused, and demoralized. The North's acquiescence in white supremacy heightened their sense of isolation and vulnerability. The campaigning black journalist T. Thomas Fortune, editor of the *New York Age*, put the problem in a nutshell: "The deuce of the matter is that Southern white men had educated Northern white men so that they have no faith whatever in black men." Upon leaving the House of Representatives in 1901, George H. White—the last black congressman from the South for seventy years—lamented that "at no time in the history of our freedom has the effort been made to mold public sentiment against us and our progress so strongly as is now being done." White settled in New Jersey: "I can no longer live in North Carolina and be a man."[31]

Blacks responded to the establishment of white supremacy in three ways. The first was to leave the South. Aspiring novelist Charles W. Chesnutt quit his North Carolina teaching job in 1883 and moved to New York, finally settling in Cleveland. He could no longer abide the racism of white Southerners. "I hear colored men write of their 'white friends.' I have no white friends. I could not degrade the sacred name of 'Friendship' by associating it with any man who feels himself too good to sit at table with me, or to sleep at the same hotel." For the great majority of black Southerners, however, migration was not a realistic option. Possessing only basic agricultural skills and often illiterate, they were ill-equipped to survive in the large cities of the North. In any case, Northern industry, both employers and unions, excluded black labor.

Some blacks sought freedom in the West, pursuing the Jeffersonian dream of landownership and economic independence. In 1879, "Kansas Fever" lured thousands from Louisiana and Mississippi in search of free homesteads, and a freer life. A much larger number contemplated moving but failed in the attempt. Oklahoma then became a favored destination: by 1910 black migrants had founded twenty-five all-black towns there. The stream of blacks leaving the South remained small, however, consisting mainly of the skilled and educated.[32]

Some doubted that the Negro could receive justice anywhere. "Whether North, South, East, or West be his ambition," thought William H. Councill, the head of a black school in Alabama, "his aspirations are chained to a stake, are circumscribed by Anglo-Saxon prejudice and might." Bishop Henry M. Turner, the foremost advocate of emigration to Africa, argued that "three or four millions of us should return to the land of our ancestors, and establish our own nation." But if migration was difficult, emigration was virtually impossible. The plain fact was that most blacks had to deal with life as they found it on their doorsteps, in the South.[33]

The second response to white supremacy was to protest, openly and vigorously, against violence, injustice, and discrimination. Throughout the South, blacks held "indignation meetings," formed equal rights leagues, filed lawsuits to combat discrimination, and boycotted the newly segregated streetcars. But these actions were sporadic and uncoordinated. Opposition to lynch law, disfranchisement, and Jim Crow required a new degree of black unity. The elderly leader Frederick Douglass, a former slave and abolitionist, urged blacks not to abandon their traditional political loyalty: the Republican Party was the ship, everything else was the hostile sea. But others concluded that the Republicans had betrayed blacks, who must now act independently. As T. Thomas Fortune put it, "We can't trust white men North or South to shape thought for us, we must do it ourselves. That is a dead open and shut."[34]

In 1890 Fortune formed the Afro-American League with the dual aim of uniting blacks against injustice and promoting black economic and educational progress. At the League's founding convention in Chicago, which attracted one hundred delegates from twenty-three states, Fortune argued for a black-only organization:

Ladies and gentlemen, it is time to call a halt. It is time to fight fire with fire. It is time to stand shoulder to shoulder as men. It is time to rebuke the treachery of friends in the only way that treachery should be rebuked. It is time to face the enemy and fight him inch by inch for every right he denies us. . . . Let this League be a race League. To make it anything else is to sow the seeds of discord, disunion, and disaster.

The League elected as its president Joseph C. Price, a bishop of the African Methodist Episcopal Zion (AMEZ) Church and president of Livingstone College in North Carolina. Only thirty-five years old, Price enjoyed wide respect as an orator, temperance advocate, educator, and race leader.

The Afro-American League set its sights on every facet of racial oppression. It denounced lynching and mob violence, complained about unequal schools, deplored discrimination on railroads, opposed the exclusion of blacks from jury service, and decried the cruel treatment of black prisoners under the South's convict-lease system. It vowed to attain its objectives by influencing public opinion, by appealing to the courts, and by pursuing an independent political course. Fortune was even prepared to think the unthinkable: support Democratic candidates.

The League quickly foundered, however. J. C. Price might have become a leader of the first rank, but he died in 1893 at the age of only thirty-nine. The volatile, irascible Fortune, despite his intellectual brilliance and journalistic talent, lacked the temperament to be an inspiring leader. In addition, the League was beset by schisms. At its second meeting it split, a group of dissenters forming the American Citizens Equal Rights Association. The waters were further muddied by the appearance of a third organization, the National Citizens Rights Association (NCRA), led by Albion W. Tourgee, a former carpetbagger from North Carolina now residing in Chicago, and the author of *A Fool's Errand,* a bestselling novel about Reconstruction. The NCRA included both blacks and whites. In a climate of intensifying racism, however, the struggle for civil rights could not afford the luxury of competing organizations and clashing egos. By 1893 the Afro-American League was defunct. The other two groups expired a few years later.

The failure to achieve black unity, however, had deeper causes. In a situation of increasing racial discrimination, when the white majority seemed solidly arrayed against blacks, protest and agitation appeared increasingly futile. Fortune's proposal that blacks adopt an independent political strategy was equally unproductive: bad as the Republicans were, the Democrats proved worse. The Populists appeared to be promising allies, but they, too, threw black voters to the wolves when it suited them. Blacks faced a problem for which there was no ready solution—no wonder they found it impossible to agree on strategy and tactics.

The third response to white supremacy, accommodationism, began with the assumption that blacks ought to accept the new status quo and make the most of existing opportunities. Accommodationists believed that politics had failed blacks and that agitation was not only unproductive but also dangerous. They believed that blacks in the South ought to focus their energies on self-improvement. Even without the vote, blacks could learn to read, develop skills, buy land, build businesses, support churches, and lead sober and industrious lives. Moreover, instead of resenting Southern whites as oppressors, blacks should make their peace with them—regard them as potential friends, or treat them as such, in the hope of gaining protection and assistance. Accommodationism was a survival strategy, a way of adjusting to harsh reality. It appealed especially to the emerging black middle class—members of which sometimes described themselves as the black "better class"—who expected to gain most by concentrating on the acquisition of wealth. As William C. Smith, editor of the *Charlotte Messenger*, put it, "Get knowledge. Get money. Get land. Use these things properly taking Christ as our guide, and all will be well."[35]

Teachers and ministers, the bedrock of the black middle class, espoused accommodationism most vocally. The motives and interests of these two groups were rather different. Black education suffered from declining support from the Northern missionary associations and received no support from the federal government. Black teachers were therefore more dependent than ever upon the support of Southern whites—planters, politicians, businessmen, and other men of influence—and they became increasingly careful not to offend them. Blacks needed "the intelligent and sympathetic direction of the white race," affirmed North Carolina teacher Charles N. Hunter in 1889, "and the sooner we see this and act upon it the better for us." Edward L. Blackshear, president of Prairie View College in Texas, stressed the need for patience, explaining that "Perhaps it is the duty of the stronger race to prescribe the conditions . . . under which the weaker are to be admitted to the privileges of universal civilization."[36]

Ministers, in contrast to teachers, enjoyed a great deal of independence. Indeed, the church had become the mainstay of the black community, the most important institution owned and controlled by blacks themselves. It was only to be expected that after the Civil War the freedmen would quit the white-controlled Southern denominations—Baptists, Methodists, Presbyterians, and Episcopalians—that had supported slavery. Surprisingly, however, few chose to join the Northern branches of those denominations, despite the Northern churches' abolitionist credentials and support for black education. The ambitions of black preachers, the preference of black Christians for an expressive style of worship, and a strong desire for community autonomy proved decisive. By 1870, with relatively few exceptions, black Southerners worshipped in their own churches, pastored by black ministers. Many affiliated with Northern black denominations such as the African Methodist Episcopal Church (AME) and the African Methodist Episcopal Zion Church (AMEZ). An even larger number formed independent Baptist churches.

Yet ministers also moved toward accommodationism during the 1880s and 1890s. During Reconstruction many black ministers had served as Republican leaders. Like other blacks, however, they were influenced by political realities, especially the seeming impregnability of the Democratic Party in the South. "Shall we live with the hope that the general government will bring us a panacea for all our ills?" asked Kentucky Baptist W. J. Simmons. "Let us cast our votes for liberal men who will help us. We cannot expect those against whom we vote to do so." By the 1890s many black ministers advocated withdrawing from political activity altogether.

Some ministers interpreted the triumph of white supremacy as a rebuke from God to the colored race, a lesson in humility after the prideful experience of Reconstruction. Trying to account for disfranchisement, Memphis pastor S. N. Vass argued that "After the war we took to politics instead of books, and God is using the white man to bring us back to where we ought to have started." Others lamented blacks' failure to lead moral, Christian lives. "The Negro has been departing from God," thought Bishop John Walker Hood of North Carolina. "Now God has departed from the Negro." Ministers placed more stress than ever upon moral improvement, arguing that character and integrity, not legislation, would eventually conquer white prejudice. "The strength must be infused in the man," insisted Rev. Theophilus G. Steward of Georgia. "He must be made strong. This will only come from labor, study, and thought." As they retreated from party politics, many black ministers fervently embraced the temperance movement.[37]

The division between accommodationism and protest was a blurred one. The two tendencies warred against each other without producing either a clear-cut division or a decisive resolution. Buffeted by unexpected and disorienting setbacks, many blacks oscillated back and forth between the two positions.[38]

After 1895, however, the tension between accommodationism and protest increased sharply, producing a more visible—and bitter—division between the two. The cause of this polarization was the continuing decline in the status of blacks, which evoked both intensified protest and a more determined effort to make peace with the white South. The two outstanding black leaders of the 1890s, Ida B. Wells and Booker T. Washington, personified these conflicting responses to oppression.

Ida B. Wells, circa 1893

Department of Special Collections, University of Chicago Library

2

Ida B. Wells and the Campaign
Against Lynching

Lynching was the dark heart of the new racial order that emerged in the South at the end of the nineteenth century. Nothing more starkly illustrated the decline in the status of black Americans than the steep rise in the number of blacks who were killed by white mobs, sometimes in broad daylight, and often with the general approval of the white community. Nobody knew for certain how many blacks were being shot, hanged, burned, and tortured to death. The best estimate is that between 1880 and 1930, Southern lynch mobs summarily executed, without recourse to legal niceties, 3,320 blacks and 723 whites. Yet white Southerners defended lynching with a vehemence that bordered on the irrational, and blacks opposed it at their peril.

In 1892, however, a young black woman from Memphis, Tennessee, Ida B. Wells, denounced lynching in such forthright terms—compelling her to flee the South—that the issue became a national, and then an international, *cause célèbre*. Black women's clubs, which in 1896 formed a national movement, then took up the question. The National Association for the Advancement of Colored People (NAACP), founded in 1909, subsequently campaigned to make lynching a federal crime. The long fight to end lynching was the starting point of the modern civil rights struggle—the beginning of the fight-back against white supremacy.

THE RISE OF LYNCHING, 1880–1910

Lynching had long been a form of frontier violence in America, and it used to claim many more white victims than black ones. In the late 1880s, however, its character changed: a wave of lynching swept across the South, and blacks accounted for most of the dead. Between 1880 and 1930 the proportion of lynchings that took place in the South increased from 82 percent to 95 percent of the national total; the proportion of victims who were black grew from 68 percent to 91 percent. The 1890s was the worst decade: the yearly total only twice dipped below 100; in 1892, the peak year, mobs lynched 161 blacks.[1]

Judged alongside other racial and ethnic atrocities of the modern era, the death toll from Southern lynching might seem relatively modest. The likelihood of a black Southerner being lynched was statistically small. Indeed, when lynching declined sharply after 1920, some blacks criticized the NAACP for expending too much of its energy on the problem. Raw numbers, however, did not fully explain the power of lynching to both terrify blacks and incite whites to further oppressions. And the figures themselves did not account for the prominence of lynching as a political issue.

The most important fact about lynching was not the number of blacks who were killed but the ability of whites to kill, and torture, with impunity. Often composed of respectable citizens and defended by politicians and newspaper editors, lynch mobs acted without fear of arrest or punishment. Indeed, law enforcement officers often released black prisoners into their hands. Confident of community approval, lynchers—men, women, and children—often posed for photographers in front of charred corpses and dangling bodies. White juries, even when they knew the lynchers' identities, routinely declined to indict them, blithely stating that their victims "died at the hands of persons unknown." Lynching thus illustrated, most cruelly and starkly, the vulnerability of black Southerners at the hands of the white majority.

Lynching proclaimed to the world that blacks were not entitled to the protection of the law—not even the law as harshly administered by whites. It demonstrated that whites placed such a low value on the lives of black Southerners that they would not deem the killing of blacks a crime. Thus lynching placed the highest black person at the mercy of the lowest white. It did not require large masses of victims, therefore, to underline the precariousness of life for all black Southerners, whatever their rank and station. As the black educator Robert R. Moton explained to a white Southerner: "I, or any one of us, may be taken from a train or elsewhere and lynched without Judge or jury, should we come near the description as given of a Negro charged with a crime in that locality. . . . When I tell you that our most intelligent and upright Negroes ever are conscious of the fact that at any hour they may be hurled into eternity . . . you get some idea of what we face." Of the manifold oppressions inflicted upon black people in the name of white supremacy, lynching was the worst.[2]

There was another reason why lynching aroused such passions in both blacks and whites: it reflected a view of black people as subhuman brutes. As whites stripped blacks of political power and passed Jim Crow laws to forcibly segregate them, their view of blacks became increasingly harsh. "As a race," stated James K. Vardaman, governor of Mississippi, "they are deteriorating every day." Senator "Pitchfork Ben" Tillman of South Carolina insisted that blacks were regressing toward "barbarism, savagery, cannibalism and everything which is low and degrading." The most obvious sign of black retrogression, many believed, was the increase in black crime. In Mississippi, for example, where blacks constituted 56 percent of the population but 90 percent of the criminals, cases of murder and manslaughter increased fivefold between 1880 and 1910; rape cases tripled. "It is a lamentable fact," Vardaman told the U.S. Senate, "that the negro in America is more criminal to-day than he was in 1861." It was an article of faith among white Southerners that the rape of white women by black men had been unknown under slavery, and that "these crimes are not only increasing in frequency, but in their horror and brutality."[3]

It was the purported threat from black rapists that gave whites their most persuasive defense of lynching. Only swift, certain, and terrible punishment, whites argued, could prevent black rape from reaching epidemic proportions. The courts were slow and unreliable; in any case, to ask female victims to relive their ordeal in the witness box was unthinkable. Hallie Erminie Rives, a Kentucky woman who wrote a passionate defense of lynching in a best-selling novel, defined the practice as a "lurid object lesson necessary to impress the ignorance and passion that gave it cause." To white Southerners, lynching was a necessary means of law enforcement aimed at a specific threat from a brutalized race. "There is only one crime that warrants lynching," vowed Ben Tillman, "and Governor as I am, I would lead a mob to lynch the negro who ravishes a white woman."[4]

Black rapists were not a white invention, and allegations of rape prompted at least half of all lynchings in the 1880s. Yet even when, after 1890, the victims of lynching were more likely to be accused of other crimes, rape remained central to the white defense of lynching. White women in the South lived "in a state of siege," Ben Tillman told the U.S. Senate in 1913. "I have but three daughters, but, so help me God, I had rather find either one of them killed by a tiger or a bear . . . than to have her crawl to me and tell me the horrid story that she had been robbed of the jewel of her womanhood by a black fiend." No black rapist merited the luxury of a trial, only "death, speedy and fearful," at the hands of avenging whites. "It is only because lynching for rape is excused," wrote North Carolinian Clarence Poe, editor of the *Progressive Farmer*, "that lynching for any other crime is ever attempted."[5]

The white obsession with rape was out of all proportion to the danger. Yet as the journalist Wilbur J. Cash argued in his classic analysis *The Mind of the South*, the "Southern rape complex" performed the crucial task of reinforcing both white supremacy and white patriarchy. Whites could maintain their dominance only by preventing blacks from entering the white group through marriage, and also by excluding all children born of black-white unions. Under slavery, the mulatto child of a white man inherited the legal status of the slave mother. After slavery, whites reconstructed their superior status by excluding all racially mixed people from the privileges of "whiteness." By the end of the nineteenth century state laws had criminalized "miscegenation" and, under the "one-drop rule," defined as "colored" any person who had even a small fraction of "Negro blood." Some white men continued to have sexual relations with black women, but the law defined the offspring of such liaisons as "colored."

If white men could be attracted to black women, logic suggested that white women might find black men attractive. However, if white women bore mulatto children, racial segregation would break down, and so would the patriarchal authority of white men. White men therefore rationalized their own interracial liaisons by portraying black females as libidinous, promiscuous, and sexually precocious. At the same time they constructed an idealized image of the white woman as a chaste maiden, high on a pedestal, devoid of sexual passion, thus banishing the idea that white women and black men could ever engage in consensual sex. As W. J. Cash put it, white men took refuge in fiction, casting themselves as chivalrous defenders of hearth and home, deifying the Southern Woman. "There was hardly a sermon that did not begin and end with tributes to her honor," wrote Cash, "hardly a brave speech that did not open and close with the clashing of shields and the flourishing of swords for her glory." The logical conclusion of this flight into fantasy was the belief that all sex between black men and white women (except prostitutes) must be, by definition, rape. By the same token, all black men were potential rapists. "The negro man aspires to the white woman," stated former Confederate officer Charles H. Smith, "and if he cannot get her he will take her child."[6]

Most white Southerners therefore viewed blacks, men and women both, as lascivious, lewd, and debauched. "I don't know that it ever occurred to any of us that a Negro girl was capable of virtue," wrote Rollin Chambliss, who grew up in south Georgia, in 1934. "The Negro . . . is sexually completely free and untrammelled," thought Mississippi author David Cohn. " 'When I wants me a woman, I gits me a women.' . . . Sexual desire is an imperative need, raw and crude and strong. It is to be satisfied when and wherever it arises. It is not embroidered with the roses and raptures of romantic love . . . but flies straight to its mark with the blind compulsion and devouring intensity of a speeding bullet." Even scholars viewed blacks as slaves to sexual passion. "The point where the Negro American was furthest behind modern civilization was in his sexual mores," wrote Arthur W. Calhoun, pioneer historian of the American family. "Immodesty, unbridled sexuality, obscenity, social indifference to purity were prevalent characteristics."[7]

This brutish image bore little relationship to the realities of black family life. For whites, however, black hypersexuality was a necessary myth. The rape threat justified denying blacks the vote and excluding them from juries. It justified job discrimination, for black men could not be allowed to work alongside, let alone in authority over, white women. Above all, white Southerners explained the need for strict segregation by stressing black sexuality and the awful consequences of "social equality"—be it travelling in the same railway car as black passengers or addressing a black person as "Mr." or "Mrs." "Social equality" was fraught with danger, for it would inevitably lead to miscegenation—interracial sex—and the destruction, or "mongrelization," of the white race. "If we sit with Negroes at our tables, if we entertain them as our guests and social equals, is it possible to maintain it fixedly in the sexual relation?" asked William Benjamin Smith in his book *The Color Line* (1905). White Southerners interpreted black claims to equality as an attack on white women.[8]

Despite routinely passing resolutions denouncing "lynch law," black organizations failed to mount a forthright campaign against lynching during the 1880s. For one thing, the constant white complaints about the rising crime rate among blacks placed them on the defensive. They had to rebut the charge that crime among blacks was unknown under slavery and that the race was degenerating. Slavery had been a giant prison, explained the black educator Booker T. Washington. "To say that the Negro was at his best, morally, during the period of slavery is about the same as to say that the two thousand prisoners . . . in the city of Boston are the most righteous two thousand people in Boston." Black leaders also contested the crime figures, arguing that the judicial system treated black people with singular harshness while giving white offenders "100 chances to 1 to evade the law and to escape punishment." They complained, too, that the infamous convict-lease system made prisoners profitable: blacks were arrested for trivial offenses—stealing "a few stalks of sugar-cane or a couple of watermelons"—in order to supply cheap labor to white employers. Blacks even had to counter the fallacious argument that educated blacks were more likely to commit criminal acts than illiterates.[9]

The specific accusation of rape, however, caused black leaders the most trouble. White opponents of lynching such as Bishop Atticus G. Haygood often shared the contention of lynching's defenders that the root of the problem was "the assaulting of white women by negro men"—a crime regarded as "so monstrous" as to be outside "the ordinary categories of crimes." Haygood was no extreme racist: he supported black education and wrote a book called *Our Brother in Black*. Nevertheless, he believed that the cure for lynching lay in the hands of black people themselves. Lynching would cease when the crime of rape ceased. If only black leaders would "use their influence as they can and ought—denouncing rape as much as they do lynching—the crime will be less common in a few weeks; by and by it will be so rare that lynchings will come to an end."[10]

Such arguments put black leaders in a cleft stick. If they discounted the rape issue entirely—and if they hinted that some charges of rape might have originated in consensual sex—they risked severe retribution if they lived in the South. As Haygood put it, "A single word questioning the purity of Southern women has cost many a man his life." Black denunciations of lynching, therefore, tended to be cautious and apologetic—verbal balancing acts that in the mere effort of evenhandedness seemed to tilt toward the lynchers. They deplored mob violence because it undermined respect for law and order; but they condemned, with equal severity, the high rate of crime among blacks, never failing to condemn "assault upon white women."[11]

The Rev. Elias Camp Morris, president of the National Baptist Convention for its first twenty-seven years, typified the equivocation of many black spokesmen. In 1899 he condemned the "shameful work" of mobs that "hang, shoot down, and burn helpless Negroes," but diluted his statement by denouncing "all classes of crime" and pointing out that strikes and labor violence made "mob violence" a national problem. Four years later he repeated his abhorrence of mob violence, but declared "no sympathy . . . for the wretch who has fallen so low as to commit an outrage against any woman." The ultimate solution to lynching, Morris argued, was to uplift the religious and moral standards of the race to a level "that will make impossible the heinous crimes with which so many hitherto have been charged." In short, even when blacks criticized lynching, they often accepted the premise that lynching was a response, albeit a deplorable one, to rape.[12]

IDA B. WELLS MAKES LYNCHING
AN INTERNATIONAL ISSUE

Ida B. Wells was an outspoken black journalist who, after the murder of a friend, challenged the association of lynching with rape—even denying that lynching had anything to do with black crime. Her bold assertions and fearless manner so incensed white Memphians that they threatened to kill her, forcing her to quit the South. But Wells refused to be intimidated into silence. In refuting the white justification for lynching, she attacked the core of racist ideology. And in stirring the anger of white Southerners to fever pitch, she forced a national debate on lynching and aroused international condemnation of American mob violence.

Born a slave during the Civil War, Ida Bell Wells shared some of the advantages that enabled a minority of black Southerners to evade the bondage of tenancy and prosper in freedom. James Wells, her father, was the mulatto son of his master, and the latter arranged for James to become a carpenter, permitting him to live in the town of Holly Springs, Mississippi, as a hired-out slave. Ida's mother, Elizabeth Warrenton, also of mixed blood, was a cook at the home of James Wells's employer. As urban slaves, James and Elizabeth acquired knowledge and experience that stood them in good stead when freedom came, giving them distinct advantages over the mass of rural slaves. After emancipation, skilled freedmen such as the Wellses formed the nucleus of the emerging black middle class.[13]

Living in Holly Springs, the Wellses were able to send Ida to Rust University, which was typical of the schools established by Northern missionaries after the Civil War. Sponsored by the Northern branch of the Methodist Episcopal Church—the denomination had split along sectional lines in the 1840s—Rust's interracial, but mainly white, faculty taught children and young adults of widely varying ages and abilities. Doubling as both an elementary and a high school, Rust also served as a normal school, for teachers at the time needed no more than a high school education (and often got away with less). Foreshadowing later personal clashes, Ida B. Wells fell out with Rust's president, W. W. Hooper, a white man, who decided to expel her from the college. The reasons for her expulsion are obscure. Wells later confided in her diary that she had been consumed by "childish rage and jealousy" over Hooper's apparent preference for another female student, one of lighter complexion than her. But she concluded that the root cause of her academic failure had been "tempestuous, rebellious, hard headed willfulness, the trouble I gave, the disposition to question [Hooper's] authority."[14]

In 1878 a yellow fever epidemic devastated Wells's family. Both her parents died within a day of each other, orphaning the sixteen-year-old girl and her six younger siblings. Tragedy struck again a few days later when yellow fever took away a nine-month-old brother. Showing great strength of character, Wells refused to permit strangers to adopt her siblings and assumed the responsibility for keeping her family together. In 1881, after teaching in rural schools for three years, Wells took a teaching job in Memphis, a rambunctious riverfront city which, after the yellow fever disaster, was growing and prospering. Her salary, although much higher than the pay in rural schools, scarcely kept her above genteel poverty. But her job accorded her middle-class status, and she threw herself with gusto into the bustling social life that connected black teachers, ministers, journalists, and businessmen.

Wells's combative personality, and her belief that in standing up for herself she stood up for all black people, embroiled her in another clash with white authority in 1883. When a white train conductor attempted to drag her out of the first-class carriage, she dug in her heels and bit his hand, actually drawing blood. Leaving the train rather than conceding her right to travel first-class, Wells refused to let the matter drop: she sued the railway company and won $200 in damages in a state court. The following year, after a second eviction from a first-class carriage, she sued again, and Judge James Pierce awarded her $500. These widely publicized incidents earned Wells a reputation as a doughty fighter. In 1887, however, the Tennessee Supreme Court decided in favor of the railway company on appeal. Wells was downcast. "I have firmly believed all along that the law was on our side and would, when appealed to it, give us justice. I feel shorn of that belief and utterly discouraged. . . . O God is there no redress, no peace, no justice in this land for us?"15

Wells found teaching young children tedious and unrewarding. Her real passion was journalism. Starting as an unpaid contributor to a local newspaper owned by two black ministers, she was soon selling articles to such well-known black newspapers as the *American Baptist,* the *Indianapolis World,* the *Kansas City Dispatch,* and the *New York Freeman.* In 1889 she became editor and part-owner of the *Memphis Free Speech.* Two years later, after she criticized the city's public schools, the school board refused to renew her contract, transforming Wells into a full-time journalist. Boosting the circulation of the *Free Speech,* she replaced her lost salary and enhanced her reputation. Writing under the pen name "Iola," Wells expressed her opinions in a blunt, trenchant manner. A rare woman in the masculine, rough-and-tumble world of journalism, she delighted in the nickname "Princess of the Press."

Wells was no respecter of persons. She did not hesitate to chide black politicians, black ministers, other black journalists, and the black masses generally. But her complaints about the failings of her own race were largely animated by her anger over injustice. "The world at large spits upon us with impunity," she complained, because blacks were a "disorganized mass." As the status of blacks deteriorated, Wells lamented their refusal to resist white violence. When blacks in Georgetown, Kentucky, replied to the lynching of James Dudley by setting fire to white properties, she applauded them for showing the "true spark of manhood." Stopping lynching might require blacks "to burn up whole towns."[16]

When Wells openly disputed the notion that black men raped white women, whites in Memphis retaliated against her. But although whites suppressed her newspaper and forced her to leave Memphis, they failed to silence her. Indeed, by forcing her into exile, they helped Wells to publicize lynching as a national scandal.

The train of events leading to the destruction of Wells's newspaper began on March 9, 1892. The three black owners of a grocery store in Memphis—Calvin McDowell, Will Stewart, and Thomas Moss—were abducted from jail by a group of white men and shot dead. The triple lynching originated in the resentment of a neighboring grocer, Thomas H. Barrett, a white man, who saw his business decline after the three blacks opened their store, the People's Grocery Company. Tensions escalated from children brawling to a fistfight between Barrett and McDowell to the shooting of three sheriff's deputies by armed black men who were guarding the People's Grocery Company. The three black businessmen were arrested; a state judge ordered the disarming of the Tennessee Rifles, a black militia regiment, and forbade store owners to sell arms to blacks. After three days in jail, McDowell, Stewart, and Moss met their deaths.

The killings shocked black Memphis. Wells, out of town at the time, was "stunned." She knew one of the victims well: Thomas Moss was a letter carrier who delivered mail to the *Free Speech*—"a finer, cleaner man than he never walked the streets of Memphis." Wells urged blacks to leave Memphis and to settle in Oklahoma; she also supported a boycott of the local street railway company. "For the first time in their lives," she recalled, "the white people of Memphis had seen earnest, united action by Negroes which upset economic and business conditions." But she flayed black leaders for fattening themselves on federal patronage "when the race is being burnt, shot and hanged." On May 21, 1892, ten weeks after the deaths of Moss, McDowell and Stewart, the *Free Speech* published an unsigned editorial that denounced lynching as plain murder. "Nobody in this section of the country believes the old thread-bare lie that Negro men rape white women." Throwing caution to the wind, Wells added that "If Southern white men are not careful they will over-reach themselves and . . . a conclusion will then be reached which will be very damaging to the moral reputation of their women."

Furious whites condemned Wells's "obscene intimations" against the honor of white women. Southern white men would not put up with "such loathsome and repulsive calumnies," warned the *Memphis Daily Commercial.* The *Evening Scimitar* called for the author of the *Free Speech* editorial (assumed to be a man) to be tied to a stake, branded on the forehead, and castrated. Fortuitously, Wells was journeying to New York when these incitements to lynching appeared. Her business partner fled Memphis; Wells never returned there. The *Free Speech* ceased to exist.

In her posthumously published autobiography, Wells explained how the murder of Moss, McDowell, and Stewart had clarified her thinking about lynching. "Like many another person who had read of lynching in the South, I had accepted the idea . . . that although lynching was irregular and contrary to law and order, unreasoning anger over the terrible crime of rape led to the lynching; that perhaps the brute deserved death anyhow and the mob was justified in taking his life." But here were three lynchings that stemmed from the determination of a white grocer to destroy his black business rivals. Rape had nothing to do with it. Spurred to investigate the circumstances of other lynchings, she "stumbled on to the amazing record" that whites had charged rape upon the discovery of voluntary relationships between white women and black men. She concluded that the true purpose of lynching was to "get rid of Negroes who were acquiring wealth and property and thus keep the race terrorized."[17]

Wells continued her attack on lynching in the pages of the *New York Age,* edited by T. Thomas Fortune. In column after angry column, Wells described the murders that took the lives of "three of the best specimens of young since-the-war Afro-American manhood . . . peaceful, law-abiding citizens and energetic business men." She then sought to demolish the standard white defense of lynching, recounting case after case in which rape had been alleged, but which actually had nothing to do with rape. "White men lynch the offending Afro-American," she asserted, "not because he is a despoiler of virtue, but because he succumbs to the wiles of white women." Citing white women whose relationships with black men were uncovered—sometimes by the birth of a mulatto child—Wells claimed "there are thousands of such cases throughout the South." But for antimiscegenation laws, "many" white women would marry black men. In 1895 she published *A Red Record,* a compilation of lynchings over a three-year period, in which she demonstrated that less than a third of black victims of lynching were accused of rape. Even those accusations, she argued, were mostly fictitious.[18]

Wells also took to the lecture circuit. A quiet-spoken but powerful speaker (she had once paid for elocution lessons) she took her antilynching message to Boston, Philadelphia, Washington, and several smaller cities in the Northeast. But she was preaching to the converted; she was failing to get her message across to white Northerners because white newspapers generally ignored her. In 1893, however, Wells was invited to Great Britain by two Scottish reformers, Isabelle Fyvie Mayo and Catherine Impey. She jumped at the chance to arouse British public opinion.

During two speaking tours of England and Scotland in 1893 and 1894, Wells met clergymen, members of Parliament, newspaper editors, trade union leaders, and reformers of all stripes. Her lectures—during her 1894 tour she gave over one hundred—had a profound impact on British audiences, and they were widely reported in the British press. "The American citizen in the South is at heart more a barbarian than the negro whom he regards as a savage," the *Birmingham Daily Gazette* stated. "Lynch law is fiendishly resorted to as a kind of sport." Praising Wells's "quiet, refined manner" and her "intelligence and earnestness," the *Manchester Guardian*, the beacon of British liberalism, found her to be a "powerful and convincing advocate." Influential people were moved to take action. Her first tour prompted Mayo and Impey to organize the Society for the Recognition of the Brotherhood of Man. The 1894 tour spurred the formation of a more weighty body, the Anti-Lynching Committee, headed by Sir John Gorst, also a member of Parliament. British criticism of American barbarity provoked the predictable countercharge of hypocrisy. Nonetheless, it profoundly embarrassed the United States.[19]

THE BLACK CLUBWOMEN'S MOVEMENT

Wells's most important allies in America were other black women. In the 1890s, women's clubs, black and white, emerged as influential national movements. White women's clubs, often based on alumni groups, were first organized in the late 1860s. Starting life as literary societies, over the following decades they broadened their activities, doing charity work, advocating temperance, improving sanitary conditions in towns and cities, attacking prostitution, fighting "boss rule," opposing child labor, and extolling the ideal of motherhood. In 1890, white clubwomen established the General Federation of Women's Clubs to promote national unity and enhance their influence. Black women's clubs emerged later in the 1890s, and their activities to some extent paralleled those of the white clubs. In 1896 they also banded together, forming the National Association of Colored Women (NACW). By 1900 the NACW boasted 18,000 members in 300 local clubs.

Despite the similarities, however, there were important differences between white and black clubwomen. For one thing, black clubwomen were acutely aware that they labored under a double burden of sex discrimination and race discrimination. As Fannie Barrier Williams of Chicago put it, "Colored

women have been . . , the most ill-favored class of women in the country."
Hence, although they sought to carve out a sphere of autonomous female activity, they did not separate their status as women from their status as blacks:
the struggle for racial equality was an ever-present priority. Thus the
NACW's founding platform included the goal "To secure and enforce civil
and political rights for ourselves and our group."

Second, while black clubwomen were, like their white counterparts, overwhelmingly middle class, the flatter class structure of the black community
meant that the black middle class was not only less secure than the white middle class, but it was also far less removed from the poor. While black clubwomen valued middle-class respectability, they understood that they would
sink or swim according to how the race as a whole fared. Self-interest, not al-
truism alone, prompted their concern with the masses. According to
Williams, "The club movement among colored women reaches into the sub-
social condition of the entire race. . . . It is the force of a new intelligence
against the old ignorance . . . [t]he struggle of an enlightened conscience
against the . . . social miseries born out of the stress and pain of a hated past."
The slogan adopted by the NACW encapsulated its lofty but inclusive vision:
"Lifting As We Climb."[20]

Ida B. Wells not only found a keen audience among black women in the
North, but she also played an important role in the birth of the clubwomen's
movement itself. A testimonial dinner in New York City, organized by Victoria Earle Matthews, a colleague of Wells's on the *New York Age,* and Maritcha
Lyons, a Brooklyn schoolteacher, launched Wells's lecturing career and led to
the founding of the Women's Loyal Union. Antilynching meetings in Boston,
New Haven, Chicago, and elsewhere also provided the initial impetus for the
formation of black women's clubs. The clubs then sustained Wells's antilynching work by organizing public meetings, arranging speaking tours, and
raising money to finance the publication of her *New York Age* articles in pamphlet form, entitled *Southern Horrors: Lynch Law in All Its Phases.*

Black clubwomen took to heart Wells's attack on lynching, echoing her denial that rape was either a cause or justification. Indeed, Wells's agitation was
an indirect cause of the NACW's birth. In raising the subject of interracial sex
in such a frank manner, Wells challenged the white stereotype of the de-
praved, lubricious Negro. Some white Southerners hit back by slandering
Wells's character and reiterating the notion that black women were sexually
promiscuous. In 1895, reacting to British criticism of lynching, the president
of the Missouri Press Association, John W. Jacks, asserted that "The Negroes
in this country are wholly devoid of morality. . . . The women are prostitutes
and all are natural liars and thieves. Out of 200 in this vicinity it is doubtful if

there are a dozen virtuous women of that number who are not daily thieving from the white women."

The article evoked outrage among black clubwomen, who called a national conference in Boston that paved the way for the NACW. Jacks's slur, of course, was merely the occasion for this initiative, not its cause. Nevertheless, a determination to refute racist stereotypes of black women—and to help blacks "strive for a higher standard of social purity" and make their homes "shrines of all the domestic virtues"—furnished the clubwomen with much of their drive.[21]

Black women had long been involved in organized self-help. The black churches depended heavily upon women, who not only made up most of the worshippers but also sustained the churches' social activities. After the Civil War women formed church-based benevolent organizations, as well as mutual benefit societies, and secret societies (female counterparts of the Masonic lodges and fraternal orders). Such groups furnished medical treatment for the sick and provided members with a respectable funeral; some engaged in business activities such as buying real estate, operating printing presses, and organizing savings banks. Black women also cooperated with white women's organizations such as the Women's Christian Temperance Union (WCTU)—the largest voluntary organization in America—and the fast-growing Young Women's Christian Association.

The NACW built upon these traditions, but also represented something new. It expressed, more than earlier self-help groups, the aspirations of a middle class that was better educated and more confident. It was also a bold assertion of female autonomy—a claim to the moral leadership of the black community. Clubwomen argued that a people could rise no higher than its womanhood, and that women, in fact, molded the generations as mothers and wives. "The Negro woman has been the motive power in whatever has been accomplished by the race," claimed Addie Hunton Williams of Chicago. Most clubwomen would also thoroughly endorse the bold statement of Iowa's Gertrude Calvert: "It is to the Afro-American women that the world looks for the solution of the race problem."[22]

Part of that conviction stemmed from the belief that men were talkers rather than doers. It also implied dissatisfaction with black ministers. Although clubwomen were invariably religious, they complained that far too many ministers were shallow, ignorant, immoral, and ineffective as leaders. Ida B. Wells, as editor of the *Memphis Free Speech,* had once printed a story about a minister who had bedded one of his church members, only to be caught by a returning husband, who "ran him out of the house in his night clothes." When the ministers' alliance threatened to boycott her newspaper, she published the names of all the preachers in the group and charged them with condoning immoral behavior. According to historian Deborah Gray White, "few NACW leaders had good things to say about preachers, especially rural itinerants." Often the women belonged to smaller, more middle-class denominations, where educated ministers preached logical sermons and conducted sedate services. They recoiled against the emotionalism, even hysteria, of lower-class worship, and deplored the theatrical excesses of the typical "shouting" sermon. Above all, clubwomen criticized ministers for exploiting the poor instead of helping them and, by focusing on heaven and hell, encouraging blacks to accept their lot on earth.[23]

Black clubwomen prided themselves as people who made a real difference to their communities. Indeed, the scope of their activities was immense. They founded schools, orphanages, clinics, hospitals, homes for the elderly, hostels for single women, and reformatories for young delinquents. They ran kindergartens, organized Mother's Clubs, and mounted public health campaigns. They petitioned white authorities to suppress bars and brothels; they campaigned for them to provide schools, playgrounds, paved streets, and police protection.[24]

Clearly, the work of the NACW reflected the reforming impulses of the Progressive Era. Yet black clubwomen were also providing leadership of particular importance in the black community, a role rather different from that of their white counterparts. Disfranchisement abolished black politicians and reduced black men to the same level of political powerlessness as that of black women. Women, however, were now better organized than men, having created extensive social networks outside the political sphere. Moreover, whites tended to regard black women as less threatening than black men; thus women often became the principal agents of communication and cooperation between the two communities. Black women became "spokespeople for and motivators of black citizens," writes historian Glenda Gilmore, and the "deep camouflage of their leadership style—their womanhood—helped them remain invisible as they worked toward political ends."[25]

The black clubwomen's movement, however, failed to arrest the decline in the status of the South's black population. That was simply beyond its power. Although the NACW routinely denounced lynching, disfranchisement, the convict-lease system, and other oppressions, it lacked the means to oppose them effectively. Disinclined to content itself with angry rhetoric and the passage of resolutions, the NACW focused its energies on uplift rather than protest. Yet despite the wide-ranging nature of their activities, black clubwomen commanded too little political influence and mustered too few financial resources to effect much overall improvement in the lives of the poor.

The clubwomen's movement also betrayed internal weaknesses. Although its membership reached 50,000 by 1915, it did not attempt to become a mass movement. For one thing, concern for middle-class respectability encouraged black clubwomen to look down upon the lower classes. They thoroughly disapproved of such pursuits as gambling, drinking, and sensual dancing; clubwomen preferred to listen to Beethoven, read Shakespeare, discuss Socrates, and study the Bible. Prizing chastity, they frowned upon the common-law marriages of the poorer classes. Their moral intolerance can be inferred from the minutes of a typical meeting of Atlanta's Neighborhood Union: "Mrs. Barnett succeeded in getting two families out of her district who indulged in doing things that were immoral such as breaking the Sabbath and gambling." As Deborah Gray White has noted, their moral orthodoxy was "bound to drive a wedge between themselves and the masses of black women."[26]

Failing to recruit beyond its middle-class base, the clubwomen's movement lost much of its crusading zeal, and its members frittered away more of their energies on social climbing and internal politics. Class snobbery became rampant as clubwomen competed with each other to display the best clothes, attend the most fashionable social events, and join the most favored cliques. Elections to official posts—especially the biggest plum, the presidency of the NACW—aroused bitter faction fights and venomous personal rivalries. The election of 1899, in which Mary Church Terrell won a second term as NACW president, proved especially contentious: it created resentments that festered for decades.[27]

IDA B. WELLS AND THE DECLINE OF LYNCHING

Wells faced the agonizing choice that confronted nearly all educated women of the time: to work or to marry. Feminist Susan B. Anthony tried to dissuade her from marriage, pointing out that she possessed a "special call for special work." Yet Wells was discouraged by what she saw as a lack of support from other blacks, and tired of the innuendoes that her status as a single women generated. In 1895 she married Ferdinand L. Barnett, a lawyer and newspaper publisher in Chicago. It was a happy choice, for Barnett shared her passion for politics, protest, and racial uplift, and encouraged Wells—now calling herself Wells-Barnett—to continue her public activities. With a baby on her arm, she attended the founding meeting of the NACW. In 1898, as part of a delegation from Chicago, she pleaded with President McKinley to punish the lynchers of Frazier Baker, a postmaster in Lake City, South Carolina, and to indemnify the victim's family. She also urged that lynching be made a federal crime. In 1899 she became secretary of the Afro-American Council (a revival of Fortune's Afro-American League), which condemned McKinley's silence and reiterated the demand for an antilynching law.

A combative, outspoken woman, Ida B. Wells did not hesitate to denounce the high and the mighty if they failed to oppose lynching. Her targets included the sainted Frances Willard, leader of the Women's Christian Temperance Union, and Dwight L. Moody, the internationally acclaimed evangelist. However, her outspokenness accompanied a sensitive personality; she offended others easily, but was herself easily offended. Wells consequently found it difficult to work in groups, especially alongside other strong-willed women. Her commitment to raising a family—she bore four children—and her prickly personality combined to limit her influence within the NACW, the Afro-American Council, and other organizations. As the years went by, Wells became increasingly bitter over what she perceived as slights, insults, and lack of recognition.[28]

Still, Wells made an enormous contribution to the modern civil rights struggle. Her most recent biographer, Linda McMurry, notes that "Wells was not the first to expose rape as a mythical cause of mob action, but she soon became the loudest and most persistent voice for truth." According to historian Allan H. Spear, Wells was "militant long before militancy found a national spokesman." She pioneered a brand of protest—unequivocal, outspoken, determined—that anticipated the NAACP.[29]

Did her campaign against lynching achieve anything? It may be no more than coincidence that lynchings declined in number after 1892, the very time that Wells began her campaign. Historians of lynching are loath to attribute that decline to Wells's agitation. They agree that lynching remained endemic in the South for many decades, and point out that even as the yearly lynching totals diminished, lynch mobs were often bigger, more brazen, and more sadistic. Moreover, white politicians continued to defend lynching as a necessary response to black rapists. Well into the twentieth century, lynching remained an elaborate public ritual, an act that celebrated white solidarity and perpetuated an image of black bestiality. As historian Vincent Vinikas has written, "lynchings were essentially state sanctioned events."[30]

The causes of lynching's gradual decline were complex. Yet Wells's activities did have an effect. Her two tours of Britain aroused enormous interest and controversy. By taking Wells seriously and according her respect, British public opinion compelled white Americans to confront her antilynching message. Newspapers that had once ignored her now responded to her British crusade. Northern newspapers, writes historian Gail Bederman, "stopped treating lynching as a colorful Southern folkway. They dropped their jokey tone and piously condemned lynching as 'barbarous.' " Even Southern newspapers, many of which had defended lynching with shocking irresponsibility, were put on the defensive. A growing number of Southern editors now denounced it.[31]

Although white leaders in Memphis regularly attacked Wells, their actions paid tribute to her effectiveness. After six blacks were lynched in 1894, "businessmen called a public meeting in the Merchants Exchange, where they adopted resolutions censuring the 'wicked, fiendish and inexcusable massacre.'" A grand jury expressed horror over the murders and indicted thirteen white men. The *Memphis Commercial Appeal* demanded punishment for the crime. Alas, the lynchers went free. However, no further lynchings took place in Memphis until 1917, and that turned out to be the last.

Elsewhere in the South, white opposition to lynching also grew. Some politicians, like Governor Jeff Davis of Arkansas, continued to appeal to the basest racism, virtually encouraging racial murder. Yet in Kentucky, Virginia, and other states, governors took forceful actions to protect black prisoners and curb mob violence. When black migration during World War I threatened employers with the loss of their labor force, more white leaders joined the antilynching cause. Support for lynching became the exception rather than the rule. While the forces behind lynching's decline were far bigger than Wells, the verdict of historian David M. Tucker is sound: "In the long struggle against lynching, Ida B. Wells deserves more credit than any other individual for having brought this practice before the eyes of the world and, in so doing, having accelerated the establishment of law and decency in the American South."[32]

The fact that Wells was forced to conduct her antilynching campaign in the North, however, underlined the damaging impact of white repression upon Southern black leadership. By the 1890s the South was becoming intolerant of militant agitation by blacks. The new racial order of white supremacy encouraged, and even demanded, a more subservient attitude. In 1895, the year of Frederick Douglass's death and Ida B. Wells's marriage, a black college president from Alabama delivered a speech that crystallized the growing trend toward accommodationism. In what came to be known as the Atlanta Compromise, Booker T. Washington urged blacks to abandon agitation, forget about politics, trust white Southerners, and "dignify and glorify common labor." He won national acclaim, from whites and blacks alike, as the new leader of his race.

Booker T. Washington, circa 1910

Library of Congress, Prints and Photographs Division,
Booker T. Washington Collection

3

Booker T. Washington and the
Strategy of Accommodation

Born in a squalid cabin in Virginia in 1856, the son of a white man whose identity he never knew, Booker Taliaferro Washington was a legendary American success story: his autobiography, *Up from Slavery,* has never been out of print. Through sheer ability and force of character, Washington lifted himself from the depths of bondage to the pinnacle of world fame. A living refutation of America's degrading image of black people, he created Tuskegee Institute, a black school in Alabama that symbolized the achievement and potential of his race. In addition, his unflagging efforts to mend the rift between black and white earned him the reputation of statesman as well as educator. Between 1895, the date of his famous speech to the Atlanta Cotton States and Industrial Exposition, and 1915, the year of his death, Washington was the most powerful black leader in America.

In his Atlanta Exposition address, Washington proposed a new settlement between the races in the South. Economic cooperation, he argued, should supersede political conflict. He asked for just treatment from white Southerners and offered two concessions on behalf of his fellow blacks.

Washington's first concession was the admission that Radical Reconstruction had been a mistake. Blacks had started freedom "at the top instead of at the bottom," devoting too much energy to politics and neglecting the skills and habits of industry that would enable them to earn a decent living. The second concession to white opinion was an assurance that blacks were not at all interested in "social equality." What social equality meant was not clear, but it obviously included intermarriage and sexual relations, and many whites read it as a general endorsement of racial segregation. .

Having verbally eliminated the basic causes of racial antagonism—apart from racism itself, to which he referred in only the most oblique terms—Washington put forward a positive program for economic cooperation. He urged blacks to stay in the South, concentrate on working hard rather than agitating for their rights, and cultivate "friendly relations with the Southern white man." Whites, for their part, should regard blacks as an economic asset rather than a political threat, according them fair treatment as loyal workers. If whites treated blacks justly instead of oppressing them, Washington promised, "we shall stand by you with a devotion that no foreigner can match." If blacks and whites worked together, while at the same time acknowledging each other's racial integrity, the South's economic prosperity would be assured, and both races would share in it. "In all things that are purely social we can be as separate as the fingers, yet as one hand in all things essential to mutual progress."[1]

Hailed by both races as an expression of farsighted wisdom, Washington's "Atlanta Compromise" marked the beginning of a new era in race relations. However, as the nineteenth century gave way to the twentieth, and the oppression of black people did not abate, Washington became the object of bitter censure by a small but influential black minority. The Atlanta Compromise, these critics charged, was not a compromise at all: blacks made all the concessions and whites gave nothing in return. Indeed, because the Atlanta Compromise appeared to usher in the consolidation of white supremacy, some charged that Washington had betrayed the Negro race to its enemies.

That judgment was far too harsh. Whatever his limitations, Washington struggled with great energy and integrity to keep alive the ideal of racial equality at a time when blacks were being subjected to the most intensive ideological assault on their humanity that they had ever experienced. His persistent and largely futile campaign to persuade whites to spell "Negro" with a capital "N" typified his insistence that black people deserved respect. So did his refusal, when he controlled the *New York Age,* to carry advertisements for hair straighteners and skin lighteners. However much Washington compromised in politics, he never conceded the arguments of white racists.

Although some white Southerners heaped praise upon Washington, others suspected that he was a Trojan Horse for racial equality. Many were outraged when Washington dined with President Theodore Roosevelt at the White House in 1901. The incident betrayed Washington's "deep down antipathy to white supremacy," complained an Arkansas schools superintendent. "Afar off he sees a vision of equality," warned Ben Tillman of South Carolina.

"The action of President Roosevelt in entertaining that nigger will necessitate our killing a thousand niggers in the South before they will learn their place again."[2]

Such comments contained a basic insight. Washington's ethic of hard work, self-improvement, and Christian morality may strike us as apolitical and excessively individualistic, yet those very virtues, Washington believed, would "give the lie to the assertion of his enemies North and South that the Negro is the inferior of the white man." The average Negro child, he insisted, was the intellectual equal of the average white child. In his autobiography Washington struck a note of almost defiant moral superiority:

> From any point of view, I had rather be what I am, a member of the Negro race, than be able to claim membership with the most favoured of any other race. I have always been made sad when I have heard members of any race claiming rights and privileges . . . on the ground simply that they were members of this or that race, regardless of their own individual worth or attainments. . . . Every persecuted individual and race should get much consolation out of the great human law, which is universal and eternal, that merit, no matter under what skin found, is, in the long run, recognized and rewarded. This I have said here, not to call attention to myself as an individual, but to the race to which I am proud to belong.

Washington's own attainments defied the conventional wisdom that black people were inherently inferior.[3]

WASHINGTON AND BLACK EDUCATION

Washington's fame, as well as his strategy for black progress, rested upon Tuskegee Institute and the idea it represented. Tuskegee Institute was an impressive achievement. Arriving in Alabama in 1881, Washington transformed a few tumble-down shacks in an Alabama field into a gleaming school of solid red brick (the bricks were fired by the students themselves in Tuskegee's own kiln). A tireless fundraiser who spent several months each year on the road cultivating Northern benefactors, he built up a $2 million endowment and acquired thousands of acres of land for the school.

Tuskegee Institute was staffed and administered entirely by black people: Washington insisted upon it. "I knew that . . . we were trying an experiment—that of testing whether or not it was possible for Negroes to build up and control the affairs of a large educational institution." In creating a black-run school, Washington made a statement about racial equality that was far more powerful than words. "Tuskegee alone is the fruit of a black man's heart and brain and effort and administrative skill," wrote Roscoe Conkling Bruce, one of its teachers. "Tuskegee Institute is . . . proof of the black man's capacity for the tasks of civilization." Washington made Tuskegee Institute the most famous Negro school in the world. To black people in America, and to black Africans and West Indians as well, Tuskegee was a proud symbol of what their race could achieve. It was a beacon of hope.[4]

Tuskegee was more than a school: it also represented a philosophy of racial progress through education. The "Tuskegee Idea" was this: The vast majority of blacks were not going to better their position by means of politics, protest, or higher learning. Their salvation lay in mastering basic work skills and applying them, with honest sweat, to the demands of the South's agricultural economy. Four-fifths of the South's black population lived in the rural areas; most of them farmed white-owned land as renters or sharecroppers. Whatever their hardships and problems, therefore, blacks in the South began life with one inestimable advantage: Whites needed their labor. Building upon this foundation, they would be able to pull themselves up by their own bootstraps. Washington envisaged them becoming landowners, artisans, and small businessmen.

In stressing the economic opportunities available to blacks who worked hard and possessed the right skills, Washington persistently downplayed white racism. Yes, he told a New York audience in 1890, he knew all about lynching, ballot-box stuffing, and intimidation: the reports were "generally true." But he pointed to "an absence of prejudice against the colored man in the South in the matter of business that counts for a great deal." Blacks could utilize white self-interest as the "entering wedge" to equality. If they proved themselves to be loyal, willing, and efficient workers, if they made themselves indispensable to the Southern economy, whites would respect them and treat them fairly. Blacks would erode white prejudice just as the action of water makes rough stones smooth. In time, whites would willingly accord them full citizenship rights, including the right to vote.[5]

"Industrial education," Washington believed, would best prepare blacks for surviving and prospering in the New South. As applied to the education of freedmen by Washington's mentor, Samuel Chapman Armstrong, the former missionary and Union general who founded Hampton Institute in Virginia, industrial education meant teaching practical skills in agriculture and the "mechanic arts" that would equip blacks to earn a living in the rural South. The regime at Hampton Institute, and later at Tuskegee Institute, required all students to perform manual labor about the school: cooking, cleaning, farming, printing, building, gardening, and so on. Such labor enabled Washington to build and maintain Tuskegee on the cheap, and helped impecunious students to work their way through school. But manual labor also served a higher moral purpose: "The students themselves would be taught to see not only utility in labour, but beauty and dignity; would be taught . . . how to lift labour up from mere drudgery and toil, and would learn to love work for its own sake." Industrial education did not train blacks to enter industry, but rather taught them to be industrious. To reinforce this character-building mission, both Hampton and Tuskegee subjected students to strict rules and military-style discipline.[6]

Hampton and Tuskegee deliberately distinguished themselves from the many colleges and universities established in the South after the Civil War by Northern churches and missionary societies. Although these institutions had done pioneering work in educating the freedmen, and had trained the first generation of Southern black teachers, they were ill-suited to the needs of the black population as a whole. In reality, the black universities were mainly elementary and secondary schools, with only a handful of students taking college-level courses. Yet, emulating the colleges of New England, they laid great stress on the classics, modern languages, and other staples of nineteenth-century higher education. Many whites, and some blacks, criticized the black universities for being pretentious and overambitious, complaining that their rarefied curriculum equipped blacks to be teachers, preachers, and politicians, but had little to offer the toiling masses. It had been folly to begin "at the apex of the educational fabric instead of at the base," wrote T. Thomas Fortune in 1884; money had been lavished on black colleges when "ordinary common schools were unknown." Blacks in the South were most in need of elementary and individual education—"preparation for the actual work of life." Hampton and Tuskegee attempted to fill that need. Pointedly, they did not teach Latin or Greek, nor did they offer degrees.[7]

A host of black critics, and generations of historians, have lamented Washington's influence over black education. Samuel Chapman Armstrong, they argue, conceived of industrial education as a means of adjusting blacks to a subordinate position in the New South. "He believed that blacks should be taught to remain in their place," writes historian Donald Spivey, to "stay out of politics, keep quiet about their rights, and work." Industrial education meant, in practice, training blacks for nothing better than low-grade, low-paid jobs, equipping them to be cooks, servants, sharecroppers, and laborers—the "hewers of wood and drawers of waters" so beloved of Southern whites. True, Hampton Institute trained its students to be teachers, not farmers or laborers; so did Tuskegee Institute. By molding black teachers, however, Armstrong attempted to mold the black masses. Booker T. Washington, his star pupil, absorbed his ideas and perpetuated them at Tuskegee, which trained further cohorts of conservative teachers. Spivey likened Washington to the black slave-driver who, "given the position of authority over his fellow slaves, worked diligently to keep intact the very system under which they both were enslaved."[8]

What angered Washington's opponents was not so much the idea of "industrial education" itself—there was widespread agreement that black children would benefit from being taught practical skills—as the fear that blacks would be denied all but the most rudimentary schooling, thereby perpetuating their second-class citizenship. Washington vigorously denied that he sought to place a ceiling upon black achievement. Yet his white supporters viewed industrial education in precisely that way, and they used Washington's ideas to justify a dual standard of education: a superior one for whites and a grossly inferior one for blacks.

Washington disclaimed any hostility to higher education for blacks, explaining simply that the great mass of the black population required elementary and secondary schooling of a practical bent. But many of Washington's white supporters spoke as if far too many blacks were receiving college training and argued that black universities were virtually useless. In reality, the black universities had fewer than 2,500 college-level students at the end of the nineteenth century; they had granted fewer than 2,000 degrees. Yet the impression took hold that black colleges were producing hordes of overeducated idlers. The Latin-quoting, cigar-smoking, top-hat-wearing black college graduate became a stock figure of fun in white eyes. In the ruthless struggle for white funding, Washington, in propagating his back-to-basics approach, was not above invoking this unflattering stereotype himself. "However variant may have been the interpretations of the meaning of industrial education," wrote the black scholar Kelly Miller, a contemporary of Washington's, "there was a general agreement to discredit the higher culture of the race."[9]

By 1900, industrial education and higher education appeared to be philosophies in conflict—waging a war for supremacy—rather than differing approaches that complemented each other. Blacks who had formerly admired Tuskegee Institute now feared that powerful whites were using industrial education as a cover for destroying the black universities. Southern white politicians forced state-funded black colleges to drop Latin and stop teaching foreign languages. "I do not believe in the higher education of the darky," stated Allan D. Candler, a former governor of Georgia, in 1901. "He should be taught the trades, but when he is taught the fine arts he gets educated above his station and it makes him unhappy." Many of the Northern businessmen who funded and directed the new philanthropic foundations agreed. The General Education Board, for example, which was financed by John D. Rockefeller, denied money to black universities and pressured teacher training schools to dilute their academic programs and institute classes in farming, sewing, and cooking. Industrial education was becoming a rigid orthodoxy that threatened to stifle higher education.[10]

At stake, many believed, was the very principle of racial equality. If industrial education, as defined by whites, prevailed, then no black person, however talented, could aspire to the same level of training that was open to the ablest whites. Without a "talented tenth" of college-educated blacks, moreover, the black masses, leaderless and directionless, would stagnate and even regress. "Despite frequent disclaimers and against his own desires," writes historian Robert Sherer, "Washington bartered off quality collegiate training for generations of black leaders for the upbuilding of Tuskegee and his own reputation."[11]

WHITE ATTITUDES TOWARD BLACK EDUCATION

Such harsh criticisms, however, ascribe far too much influence to Washington, and they fail to appreciate the depth of white opposition to black education. In the 1890s black education was in a parlous state. The South's public school system generally was undeveloped, underfunded, and in many areas nonexistent. The region was poor and rural; whites had a deep-seated reluctance to spend money on public services, and the Democrats who came to power after Radical Reconstruction slashed spending on education. A glimmer of light appeared in 1883, when Congress debated the Blair Bill, which proposed using federal funds to subsidize public schools. Because the measure envisaged allocating money to individual states according to their rate of illiteracy, the South would have benefitted more than any other region. However, the bill never passed.

The best schools for blacks, and virtually the only ones that offered education beyond the elementary level, were private academies, colleges, and universities. The many black-run private schools depended upon constant sacrifices by their teachers, never-ending fundraising appeals, and financial support from parents who could ill afford the tuition fees. Most collapsed after a few years. The schools and colleges founded by Northern churches and missionary associations enjoyed a more stable existence. However, as Republican idealism declined and interest in the South waned, Northern funds diminished. "By the turn of the century," writes James D. Anderson, "the mission societies were virtually bankrupt." Even prestigious universities like Fisk and Atlanta tottered along precariously, living hand-to-mouth.[12]

Blacks also faced white prejudice against the very concept of education for blacks. Schooling for blacks was inseparably associated in the minds of white

Southerners with Radical Reconstruction, during which, according to the newspaper editor and white supremacist Josephus Daniels, the teaching of Northern missionaries produced a "vicious attitude among some of the worst young negroes." Reconstruction was long gone, but whites resented even a portion of their taxes being expended on black children—so much so that they often refused to vote school taxes at all, thereby crippling their own children's education in denying schools to blacks. As a Louisiana school official put it, "A little learning with the negro is a dangerous thing. Why should the white race be forced to aid *a dangerous thing?*"[13]

As white politicians aggressively advocated, and then implemented, the total disfranchisement of black voters, many questioned the utility of educating blacks at all. Governor James Vardaman of Mississippi pronounced black education a failure. "The knowledge of books does not seem to produce any good substantial result with the negro, but serves to sharpen his cunning, breed hopes that cannot be fulfilled . . . creates an inclination to avoid labor, promotes indolence, and in turn leads to crime." Stripped of such sophistry, the basic objection was that educated blacks threatened to impair or undermine white supremacy. Whites did not want to equip blacks with skills that would enable them to compete with whites in the economy. They did not want blacks to circumvent disfranchisement by passing the literacy tests. Above all, ignorant blacks made the cheapest and most reliable laborers. "Educate a nigger," the saying went, "and you spoil a good field hand." Governor Hoke Smith of Georgia put the matter more elegantly but no less bluntly: "Mere instruction from books will accomplish nothing for him. . . . The best educator he can have will be found in the white man who will control and direct him.[14]

In 1895, the year that Washington's speech at the Atlanta Exposition propelled him to national prominence, most black children in the South did not attend school. Those who did walked to shacks and churches that often lacked adequate lighting, heating, toilets, washing facilities, and even basic items like desks and tables. In such schools a solitary teacher, usually a young woman with little more education than her pupils, struggled with classes of as many as seventy children spread over eight grades. To make matters worse, there loomed a real possibility that whites would reduce or even abolish the pittance that they allocated to black public schools. Whites even had the power, if they chose to use it, to cripple black private schools. In the 1890s the question was not so much what kind of education blacks were going to receive, but whether they would receive any education at all.

If black schools were to survive, Washington knew that white opposition to black education had to be neutralized. One way he tried to do this was by divorcing education from its association with Radical Reconstruction, denying that blacks regarded education as a means of challenging white political control. He also stressed that "industrial education" trained blacks to do "practical and useful" tasks, and that schooling "makes the Negro not an idler or spendthrift, but a more industrious, thrifty, lawabiding and useful citizen." Above all, Washington strove to overcome the objection that "when he is educated [the Negro] ceases to do manual labor." Students at Tuskegee, he never tired of boasting, were employed in gardening, carpentry, printing, bricklaying, sewing, laundering, housekeeping, and other down-to-earth skills. Blacks educated in this manner, he insisted, would stay in the South and contribute to the rural economy. Schooling would not induce blacks to quit farming and rob white planters of their labor force.[15]

But there was a large degree of subterfuge in Washington's use of the term "industrial education." White Southerners praised Washington in the mistaken belief that Tuskegee turned out cooks and servants. In fact, Tuskegee Institute admitted blacks who were all but illiterate and taught them to read. It then introduced them to "book learning." The ablest students proceeded to an academic program and graduated; most of them became teachers. As historian Richard Ralston has described it, Tuskegee's "complicated but effective" program "provided an almost infinite number of class levels to match up with individual abilities and preparation." Although Tuskegee did not provide higher education along the lines of Fisk or Atlanta, many of its students went on to university. "When I got to Tuskegee," recalled Alfred B. Xuma, "I found that you could be doctors, lawyers, anything you wanted to be." After leaving the Institute, Xuma qualified as a doctor and became president of the African National Congress. In short, whites wanted industrial education to keep blacks down, but Washington used it to raise them up. His aim, concluded biographer Louis Harlan, was to create "small independent businessmen, farmers, and teachers rather than wage-earners or servants of white employers."[16]

A vague, ambiguous concept, industrial education could mean all things to all men. Southern whites assumed that it meant providing blacks with separate and inferior schools, a watered-down curriculum, and training in only the most rudimentary skills. Washington let them believe that. "The white race saddles its own notions and feelings upon him," Kelly Miller noted, "and yet he opens not his mouth." Washington, however, pointed to the "two hundred years' schooling in prejudice . . . which the ex-slaveholders are called upon to conquer." Industrial education, he reasoned, "kills two birds with one stone: it secures the cooperation of the whites, and does the best possible thing for the black man."[17]

The progressive white Southerners whom Washington cultivated believed, almost to a man, that black schools should be separate and unequal. John

Herbert Phillips, for example, the superintendent of schools in Birmingham, Alabama, was widely respected as one of the best school officials in the South. Yet Phillips believed that the "negro brain" stopped developing after puberty, and that education was largely wasted on blacks after the ages of 12–14. "The industrial methods of Hampton and Tuskegee must be extended downwards," he argued, "and applied to the masses in the elementary schools." To Phillips, industrial education for black children meant the study of hygiene, home sanitation, domestic science, woodworking, gardening, and stock-raising; "the subjects of the academic course should be simplified." Yet in practice Phillips went beyond his own racial theories in supporting black education. For example, he backed the establishment of a black high school at a time when most whites frowned upon secondary education for blacks. Through the herculean efforts of its principal, Arthur Harold Parker, Birmingham Industrial High School evolved into one of the best black public schools in the South.[18]

WASHINGTON AND NORTHERN PHILANTHROPY

Tuskegee Institute was founded as a state-supported "normal school" (teacher-training school) after Lewis Adams, a former slave and local Republican leader, agreed to support two white Democrats, Colonel Wilbur F. Foster and Arthur L. Brooks, in the election for state legislature. The Democrats won handily, receiving substantial black support. In 1881 they repaid their debt to Adams by persuading the legislature to charter Tuskegee Institute and give it an annual appropriation of $2,000. All over the South, blacks were striking similar deals with Democratic opponents.

As blacks lost political influence, however, state funding became increasingly precarious. For all his talk about Southern whites being the "best friends" of the Negro, therefore, Washington looked North to augment Tuskegee's income and place its finances upon a stable basis.

His annual summer fundraising trips at first took him mainly to Boston and New England, the former heartland of the abolitionist movement. Over the years, however, he spent more and more time in New York, the nerve center of industrial America. Industrial capitalism was generating fabulous profits; moreover, despite the size and complexity of the new corporations, control was concentrated in relatively few hands. The freebooting capitalists who bestrode the business behemoths formed a new aristocracy. They were wealthy beyond imagination, and some of them, from a variety of motives, wished to help good causes. Washington secured thousands, then tens of thousands, and ultimately millions of dollars from the likes of Collis P. Huntington, master of the Central Pacific Railroad; William H. Baldwin, director of the Southern Railway; Andrew Carnegie, retired colossus of the steel industry; and Henry H. Rogers, the Standard Oil magnate. The support of these capitalists enabled Washington to abolish Tuskegee Institute's financial dependence on the state of Alabama, establishing an autonomous power base that made him the most influential black educator in the South.[19]

Yet the new industrial philanthropists were far less sympathetic toward blacks than the churches and missionary societies had been. They regarded Radical Reconstruction as a mistake, doubted that blacks had the same innate intelligence as whites, were skeptical about the value of higher education, and had little interest in supporting black claims to equality. Hardheaded businessmen, they contrasted their own "practical" approach to the race question with the "sentimental suggestions of theorists." In practice, these Northern benefactors accepted the white South's insistence that racial segregation, accompanied by disfranchisement, was the only workable solution to Dixie's race problem, and that blacks should continue to make up an economic substratum of farmers, laborers, and domestic servants.[20]

William H. Baldwin's blunt description of the black's correct status summed up the views of the new philanthropy:

Properly directed he is the best possible laborer to meet the climatic conditions of the South. He will willingly fill the more menial positions, and do the heavy work, at less wages than the American white man or any foreign race which has yet come to our shores. This will permit the Southern white laborer to perform the more expert labor, and to leave the fields, the mines, and simpler trades for the negro.

To Southern blacks, Baldwin advised:

Avoid social questions; leave politics alone; continue to be patient; live moral lives; live simply . . . learn that it is a mistake to be educated out of your necessary environment; know that it is a crime for any teacher, white or black, to educate the negro for positions which are not open to him.

Such views were in complete accord with those of the South's white supremacists.[21]

Here was Washington's great dilemma. By loosening the pursestrings of Northern philanthropists he could rightly claim to be helping black schools in the South. But if these philanthropists endorsed white supremacy, and supported industrial education to perpetuate the economic subordination of blacks, then their dollars came in a poisoned chalice. Education for second-class citizenship was, in the eyes of some blacks at the time—and in the opinion of many historians since—no education at all. Washington's alliance with Northern philanthropists and Southern whites was a Faustian pact: they used him more than he used them. In Louis Harlan's damning verdict, "By the white men's indirect rule, he was 'the king of a captive people.'"[22]

The most telling evidence that Washington failed to improve the level of black education was the widening disparity between black and white schools. Despite white philanthropy, and despite the commitment of Southern progressives to the cause of public education, black schools stagnated while white schools underwent dramatic improvement.

Before 1900, white schools in the South had been so poor that they often resembled black schools; public spending was so low that it hardly permitted gross discrimination. As Harlan put it, "Whites and blacks shared scholastic poverty relatively equally." Moreover, blacks successfully resisted proposals to divide school tax revenues according to race—many whites reasoning that they would be massively subsidizing black schools, and that blacks would be incapable of supporting them by themselves. After 1900, however, as spending on public schools massively increased, so did racial discrimination. In North Carolina, for example, blacks comprised 34 percent of the school-age population in 1900 and received 28 percent of the school funds. By 1915 their share of school funds had fallen to 13 percent. In South Carolina, for every dollar spent on a black child in 1900, a white child received $5.75; in 1915 that white child received *twelve times* as much as the black child. In 1901, a white teacher in Mississippi was paid about 50 percent more than a black teacher; in 1910 that white teacher received double.[23]

The disfranchisement of black voters facilitated and encouraged such discrimination. So did the policies of the Northern philanthropists. To Washington's immense disappointment, the Southern Education Board (SEB), organized in 1901 and funded by John D. Rockefeller's General Education Board (GEB), decided to promote white public schools, not black. Frightened by the strength of Southern racism, the SEB feared that whites might refuse to back its crusade for public schools if they emphasized black schools "too much." It then decided to ignore black schools altogether, reasoning that, in the words of Charles W. Dabney, president of the University of Tennessee, "the superior, the dominant part of this society, must be educated first before they could possibly be induced and made able to do their duty to the less fortunate race." Thus black public schools languished while tens of millions of dollars were spent on new schoolhouses for white children. Between 1902 and 1909 John D. Rockefeller gave $58 million to the GEB to be spent, on the advice of the Southern Education Board, on the South's schools and universities. Virtually none of it benefitted black education.[24]

The education movement of the 1900s was, in effect, an alliance of Northern philanthropists and Southern white progressives from which blacks were excluded. Indeed, Washington suffered the personal humiliation of being paid a salary by the Southern Education Board as one of its "agents," but being banished, as a black man, from the SEB's meetings. He complained about his exclusion. He protested that nothing was being done for black schools. But the white bureaucrats of the SEB and the GEB—who formed an interlocking directorate—fobbed him off with excuses. Washington did not so much shape the policies of the Northern philanthropic foundations as acquiesce in them. Blacks were getting the crumbs from the table.[25]

Yet Washington's patience enabled him to acquire influence. His intimate knowledge of the white power structure, including the vanities, prejudices, and foibles of the ruling class, eventually translated into tangible benefits for black education. When the GEB excluded blacks from its largesse, he sought help elsewhere. By courting the charitably inclined nouveau riche, Washington attracted money not only to Tuskegee but also to other schools and colleges. Through Washington, Henry H. Rogers subsidized dozens of black schools. Through Washington, Andrew Carnegie helped "practically the whole list of black colleges and universities."[26]

Washington's crowning achievement was to interest Julius Rosenwald, a Jewish businessman who made his fortune running the Chicago-based Sears, Roebuck mail-order firm, in the improvement of black public schools in the South. The Rosenwald school-building program started in 1912 as a modest pilot project in Macon County, Alabama. Under Washington's supervision, the money donated by Rosenwald, matched by money raised locally by blacks themselves, built half a dozen one-room schoolhouses. In 1914 Washington persuaded Rosenwald to subsidize a further 100 schoolhouses in Alabama. By 1932, seventeen years after Washington's death, the Rosenwald Fund had subsidized the construction of 5,358 black schools to the tune of $22 million. Washington's biographer, Louis Harlan, concluded that in building up Tuskegee, Washington also directly helped the broader cause of black education. "In a skillful and broad-gauged way he brought the money of the philanthropists into conjunction with the areas of need at every level of black education."[27]

THE RISE OF OPPOSITION TO WASHINGTON

If Washington gave black Southerners a strategy for survival, self-respect, and individual self-improvement, he devised no realistic strategy for breaking the chains of racism and poverty that shackled the great mass of black people.

He insisted that industrial education, wedded to sobriety and thrift, and assisted by white good will, would eventually solve the race problem. It was a simplistic belief. Education was a necessary but hardly sufficient condition for black progress. Moreover, the widening gap between black and white schools offset many of the educational gains secured by Washington and other black educators.

Although a small black middle class of businessmen, teachers, and professionals prospered under Jim Crow, economic progress eluded the great majority. Most black farmers failed to realize the dream of landownership; sharecropping screwed down their living standards to levels of unimaginable wretchedness. In the towns and cities blacks were barred from many trades and industries, excluded from white-collar jobs, and banned from entire sectors of the urban economy. Most black city-dwellers earned less than a dollar a day working as menial laborers or domestic servants. Washington placed too much faith in the capacity of Southern whites for fair play. The people he described as the "best friends" of the Negro had no intention of facilitating black economic progress. Whites wanted cheap, obedient labor, and plenty of it.

The gains blacks made through education and self-help could not compensate for Jim Crow laws, disfranchisement, lynching, employment discrimination, and manifold other oppressions. After 1900, Washington's talk of racial progress rang increasingly hollow. Indeed, the thing that infuriated his critics most of all was Washington's dogged insistence that things were actually getting better for blacks. With his extraordinary patience, perpetual optimism, and willingness to endure insults, he appeared to be explaining away the South's racism. "I worry over your unconscious habit of apologizing for the shortcomings of white men," scolded T. Thomas Fortune.[28]

Two facts, in particular, damaged black confidence in Washington's policy of conciliating the white South. One was his endorsement of educational and property qualifications for voting, with the proviso that these restrictions "apply with equal and exact justice to both races." Given the avowed intention of white proponents of disfranchisement that blacks, not whites, be the targets of these new qualifications, Washington's position was untenable. To nobody's great surprise, literacy tests were applied with great prejudice, practically wiping out the black vote. The persistence of lynching also damaged Washington's influence. It not only contradicted his contention that Southern whites could be relied upon to protect blacks, but it also exposed him to the further criticism that he failed to denounce lynching with sufficient passion. After the gruesome public burning of Sam Hose in Newnan, Georgia, in 1899, Washington refused to comment: "I feel constrained to keep silent and not engage in any controversy that might react on the work to which I am now lending my efforts." Although Washington's condemnations of lynching became increasingly forthright as the years passed, they always appeared reluctant. There was a time and a place for righteous anger, but Washington declined to express it.[29]

By 1899 Washington's contacts in the North warned of a definite rise in hostility toward the "Wizard of Tuskegee." The editor of the *Boston Transcript* was shocked to hear Washington's name "hissed" at a black meeting in Boston. Samuel Laing Williams, Washington's loyal supporter in Chicago, reported that "Some of the colored folks seem to be quite stirred up by what they seem to think is a surrender on your part to all the meaner forces in the South." In the nation's capital some 1,500 blacks heard a visiting speaker condemn Washington as a "sham and a traitor." The audience was receptive.[30]

Frustrated by Washington's refusal to take the lead, many blacks, and some whites, yearned for a new movement that would vigorously oppose disfranchisement and lynching. "The time is drawing near," wrote John Milholland, a wealthy white industrialist and fervent equal rights advocate, "when these rose water methods of dealing with a dangerous situation will be . . . relegated to their proper place, because the majority of the people of this country still believe that the Constitution of this country means something and its provisions are operative south of the Mason and Dixon line." Other critics, impatient with words, were more direct and even reckless in their opposition. When Washington addressed a meeting at Boston's Zion AME church in July 1903, a group of black men tried to shout him down. In the ensuing fracas, five people were arrested. One of them was a Harvard graduate called William Monroe Trotter, who for two years had edited the *Boston Guardian,* the most vehemently anti-Washington organ among the nation's approximately two hundred black newspapers.[31]

For a time Washington could neutralize his out-and-out critics, who were relatively few, through clever politicking and astute string-pulling. But the opposition could not be contained for long. In July 1905, twenty-nine blacks, most of them college-educated professionals—teachers, doctors, lawyers, journalists—met on the Canadian side of Niagara Falls to encourage "organized, determined and aggressive action on the part of men who believe in Negro freedom and growth." The twenty-nine, all men, were led by Trotter and W. E. B. Du Bois. The others included Frederick McGhee, born a slave in Mississippi and now a criminal lawyer in St. Paul, Minnesota; Charles E. Bentley, a Chicago physician; Clement Morgan, a Harvard classmate of Du Bois and now a lawyer in Boston; Alonzo F. Herndon, a former slave who parlayed a barbering business into the Atlanta Life Insurance Company; and

Harry C. Smith, editor of the *Cleveland Gazette*. It was a distinguished group and included eight people from the South.[32]

The Niagara Movement set out many goals, some of which could win the hearty endorsement of virtually all blacks. But its core demand, "the abolition of all caste distinctions based simply on race and color," clearly set it apart from Washington's position. The language of its "Declaration of Principles" accentuated the difference. In words intended to draw a line in the sand, the Niagarites explained that "to ignore, overlook, or apologize" for wrongs was "to prove ourselves unworthy of freedom." The signatories vowed "to complain, and to complain loudly and insistently," because "persistent manly agitation is the way to liberty."[33]

The conflict between the Niagara Movement and Washington and his supporters embodied an ideological struggle that concerned all black Americans. It was also an ill-tempered clash of personalities, with Washington and Du Bois—who quickly surpassed Trotter as the leading anti-Washington spokesman—developing a profound mutual loathing. On both levels, the conflict between Du Bois and Washington tugged educated blacks in opposite directions. Black teacher, songwriter, diplomat, and future NAACP leader James Weldon Johnson recalled that the Niagara Movement "marked a split of the race into two well-defined parties," between which "there were incessant attacks and counter-attacks." The war of wills and ideologies was conducted through speeches, letters, pamphlets, books, meetings, organizations, and secret maneuverings. The polarization was never total, and many blacks, like Johnson himself, had a foot in both camps. Nevertheless, it was difficult to avoid taking sides, and the split produced intense bitterness.[34]

In theory, the two sides could have cooperated. Washington well knew that blacks, with good reason, were becoming angry and impatient. Intellectually, he could appreciate the necessity for protest and agitation, "work . . . which no one placed in my position can do, which no one living in the South perhaps can do." A division of labor between protest in the North and accommodationism in the South might have been devised. "I realize fully," Washington admitted, "that there are two lines of work—one is in the direction of radicalism and the other is in the line of education."[35]

Yet Washington proved incapable of reacting to his black critics in a constructive manner. Like many leaders who are driven by a sense of mission and who have accumulated great power, he found it impossible to accept the sincerity and integrity of his critics. He could only attribute base motives to them—jealousy, spite, political ambition, and a desire for publicity. A few friends tried to disabuse him of this belief. "Your following may be equal in number to those who are arrayed against you," wrote Theodore W. Jones from Chicago, "but they are far outclassed by brain, tact, and influence."

Washington's critics included "some of the brainiest lawyers, best physicians, dentists, druggists, clerks, teachers, and good moral citizens: men and women whose influence is felt." Washington could have seen from the example of his own friend Charles W. Chesnutt, a successful businessman as well as a distinguished novelist, that at least some of the doubters were both successful and sincere.[36]

But Washington refused to make the logical connection between black impatience, which he knew to be well-founded, and vocal opposition, which he dismissed as fabricated. He classed most of his critics as useless agitators who should not be taken seriously. For one thing, they lived in the Northern cities—an "artificial" civilization, to Washington—whereas the black masses resided in the rural South. "Having never come into contact with the rank and file . . . [they] cannot in any appreciable degree touch or influence the real heart of the people." Their privileged backgrounds further estranged them from the realities of black life. Unlike Washington, who had struggled to work his way up from the bottom, "their growth has been artificial rather than natural." These urban intellectuals, Washington alleged, were a tiny, unrepresentative minority who lived in a rarefied atmosphere remote from the lives of ordinary blacks.

For Washington, life was all about overcoming adversity, not whining about it. Dwelling upon prejudice simply made people "unhappy," "miserable," and "unbalanced"; it blocked them from achieving, and soured them against the world. The agitators were chronic complainers, impractical dreamers, failures in life. Worse, they were a "class of colored people who are ashamed of the race to which they belong and are angry because they are not white people."[37]

In his pettiness and lack of vision, Washington proved incapable of building bridges to his critics. Instead, he furtively sought to traduce them. He used spies and informers. He pulled strings to deny his critics employment and exclude them from white philanthropy. He planted malicious editorials in the newspapers he controlled. The malign maneuverings of the Tuskegee "Machine" reveal Washington at his worst.

Washington could not make common cause with Du Bois and the Niagarites, of course, without surrendering some of his own power. Yet it was that very power, hard-won and jealously guarded, that fuelled the conflict. Washington created a myth that he represented black America; he then attempted to monopolize black leadership. White Americans supported the myth, using Washington to advance their own racial agendas and attack black dissenters. As Thomas Sowell has put it, "The tragedy of the Du Bois–Washington conflict was not simply that one man was wrong on this point and the other was wrong on another point. That is inevitable among human beings. The tragedy was that one man—Booker T. Washington—was regarded by white

America as 'the' black spokesperson, and all opposing ideas from other blacks, such as Du Bois, were disregarded, deflected, or stamped out."[38]

Blacks who advocated alternative strategies were thus all but compelled to attack Washington. "Things came to such a pass," Du Bois recalled in later life, "that when any Negro complained or advocated a course of action, he was silenced with the remark that Mr. Washington did not agree with this. Naturally, the bumptious, irritated young black intelligentsia of the day declared: 'I don't give a damn what Booker Washington thinks! This is what I think, and *I have a right to think*.'"[39]

Washington's involvement in politics also provoked criticism. Although he deprecated politics and endorsed partial disfranchisement, Washington sought political influence. In local politics a Democrat, in national politics he was a staunch Republican. After gaining the ear of President Theodore Roosevelt, he offered advice to the president on racial matters. Roosevelt, in turn, consulted him with regard to federal patronage in the South.

For the most part, Washington used his relationship with Roosevelt in a disinterested and constructive way. He sought to dissuade Roosevelt from supporting the "Lily White" Republicans in the South—a faction that advocated the purging of blacks from the party and the elimination of all black officeholders—and to accord black Southerners political recognition. He advised Roosevelt not to endorse racial segregation by condemning "social equality," carefully explaining that "the Southern white man is constantly confusing civil privileges with social intercourse." Blacks did not object to separation of the races in itself, he told Roosevelt, "but [the Negro] knows by experience that in nine times out of ten . . . the colored man pays the same fare as the white man on the railroad trains but gets an accommodation that is far from equal."[40]

Yet Washington's position as presidential adviser was more symbol than substance. Washington failed to prevent Roosevelt from adopting increasingly critical, even hostile, views about black people. Visiting Tuskegee in 1905, Roosevelt endorsed industrial education but implied that blacks should not aspire to anything higher. Roosevelt repeatedly scolded blacks for their high rate of crime, and in 1906—against Washington's advice—told Congress that "the greatest existing cause of lynching is the perpetration, especially by black men, of the hideous crime of rape."

The Brownsville Affair cruelly exposed Washington's inability to intercede with Roosevelt on behalf of black people. On August 15, 1906, Roosevelt received reports that black soldiers of the Twenty-fifth Infantry Regiment—the famous Indian-fighting "Buffalo Soldiers"—had raided the town of Brownsville, Texas, on the Mexican border. Two white men, a bartender and a policeman, were killed by the raiders' wild, indiscriminate shooting. After an army investigation failed to identify the culprits, assumed to be about twelve in number, Roosevelt ordered that three entire companies be dishonorably discharged from the army. The order affected 176 men, six of whom held the Congressional Medal of Honor. They lost their pension rights and were barred from all federal employment. Washington pleaded with Roosevelt to delay his decision until they could discuss the matter. Roosevelt would not listen. In a public message, Roosevelt labeled the incident a "black and dastardly crime" and warned blacks that "shielding an evil doer because he is a member of their race . . . means ruin to the black race."

The true facts of the Brownsville raid were never established, and the army failed to prove the guilt of a single soldier. Yet the innocent, along with those presumed to be guilty, were punished without the benefit of any judicial process. Blacks were outraged by the injustice of Roosevelt's action. "I have never seen a time when the whole race has been so stirred up and hurt," Washington privately admitted. After his private intercession failed, however, Washington refused to publicly criticize Roosevelt. "The colored people of this country," he explained, "cannot afford to place themselves in continued opposition to the President of the United States, no matter who he is." No other event did more to spread disillusionment with Washington's leadership.

For white liberals like John Milholland, president of the Constitution League, and Oswald Garrison Villard, proprietor of the *Nation* and the *New York Evening Post,* Brownsville was proof positive that Washington's approach was inadequate. Militant agitation, in the tradition of the abolitionist movement, was an urgent necessity. For black moderates like Mary Church Terrell, a leader of the clubwomen's movement, and Archibald Grimké, a prominent lawyer in Washington, D.C., Brownsville was also an epiphany. Distrustful of the Niagara Movement, and respectful of Washington as an educational leader, they nonetheless realized that a strategy of protest was unavoidable.[41]

Washington never saw the inconsistency of dabbling in politics while belittling the importance of the vote. "Practically," he wrote Charles Chesnutt, "the matter of earning your daily bread and banking your money is a matter of the first consideration. You vote perhaps one in two years." Chesnutt ridiculed such fatuous reasoning:

The importance of a thing is not to be measured by the number of times you do it. Some of the most important and vital things of life are done only once. A man is born only once, but on that act depends his whole

life; he dies only once, which ends all his hopes and fears and useful-
ness. . . . It is not the *act* of voting I speak of—it is the right of every citizen to have some part in the choice of those who rule him, and the only
way he can express that choice is at the polls. It is just as effective if he
votes once in five years as once a day.

Washington never accepted the point. A man with "property, education, and
high character," he insisted, had political influence in his community whether
he voted or not. Washington was unable to see that blacks suffered economic
exploitation in part because they lacked political rights.[42]
Despite all the time they consumed and the criticism they engendered,
Washington's political activities were largely futile. With black voters fast
disappearing, the Republican party paid less and less heed to black concerns.
Roosevelt appointed fewer blacks to public office than McKinley, and
William Howard Taft, elected in 1908, fewer still. When Woodrow Wilson, a
Southern-born Democrat, entered the White House in 1913, only a handful
of black officeholders survived.

WASHINGTON'S ACHIEVEMENTS

His most thorough biographer, Louis Harlan, portrayed Washington as a
master manipulator whose relentless pursuit of power, and skill at disguising
his real emotions and opinions, produced spiritual emptiness and political
corruption. Washington emerges from Harlan's pages as a despotic, devious,
and rather sinister figure—and above all as a failure. "Seeking to be all things
to all men . . . Washington 'jumped Jim Crow' with the skill of long practice,
but he seemed to lose sight of his dance."
However, the Washington that looms across the massive bulk of his collected papers—which, ironically, Harlan himself edited—is an altogether different character. As historian Virginia Denton has argued, far from showing a
power-obsessed enigma, Washington's letters and speeches disclose a man
unselfishly committed to the social, educational, and economic uplift of his
race. "Washington was dominated by purpose, not power." Judged by his
best, Washington was an admirable leader. He addressed the most pressing
needs of black Southerners and showed them a way of coping with their situation, and even prospering, in a climate of extreme racism. Using a combination of flattery, persuasion, and guile, he gradually wore down Southern white
opposition to black education. When blacks in the South were abandoned by
the Republican Party, Washington built alliances with Northern capitalists

and philanthropists. His much-criticized relationship with President Roosevelt had important symbolic value, for it told Southern blacks that they had a foot in the White House door.[43]

Washington's economic vision strikes us as unrealistic. At a time of pell-mell urbanization, Washington urged blacks to stay in the countryside. In an age of breakneck industrialization, he envisaged blacks as yeoman farmers, self-employed artisans, and independent entrepreneurs. At the time, however, Washington's message did not seem irrelevant. To the emerging black middle class of teachers and small businessmen it was an inspiration. To black farmers, it offered a road map out of tenancy and debt. Indeed, by 1900, about one black farmer in four—some 193,000 people—were landowners. They achieved this, moreover, despite Congress's refusal to apportion land to the freedmen, despite the obstacle of discrimination, and despite a credit system that made it extremely difficult to accumulate capital.[44]

This golden age of agriculture did not last. Even at its height, blacks, who comprised 28 percent of the South's farmers, accounted for only 14 percent of the region's farm owners. Moreover, the era of the small farmer was drawing to a close. Washington failed to predict how economic change, abetted by government policy, would completely transform American agriculture. Still, he was hardly the only person who lacked a crystal ball. Not even the experts predicted that most farmers, white as well as black, would be swept from the land in a matter of decades.[45]

Washington's reputation as a Victorian moralist who constantly berated blacks for their shortcomings still persists. His priorities were hardly misplaced, however. Washington sought to raise the standards of people who had been denied legal marriage, refused education, clothed in rags, and housed in squalor. His seeming obsession with cleanliness, for example—famously exemplified by his praise of the toothbrush as a civilizing influence—strikes us today as ridiculous. In the context of his age, however, such concerns were not so absurd. Reformers on both sides of the Atlantic were vitally interested in sanitation and public health. Black Americans suffered an especially high mortality rate: eliminating dirt meant eliminating disease. Hygiene was a matter of life and death. It was typical of Washington that after one visit to Fisk University, he complained to the president that the outhouses were filthy and that the students had no place to bathe. His concern for cleanliness led him to support Negro Health Week, launched at Tuskegee in 1915, a major effort to reduce mortality in the black community.[46]

Washington criticized but never belittled the black community. Blacks might be ignorant, he argued, but they were not degraded. Far from being indolent, he told whites, "the masses of the colored people work hard, but . . . someone else receives the profits." To those who alleged that blacks had little reverence for family life, Washington pointed out that blacks took care of their dependents to a greater degree, perhaps, than any other race. "In all my experience in the South, I do not think I have ever seen a little child suffering by reason of the fact that no one would take him into his family." While criticizing many black ministers for being ignorant and immoral—valid criticisms—he praised the sincerity and passion of black religious faith. Educated blacks often cringed when Washington put on a thick dialect and told "darky" stories. But Washington understood that blacks, like most groups, were quite able to laugh at themselves if the joke were funny and it came from the right person.[47]

Did Washington concede too much? Did he, by his failure to join the forces of protest, aid and abet the white supremacy movement? Although only two states, Mississippi and South Carolina, had actually disfranchised blacks by 1895, disfranchisement was an unstoppable movement. As for segregation, blacks and whites already lived separate social lives, hardly ever intermarried, worshipped at separate churches, and attended separate schools. Separation was also the custom in saloons, hotels, restaurants, and other public accommodations. These forms of separation, moreover, were by and large accepted by blacks, some more grudgingly than others. The main area of contention was public transportation: blacks bitterly resented being relegated to filthy railway carriages and assigned to the back seats of streetcars. Like disfranchisement, however, the onward march of Jim Crow was irresistible. W. E. B. Du Bois, then a professor at Atlanta University who became Washington's most influential critic, charged that conciliation of the white South had made a bad situation worse. On the other hand, Kelly Miller, who taught at Howard University, argued that "no human power could stay the wave of race hatred now sweeping over the country."[48]

There is ample evidence that Washington harbored deep anger about lynching, peonage, convict labor, Jim Crow laws, the neglect of black schools, and what he called the "cancer of discrimination." As historian Donald J. Calista put it, "beneath his ingratiating manner boiled a man filled with contempt for the injustices done to his race by whites." Behind the scenes, Washington fought disfranchisement, challenged railroad segregation, attacked peonage, and opposed the exclusion of blacks from juries.[49]

From Washington's point of view, however, a strategy of open protest— as practiced by Ida B. Wells, for example—would be barren of results and may even, by antagonizing white Southerners, make life even more difficult for blacks in the South. "It takes more courage, in my opinion, for one to keep his mouth closed than to open it," he once explained, "especially when he is a thousand miles from the seat of real danger." Washington knew the precariousness of his own position, and that of Tuskegee Institute. Despite Tuskegee's relative independence, its autonomy was not absolute; the state legislature could wreak serious damage if it chose to do so. And no black person in the South, however well-connected, was beyond reach of white retribution.[50]

The cost of militancy was vividly illustrated by the experiences of two other men who headed black colleges in Alabama. William H. Councill, black president of State Normal and Industrial School in Huntsville, was forced to resign in 1887 after he sued the Atlantic Railroad Company for racial discrimination in evicting him from a first-class carriage. In the same year, in the town of Marion, black students from Colored University fought with white students from Howard College, and black townspeople boycotted white merchants. The Alabama legislature thereupon punished William B. Paterson, the white president of Colored University, by abolishing his school. Councill eventually got his job back, and thereafter accorded Alabama's Democrats unswerving devotion. Paterson succeeded in reestablishing his school in Montgomery, but the legislature denied it the name of "university." These happenings reinforced what Washington already knew: if he forcefully and repeatedly criticized racial discrimination, his position in Alabama would become untenable.[51]

Washington, then, was a product of black powerlessness. Black political leadership was headed toward extinction, and Washington stepped into the opening vacuum. He proposed a strategy for dealing with the unenviable situation in which black Southerners found themselves. He tried to find a means whereby blacks could find a secure economic niche in the New South, even if they had to surrender their political rights and some of their civil rights. Despite his conservatism, however, Washington never renounced the ultimate goal of equality. He advocated a tactical retreat in order to prepare the way for a strategic advance.

Yet did the gains secured by Washington justify the refusal to protest, the abandoning of politics, and the apparent endorsement of segregation? Many doubted it. Charles W. Chesnutt complained to Washington that "you Southern educators are all bound up with some special cause or other, devotion to which sometimes warps your judgment as to what is best for the general welfare of the race. Your institution, your system of education . . . is apt to dwarf everything else and become the sole remedy for social and political evils which have a much wider basis." Even staunch ally T. Thomas Fortune felt uneasy about Washington's denigration of politics and lack of vigor in opposing disfranchisement. "It is not necessary to give away the *whole* political case in order to propagate the industrial idea."[52]

Many blacks found Washington's accommodationism deeply humiliating. "If we are not striving for equality, in heaven's name for what are we living?"

asked black teacher John Hope in 1896. "If money, education, and honesty will not bring to me as much privilege, as much equality as they bring to any American citizen, then they are to me a curse, and not a blessing." Even if Washington's accomplishments are taken into account, therefore, they need to be balanced by the psychological damage that the policy of appeasing the white South may have inflicted upon both individuals and the race as a whole. As historian Lawrence J. Friedman has suggested, the "material gains may have been dwarfed against the psychic gains he could have rendered blacks had he been openly defiant and patently courageous." Friedman also speculated that his repression of anger and masking of feelings "may have . . . inflicted physical as well as psychological damage" upon Washington himself.[53]

For many black Southerners, however, and for Washington himself, the strategy of accommodation provided self-respect and psychological comfort. Washington was correct in sensing that few people could base their lives upon agitation and protest. Protest meant defining oneself in opposition to whites, and continually dwelling upon the negative effects of discrimination. Nothing was more frustrating and discouraging, moreover, than engaging in protest when circumstances made it barren of results. To Washington, agitation wasted energy that could be better devoted to self-improvement and racial uplift. "If one wants to be made to feel real sick and disconsolate he needs but to share the experience of sitting in an Afro-American meeting and hear two or three Negro speakers speak for two or three hours describing the ills of the Negro race. . . . In some places the race makes no effort to go forward in the direction that other races are working because it has gotten into the habit of crying and can do nothing else." Writing to his daughter Portia, then studying in the North, he warned her not to "dwell too much upon American prejudice, or any other race prejudice. The thing is for one to get above such things." Washington's message of self-help held such a powerful appeal to many black Southerners, especially the middle class, because it coincided with aspirations and beliefs they already held.[54]

Washington believed that he spoke to, and for, the black masses. It was not such a vain delusion: he was the only black leader of his age who could consistently attract large and enthusiastic audiences. Writing in 1937, historian Horace Mann Bond tried to analyze Washington's appeal:

> Those persons who have praised Booker T. Washington most loudly in the past . . . by far underestimate him. To them Booker T. Washington is a sort of mythical figure who preached humility and manual labor for Negroes. To me he is a man who came to understand the American culture—and that of the South—as no man before or since him could.

More, in his life and person he translated that understanding into action, by means of a personality so rare and compelling that he could appeal with equal force, not only to Northern financiers and scholars, but also to the most illiterate Negroes in the lower South.

Not until Martin Luther King, Jr., achieved fame forty years later would another Southern black leader command such influence and popularity.[55]

Washington's very eminence, however, exposed him to the full force of black disappointment and anger. "When a people are smarting under wrongs and misfortunes inflicted from many quarters, it is but natural that they should look for some individual on whom to lay the blame for their seeming misfortunes, and in this case I seem to be the one." But Washington was more than a scapegoat. Well before 1915, the year of his death, it had become painfully clear that his policy of conciliating Southern whites had done little to soften racial discrimination. The tenacity with which he clung to this policy caused many blacks to conclude that he had yielded the fight for racial equality, accepting a status of across-the-board inferiority for black people. When Washington died, effective leadership in the struggle for black equality had already passed to the National Association for the Advancement of Colored People.[56]

W. E. B. Du Bois, circa 1915

*Library of Congress, Prints and Photographs Division,
Visual Materials from the National Association
for the Advancement of Colored People Records*

The Rise of the NAACP

THE FOUNDING OF THE NAACP

On August 14, 1908, white citizens in Springfield, Illinois, incensed by the rape of a white woman by a black man, formed a mob that wreaked indiscriminate vengeance upon the town's black community, a vulnerable one-tenth of the population. Two black people were lynched, six shot dead, and scores injured. Hundreds of black families fled in terror.

When William English Walling visited Springfield in the aftermath of the riot, the absence of guilt or even regret on the part of the local whites appalled him. The *Illinois State Journal* even blamed the trouble on "the negroes' own misconduct, general inferiority, or unfitness for free institutions." Walling was a young white man who descended from Kentucky slaveholders. A Socialist, he detested racial oppression. In a magazine article, "The Race War in the North," Walling predicted a grim future for the United States—perhaps the death of democracy itself—if Southern methods of racial oppression became universal. Walling called for a revival of "the spirit of the abolitionists" lest Springfield become a harbinger of greater calamities.

To whites who still believed in racial equality, Walling's article was a veritable "wake-up call." It underlined the point that race was a national problem, not a sectional one. And it showed that the tide of "progressive" reform then sweeping America, despite its fervent desire to eradicate flaws in American society, had done little to address the problem of racial discrimination. A small group of people helped Walling organize a "large and powerful body of citizens" to come to the aid of blacks. On Abraham Lincoln's birthday in 1909, invitations went out to more than one thousand people. "We call upon all believers in democracy to join in a national conference for the discussion of present evils, the voicing of protests, and the renewal of the struggle for civil and political liberty."[1]

The two other prime movers were steeped in the traditions of abolitionism and already deeply interested in the cause of racial justice. Mary White Ovington was the granddaughter of abolitionists and grew up on stories of fugitive slaves and the Underground Railroad. Brooklyn-born and Radcliffe-educated, she became a settlement house worker in New York City, "the first professionally trained social worker in the United States to devote her career to the cause of the Negro," according to historian John Hope Franklin. Working among black migrants, she had helped to organize a "Committee for Improving Industrial Conditions of Negroes in New York," a precursor of the National Urban League. In 1911 she published *Half a Man: The Status of the Negro in New York,* one of the earliest studies of its kind. Ovington had also travelled throughout the South, visiting black schools and colleges. She knew black people from all walks of life and was a close friend of W. E. B. Du Bois.

Oswald Garrison Villard was the grandson of abolitionist pioneer William Lloyd Garrison. A wealthy, Harvard-educated Republican, he had visited the South in 1902 and had been shocked by what he saw. "I feel as if I had emerged from darkest America," he wrote after a trip to Alabama, "and the sense of the wrongs of the people of color is strong upon me." An enthusiast for industrial education, he became a strong supporter of Booker T. Washington. By 1909, however, Villard believed that Washington's optimistic statements about Negro "progress" grossly misrepresented the real situation, which in vital respects was getting worse, not better. "I grow very weary of hearing it said that Hampton and Tuskegee are the absolute solution," he complained of Washington. "It is always the same thing, platitudes, stories, high praise for the Southern white man." Although he stayed on good terms with Washington, Villard was convinced of the need to be, in the famous words of his grandfather, "as harsh as truth, and as uncompromising as justice." He enthusiastically endorsed the proposal for a national defense committee to protect Negro rights. Villard's backing for the conference was invaluable: he not only commanded respect as a reformer but also wielded influence as a publisher, having inherited the *New York Evening Post* and *Nation* magazine from his father, railroad magnate Henry Villard. It was Villard who drafted the Lincoln's birthday "call" that initiated the NAACP.

On May 31, 1909, a galaxy of eminent Americans gathered in New York City to attend the National Conference on the Negro. Denouncing the "ever-growing oppression of our 10,000,000 colored fellow citizens," they invoked the moral passion of the abolitionist movement to describe what black people were enduring and warn about the consequences of oppression:

> Often plundered of their just share of the public funds, robbed of nearly all part in the government, segregated by common carriers, some murdered with impunity, and all treated with open contempt by officials, they are held in some States in practical slavery. The systematic persecution of law-abiding citizens and their disfranchisement on account of their race alone is a crime that will ultimately drag down to an infamous end any nation that allows it to be practised.

This statement marked the birth of the National Association for the Advancement of Colored People. The NAACP became the spearhead of the black struggle for equality and one of the most influential reform organizations in American history.[2]

The Character of the NAACP

The men and women who founded the NAACP were in many ways typical products of the Progressive Era (1890–1917), when reform movements were often led by businessmen, social workers, teachers, writers, and journalists. The whites fit the Progressive profile perfectly: they were affluent and college-educated, "old stock" Americans rather than recent immigrants, Protestants rather than Catholics, Republicans and Socialists rather than Democrats. They lived in the big cities—New York, Boston, Chicago, Philadelphia— rather than the small towns or countryside. A fair number, like Ovington and Villard, were descended from abolitionists; a handful were elderly veterans of the fight against slavery.

The blacks at the National Conference on the Negro were also well-educated, politically active, and of relatively high economic standing. William S. Scarborough, professor of classics at Wilberforce University, a black college in Ohio, had long been an eloquent defender of higher education for black people against the onslaught of the "Tuskegee Idea." William L. Bulkley, a rare black Ph.D., was the only black public high school principal in New York City. Two medical men were present: Charles E. Bentley, the most eminent black physician in Chicago, and William Sinclair, a doctor in Philadelphia. Among the clergymen were Bishop Alexander Walters of the AMEZ Church, formerly head of the Afro-American Council, and Bishop Robert R.

Wright, Jr., of the AME Church. Antilynching crusader Ida B. Wells-Barnett attended, as did women's club leader Mary Church Terrell. William Monroe Trotter was there, as, of course, was W. E. B. Du Bois.

These founders of the NAACP differed from other "progressives," however, in one all-important way. Most white reformers of the Progressive Era had little interest in black Americans. If they thought about race at all, they tended to agree with Southern whites that black people were racially inferior, morally deficient, and politically unqualified—that blacks themselves were the main cause of the "race problem." In the South, nearly all progressives were committed white supremacists who regarded disfranchisement and segregation as rational, forward-looking reforms. The man who more than anyone else served as the national symbol of progressivism, Theodore Roosevelt, inclined to this view.

The National Conference on the Negro's ideological starting point was a total rejection of racism. In the 1900s, despite the pioneering work of anthropologists such as Franz Boas in disputing the notion of racial-biological hierarchies, the proposition that race was a fundamental determinant of human inequality commanded widespread support among scientists and other scholars. The National Conference on the Negro therefore fielded some of the best minds in America to refute this view. The word "race" was "in hopeless disrepute," argued Livingston Farrand, professor of anthropology at Columbia University; variations within human groups were "so wide as to cause overlapping in every direction." Addressing the thorny subject of the "Negro Brain"—widely believed to be inferior to the white brain—Burt G. Wilder, professor of neurology and vertebrate zoology at Cornell University, asserted that nobody had found a reliable way of distinguishing one from the other. Philosopher John Dewey contended that environment, not biology, molded human characteristics, and that "all points of skill are represented in every race." Political economist Edwin R. A. Seligman put it most simply of all: "The human race is about the same all over."

Booker T. Washington had declined his invitation to the National Conference on the Negro. Still, his unseen presence hovered over the proceedings. None of the speakers referred to him by name, but all knew that the meeting was a repudiation of Washington's leadership. Lest anyone doubt the point, the remarks of Du Bois, Washington's best-known critic, were explicit. Du Bois refuted the view that "the economic development of the Negro . . . demanded his exclusion from the right of suffrage at least for the present." He denied that a program of "industrial training and property getting" could advance the mass of Negroes when one-half of the working class could vote but the other half could not. Disfranchisement, he insisted, far from calming racial tension had accentuated race prejudice: "The voteless Negro is . . . an invitation to aggression, a plaything for mobs, and a bonanza for demagogues." As for remedying the lamentable situation in which black people found themselves, Du Bois called for "open, frank agitation" instead of "secrecy and machine methods."[3]

Villard unveiled the blueprint for the NAACP. He proposed a "permanent, incorporated national committee, to forward the interests of the Negro and to combat race prejudice." Through an education bureau, the organization would disseminate the truth about race relations, for "the masses are sound . . . if we can but get the facts to them." The NAACP should investigate lynchings, publicize injustices, and advertise the "marvellous achievements of the colored people." Above all, this was to be a fighting organization—a "scientifically planned and aggressive movement on behalf of the Negro's rights." Its main task was to take "case after case" to the Supreme Court, using the best lawyers available, forcing "that shifting and evasive body . . . to decide whether there shall be two degrees of citizenship in this country . . . and whether the Constitution of the United States shall be permanently violated."

In molding an organization from the raw material of the conference, blacks and whites had to work in harness, if not in harmony. This was a sensitive and difficult matter; blacks and whites did not work easily together. Apart from the abolitionist movement, the Republican Party (not a happy model), and the United Mine Workers Union, there were few historical precedents for interracial organization in the United States. Moreover, the new organization ran the danger of being dominated by white people. Whites had initiated the idea of the NAACP; blacks were a distinct minority at the founding conference. "Some of the colored people were distrustful of us," Mary White Ovington recalled. Were the whites going to be "namby-pamby . . . and counsel halfway measures?"

The resolutions adopted by the conference, their wording stiffened after much wrangling, were sufficiently forthright to satisfy most of the blacks. They demanded the strict and impartial enforcement of the Constitution: blacks should be guaranteed all the rights ensured to them—equal treatment before the law and equal access to the ballot box—by the Fourteenth and Fifteenth Amendments. The conference also demanded "equal educational opportunities for all," insisting that "public school expenditure be the same for the Negro and white child." This brief agenda kept the NAACP fully occupied for the better part of a century.[4]

When it came to selecting a Committee of Forty to steer the new organization, the most vocal black militants, William Monroe Trotter and Ida B. Wells-Barnett, found themselves excluded. Their omission from the list of a dozen black committee members was no oversight. Villard did not wish to antagonize Booker T. Washington—whose opposition, he feared, might prove fatal to the new organization—by including Washington's most uncompromising critics. There was probably another consideration. As Mary White Ovington later explained, Trotter and Wells-Barnett were headstrong individualists who were incapable of accepting the "restraints of organization." Trotter, in particular, was famously difficult, and had instigated much of the internal wrangling that caused the Niagara Movement to collapse. The omission of Wells-Barnett was more unfortunate, for the new organization sorely needed the participation of black women. Her name was belatedly added to the committee, but the damage was done. Wells-Barnett never got over the slight, and the NAACP had to do without her wholehearted support. Nevertheless, most members of the Niagara Movement followed Du Bois into the NAACP.[5]

From the beginning, the NAACP was a rather unbalanced and somewhat uneasy alliance between blacks and whites. As the organization formed local branches, most of the ordinary members, who paid an annual subscription of two dollars a year to join, were black people. Blacks were also well represented on the thirty-member board of directors. Yet whites monopolized the three key leadership positions of president, chairman, and treasurer. The organization also depended upon white lawyers, of whom one—the distinguished Boston attorney Moorfield Storey—served as the NAACP's first president. Moreover, board meetings—always held in New York City—were often poorly attended, a fact that augmented the authority of the permanent officers.

Thus during the NAACP's first two decades, a handful of whites dominated the organization. Oswald Garrison Villard served as chairman and treasurer. For the first few years, writes historian James M. McPherson, Villard "carried the association almost single-handedly, dipping into his own pocket to meet its frequent deficits and providing office space in the *Evening Post* building." Mary White Ovington served as a full-time, unpaid volunteer, becoming a permanent fixture at the organization's New York headquarters. A younger white woman, May Childs Nerney, joined the staff in 1912 as a salaried secretary. She stayed only a few years, but was a driving force behind the NAACP's early development.

During this formative time another white person, Joel Elias Spingarn, exerted a strong influence. An urbane, intense, elegant-looking man in his thirties, Spingarn threw himself into NAACP work after his dogged defense of academic freedom led Columbia University to dismiss him from its chair of comparative literature in 1911. A poet, essayist, and publisher, and man of independent means, Spingarn developed a close friendship with Du Bois, who saw in him an intellectual equal—both men were Harvard graduates and held Ph.D.'s—and a kindred spirit. With his brother Arthur, a lawyer, Spingarn became an NAACP stalwart. His energetic speaking tours between 1912 and 1915 were crucial in giving the NAACP an organizational foothold outside the Northeast.[6]

The fact that the NAACP appeared top-heavy with white people made it an easy mark for black critics like Trotter. Fortunately, the whites who stuck with the organization were men and women of integrity. They were paternalistic and at times overbearing—Villard notoriously so—but their sincerity was not in doubt. It was the support of W. E. B. Du Bois, however, that gave the NAACP visibility and credibility as an interracial organization. Joining the staff in 1910 as director of research and literature, Du Bois founded and edited the association's monthly magazine, the *Crisis*, and established himself as a forceful presence within the organization. Du Bois's prominent position furnished the best evidence that the NAACP's commitment to racial equality was genuine.

W. E. B. Du Bois, *The Souls of Black Folk*, and the Niagara Movement

The NAACP was far more than W. E. B. Du Bois. Indeed, the organization and the man had a stormy relationship, and Du Bois twice resigned. Nevertheless, the NAACP would have been inconceivable without him. By 1909 Du Bois had become, to quote biographer David L. Lewis, "the dynamo charging a new energy field in American race relations."[7]

To call W. E. B. Du Bois an intellectual is rather like calling Albert Einstein a mathematician—a true, but utterly inadequate, description. It is hard to do justice to the sparkling brilliance, profound originality, passionate humanity, incredible versatility, and sheer industry of a life that spanned almost one hundred years of American history, from Reconstruction in the 1860s to the civil rights movement of the 1960s. Du Bois was one of the great polymaths of the modern age: he wrote pioneer works of black history and milestone studies in black sociology; he published poems, novels, and several autobiographies; he was a brilliant polemicist and, as editor of the NAACP's *Crisis* magazine, a dazzlingly effective propagandist.

Du Bois and Washington could hardly have been more different. For one thing, they came from radically dissimilar backgrounds. Washington was born to a slave mother and an unknown white man in the South; he knew next to nothing about his other forebears. Du Bois was born in the North, his ancestors had been free for a hundred years, and he could trace his family tree over several generations. Washington was a man of the soil, a self-confessed rustic, who regarded pigs, chickens, cotton, and corn as the most valuable measures of earthly achievement. Du Bois was an urban intellectual, a man of letters, to whom truth, beauty, and culture were the noblest of ideals. Washington, who started life at the bottom, had a seemingly infinite capacity to absorb insult and injustice without complaint; he thought blacks should adjust to their environment. Du Bois, who began life at the top, for a black person, was cut to the quick by racial discrimination, exhibited a notoriously prickly exterior, and regarded acquiescence in second-class citizenship as blasphemy. Poles apart, the two men approached the black experience from vastly different perspectives. Small wonder they clashed.

Born in 1868, Du Bois grew up in Great Barrington, Massachusetts, a town with only a few black families who suffered relatively little discrimination. Du Bois's family worshipped in a Congregational Church, surrounded by white people; Du Bois himself was the sole black pupil at Great Barrington High School. With the flying start of a Massachusetts public school education, Du Bois attended Fisk University in Nashville, Tennessee, gained an M.A. from Harvard, and then, with the support of former president Rutherford B. Hayes, head of the Slater Fund, won a graduate fellowship to continue at Harvard as a doctoral student. Du Bois gained his Ph.D. in 1895, having studied for two years at the University of Berlin; his dissertation, "The Suppression of the African Slave Trade," was published as the first volume of Harvard Historical Studies. Taught by some of the greatest historians, philosophers, economists, and sociologists, Du Bois honed his intellect into a powerful tool of analysis and expression. Inspired by the example of Bismarck's Germany, and convinced by Hegelian philosophy that ideas had the power to transform reality, he viewed himself as a world-historical individual. "These are my plans," he wrote to himself: "To make a name in science, to make a name in literature and thus to raise my race."[8]

On the face of it, Du Bois was a rather unlikely spokesperson for black Americans, for his background and education were so atypical. Yet Du Bois was uniquely qualified to describe and analyze the situation of black Americans. Before he went to Fisk University, Du Bois was a stranger to the South and knew little of how the vast majority of black Americans actually lived. His undergraduate years, therefore, and his twelve-year tenure as a professor at Atlanta University, constituted a voyage of discovery—of both himself and of the black way of life. Du Bois was participant and observer, living within the black community and studying its social structure. He struggled to define the essence of the black experience, combining his own quest for self-identity with a broader search for the meaning, individual and collective, of what it meant to be black in America. Unlike Washington, Du Bois could never matter-of-factly accept the question of racial identity as a "given." His searching, speculative mind constantly probed the nature of existence, and questions of race and identity preoccupied him for much of his life.

Du Bois illuminated the black experience as no one else had done. A social scientist, he brought his analytical powers to bear upon the black church, the black family, and the black school in ways that challenged the racist obfuscations of most white academicians. But in *The Souls of Black Folk,* published in 1903, he did much more. His open criticisms of Booker T. Washington aside, what gave *Souls* its potency was the combination of sensitivity and detachment that enabled Du Bois to describe black life in all its broad humanity while at the same time brilliantly exploring the psychological tensions of being an individual black person. A self-confident egoist, he framed the black experience within his own inner struggles. Yet the effect was far less self-serving than the rags-to-riches story that Washington served up in his anodyne autobiography, *Up from Slavery.* Washington peddled superficial certainties; Du Bois offered ambiguity and profound insight:

> The Negro is sort of a seventh son, born with a veil, and gifted with second-sight in this American world,—a world which yields him no true self-consciousness, but only lets himself see himself through the eyes of others. It is a peculiar sensation this double-consciousness, this sense of always looking at one's self through the eyes of others, of measuring one's soul by the tape of a world that looks on in amused contempt and pity. One forever feels his two-ness,—an American, a Negro; two souls, two thoughts, two unreconciled strivings; two warring ideals in one dark body, whose dogged strength alone keeps it from being torn asunder.

Washington avoided the problematic. Du Bois placed it at the heart of black existence.[9]

Although irony and ambiguity pervaded *Souls,* Du Bois also gave blacks a political compass. If blacks were to gain the right sense of direction, he believed, they needed a correct understanding of their history. For that reason, it was extremely important to repudiate the notion that the egalitarian ideals of Reconstruction had been misguided. Whereas Washington told blacks that Reconstruction had been a mistake, Du Bois stoutly defended it. He praised the work of the Freedmen's Bureau, lauded the devotion of the Yankee schoolteachers, and described the Reconstruction legislatures as democratic governments whose achievements outweighed their errors. Such judgments now seem unexceptionable. In 1903, however, they were far ahead of their time. By insisting upon the validity of the Reconstruction experiment, Du Bois linked the postbellum struggles for equality with the present-day defense of the ballot, higher education, and equal citizenship. Washington's policy of "submission," he contended, was out of step with the tradition of black leadership, which had always aspired to "self-assertion and self-realization."

The Atlanta Compromise, not Radical Reconstruction, was the historical aberration.[10]

Souls exuded erudition. With its Latin tags, references to Greek myths, and quotations from Byron, Swinburne, Tennyson, Schiller, and Elizabeth Barrett Browning, Du Bois ostentatiously paraded his learning. But this was more than an egotistical show. Du Bois was asserting the principle of racial equality in the most profound way he knew. The ignorant "darky" who naively aspired to learn Latin and Greek was a standard caricature in the repertoire of racist stereotypes. Du Bois recognized the sneer for exactly what it was: an attack on the very idea of equality. He found it unforgivable that Washington should pander to white prejudice by disparaging "dead languages." After all, it was not as if the siren calls of Homer and Virgil were denuding the cotton fields of black labor: the number of blacks receiving a college-level education was tiny.

In attacking the classics, moreover, opponents of black higher education sought to rob blacks of their intellectual inheritance. Black Americans were as much a product of European culture as of African culture. The quotations that headed each of *Souls*'s chapters—a literary quotation from a European or white American poet, a musical quotation from a slave spiritual—illustrated the "two-ness" of the American Negro. They also showed that ideas and culture were the common property of all: the life of the mind knew no color line. "I sit with Shakespeare . . . I move arm in arm with Balzac and Dumas . . . I summon Aristotle and Aurelius." To deny blacks culture, whatever its source, was to deprive them of truth. "Is this the life you long to change into the dull red hideousness of Georgia? Are you so afraid lest peering from this high Pisgah, between Philistine and Amalekite, we sight the Promised Land?" The reader he addressed was also, of course, Booker T. Washington.[11]

Like Alexander Crummell, the aged and learned Episcopalian minister who founded the American Negro Academy in 1897, Du Bois insisted that culture and leadership were inseparable. Crummell had scorned the idea that true emancipation could come through economic striving alone. Only "scholars and thinkers" could guide and lead the unlettered masses. From Crummell's conception of leadership came Du Bois's idea of a "Talented Tenth": a cultured, broad-minded leadership that would fight for equal rights. "Progress in human affairs is more often a pull than a push," Du Bois explained, a "surging forward of the exceptional man, and the lifting of the duller brethren slowly and painfully to his vantage-ground." Without access to higher education, leaders of vision and intellect would be lacking. Du Bois likewise echoed Crummell's critique of the shallow materialism that pervaded the age, and which Washington's "get rich" philosophy reflected. No amount of material wealth could compensate for loss of the vote, inferior education, and the "emasculating effects of caste distinctions."[12]

In words of beauty and power, *The Souls of Black Folk* expressed what many educated black people were already thinking. The book made its author, virtually overnight, the intellectual leader of a renascent struggle for equal rights. Du Bois had once supported the Atlanta Compromise. But after much hesitation, he repudiated Washington's leadership—a decision that made all the difference to the anti-Washington opposition. Du Bois provided the intellectual force that transmuted the carping criticism of a few individuals into something much more powerful: an organized movement with a clear program and a coherent ideology.

The Niagara Movement, which Du Bois instigated in 1905, was described by historian David Levering Lewis as "the first collective attempt by African-Americans to demand full citizenship rights in the twentieth century." Yet it failed to become an effective vehicle of black protest, and its demise revealed some of Du Bois's own flaws as a political leader and organization builder.[13] Although most of its members lived in the Northern states, the Niagara Movement needed to take root in the South, the home of nine-tenths of America's blacks, in order to establish its relevance. The potential for a Southern protest movement was clear. Resentment against segregation in public transportation, for example, was as strong as ever, and blacks showed remarkable persistence in opposing it. They held mass meetings, petitioned state legislatures, and got up legal challenges. In New Orleans, a group called the Citizens Committee had brought the suit against railway segregation that led to the 1896 *Plessy v. Ferguson* decision. Even after that disastrous judicial reverse, blacks refused to admit defeat. When a new wave of Jim Crow laws mandated segregated seating on streetcars, blacks organized boycotts. According to one tally, boycotts of streetcars took place in twenty-seven cities between 1900 and 1907—virtually every city in the South. These protests commanded widespread support, and were often backed by the very teachers, ministers, professionals, and businessmen who were Booker T. Washington's most ardent admirers. For many black Southerners, in fact, there was no contradiction between support for Washington's self-help doctrine and agitation for equal rights.[14]

The Niagarites, however, had little conception of how to organize a mass movement. Indeed, it was not even clear that they wanted such a movement. The words of historian Elliott Rudwick are cruel but not inaccurate: Du Bois was "the College Professor of Niagara—giving lectures here, writing papers there, and expecting all the while that his 'students' would carry his ideas far and wide. He seemed oblivious of the fact that the Talented Tenth were not the 'leaders' of the race." An eloquent propagandist, Du Bois failed to develop a strategy beyond mere agitation. Surprisingly, the Niagara Movement failed to support the streetcar boycotts, even though one was taking place in Savannah, Georgia, in Du Bois's own state. The movement's only practical proposal for attacking discrimination was legal action, but that differed not at all from Washington's own methods. In the end, the Niagara Movement failed to raise sufficient money to finance a litigation strategy.

The vicious race riot that broke out in Atlanta in September 1906, leaving twenty-five people dead, was a demoralizing setback for the Niagara Movement and for Du Bois personally. This bloody outbreak of white mob violence, sparked by a political campaign to disfranchise black voters and inflammatory newspaper stories about alleged black rapists, intimidated the black community and quashed the Niagara spirit. Black leaders were not only shocked by the violence but also personally endangered by it. Dr. John Bowen, president of Gammon Theological Seminary, was beaten up by white militiamen. J. Max Barber, editor of the militant *Voice of the Negro,* fled to New York and his newspaper folded. Black leaders aimed to prevent further outbreaks by seeking the protection of the white upper class. Booker T. Washington visited the city and urged caution, restraint, and cooperation with the "best white people." If the riot gave Washington an opportunity to reassert his leadership, it underlined Du Bois's powerlessness and shook his self-confidence. It also placed a question mark over Niagarite methods.[15]

Du Bois doggedly defended the value of agitation for its own sake, but the Niagara Movement was running out of steam. In addition to the conundrum of strategy, it faced numerous other difficulties. It initially excluded women, needlessly depriving itself of an important source of support. Personality conflicts within the leadership group, especially tensions caused by the egocentric and volatile William Monroe Trotter, were debilitating. Absence of white participation proved a weakness; it denied the movement financial support and isolated the group from the mainstream of progressive reform. Washington's covert efforts to undermine the group exacerbated the existing problems and created some new ones. By 1908 the Niagara Movement was on the point of expiring.[16]

The band of Niagarites, nevertheless, were important pioneers. They reasserted the fundamental belief, eclipsed by the rise of Washington, that blacks were entitled to all the rights bestowed upon them by the Constitution, and that blacks should campaign for their immediate restoration. By 1909, moreover, Washington's black support was fast eroding, and many more white liberals were ready to endorse a Niagara-type program. Thus, while the Niagara Movement revealed the limitations of a black-only protest movement, it also blazed a trail for the NAACP. The Niagara years, moreover, gave Du Bois an apprenticeship in campaigning journalism—he edited two magazines, the *Moon* and *Horizon*—that stood him in good stead when he became editor of the *Crisis,* the official voice of the NAACP.

Du Bois and the *Crisis*, 1910–15

The first issue of the *Crisis*, with an initial print run of 1,000 copies, appeared in November 1910. It was an overnight success. By 1911 it was selling 16,000 a month. In 1919 the *Crisis* reached a circulation of 100,000, a number double that of the NAACP's paid membership. "With this organ of propaganda and defense," Du Bois recalled in his old age, "we were able to organize one of the most effective assaults of liberalism upon reaction that the modern world has seen." Du Bois was never one to undervalue his own achievements.[17]

Other leaders of the NAACP were more skeptical about the *Crisis*. Oswald Garrison Villard, the chairman of the board of directors, criticized the amount of time and energy that Du Bois devoted to the magazine to the detriment of his other duties as the association's director of research and publicity. Du Bois's insistence upon treating the *Crisis* as his personal mouthpiece rather than as the official organ of the NAACP further angered Villard. Colleagues also worried that his editorial attacks upon white philanthropists, black ministers, and anyone else who failed to match up to Du Boisian standards of militancy were divisive and offensive. A haughty, obstinate, prickly personality added fuel to the flames: the bloodiest board meetings in the early years of the NAACP concerned Du Bois and the *Crisis*.

Fortunately for the NAACP, the rows over the *Crisis* always blew over, with Du Bois continuing to go his merry way, albeit with an editorial committee peeking over his shoulder. The refractory editor might drive Villard to distraction—eventually provoking his departure from the NAACP's leadership—but Ovington and Spingarn realized that Du Bois was far too valuable to lose. "He does do dangerous things," Ovington admitted. "He strikes at people with a harshness and directness that appalls me, but the blow is often deserved and it is never below the belt. . . . He is head and shoulder above any other colored man we could find to fill his place."[18]

Du Bois fully understood the importance of the NAACP's organizational work, especially its legal challenges to Jim Crow. Litigation, however, would not stir the black masses, and efficient organization meant nothing if the NAACP's message failed to reach a wide audience. Du Bois saw his own work as altogether larger and more fundamental: he was battling for the hearts, minds, and allegiance of black America. That meant winning over the "Talented Tenth." He could not match the financial largesse that Washington commanded through his connections with white philanthropists. Yet the *Crisis* enabled him to speak directly to the educated Negro throughout the nation.

Attractively laid out, with pungent cartoons and striking covers, the *Crisis* reflected the highest technical and professional standards of the American magazine, then in its heyday. More important, the message of the *Crisis* struck a chord with black Americans. Sick of Washingtonian obfuscation, blacks were thrilled by a magazine that pulled no punches. Issue after issue, the *Crisis* flayed discrimination, pilloried prejudice, denounced Jim Crow, and attacked lynching. It mounted a sustained frontal attack on the dogmas, totems, and shibboleths of race prejudice. No hallowed institution, hoary idea, or respected person was safe from its assaults.

For a short time, largely at Villard's insistence, the *Crisis* avoided gratuitous criticism of Washington. When it became evident, however, that Washington's cooperation was not forthcoming, such reticence ended. At every turn, Du Bois poured scorn on the "tactfully conciliatory attitude" associated with Tuskegee. When a white reader criticized Du Bois for being "bitter," the editor's riposte was withering:

> For now nearly twenty years we have made of ourselves mudsills for the feet of this Western world. We have echoed and applauded every shameful accusation made against 10,000,000 victims of slavery. Did they call us half-beasts? We nodded our simple heads and whispered: "We is." Did they call our women prostitutes and our children bastards? We smiled and cast a stone at the bruised breasts of our wives and daughters. Did they accuse of laziness 4,000,000 sweating, struggling laborers, half paid and cheated out of much of that? We shrieked: "Ain't it so?" We laughed with them at our color, we joked at our sad past, and we told chicken stories to get alms.
>
> And what was the result? We got "friends." I do not believe any people ever had so many "friends" as the American Negro today! He has nothing but "friends" and may the good God deliver him from most of them, for they are like to lynch his soul.

The *Crisis* simply spoke the truth. "If this be bitterness, we are bitter."[19]

Different Du Bois biographers have tried, with varying success, to capture the flavor of the *Crisis*. To Arnold Rampersad, the key to the magazine's impact was Du Bois's editorials, which combined "poetic rhetoric, tearful tribute, sober assessment, and stern rebuke." Francis Broderick praised them for their "brevity, luster, and pungency," noting how Du Bois "clothed his facts with wit, paradox, indignation, and a call to arms." David Levering Lewis thought that Du Bois's "pulsating prose" infused his message "with a mystical fervor that bordered on the religious." The magazine's distinctive voice "was one of grievance ennobled and pride stiffened." However, Du Bois was no mean hand at ridicule. "When it was not hurling thunderbolts," writes Lewis, "the *Crisis* dripped acid. . . . Mordant observations and gratuitous asides filled its pages."[20]

Lynching provoked Du Bois's most wrathful condemnations. The NAACP sent white staff members and sympathizers to investigate lynchings, and the *Crisis* published the results. Elizabeth Freeman, for example, reported on the burning alive of Jesse Washington before thousands of onlookers in Waco, Texas. Du Bois put a photograph of Washington's charred corpse on the magazine's front page. Through reports, statistics, cartoons, and gruesome pictures, the *Crisis* gave a much stronger focus to the campaign against lynching.[21]

Du Bois's editorials on the "lynching industry" stretched irony to a grotesque extreme. After a black man was burned alive in Coatesville, Pennsylvania, he wrote:

> Let the eagle scream! Again the burden of upholding the best traditions of Anglo-Saxon civilization has fallen on the sturdy shoulders of the American republic. . . . The flames beat and curled against the moonlit sky. The church bells chimed. The scorched and crooked thing, self-wounded and chained to his cot, crawled to the edge of the ash with a stifled groan, but the brave and sturdy farmers pricked him back with the bloody pitchforks until the deed was done.
> Let the eagle scream!
> Civilization is again safe.

When a mob murdered a black man who worked as a janitor at the University of Missouri, Du Bois praised the institution's new course in "applied lynching"—"we are expecting great results from this course of study at one of the most eminent of our State Universities." When the lynching of two Italians elicited a futile protest from the government of Italy—it transpired that both victims were naturalized Americans—Du Bois dryly noted the advantage of U.S. citizenship. "The inalienable right of every free American to be lynched without tiresome investigation and penalties is one which the families of the lately deceased doubtless deeply appreciate."

The *Crisis* boldly advocated armed self-defense in the face of lynch mobs. Lynching would only cease, Du Bois warned, when white mobs ran up against black people who were "determined to sell their souls dearly." He berated blacks for cowardice and inertia. "We have been cheerfully spit upon and murdered and burned. If we are to die, in God's name let us perish like men and not like bales of hay." He exhorted black men to "kill lecherous white invaders of their homes and then take their lynching like men. It's worth it!"[22]

The *Crisis* was more than a superb vehicle of black protest. The *Crisis* instilled pride of race, extolling blacks' accomplishments, showcasing black history, art, scholarship, and literature. It placed the struggle of blacks in the context of world events and broad social currents. It campaigned for women's suffrage and supported the rights of labor. Booker T. Washington, for one, had no doubt that the popularity of the *Crisis* was a pretty accurate guide to the fortunes of the NAACP. He watched its circulation like a hawk, noting in July 1911—just six months after its launch—that the *Crisis* was outselling the Bookerite *New York Age* two-to-one. Washington encountered the *Crisis* not only in New York barbershops, but also, more worryingly, "in nearly every portion of the South."[23]

THE NAACP's EARLY CAMPAIGNS

The NAACP had to show that it could act as well as talk. In line with Villard's strategy of aggressive litigation, the NAACP fought discrimination in the courts, notching up some important victories. The New York City branch successfully defended a black man accused of rape and won an injunction against a theater that refused to seat blacks. In 1915, in *Guinn v. United States,* the Supreme Court knocked out Oklahoma's "grandfather clause," which had exempted prospective voters from taking a literacy test if they were "lineal descendants" of people who had been qualified to vote on January 1, 1866. Only whites, of course, could get through this loophole. The NAACP persuaded the solicitor general, John W. Davis, to challenge the "grandfather clause," and Moorfield Storey, the NAACP's president, supplied the Court with an incisive brief. It was the first time that the Court struck down a disfranchising device. Two years later, in *Buchanan v. Warley,* the NAACP won another victory: the Supreme Court ruled that an ordinance passed by the city of Louisville, Kentucky, that established black and white zones of residence, was unconstitutional.[24]

These legal triumphs were less clear-cut than they seemed, for Supreme Court rulings had very little effect on the daily realities of race relations. Racial zoning laws might be unconstitutional, but politicians and planners had plenty of less-obvious methods of encouraging segregation. Moreover, housing discrimination by builders, realtors, and private owners was quite legal. Similarly, when the Supreme Court eliminated the "grandfather clause," whites simply used other means of keeping blacks disfranchised.

Even on paper, the NAACP lost many more battles than it won. It failed, most notably, to stop the introduction of segregation within the federal government. In 1913 Postmaster General Albert Burleson, a Texan, proposed that blacks and whites in the Railway Mail Service, who at the moment worked side by side, should henceforth be separated. The cabinet assented, and a pattern of segregation quickly spread to other government departments. Black federal employees found themselves banished from canteens where they had previously eaten, assigned to separate toilets and lockers, and confined to separate work rooms. Moreover, from 1914 all applicants to the civil service were required to submit photographs; the proportion of black government employees subsequently fell.

To the immense bitterness of NAACP leaders like Villard and Du Bois—who in 1912 had deserted the Republican Party in the hope that Woodrow Wilson would treat blacks, in his own words, with "justice executed with liberality and cordial good feeling"—the Southern-born president publicly approved of the segregation policy. When a black delegation led by the undiplomatic William Monroe Trotter complained, Wilson angrily dismissed the group, declaring he would not be "blackmailed."[25]

The NAACP also lost one of its most fervent propaganda battles: the campaign to stop movie theaters from showing *The Birth of a Nation*. A racist caricature of the Reconstruction period inspired by Thomas Dixon's white supremacist novel *The Clansman*, D. W. Griffith's epic film, released in 1915, turned history upside down by depicting blacks as the oppressors and whites the oppressed. It dramatized black men as brutes and rapists who lusted after white women, and it glorified the Ku Klux Klan as heroic saviors of civilization. In short, it distorted history and purveyed the most vicious white stereotypes of black people. The fact that *Birth of a Nation* was a cinematic masterpiece magnified its influence: vivid, spectacular, fast-paced, and dramatic, it held audiences spellbound for over two hours. Woodrow Wilson, after a private screening in the White House, declared, "It is like writing history with lightning. And my only regret is that it is all so terribly true." The NAACP denounced the film as a vile slander. But despite one or two local victories—the film was temporarily banned in Illinois, for example—the NAACP's effort to have *Birth of a Nation* suppressed or drastically censored failed.[26]

In one sense, however, the NAACP triumphed even in defeat. Simply by creating public controversy, the Association forced whites to pay attention. Stung by the almighty row over *Birth of a Nation*, Woodrow Wilson distanced himself from the film. Embarrassed by the dispute over segregation in the civil service, the federal government backed off from making racial segregation an official policy. Plans for a completely segregated postal service, for example, were quietly dropped. Although the NAACP failed to persuade Congress to make lynching a specific federal crime, it generated, through the cooperation of Leonidas C. Dyer, a Republican representative from St. Louis, congressional debate on the issue that brought home to Southern white leaders the possibility of federal intervention if they failed to curb lynching.

Win or lose, moreover, the NAACP's campaigns, conducted with fire and vigor, stirred black people and recruited new members. Despite the early success of the *Crisis,* the NAACP's growth was painfully slow at first. Until 1912 its only branches were in Boston, New York, and Washington, D.C., with a combined total of 329 members. At the beginning of 1914 the NAACP still lacked functioning branches in Chicago, St. Louis, and Detroit, and it had yet to organize a single branch in the South. By 1916, however, membership had jumped to 8,785, with sixty-eight branches in the North and three in the South. Paradoxically, writes David Lewis, "*The Birth of a Nation* and the NAACP helped make each other."[27]

In 1917 the NAACP hired a full-time field secretary who, over the next dozen years, did as much as anyone to strengthen the NAACP. James Weldon Johnson was a native of Florida rather than Massachusetts, but he had much in common with W. E. B. Du Bois. Like Du Bois, Johnson was a light-complexioned mulatto whose family had been free before the Civil War. Like Du Bois, he was artistic, accomplished, and versatile.

After graduating from Atlanta University, Johnson taught school for ten years in his hometown of Jacksonville. He also qualified as a lawyer, wrote poetry, founded a newspaper, published a bestselling novel, and served as a U.S. consul in Venezuela and Nicaragua, where he lived through a revolution. Johnson was also, famously, part of the songwriting trio "Cole and Johnson Brothers"—the others being Rosamond Johnson and Bob Cole—that turned out a stream of popular hits, such as "The Maiden with the Dreamy Eyes," "Under the Bamboo Tree," "Congo Love Song," and "Oh, Didn't He Ramble." After triumphs on Broadway, Cole and Johnson took their musical show on the road, touring America and headlining in London and Paris. In 1904 they wrote Theodore Roosevelt's campaign song, "You're All Right, Teddy," a favor that smoothed James Johnson's appointment—on Booker T. Washington's recommendation—to the State Department.

Johnson's most famous lyric was "Lift Every Voice and Sing." Rosamond's soaring melody accompanied the words:

> *God of our weary years,*
> *God of our silent tears,*
> *Thou who hast brought us thus far on our way;*
> *Thou who hast by Thy might*
> *Led us into the light,*
> *Keep us forever in the path, we pray.*

In his autobiography *Along This Way* (1933), Johnson recalled the "transports of the poet's ecstasy" as he had penned these lines. "I could not keep back the tears, and made no effort to do so." It was adopted as the official song of the NAACP, and became known as the "Negro National Anthem."[28]

Although Johnson and Du Bois had much in common, they were, temperamentally, chalk and cheese. Johnson was easygoing and worldly wise. Having attained and enjoyed success, he was not so exclusively obsessed with race. A latecomer to protest, he had shown no interest in the Niagara Movement and had not been involved in founding the NAACP. Indeed he had been in the Washington camp. Once committed to the NAACP, however, Johnson's personal skills, honed in the diplomatic service, proved invaluable. He was a good organization man, felt comfortable with white people, and proved highly successful in selling the NAACP to blacks.

Johnson made his first task that of organizing the South. A speaking tour of the east coast took him from Richmond, Virginia, to Tampa, Florida, and left a string of new branches in its trail. The meeting in Atlanta, held in a black theater with white policemen looking on, was especially memorable. Johnson had to squeeze through a tightly packed throng to reach the stage. "The leading colored men of the city" were there, recalled Johnson: "lawyers, doctors, college professors, public school teachers, editors, bankers, insurance officials, and businessmen." Johnson spoke calmly but compellingly of how race prejudice destroyed both victims and perpetrators. Others were more impassioned. A young insurance agent who had organized the meeting, Walter White, raised one of the biggest cheers by declaiming, "We have got to show these white people that we aren't going to stand being pushed around any longer. As Patrick Henry said, so must we say, 'Give me liberty, or give me death!'" Johnson promptly put the young man—a future NAACP leader—on the staff.[29]

The NAACP had arrived. It was a going and growing concern. Booker T. Washington had tried to derail it, but failed, and his death in 1915 removed any coherent opposition among blacks. The Amenia Conference of August 1916, held at Joel Spingarn's estate, brought together black leaders of all opinions, and they agreed on a common set of principles that should guide the struggle for equality. In fact, the unity that emerged at Amenia was superficial; many blacks in the South, especially, remained fearful and skeptical of open agitation. But at least the bitterness of the old Washington–Du Bois schism had passed away.

Moreover, a political and economic convulsion was underway that quickly made the Age of Booker T. Washington seem like ancient history. Southern blacks were streaming northward in unprecedented numbers to work in labor-starved factories. The rhetoric of patriotism and democracy echoed across the land. The First World War was shaking America, and it inspired blacks with the hope that they could strike a decisive blow against racial tyranny.

Black soldiers building a railroad in France, circa 1918

National Archives at College Park, Still Picture Branch, (NWDNS)

5

The Great War and Racial Equality

The shots that killed Archduke Franz Ferdinand of Austria-Hungary as he drove across a bridge in Sarajevo on June 28, 1914, sparked the bloodiest war in the history of mankind. For Europe, the "Great War" was an unmitigated disaster, inflicting hunger, pestilence, and mass slaughter upon entire populations. The defeated nations were shattered, their political structures swept away in a tide of despair and revolution. The main victors, Britain and France, were traumatized, debilitated, and impoverished.

The United States had a less punishing war. Neutral for the first two and a half years, America enjoyed an economic windfall produced by the enormous volume of Allied war orders. In actual combat for only a few months, American troops incurred relatively few casualties. Suffering no war damage, no hunger, no deep economic stress, America avoided the political upheavals that wracked Europe. She emerged from the war stronger, not weaker, and with the feeling, moreover, that America, alone among the great powers, could represent the cause of democracy in a disinterested way.

Yet the First World War, although relatively short and benign for the United States, affected Americans profoundly. The Wilson administration approached the conflict with ruthless efficiency and sweeping power. The entire population was enlisted in the struggle: people were ordered to "work or fight." Every adult male registered with a draft board, and an army of two million men was mobilized and sent to France. The federal government commandeered the railroads and placed basic industries on a wartime footing. To a symphony of patriotic propaganda, the federal government regimented, exhorted, browbeat, and borrowed large sums of money from the American people. In return, the masses of the American people expected to see improvements in their lives.

The war brought unexpected and welcome opportunities for black Americans. Inspired by patriotism and encouraged by President Wilson's idealistic rhetoric, blacks embraced the "War for Democracy" with the hope that white America would reward their loyalty and service. This conflict, it seemed, presented a heaven-sent chance to strike a blow against racial discrimination in the United States—even to fight the colonial oppression of colored peoples overseas. Just as the Civil War ended slavery, so might the Great War undermine white supremacy. "It is the business of the Negro not to sit idly by and see this rearrangement of the world, hoping that something good will come out of it for him," lectured Du Bois in the *Crisis*. "It is rather his business actually to put himself into the turmoil and work effectively for a new democracy that shall know no color."[1]

THE GREAT MIGRATION

The first and most visible effect of the First World War on black Americans was a dramatic movement of people from the South to the North—the Great Migration. For half a century after emancipation, economic circumstances had trapped the vast majority of blacks in the former slaveholding states, where the bulk of the black population remained on the land. Blacks in agriculture often moved from farm to farm and county to county in search of better land and better landlords. Some were lucky enough to find temporary prosperity in new areas of cotton cultivation such as the Mississippi Delta. The gains of moving, however, were usually temporary and slight; the profits made from cotton rarely trickled down to tenants and sharecroppers. However, even when their farms were inundated by Mississippi floodwaters, and their crops ravaged by the boll weevil—a cotton-eating pest that crossed the Rio Grande in 1892 and marched steadily eastward, reaching Alabama by 1913—black farmers had little option but to stay in the South.

It would be wrong to say that blacks were completely excluded from Southern industries. The coal mines and iron mills of Alabama employed black workers, as did the tobacco factories of North Carolina and Virginia. Southern railroads employed black firemen and brakemen. Compared with Northern industries, however, these enterprises were small. Moreover, the South's biggest and fastest-growing industrial enterprise, textiles, barred blacks entirely. When they moved to towns and cities, therefore, blacks were usually restricted to do-mestic service if they were women, common labor if they were men.

For black Southerners, there were formidable obstacles to quitting the South, including lack of skills, lack of money, and lack of friends and relations in the North who might smooth their passage. However, racial discrimination in employment was the biggest deterrent. Through tacit and sometimes ex-plicit collusion between bosses and workers, blacks were excluded from most Northern industries, and widespread discrimination in the rest of the econ-omy relegated blacks to certain categories of low-wage, unskilled jobs. Partly as a reaction to the use of blacks as strikebreakers, partly through racial preju-dice, most labor unions excluded blacks, with only a handful of unions stand-ing out against the pattern. The largest of the exceptions, the United Mine Workers of America, accounted for half of all the black unionists in the Amer-ican Federation of Labor. Twelve unions, including the four powerful railroad "brotherhoods," explicitly barred blacks, and many more practiced covert discrimination to keep them out.

Only about 200,000 black people quit the South altogether during the grim decades between 1890 and 1910. Although this seems like a substantial number, it barely dented the South's black population of ten million. And it only slightly diminished the proportion of the black population that lived in the South, from 91.5 percent in 1870 to 89 percent in 1910.[2]

Yet in 1915 the northward trickle suddenly swelled. Nobody knows pre-cisely how many blacks deserted the South during the First World War. The best-informed estimate is about 330,000. By the standard of the 1940s and 1950s, this Great Migration was but a modest shift of population. Compared to the vast numbers of European immigrants—a million a year between 1910 and 1914—it was a drop in the ocean. To many observers at the time, how-ever, the flow of black Southerners to New York, Philadelphia, Chicago, and every other big Northern city seemed like a raging, uncontrollable flood. And all agreed that it represented something profoundly significant.

Clearly, blacks were quick to take advantage of economic opportunities that had never before been open to them. The outbreak of war in Europe cre-ated an acute labor shortage in the North. Britain and France needed muni-tions and supplies, and America's factories were straining to fill Allied orders. The fighting, moreover, virtually cut off the supply of new immigrants from Europe. "Labor was needed in railroad construction," wrote historian Ben-jamin Brawley, "in the steel mills, in the tobacco farms of Connecticut, and in the packinghouses, foundries, and automobile plants."[3]

Industries that had previously excluded blacks—often cynically hiring them only when a strike needed breaking—now opened their doors to black workers. Packard became the first automobile manufacturer in Detroit to hire blacks in large numbers. The other employers, including Ford, soon followed. Some factories even sent labor agents into the South, instructing them to actively recruit blacks and pay their train fare north. Black women, too, found more jobs in the North, filling positions in kitchens and laundries previously held by immigrant women, many of whom now worked in stores and factories. It would be wrong to say that racial prejudice was diminishing—black women found it difficult to find employment except as servants and washerwomen. But for the time being, at least, prejudice took a back seat to profit and necessity.[4]

Many Southern whites refused at first to take the black exodus at face value. They attributed it to the natural credulity of the Southern plantation Negro, who naively believed the alluring descriptions of the North that appeared—often in the convincing form of letters from migrants—in black newspapers like the *Chicago Defender.* Whites knowingly predicted that the trek North would cease once blacks had shivered through a winter in Chicago or New York. Democratic politicians in Northern cities suspected that the migration might be a Republican plot to import illegal voters. Instructed by the Wilson administration to investigate possible election fraud involving Southern migrants, agents of the Justice Department questioned the families that migrants left behind. "They are loath to tell where these people have gone," reported one official; "they are secretive by nature." The agents found no evidence, however, of any political scheme behind the migration. Blacks were going North because they could earn two or three times what they made in the South.[5]

Yet there *was,* in the broader sense of the word, a "political" dimension to the Great Migration. An investigator from Tuskegee Institute, working for the Department of Labor, was emphatic: "The treatment accorded the Negro always stood second, when not first, among the reasons given by Negroes for leaving the South." The accumulated oppression of decades—lynching, segregation, disfranchisement, inadequate schools, vagrancy laws, the convict-lease system, insults, humiliation, and danger—accounted for the eagerness with which blacks moved North. It was plain from the letters of migrants and would-be migrants that they were not only embracing the North but also rejecting the South. "I myself is anxious to leave this part of the country and be where a negro man can appreshate beaing a man," wrote a job-seeker from Alabama. "I am in the darkness of the south," pleaded another. "O please help me to get out of this low down country [where] I am counted no more thin a dog." Blacks were voting with their feet—and, deep down, Southern whites knew it.[6]

BLACK AMERICANS SUPPORT THE "WAR FOR DEMOCRACY"

When the United States entered the war on April 6, 1917, blacks supported the war effort with the patriotic fervor that the Wilson administration demanded of all Americans. But the thought of attacking racial discrimination—the very negation of democracy—was never far from their minds. They believed that the "War for Democracy" should be a fight against racial tyranny at home, not merely a struggle against German autocracy abroad. The war heightened their resentment of racial discrimination and increased their readiness to speak out against it. Support for the NAACP skyrocketed. In 1914 the organization boasted 54 branches; four years later the number stood at 117.[7]

The federal government, by enlisting black support on every level, inadvertently encouraged black militancy. A Democratic administration previously deaf to black grievances now appointed black advisers in Washington, enlisted blacks in the Liberty Loan fundraising drives, and encouraged Southern whites to formally consult black leaders. The black community received a degree of respect and recognition. As historian Judith Stein put it, "Popular demands summarily rejected in prewar years became negotiable." A system of white supremacy that had seemed set in stone suddenly appeared vulnerable.[8]

Blacks appropriated the war's idealistic rhetoric to press for change. The Reverend Adam Clayton Powell, pastor of Abyssinian Baptist Church in Harlem, New York City, captured the black mood:

> While we love our flag and our country, we do not believe in fighting for the protection of commerce on the high seas until the powers that be give us at least some verbal assurance that property and lives of the members of our race are going to be protected on land from Maine to Mississippi. Let us have the courage to say to the white American people, "Give us the same rights which you enjoy, and then we will fight by your side with all of our might for every international right on land and sea."

Petitioning President Wilson, black newspaper editors explained that the government could make the Negro "an efficient fighter for victory" by redressing some of his grievances. Specifically, they asked for "better conditions of public travel," greater employment opportunities, and "the immediate suppression of lynching."[9]

The treatment of black soldiers became a test of racial progress. Would blacks be allowed to serve as combat troops? And would black servicemen be accorded the same treatment as whites? The first question should not have needed asking: blacks had fought with distinction in the Civil War; black regulars, the famous "Buffalo Soldiers," had proven to be effective Indian-fighters; in the Spanish-American War, black troops had charged up San Juan Hill alongside Teddy Roosevelt's "Rough Riders"; when America occupied the Philippines, the black regiments bore the brunt of putting down the native insurrection led by Emilio Aguinaldo.

Yet white Southerners had long resented black soldiers, regarding them as a threat and an insult. By the 1900s, when the South was systematically stripping blacks of their rights, their dignity, and their manhood, black men in uniform had become an affront to white supremacy. White concerns were not irrational. Even in segregated regiments commanded by white officers, black soldiers assumed a rough equality with their white comrades-in-arms. Military service stiffened backbones: black soldiers who had chased Geronimo and his Apaches through the deserts of Arizona were liable to answer back—and hit back—when they encountered discrimination and abuse. The Brownsville incident of 1906 had dramatically illustrated the growing tension between black military pride and Southern white racism. Many whites feared an explosion of Brownsvilles. "If you put a boy from Mississippi in a Negro regiment from Massachusetts," warned a South Carolina congressman, "you won't have to go to Germany to have war. You will have it right here."[10]

But the nation needed all the manpower it could get, and the Selective Service Act, drawing no distinction of race, cast a wide net. Well over two million black men eventually registered with local draft boards, of whom 367,000 were conscripted into the army. When the army took no steps to train black officers, Joel Spingarn, the chairman of the NAACP, campaigned to make the War Department change its mind. His proposal for a black-only officer training camp flew in the face of the NAACP's opposition to segregation, and many blacks condemned Spingarn for aiding and abetting Jim Crow. Spingarn retorted that the only alternative was no camp at all. Getting black officers commissioned should be the paramount goal: that in itself would help to undermine discrimination. His close friend Du Bois agreed. "We must make the choice else we play into their very claws. It's a case of camp or no officers. Give us the officers. Give us the camp."

Spingarn's lobbying paid off. Camp Des Moines opened in June 1917, and in time it trained over 2,000 black officers. Trawling the editorial columns of Southern newspapers, Du Bois detected a distinct softening of Southern white hostility to black troops. The Negro "is measuring up to the full valuation of a citizen and a patriot," he quoted from the *Charlotte Observer* in the *Crisis*. "There has been nothing wanting about him."[11]

Du Bois himself, carried along by the wave of patriotism sweeping the nation, and thrilled by the apparent shift in white attitudes, brimmed with optimism. After fifty-four years of relentless oppression, the tide was finally turning, he informed readers of the *Crisis* in December 1917. "From now on we may expect to see the walls of prejudice gradually crumble before the onslaught of common sense and racial progress." Du Bois now calculated that unconditional patriotism would advance the Negro's cause far more effectively than complaints and protests. In July 1918 he urged blacks to "forget our special grievances" and "close ranks" behind the war effort. "We shall not profiteer with our country's blood," he explained. "We want victory for ourselves—dear God, how terribly we want it—but it must not be cheap bargaining, it must be clean and glorious, won by our own manliness, and not by the threat of the footpad." As he penned these stirring words, black soldiers were fighting and dying in the Argonne forest, helping to blunt one of the last German offensives on the Western Front.[12]

THE WHITE BACKLASH IN 1917

Du Bois's "Close Ranks" editorial came back to haunt him. Black Americans soon discovered that the wartime spirit of patriotic cooperation was utterly superficial. If the war made blacks increasingly resentful of discrimination, it also underscored the fact that whites of all classes were still determined to keep blacks in their place. Whites accepted black participation in the war effort, but only on Jim Crow terms. Rather than bring about change, the forces unleashed by the war—black migration, black militancy, and black military service—provoked a violent white backlash.

The *Chicago Defender* told blacks in Dixie that the North was a land of freedom. The riot in East St. Louis, Illinois, presented horrible evidence that it was not. In East St. Louis, the "Pittsburgh of the West," thousands of Southern blacks from Louisiana and elsewhere found jobs with the railroads, factories, foundries, stockyards, and meatpacking houses. But if industrial employers regarded the stream of cheap black labor as a boon, white workers feared and resented the migrants, viewing them as an immediate threat to their social status, political influence, and living standards.

Even under the best of circumstances such a large and sudden influx, which doubled the black population virtually overnight, would have strained the city's social fabric. When the Aluminum Ore Company utilized the newcomers to break a strike and destroy a labor union, white workers ripped the social fabric apart. Summoning a public meeting of white unionists to protest against "this influx of undesirable negroes," labor leaders proposed "drastic action." They wanted not only "to retard this growing menace" but also to "get rid of a certain portion of those who are already here." Contemptuous of a frightened, incompetent mayor, and undeterred by a corrupt, inefficient police force, whites proceeded to do just that.

On July 2, 1917, gangs of white men roamed through downtown East St. Louis and randomly but systematically beat, shot, hanged, and burned black people. They pulled blacks off streetcars, and, egged on by cheering spectators, kicked, clubbed, and pelted them with rocks. Congealing into larger mobs, they torched black homes and shot their fleeing residents. They lynched some blacks from telephone poles.

Women and children joined in. Nathaniel Cole, a twenty-two-year-old foundry worker, was travelling to the city from Alton on an interurban streetcar. He arrived in East St. Louis oblivious to the danger:

> I saw a crowd of whites hollering, "Stop the car and get the nigger." The car was pulled off and a Negro man pulled out and beaten. In the meantime a white child called "There's another nigger." I was then pulled off the car, beaten and left in the street. . . . I ran into a white neighborhood and a woman hollered, "Stop that nigger. Stop that nigger." . . . They then hemmed me in a yard, where a carpenter was at work and began beating me. The carpenter then asked the rioters not to beat me up there, but to turn me over to the police if I had done anything to deserve it. The rioters replied, "The nigger takes the white man's job." . . . I was beaten into insensibility and when I came to they were taking stitches in my head at St. Mary's Hospital.

A white newspaper reporter saw rioters beat a black man to death. They clubbed him to the ground and then moved in for the kill. "'This is the way,' cried one. He ran back a few paces, then ran at the prostrate figure at full speed and made a flying leap." His heels came down on the man's head. A girl then kicked the man in the face. The police fraternized with the rioters. Soldiers of the Illinois National Guard shot black people but never once opened fire on whites. At least forty blacks and eight whites died in the riot.[13]

Seven weeks later, however, a shocking instance of black violence erupted when a hundred soldiers of the Twenty-fourth U.S. Infantry, stationed in Camp Logan, Texas, wreaked vengeance upon whites in Houston for subjecting them to Jim Crow rules and general discrimination. These hard-bitten regular troops in a fit of drunken anger defied their officers, seized weapons, shot a soldier guarding the ammunition supply, and marched on downtown Houston. Corporal Charles W. Baltimore, who earlier in the day had been beaten by white policemen, led the contingent. Opening fire on the police station, the soldiers killed five policemen and twelve other white people—including a small girl, who was killed by a stray bullet as she lay sleeping. Two black soldiers also met their deaths.

The NAACP sent Martha Gruening to investigate the affair. Her report tried to shift the blame for the violence onto Houston's whites. "The primary cause of the Houston riot," she told *Crisis* readers, "was the habitual brutality of the white police officers . . . in their treatment of colored people." Given the deadly response of the soldiers, such an interpretation smacked of special pleading—it attempted to defend the indefensible. However, the execution by hanging of nineteen soldiers for mutiny and murder struck black Americans as grotesquely unfair. The swift court martials, and the speed with which the death sentences were carried out, smacked of Jim Crow justice. The first thirteen condemned men were hanged without any opportunity to appeal their sentences. Blacks were so angry and appalled that President Wilson, after the NAACP appealed for clemency, commuted ten of the remaining sixteen death sentences. All told, fifty men received life terms.

The army privately admitted that the "ultimate cause" of the Houston riot was the resolve of black troops to "assert what they believe to be their rights as American citizens and United States soldiers" in the face of white hostility. For Southern whites, however, and for the federal government as well, the principle of racial segregation was not negotiable. If black troops resented segregation and by their very presence irritated Southern whites, the logic of white supremacy pointed to the restriction and removal of the troops. The desire to keep black soldiers out of the South helps to explain why the army assigned its regular black units to America's periphery—the Mexican border and the Philippines—and why it shipped black conscripts to France after the most perfunctory training.[14]

BLACK SOLDIERS IN FRANCE

The story of black American soldiers on the Western Front was very much like that of America's white soldiers. Green troops, poorly equipped, often badly led, and with no experience in modern warfare, were pitched against battle-hardened Germans—the world's most skillful practitioners of trench warfare and shock-assault tactics—and were severely mauled. After a good deal of panic, confusion, and incompetence, the Americans learned how to fight effectively. American troops, black and white, helped to push the Germans out of France in the war's final, decisive, Allied offensive.

But America's black soldiers received little credit for their heroism and sacrifice. On the contrary: a myth spread that black soldiers invariably broke and ran, and that black officers were abject failures. White officers, many of them Southern-born, were the source of the myth. "Poor Negroes!" General Robert Bullard wrote in his diary. "They are hopelessly inferior." Condemning the 368th Regiment—whose first experience in battle had been a fiasco—as "rank cowards," Major J. N. Merrill explained that "the Negro race, as to cranial capacities . . . has reached a state that will not improve and cannot improve." Colonel Allen J. Greer's judgment was equally categorical. "It is an undoubted fact, shown by our experience in the war, and well known to all people familiar with negroes, that the average negro is naturally cowardly."[15]

Whites were scathing about most of the black officers turned out by Camp Des Moines. Faced with the undeniable fact that some at least were brave and competent, whites had a ready explanation: these able few were "exceptional mulattoes." Colonel Charles H. Young, America's highest-ranking black officer, had been denied an active service commission on the grounds of ill health—despite making a quixotic horseback ride from Ohio to Washington—to the immense disappointment of black people everywhere. But he rallied to the defense of black officers, pointing out that nine out of ten Negro Americans were of mixed blood. In any case, Young added, blood had nothing to do with military prowess: Toussaint L'Ouverture, "who routed the best troops of Napoleon Bonaparte, was a pure Negro."[16]

But the training, deployment, and treatment of black troops in France made it obvious that the army had already made up its mind that blacks were inferior. Fully 80 percent of the black conscripts were assigned to labor battalions, accounting for a third of all the army's pick-and-shovel workers. "The poorer class of backwoods negro has not the mental stamina and moral sturdiness," explained one officer, "to put him in the line against opposing German troops." Treating black soldiers as laborers, moreover, might allay some of the "prejudice against colored troops [that] exists more or less in southern States."[17]

The army not only exported white supremacy to France, it also tried to have the French practice racial segregation. Lest the free-and-easy French fraternize with America's black soldiers, the army circulated a leaflet, "Secret Information Concerning Black American Troops." White Americans were of the unanimous opinion, it explained, that blacks must be strictly segregated in order to avert the "menace of degeneracy." French officers, if they were to avoid "estranging American opinion," should not become too friendly with black officers, refrain from commending black soldiers too highly—"particularly in the presence of [white] Americans"—and make a point of preventing French civilians from "spoiling the negroes." Alleging that black troops had committed more rapes than "all the rest of the army," the directive lectured the French that "the vices of the Negro are a constant menace to the American who has to repress them sternly."[18]

Like all myths, the belief that black soldiers had been "failures" acquired a life of its own. It received a powerful boost when psychologists interpreted the results of IQ tests, administered to 1.7 million conscripts, as further evidence of black inferiority. In reality the test scores were closely related to education and income: black recruits from Ohio, for example, outperformed white recruits from eight Southern states. Yet the initial, racially biased, interpretation accorded too closely with what many whites already believed about black people. Even when the white psychologists repudiated their earlier conclusions, the army continued to regard black conscripts as inferior. When America entered the Second World War, the army's policy on black troops was even more discriminatory than the one it had practiced during the first. It refused to assign them to combat duty at all.[19]

By the end of the First World War, black soldiers in France were seething with discontent. After the Armistice, President Wilson authorized Robert R. Moton, Booker T. Washington's successor at Tuskegee Institute, to investigate racial tensions in France. Moton knew very well that the record of black troops reflected on the reputation of the race as a whole, and he assiduously tracked down allegations of black incompetence and misconduct. His report to the secretary of war, Newton D. Baker, refuted the charge that black officers were failures and black soldiers cowards. He also demonstrated from trial records that only a handful of black soldiers—contrary to widespread belief—had been convicted of rape. Speaking to white officers, Moton pleaded for returning black soldiers to "have a fair and absolutely equal chance with every other American citizen." His words to the black men in uniform, however, seemed calculated to dampen down expectations of change. "I hope no one will do anything in peace," he told them, "to spoil the magnificent record you have made in war."[20]

Moton's soothing bromides, however, were out of tune with the black mood in 1918–19. America's entry into the First World War had nurtured a new crop of radicals. Challenged from the left by younger men like the socialist A. Philip Randolph, Du Bois saw an opportunity to redeem his radical credentials—which had suffered badly when it became known that his superpatriotic *Crisis* editorial, "Close Ranks," might have been linked to his desire for an army commission. Du Bois now blasted the army's treatment of black soldiers and charged Robert Moton with showing less interest in uncovering discrimination than in telling the black troops how to comport themselves when they returned to America. Moton allegedly advised the soldiers to forget about gaining the right to vote or upsetting Jim Crow.[21]

As usual, Du Bois exaggerated. Nevertheless, his attack hit home. Millions of blacks seethed with indignation over Moton's speech to the black soldiers. One wrote to Moton to express his disgust: "You ought to have gone over and fired the boys with the thought that they . . . demand their rights as men and citizens. The rights of a white man. Equal rights. . . . [T]hey say you are 'white folks nigger.' That you are in the gang that helps to keep the Negro down." After his own investigation in France, Du Bois stated the matter with his customary bluntness. "A nation with a great disease set out to rescue civilization; it took the disease with it in virulent form and that disease of race-hatred and prejudice hampered its actions and discredited its finest professions."[22]

"WE RETURN FIGHTING"

"We return fighting," proclaimed Du Bois in May 1919. Having fought for democracy in Europe, "we are cowards and jackasses if . . . we do not marshal every ounce of our brain and brawn to fight a sterner, longer, more unbending battle against the forces of hell in our own land." It was presumptuous of Du Bois to speak on behalf of black veterans, especially as he had failed to obtain a captain's commission in the army. Still, his fighting words accurately summarized the mood of many black veterans. Black soldiers returned from Europe with broadened horizons and greater political awareness, some of them with combat experience. They also brought home bitterness over their treatment in the army, warm feelings toward the French people, and, despite Moton's words of caution, a resolve to assert their rights in the United States. And the veterans conveyed that mood to the rest of black America. "Beyond a doubt," stated a military intelligence analyst, "there is a new negro to be reckoned with in our political and social life."[23]

The new black militancy was most evident, perhaps, in New York City, the intellectual capital of black America, a meeting place of Africans, West Indians, and black people from across the United States. From 1917 on, a black New Yorker could buy a copy of the *Messenger*—in its own words, "the only magazine of scientific radicalism in the world published by Negroes." Mixing Marxist theory, sparkling prose, and blistering attacks on virtually every established black leader, the two young editors, Owen Chandler and A. Philip Randolph, aimed to provoke. They condemned the war as a fight between capitalists, ridiculed Du Bois as a naive opportunist, denounced the NAACP as antilabor, condemned the black church as "a business . . . run primarily for profits," and dismissed black politicians as "the worst enemies of the Negro race." They labelled Woodrow Wilson a narrow-minded bigot and lambasted Theodore Roosevelt as a "leader of American imperialism, militarism, and capitalism." Hailing the Bolshevik Revolution, they exulted in the spread of communism and praised the "titanic strikes" that were sweeping America. Soviet government "bids fair to sweep over the whole world," the *Messenger* predicted. "The sooner the better. On with the dance!"[24]

Not far from the Lenox Avenue offices of the *Messenger*, at Mother Zion AME Church, a portly, round-shouldered, dark-skinned Jamaican, Marcus Mosiah Garvey, enthralled 3,000 people with spellbinding oratory. Garvey had arrived in America in 1916. The founder and president of the Universal Negro Improvement Association (UNIA), and an admirer of Booker T. Washington, he came to raise funds for a Tuskegee-type school in Jamaica. He soon discovered, however, that most blacks in the North were far more militant than Washington. Then the war changed the political landscape and transformed black aspirations. Quick-witted and quick-tempered, Garvey attuned himself to the new mood. By 1917—after the East St. Louis riot—his speeches sizzled with angry rhetoric. Drawing bigger and bigger crowds, he berated white people for their racial cruelty and called upon black people everywhere to unite under his leadership. The membership of the UNIA grew by leaps and bounds.

Black militancy had an international dimension. Woodrow Wilson's insistence that national self-determination be the cornerstone of the postwar world stirred black Americans, who wanted that principle applied to Africa. Blacks across the political spectrum looked forward to the Paris peace conference with great hope, and they expected to see black delegates at the negotiating table. "This war ought to result in the establishment of an independent Negro Central African Republic," wrote Du Bois, "composed, at least, of the Belgian Congo and German East Africa, and, if possible, of Uganda, French Equatorial Africa, German Southwest Africa, and the Portuguese territories of Angola and Mozambique." Du Bois organized a Pan-African Congress that met in Paris and submitted proposals to the Allied powers. Marcus Garvey went further, demanding that "Africa must be for the Africans" and promising to "organize the Negroes of the world." If "the white man" refused to "clear out" of Africa, then blacks should be prepared, like the Irish, to fight and die to establish their independence. "We pledge our life's blood, our sacred blood, to the battlefields of Africa."[25]

The new militancy affected blacks in the South as well. In April 1919 the University Commission on Southern Race Questions, a group of white men from eleven state universities, met with black faculty members at Nashville's Fisk University to "hear from the negroes themselves exactly what negroes were thinking about, what they wanted and how they felt they were being treated." The blacks did not mince words. "It would astonish you to know the depth of the bitterness that is in the hearts of the negroes in the South today," said one of the teachers, Reverend Thomas M. Brumfield. "As long as there are Jim Crow laws and practices in the South, so long will there be distrust of the white man." Then Professor Isaac Fisher—a protégé of Booker T. Washington—presented a list of demands. Blacks wanted equal education facilities, the opportunity to vote, fairer treatment in court, black jurors, more protection for black women, an end to lynching, an end to employment discrimination, and an end to Jim Crow. "Segregation in every one of its forms must be abandoned before right relations will be effected. Separation is a sign of inferiority and the negro is bitter about it. We object to the fact of segregation, not to the condition of the Jim Crow car. We want to ride at will . . . on exactly the same terms and conditions as the white man."[26]

The expansion of the NAACP in the South testified to the fact that the era of Booker T. Washington was well and truly over. In 1914 the NAACP boasted only three Southern branches. By 1919 the South accounted for 131 of the NAACP's 310 branches. In 1919 alone the organization gained 85 new branches, nearly all of them in the South, and 35,000 new members.

The network of black women's clubs contributed mightily to the NAACP's growth. "Negro women enjoy organization," wrote Mary White Ovington. "They are ambitious, often jealous, and sensitive. But they get things done." The First World War tapped women's organizational skills and drew black clubwomen closer to the national civil rights struggle.[27]

Mary Burnett Talbert was typical of the middle-class women who helped to strengthen the NAACP. Born in Oberlin, Ohio, and educated at Oberlin College—the first coeducational college in the United States and a center of the abolitionist movement—Talbert taught in the public schools of Little Rock, Arkansas, before marrying and moving to Buffalo, New York. She then directed her energies toward her family, her Baptist church, and the women's club movement, serving as president of the NACW between 1916 and 1920. During the war she served in France as a Red Cross nurse and YWCA secretary. In 1918 she joined the board of the NAACP and in the autumn of that year toured Louisiana and Texas to found new branches and drum up members.

The efforts of Talbert and local clubwomen paid off handsomely. In Texas, where the NAACP had been completely unorganized, blacks founded twelve branches in 1918 and a further twenty-one in 1919. Within the space of one year, the original membership of 2,774 swelled to 7,692. In most of the new Texas NAACP branches, women made up at least a quarter of the charter members. The raw numbers, of course, were still small, but the people drawn into the NAACP fairly reflected the state's black population. There were doctors and businessmen and teachers, but the bulk of the membership, according to historian Steve Reich, came from the black working class. Most of the rural members were farmers and laborers. In the port city of Galveston, black longshoremen organized the branch. In other towns, Reich notes, "janitors, laborers, butlers, letter carriers, housekeepers, laundresses, seamstresses—even the butler at the governor's mansion—joined the ranks of the NAACP."[28]

. The new militancy affected every class of black Americans. Surging support for the NAACP—and for Marcus Garvey's UNIA—reflected the aspirations of workers and poor people, not just the educated middle class. A heightened sense of class consciousness and a new interest in unions went hand-in-hand with a greater determination to achieve racial equality. Just as the Great War encouraged blacks to expect racial equality, it also encouraged all workers, black and white, to expect higher wages, better conditions, and union recognition. Anxious to speed up industrial production, the Wilson administration made important concessions to organized labor, and private employers reluctantly followed suit. The labor movement thus enjoyed a rare interlude of dynamic growth: between 1915 and 1920 union membership increased from 2.6 million to 5.1 million. Wartime inflation, however, eroded wages, and when the government relaxed its supervision of the economy after the Armistice, workers staged strikes in one industry after another. Although largely shut out of the American Federation of Labor, many black workers were eager to organize and ready to strike.

Blacks joined what unions they could and sometimes formed unions of their own. In Alabama, black miners joined the United Mine Workers, one of the few AFL unions that welcomed blacks, and took part in the strike of 1919. Black longshoremen, organizing themselves into separate locals, staged a series of strikes in the ports of the South, sometimes in cooperation with the white longshoremen. In the Louisiana lumber mill town of Bogalusa, the International Union of Timber Workers, in alliance with the United Brotherhood of Carpenters and Joiners, started an organizing drive that embraced blacks as well as whites. In the cotton flats of Phillips County, Arkansas, black sharecroppers and tenant farmers, tired of being annually shortchanged by their white landlords, joined the Progressive Farmers Union and hired lawyers to negotiate for them. In Baltimore, black schoolteachers formed a union.

THE "RED SUMMER" OF 1919

Within days of the signing of the Armistice, however, the climate of national unity that had fostered cooperation between races and classes dissolved. The very changes that had given black people grounds for optimism—the Great Migration and the wartime mobilization—now produced a renewed determination on the part of whites to keep blacks in their place. Left-wing ideas and labor militancy challenged racial divisions. But employers, backed by the federal government and abetted by racism, crushed one strike after another, leaving the AFL enfeebled. A broader backlash against blacks accompanied the employer offensive. James Weldon Johnson dubbed the epidemic of racial violence that marred 1919 the "Red Summer," and the name stuck.

Arriving back in the South, black veterans ran into a brick wall of suspicion and hostility. From the Division of Military Intelligence in Washington, D.C., which warned that black veterans would be "inclined to impudence and arrogance," to the county sheriffs who wielded actual power of life and death, white officials struck hard against militancy. Southern whites swiftly disabused black veterans of any pretensions to equality. "In many a local community," recalled Benjamin Mays, then a young student from South Carolina, "Negro soldiers were told, 'Take off those uniforms and act like a nigger should.'" In one instance the mere sight of a uniformed black man led whites to lynch the offending veteran. While the thirty-six lynchings recorded in 1917 represented the lowest annual total since the Tuskegee Institute first began gathering statistics in 1882, the number of victims in 1919 soared to seventy-six. Whites offered excuses. "Negro soldiers returning from the war inflamed their people with stories of race equality in Europe," commented one newspaper, "especially the lack of discrimination in social intercourse."[29]

The climate of intensified repression also sparked race riots across the nation—twenty-six of them by one count—that left untold numbers dead, wounded, and homeless. Despite the entreaties of the NAACP, the federal government did nothing to curb this vicious anarchy. After much delay and with evident reluctance, Woodrow Wilson eventually issued a statement condemning mob violence. It was an utterly inadequate response to a national crisis.

The government then compounded its action during the "Red Summer" by whipping up a "Red Scare." Trading on the fear and confusion generated by Russia's Bolshevik Revolution, Attorney General A. Mitchell Palmer depicted America's own tiny radical fringe as a serious revolutionary threat. Unrestrained by Woodrow Wilson—who was enfeebled by a stroke, and in any case bitterly hostile to Bolshevism—Palmer unleased the Bureau of Investigation against suspected Socialists, Communists, anarchists, and unionists. After a coast-to-coast raid, the government deported hundreds of alien radicals. State and local authorities, taking their cue from Washington, cracked down on homegrown radicals. They not only smashed America's indigenous revolutionaries, the Industrial Workers of the World—who advocated "one big union"—but they also tried to suppress every shade of left-wing thinking. The New York legislature even expelled elected members of the peaceable Socialist Party. Many states outlawed "criminal syndicalism," a catchall offense that made advocacy of revolution illegal and rendered any expression of radicalism, however innocuous, vulnerable to prosecution.

Blacks escaped Palmer's dragnet because they were American citizens. But the Justice Department treated black militancy as subversion, and anybody who opposed white supremacy ran the risk of being targeted as a dangerous radical. "Bolshevism" was an easy explanation for black unrest and a quick excuse for antiblack violence. Many whites—and not only those in the South—justified the wave of lynchings and race riots in the name of patriotism. As the *New York Times* put it, "Bolshevist agitation has been extended among the negroes, especially in the South, and . . . is bearing its natural and inevitable fruit." The combination of the "Red Summer" and the "Red Scare" created a white backlash of peculiar ferocity.

Blacks were in no mood to accept white repression passively. Claude McKay's poem "If We Must Die" captured the imagination of black Americans in 1919. It ended with the lines:

Oh, kinsmen! we must meet the common foe!
Though far outnumbered let us show us brave,
And for their thousand blows deal one deathblow!
What though before us lies the open grave?
Like men we'll face the murderous, cowardly pack,
Pressed to the wall, dying, but fighting back!

Even the law-abiding NAACP encouraged blacks to defend themselves. "When the mob moves," Du Bois exhorted, "we prepare to meet it with bricks and clubs and guns."[30]

In many instances, blacks *did* fight back, especially in the cities of the North. NAACP official Walter White learned this reality most alarmingly when he walked through Chicago's South Side during the race riot. He saw a black man, shielded by a tree, take aim at him with a revolver. "I ducked as a bullet wanged into the side of the building exactly where my head had been a fraction of a second before." White, a black man, thought he would be safe from the riot if he stayed inside the black ghetto. But he looked like a white man, and became a target.[31]

In a race war, however, blacks could not possibly win. They would be outnumbered and outgunned. Whites controlled the police, the courts, and the prisons. Whites could also draw upon the might of the federal government. The Elaine, Arkansas, riot of October 1919 showed that when blacks resorted to violence, even in self-defense, whites would deploy overwhelming force to crush them.

A confused shooting incident—there are two versions of what happened and who fired first—sparked this bloody explosion of violence. The roots of the riot, however, lay in the perennial economic conflict between black farmers and white landlords. Black tenants and sharecroppers in Phillips County had formed an organization, the Progressive Farmers and Household Union of America, to strengthen their hand in dealing with landlords, who, they believed, systematically cheated them at the annual settling up of accounts. Taking advice from lawyers in Little Rock, they decided to demand itemized statements of accounts, and if the landlords refused, to take them to court. They also planned to "refuse to pick cotton then in the field or to sell cotton belonging to them for less than the market price."[32]

On the evening of September 30, black farmers met at a black church in a hamlet called Hoop Spur to discuss their dispute with the landlords. Some brought their shotguns and kept a wary eye out for attacks. Unexpectedly, a car carrying two white men and a black man—a deputy sheriff, a railroad agent, and a prison "trusty"—pulled up outside. Whether the car stopped by accident or design is not clear. Deputy sheriff Charles W. Pratt claimed that they were en route to Elaine to arrest a bootlegger when their car broke down; they were then fired upon from the church. The black farmers claimed that they fired only in self-defense, that the whites were the aggressors. In any case, after a fusillade of bullets the railroad agent lay dead and the deputy sheriff was wounded. An army intelligence officer used a revealing choice of words to describe the incident. "The negroes, not knowing the real mission of these officers, looked upon them as Russian revolutionists would have looked upon the secret police that the czars employed."[33]

Horror-struck whites convinced themselves blacks were about to launch a full-scale insurrection. The cry went up that blacks were plotting to kill the planters, seize their lands, and then massacre all whites. The governor of Arkansas requested federal troops to suppress the alleged revolt, and the army was glad to oblige. "The disorder had been brought about by radical influence," claimed Captain John B. Campbell of military intelligence, "which is part of the organized campaign of terrorism of the I.W.W. and joint radical organizations."[34]

Scouring the woods and canebrakes around the town of Elaine, six hundred federal troops helped local whites "round up and disarm" suspected insurrectionists. One soldier and four other white men lost their lives in sporadic shooting. Nobody knows how many black people died. According to the NAACP, as many as 250 may have perished at the hands of the soldiers and the white posse. The true number was probably smaller. Even so, the army admitted to killing "about twenty negroes . . . for refusing to halt when so ordered or for resisting arrest." The white posse killed others. Hundreds of blacks were summarily arrested and roughly interrogated. If employers and landlords could affirm that they were "good negroes," the army released them. The Phillips County grand jury indicted 122 blacks, charging 73 of them with murder. Twelve received death sentences.[35]

The NAACP resisted the baleful consequences of the Red Summer with all the means at its disposal. In 1917, after the riot in East St. Louis, the NAACP mounted a protest parade down New York City's Fifth Avenue, conducting it in total silence but for the sound of muffled drums. In the same year it took out a full-page advertisement in the *New York Times,* paid for by black clubwomen, that condemned lynching as "The Shame of America." In 1919 the NAACP held a conference on lynching at Carnegie Hall in New York City that featured speeches by, among others, Charles Evans Hughes, a former Supreme Court Justice, and Emmett O'Neal, a former governor of Alabama. The NAACP also caused an antilynching bill to be introduced in Congress and seriously debated. The NAACP even saved the lives of the twelve men condemned to death for their alleged role in the Elaine riot: in *Moore* v. *Dempsey* (1923) the U.S. Supreme Court decided that the trials had been "dominated by a mob." Southern white leaders, fearing federal legislation, and worried that combined black migration would cause a shortage of cheap labor, finally took steps to curb mob violence. After 1920, lynching declined sharply.[36]

The Red Summer, however, shattered the NAACP's hopes of becoming a mass organization with roots and branches throughout the South. A single incident, the beating of John R. Shillady, illustrated the reason why: whites were not prepared to tolerate an organization that openly challenged racial inequality.

Shillady, a white man, was the NAACP's first executive secretary. A former social worker and a man of good will and optimism, he believed in putting the NAACP's case honestly and openly before Southern white people, appealing to their reason, democratic instincts, and enlightened self-interest. But when he travelled to Austin, Texas, to talk with state officials who were threatening to suppress the local NAACP branch, he was savagely beaten by three white men, in broad daylight, outside his hotel. One of his assailants, a county judge, explained that "The main object of this man's visit was to sow discontent among the Negroes, and I thought it was my duty to stop him. And we not only stopped him but have gotten him out of the community." Shillady returned to New York, physically intact but mentally broken. He resigned his job in 1920 and died soon afterwards—as much a casualty of Southern racism, Walter White believed, as if he were the victim of a lynch mob.[37]

THE CONSOLIDATION OF WHITE SUPREMACY, SOUTH AND NORTH

If John Shillady's beating had been condemned by Southern whites, the NAACP might have passed it off as an unfortunate but isolated incident. Instead, white leaders in the South applauded the beating, treating it as an object lesson in how to deal with the NAACP. Men like Shillady were a "public menace," commented a Rome, Georgia, newspaper; they should be "kept in jail." The New York–based NAACP was "only breeding trouble, intensifying racial feeling and provoking clashes," wrote the *New Orleans States*. "The sooner it ceases its activities in this section . . . the better." In Texas, the NAACP's explosive growth came to a sudden halt, and then went into reverse. Only a few of the people who had signed up in 1918–19 chose to renew their memberships in 1920; most branches became dormant. But the chilling effect of Shillady's beating went far beyond the Lone Star State. Throughout the South, NAACP branches shrank or folded. By the mid-1920s the NAACP had virtually collapsed outside the major cities. The few functioning branches trod very cautiously indeed.[38]

The Commission on Interracial Cooperation (CIC), founded in Atlanta in 1919, came into being as an effort to discourage racial violence. Besides ameliorating racial tension, the CIC did much other good work. It fought the Ku Klux Klan, which was revived in 1915, seeking to expose and discredit it. It encouraged whites to take practical steps to improve black education, health, and living conditions. It campaigned against lynching by organizing the moral influence of Southern white women, who tried to shame the South's politicians and sheriffs into protecting black prisoners and curbing mob violence. The CIC turned out a steady stream of informed research on the South's social, economic, and racial problems. (Its studies of lynching, and of the plight of tenant farmers and sharecroppers, became instant classics.) It produced

textbooks and provided visiting speakers for college courses on "race relations." Above all, the CIC succeeded in bringing Southern whites and Southern blacks together where the NAACP had failed.

The existence of the CIC proved acceptable to Southern whites, however,
only because the commission accepted the basic structure of white supremacy. It assumed that Northern black leadership only provoked Southern hostility, and that improvements in race relations would only come about with the
consent of Southern white people. It did not, therefore, campaign for the
reenrollment of blacks as voters. Nor did it advocate an end to segregated
schools, trains, streetcars, and public accommodations. Although the CIC
was interracial, whites dominated its leadership, and it brought blacks and
whites together only in the most carefully circumscribed settings, eschewing
anything that could be construed as "social equality." The CIC made no attempt, moreover, to build a popular base. Anxious not to arouse the passions
and prejudices of the masses, black or white, it enlisted the support of the
middle and upper classes—the "best elements" of each race. The CIC, therefore, was no substitute for the NAACP. Indeed, it sought to divorce Southern
blacks from the NAACP's militant program of racial equality. "For the Negro
himself," explained CIC staff member Thomas J. Woofter, "the need is for
patience."[39]

In the North, too, the aftermath of the Red Summer proved gravely damaging to the NAACP's cause. Chicago provided a microcosm of how a Northern version of white supremacy consolidated itself after the violence of
1919. Even before the Great Migration, white Chicagoans had resented black
newcomers, viewing them as unwelcome competitors for jobs and housing. In order to defend their turf, whites had formed neighborhood associations, pressured landlords and realtors, and even bombed the homes of
black people who crossed invisible racial boundaries. When racial violence
exploded on July 27, 1919, the ensuing riot claimed thirty-eight lives. But
the long-term consequences were far worse. In the words of historian
Allan Spear, the riot "destroyed whatever hope remained for a peacefully
integrated city." Chicago's politicians and businessmen concluded that only
racial segregation could ensure racial peace. In 1921 the city's realtors
adopted the "restrictive covenant," which prohibited the white home buyer
from reselling or renting the property to blacks. Restrictive covenants soon
covered most of the city's housing. Black Chicago congealed into a gigantic
ghetto.[40]

The Chicago pattern served as a model for the rest of the North. While the
Supreme Court consistently struck down municipal laws that carved cities
into black and white residential "zones," private discrimination, backed up by

intimidation and violence, created such zones anyway. Housing became strictly segregated. School enrollments then followed housing patterns, keeping black and white children apart. The actions of public officials, overt and covert, reinforced racial segregation at every turn. Some Northern cities, for example, adopted school segregation as official policy. One quarter of the black children in Philadelphia attended schools officially designated as Negro. The City of Brotherly Love also decided never to employ black teachers outside all-Negro schools. By 1929 Indianapolis had implemented a thoroughgoing policy of school segregation that remained in place for twenty years. Even in cities that never officially adopted school segregation, politicians, administrators, principals, and parents colluded to bring about single-race schools through the use of transfers and attendance zones.[41]

The Catholic Church became another bulwark of segregation in the cities of the North. An immensely powerful institution by the 1920s—almost a state within a state—the Church reflected the clannishness and prejudices of its immigrant clientele. But most of the hierarchy, from priest to archbishop, also felt indifferent or hostile to black people. The Church organized separate parishes for black worshippers, but in 1930 boasted only one black parish priest. Catholic lay institutions like the Knights of Columbus refused to accept blacks as members. Apart from maintaining a "colored" university in New Orleans, Xavier, patronized for the most part by mixed-race "creoles," the Church barred blacks from its seminaries and colleges. Catholic hospitals, wrote one of the Church's lay critics, "had no place for Negroes either as physicians, interns, nurses, or patients."[42]

The Red Scare, and the defeat of the 1919–20 strikes, also played a part in consolidating white supremacy. Left-wing radicals offered class solidarity as a political alternative to ethnic and racial bigotry. Socialist-minded labor leaders tried to implement class solidarity as a practical strategy for unionizing entire industries. But the Red Scare helped employers suppress radical thinking and defeat interracial unions. In Bogalusa, Louisiana, the Great Southern Lumber Company unleased armed vigilantes, who killed three union leaders and forced others to flee. In Chicago, the meat-packers persuaded most of their black employees to cross union picket lines, undermining a strike. It did not greatly matter whether employers played the race card, cried "Bolshevism," or resorted to force: the end result was the same. White union members became more convinced than ever of the futility of attempting to organize blacks. Black workers had their distrust of white-led unions confirmed.

The Great War had failed to end colonialism abroad and failed to end white supremacy at home. Two years after the Armistice, the goal of racial equality seemed no closer than it had been in 1915, the year of Booker T.

Washington's death and the start of the Great Migration. The somber words of John Shillady upon resigning from the NAACP reflected a creeping pessimism: "I am less confident than heretofore . . . of the probability of overcoming, within a reasonable period, the forces opposed to Negro equality."[43]

Marcus Garvey in 1923

Library of Congress, Prints and Photographs Division, NYWT&S Collection

Marcus Garvey and the UNIA

In its glorious heyday, the United Negro Improvement Association put on a breathtaking display of pageantry. Parading through Harlem on August 2, 1920, the UNIA's massed ranks took three hours to pass by. A chauffeured automobile, preceded by four mounted policemen, conveyed Marcus Garvey, the Provisional President of Africa, in the manner befitting a head of state. Resplendent in brocaded uniform and cocked hat, Garvey acknowledged the cheering onlookers with a regal wave of the hand. More cars trailed behind him, carrying regalia-attired lesser officials, including the Knight Commanders of the Distinguished Order of the Nile.

Then came thousands of walking rank-and-file. Uniformed contingents marched in proud lockstep: the Black Star Line Choir, the Philadelphia Legion, the Black Cross Nurses, the Black Eagle Flying Corps, the African Motor Corps. Swaying bands from Norfolk and New York City "whooped it up." Then a forest of banners, each emblazoned with a slogan—variations on "Africa for the Africans!"—snaked its way down Lenox Avenue. They were borne aloft by UNIA members who came from Liberia, Canada, Panama, British Guiana, the Caribbean islands, and a dozen states of the Union. Hundreds of cars and more mounted policemen ended "the greatest parade ever staged anywhere in the world by Negroes."[1]

Black Americans were accustomed to being satirized for imitating the ways of white people, and the UNIA was an easy mark. With its garish uniforms and pompous titles, the Garvey movement seemed like a grotesque parody of the British Empire, a bizarre black Ruritania. Marcus Garvey's own

Napoleon-sized ego attracted savage ridicule. It is tempting to portray Garveyism as an escapist fantasy, a pathetic expression of black political naivete, or a popular fad of a type all too common in the 1920s—when millions of Americans, whites and blacks, donned exotic hats and robes to become Masons, Elks, Oddfellows, and Shriners.

Garveyism, however, was more than a superficial phenomenon of a shallow decade: contemporaries took it very seriously indeed. White governments that held sway over black populations found the rise of the UNIA profoundly disturbing. Great Britain feared that Garveyism might destabilize its colonial empire in Africa and the Caribbean. The government of the United States viewed Garvey as a powerful agitator who—alone among black leaders—had the magnetism and mass following to endanger white supremacy. Other black leaders variously admired him, envied him, feared him, and opposed him. Some concluded that he was an unscrupulous demagogue who had to be stopped at all costs. The passions he aroused and the opposition he evoked suggest that Garvey represented something important and disturbing.

Marcus Garvey did not invent black nationalism in the United States: the idea that blacks should form their own Negro republic because they could never achieve justice in America was almost as old as the United States itself. However, Garvey was the first black nationalist—the only one before or since—to create a mass movement. The exact size of that movement is impossible to determine. Garvey extravagantly boasted of two million, four million, six million "members." Du Bois, his archenemy, ridiculed these grandiloquent claims, reckoning that the UNIA at its peak had only 80,000 dues-paying members. Yet even if Du Bois were right, the UNIA still outstripped the NAACP. Moreover, Garvey could count millions of blacks as followers in spirit and sympathy. No other black leader generated such enthusiasm and adulation.

Garvey gave black Americans something they had never before felt so clearly and unequivocally: the sense that they were a people—a nation—with a proud past, a heroic present, and a magnificent future. He insisted that blacks were Negroes first and Americans second. If the 400 million people of African descent came together, he argued, they could liberate Africa—by war if necessary—from the yoke of white colonialism. They could then create a great African Empire that would embrace the native Africans, the American Negroes, and the blacks of Central America and the Caribbean.[2]

In readiness for that day, Garvey created a government-in-waiting and endowed it with the trappings and symbols of nationhood. UNIA members saluted a flag of red, black, and green—symbolizing the blood shed for liberty, the color of the Negro race, and the verdant flora of the African motherland. They sang a national anthem, "Ethiopia, thou land of our Father." They repeated a motto, "One God! One Aim! One Destiny!" They chanted a slogan, "Africa for the Africans!" The UNIA boasted a diplomatic corps, a Great African Army, and, in the steamships of the Black Star Line, a navy of sorts. In its African Orthodox Church, worshippers could pray to a black Jesus and a black God.[3]

GARVEY'S WEST INDIAN BACKGROUND

It seems astounding that a native of Jamaica, who did not set foot in the United States until 1916, could eclipse America's established black leaders in so short a time. In fact, immigrants from the Caribbean islands were prominent in American radical and black nationalist circles, out of all proportion to their numbers, in the early twentieth century. As historian Winston James has argued, West Indian immigrants tended to be more militant than native-born Americans. They were unaccustomed to being a minority and had never experienced legalized racial segregation. Racial terrorism such as lynching did not exist in their home islands. Although ruled by colonial officials, they recalled a long tradition of armed resistance to slavery.[4]

Garvey's West Indian background thus equipped him with experiences and insights that gave him an enormous advantage over American-born blacks. He grew up in a majority-black society, which, paradoxically, combined an easygoing racial tolerance with deep racial inequality. He played with white children until he was fourteen years old, received an "English" education, and cultivated the friendship of white teachers, ministers, and colonial officials. "We have no open race prejudice here," he noted, "and we do not openly antagonize one another." Jamaica's Anglocentric culture left a profound impression on him. His favorite poet was that laureate of Victorianism, Alfred Lord Tennyson. His heroes from history were the nation-builders of Britain and Europe: Marlborough, Pitt, Wellington, Napoleon, Bismarck. His vision of a great Negro empire made the ambitions of America's black leaders seem parochial. His imperial dreams caught the imagination of the masses.[5]

Jamaica also bequeathed to Garvey a vehement hostility to all forms of "shade prejudice" among blacks. Like other Caribbean and Latin American societies, Jamaica had a three-tier caste system consisting of a very small white minority, a larger minority of "coloreds," and a very large black majority. The coloreds were mulattoes—the descendants of unions between whites and blacks—and they enjoyed a status that was distinctly superior to that of the blacks. The small size of the white population, the legality of racial intermarriage, and the favored position of the coloreds all contributed to a softening of the latent antagonism between black and white.

But Jamaica's racial fluidity also militated against the formation of a strong sense of identity among the black majority. Even though they suffered from exploitation and discrimination, the blacks lacked unity. The coloreds formed a kind of buffer between them and the whites. The coloreds identified with the whites; the blacks saw the coloreds' privileged position as evidence that Jamaica did not operate a rigid color line. Thus the whites manipulated the coloreds, and both groups oppressed the blacks. According to Garvey, "The black man naturally is kept at the foot of the ladder and is trampled on by all the shades above."

Garvey, a very dark-complexioned Negro with little or no white ancestry, deplored the fact that the colored Jamaicans—the very people who could provide blacks with strong leadership—"made the mistake of drawing and keeping themselves away from the race." They deluded themselves into believing that whites would accept them as equals. "It is useless for any pompous man of color to think because his skin is a little paler than that of his brother that he is not also a Negro." He urged Negroes of all shades to unite.

Jamaica left Garvey with another strong conviction. Because there was no hard-and-fast color line in Jamaica, he believed that black people were hampered by their own lack of ambition and achievement rather than by prejudice and discrimination. The Negro was handicapped by difficult circumstances, true enough, "but no one is keeping him back. He is keeping back himself." Whites had indeed created an advanced civilization, but they had done it through deeds of glory and heroism. The only way for blacks to overcome their own backwardness, Garvey believed, was to emulate whites and match their achievement. "If the Negro were to try to raise himself in the civilized cosmos, all the other races would be glad to meet him on the plane of equality and comradeship." The respect of whites had to be earned.[6]

To Garvey, therefore, the advancement of the black race was above all a matter of will:

The will is the thing that rules men; the will is the thing that rules the world. The human will is that force . . . that the white races have used to make themselves the giants that they are in this world today; and because we fail to use that human will, that accounts for our being pigmies as a race. . . . We are believing that we are still too humble to soar to the heights of independence and freedom and liberty.

Blacks must be builders rather than complainers. Consciousness of race and a willingness to work and sacrifice for a common cause were the hallmarks of national greatness.[7]

Small wonder, then, that as a young, would-be race leader in the years before the First World War, Marcus Garvey was an unabashed admirer of Booker T. Washington. The Wizard of Tuskegee was a builder par excellence: Jamaica had no comparable example of black achievement. Even when the war radicalized American blacks, and the "old-time cringing Negro passed from the stage," Garvey continued to believe that nothing stimulated race consciousness more effectively than the building of black-owned, black-controlled institutions. Washington had his Tuskegee Institute, Garvey his Black Star steamship line.[8]

THE EVOLUTION OF A BLACK NATIONALIST

By 1919 Garvey had years of experience as a soap-box orator, political journalist, and street-corner philosopher. At the age of eighteen he led a strike of printers in Kingston, Jamaica. In Costa Rica and Panama, he did battle on behalf of West Indian plantation workers employed by the United Fruit Company. In London, where he lived between 1912 and 1914, he appeared regularly at Speaker's Corner in Hyde Park.

Between 1910 and 1914, years of almost constant travel, Garvey saw how blacks were treated in a dozen countries on both sides of the Atlantic. Everywhere, they lived like "peons, serfs, dogs, and slaves." In London, his first-hand observation of Parliament— which he admired—made him even more aware of the contradiction between British democracy and British colonialism. In London, too, he became an avid reader of *African Times and Orient Review*, published by Duse Mohammed Ali, an Egyptian nationalist and influential foe of racial prejudice. Ali introduced Garvey to the writings of Edward Wilmot Blyden, a Liberian scholar who extolled the glories of Ethiopia, and to his own histories of ancient Egypt. By 1914, Garvey recalled, "I could not remain in London any more. My brain was afire." He resolved that "the black man would not continue to be kicked about by all the other races of the world."

On his passage to Jamaica, Garvey encountered a fellow West Indian who had married a Basuto woman. The man told such "horrible and pitiable tales" about native life in Africa, he recalled, that "my heart bled within me."

Retiring to my cabin, all day and the following night I pondered over the subject of that conversation, and at midnight, flat on my back, the vision and thought came to me that I should name the organization the Universal Negro Improvement Association and African Communities (Imperial) League. Such a name I thought would embrace the purpose of all black humanity.

In a hotel room in Kingston, with the help of Amy Ashwood, who became his first wife, he founded the UNIA. It attracted little interest and less support. In March 1916, frustrated by the tepid response in Jamaica, he arrived in New York to organize an American branch.[9]

Wartime Harlem boasted any number of street-corner agitators, from radical socialists like A. Philip Randolph to black nationalists like Hubert H. Harrison, and it took several years for Garvey to separate himself from the pack. He had his share of speaking disasters—at one meeting falling off his soapbox—and his first two attempts to foster a branch of the UNIA in New York met with failure. "Harlem ignored him," wrote Roi Ottley. "Worse, he was dismissed as an ignorant carpet-bagger." In 1918, however, Garvey decided to make America, rather than Jamaica, his principal base. He took over personal direction of the New York branch of the UNIA, and founded a newspaper, the *Negro World.* The UNIA grew by leaps and bounds. By 1919 the New York branch boasted more than 5,000 members, and about thirty other branches had been established. In August, the UNIA held a hugely successful meeting in Carnegie Hall.[10]

What accounted for Garvey's extraordinary rise? It could not have been his physical appearance. Short and pudgy, not even admirers considered him handsome. Journalist John E. Bruce called him a "little, sawed-off, hammered-down man." Du Bois, in words that became notorious, described him as a "little, fat black man, but with intelligent eyes and big head." An FBI agent, after recording his age (thirty-two), height (five feet, seven and a half inches), and weight (170 pounds), noted Garvey's "very dark complexion, . . . marked round shoulders, [and] small oriental eyes."[11]

That Garvey was a powerful speaker is undeniable. One admirer attested that he "could throw his voice around three corners without batting an eyelash." Du Bois, an opponent, admitted that he was a "facile speaker, able to express himself in grammatical and forceful English." Even his nemesis, the young J. Edgar Hoover, conceded that "He is an exceptionally fine orator." By turns angry, sarcastic, erudite, funny, and statesmanlike, he delivered his speeches with a staccato, rapid-fire delivery that evidently transported audiences. Yet the only surviving sound recordings of Garvey reveal a curious monotone that strikes the modern ear as repetitive and dull.[12]

What Garvey said was more important than how he said it. To state that he preached racial pride and ambition, and that black Americans responded with enthusiasm, is to grasp an important truth—but it is only a partial explanation for Garvey's astonishing popularity. Nearly every American black leader of note had sought to instill racial pride, and to rebut accusations of black inferiority. Yet such was the climate of racism in overwhelmingly white America that their protestations of equality had invariably sounded an apologetic note. Booker T. Washington had been notorious for scolding blacks for their moral shortcomings. Even the militant proclamations of Du Bois betrayed a touchy defensiveness. Garvey, perhaps because he grew up in Jamaica, was far less preoccupied with the white supremacist ideas that had bedeviled black American leaders. Moreover, because he pitched his arguments solely to black people—unlike the interracial NAACP—the UNIA openly fostered black chauvinism.

A vision of "Africa for the Africans" was the heart of Garvey's black nationalism, the emotional core of his popular appeal. Blacks in the New World had been robbed of their African language, culture, and identity. Africa itself had been carved up by the European powers, leaving only two independent nations, Liberia and Ethiopia, governed by black people. In Garvey's era, moreover, virtually every depiction of black Africa that appeared in Europe and America was a negative one. Whites referred to black Africans as backward, primitive, and savage. They portrayed Africa as a place without a history, without any record of civilization. Heathen and barbarous, unfitted for self-government, Africans were destined to be ruled by white people for the foreseeable future. Small wonder that blacks in the American diaspora felt little kinship with, or interest in, their ancestral homeland. The image of Africa as the "Dark Continent" rammed home the message that black people were inferior.

The UNIA sought to demolish that image. Like today's "Afrocentric" scholars, the Garveyites depicted Africa as the cradle of civilization. The ancient Ethiopians, a black people, influenced the ancient Egyptians; indeed, the two peoples shared a common culture. "When Europe was still a continent of barbarians," Egypt developed a written language, practiced a flourishing agriculture, acquired advanced knowledge in medicine, mathematics, and astrology, and built magnificent temples and pyramids. Through Egypt, the Ethiopians transmitted civilization to ancient Greece. Even in modern times, when they had "lapsed into a wild and nomadic life," black Africans cultivated crops, wove cloth, smelted iron, practiced medicine, and retained a stable and orderly social structure. Far from being barbarous heathens, native Africans were "the most moral people in the world," with "very clear ideas about God, or gods," and carefully observed religious rites.

Given the fact that most black Americans were Christians, the UNIA took pains to refute racist interpretations of the Scriptures. Garveyite ministers insisted that the Biblical passage invoked by whites to justify Negro slavery— "Cursed be Canaan," Noah had said, "a servant of servants shall he be unto his brethren"—had *not* referred to the dark-skinned Cushites or Ethiopians. They maintained that the Bible actually described the ancestors of black Africans in respectful terms. "Simon, the Cyrenean, a Negro," carried the cross of Jesus to Mount Calvary. Garveyites treasured this verse from Song of Solomon: "I am dark, but comely, daughters of Jerusalem." And they took the famous words from Psalm 68—"Princes shall come out of Egypt, Ethiopia shall stretch out her hand unto God"—as a Biblical prophecy that Africans would create their own nation and government.[13]

Garvey's nationalism was uncompromisingly problack. It was also, at times, aggressively antiwhite. Indeed, in reversing the logic of white racism, he at times sounded like a black racist. Nationalism feeds on some of the ugliest human emotions: xenophobia, racism, ethnic hostility, and religious intolerance. Garveyism sometimes whipped up these emotions.

It was Garvey who first popularized the term "white devils" as a synonym for white people. "They tell us that God is white," he thundered. "That is a lie. They tell us that all of His angels are white, too. To my mind, everything that is devilish is white. They told us that the devil was a black man. There isn't a greater devil in the world than the white man." Garvey and his followers never tired of uttering bloodcurdling threats of warfare against "Anglo-Saxons" and retribution against "Southern Crackers." As one Garveyite orator—a minister—put it, "Not only will we seek an opportunity to revenge our wrongs, but every man that lifts a hand against a Negro must die with that Negro." Such statements were infrequent, but not untypical.[14]

Yet, for the most part, Garvey avoided the meaner impulses of nationalism. He intended "white devils" as a political metaphor, not a literal truth. Similarly, the UNIA constructed its "black God" as an imaginative device rather than an exclusive deity. In fact, the UNIA's "Negro Catechism," written by Rev. George Alexander McGuire, was more universalistic than the Christian theology of the mainstream white churches. God made no group or race superior to another: "He created all races equal and of one blood, to dwell on all the face of the earth." God had "neither color, nor other natural parts"— blacks could envisage him as black, just as whites imagined him to be their own color. Garveyism looked for a world order in which blacks would attain parity with whites, not strive for superiority.[15]

Above all, it was sheer timing that accounted for the rapidity of Garvey's rise. In the first place, the death of Booker T. Washington had removed the primary symbol of black self-help and racial pride. Neither the NAACP nor the National Urban League (founded in 1911 to assist black migrants in the North) could replace that symbol: they were too narrowly focused, and white people were too prominent among their leaders. "There was no one with a positive and practical uplift program for the masses," recalled Amy Jacques

Garvey. "There was no all-Negro organization with a program or plan for the race beyond equality and citizen's rights." The UNIA stepped into this vacuum, appealing to the ever-present yearning for racial solidarity.[16]

In the second place, Garvey skillfully exploited the extraordinary political ferment unleashed by the Great War. The first year of peace, 1919, witnessed the return of black soldiers from France, bitter over their treatment by the army; widespread labor unrest marked by a wave of strikes; an upsurge of nationalism in Europe, including open rebellion in Ireland against British rule; and a stirring of anticolonial consciousness among colored peoples in India, Africa, and the Caribbean. Accompanying this crisis of the *ancien régime* was a powerful tide of conservative resistance to change, some of it specifically directed against blacks: the revival of the Ku Klux Klan, race riots in Chicago and elsewhere, an increase in lynching, and the determination of white Southerners to maintain Jim Crow. The clash of heightened expectations and continuing oppression made black opinion extremely volatile. "Garvey leaped into the ocean of black unhappiness at a most timely moment for a saviour," wrote newspaper reporter Roi Ottley.[17]

THE UNIA's VISION OF AFRICAN LIBERATION

Contrary to popular belief, Garvey did not advocate wholesale emigration "back to Africa" as a cure-all for the problems of black Americans. True, he held out the prospect that they should, at some distant and indeterminate point in the future, return to Africa. But he never pretended that emigration was, in the short term, a realistic option for most black Americans. Rather, Garvey saw the establishment of a "free and independent Africa" as the key to improving the position of blacks in the New World.[18]

Garvey knew that white immigrants in America had been powerfully assisted by the rise of European nationalism. The lynching of Italians in New Orleans had provoked a diplomatic crisis between the United States and Italy. Discrimination against Japanese immigrants in California had evoked vigorous protests from the government of Japan. The rise of the Irish in America paralleled the advance of nationalism in Ireland. Blacks, however, could exert no such external pressure. Hence whites lynched them with impunity. But when the "big black African Republic" was established, Garvey predicted, black people in the Americas would have a formidable ally. "Make Africa a first-rate power, a first-rate nation, and if you live in Georgia, if you live in Mississippi, if you live in Texas, as a black man I will dare them to lynch you, because you are an African citizen and you will have a great army and a great navy to protect your rights."[19]

Garvey's vision appeared absurdly grandiose. Yet blacks in the United States drew hope from the international situation. In 1919 nationalism was flowing at high tide. The Great War had destroyed old empires—Russia, Germany, Austria-Hungary, Turkey—and new nations rose up from their ruins. The Paris Peace Conference endorsed the principle of "self-determination." Britain, it is true, claimed a wholesale exemption from that principle, seeking to protect—and expand—its far-flung empire. Yet in 1919 even British colonialism appeared shaky, with independence movements gathering strength in Egypt and, especially, in India. In the Caribbean, strikes shook Trinidad and Jamaica; rioting, initiated by returning soldiers resentful of racial discrimination, erupted in British Honduras.[20]

The most serious challenge to Britain, and the one giving the UNIA its greatest inspiration, was the rebellion in Ireland. Britain's brutal reprisals after the 1916 Easter rising, and its ham-fisted extension of wartime conscription to the Emerald Isle, killed the old Home Rule party stone dead. In 1918 a new nationalist party, Sinn Fein, captured the allegiance of the majority of the Irish people on a platform of complete independence from Britain. In tandem with the Irish Republican Army, Sinn Fein proceeded to render British rule unworkable. Meanwhile, Eamon De Valera, president of the independent republic proclaimed by Sinn Fein, escaped from a British jail and embarked upon a triumphant tour of the United States.

Could any of this help to pry loose white rule over black Africa? That Germany would lose her African colonies was a certainty. Du Bois argued that those colonies should be placed under international administration; Garvey campaigned for the total extinction of colonial rule. The Treaty of Versailles, however, turned out to be a bitter disappointment. It placed Germany's former possessions under the "mandate" of the victorious powers—in effect simply transferring them from one white government to another. The peace treaties took no cognizance whatever of the wishes of the indigenous Africans. The empires of Britain, France, Belgium, Holland, and Portugal were not touched.

Garvey was sufficiently prescient to understand that the postwar settlement would not last. A new era of rivalry among the great powers and commercial competition, he believed, would lead to another war, and to the ultimate destruction of European colonialism. Japan, already a great power, harbored imperial ambitions and posed a clear challenge to white power in Asia. Allied to independence movements in India, Indochina, and elsewhere, Japan would be a formidable foe.[21]

The coming war, Garvey predicted, would pit the "yellow and brown peoples of Asia" against the whites of Europe and America. And 400 million black people would decide the outcome of that conflict. No longer would blacks fight in the service of their white oppressors: this time they would fight for African liberation. "We have been dying for the last five hundred years—and for whom? For an alien race. The time has come for the Negro to die for himself. We pledge our life's blood, our sacred blood, to the battlefields of Africa."[22]

The UNIA needed more than saber-rattling verbosity, however, to sustain its vision of African liberation. The Black Star Line (BSL) Steamship Corporation, formed in the summer of 1919, was a propaganda masterstroke. "Ships were the preeminent symbols of national power," noted historian Judith Stein. The BSL offered an exciting, romantic, and visible expression of black ambition. Moreover, by selling stock in the company, the UNIA offered black Americans a tangible stake in the building of an all-black merchant marine. The BSL would provide black passengers with nondiscriminatory service throughout the Caribbean, and its ships would, in time, reap rich financial pickings from trade with Africa.[23]

Garvey's scheme was perfectly attuned to the speculative mood of the time. Many people of quite modest means, blacks as well as whites, had purchased Liberty Bonds during the war and accumulated savings. They were now lured into buying stock in the belief that profits were all but guaranteed. An agent of the Bureau of Investigation (forcrunner of the FBI) attended a UNIA meeting in New York's Madison Square Garden and watched in amazement as Garvey's appeal for funds elicited a "shower of five, ten and even one hundred dollar bills," soon filling "a leather bag of large size to the top." The BSL quickly sold almost 100,000 shares.[24]

Within a year, the Black Star Line had acquired three vessels: the *Yarmouth*, its flagship, a merchantman; the *Shadyside*, an excursion boat that offered trips along the Hudson River; and the *Kanawha*, a yacht that had been converted to steam. In 1921 Garvey toured the Caribbean aboard the *Yarmouth*, stopping in Cuba, Jamaica, Panama, Costa Rica, and Belize. Meanwhile, the UNIA hatched plans to acquire a transatlantic steamer. "The Black Star Line," wrote Judith Stein, "transformed Garvey into an international leader of black communities on three continents."[25]

Liberia now became the focus of the UNIA's African ambitions. Founded in 1847 by the American Colonization Society as a homeland for freed slaves, it was the only African nation, with the exception of Ethiopia, that had escaped white colonial rule. Ethiopia was landlocked, remote, and utterly foreign. Liberia, on the other hand, was accessible by sea and had cultural ties to the United States. A small English-speaking elite, most of them the descendants of former American slaves, ruled the country from Monrovia, the capital, and other coastal towns. About half a million native Africans inhabited the interior. In 1920 the UNIA proposed to invest $2 million in Liberia's ailing economy, money that would be raised in the U.S. through the sale of "Liberian Construction Bonds." A UNIA loan would not only safeguard Liberia's political independence, but also give the Garveyites a vital foothold in the African continent.[26]

In 1920–21 Marcus Garvey was at the height of his power and influence. "The UNIA was the major political force among blacks in the postwar world," writes historian Robert Hill. The *Negro World* sold 75,000 copies a week, and, with articles in French and Spanish as well as English, was circulated throughout the Caribbean and Central America. With over 400 branches, the UNIA dwarfed the NAACP.

Who were the Garveyites? At the leadership level, Garvey attracted an array of talented individuals to beef up the UNIA's organization. Top supporters included T. Thomas Fortune, veteran newspaper editor, civil rights activist, and a former ally of Booker T. Washington; William H. Ferris, a Harvard graduate and author of books on African history; John E. Bruce ("Bruce Grit"), one of the best-known writers in the black press; and Henrietta Vinton Davies, an actress and elocution teacher, who, according to one federal agent, "has personality, and a very forceful way of expressing her views." The UNIA also recruited a clutch of prominent ministers, among them George Alexander McGuire, a former Episcopalian who founded the African Orthodox Church; and James Walker Hood Eason, the pastor of People's Metropolitan AMEZ Church in Philadelphia, whose homiletic skills earned him the sobriquet "silver-tongued Eason." Almost half of the UNIA's most prominent leaders were immigrants from the Caribbean islands.[27]

But most of the rank-and-file UNIA members were native-born Americans. Far from being ignorant riffraff, they were, according to Judith Stein, "physically mobile and ambitious." The UNIA attracted ministers, businessmen, lawyers, politicians, and scholars, as well as West Indian immigrants (who had a very high rate of literacy) and a cross-section of the black working class. "They were not the people of the slums," recalled Saunders Redding, who grew up in Wilmington, Delaware. "They were men with small struggling clothes-pressing shops and restaurants, personal servants, and . . . 'black yeomen,' unlearned but percipient."[28]

Although it was a male-dominated organization that exalted masculine values, the UNIA appealed to women and, to a greater extent than many other black organizations, utilized their skills. Unlike the NAACP, for example, the UNIA counted black women in its top leadership. Garvey's first wife, Amy Ashwood, helped to found the UNIA; his second wife, Amy Jacques, helped to edit the *Negro World*. Charlotta Bass (later a successful newspaper publisher and left-wing activist) headed the UNIA in California. Henrietta Vinton Davis was a senior UNIA officer throughout the 1920s; she travelled throughout America and the Caribbean, speaking, singing, fundraising, and organizing.[29]

The NAACP, which feared and distrusted Garvey, respected his influence. Indeed, despite their reservations, some could not help but admire him. As NAACP official William Pickens privately admitted,

Garvey has the right idea that ALL NEGROES of all countries and especially of the Western World, should be in touch and organized with each other. . . . The idea he has injected into the Negro masses will stay, even if Garvey should be jailed or hung. The white world today . . . are more concerned over the "Garvey idea" than over any other move the Negro has ever made for power in the modern world. They know that to effect an international organization is to reach out for REAL power.

The sheer bravado of Garvey's vaulting ambition evoked awe. "The signal honor of being Provisional President of Africa is mine," he told the readers of the *Negro World.* "It is a political job calling for me to redeem Africa." Like Napoleon, Garvey boasted, he had an empire to win.[30]

GARVEY EMBRACES RACIAL SEGREGATION

Like Napoleon, however, Garvey had his Waterloo. By 1922 Garvey's ambitious plans had gone seriously awry: the Black Star Line foundered; the Liberian venture failed; and Garvey himself faced prosecution by the federal government for mail fraud. Moreover, the revolutionary tide of 1919 had receded, and with it the prospects of African liberation. The UNIA faced unremitting hostility from ruling governments both at home and abroad. White rule seemed once again secure. Garvey also had to contend with a crescendo of internal dissent and external criticism from blacks in America. Garvey's methods of dealing with these setbacks, however, only made them worse.

The Black Star Line, far from being a gold mine, turned out to be a white elephant. The BSL's ships lost money from the start—the *Yarmouth* proved to be unseaworthy—and the company's difficulties were compounded by Garvey's business inexperience, administrative incompetence, and poor judgment of character. When negotiations with the U.S. Shipping Board for the purchase of the *Orion,* an ocean-going steamer, eventually failed, the Black Star Line collapsed. Money to pay the UNIA's bloated staff of four hundred people all but dried up; the Black Star Line had bled the organization dry. In January 1922 a federal grand jury indicted Garvey and three other BSL officers on charges of mail fraud. Garvey faced possible deportation.

The Black Star Line's failure seriously weakened Garvey's prestige and authority. The UNIA held its 1922 convention in an atmosphere of dissension and recrimination. Latent tensions bubbled to the surface. American-born blacks angrily charged West Indian immigrants with being too clannish, too assertive, and too influential. Women for the first time openly complained of being relegated to the sidelines. Garvey himself became the target of withering criticism.

The failure of the UNIA to secure a foothold in Liberia put paid to Garvey's African ambitions. In fact, the UNIA betrayed a vast ignorance of African realities. The UNIA members who journeyed to Liberia were astonished by the gulf between African and American conditions; the corruption, exclusiveness, and xenophobia of the Liberian ruling class appalled them. Cyril Henry experienced a bewildering sense of cultural confusion in dealing with blacks who were "more Oriental than Occidental." Laying constant "traps and pitfalls for the foreigner," Henry complained, "a mere handful of partly Westernized Negroes" treated government as a means of self-enrichment. "'You are welcome,' they say, 'but your numbers, your influence and combined power should not be sufficient to supplant our political preferments. . . . You must adopt our ways, be scattered amongst us, not combined, be not-overzealous about the welfare of the aborigines—us first! And do not place us at odds with the white governments from whom we expect favors.'" The corrupt Liberian elite had no intention of conceding power to an organization of American blacks. In 1924, after President C. D. B. King granted sweeping concessions to the Firestone Rubber Company, Liberia excluded the UNIA altogether. The Garvey movement suffered a crippling setback.[31]

Faced with this sea of troubles, the "Provisional President of Africa" became increasingly autocratic. Garvey responded to his UNIA critics by trying to bully them into silence; failing that, he removed them. The UNIA was wracked by splits, defections, and expulsions. When James W. H. Eason quit the UNIA and set up his own organization, two Garveyites shot him at a public meeting in New Orleans. He died four days later. As the Justice Department developed its case against Garvey, a string of embittered, disillusioned, and frightened colleagues volunteered damaging evidence against him.[32]

As he fought to escape conviction and possible deportation, Garvey embarked upon the most controversial phase of his career. With his vision of the future fixed firmly on Africa, and more convinced than ever that blacks could not win equality in America, he enunciated what he had previously only hinted at: American Negroes should seek a complete separation of the races. "This is going to be a 'white man's country,' sooner or later," he predicted, "and the best thing possibly we can do is find a black man's country." When President Warren Harding told an Alabama audience that neither race sought "social equality"—a statement roundly condemned by other black leaders as an endorsement of segregation—Garvey agreed with him. Advocating strict "racial purity," he argued that blacks should seek an accommodation with white supremacists, and, in a curious echo of Booker T. Washington's Atlanta Compromise, insisted that "the Southern White Man is the best friend the Negro ever had."[33]

Garvey's advocacy of racial separation stemmed from a cold-eyed assessment of how racial groups behaved. Like every other black leader, he condemned the riots and lynchings perpetrated by white people. But the very ubiquity of such atrocities—1919 saw whites rioting against black people in London, Liverpool, and Cardiff, as well as in Chicago, Washington, and Omaha—suggested that a universal law of race was at work. Man's sinful nature made the Christian ideal of the "brotherhood of man," however laudable, impossible to attain in this world. "From the action of man today, I can see that everyone is looking out for himself where the question of race comes in. The white race is looking out for the white race; the yellow race is looking out for the yellow race. . . . The time has come when the Negro should look out for himself and let the others look out for themselves."[34]

Crucial to Garvey's analysis was a firm conviction that conditions for black Americans would get worse, not better. In the South, white supremacy was inviolate. In the North, the promise of the Great Migration was turning sour. Race riots, the growth of ghettos, rampant job discrimination, and the exclusion of blacks from labor unions all pointed to the same conclusion: whites in the North were no more willing to accept blacks as equals than whites in the South. Did the migration mean that "there is a new heaven opening up for the Negro?" asked UNIA supporter Rev. J. G. Brooks. "No, sir. Does it mean that folks, North, East, and West are more gracious to us because we are Negroes? No, sir. It does mean that it is almost like jumping out of the frying pan into the fire." It was no coincidence that the UNIA flourished at precisely the time when the Ku Klux Klan, reinvented in Atlanta in 1915, gained millions of members in the cities and states of the North.[35]

Given their lack of alternatives, Garvey's argument that blacks should make a virtue out of necessity possessed an obvious logic. The NAACP had scarcely made a dent in the walls of discrimination and segregation. Socialists like A. Philip Randolph and Chandler Owen were voices in the wilderness. Politically, blacks had virtually no influence whatever. For many blacks, therefore, the UNIA's strategy of unity, racial pride, entrepreneurship, and, ultimately, separatism was no more unrealistic than the NAACP's pursuit of integration or the *Messenger*'s goal of working-class unity. Indeed, from the perspective of Harlem or South Side Chicago, it made a good deal more sense. Garvey's acceptance of segregation was a calculated accommodation to the conservative and racist climate of the 1920s. Perhaps, too, Garvey sought to emulate Booker T. Washington's Atlanta Compromise—hoping to extend UNIA influence in the South (where so far it had made few inroads) by reassuring whites that it would not threaten Jim Crow.

Whatever his motives for endorsing a policy of "racial purity" and racial segregation, Garvey demonstrated spectacular lack of judgment in aligning himself with people whom blacks had traditionally regarded as their worst enemies. In New Orleans, he argued that "lynching did more to arouse consciousness in the Negro than anything else" and claimed arch–white supremacists Hoke Smith and Ben Tillman as the "Negroes' best friends." In North Carolina, he again "thanked" Southern whites for having "lynched race pride into the Negro." Such statements, delivered without irony, were profoundly offensive to many blacks. A few months later, Garvey withdrew his support from the NAACP's campaign against lynching, saying that even if Congress did pass an antilynching law, white officials would never enforce it.

In June 1922 Garvey committed what many deemed his most egregious blunder: he admitted to holding secret talks in Atlanta with the "imperial wizard" of the Ku Klux Klan, Edward Clarke. Agreeing with the Klan's opposition to miscegenation, Garvey condemned the civil rights policies of the NAACP as a thin disguise for "miscegenation and race suicide." Most of the NAACP's leaders, he charged, were light-skinned mulattoes who hated their African ancestry. They sought to "wipe out the Negro race and make a new race which will not be Negro in any degree."[36]

THE "GARVEY MUST GO" CAMPAIGN

Du Bois and others had long regarded Garvey as a crook, suspecting that the Black Star Line was a cynical racket to fleece gullible Negroes of their hard-earned savings. Only when Garvey embraced segregation, however, did his critics combine against him. They did so with a vengeance.[37]

Outraged by Garvey's dealings with the Klan, the *Messenger* declared that "Garvey Must Go" and launched a "campaign to drive Garvey and Garveyism in all its viciousness from the American soil." Led by A. Philip Randolph and Chandler Owen, and supported by NAACP officials William Pickens and Robert Bagnall, the anti-Garvey movement launched a series of public meetings in which Garvey was denounced as a liar, a fraud, "a race baiter and a race traitor." In January 1923, Owen, Pickens, Bagnall, and five others wrote to Harry M. Daugherty, the U.S. attorney general, asking him to "disband and extirpate this vicious movement," and to "speedily push the government's case against Marcus Garvey for using the mails to defraud."

The war between Garveyites and anti-Garveyites made the old quarrel between Washingtonians and Du Boisites seem like a gentlemanly debate. Each side appealed to fear, made threats, exploited prejudice, and traded personal abuse. Garvey, the target of the campaign, was perhaps more sinned against than sinner. It was difficult to surpass the gratuitous nastiness of the attacks hurled by the "Garvey Must Go" spokesmen—who seemed to vie with each other in plumbing the depths of bad taste. "A Supreme Negro Jamaican Jackass," was a milder *Messenger* headline. Chandler Owen called Garvey "the nefarious Negro lizard" and his followers "universally ignorant Negro savages." The NAACP's Bagnall described Garvey as "squat, fat, and sleek, with protruding jaws, and heavy jowls, small pig-like eyes and rather bull-dog-face." After a string of abusive epithets—"boastful, egotistic, tyrannical, cunning, shifty, smooth and suave, avaricious"—Bagnall concluded that Garvey was either a "demogogic charlatan" or "insane." In a *Crisis* editorial entitled "A Lunatic or a Traitor," Du Bois demanded that "this open ally of the Ku Klux Klan should be locked up or sent home."[38]

But Garvey gave as good as he got. To the attorney general, he denounced his detractors as "Socialists and Bolsheviks." To his own followers, he attacked them as "liars and fabricators" and "good old darkies." Rounding on them one by one, he ran through the list: a "business exploiter," a "race defamer," a "real estate shark," a "hair straightener and face bleacher," a "grafter Socialist," a "turn coat and a lackey," an "unscrupulous politician," and the pastor of a "Blue Vein Society Church." Six of the eight signers of the missive to the attorney general, he acidly noted, were "Octoroons and Quadroons." Garvey reserved his most vituperative insults for his most formidable foe. "A colored man who hates the drop of Negro blood in his veins," the light-skinned Du Bois despised black people as ugly, Garvey said. "That is why he likes to dance with white people, and dine with them and sometimes sleep with them."[39]

Garvey's choice of abuse helps to explain the bitterness of his critics. There had been an unwritten rule among educated blacks that color differences among Negroes should be downplayed or ignored. This was not because blacks were unconscious of color differences—far from it—but because they recognized how destructive and divisive it would be if dark-skinned blacks turned against light-skinned mulattoes.

The fact that skin color and class status were closely related made the mulatto issue potentially explosive. Most members of the small black middle class, and the even smaller black upper class, were mulattoes—descendants of the antebellum class of "free Negroes," or "free people of color." Before the Civil War the "free Negroes" had enjoyed a special status: inferior to whites, to be sure, but distinctly superior to the mass of slaves. Most had been manumitted by white fathers, who, in many cases, continued to favor them. As a class, the free Negroes had prospered in the antebellum South. Many became literate;

some even owned slaves. In the post–Civil War South, the former free Negroes enjoyed a decided advantage over the mass of newly emancipated freedmen. Mulattoes supplied a disproportionate number of the black politicians, teachers, ministers, businessmen, and landowners. Historically, many of the most prominent black leaders—Frederick Douglass, Ida B. Wells, Booker T. Washington, James Weldon Johnson, and Du Bois himself—were mulattoes.

The division between free Negroes and slaves lingered on into the twentieth century. In some cities mulattoes formed a distinct social grouping, worshipping in the same churches and marrying among themselves. The light-skinned Creoles of New Orleans, for example, were notoriously clannish, regarding themselves as quite different from other blacks. The mulattoes of Charleston were similarly exclusive. Mulattoes prospered, many believed, because they stuck together, "married light," and received more favorable treatment from whites. In the words of a rhyme that became part of black folklore: "If you're white, all right. If you're brown, stick around. If you're black, stay back." Even some well-educated blacks shared a suspicion of mulattoes. "I have a bit of white blood in me," confessed J. Max Barber, "but somehow I never warmed up to—never quite trusted—a half white or near white Negro. He is under a diversity of complexes which do not help his soul."[40]

Garvey's appeal to resentment on the basis of color, however, cut across the grain of American realities and did his cause more harm than good. Mulattoes in the United States, unlike those in Jamaica, did *not* enjoy special privileges: because of the so-called "one-drop rule," the law defined mulattoes, however light-skinned, as Negroes. They were subjected to the same kind of prejudice and discrimination as the darkest-skinned blacks. The sheer weight of white racism had forced the mulattoes, willy-nilly, to identify with the darker Negroes. Consciousness of color, therefore, was far more muted than in Garvey's native Jamaica. Moreover, by the 1920s intermarriage between blacks and mulattoes was increasingly common. Only a minority of blacks had no visible trace of white ancestry, and brown—rather than black or very light—was becoming the most common phenotype. As historian Joel Williamson put it, "blacks and mulattoes were melting together physically." Opponents were correct to condemn Garvey's attacks on "Negro-hating mulattoes" as a demagogic ploy of the most dangerous kind.[41]

Locked in a desperate battle for survival, however, Garvey's foes also appealed to prejudice. They characterized Garvey's followers as the "most primitive and ignorant element" of the black population. They constantly referred to Garvey as a Jamaican, a West Indian, and a foreigner. And they persistently charged that West Indian immigrants, whom Du Bois described as "peasants," dominated the UNIA. Without a trace of irony, they then charged

Garvey with fostering antagonism between West Indians and Americans. That Garvey's critics colluded with the federal government to convict Garvey on a trumped-up charge, and to deport him as a foreigner, was the most discreditable act of a disreputable campaign. The fact that they aided and abetted the Federal Bureau of Investigation, an inveterate foe of black rights, made their collusion all the more reprehensible.[42]

In justifying such a desperate action, the anti-Garveyites appealed to fear—physical fear. Their concerns were not groundless. As so often happens with nationalist movements headed by strong, charismatic leaders, the UNIA acquired thuggish, violent overtones. Tony Martin, a sympathetic Garvey biographer, has described the ugly response that the "Garvey Must Go" meetings evoked. "In New Orleans, Chicago, Toronto, Harlem, and elsewhere, [opponents of Garvey] were subjected to threats, harassments, and intimidations by Garveyites. Their meetings regularly had to be held under police protection." Du Bois and others were convinced that Garvey had a hand in the murder of James Walker Hood Eason.[43]

THE DECLINE OF THE UNIA

In 1923 Garvey was convicted of mail fraud. In 1925, having exhausted his appeals, he entered the federal penitentiary in Atlanta to begin a five-year sentence. Two years later, after President Calvin Coolidge commuted the rest of his term, Garvey boarded a Jamaica-bound ship in New Orleans and never again set foot in the United States. With Garvey stranded in Jamaica, the UNIA disintegrated into quarreling factions of ever-decreasing size and significance. Black nationalism survived into the 1930s, but as a diminished, fragmented, and leaderless force. As a mass movement, it was finished. Garvey moved to London in 1935 and died there in 1940.

On the face of it, Garvey and the UNIA posed little threat to the American social order. Garvey condemned communism, criticized unions, and praised capitalism as "necessary to the progress of the world." His advocacy of "racial purity" ought to have disarmed the most vehement white supremacists—indeed, while in jail Garvey won the support of the White America Society and the Anglo-Saxon Clubs of America, both Virginia organizations that campaigned for stricter segregation and antimiscegenation laws. By the time the federal government prosecuted Garvey, the UNIA was past its peak; when it deported him, the movement was a shambles. More than anything else, perhaps, Garvey's prosecution and expulsion illustrated the militantly anti-black policies of the FBI, which, according to historian Kenneth O'Reilly, "dismissed every black dissident as a subversive." The FBI's rising star, J. Edgar Hoover, targeted Garvey in particular because he, as an alien, could be deported.[44]

Yet the *potential* power of the UNIA was incalculable. As Judith Stein notes, "Garvey was a threat not because of what he did but because of what he might inspire." As early as 1919, the British government noted with alarm that the *Negro World* was circulating in Africa, Central America, and the West Indies: "The Negro agitation is beginning to assume international proportions." By 1921 the colonial authorities had banned the newspaper in British Honduras, British Guiana, St. Lucia, St. Vincent, St. Kitts, Nevis, Antigua, Dominica, Trinidad, Grenada, the Gold Coast, and Sierra Leone. The American government, too, recognized the extent of Garvey's influence. In 1926 Attorney General John S. Sargent noted that "Garvey undoubtedly holds today an important and controlling influence over many thousands of the Negro race in the United States," and that "he might become an even greater menace" if released from jail. Only the certainty of deportation, wedded to his fear that Garvey's continued imprisonment was creating serious unrest among blacks, persuaded Sargent to approve Garvey's early release.[45]

Garvey's opponents were a motley crew of Socialists, conservative businessmen, NAACP officials, rival black nationalists, UNIA defectors, and Justice Department officials. They acted, to quote Judith Stein, from "a witch's brew of principle and opportunism, righteousness and revenge." If the leaders of the "Garvey Must Go" campaign agreed upon anything, it was the conviction that Garvey's program of racial separatism was not only utterly impractical, but also threatened to undermine every effort to gain racial justice and equality for black people within the United States. They believed that Garvey, by attempting to effect a rapprochement with the white South and an alliance with the Ku Klux Klan, was betraying the interests of black Americans and sowing the seeds of a race war that blacks would only lose. But his opponents also had a more selfish interest in bringing him down: Garvey was simply too powerful a rival. As Owen and Randolph privately acknowledged, "As long as he gets the vast sums [of money] that he does, no other negro movement can prosper."[46]

In the long run, the critics may have been correct: perhaps Garveyism was such a massive roadblock to black progress that it had to be removed. Yet it took more than half a century for the NAACP to achieve even minimal implementation of its own basic program. Set against this time scale, it was not so apparent to most black Americans in the 1920s that Garvey was leading them down a blind alley.

In destroying the UNIA, moreover, Garvey's foes destroyed something of great value to black Americans. Garvey's depiction of the NAACP as a white-controlled institution was, at best, a half-truth, but it made an important point. The UNIA was entirely led, controlled, and financed by black people. That was no mean achievement. The UNIA fostered racial pride in ways that the NAACP simply could not. The UNIA also gave large numbers of black people an opportunity for participation and leadership. Garvey "personified the possibility of the fulfillment of a dream latent in the heart of every Negro," recalled James H. Robinson. "I remember as a lad in Cleveland, Ohio, during the hungry days of 1921, standing on Central Avenue, watching a parade one Sunday afternoon. . . . When Garvey rode by in his plumed hat, I got an emotional lift, which swept me up above the poverty and prejudice by which my life was limited."

The "Garvey Must Go" campaigners destroyed Garveyism as a mass movement but failed to put anything in its place. Indeed, their disdainful descriptions of Garvey's supporters ("ignorant Negro fanatics," "the lowest type of Negro") suggests that Garvey's black opponents actually feared mass politics. Few former Garveyites joined the NAACP; the NAACP made little effort to recruit them. The collapse of the UNIA, therefore, left a demoralizing void in black America. That void was not really filled until the civil rights struggle of the 1950s and 1960s created a very different kind of mass movement.[47]

Scottsboro protesters march by the White House, circa 1933

Bettmann/CORBIS

The Radical Thirties

The names of Alabama towns are milestones along the path to black freedom. Tuskegee is forever linked with the name of Booker T. Washington and his crusade for education. Montgomery, Birmingham, and Selma were the sites of decisive civil rights campaigns led by Martin Luther King, Jr. Between the eras of Washington and King, another Alabama town, Scottsboro, cast off its anonymity to become an unwitting symbol of race relations in the American South.

In the 1930s, "Scottsboro" was a synonym for white bigotry and injustice. Scottsboro was also a metaphor for the left-wing currents of the Depression Decade, a time when workers eagerly signed up to join labor unions, when artists and intellectuals proudly espoused Marxism, and when critics of capitalism found willing listeners and eager followers. Astonishingly—dismayingly for some but nevertheless undeniably—it was America's Communist Party, the CPUSA, that turned Scottsboro into a worldwide *cause célèbre*, the rallying-cry of a new, militant, confrontational challenge to the South's caste system.

THE SCOTTSBORO AFFAIR

The Scottsboro affair began on March 25, 1931, during the downward plunge into the Great Depression. Eighteen months after the stock market crash on Wall Street, ragged hosts of Americans were in stumbling flight from joblessness, homelessness, hunger, and family breakdown. Perhaps two million people lived in the shantytowns, or "Hoovervilles," that sprouted like mold on rotting cities—in derelict factories, under bridges, and in city garbage dumps. This human flotsam and jetsam washed back and forth across the land, following the pull of seasonal tides. Dubbed "itinerants" and "vagrants," "hoboes" and "bums," "Okies" and "Arkies," famished and uprooted people roamed the land, searching desperately for food and work. Travelling singly or in families, they formed unstable groups that huddled together for warmth, company, and survival as they tramped the highways. Huge numbers, in search of faster transportation, "rode the rails" illegally. Perhaps 200,000 people could be found aboard freight trains at any given hour. Leaping on and off moving wagons—or travelling under them—they risked injury, death, and savage beatings by railroad "bulls."

Even in this rough democracy of poverty, blacks and whites eyed each other warily. When four white boys hopped aboard a Chattanooga-to-Memphis freight train as it slowly clunked and swayed through the hills of northern Alabama, they encountered an equal number of black boys already aboard. Who started the ensuing fight is unclear. It probably began with a racist epithet and an aggressive rejoinder: "Nigger bastard, this is a white man's train. You better get off. All you black bastards better get off!" "You white sonsabitches, we got as much right here as you!" After a skirmish of insults and rock-throwing, the black hoboes, now nine in number—five more had joined the train—pressed home their tactical advantage. "We outmanned them in hand-to-hand scuffling," recalled Haywood Patterson, who was nineteen at the time. They then pitched three of the whites off the train, pulling the fourth back on board after the train began to pick up speed. The bruised and humiliated whites, however, went straight to the nearest station and alleged that they were the victims of an unprovoked attack.[1]

When a sheriff's posse searched the train as it stopped in Paint Rock, Alabama, the white deputies prized a motley collection of drifters from the forty-two wagons. Blinking in the sun before the grim-faced possemen were nine black youths, ranging in age from twelve to twenty, one white boy, and two white females, twenty-one-year-old Victoria Price and her seventeen-year-old companion, Ruby Bates. All of these drifters, including the girls, wore grubby overalls. Twenty minutes later, as the nine blacks were about to be carted off to the Jackson County jail in Scottsboro, Ruby Bates and Victoria Price told deputy sheriff Charlie Latham that they had been raped, repeatedly, by the Negroes.

Levelled against black men by white women, the charge of rape often meant certain death for the accused, either by lynching or legal execution. To prevent a mass lynching, Alabama governor Benjamin M. Miller took swift action and dispatched a contingent of state militiamen to Scottsboro. This kind of vigorous action by Southern sheriffs and governors had brought about a sharp decline in lynching since 1920. Indeed, white Alabamians who opposed lynching took grim pride that "the law would be allowed to take its course." Although a crowd of several thousand white people ringed the courthouse when the case of the "Scottsboro boys" came to trial, they were not about to challenge the bayonets and machine guns of the National Guardsmen, who searched everyone who entered the building.

The word of Victoria Price and Ruby Bates was enough to condemn the boys: they were adamant that the defendants had raped them. In the case of thirteen-year-old Roy Wright, the judge declared a mistrial. However, juries of white men (women were automatically exempted from jury duty) found the other eight boys guilty. "Instantly," wrote Stephen Roddy, one of the boys' lawyers, "a wild and thunderous cheer went up from the audience and was heard by those in the court house yard where thousands took up the demonstration and carried it on for fifteen or twenty minutes." Judge Alfred E. Hawkins betrayed not the slightest hesitation as he sentenced the eight to death. The white crowd, entertained by a brass band, celebrated until after dark.[2]

The standard of justice dispensed at Scottsboro was no worse—perhaps better—than what blacks accused of rape could expect in a Southern courtroom in the 1930s. But the atmosphere of intimidation, the speed of the proceedings, the hostility of the judge, and the inadequacy of the defense had militated against a fair trial. The boys' two lawyers had had no time to prepare their defense. Judge Hawkins showed evident sympathy for the prosecution and concluded the trials in four days. Worst of all, the guilty verdicts flew in the face of the forensic evidence, for when doctors in Scottsboro examined the two young women they found no bleeding, no lacerations, and no bruising around their private parts. What semen the doctors recovered was "nonmotile" (old and dead), which squared with the fact that both women had had intercourse, with white men, before boarding the train. What little bruising and scratching the doctors saw could easily be attributed to normal, everyday physical activity. The women were calm, their pulses normal. The police found no signs of semen—no wet or damp spots—on the clothes of the accused boys.[3]

However, the entire machinery of the law, controlled and staffed from top to bottom by white people, seemed bent on reaching a guilty verdict. Eight young Negroes were convicted and sentenced to death on the unsubstantiated testimony of two white women who, in the words of NAACP executive secretary Walter White, were nothing more than prostitutes. But Southern white men rarely disputed the word of a white woman if she accused a black man of rape. Birmingham congressman George Huddleston made this thunderingly clear when he angrily rejected White's entreaties on behalf of the Scottsboro boys:

> I don't care whether they are innocent or guilty. They were found riding on the same freight car with two white women, and that's enough for me! It doesn't matter to me what the women had done previously. I'm in favor of the boys being executed just as quickly as possible! You can't understand how we Southern gentlemen feel about this question of relationships between negro men and white women.

What comfort could black people derive from the decline of lynching if white juries treated the matter of evidence as irrelevant?[4]

White's visit to Alabama left him confused and pessimistic. "Mister, before God, we're innocent," the boys protested. Yet White was repelled by them. The NAACP liked to defend people who showed the race to its best advantage—pious, hard-working, virtuous, educated. But the Scottsboro boys were ignorant, illiterate, and had "exceedingly bad" reputations. Perplexed by a case he found "tangled and ugly," White moved cautiously. As the NAACP hesitated, however, the Communist Party stole a march on it.[5]

The ILD and Scottsboro

"Two guys from New York, head men from the International Labor Defense [ILD], brought us pops and candy and gave them to us in the visiting room," recalled Haywood Patterson. "They were Jewish. Which was okay with me. . . . They told us the people were up in arms over our case in New York and if they had our say-so they would like to appeal our case."[6]

The Communist Party seized on the Scottsboro case as a heaven-sent opportunity. Acting swiftly and decisively, it persuaded the boys and their parents to let the Communist-controlled ILD represent them. At the same time, the party launched an energetic campaign of public agitation to save the boys from "cold blooded illegal lynching."

Walter White was appalled by the ILD's entry into the case, and the case became a tug-of-war between the two organizations. Ruling out cooperation, White argued that "it would be suicidal for us to be tied up in any way with that outfit of lunatics"—the Communists—and he rebuked an NAACP official, William Pickens, who wrote to the *Daily Worker* praising the ILD. "It is Communist strategy to try to destroy and discredit every organization except their own," he explained. The Communists were more interested in discrediting the "capitalist courts," White believed, than in securing justice for the boys; indeed, some would prefer to see them executed. White visited the parents of the boys and urged them to repudiate the ILD, warning one mother that "she would practically insure her boy's execution by remaining tied up with the Communists." White delivered the same stark message to the jailed lads. "He told us we were doomed if we let the ILD lawyers defend us," Clarence Norris recalled. But after some dithering, the boys decided to stick with the ILD.[7]

Springing into action overnight, Communists organized meetings, marches, parades, and petitions. They flooded Alabama officials with letters and telegrams. They sent mothers of Scottsboro boys around America and Europe on speaking tours. At the flick of a political switch, the party mobilized members and supporters throughout the world. People marched in London and Amsterdam as well as in Chicago and New York. The massive German Communist Party—then embroiled in a life-and-death struggle against the Nazi Party—organized enormous demonstrations in Berlin, Dresden, Chemnitz, and Lustgarten. "On a single day," writes historian Hugh Murray, "there were Scottsboro demonstrations in San Salvador, Johannesburg, Montevideo, Santo Domingo, and Santiago de Cuba." On November 7, "International Scottsboro Day," Communists all over the world expressed solidarity with the nine boys.[8]

The complex nature of the Communist movement amplified its voice. Controlling a plethora of labor unions, defense committees, cultural organizations, and other "fronts," the party made its Scottsboro campaign seem far more spontaneous and broadly based than it actually was. As James Goodman has written, "Postcards, letters, and petitions from Communists, and mail from organizations that smelled radical or foreign or red, far outnumbered all the others." When the Berlin Transport Workers Union wired a telegram to the governor of Alabama—the first of the foreign flood—it is fair to assume that a party directive, not the spontaneous anger of German trolley-drivers, prompted its dispatch. The vigor of the Scottsboro campaign testified to the centralized, disciplined, and international character of the Communist movement.[9]

Yet large numbers of non-Communists also supported the ILD-led campaign. Tens of thousands of ordinary citizens, prompted by anger and shame, attended rallies, donated money, and wrote letters of protest. The cause drew in eminent artists, writers, scientists, intellectuals, and political leaders. "Albert Einstein, Maxim Gorki, Mme. Sun Yat Sen, Jomo Kenyatta, André Malraux, and Theodore Dreiser all petitioned for the release of the defendants," writes Hugh Murray. Communist propaganda turned Scottsboro into the most talked about American news story in 1931–32. The party had taken a gross example of manifest injustice and turned it into what was, according to historian Harvard Sitkoff, "the most searching indictment of Jim Crow yet to appear in the United States."[10]

In 1932 ILD lawyers won a stunning victory when they appealed the Scottsboro verdicts to the United States Supreme Court. In *Powell* v. *Alabama*, the Court ruled the boys' defense counsel had been so inadequate that the defendants had been denied the Fourteenth Amendment right to "due process of law," a fair trial. The Court set aside the guilty verdicts, granting the defendants the right to new trials. The ILD prevailed upon one of the best criminal lawyers in America, Samuel L. Liebowitz of New York, to head the boys' defense when they faced a different judge and jury.[11]

The second trial of the Scottsboro boys, held in Decatur under the gavel of Judge James E. Horton, became one of the most politicized trials in American history. The technical matter of establishing the guilt or innocence of the defendants became intertwined and confused with a three-way political battle between Southern conservatism, Northern liberalism, and international communism.

The ILD represented, in an extreme form, everything that white Southerners—the ILD would say the "white ruling class"—feared and despised. It was culturally alien, avowedly revolutionary, and militantly antiracist. The chief defense counsel, Samuel Liebowitz, was a Jew from New York; his ILD associate, Joseph Brodsky, was a Jew and a Communist. The ILD was a Communist organization that damned the South as a hellhole of oppression, dismissed the charge of black rape as a racist lie, and exhorted the "toiling masses," black and white, to overthrow their capitalist exploiters. White Southerners correctly viewed the intervention of the Communist Party as an indirect attack upon the South's political and economic order.

For many Southern whites, the case also became a chivalrous defense of Southern white womanhood, whose honor was being impugned. White juries were rarely inclined to credit black defendants in rape cases involving white women. Thus the political character of the Scottsboro case made the defense's task doubly difficult, and Liebowitz further outraged Southern whites by depicting the testimony of Victoria Price, the chief prosecution witness, as the "foul, contemptible, outrageous lie . . . [of] an abandoned, brazen woman." The state prosecutors had a field day, urging the jurors to show that "Alabama justice cannot be bought and sold with Jew money from New York." The jury duly found Haywood Patterson, the first of the defendants to be retried, guilty of rape, and fixed the punishment as death.[12]

In an astonishing turn of events, however, Judge Horton set aside Patterson's conviction, deeming Victoria Price's uncorroborated testimony as unreliable, improbable, and overwhelmingly contradicted by other evidence. The alleged rapes, he concluded, did not take place. "History, sacred and profane, and the common experience of mankind teaches us that women of the character shown in this case are prone for selfish reasons to make false accusations of rape."[13]

But the Alabama authorities refused to give up. They proceeded to try the other defendants, and put Haywood Patterson on trial for a third time. Moreover, they persuaded Horton to withdraw from presiding over the other trials and allocated the cases to Judge William Washington Callahan, a man completely in sympathy with the prosecution and determined to obtain convictions as speedily as possible. "His robes might as well have been those of the Ku Klux Klan," recalled Clarence Norris. "It didn't matter to him if we were innocent or guilty, he was determined to send us to the electric chair." Displaying unconcealed hostility toward Liebowitz, disallowing any questions with regard to Victoria Price's character or sexual activities before the alleged rape, Callahan advised the jury that it was perfectly permissible to convict on the basis of Price's uncorroborated testimony. When instructing the jury on the verdicts that were open to them, he neglected to mention acquittal until prompted by the defense. Once again, all-white juries declared Patterson and Norris guilty of rape and decided upon the death sentence.[14]

For a second time, however, the United States Supreme Court agreed to review a Scottsboro conviction. Liebowitz, establishing that no blacks within living memory had served on juries in either Jackson County or Morgan County, argued that both the indictment and prosecution of the Scottsboro boys had been unconstitutional—that blacks had been deliberately excluded from jury service on the basis of race. In *Norris* v. *Alabama* the Supreme Court agreed, citing clear evidence of racial discrimination. Incredibly, although dropping charges against four of the boys, state prosecutors tried Patterson for a fourth time, Norris a third, and three others a second. Guilty verdicts duly followed. Norris received a death sentence, Andy Wright, Haywood Patterson, and Charlie Weems jail sentences of ninety-nine years, seventy-five years, and seventy-five years respectively. The state prosecuted Ozzie Powell for assaulting a sheriff rather than rape; he received a twenty-year sentence.[15]

The NAACP could claim partial credit for this limited victory. After two ILD lawyers were caught attempting to bribe Victoria Price, Liebowitz angrily insisted that the Communist Party bow out of the case; the Scottsboro Defense Committee (SDC), a coalition backed by the NAACP and chaired by clergyman Allan Knight Chalmers, thereafter organized the boys' defense. But although Governor Bibb Graves commuted Norris's sentence to life imprisonment, the SDC failed in its behind-the-scenes negotiations to secure pardons for the boys. The five left prison at different times; Charlie Weems, the first, in 1943; Andy Wright, the last, in 1950.[16]

Throughout the campaign to free the Scottsboro boys, the NAACP and the Communist Party had traded political blows and verbal abuse. The Communists flayed the NAACP as "bourgeois misleaders," allies of the capitalists, and enemies of the working class. The ILD's William Patterson ridiculed the NAACP's reliance upon legalism, belittling its Supreme Court victories as "concessions for the top layer of well-to-do Negroes" that "meant nothing to the masses." Patterson argued that every legal victory in the Scottsboro cases had been due to the "tremendous mass pressure developed by the ILD," not through any principle of fairness within the legal system itself. Judge Horton—much praised by liberals for his fair-mindedness—was "part and parcel of the lynching machinery," and the Supreme Court's decision in *Powell* v. *Alabama,* hailed by liberals as a triumph for justice, was merely a guide to the Alabama authorities on "how 'properly' to carry through such lynch schemes."

The NAACP responded in kind. It accused the Communist Party of being more concerned with discrediting the legal system, attacking their political opponents, and winning converts to communism than in defending the boys. The Communists' tactics, moreover, actually hurt the cause of the Scottsboro boys. "If the Communists want these lads murdered," Du Bois charged, "then their antics of threatening judges and yelling for mass action on the part of white Southern workers is calculated to insure this." The association also accused the Communists of swelling the party treasury by exploiting the case. "Never have I seen such a bald-faced piece of racketeering," wrote Walter White.[17]

Charges of opportunism and bad faith, however, ran up against one incontrovertible fact: But for the ILD's tenacious defense of them, backed up by a worldwide campaign of mass agitation, the Scottsboro boys would probably have died in the electric chair. The fact that the Supreme Court reversed the verdicts of the first trials because the defendants had been denied adequate legal counsel underlines this point. As Hugh Murray points out, the boys' inadequate counsel had been supplied by the NAACP: if the NAACP had argued the appeals, it would scarcely have cited its own lawyers as grounds for reversal. As the NAACP's Charles Houston admitted, the Communists' "uncompromising resistance to southern prejudice set a new standard for agitation for equality" and "fused all the elements of the Negro population into a common resistance."[18]

AMERICAN COMMUNISM IN THE 1930s

Today, it is hard to understand how the Communist Party, with its slavish devotion to the Soviet Union and idolatry of Stalin, could have been so influential in the 1930s. Stalin, the "God that failed," turned out to be a mass murderer. Corruption, inefficiency, and oppression, the seeds of communism's destruction, bore fruit in the 1980s and 1990s with the collapse of communism in Eastern Europe and the breakup of the Soviet Union. Surviving only in China, Cuba, North Korea, and Vietnam, Marxism is a discredited ideology around most of the globe, and communism, as an international movement, is a spent force. Like the Habsburg, Ottoman, or British empires, the Soviet Union is a relic of history. Communist parties across the globe, their umbilical cord to Moscow severed, have shrivelled and died. The CPUSA is a strange historical fossil, as remote from present-day reality as the Know-Nothings or the Populist Party.

In the middle of the Great Depression, however, legions of Americans from all walks of life were bitterly disillusioned with capitalism. The nation was a vast echo chamber for radical voices; rhetoric of class warfare that fell on deaf ears in the "Roaring Twenties" found an appreciative audience among the hungry, the bankrupt, and the unemployed. Demagogic politicians like Huey Long attracted an army of followers by attacking the rich and promising to "Share Our Wealth." Even President Roosevelt, weaned on a silver spoon, lashed out against the "royalists of the economic order" who believed in "economic slavery."   ‹

Compared with America's desperately flawed capitalism, Soviet communism did not seem so terrible—the Soviet economy was apparently surging to modernity under the "Five-Year Plan." Not many people actually joined the Communist Party, which at the peak of its strength in the late 1930s had probably fewer than 100,000 members. Yet this number exceeded the membership of the NAACP at the time. Moreover, for every worker or intellectual who became a Communist Party member, there were many more who admired the party, respected it, or sympathized with at least some of its goals.

Historians disagree vigorously and often vehemently about communism's contribution to the betterment of American society. Most, until recently, condemned the Communist Party as the tool of a foreign power. If the party supported civil liberties, labor unions, and racial equality, it did so for cynical reasons; its primary interest was always in furthering the Soviet cause. Even granting the Communists sincerity in defending the Scottsboro boys, their tactical flip-flops showed that they danced to the tune of a Kremlin-dictated "party line." To critics such as Wilson Record, Theodore Draper, and Harvey Klehr, the Communist Party was secretive, devious, manipulative, authoritarian, and fundamentally insincere. It was not a legitimate political party because it had no commitment to democracy and no loyalty to the United States. According to this diabolical image, there were no lows to which Communists would not stoop in order to lure gullible blacks into joining the party—even tempting them with the bait of interracial sex.[19]

The Vietnam War, however, caused many Americans to question the Cold War consensus, and a growing number of historians became convinced that McCarthyism, the supposed cure, had been worse than communism, the disease. The view that McCarthyism—taken to mean all forms of anti-communism—had been a disaster for the cause of racial equality and social justice then prompted a more sympathetic appraisal of the Communist Party. True, the party's dependence upon the former Soviet Union can now be documented in the Russian archives. But scholars such as Harvard Sitkoff, Fraser Ottanelli, and Robin D. G. Kelley, while not discounting American communism's dependence upon Soviet guidance, have disputed the Cold War image of the CPUSA as sinister, unprincipled, and un-American. In reality, they argue, the party was a complex mixture of cynicism and idealism, fanaticism and patriotism. Most Americans who became Communists acted out of a passionate commitment to social and economic justice; many were Communists despite the zig-zagging "party line," not because of it. Communists saw themselves as loyal Americans even as they myopically admired the Soviet Union. They sincerely opposed racial prejudice, but were happy to denounce the NAACP if the party instructed them to do so.[20]

One issue on which the Communist Party *did* display principled consistency was opposition to racial discrimination. The party regarded black Americans—oppressed and largely propertyless—as natural recruits to communism. But it also recognized that the situation of blacks differed from that of white workers. It therefore not only denounced racism as a capitalist device to divide the working class, but also adopted policies that were specifically designed to attract black support. Impressed by the vast popularity of Marcus Garvey and his brand of black nationalism, the party adopted a position that blacks in the Deep South constituted an oppressed nation. "Where the Negroes form a majority of the population," declared the Sixth World Congress of the Communist International (Comintern) in 1928, they possessed "the right . . . to national self-determination."

Although the policy of "national self-determination" won support from a handful of American blacks—notably Harry Haywood and Cyril Briggs, who joined the Communist Party via an organization called the African Blood Brotherhood—it would never have been adopted but for Comintern's insistence. It was Stalinist dogma that flew in the face of American reality. The idea that 279 counties in the South's Black Belt could form a separate black nation was fanciful—"so preposterous," sneered Roy Wilkins of the NAACP, "that only the worst dunderheads paid any attention to it."

Still, the policy of "self-determination" powerfully symbolized the Communists' commitment to racial equality; to quote historian Mark Naison, it "endowed the black struggle with unprecedented dignity and importance." The party underlined its commitment by promoting blacks to leadership positions. In 1932 it selected William L. Patterson to head the ILD and nominated James W. Ford as its candidate for vice president of the United States—the first political party ever to do so. The party also vigorously opposed racial prejudice—what it termed "white chauvinism"—within its ranks. In one famous case it accused a Finnish-American member, August Yokinen, of racial prejudice, and, after a public "trial" in Harlem, expelled him from the party.[21]

"More than ever," writes Naison, "interracialism became the trademark of the Communist left":

> It meant a Workers Alliance office in Birmingham, Alabama, which re-
> fused to maintain separate toilets for black and white members; a coop-
> erative housing project in the Bronx that welcomed interracial couples . . .
> picket lines at baseball parks demanding the integration of major league
> baseball; interracial marches through Harlem celebrating Joe Louis's
> victories; pageants celebrating black history and concerts extolling the
> black contribution to U.S. popular music.

Small wonder that idealistic whites, as well as blacks, were attracted to communism. The CPUSA was the *only* political party that took racial equality seriously. To a young Southerner like Junius Scales, a student at the University of North Carolina (and grandson of a Confederate general), joining the Communist Party seemed obvious. "When it came to opposing white supremacy," he remembered, "there was nowhere else to turn."[22]

The Communist Party opposed the racial and economic oppression of black people with greater energy, militancy, and imagination than any other organization. In the cities, it mounted demonstrations of unemployed people. In Alabama and Louisiana, it formed sharecroppers' unions. As well as maintaining the ILD as an organization devoted to black rights, the Communists helped to establish civil organizations that drew in supporters from across the political spectrum. The National Negro Congress (NNC, 1935) was a broad coalition that embraced labor unions, churches, fraternal organizations, and civic groups. The student-oriented Southern Negro Youth Congress (SNYC, 1937) won the backing of relatively conservative black college presidents.

The Southern Conference for Human Welfare (SCHW, 1938) brought together liberals and radicals of both races.

Communist influence in these organizations varied, and historians differ over its extent and meaning. Some believe that the NNC, and SNYC, and even the SCHW were Communist "fronts," created by the CPUSA in response to the Comintern's call, in 1935, for a broad alliance of antifascist forces. Others insist that they were genuine coalitions, in which Communists participated but did not dominate. But as Roi Ottley argued at the time, for many blacks the degree of Communist control was not an important issue. What mattered to them was that by joining "organizations in which the party's influence was a factor . . . Negroes discovered themselves, once given opportunities for self-expression beyond the Negro world."[23]

Communists provided much of the drive in the campaign launched in 1935 by the Congress of Industrial Organizations (CIO) to unionize workers in America's mills, mines, factories, packinghouses, ports, merchant marine, and street railways. The American Federation of Labor either relegated black workers to segregated unions or excluded them altogether. The CIO, in contrast, made it a cardinal principle to organize blacks and whites together. The CIO had a sound pragmatic reason for adopting an interracial approach: the opposition of black workers would have made it impossible to win strikes and gain bargaining power. Still, it was in large part due to Communist influence that the CIO opposed racial discrimination. And although in practice many CIO unions, especially in the South, gave white workers more favored treatment, when Communists gained control or exerted a strong voice they gained a deserved reputation for treating blacks fairly.

"While other political groups talked, Communists acted," writes historian Ellen Schrecker. "For many idealistic and energetic young men and women . . . joining the Communist Party seemed to make a lot of sense." The party made members of bright black college students like James E. Jackson, Esther Cooper, and Edward S. Strong. It recruited sharecroppers like Clinton Clark, steelworkers like Hosea Hudson, and auto workers like Coleman Young. The party boasted a stellar array of black artists and intellectuals, including the writers Claude McKay, Langston Hughes, and Richard Wright, whose 1940 novel *Native Son* shocked America and established itself as a literary classic.[24]

The party's biggest catch was undoubtedly the charismatic and multitalented Paul Robeson. Rendering Negro spirituals in his magnificent bass, singing the definitive version of "Ol' Man River" in the musical *Showboat,* starring in movies like *The Emperor Jones,* taking the London stage by storm in *Othello,* Robeson was an international star. Handsome, magnetic, intelligent, and articulate, he was also, by the mid-1930s, a passionate Communist.

He visited the Soviet Union, entertained Republican troops in Spain, and won the hearts of Welsh miners by supporting their struggle for economic justice. Although he never carried a party card, Robeson became the best-known Communist sympathizer in America.

Black newspaper editors, usually sensitive barometers of the mood of black America, testified to the impact of the Communist Party in the early 1930s. It "appears to be the only party going our way," wrote Carl Murphy of the *Baltimore Afro-American*. "They are as radical as the NAACP were twenty years ago." Even such a staunch NAACP supporter as Roy Wilkins, editor of the *Kansas City Call*, praised the Communists' flair for "sending out publicity and generally whooping it up." It was Scottsboro, of course, that made the Communist Party a household name in black America. Writer and teacher Saunders Redding recalled a meeting addressed by Alice Dunbar-Nelson, widow of the poet Paul Laurence Dunbar, that typified the electrifying effect of the Scottsboro campaign. "In the end, with tears in her eyes, she stretched out her gloved hands and cried, 'Thank God for the Scottsboro case! It has brought us together.'"[25]

When Comintern dropped the ultrarevolutionary doctrines of the period 1928–34 in favor of a "popular front strategy," the CPUSA greatly increased its support. Its membership increased from 26,000 in 1934 to 85,000 in 1939, and the number of black members more than doubled, reaching 7,000.

But the Communist Party failed to establish a mass movement for black liberation. People admired the Communists' militancy, recalled Hosea Hudson, "but many times they wouldn't join us." To become a Communist, especially in the South, was a dangerous business; members risked beatings, jailings, and death. In Alabama and Louisiana, the party's sharecropper unions met with violent repression from planters and sheriffs. Few blacks wished to associate with the Communist Party too closely. According to historian George Fredrickson, "African-American membership . . . remained disproportionately small in relation both to total party membership and to the total number of politically active blacks."[26]

In the North, ironically, it was the party's *success* in entering the political mainstream that hampered its expansion. As Mark Naison argues, between 1935 and 1939 Communists attained influence within unions and other non-Communist organizations by concealing their party membership and watering down their policies. The Popular Front, he believes, was a Faustian pact that "rested on the most fragile and vulnerable political foundations." The Communist Party's conspiratorial methods, authoritarian style, and exacting discipline gave it energy and direction, but kept membership small.[27]

The party also committed serious tactical errors that cost it support.

Abrupt policy shifts inspired distrust and cynicism, frittering away much of the credit it had garnered from Scottsboro. In particular, the party's endorsement of the Nazi-Soviet Pact in 1939 badly dented its prestige, moral authority, and political credibility. Many non-Communists who once respected the party became bitterly anti-Communist. Even in their stronghold of Harlem, writes Naison, Communists "lost their ability to shape the goals and tactics of the civil rights movement."[28]

BLACKS AND LABOR: WORKING-CLASS UNITY OR RACIAL SOLIDARITY?

The issues that confronted black leaders and organizations in the 1930s were complex and vexing, but they offered exciting challenges. The Depression made poverty, unemployment, and economic reform matters of overwhelming political urgency. Franklin Roosevelt became president in 1933 promising a "New Deal for the American people." When he assumed sweeping powers to promote economic recovery and alleviate suffering, black people realized that the actions of the federal government, which had previously played a minimal role in their lives, now vitally affected them. In fact, because they were worst hit by the Depression, blacks stood to gain most—or least—from the New Deal. They began to rethink their attitude toward the Democratic Party. They needed a voice, or at least a sympathetic ear, within the Roosevelt administration.

The Depression also caused many blacks to become more class-conscious, viewing their situation in a new light. There had always been Socialists and Populists who blamed the oppression of blacks on capitalism rather than white people. But when poor whites made up the lynch mobs, when white trade unions were vehemently antiblack, and when white capitalists were the ones endowing black education and supporting interracial cooperation, this class analysis did not seem very convincing.

The Great Depression, however, was a great leveller: it reduced whites as well as blacks to abject poverty. With hunger stalking the land, blind to race or color, many black people concluded that their economic plight stemmed from a failing economic system, not merely from white prejudice. It became a commonplace among blacks, especially younger intellectuals like Abram Harris and Ralph J. Bunche, that the problems of the race were primarily economic and that all workers shared common interests. At the Amenia Conference of 1933, convened by NAACP chairman Joel Spingarn, black activists called for a "new labor movement" to organize "the great mass of workers both skilled and unskilled, white and black."

The NAACP seemed out of touch with the new mood. Despite regularly acknowledging the need to address economic problems, it stuck to its emphasis on civil rights, relying upon tried-and-trusted methods of lobbying Congress, publicizing racial injustice, and using the courts to challenge racial discrimination. The NAACP had certainly won important legal victories. It had also flexed its political muscle, in 1930 preventing the appointment of a North Carolina white supremacist, John J. Parker, to the Supreme Court. The NAACP's courtroom triumphs, however, barely affected the lives of ordinary black people, and whites invariably found ways of evading judicial rulings. The Parker victory, while gratifying, could not disguise the NAACP's inability to end the disfranchisement of black voters in the South.

The Communists damned the NAACP for being a tool of the "white ruling class" and for opposing "any alliance of the Negro and white masses." On the face of it, the charge was absurd—the kind of propaganda one would expect from the Communist Party during its most "revolutionary" phase. But the NAACP also received criticism from friends, who pointed out that the Depression made the organization's stress on individual rights appear more attuned than ever to the interests of the black middle class. NAACP special counsel Charles H. Houston called the organization "top heavy with white-collar interests and attitudes." What was it doing for workers, sharecroppers, and the jobless? Not much, thought a special NAACP committee chaired by Howard University economist Abram Harris. Even if the NAACP achieved its goal of "full citizenship rights," black people would remain "a landless proletariat in the country and a propertyless wage-earner in the city." Like the Amenia Conference, the Harris Committee urged the NAACP to adopt an economic program that focused on building an interracial labor movement.[29]

The new labor movement of the 1930s went some way toward compensating for the shortcomings of the NAACP. Between 1935 and 1945 the CIO created industrial unions on the basis of interracial memberships, forging an unprecedented degree of working-class unity. The CIO unions substantially improved wages and conditions for black and white workers. They gave black workers, in particular, new opportunities for leadership, education, and self-expression. And they provided lessons in mass action that could be applied to the struggle for racial equality.

However, the labor movement could not, in itself, bring about racial equality. For one thing, working-class unity rarely extended beyond the workplace. Whites remained hostile to associating with blacks outside the factory gate, and they were reluctant to embrace the wider cause of black civil rights. In the face of white conservatism and prejudice, the CIO unions often compromised their egalitarian principles, permitting a degree of racial segregation, formal or informal, inside the workplace and inside the union. Secondly, the CIO made few inroads in the South, the most bitterly antiunion region of the country. Here, of course, still resided the bulk—three-quarters in 1940—of America's black population. The new labor movement directly affected only a small portion of the black workforce, most of whom still toiled in the South's cotton-fields and kitchens.

If "mass action" was the clarion call of the 1930s, some believed that black people ought to act for themselves. Such a view was not confined to the black nationalists in Harlem and Chicago who organized "Don't Buy Where You Can't Work" campaigns—boycotts of white-owned department stores that refused to employ black people. It was also shared by W. E. B. Du Bois, who dismissed the politically fashionable argument that black advancement should come about through a union of black and white workers. "A mud-sill of black labor is essential to white labor's standard of living," he believed, and, despite the Depression, there was no prospect of a "united class-conscious proletariat." Ironically, the Communists' very success in "completely obliterat[ing] the color bar within their own party ranks" undermined their capacity to attract white workers. "It is impossible to get solidarity over race lines today."

Blacks must therefore look to their own devices, Du Bois believed, in order to achieve any economic and political progress. In 1934 he criticized the NAACP's opposition to racial segregation as dogmatic, myopic, and unrealistic. The true situation facing blacks, he explained, was usually a choice between segregated institutions or none. Such had been the case with Camp Des Moines, the wartime training camp for black officers, and with the Veterans Hospital in Tuskegee that opened in 1922 with black nurses, doctors, and administrators. Such was the case, too, with public schools in the South. Arguing that segregated schools in the South were sometimes superior to integrated schools in the North, Du Bois claimed that "Most Negroes would prefer a good school with properly paid teachers for educating their children, to forcing children into white schools which met them with injustice and discouraged their efforts to progress." If whites barred their way to integration, Du Bois concluded, blacks should "voluntarily and insistently . . . organize our economic and social power, no matter how much segregation it involves."[30]

Although his belief that blacks could establish a "co-operative common-wealth" was far-fetched, in some respects Du Bois's analysis was clear-sighted. Blacks had long ago formed their own churches, societies, and social clubs. These institutions were sources of community pride and strength: nobody suggested that they should be abandoned. At the same time, *involuntary* segregation was on the increase: racial ghettos were growing, not breaking up, and the New Deal was extending segregation into new areas such as public housing. A combative intellectual who readily admitted his incapacity for popular leadership, Du Bois made few converts. Worse, his *Crisis* editorials arguing for segregation brought to a head his simmering rivalry with Walter White. The dispute was only resolved by Du Bois's embittered resignation from the NAACP.

Yet many blacks were already pursuing collective action as a matter of common sense and practical self-interest. Black workers, for example, often experienced particular problems of racial discrimination, either from employers or white unions, and formed their own organizations in self-defense. Black postal workers had created their own union, the National Alliance of Postal Employees (NAPE), as far back as 1911. NAPE flourished in the 1930s, greatly increasing its membership and becoming an important source of support for the NAACP. In New Orleans and other Gulf Coast ports, black dockworkers stuck with the segregated International Longshoremen's Association rather than the integrated International Longshoremen and Warehousemen's Union, reasoning that they had greater bargaining power and autonomy if they were organized into all-black locals.

The most powerful example of autonomous action by black workers was the Brotherhood of Sleeping Car Porters (BSCP). Its members were the men who waited on the passengers (mostly white) who travelled and slept aboard the luxury Pullman railroad cars. The Pullman Company, which employed the porters and built the cars, symbolized the authoritarianism of American Big Business. George Pullman, the company's founder, saw himself as a benevolent paternalist, erecting a company town near Chicago (named, naturally, "Pullman") that catered to all his workers' needs. But his employees hated the company town and regarded George Pullman as a tyrannical autocrat. The famous Pullman strike of 1892 precipitated a nationwide railway strike, but failed.

Although the Pullman Company relied upon white workers to build its sleeping cars, it hired only blacks to staff them. The model of a Pullman car porter was an attentive, deferential Negro who carried and stowed luggage, made up beds, served drinks, waited on tables, pressed clothes, and shined shoes. The tradition of black servants waiting upon white people was, of course, a Southern one, and George Pullman originally hired ex-slaves on the grounds that they were already trained in the art of flattering and serving whites. Yet given the other alternatives for earning a living—laboring, sharecropping, and domestic service—working on the Pullman cars was relatively attractive. The job was less physically demanding than most. Porters enjoyed steady work, had ample opportunity to earn tips, and travelled extensively. Along with postal workers and longshoremen, Pullman porters made up the aristocracy of black labor.

But the job also had many drawbacks. Porters spent long hours away from home—as many as 400 a month—for a top monthly wage of $59. Hours spent in the railway yards preparing the cars went unpaid. Porters wore smart uniforms, but they had to purchase them. They enjoyed social prestige in the black community, but received little respect from managers and passengers. The custom whereby passengers addressed all porters as "George" symbolized the smell of slavery that still clung to the job. In 1925 the Brotherhood of Sleeping Car Porters hired A. Philip Randolph, editor of *The Messenger,* as its chief organizer. Randolph set about unionizing the porters and wresting a contract from the company. He faced an uphill struggle.[31]

The Pullman Company was vehemently antiunion, but in line with best industrial practice of the 1920s, it used the stick-and-carrot approach. On the one hand it fired "disloyal" porters and threatened to replace blacks with Mexicans and Filipinos. On the other hand it set up an "employee representation plan" (a company union) in order to undermine the Brotherhood. It also cultivated an image as a good employer—the biggest employer of black labor in the country—by quietly spreading cash among "influential" black leaders. Thus, black ministers denounced Randolph as an atheist; black newspapers attacked him as a Bolshevik; black politicians traduced him as an unprincipled demagogue.

In 1929 the Brotherhood held a strike vote. It was a disastrous miscalculation. Although the "Yes" votes comprised a large majority, the union was still too weak, and it failed to win backing from the AFL. When Randolph "postponed" the action, writes Saunders Redding, "Union morale dropped like a lowered curtain, dues dwindled. . . . Union headquarters gave up its telephone, it gave up its electric light." *The Messenger* ceased publication. The Brotherhood lay at death's door.[32]

What Randolph lacked as a tactician, however, he made up for with integrity, determination, vision, and ability to inspire. A native of Florida who moved to New York at age seventeen, Randolph was a tall, handsome man whose dignified bearing, stentorian voice, and Shakespearean elocution—a cross between Harvard and Oxford that he acquired at acting school—made him an orator of considerable power. If Randolph sometimes betrayed the pedantry and pomposity of the autodidact, his years of study and street-corner activism in the radical circles of prewar New York gave him a deep understanding of history, economics, and politics. Well-versed in Marxist theory, the young Randolph was an ardent Socialist, passionate opponent of the war, and disdainful critic of "old crowd Negro leaders." By 1925, however, Randolph was older, wiser, and more pragmatic. Recognizing the need to build broad public support for the Brotherhood, he won backing from the NAACP, the National Urban League, and the Improved and Benevolent Order of Elks of the World, an influential black fraternal society. When important white church denominations endorsed the Brotherhood, opposition from black ministers crumbled.

If Randolph sometimes appeared to be an other-worldly intellectual—remote, aloof, uninterested in the nuts and bolts of administering the Brotherhood—his incorruptibility was an inspiration. Legend has it that the Pullman Company tried to bribe him by sending, via a circuitous route, a nontraceable check for a very large sum of money. In one version of the story, Randolph returned the check by registered mail; in another, he had the check framed and hung it on his wall. A third version holds that the check was, in fact, a blank one. Whatever the version—and the story may be apocryphal—the moral is the same: Randolph could not be bought.

The New Deal gave the BSCP a final push toward victory. The Roosevelt administration was more sympathetic to unionism than any previous government. In 1934 Congress passed a Railway Labor Act that outlawed company unions and guaranteed workers the right to organize collectively without penalty or interference. The Pullman Company "reformed" its company union, the Pullman Porters and Maids Protective Association (PPMPA), so that it complied with the letter of the new law. But in 1935 the BSCP defeated the PPMPA by 5,931 votes to 1,422. Two years later, the company ran out of delaying tactics and signed a contract with Randolph's union. Porters immediately gained substantially increased pay, a shorter working month, and a reduction in the number of miles they had to travel. The contract of 1937 marked a triumphant conclusion to one of the longest struggles for recognition in the history of the American labor movement. "For twelve years," writes historian William H. Harris, the porters had "fought against overwhelming odds and had weathered the worst depression in the nation's history, and they had won."[33]

That victory made the Brotherhood of Sleeping Car Porters a national symbol of black solidarity, giving it prestige and influence far beyond its small (and declining) membership. It also made A. Philip Randolph a leader of national stature—one of the very few to possess an institutional power base in the black community. Randolph was as convinced of the need for working-class unity as any good Socialist should be. In Harris's words, he viewed the BSCP as a "pioneering wedge that would open the doors of the American labor movement for Afro-Americans." After years of petitioning the notoriously racist AFL, the Brotherhood finally won an international charter—the first black union to gain full AFL recognition. For the rest of his long career as a union leader, Randolph was a tireless campaigner against racial discrimination in the labor movement, a persistent thorn in the side of the AFL.[34]

The BSCP's victory embodied a contradiction between means and ends that bedevilled the struggle for racial equality. "If it demonstrated the Negro's ability to organize on racial lines and move toward democratic goals," explained Saunders Redding, "it proved as well the continuing necessity to do this." In other words, the Brotherhood had gained its victory through the solidarity of black workers, rather than the union of black workers with white. This lesson saddened Randolph, but he learned from it. The BSCP's achievement, he believed, could be used as a model: racial unity wedded to mass action represented the way forward for black Americans. In a veiled criticism of the NAACP, he stated that "The old policy of defending Negroes' rights is well nigh bankrupt. . . . Fundamental rights don't mean a thing if you can't exercise them." He urged blacks to "take the offensive and carry the fight for justice, freedom, and equality to the enemy." For the next ten years, Randolph attempted to implement his strategy of united mass action by and for black people.[35]

THE NATIONAL NEGRO CONGRESS AND
THE MARCH ON WASHINGTON MOVEMENT

T. Thomas Fortune's Afro-American League and the Amenia Conferences of 1916 and 1933 had tried, and failed, to forge black unity. In 1935 John P. Davis, a graduate of Harvard Law School who headed a small but widely respected committee that exposed and fought racial discrimination in New Deal programs, believed that the time was ripe for a fresh effort. At a convention in Chicago in February 1936, 817 delegates backed the formation of the National Negro Congress (NNC), electing A. Philip Randolph as its president. Gathering together in a broad coalition virtually every black organization of any importance, the NNC was the most ambitious effort to coordinate black power yet undertaken. It represented a coming together of left-wing radicalism, labor militancy, and heightened racial consciousness.

External events contributed to the NNC's birth. In 1935, Italy, led by the Fascist dictator Benito Mussolini, attacked Ethiopia. Rarely has there been a clearer example of unprovoked aggression and ruthless colonialism. Black Americans were outraged, interpreting the attack as a deliberate and specific assault on their racial group. Ethiopia was, in effect, the last surviving independent black nation in Africa (Liberia, founded by whites, governed by

English-speaking mulattoes, and dominated by the Firestone Rubber Company, did not really count). Black nationalists had always regarded Ethiopia, a nation of great antiquity, as the fount of civilization and the symbol of black greatness. Blacks of all political hues embraced Ethiopia's cause. They held pro-Ethiopia demonstrations, petitioned the League of Nations, and raised money for relief and medical supplies. Some blacks volunteered to fight in Ethiopia's army (an effort that the federal government did its best to frustrate). "The survival of the black nation became the topic of angry debate in pool-rooms, barber shops, and taverns," recalled black journalist Roi Ottley. "I know of no other event in recent times that stirred the rank-and-file of Negroes more than the Italo-Ethiopian War."[36]

The second foreign event, the victory of the rabidly anti-Communist Nazi Party in Germany, also had a direct impact on American politics. After gaining power in 1933, the Nazis suppressed all political opposition, including the largest Communist Party in Europe. This massive setback for communism revealed the utter futility of the Soviet policy, imposed on all foreign Communist parties, of treating Socialists and other reformists as enemies of the working-class to be denounced and opposed. By promoting divisions on the Left, the Communists had played into the hands of the Nazis. Seriously alarmed by the mounting threat from fascism, the Soviet Union retreated from its strategy of revolution and called for a "broad people's anti-fascist front." This sea change in Communist policy had immediate repercussions in black America. The CPUSA called off its war against the NAACP and ceased abusing the middle classes. Suddenly the acme of cooperation and sweet reason, it sought to build the broadest possible center-left coalition, a "popular front" against fascism. The party was therefore instrumental in founding the National Negro Congress.

Randolph's first speech as president of the NNC was a hard-hitting, radical manifesto that bristled with the language of socialism and class struggle. Disparaging the Republicans and Democrats as "political committees of Wall Street," he lauded the "struggle of the workers against exploitation of the employers," the "struggle . . . of the exploited sharecropper and tenant farmers," and the "struggle of the workers against Fascism." While he welcomed alliances with whites, however, Randolph urged blacks not to depend upon them. "In the final analysis, the salvation of the Negro, like the workers, must come from within":

True liberation can be acquired and maintained only when the Negro people possess power, and power is the product and flower of organization—organization of the masses, the masses in the mills and mines, on the farms, in the factories, in churches, in fraternal organizations, in homes, colleges, women's clubs, student groups, trade unions, tenants' leagues, in cooperative guilds, political organizations and civil rights organizations.

He proposed not to merge these disparate groups, but to "integrate and coordinate" them, forming a black "United Front" to fight for civil and political rights through mass action. The Scottsboro campaign, the Ethiopia campaign, and the labor movement illustrated the kind of techniques that should be utilized: "parades, picketing, boycotting, mass protest, the mass distribution of propaganda literature, as well as legal action."[37]

A. Philip Randolph was no Communist. But like CIO chief John L. Lewis—who famously retorted, on being asked about his employment of Communist organizers, "Who gets the bird, the hunter or the dog?"—Randolph was willing to harness Communist energy and savvy to further his own cause.[38]

It was a dangerous strategy, however. By 1940, when the NNC held its third convention (it did not meet in 1938 or 1939), the Communist Party had effected another about-face, dutifully endorsing the Hitler-Stalin pact and all but abandoning the "Popular Front" against fascism. As Germany swallowed up Czechoslovakia, conquered France, and threatened Britain with invasion; as the Soviet Union attacked Finland; and as the two dictatorships carved up Poland, Communists energetically campaigned for peace and neutrality. The Communists finally revealed their hand inside the NNC when the organization passed a motion condemning the "imperialist war," criticizing American "partiality" toward Britain and France, and urging the United States to stay out. A disgusted Randolph—who believed that the Allies' cause should be America's—resigned as president. Taking a swipe at the white-dominated Communist Party, he explained that the NNC could not accurately be called a "Negro Congress" since, of its 1,200 or more delegates, over 300 were white.[39]

Communist manipulation alone did not doom the NNC to impotence. Black unity of the kind the Congress aspired to was a will-o'-the-wisp, for black organizations guarded their own "turf" too zealously to permit effective cooperation. Walter White treated the NNC with studied suspicion, ensuring that the NAACP withheld its support. The National Urban League, under Lester Granger, also viewed it as a potential rival. In addition, the NNC's radical agenda of 1935, which included rejection of the New Deal and support for independent political action, quickly became dated. Roosevelt's landslide victory of 1936, and the fact that a majority of black voters, for the first time ever, supported the Democratic Party, made a third-party strategy futile. The possibilities for radical change were receding; blacks had to work within the political landscape created by Roosevelt and the New Deal. Even before Communist influence became irreparably divisive, it was plain that the National Negro Congress was too unwieldy and too ambitious; its reach far exceeded its grasp.[40]

Randolph still aspired to lead a mass movement. In January 1941, as the Roosevelt administration made the United States "the arsenal of democracy," commencing a rearmament program that finally pulled the economy out of Depression, Randolph complained that "the whole national defense set-up reeks and stinks with race prejudice, hatred, and discrimination." He then hurled a bombshell. "Let us march 10,000 strong on Washington, D.C." to demand the "Right to Work and Fight for Our Country." Over the following weeks and months, Randolph's rhetoric intensified and his threatened numbers increased—to 25,000, 50,000, and finally 100,000. "An 'all-out' thundering march on Washington, ending in a monster huge demonstration at Lincoln's monument, will shake up white America. It will shake up official Washington. . . . It will gain new respect for the Negro people."

The "March on Washington" (MOW) electrified black America. The tactic itself was imaginative, dramatic, and easily understood. "Mass action . . . places human beings in physical motion which can be felt, seen and heard," Randolph argued. It enabled ordinary people to strike a blow against oppression. Even the poorest, humblest, and least educated could take part. "Mass demonstrations against Jim Crow are worth a million editorials and orations."[41]

Equally important, the MOW spoke to the material conditions of black Americans, millions of whom faced an appalling situation. The expanding economy, stimulated by federal defense contracts, was soaking up the pool of white unemployed. Blacks, however, found themselves excluded from all the well-paid "skilled" jobs in the defense industries. The discrimination was quite blatant and could be found North and South. Over half of the firms replying to a government questionnaire flatly stated that they would not hire blacks. In the aircraft factories of Detroit, whites manned the production lines—blacks were hired for "mop-and-broom" work only. Ten New York factories that employed a total of 29,215 people gave work to only 142 blacks. None of the booming shipyards of the Gulf Coast employed black welders. The six-thousand-man workforce of the Delta Shipyard in New Orleans, for example, included only sixty blacks, half of them office porters and half "common laborers." To make matters worse, the government was terminating New Deal relief programs, making the plight of the black jobless desperate.

Randolph's insistence that the MOW should be an all-black endeavor amplified its appeal. "The reason for this policy," he explained, "is that all oppressed people must assume the responsibility and take the initiative to free themselves." Jews, Catholics, and Protestants, for example, each had their own organizations; so did workers. The MOW was "pro-Negro but not anti-white, or anti-semitic, or anti-labor, or anti-Catholic." Randolph was not a black nationalist—he had been one of Marcus Garvey's most vehement critics. But living in Harlem, still a hotbed of black nationalism, he could see the enduring emotional force of Garvey's appeal to racial solidarity and pride. It was astonishing, for example, that the Ethiopia Peace Movement, a Garveyite remnant led by Mittie Maud Lena Gordon, could secure hundreds of thousands of signatures in support of a bill sponsored by Senator Theodore G. Bilbo of Mississippi to repatriate blacks to Africa. Randolph knew that an all-black MOW would attract many blacks who would otherwise have distrusted it.[42]

Randolph had another motive for excluding whites: he was determined to minimize Communist influence. Communist participation would have been disastrous. The CPUSA opposed any preparation for war, including conscription and rearmament, and it denounced Randolph as a "war-monger." Black Communists could participate in the MOW as individuals. Shutting out white organizations, however, made it impossible for the Communist Party to send blocs of delegates, representing "front" organizations, in order to manipulate the movement. Randolph's explicit anticommunism safeguarded his control of the MOW and also made it easier for groups like the NAACP to endorse it.[43]

Roosevelt shuddered at the prospect of Randolph's mass march, scheduled for July 1, 1941. Governments have always hated public demonstrations in Washington, regarding them as coercion at best and insurrection at worst. "Coxey's Army" of 1894, a march of the unemployed, had been broken up before it ever reached the capital. The "Bonus Marchers" of 1932, unemployed war veterans who camped out on Anacostia Flat, were driven away by the army on the orders of President Herbert Hoover. A mass demonstration of *black* marchers held the additional danger of racial violence; memories of the 1919 Washington race riot were still fresh. (Washington, D.C., was a "Southern" city in customs and attitudes, with strict segregation, a police force dominated by Southern whites, and an unelected government controlled by Southern congressmen.)

Roosevelt, whom many blacks resented for failing to oppose racial oppression—he refused, for example, to support antilynching legislation—shrewdly dispatched three prominent racial liberals to intercede with Randolph. Eleanor Roosevelt, who was widely respected by blacks for her outspokenness in opposing racial discrimination, warned Randolph that "there may be trouble if the march occurs." Aubrey Williams, director of the National Youth Administration, and Fiorello LaGuardia, mayor of New York City, agreed that the march should be cancelled. Randolph refused to budge unless the government took definite action against discrimination. Summoned to the White House on June 16 for a conference with the president himself, he resisted the famous "Roosevelt charm" and refused to call off the march. "Buses were hired, special trains chartered, and . . . thousands of dollars spent," wrote Roi Ottley. "And those efficient couriers—the Pullman porters—carried the word to Negro communities throughout the country."[44]

Historians have speculated that Randolph might have been bluffing, that he had no intention of actually holding the march. If so, it was a very good bluff, for on June 25 Roosevelt folded. Executive Order 8802, bearing the president's signature, stated that "there shall be no discrimination in the employment of workers in defense industries and in Government because of race, creed, color, or national origin." Henceforth, all government defense contracts were to contain antidiscrimination clauses. The government promised "special measures" to eliminate discrimination in its defense training programs. The order obliged employers and unions to provide for "full and equitable participation of all workers in the defense industries without discrimination." It created a Fair Employment Practices Committee (FEPC) to investigate complaints of discrimination and recommend appropriate action.

Blacks across America were jubilant. Executive Order 8802 appeared to be an economic breakthrough. Some New Deal agencies had taken feeble steps to combat racial discrimination, but never before had the government made fair employment a national policy, and never before had a president made such a firm commitment to racial equality. Predictably, however, racial discrimination was too deeply rooted to eliminate by government fiat. Fair employment policy foundered on the rocks of union and employer resistance; white Southerners fought the FEPC every step of the way and eventually succeeded in abolishing it. Roosevelt, unfortunately, all but nullified his own policy by downgrading the FEPC and showing little further interest in the issue. For the moment, however, celebration was in order. Once again, A. Philip Randolph was the hero of the hour. "For a few months," wrote Arna Bontemps, "he could scarcely enter a crowded place without seeming to put a spell on it. . . . [S]ome of his more ardent admirers began comparing him to Gandhi."[45]

Randolph now tried to fashion a permanent organization from the march that never took place. "The central principle of the struggle of oppressed minorities," he pointed out, "is not only to develop mass demonstration maneuvers, but to repeat and continue them. The workers don't picket firms today and fold up. They practice the principle of repetition." Instead of disbanding the MOW, therefore, he converted it into the March on Washington *Movement* (MOWM), proposing more marches, rallies, picket lines, and demonstrations. The MOWM aimed "actually to organize millions of Negroes . . . so that they may be summoned into action over night and thrown into physical motion."

Randolph laid out an eight-point program that demanded the right to vote, abolition of the poll tax, and the abolition of segregation in transportation, schools, housing, public accommodations, and the armed forces. He addressed mass rallies in New York, Chicago, and St. Louis, as well as dozens of smaller meetings. America's entry into the war after Pearl Harbor did nothing to tone down his plans. Indeed, in 1942–43, inspired by Gandhi's Indian independence movement, he mooted plans for a campaign of civil disobedience. Blacks in the South should register their opposition to Jim Crow, he suggested, by staging one-day boycotts of segregated schools, buses, streetcars, and railroads.

In the summer of 1943, however, the March on Washington Movement all but fizzled out. In large part, the war was to blame. Randolph's calls for mass protest appeared increasingly inappropriate when America was bending all its energies to winning the struggle against Germany and Japan. Although black newspapers and organizations pointedly refused to keep silent about racial discrimination, they, too, rallied behind the war effort. The drive for national unity, fuelled by government propaganda as well as straightforward patriotism, overwhelmed Randolph's campaign.

For all his militant rhetoric, moreover, Randolph proved unable to translate his belief in mass action into a practical program. When Secretary of the Interior Harold Ickes denied Randolph use of the Lincoln Memorial, Randolph's failure to challenge the decision exposed his "March on Washington" threat as an empty one. Randolph could pack Madison Square Garden, in New York City, but mass meetings soon became stale—a way of letting off steam rather than an effective means of protest. In calling for a campaign of nonviolent direct action, Randolph was influenced by young pacifists like Bayard Rustin, Bernice Fisher, and James Farmer, who in 1942 founded the Congress of Racial Equality (CORE) to apply Gandhian techniques to the race question. But CORE confined itself to the North, and it involved very small numbers. In the South, Randolph's call for mass boycotts elicited a muted response; nonviolent protest seemed suicidal. By 1943 many had concluded that Randolph was all talk and no action. "Mass leadership in times like these . . . requires a little more guts than any of the Negro leaders possess," wrote black journalist George Schuyler. "I know of none willing, like Nehru and Gandhi, to go to jail."[46]

The radicalism of the 1930s had about run its course. The Communist Party enjoyed a brief honeymoon with America when, between June 1941 and May 1945, the United States and the Soviet Union were allies in the war against Nazi Germany. But the Cold War, and the anti-communist repression known as McCarthyism, eliminated communism as an organized force in American political life. Randolph's March on Washington Movement expired altogether in 1946. The South weathered the challenges of the New Deal era with its system of white supremacy virtually intact. In attacking racial inequality, blacks in the South had to play a longer and more cautious game. And it was the NAACP, not the Communist Party, that enabled them to make the first real breakthroughs in the struggle for black freedom.

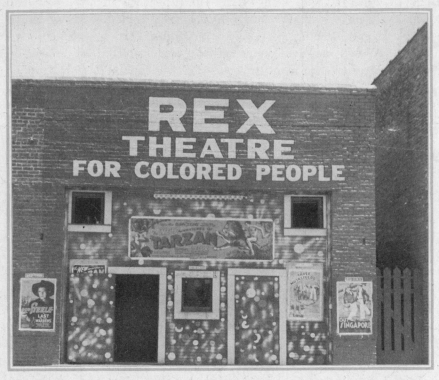

The Rex Theatre for Colored People, Leland, Mississippi, 1937

8

Blacks in the Segregated South,
1919-42

In 1939, Gunnar Myrdal, a Swedish economist engaged in a "comprehensive study of the Negro in America" on behalf of the Carnegie Foundation, interviewed the president of the NAACP in one of the state capitals of the Deep South. "The NAACP stands firm on its principles and demands our rights as American citizens," explained the activist, whom Myrdal left unnamed, "but it accomplishes little or nothing in this town because it arouses a good deal of anger in whites." Another local organization, however, the League for Civic Improvement, was "humble and pussyfooting, begs for many favors from the whites, and succeeds quite often." Asked by Myrdal who headed this civic improvement league, the NAACP president—an elderly and distinguished-looking man—admitted that he did. "We are all the same people in both organizations."[1]

The struggle for racial equality can be chronicled in terms of agitation and protest, of courtroom confrontations and bus boycotts, and of the history of civil rights organizations like the NAACP. Such a narrative, however, would leave much of the story untold. In the segregated South during the heyday of white supremacy—from about 1910 to about 1950—blacks could rarely, if ever, openly challenge white people without fear of retaliation. Sharecroppers could be evicted, employees fired at will, and businessmen refused credit without ever being told why. Whites could also employ more drastic sanctions—arrest, beating, banishment, and murder—with virtual impunity.

Short of migration, black Southerners had little choice but to make the best of a bad situation. They said what white people wished them to say, but also tried to manipulate them. They flattered and kowtowed, but also cultivated pride and self-respect among themselves. Hemmed in by walls of prejudice, blacks created havens of security within families, communities, and churches. In a sense, they were reverting to the strategy of accommodation devised by their slave forebears and dusted off by Booker T. Washington—just as whites were trying to re-create the next best thing to slavery.

Throughout these grim decades, however, blacks did more than merely survive. For all its violence and ugliness, the South of the first half of the twentieth century differed in crucial essentials from the antebellum South. Although historians like U. B. Phillips might rewrite history to depict slavery as a beneficent institution, Southern whites could not resurrect human bondage. Despite the cult of the Lost Cause—symbolized by thousands of stone Confederate soldiers that watched over courthouse squares—the South could not seal its borders as if the Confederacy had triumphed. The slaveholders censored the mails and suppressed abolitionist propaganda; in the segregated South, copies of the *Crisis,* the *Chicago Defender,* and the *Pittsburgh Courier* freely circulated, as did Southern black newspapers like the *Norfolk Journal and Guide,* the *Louisiana Weekly,* and the *Houston Informer.* If sharecropping sometimes shaded into peonage, the majority of sharecroppers, unlike slaves or peons, were free to move and frequently did so. Even within the confines of white supremacy, therefore, black Southerners enjoyed a measure of freedom.

One way blacks used this freedom was to organize under the banner of "racial uplift." Behind the wall of segregation, they built and strengthened parallel institutions—churches, societies, businesses, unions, newspapers, and professional associations. They also enlisted white cooperation and support for ostensibly "nonpolitical" causes like education and public health.

"Racial uplift" entailed a compromise with Jim Crow, and many blacks, without a doubt, became resigned to segregation and second-class citizenship. Viewed from a different angle, however, racial uplift represented one step backward in preparation for two steps forward. Unable to attack segregation head-on, blacks adopted tactics of indirection. Without abandoning the ultimate goal of full citizenship, they worked for short-term improvements within their segregated sphere. Moreover, because the gap between "separate" and "equal" was so vast, blacks did not yet have to choose between the NAACP's platform of equal rights and the Washingtonian strategy of racial uplift. They could endorse the first while pursuing the second. By enduring the daily humiliations of segregation, two generations of black Southerners made a second Reconstruction—the Civil Rights Movement of the 1950s and 1960s—a historical possibility.

RACIAL UPLIFT AND INTERRACIAL COOPERATION

The concept of "racial uplift" is easily mocked. It reeks of the condescension and snobbery with which middle-class reformers so often treat the objects of their charity, the great unwashed. It conjures up images of bustling busybodies scolding the poor for intemperance, lecturing them on thrift, and teaching them domestic arts such as needlework and the correct placement of the doily. "Uplift" reeks of self-regard and social striving on the part of the "best elements" of the race. "'Uplift' occasions were teas and afternoon programs to which we went in nice little dresses and with our hair freshly pressed or touched up," recalled Mamie Garvin Fields of her childhood in Charleston, South Carolina. "At 'uplift' occasions we met ladies with smooth faces and silken dresses, soprano voices 'soooo happy to see you,' and resounding kisses which smelled of powder and cologne."[2]

Yet under the innocuous cover of "uplift," blacks gained white support for activities that directly improved the lives of poor people. Public health, for example, had long been a major interest of black women's clubs, and in 1915 Booker T. Washington strengthened and focused these efforts by initiating National Negro Health Week. Washington and his successor, Robert Moton, skillfully appealed to white self-interest by stressing that germs crossed the color line with alacrity. "If we die, they die," said Moton. "If we get diseased, they will get diseased, and they know it."

Few whites cared to dispute that argument. Through local committees of the Commission on Interracial Cooperation (CIC), founded in 1919, whites encouraged and supported the black public health campaign. State and local officials rendered help. In 1932 the United States Public Health Service created the Office of Negro Health Work, which, under Dr. Roscoe D. Brown, a graduate of Howard University Dental School, assumed responsibility for what now became known as the National Negro Health Movement. Through lectures, leaflets, films, clinics, inoculations, and neighborhood "clean-up" campaigns, Negro Health Week reached millions. White people encouraged such activities, of course, because they seemed fundamentally nonpolitical, presenting no threat at all to their racial domination. Yet as historian Susan L. Smith astutely notes, "the assertion of black health needs was itself a political expression." Blacks used the public health issue to make political claims upon the state and to subtly criticize segregation. In Charleston, for example, the Federation of Colored Women's Clubs carried out a housing survey in 1932 which, by identifying the worst slums, influenced the siting of the city's first public housing.[3]

Ostensibly led by male doctors, the public health campaign provides one example of how, at the state and local level, middle-class women did most of the work in building the organizational networks that lobbied for black interests. Women were already highly organized through churches and clubs, and the hardening of white supremacy further enhanced their relative importance within the black community. Disfranchisement stripped black men of the vote and denied them any role as political leaders, and while segregation applied to both sexes equally, it bore down more harshly upon black men. Black women, accustomed to being voteless, but skilled in the techniques of voluntary organization, were better able to adapt to the new racial order. They found it easier to work in a nonconfrontational manner, acting as mediators between the two communities. Yet because whites viewed them as less threatening, black women could also express themselves with greater forthrightness than black men. Among whites, moreover, white women were the keenest supporters of interracial cooperation. It would be too much to argue that black and white women shared a sense of "sisterhood" in the feminist sense of that word. Yet they did recognize common concerns as women, mothers, and Christians.

The most important women's initiative took place in 1920 when two white Methodist laywomen, Sara Estelle Haskin and Carrie Parks Johnson, journeyed to Tuskegee Institute to meet with ten leaders of the National Association of Colored Women. Encouraged by wartime cooperation within the Young Women's Christian Association, the women talked of ways to promote interracial understanding.

The meeting, held at the home of Margaret Murray Washington, Booker T. Washington's widow, was tense and awkward. One of the black women, Charlotte Hawkins Brown, suspected, cynically, that whites had called them together in order to discuss the servant problem. "There was a gulf of distance, of mistrust and suspicion," admitted Carrie Johnson. "I wanted to speak with them but didn't know how." After prayers and heart-searching, the women finally began to communicate across the walls of race and history. For the whites, this emotionally charged meeting was a revelation. As Johnson recalled, the black women "poured out their hearts, showing us how inconsiderate the white man is, and the white woman is, how unconcerned as to their homes, the streets on which they live, telling of their unprotected childhood and girlhood." As they unburdened themselves, "these women looked into my face and saw the pain of the southern white women."

The black women received invitations to a special meeting, jointly sponsored by the Commission on Interracial Cooperation and the Women's Missionary Council of the white Methodist church, of about one hundred

Southern white women in Memphis. The white women were veterans of the temperance movement and of the campaign for women's suffrage. Many were active in their churches' social programs. A good number participated in the YWCA and the white women's club movement. Still, the white female wing of Southern progressivism was no more sympathetic to racial equality than the white male wing. White suffragists heartily endorsed black disfranchisement. Perhaps half of the white women belonged to the United Daughters of the Confederacy. One of them was the sister of Colonel Alfred M. Waddell, the former Confederate officer who led the bloody Wilmington riot of 1898.

Astonishingly, when the black women entered the meeting room of the Memphis YWCA, the white audience rose to its feet; as they walked down the aisle, Belle Bennett, president of the Methodists' women's council and the daughter of a Confederate general, began to sing "Blest Be the Tie That Binds." By the time Margaret Murray Washington, Elizabeth Ross Haynes, Jenny B. Moton, Mary McLeod Bethune, and Charlotte Hawkins Brown reached the front of the room, "everyone was singing and everyone was crying." When the room became silent, Carrie Johnson invited the black women to "tell us your story and try to enlighten us. You probably think we're pretty ignorant, and we are, but we're willing to learn."

After carefully measured speeches by Washington and Haynes that appealed to the white women as wives and mothers, Charlotte Hawkins Brown threw diplomacy to the winds. Angry and impassioned, she described the humiliation she had suffered en route to the meeting. Booked into a railway sleeping car, she had been forced to quit her berth and sit in the Jim Crow carriage when a group of white men objected to her presence.

Will you put yourself in my place? Just be colored for a few moments and see yourself sitting down in a seat, helpless, with twelve white men sitting around. A young man leaned forward and said, "We have wired ahead to have you taken off this train. Now, we give you your choice, to get off this car right away and go into the day coach, or be taken off."

She ended her speech by invoking their common Christian faith. The audience rose and belted out a hymn.[4]

The Memphis meeting was a genuine landmark: Southern white women listened respectfully to black women leaders and sought an honest understanding of their grievances. It unleashed a burst of energy and enthusiasm for interracial cooperation. The meeting prompted the Commission on Interracial Cooperation, hitherto a men-only operation, to form a Committee on Women's Work with a paid, full-time staff member. State and local women's committees multiplied, most of the latter organized under the wing of the Methodist church. By 1927, writes Jacqueline Hall, over six hundred local committees were engaged in some kind of interracial work, much of it geared toward improving black living conditions. "They helped establish dental and health clinics in public schools, secured library and hospital privileges, and set up municipal playgrounds."[5]

The initial burst of energy and enthusiasm unleashed by the historic Memphis meeting inevitably ran out of steam. By the late 1920s, Hall notes, "interracial gatherings had begun to lose their symbolic impact. The novelty of meeting educated black women had worn off." State and local committees became dormant.[6]

Yet in 1930 a group of twenty-six women initiated the most significant campaign against racial oppression yet undertaken by white Southerners. The Association of Southern Women for the Prevention of Lynching (ASWPL), headed by Jesse Daniel Ames, an energetic and strong-willed Texan, disputed the argument that lynching protected white women from rape, named and shamed law enforcement officials who turned prisoners over to the mob, and tried to prevent threatened lynchings from happening. The drastic decline of lynching during the 1930s had many causes, including the NAACP's widely publicized campaign to persuade Congress to make lynching a federal crime. The ASWPL actually opposed federal action, and Southern congressmen managed to defeat successive antilynching bills. Yet the *threat* of federal intervention made the ASWPL's argument for state action against lynching increasingly persuasive. By 1941, writes Jesse Ames's biographer, the ASWPL had secured signed "pledges" to prevent lynchings from 1,355 Southern sheriffs and policemen. In a single year, law enforcement officers frustrated at least forty lynch mobs by ensuring the safety of black prisoners.[7]

In the 1930s, however, the limitations of both racial uplift and interracial cooperation became increasingly apparent. When America slid into Depression, local fund-raising for black causes became virtually impossible. The Depression also revealed the vulnerability of black institution-building, as black-owned banks failed, insurance companies folded, and fraternal societies defaulted on their benefit payments. The Depression, moreover, undermined the whole principle of voluntarism: only the federal government had the resources to alleviate unemployment, build public facilities, and improve the living conditions of the poor. By the mid-1930s more and more blacks were looking to the Roosevelt administration to relieve their suffering and change the situation in the South for the better.

The interracial cooperation movement had always been a poor substitute for political action. From the time of its formation in 1919, the Commission on Interracial Cooperation drew criticism from blacks for being weak, ineffective, and conservative—an organization devoted to preserving the status quo rather than changing it. Certainly, the CIC deliberately avoided challenging the basics of white supremacy: it did not seek political rights for black Southerners, and it failed to question racial segregation. The CIC's caution stemmed in part from a calculation, based on a hardheaded assessment of Southern political reality, that to attack the Jim Crow system head-on would rekindle white nightmares of Reconstruction, evoking even greater violence and repression.

The necessity to appease Southern whites exposed a basic contradiction at the heart of the "interracial cooperation" idea. Whites in the CIC contended that black progress could be facilitated within the confines of segregation. Up to a point, that was true. But segregation and true equality were incompatible: white superiority was the very essence of racial segregation. Hence, most white Southerners remained suspicious of interracial cooperation, insisting that every interracial contact should explicitly underline black inferiority.

The white custom of withholding courtesy titles from black people epitomized this determination. "It is our policy not to refer to negro men or negro women as Mr. or Mrs.," explained one newspaper editor in 1941. "This policy," he added, "I have no idea of changing." Edwin Morgenroth, a Rosenwald Fund researcher in Arkansas, received an impassioned lecture on the subject by the president of the local school board:

No one down here calls a nigger Mr., Miss or Mrs. You just can't do it. You mustn't. Another thing, don't say "thank you" to a nigger. You can say "that is fine," "I like that" but never say "Thank you." You must make him feel that you are superior. . . . If you go around "mistering" a nigger he will have less respect for you than if you cuss him and order him around.

Even when expressing what they perceived as their most generous sympathies, whites made it plain what they expected of blacks. In 1927 the white citizens of Natchitoches erected a statue dedicated to "the good darkies of Louisiana." It depicted a black man with stooped shoulders and doffed hat in the act of bowing.[8]

The CIC's unwillingness to confront white supremacy also reflected the conservatism of its white supporters. The famous interracial women's meeting of 1920, for example, failed to produce a common program because the demands presented by the black women proved too radical for the whites. The blacks had prepared a statement calling for better schools, child welfare, more accurate and respectful treatment of black people by white newspapers, more equitable transport facilities, the protection of black girls, especially domestic servants, the suppression of lynching, and the franchise. But when Carrie Johnson read out the statement she omitted the suffrage section, and added to the lynching section a sentence that condemned "any action on the part of Negro men which excited mob spirit." She also, revealingly, left out a sentence in the preamble that demanded for Negro women "all the privileges and rights granted to American womanhood." Over the next twenty years, white women in the CIC never reached the point of working *with* black women on a platform of racial equality.[9]

The conservative instincts of influential white supporters such as Thomas Jesse Jones and Edgar B. Stern underlined the limitations of the CIC's racial liberalism. Jones, head of the Phelps-Stokes Fund, decried the "overemphasis on *conflict* that seems to me to characterize the attitude of Negro intelligentsia." A long-standing critic of Du Bois, Jones tried to promote Robert Moton as the "outstanding American Negro." Stern, a New Orleans cotton broker and the son-in-law of philanthropist Julius Rosenwald—whose foundation helped to finance the CIC—firmly believed in racial segregation. Instrumental in the founding of Dillard University in 1935, Stern argued that only a white president ought to run a mixed faculty: a black person should not be placed in authority over whites. Moreover, he insisted that the president "avoid giving offense to southern tradition" by refraining from "social contact" with black students and faculty members. If ever the white president of Dillard allowed his wife to dance with Negro men, Stern warned, he would resign forthwith from the board of trustees.[10]

In the 1930s, recognizing that "interracial cooperation" had reached the point of diminishing returns, the more advanced liberals in the CIC looked to influencing the Roosevelt administration as a strategy for promoting change in the South. Although anchored to a party in which the white South held enormous power, Franklin Roosevelt's administration was open-minded, politically catholic, and willing to experiment. Roosevelt "energized the political process," wrote historian Patricia Sullivan, "giving full play to a wide range of ideas, personalities, and interests."[11]

In addition to the usual Southern conservatives and machine politicians from the North, his cabinet included a Republican from Chicago, Harold Ickes. A former president of the Chicago branch of the NAACP, Ickes brought to the New Deal a concern for racial justice that ran counter to the Democratic Party's historic opposition to black rights. As secretary of the interior, with control over some of the biggest New Deal spending programs, he exercised considerable influence. Ickes set a notable precedent by prohibiting racial discrimination in the Public Works Administration, insisting that every building contract include a fair-employment clause. He imposed racial quotas in an effort to enforce the policy. Equally important, Ickes led the way in making the government accessible to black opinions. Black leaders criticized his appointment of a white man, Clark Foreman, as his "special adviser on the economic status of Negroes." Nevertheless, Foreman, a native of Georgia, was a strong supporter of racial equality who had demonstrated his commitment by working for the CIC and the Rosenwald Fund. His successor, moreover, was a black man, Harvard-educated economist Robert C. Weaver.[12]

By the mid-1930s the New Deal had established a tier of black advisers in government departments and agencies. This so-called "Black Cabinet" did not function as a policy-making body and was not really a unified group. Nevertheless, black advisers exercised considerable influence over the implementation of New Deal programs, especially when they worked for racial liberals like Will Alexander, head of the Farm Security Administration, Aubrey Williams, director of the National Youth Administration (NYA), and Ickes himself. The best-known example is undoubtedly Mary McLeod Bethune, whose success in promoting black interests as head of the "Negro Division" of the NYA became legendary. Working closely with Aubrey Williams, forging a strategic friendship with Eleanor Roosevelt, and using her myriad connections with the black community, especially the women's club movement, Bethune parlayed her relatively low-level position into one whose reach extended far into the federal bureaucracy.[13]

THE AMBIGUITIES OF THE BETTER SCHOOLS CAMPAIGN

Campaigns to improve black education revealed the benefits and limitations of racial "uplift." They united the black community and elicited valuable support from whites—practically all white leaders conceded that blacks needed a modicum of schooling. Between 1917 and 1932, the Rosenwald Fund stimulated a massive effort on the part of black Southerners to donate money, land, building materials, and labor to the building of new schoolhouses. Increased state funding accompanied this drive.

Even in the 1930s, when the Rosenwald Fund curtailed its school-building program and the Depression reduced public expenditure, blacks retained a robust faith in education. "Members of a race characterized by the Whites as thriftless and improvident scheme and save and labor, sometimes for years in advance, to secure an education for their children," wrote anthropologist Hortense Powdermaker, who spent two years in Indianola, Mississippi. "Almost every mother is ardent in her wish that her child should receive more education than she did, and thus gain the prospect of a happier and easier life." Teachers and parents, especially mothers, sustained community involvement in schools through parent-teacher associations. The desire for better education also spurred black migration to the cities—usually the only places where black children could attend a public high school.[14]

Black Southerners waged a long campaign, beginning in Reconstruction, to have their public schools staffed exclusively by black teachers, an objective they had largely achieved by World War I. In Charleston, South Carolina, where whites taught in black schools long after they had been replaced elsewhere, the NAACP launched a petition drive to have them phased out. In 1919 the state legislature passed a bill to that effect, confining white teachers to white schools. Even in the white-controlled private colleges, where faculties had for decades been exclusively white, black teachers were in the majority well before 1930.[15]

In the Age of Segregation, black teachers became skilled in using organization and research to press for educational improvements. Long organized at the state level, by 1930 they had formed at least five national associations, each with a slightly different constituency, but with overlapping memberships and a common overall purpose. Teachers' groups cultivated the philanthropic foundations, influenced Southern whites through the Commission on Interracial Cooperation, criticized racism in school textbooks, decried racial stereotyping in Hollywood movies, promoted the teaching of Negro history, sought recognition from the National Education Association (NEA), and lobbied the federal government. During the 1930s there was still a clear sense that education was a "movement" for racial progress and equality. Moreover, black teachers demanded that black schools and colleges be accredited on exactly the same basis as white institutions—a clear rejection of white supremacist assumptions.

The campaign for better education, however, also involved costs and compromises. Most obviously, black teachers had to bend to the ideological demands of segregation. After disfranchisement, triumphant white supremacists tightened their control over state-funded black colleges: the men at their helms had to abandon politics or suffer unceremonious dismissal. Black educators also faced continual pressure to keep academic standards low. For example, when Nathan B. Young took Florida Colored Normal School too far from vocationalism, he found himself on the sharp end of a political campaign that forced his resignation. Others, like Richard R. Wright, longtime president of Georgia State Industrial College in Savannah, quit the South in discouragement and disgust. White support for black education was contingent upon black acquiescence in white supremacy.

Although Southern whites recognized black educators as "leaders," teachers were leaders in a very narrowly defined sense. Nobody elected them, and in the public sector they were beholden to white school boards and state officials. Blacks could not demand, bargain, or negotiate. In order to secure white support, therefore, they often resorted to devious, self-abasing stratagems. Whites expected deferential behavior and were in a position to demand it.

"I was struck by the roundabout fashion in which by various subterfuges Negro education has been improved," wrote John J. Coss, a board member of the Rosenwald Fund, and professor of philosophy at Columbia University, when he visited Georgia in 1936. The teachers who succeeded in influencing white leaders were "almost miracles," thought Coss. They "have come through the state of the despised or tolerated, been subject to condescension, and still have kept their steady goodness without bitterness." Coss cited the example of W. H. Hubbard, principal of a two-year normal school in Forsyth, Georgia. "Slow, soft-spoken, plodding but patient and humble and beloved by many of the white town folks," Hubbard was particularly adept at cultivating the principal of a white Baptist girls' college. He sent his boys to do odd jobs at the college, and, in return, received periodic donations of dogeared books and worn-out equipment.[16]

Even private schools that were independent of public funds could only survive with the consent of local whites, and their principals went to great lengths to obtain it. They secured protection and approval by prevailing upon local bankers, planters, and merchants to serve as school trustees. They also emulated the dissembling of public school principals. Laurence C. Jones, who founded the famous "Piney Woods School" in Mississippi in 1909, and headed it for sixty years, "was careful to heed the will of his white friends, seeking their advice and sanction frequently and staying away from politics." His habit of donning work overalls whenever he visited state officials in Jackson was an extreme form of role-playing that other black teachers found gratuitously demeaning.[17]

Ironically, as the Hubbards and Joneses of the South succeeded in improving black schools they became even more dependent upon whites—and thus increasingly trapped in their accommodationist role. Philanthropic money and increased state funding brought about improvements in black education, but at the cost of greater bureaucratic control by Southern whites. School buildings owned by blacks had to be deeded to county education boards in order to qualify for Rosenwald money. Some black colleges that started as private initiatives only survived by accepting state money and control. The state agents of Negro education appointed by the General Education Board worked within the state governments: they did not—could not—challenge white supremacy. Black teachers, once chosen by black school trustees, were now appointed by white county school superintendents. "Negro teachers at all levels," Gunnar Myrdal noted, "are dependent on the white community leaders."[18]

That was especially true of the principals of the new high schools, or "training schools," that were being established, mainly in the towns and cities, during the 1920s, 1930s, and 1940s. In Charleston, South Carolina, writes Edmund Drago, the school board "closely monitored the black principals' work [and] their after-school activities." Elsewhere, superintendents and school board members sometimes treated black principals as chauffeurs, gardeners, repair men, and errand boys. They "asks you to do things," a Louisiana principal told Horace Mann Bond, "and it's right that you should do it. They give you your job. The other night I was got up at 2 o'clock in the morning doctoring on one of the school board members' horses."[19]

School superintendents also expected black principals to tell them what was going on inside the Negro community. Whites used teachers as sources of intelligence *from* the black community and messengers *to* the black community. School principals had to be racial diplomats; they often became, in Glenda Gilmore's phrase, "double agents." The problem with double agents, however, is that it often becomes impossible to tell where the person's ultimate loyalty lies. During the high tide of segregation, there was a widespread perception among blacks that teachers, along with ministers, acted as indirect agents of white control by functioning as spies and collaborators. "The temptation to sell out the group and to look out for his own petty interest is great," noted Myrdal.[20]

The position of black teachers as community leaders was therefore deeply ambiguous—some would say fatally compromised. In addition to respect, teachers also evoked cynicism and distrust. A novel by J. Saunders Redding, *Stranger and Alone,* published in 1951, offered a bitter perspective. Redding, a professor of English at Hampton Institute, gave a chilling portrait of a black teacher who possessed no idealism, no racial loyalty, and no spiritual strength; in return for preferment and privilege, he betrayed NAACP members—fellow teachers—to the white schools superintendent.[21]

Betrayal and bad faith were constant refrains in discussions of black teachers. The presidents of state-funded black colleges gained a particular reputation for "Uncle Tomism." These men—and they always were men—were characterized by their black critics as ignorant autocrats. Immune from black public opinion, wrote Lewis K. McMillan, "the president stands a surer chance of keeping his job to the extent that he is hostile to the best interests of his own people." Saunders Redding was even more damning. "Negro colleges have tended to breed fascism. . . . Victims of a tyranny imposed from without, [Negro college presidents] are tyrants within the academic group and, if given a chance, outside it too. They play the strong man and the dictator role."[22]

However, accommodationism did not necessarily imply selling out. Many teachers cynically told whites what they wanted to hear in order to manipulate them and, in Myrdal's words, "unselfishly forward Negro interests by a slow, patient, but determined plodding along against odds and difficulties." Hortense Powdermaker was astonished when she saw a black woman teacher whom she knew as a "strong self-respecting person" become the "essence of meekness" in front of her white superior. This was how she "deliberately fooled the whites," the teacher told the anthropologist. Looking back on the incident thirty years later, Powdermaker believed that "this kind of accommodation to the white power structure was realistic."[23]

In practice, black teachers often enjoyed greater freedom of speech and action than one might expect. The white school superintendents, especially in the rural South, usually paid little attention to black teachers and rarely visited black schools. Quite often they delegated the administration of black schools to the "Jeanes teachers"—black officials, nearly all of them women, who were paid by the General Education Board to promote "manual work" among black country folk. These "rural school supervisors," to give them their official title, quickly outgrew their Washingtonian job description. Soon they were hiring and firing teachers, lobbying school boards, raising funds, organizing public health campaigns, setting up PTAs, and establishing homemakers' clubs. They also acted as informal social workers and general problem solvers. At a time when blacks were excluded from politics, notes James Leloudis, and when black men could not risk being assertive, the Jeanes teachers functioned as important "liaisons to white officialdom."[24]

By the 1930s, however, many blacks were questioning whether the campaign for better schools could ever bring about fundamental social change. For one thing, educational equality seemed like a will-o'-the-wisp. According to Horace Mann Bond, during the early years of the Great Depression the South's black children were receiving "a smaller proportion of public funds" than ever before. Even as black schools improved, so did white schools, and the racial disparity remained. Secondly, no matter how good they were, schools could not change the fact that whites monopolized political power, owned nearly all the wealth, and subjected black people to discrimination, abuse, and violence. "In the restricted sense of pupil-teacher relationships within the classroom," Bond wrote in 1934, "no 'school' can . . . solve the problems of Negro health, economic dependence, or family disorganization." Whites encouraged black education, one suspects, as a means of diverting black ambitions into nonpolitical channels that could be directed and controlled.[25]

The dismal state of most rural schools, despite the Rosenwald Fund's school-building program, underlined the extent of the problem. In the 1930s most black schools were still dilapidated wooden buildings, many of them lacking blackboards, desks, libraries, and textbooks. Underpaid, poorly trained teachers—often with little more education than their pupils— struggled with classes of fifty to seventy-five children of all ages. If the schoolhouse was bad enough, observed Clark Foreman in 1932, "it can almost completely stop the educational process, as may be illustrated by one very small and dilapidated shack without windows, in which the investigators on opening the door found the school in absolute darkness and the teacher and pupils asleep."[26]

Sociologists seriously questioned whether such schools could encourage racial pride, raise cultural awareness, or teach anything beyond basic literacy. Certainly, rising overall levels of education masked an enormous residue of ignorance. In a one-teacher school in Macon County, Georgia, sociologist Arthur Raper asked a child named Booker T. Washington Williams for whom he was named. Neither he nor any of the other pupils knew. Even the teacher failed to identify Washington. In 1939 Gunnar Myrdal "hardly believed his eyes and his ears" when he questioned the students in a similar school. "No one could tell who the president of the United States was or even what the president was. . . . No one had heard of the NAACP." Asked about the Constitution of the United States, "all remained in solemn silence, until one bright boy helped us out, informing us that it was 'a newspaper in Atlanta.'"[27]

For many black children, school was a confusing, disturbing, alienating experience. After studying rural schools in six cotton counties scattered across the South, Charles S. Johnson thought he understood why. "Poorly prepared teachers . . . control their pupils more by physical fear than by the interest they can inspire." Harsh punishment, rote learning, and a "lifeless curriculum," promoted "maladjustment" to school and inhibited "proper personality development." When Johnson studied Louisiana's black schools, he printed verbatim transcripts of lessons: many were exercises in confusion that taught the children nothing. Small wonder that many children left school at the earliest opportunity, convinced that education was meaningless.[28]

City schools, private and public, were far superior to rural schools. However, neither better buildings nor the shift from white to black teachers guaranteed better education—not, at least, an education that encouraged blacks to question segregation. Schools did little to unite the black community or inspire it to fight for equality, argues Idus A. Newby. "Academic subjects became the vehicles for teaching black Carolinians to accommodate to white supremacy." State-approved textbooks—often selected by the United Daughters of the Confederacy—defended slavery, eulogized the Lost Cause, and damned Reconstruction. Black schoolchildren in Charleston learned to sing "Dixie" and "The Bonnie Blue Flag." Teachers rarely discussed racial discrimination, and what passed for "community civics" ignored the race question.[29]

Black intellectuals even wondered whether improvements in higher education were benefitting the race. The number of college students increased from 12,000 in 1928 to 37,000 in 1941, but as black colleges departed from the vocationalism of Booker T. Washington and imitated the academic programs, Greek letter societies, and sports obsessions of white colleges, they lost that sense of mission that had characterized them in the late nineteenth century. Du Bois warned that the rise of an educated elite might weaken the mass rather than raise the culture of the entire group. The "talented tenth," he complained, had surrendered to "selfish and even silly ideals." Horace Mann Bond thought that black students were conservative, elitist, and quite willing to selfishly profit from the ignorance and superstition of the masses. The Victorian assumption that the educated few could lead the black masses out of poverty and ignorance—"lifting as they climb," to use the motto of the black women's club movement—was wearing thin.[30]

Black college teachers, poorly paid and overworked, continually complained about lack of academic freedom. "The quickest way I know to become *persona non grata* in a college community is to exercise freedom of speech—to question the existing order," commented a Bennett College, North Carolina, professor. Black colleges made much of their "leadership," but "too often, they are little islands of smugness and safety." Small wonder, thought Harold Lee of Lincoln University, that the Negro college "has failed to produce a sufficient number of intelligent, dynamic Negro citizens."[31]

EDUCATION AS TRAINING FOR DEMOCRACY

Yet Gunnar Myrdal, as usual, hit the nail on the head. "The long-range effect of the rising level of education in the Negro people," he insisted in 1944, "goes in the direction of nourishing and strengthening the Negro protest."

Three decades later historian Diane Ravitch came to much the same conclusion, arguing that "Blacks were more often oppressed by the education they
did not receive than by the education that they did receive." Any education
was better than none, and more was better than less.[32]

Although black schoolteachers worked within the confines of a system
controlled by white officials, they strove to encourage racial pride and stimulate personal ambition. As civil rights leader Andrew Young recalled of his
childhood in New Orleans, "The attitude of . . . our teachers seemed to be
that we should not waste our time complaining about the way blacks were
treated—that wouldn't achieve very much. Instead, we should concentrate
our efforts on 'improving the race.'" Young retained vivid memories of how
the redoubtable Fannie C. Williams, principal of Valena C. Jones Junior High
and one of the outstanding teachers of her day, put the uplift philosophy into
practice. A woman of "legendary determination" who believed in strict discipline, Williams "invited every black celebrity who visited New Orleans to
come over to Jones School, and most came, from Joe Louis to Marian Anderson." To her students, Young remembered, "Miss Williams had the bearing
and charisma of Mary McLeod Bethune."[33]

In the 1920s and 1930s, black teachers strongly supported Carter G.
Woodson's Negro History movement. Forming local branches of the Association for the Study of Negro Life and History, they organized Negro History
Weeks. In New Orleans, for example, George S. Longe, principal of Albert
Wicker Junior High School, devised a Negro History syllabus and persuaded
the school board to approve it. Children in grades one through eleven read
poems by black authors, heard stories about black heroes, sang spirituals and
secular songs, and learned about Louisiana's free people of color.[34]

The democratic rhetoric of the New Deal and the democratic ideas of progressive educators made "democracy" and "education" inseparable. White
school officials argued that public education was essential for the survival of a
democratic society. Black teachers gladly utilized these arguments. In Virginia, for example, black high schools included full citizenship among their
stated goals. "The core of our philosophy," proclaimed one, "is an unshak-
able belief in democracy." Elementary schools spread democratic ideals simply by teaching literacy. It was no coincidence that black newspapers,
scourges of discrimination and tireless propagandists for racial equality, attained record circulation levels at precisely the time when universal schooling
finally achieved mass literacy.[35]

If black colleges were not models of democracy, they were oases of freedom
compared with the surrounding society—and compared with many white colleges as well. Some permitted students to form campus NAACP chapters.

Nearly all colleges, private and state-funded, allowed outside speakers. In 1938, for example, James Weldon Johnson, opening a new gymnasium at Prairie View State College in Texas, spoke on "The Negro: The Test of Democracy in America." Florida A&M hosted Countee Cullen, Langston Hughes, Kelly Miller, and W. E. B. Du Bois. Even in Mississippi, students at Tougaloo College could hear visiting speakers such as Langston Hughes and Paul Robeson.

Inside the classroom, teachers enjoyed a good deal of latitude. "I have used . . . first-class authors, and pictures of Du Bois and others in my classroom," a professor from South Carolina told a gathering of black educators in 1938. "People have asked, how in the world do you keep Du Bois' picture in a school sponsored by [racist governor] Cole Blease?" The governor of South Carolina, he explained, did not care what professors taught. As long as Blease trusted the college president, "then other Negroes can do what they want." Morehouse College sociologist Walter Chivers (who taught Martin Luther King, Jr.) even offered a course on "Karl Marx and the Negro." In response to one survey, most college teachers claimed that they did, indeed, encourage their students to understand and oppose racial discrimination.[36]

If black college presidents were autocratic and accommodating, they had to be. They were striving to improve black education within a political system anchored on white supremacy. Yet many were "courageous and progressive men," wrote sociologists David Riesman and Christopher Jencks, "who did as much as their situations would allow and more. . . . [They] had great personal fortitude and dignity. By drawing upon their connections with cosmopolitan whites they were able to create some breathing space in the Negro community." Students still chafed under Victorian codes of conduct, yet the very frequency of student strikes—from the 1900s through the 1940s—suggests that the black colleges were not the harsh dictatorships of legend. Rather, they were relatively benign institutions in which young people could safely challenge constituted authority.[37]

It was a student protest at Virginia State College in Petersburg that led to the formation of the Southern Negro Youth Congress (SNYC), one of the most important civil rights organizations of the New Deal era. In 1937 students organized a strike against oppressive rules, forcing the president, veteran black educator John M. Gandy, to permit a student government association. In the same year, students at Virginia Union University in Richmond petitioned the state legislature against spending cuts and racial inequality in education. Out of this ferment came the SNYC, launched in February 1937 at a conference in Richmond attended by 534 young people, average

age twenty-two, half of them women. An offshoot of the Communist-backed National Negro Congress, the SNYC was not an exclusively student movement, but much of its support came from black colleges, and most of its leaders were recent graduates. It also won support from black college presidents, including Fred L. Patterson, president of Tuskegee Institute, who welcomed the SNYC to Tuskegee's campus for its 1942 conference. During its ten-year existence the SNYC supported strikes of tobacco workers in Richmond, garbage workers in Atlanta, and teamsters in New Orleans. In 1940 it launched a Southwide "right-to-vote" campaign that featured meetings, leafleting, poll tax drives, lawsuits, citizenship classes, and attempts to register.[38]

At a time when blacks were politically powerless and physically intimidated, black college presidents, for all their caution, were important voices for democracy and human rights. Mary McLeod Bethune organized the National Council of Negro Women (NCNW) and secured an important position within the Roosevelt administration. A vociferous opponent of discrimination, she insisted upon integrated seating at public events at Bethune-Cookman College in Daytona, Florida. Sociologist Charles S. Johnson made Fisk University the nation's leading center for research in race relations. David Jones, president of Bennett College in Greensboro, North Carolina, supported the American Students Union and "instructed his students not to spend money where they were mistreated." Mary Branch, head of Tillotson College, served as president of the Austin, Texas, NAACP.[39]

Of the fifty-nine black leaders who gathered in Durham, North Carolina, in October 1942 to revive the moribund interracial cooperation movement, thirty-four were college presidents, college administrators, or college teachers. The "Durham Manifesto" was not a radical document. It opposed "compulsory segregation," but not strongly, stressing instead "current problems of racial discrimination and neglect." Nevertheless, this deliberate strategy of moderation succeeded in winning enough white support to create the Southern Regional Council (SRC), a successor to the Commission on Interracial Cooperation. The SRC itself attracted widespread criticism for its failure to condemn Jim Crow. Yet in the 1950s and 1960s the organization became a great source of information and support for the Civil Rights Movement.[40]

During the heyday of the Civil Rights Movement, black teachers attracted widespread criticism for failing to lead, and in some cases actively opposing, the fight against segregation. Yet during the decades of Jim Crow, black schools and colleges, public and private, had adamantly refused to surrender the goal of racial equality. At the very least they encouraged political awareness by teaching literacy. At their best they inspired self-worth, ambition, and a desire for liberation. For all the unheroic compromises made by teachers, black schools and colleges served, in the words of historian James Leloudis, as "vital bridges between the freedom struggles of the late nineteenth century and those of the mid-twentieth."[41]

Roy Wilkins, Walter White, and Thurgood Marshall, circa 1940

National Association for the Advancement of Colored People

9

The NAACP's Challenge to
White Supremacy, 1935–45

In 1935, in New Orleans, mailman W. W. Kerr boarded a streetcar and rode to the start of his delivery route. A fair-skinned black man, Kerr sat in the front of the vehicle—the section reserved for white passengers. When his foreman spotted him blithely ignoring the segregation law, he gave Kerr a written reprimand. It was the first of many: complaints about Kerr wound their way up and down the Post Office hierarchy. "Kerr is bold and defiant," his foreman noted. "Apparently he is determined not to obey the law," echoed his superintendent. Kerr continued to ride up front in the streetcar.

Exasperated by this insubordination, Superintendent Ralph Handlin confronted Kerr. "I want to ask you a question. Are you a white man or are you a colored man?" Kerr hesitated—unsure as to the propriety of the question—before replying, "What do you mean by colored man, and what do you mean by white man?" Utterly taken aback, the white official blurted out, "Are you a white man of the Caucasian race?" Kerr must have savored the moment as he responded, "Yes." Handlin, furious, jumped up and called Kerr a liar. "You associate with niggers, don't you? You head up a nigger organization, don't you?" Kerr explained that "my hair is smooth and dark brown, or grey, [and] my skin is as white as that of a great majority of the people in this community." Because he looked Caucasian, he added, his presence in the black section of the streetcar might cause "confusion and disorder"—the very thing that the segregation law was designed to prevent.

In 1937, despite two years of reprimands, Kerr still obstinately refused to sit behind the movable "screen" that separated white and black passengers.

"As an individual I am entitled to the protection of the Fourteenth Amendment," he explained. "As a Federal employee, I represent a function of government that cannot be circumscribed by the limitations of race, creed or color." To cap it all, he filed a formal complaint against Superintendent Handlin for having insulted and humiliated him.[1]

The protracted dispute between W. W. Kerr and the U.S. Post Office was not about a light-complexioned African American wanting to pass for white. Rather, it expressed a principled rejection of racial segregation. To Kerr, race was an arbitrary, man-made category that ought to have no place in law. As John M. Harlan, the "great dissenter" in *Plessy* v. *Ferguson*, had asserted, "Our Constitution is color-blind and neither knows nor tolerates classes among its citizens." That, of course, was the basic platform of the NAACP.[2]

Even in the Deep South during the zenith of white supremacy, some black Southerners protested against Jim Crow. In most cases, their protests were silent and indirect. Many simply refused to ride on segregated buses and streetcars, choosing to trudge long miles on hot sidewalks. A prosperous minority could travel by car—although even on the highways they faced humiliating contacts with policemen, gas station attendants, and white drivers. A few, however, elected openly to oppose racial discrimination. Those people formed a "tangible nucleus" of resistance (to borrow Abraham Lincoln's phrase) around which others could rally.

What is more, instances of calculated defiance often represented more than random acts of bravery. Overt resisters usually possessed some degree of protection from white reprisal. In the 1930s and 1940s, they often personified the growing strength of black unions—it was no coincidence that W. W. Kerr was a leader of the National Alliance of Postal Employees (NAPE). When the struggle for civil rights emerged from the shadows and came out into the open, it was the self-sufficiency of the black middle class, reinforced by organizations of the black working class, that supplied the initial impetus. The story of the early Civil Rights Movement is, in large part, the story of how the NAACP finally became a mass organization.

BLACK WORKERS AND THE EXPANSION OF THE NAACP

The NAACP did not increase its membership tenfold, from 50,000 in 1940 to almost 500,000 in 1946, without conflict—sometimes bitter class conflict—within the black community. In the 1930s the NAACP suffered from the reputation of being an elitist body dominated by wealthy businessmen and professionals. "Control of the branches," wrote political scientist Ralph J. Bunche, "rests largely in the hands of an exclusive, often class and color snobbish, self-appointed Negro upper class group, and they are run, more frequently than not, as closed corporations." The NAACP had failed dismally, he added, "to pitch its appeal so as to reach the ears of the masses."[3]

Up to a point, Bunche was correct. Young radicals like Bunche, however, underrated the crucial service rendered by the black middle and upper classes in keeping the NAACP alive during its most difficult period. The men and women who led the NAACP's Southern branches needed to be economically independent of white people if they were to operate openly. That is why the branch officers included so many ministers, lawyers, physicians, dentists, undertakers, insurance agents, barbers, and beauticians. These groups found it difficult to appeal to the lower classes and often made little effort to do so.

By the late 1930s, however, the radical tide of the Depression decade was lapping at the NAACP's doors. The resurgence of labor unions, the rise of the CIO, the agitation of the Communist Party, and the general movement of public opinion to the left presented a powerful challenge to the organization's traditional leadership. In many cities, "Young Turks," often associated with labor unions, joined the NAACP and tried to wrest control from the "Old Guard." They pressed for more open decision making, an expansion of membership, closer relations with organized labor, the use of black lawyers rather than white ones, and more assertive tactics generally.

In the South, postal workers like W. W. Kerr became key figures in orienting the NAACP more closely toward the labor movement. Black postal employees comprised, along with longshoremen and Pullman porters, the aristocracy of black labor. In the flattened class structure of black America, moreover, postal workers enjoyed a level of pay, prestige, and job security that placed them in the middle class rather than the working class. They were, in fact, unique among black wage earners: federal civil service regulations protected them from arbitrary dismissal and gave them some means of redress against discrimination. Post Office jobs were highly prized, and they attracted some of the best-educated blacks, including people who aspired to be teachers, journalists, and lawyers. By 1940, postal workers led many of the NAACP's largest Southern branches, including Norfolk, Mobile, and New Orleans.

Black postal workers were well-organized and accustomed to sticking up for themselves. In 1911 a white postal union, the Railway Mail Association, adopted a clause that restricted its membership to "Caucasians." Soon afterward, upon the election of Woodrow Wilson, the federal government tried to impose Southern-style racial segregation upon the civil service. Founded in 1913 on the initiative of Houston postal worker Henry L. Mimms, NAPE opposed these efforts to discriminate against blacks. NAPE initially represented the elite of black postal workers, the 2,500 railway mail clerks who sorted letters aboard fast-travelling trains. In 1923, however, it opened its membership to clerks, letter carriers, and all other grades. From the start, NAPE supported the NAACP. In the 1930s, as new members swelled its ranks, NAPE was strategically positioned to give black workers a greater voice within the NAACP.[4]

The NAACP's branch leaders, however, were often hostile to organized labor. The Labor Committee of the Dallas branch was headed by a vehement opponent of unions, "an active strike-breaker." The men who led the Detroit branch had long supported the antiunion policies of the automobile manufacturers. In New Orleans and elsewhere, an interlocking directorate of doctors, insurance executives, and undertakers opposed the CIO. Moreover, the rise of organized labor now entailed direct conflict between black workers and black employers. In 1935 the editorial workers of Harlem's *Amsterdam Star-News* went on strike under the banner of the American Newspaper Guild; journalist Roi Ottley called it "the first open dispute between Negro workers and a Negro employer." In 1940 insurance agents in New Orleans joined a CIO union and struck the four largest black-owned insurance companies. The strike bitterly divided the local NAACP.[5]

Black workers often lost such confrontations. But in city after city they gained a voice in the NAACP, sometimes winning outright control. For one thing, the NAACP's national leaders were determined to increase membership. They ensured that joining the NAACP was simple and cheap. They chartered "Youth Councils" that functioned alongside local branches but were largely independent of the adults. As director of branches, they appointed Ella Baker, a tireless organizer who coordinated local membership drives and helped branches band together in statewide alliances, or "conferences." Crucially, the NAACP's national leaders applauded the labor militancy of the 1930s, recognizing that unionization both secured material benefits for black workers and provided another angle of attack on racial discrimination. Inadvertently, the NAACP benefitted from the Communist Party's 1935 decision to cooperate with reformist organizations: in Richmond, New Orleans, Winston-Salem, and elsewhere, Communist-influenced unions helped to boost the organization's membership.

The results were spectacular. In Detroit, for example, membership increased from 2,400 in 1937 to 6,000 in 1939 to 12,000 in 1942. New Orleans grew from 300 in 1938 to 6,000 in 1944. Houston went from barely a hundred members in 1937 to over 5,000 in 1943. Membership in Texas as a whole reached 23,000 by 1945, the highest of any Southern state.

By the 1940s, in most cities, the NAACP had ceased to be a purely middle-class organization. To be sure, ministers, businesspeople, and professionals remained influential. But the leadership now included postal workers, Pullman porters, longshoremen, plumbers, printers, truck drivers, shopworkers, and factory workers. In 1941 Walter White travelled to Detroit to rally black support for a strike by the United Auto Workers (UAW) against that bastion of antiunionism, the Ford Motor Company. His intervention, which helped the UAW to secure victory, symbolized the new alliance between the NAACP and organized labor.

By the time of Pearl Harbor, blacks in the South were organizing more openly, speaking more confidently, and acting more militantly than they had been for a generation. Thousands of black workers had gone on strike, tasting the fruits of mass action. Black teachers, working with the NAACP's top legal strategists, had initiated a successful campaign to secure equal salaries. Black newspapers, brash and outspoken in their condemnation of racism, were breaking circulation records and reaching every nook and cranny in the South. Randolph's March on Washington had thrilled the black population and wrested Executive Order 8802 from FDR. However, there were to be no easy victories, no decisive breakthroughs.

THE SECOND WORLD WAR: EMPLOYMENT

World War II seemed to change everything. It uprooted millions of Americans from their homes and farms, sending them to factories, shipyards, and military bases. It ended unemployment, producing amazing feats of industrial production, and made the Pacific Coast an economic colossus. It changed the face of the South, accelerating out-migration and ending the primacy of agriculture. It trained women to be welders, riveters, and assembly-line workers. It put 14 million men into uniform, including more than 900,000 blacks. It increased the combined membership of labor unions from six million to fifteen million.

The war not only rededicated America to the ideal of democracy but also extended that ideal to people of all races, colors, religions, and national origins. It both defeated fascism and discredited the ideology of racism. It made the United States the most powerful nation in the world. It led to the founding of the United Nations, with its commitment to human rights for all. It gave way to the Cold War, in which the United States championed the "Free World."

All this should have added up to a turning point in race relations. Indeed, black Americans perceived the war as a great opportunity to press their claim to equal citizenship. Bitter about the promises made and betrayed between 1917 and 1919, blacks responded with enthusiasm to a slogan coined by the *Pittsburgh Courier* early in 1942: "Double V." This cryptic phrase defined the conflict as a two-front war: racial discrimination and fascism were two sides of the same coin, and blacks must fight both simultaneously. "Democracy will never survive the present crisis as a frozen or half-caste concept," thundered the black newspapers. "The struggle to preserve it must be linked with the struggle to extend it. . . . We must overthrow Hitlerism within as well as Hitlerism without." The worst mistake black Americans could make would be to set aside their grievances for the duration. As the *Crisis* argued shortly after Pearl Harbor, "Now is the time *not* to be silent about the breaches in democracy in our own land."[6]

Yet the Second World War led to a sharp increase in racial tensions while doing very little to address the basic causes of those tensions. The vast majority of white Southerners firmly resisted the notion that racial segregation was incompatible with America's war aims. Although black agitation alarmed them, whites responded by defending Jim Crow with fierce determination. Their way of avoiding racial antagonism, explained Senator John Overton, was to make it quite clear to blacks that "we have a white man's government, run by white men. . . . We permit neither social nor political equality." Whites in the South could still deal with blacks from a position of overwhelming strength. They monopolized political power, controlled the judicial process, and could use the law enforcement agencies to intimidate, punish, and if necessary kill.[7]

The story of the Fair Employment Practices Committee, created by President Roosevelt in 1941 in response to A. Philip Randolph's threatened "March on Washington," illustrated how Southern white intransigence dashed black hopes of wartime breakthroughs. "To many southern whites," wrote Merl Reed, the FEPC's thorough historian, "the committee was no less feared and hated than the enemy overseas." Greeted by blacks as the greatest victory since the Emancipation Proclamation, Executive Order 8802 ran into a storm of white vituperation. Governor Frank Dixon of Alabama called it a "crackpot reform" and described the FEPC as a "kangaroo court obviously dedicated to the abolition of segregation." The governor of South Carolina threatened to expel "any outsiders [who] come into our state and agitate social equality among the races." The mayor of Shreveport, Louisiana, rejected federal money to build a health center because the contract specified that for every hundred workers hired, twelve should be blacks. The FEPC, he complained, wanted to "cram the negro down our throats." Better to lose the health center than "accept the negro as our political or social equal."[8]

Southern employers simply ignored the FEPC, insisting that blacks were only fit for certain jobs, and that white workers would never stand the presence of blacks in the same grades. In the booming shipyards, blacks found employment as porters, janitors, and laborers, but not as welders or office workers. "We cannot put Negroes in our office," explained one employer. "Everybody would quit, beginning with the manager." Employers predicted strikes and violence if blacks worked alongside white men—and white women—as welders. Job equality was "impractical and utopian," a Mobile shipyard manager told FEPC investigator John Beecher. Nothing would change, reported a frustrated Beecher, "without strong and *immediate* measures originating in the highest quarters of the government."[9]

From the start, however, the FEPC found itself hamstrung by lack of support from the Roosevelt administration. The committee could investigate and report, but possessed no power to enforce its recommendations. Its June 1942 hearings in Birmingham, Alabama, painfully exposed its weakness and vulnerability. Faced with a hornet's nest of white criticism—"a bunch of snoopers," "halo-wearing missionaries of New Deal socialism," "dat cummittee fer de perteckshun uv Rastus & Sambo"—FEPC chairman Mark Ethridge, a white newspaper publisher, told black member Earl Dickerson that his life was in danger and that perhaps he ought to stay away. Dickerson went anyway. But when the hearings opened, Ethridge went out of his way to appease Southern racism. The FEPC had no intention of attacking segregation, he stated. Blacks must recognize the fact, he added, that "there is no power in the world—not even in all the mechanized armies of the earth, Allied and Axis—which would now force the Southern white people to the abandonment of the principle of social segregation."[10]

Shortly afterwards Ethridge resigned as chairman, and FDR downgraded the FEPC by placing it under the War Manpower Commission (WMC). The head of the WMC, Paul McNutt, then "indefinitely postponed" the FEPC's proposed investigation of the railroad industry. The FEPC limped on. Reorganized under the chairmanship of Monsignor Francis J. Haas, it held more hearings. Slowly and reluctantly, industrial employers began to hire blacks—first men, then women—as production workers. In Detroit, for example, the Ford Motor Company had refused to employ *any* black women at its giant Willow Run bomber plant. Only pressure from the FEPC, the United Auto Workers, and the NAACP induced it to abandon that policy. At the Packard aircraft factory, where 25,000 white workers walked out in a "hate strike" against the hiring of blacks, it took the FEPC four months to negotiate the employment of black women and the upgrading of black workers to the assembly lines.

In the South, FEPC directives were more likely to ignite white violence than bring about black job gains. On May 24, 1943, after months of delaying tactics, the Alabama Dry Dock Company in Mobile appointed its first black welders, twelve in number. Unfortunately, the company had neglected to inform its white employees, who erupted in violence, randomly attacking black workers and injuring fifty. The army had to quell the violence. In June 1943, white shipyard workers went on a rampage in Beaumont, Texas, an outbreak that caused three deaths and created thousands of refugees.

If white workers opposed the entry of blacks into the industrial workforce, so did employers. The state officials who ran the U.S. Employment Service in the South did their utmost to deny blacks industrial training. When the NAACP in New Iberia, Louisiana, complained to the FEPC about the absence of welding classes for black people, outraged whites delivered a sharp lesson in political reality. On the orders of the schools superintendent and the sheriff, two deputies arrested, beat, and expelled the leading NAACP "troublemakers." An investigation by the FBI led nowhere; a federal grand jury refused to prosecute anyone. "The job done by the sheriff was a job expertly done," local whites told the FBI. "The fact that these negroes were run out of town quieted the negro situation down." Best of all, there was still plenty of "colored help" for the merchants and planters.[11]

Despite conscription, migration, and the decline in cotton production, whites still tried to keep blacks in their fields and in their kitchens. World War I "work or fight" laws were dusted off. Blacks were fined for loitering and vagrancy; sometimes the police simply scoured the bars and pool halls, dispatching their occupants to the cane and cotton fields. In Mississippi, local draft boards often exempted the "best" sharecroppers. In 1943 the U.S. Department of Agriculture lent a hand, forbidding agricultural workers to leave their home counties unless a labor surplus had been officially declared.

Black women still deserted domestic service in droves, black men left the cotton fields regardless, and black children aspired to "easy jobs" despite having classes in agriculture and maid-service thrust upon them. A school official in North Carolina was horrified to discover that one black girl wanted to become a stenographer—this "most unholy ambition" typified a growing aversion to manual labor. Although the South's economic landscape was being transformed, whites held fast to the notion of separate occupational niches for black people. White-collar worker and skilled industrial worker were not among them. In 1946 the Southern Democrats succeeded in strangling the Fair Employment Practices Committee.[12]

THE SECOND WORLD WAR: THE MILITARY

Wartime upheaval enabled black Americans to challenge the "normality" of segregation. The war sent Northern blacks South, Southern blacks North, and both overseas. Moreover, the government itself, attacking the "master race" ideology of fascism, defined American democracy as assimilationist, inclusive, and tolerant. "In official government posters and proclamations, 'Americans All' closed ranks," writes historian Thomas Doherty. In contrast to the WASPish intolerance of the Great War—with its assault on German culture and "hyphenated-Americans"—government propaganda in World War II celebrated the melting pot, an "open-hearted embrace of the family of man." Hollywood reinforced the message. As commanding officer, actor Randolph Scott told his new recruits in *Gung Ho!* (1943), "cast out all prejudices—racial, religious, and every other kind."[13]

Not surprisingly, black organizations pressed hard for equality within the armed services. They viewed the military as a key institution in American life. A direct arm of the government, and a direct expression of the people, it personified the democratic values for which the United States fought. Ending racial discrimination in the armed forces would have a powerful effect on civil society. Moreover, if blacks made an equal contribution to the war effort, their claim to full citizenship would be much stronger.

The armed services presented a large and inviting target. Before the war, the military had made no pretense whatever of treating blacks equally. In 1939 the black presence in the army consisted of 3,640 soldiers and five officers, organized into segregated regiments, comprising less than 2 percent of America's soldiers. The navy employed blacks only as cooks, messmen, and servants. The marine corps and the army air corps excluded blacks altogether. At the outbreak of the war, military leaders affirmed that they had no intention of changing their racial policies. The lowly status of black soldiers, argued the generals, reflected "the position attained by the Negro in civilian life." Besides, they added, "The Army is not a sociological laboratory." Social experiments "are a danger to efficiency, discipline and morale" that could result in military disaster.[14]

The Roosevelt administration reacted to black agitation over unfair treatment by the military by enunciating a policy of nondiscrimination. In 1940 Roosevelt required the army to implement a "balanced force" principle, ensuring that the number of black soldiers reflected the proportion of blacks in the overall population, 10 percent. The army also undertook to train black officers, and the army air corps established an airfield near Tuskegee, Alabama, to train black pilots. Roosevelt also pressed the navy to assign blacks to regular sailors' posts, not just stewards' positions. To further convince blacks of his sincerity and commitment, FDR promoted Benjamin O. Davis to the rank of brigadier general—the highest-ranking black officer in the nation's history—and appointed William Hastie, a distinguished black lawyer and NAACP member, as an adviser on "Negro Affairs" to the War Department. Congress also acted, stipulating that voluntary enlistment, conscription, and military training should all be carried out without discrimination "against any person on account of race or color."[15]

Instead of mollifying blacks, however, these measures intensified their awareness and resentment of racial discrimination in the military. For one thing, both the government and the military continued to defend racial segregation—a system that blatantly contravened the official commitment to equality. Moreover, the war placed certain institutions under such physical strain that racial segregation, from the black point of view, became unworkable and intolerable.

Discrimination within the armed services probably aroused more black anger than any other issue. A traditionally conservative institution in which white Southerners were overrepresented, the military did its best to minimize the effects of Roosevelt's policies. It continued to treat black servicemen as lazy, unreliable in combat, and of below-average intelligence. Explaining why only half as many black soldiers as white soldiers were assigned to combat units, the army general staff pointed to "the lower average intelligence rating of colored selectees" and their "apparent lack of inherent natural mechanical adaptability." According to one major general, "The negro type has not the proper reflexes to make a first-class pilot." Defending the policy of assigning most blacks to service battalions, Secretary of War Henry L. Stimson emphasized that many black combat units had been "unable to master efficiently the techniques of modern warfare."[16]

The army made much of the fact that blacks did relatively poorly on its aptitude test. Tellingly, however, it rarely referred to the systematic discrimination that rendered black schools in the South so bad. Military leaders, in fact, betrayed their racial prejudice time and again, especially in their dogged defense of racial segregation. A statement by the general board of the navy explaining its refusal to assign blacks to general duties encapsulated the military's thinking:

> Men on board ship live in particularly close association; in their messes, one man sits beside another; their hammocks are close together; in their common tasks they work side by side. . . . How many white men would choose, of their own accord, that their closest associates in sleeping quarters, at mess, and in a gun's crew should be of another race? How many would accept such conditions, if required to do so, without resentment and just as a matter of course? The General Board believes the answer is "Few, if any."

The head of the marine corps, Major General Thomas Holcomb, was even more offensively blunt. Blacks were seeking "to break into a club that doesn't want them." Given the choice between 5,000 whites and 250,000 blacks, "I would rather have the whites."[17]

The policy of segregation produced a vicious cycle. Segregation produced poor morale, which often led to poor discipline and poor performance. Off-base discrimination compounded the problem: most military bases were located in the South, and blacks were required to obey local Jim Crow laws. All blacks resented the situation; blacks from the North, many of whom were totally unaccustomed to being insulted by storeowners and ordered about by bus drivers, were enraged by it. Jim Crow pursued black servicemen even abroad. In Britain, for example, the military authorities tried to discourage local civilians—who received them openly and warmly—from fraternizing with black soldiers.

This poisonous brew of segregation and discrimination ignited a rash of violence. In incidents that ran the gamut from brawls to riots, black soldiers challenged the actions of white bartenders, bus drivers, policemen, MPs, NCOs, officers, and fellow soldiers. The worst incidents verged on outright mutiny. At Camp Stewart, Georgia, black soldiers fired upon military policemen, wounding four and killing one. After a violent rampage at Camp Claiborne, Louisiana, fourteen black soldiers were court-martialed, one receiving a death sentence. At Fort Dix, in New Jersey, black soldiers exchanged fire with white MPs in a fifteen-minute battle that left three people dead.

Resentment against draconian punishments meted out by military tribunals—especially in cases involving rape allegations—added fuel to the fire. In Louisiana, for example, a court-martial imposed death sentences on three soldiers accused of raping a white waitress. Convinced of their innocence, the NAACP mounted a successful campaign to save the men's lives—in 1947 they were pardoned. The skepticism with which blacks viewed rape charges was understandable in light of the military's well-known distaste for interracial sex. As one regimental notice put it: "Any cases between white and colored males and females, whether voluntary or not, are considered rape and during times of war the penalty is death."[18]

THE SECOND WORLD WAR: THE SEGREGATION ISSUE

Arguments between black soldiers and white bus drivers highlighted the issue of segregation in public transportation. Transit systems that had been starved of investment during the Depression now faced unprecedented demand, as soldiers and workers flooded into the cities, and rationing drastically reduced the use of private cars. Passengers jammed buses and streetcars, whites and blacks jostled for space, drivers became exasperated, and tempers flared. During a twelve-month period in 1941-42, the police in Birmingham, Alabama, recorded fifty-five incidents in which black passengers defied white drivers by refusing to give up their seats or by sitting in the white section. The files of the NAACP bulged with angry letters from black people who had been ordered about, shouted at, and threatened by white drivers. Black servicemen joined the NAACP in droves.[19]

A Tampa woman recounted a typical incident involving herself, her soldier husband, and a soldier friend. The trio boarded a streetcar on a stifling July evening in 1944, only to find the rear of the vehicle "crowded thickly with Negroes standing and sitting." They moved to the fringe of the crowd, about a third of the way back, "standing quietly and annoying no one." As more blacks boarded, the driver yelled for them to move back. Seeing nowhere to move, they stayed put. The driver got up and repeated the order to their faces. "If you soldiers don't move back in the car, I'll call the MPs." Furious at being ignored, he drove on, refusing to allow any more black people to board. The threesome eventually found seats and forgot about it. The driver, however, halted the bus and summoned two military policemen, who ordered the three passengers to vacate their seats and stand at the back of the streetcar.

The number of people jailed over such incidents skyrocketed. In New Orleans, in 1943, a driver ordered a black soldier to vacate a forward seat even though the "white" section was empty. The black passengers protested so vehemently that the driver took the bus to the nearest police station and had all twenty-four arrested. In Savannah, in 1944, fifty black college students occupied the front of the bus and refused to move. Two of them were arrested and convicted of attempting to riot. Barbara Lewis was travelling on a Trailways bus from New York to Lynchburg when, upon entering Nelson County, Virginia, at the foothills of the Blue Ridge mountains, the driver ordered her to move back. Lewis refused. She refused again when a sheriff came aboard— and she hit the driver with a jack handle as he pushed her out the door. She received a four-month jail sentence for assault and disorderly conduct. In Norfolk, Sarah Morris Davis sat between two white passengers at the front of a bus. Noting that whites had taken seats in the black section, she refused to move. Arrested and fined, she filed an unsuccessful suit against Virginia's segregation law.

In a letter of protest to a transit company, the wife of a black soldier spoke for millions:

We're fighting a war now to insure freedom of opportunity to everybody. . . . If the American Negro is not going to enjoy equally the fruits of democracy, why then should our men in the armed services be maimed or die on foreign soil . . . when here in the South their lives are made a virtual "hell on earth?" Why not be maimed or die here on native soil to insure for themselves and for other oppressed groups this democratic way of life? Never let it be said that there are not many colored servicemen who ask themselves frequently, "Why not?"

Some soldiers did indeed lose their lives in quarrels over segregation. In 1942 a bus driver in Mobile shot and killed Henry Williams, a young black soldier. When Private Edward Green sat in the white section of a bus in Alexandria, Louisiana, the driver ordered him off the bus and then shot him dead.[20]

In *What the Negro Wants,* edited by black historian Rayford W. Logan and published in 1944, black leaders from across the political spectrum and from both sides of the Mason-Dixon line chorused the demand that segregation on buses, streetcars, and trains should be scrapped. This most blatant and humiliating form of Jim Crow had become a litmus test of racial progress.

It was also an enormous stumbling block. White attitudes toward racial segregation seemed inflexible; compromise on the issue proved impossible. The failure of the South's white liberals to contemplate even the *gradual* elimination of Jim Crow illustrated the problem that blacks faced. "Anyone with an ounce of common sense must see . . . that separation of the races must be maintained in the South," declared Ralph McGill, the editor of the *Atlanta Constitution.* Practically every white newspaper editor and politician in the South agreed with him. Even the most enlightened supporters of the interracial movement treated segregation as too hot to handle. Tying themselves into knots trying to finesse the issue, they argued that segregation could not be challenged until race relations improved; and that any challenge to segregation would increase racial tension. A few whites deplored the futility of this circular reasoning. "There is, as I see it, no way to get around the issue of segregation today," insisted one member of the Southern Regional Council. The SRC, however, continued to dodge the issue.[21]

Blacks had scant support from the federal government. The Roosevelt administration was not oblivious to black unrest. It was in no mood, however, to use the war as a pretext for challenging white supremacy in the South. The president himself, notwithstanding Eleanor Roosevelt's friendship with Mary McLeod Bethune and public support for organizations like the Southern Conference for Human Welfare, had never shown much interest in the race question. In any case, "Dr. New Deal" was now "Dr. Win the War"—domestic reform was a low priority. Roosevelt saw black agitation for equality as at best a nuisance and at worst a calculated attempt to undermine the war effort. He was especially irritated by the black press, and urged Attorney General Francis Biddle to prosecute editors who were guilty of sedition. Biddle resisted such pressure. Nevertheless, the FBI stepped up its surveillance of black organizations. In the South, the commanders of some military bases suppressed the *Pittsburgh Courier* and the *Chicago Defender*.

Ever the supreme politician, Roosevelt was sensitive to his increasing dependence upon the white South. "Supplementing steady Republican gains in 1938, 1940, and 1942," writes Patricia Sullivan, "southern Democrats secured the balance of power in Congress and used their position to reassert the ideology of states' rights and white supremacy." They dismantled or gutted the more radical New Deal programs, tried to purge the government of left-wingers and racial liberals, and blocked every congressional initiative to extend the vote to black people in the South. The principal victims were the Farm Security Administration, the National Youth Administration, the Works Progress Administration, and the Civilian Conservation Corps—the very New Deal programs that most benefitted black people. Bills to abolish the poll tax in federal elections, and to give absentee ballots to servicemen, fell before Southern opposition. The South's Democrats had a stranglehold on the federal government.[22]

Black militancy, therefore, posed less of a threat to Roosevelt than white backlash did. The Justice Department on occasion took action in defense of black rights, prosecuting (nearly always without success) a handful of police brutality and lynching cases. There was never any question, however, of the federal government opposing segregation, introducing civil rights bills, or prosecuting white officials who denied blacks the vote. FDR's adviser on race relations, Jonathan Daniels, was a white North Carolinian and a staunch segregationist. In 1944 he warned that any federal action against black disenfranchisement would provoke an anti-Democratic revolt among the South's white voters.

Roosevelt knew, moreover, that measures to assist black people would arouse white resentment in the North as well. In the cities of the North, the influx of black migrants made whites more determined than ever to maintain housing segregation. In Chicago, for example, "restrictive covenants" applied to nine-tenths of all the housing, and white people had organized 175 "neighborhood protective associations" to police racial boundaries. Small wonder that at a 1944 conference in Chicago devoted to Northern race relations, the white participants were visibly reluctant to support a no-holds-barred resolution condemning segregation. Such a statement, warned one, "would create such a furor that we might have trouble in our big industrial cities."[23]

Racial tensions had already sparked serious violence in the North. Some of the worst soldiers' disturbances took place in and around Fort Dix, New Jersey. In 1943 a riot broke out in Harlem. Another riot erupted in Detroit, the worst of the war, an outbreak that left twenty-five blacks and nine whites dead. Appealing to white voters, Mayor Edward J. Jeffries pinned the blame on "Negro hoodlums" and denounced "the mingling of Negroes and whites in the same neighborhoods." He was reelected in 1943 and again in 1945.[24]

By 1944 about one-third of the black population resided outside the South. The black population of New York exceeded that of Tennessee, Florida, and Arkansas. Chicago contained twice as many black people as any Southern city. Despite its growing size, however, the black vote in the North was still too small to carry much political weight. Blacks in the South, of course, were still without the ballot. FDR knew that whites constituted his power base, and he would not endanger that base. In 1944 his vice president, Henry Wallace, an increasingly outspoken champion of racial equality, ran into fierce opposition from conservative politicians at the Democratic National Convention. Roosevelt dropped him, selecting Senator Harry S. Truman of Missouri as his running mate.

"A Voteless People Is a Hopeless People"

Ending disfranchisement in the South—winning back the right to vote—was an absolute necessity if blacks were to make any real headway in their struggle for racial equality. During the high tide of white supremacy, however, the masses of black people realized that attempting to vote was futile and even dangerous; politics had become "white folks' business" and nothing could be done about it. Throughout much of the South, especially in the rural counties, blacks rarely even attempted to register.

Yet many blacks never abandoned their interest in politics. For one thing, a few pockets of black voting survived: blacks had continued to vote in border states like Maryland and Kentucky, and they voted, too, in Memphis and other parts of Tennessee. In addition, a handful of Southern black Republican leaders—Henry Lincoln Johnson of Georgia, Perry Howard of Mississippi, Robert Church of Tennessee, Robert Moton of Alabama—enjoyed access to Republican presidents during the 1920s, and wielded some influence over federal patronage.

In the 1920s a few blacks actively sought, sometimes as individuals, more often in groups, to obtain the ballot. After the passage of the Nineteenth Amendment in 1920, for example, black clubwomen in North Carolina mounted a voter registration drive that enrolled perhaps a thousand people. Civic leagues sprang up in most of the larger cities: they encouraged blacks to pay their poll tax—a basic and onerous prerequisite for voting—and then attempt to register. Not infrequently, however, the men at their helms were Republican hacks seeking personal profit and political spoils. Their selfishness and narrowness of vision often inspired cynicism rather than support. Besides, the barriers to black voting remained impenetrable.

During the 1930s black interest in voting quickened. The New Deal poured federal money into the South, making government seem much more relevant to the lives of ordinary people. President Roosevelt's vigorous leadership and evident sympathy for the "forgotten Americans" deepened the interest of *everyone* in politics, black people as well as white. Demagogues like Huey Long, the flamboyant boss of Louisiana who lashed out at the rich and proposed to "Share Our Wealth," appealed to the masses more unscrupulously. Roosevelt and Long were political enemies, yet both awakened black people to the potential of an activist government to transform their living conditions. Voting was no longer simply a matter of political patronage: it was about work for the jobless, help for the farmer, clinics for the poor, scholarships for students, decent homes instead of slums. The New Deal was a political education in itself.

Bolstered by labor unions, the NAACP, and new organizations like the Southern Negro Youth Congress, voter registration campaigns multiplied dramatically in the late 1930s. Results were usually meager. In Tuskegee, Alabama, the county registrar enrolled only ten new black voters a year. In New Orleans, registrars toyed with and humiliated applicants, then rejected them. "Some of these niggers don't even know when they were born," said one. "Oh, they're coming down here alright, but we're turning down by the hundreds because they don't qualify." Outside the big cities, applicants faced threats and violence. John Deshotels of St. Landry Parish, Louisiana, was cruelly beaten outside the courthouse in Opelousas after trying to register. In Brownsville, Tennessee, Elbert Williams was lynched after announcing a voter registration campaign.[25]

Yet some campaigns did achieve substantial black registration. In Greenville, South Carolina, a broadly based drive in 1939 united the NAACP, the Workers Alliance, and the black clergy; it increased black registration from thirty-five to 324. The Atlanta Civic and Political League, organized in 1936 by lawyer A. T. Walden and Masonic leader John Wesley Dobbs, boosted black registration from 600 to 3,000 in three years. Birmingham's Right to Vote Club achieved a comparable increase over the same period.[26]

During World War II, the campaign for the vote paralleled the explosive growth of the NAACP. Sporadic efforts to gain the franchise were now widespread, persistent, and well organized. Adopting the slogan "A Voteless People Is a Hopeless People," black civic leagues—often NAACP branches in different guise—held rallies, distributed leaflets, and proceeded in groups to the registration offices. In Washington, D.C., a white Alabama woman, Virginia Foster Durr, coordinated the National Committee to Abolish the Poll Tax, a body founded in 1941 with the support of labor unions, civil rights organizations, and liberal white Southerners.

Blacks also filed lawsuits. Hardly a year had gone by, in fact, when blacks, somewhere in the South or the border states, had not been challenging disfranchisement in the courts. An Oklahoma case prompted the Supreme Court, in 1915, to disallow the "grandfather clause," which had exempted white men from literacy tests if their grandfathers had voted. Twelve years later, ruling on a suit filed by a black doctor from El Paso, the Court decided that Texas laws excluding blacks from the Democratic Party's primary elections—the only elections that mattered—were unconstitutional. In Louisiana and Alabama, blacks sued registrars who refused to enroll them.

Lawsuits, however, failed to increase significantly the number of black voters. The South's registration laws were devilishly complex, and no sooner did blacks succeed in striking down one discriminatory device than whites substituted another. Moreover, the legal issues were murky, and the Supreme Court was not disposed to take a clear stand against disfranchisement. In *Trudeau* v. *Barnes* (1933), blacks were told that they could not sue in federal court until they had first appealed to the state authorities. In *Grovey* v. *Townsend* (1935), the Court ruled that the "white primary" in Texas no longer violated the Fourteenth Amendment because the Democratic Party was now a wholly private organization. In Alabama, registrars undermined a court challenge by enrolling the handful of plaintiffs and rendering the case moot. Litigation was a crucial weapon in the NAACP's arsenal, yet it was very hit-and-miss.[27]

CHARLES H. HOUSTON, THURGOOD MARSHALL, AND THE COURTS

The NAACP realized that its resort to the courts often amounted to firefighting—defensive litigation that might stop things from getting worse, but which failed to make things better. In 1930 it hired a top legal brain, Nathan Margold, to devise a coherent strategy, one that would achieve precedent-making courtroom victories that would advance the civil rights struggle across a broad front. Margold advised the NAACP not to fritter away its limited resources on trying to gain equality within segregation. Instead, the NAACP should "boldly challenge the constitutionality of segregation"—to "strike directly at the most prolific source of discrimination," the *Plessy* v. *Ferguson* decision itself.[28]

In time, the NAACP adopted precisely this strategy. But in the 1930s it was deemed too risky. Charles H. Houston, who in 1934 assumed the job of

NAACP "special counsel," carefully avoided attacking the constitutionality of segregation itself. To mount such a challenge and to lose in federal court—a decision that might reaffirm *Plessy* v. *Ferguson*—would be a calamity. Yet the long-term effect of pressing for equality *within* segregation, he believed, would be to undermine segregation. If the courts ruled that "separate" should indeed mean "equal," then the cost to the Southern states of maintaining two systems of public education would become prohibitive. Segregation would collapse under its own weight.

One of the founding fathers of the modern Civil Rights Movement, Charles Hamilton Houston was a brilliant and indefatigable lawyer. After graduating from Harvard Law School in 1922—he studied under Felix Frankfurter, one of the cleverest legal minds of the century—Houston became a professor at Howard University, where he acted as teacher and mentor to a generation of black attorneys. No dry academic, Houston viewed the law as a powerful tool for social change and believed that black lawyers had an obligation to use it as such—"a lawyer's either a social engineer or he's a parasite on society." He also believed that litigation and community mobilization should go hand-in-hand, and was profoundly impressed by the Communist Party's success in combining legal tactics with mass pressure in the Scottsboro campaign. "Our idea should be to impress upon the opposition and the public that we have a real program," he argued, "sweeping up from ground influence and popular demand."[29]

Houston proposed to attack Jim Crow at its most vulnerable point: public education. Here, racial discrimination was clear, gross, and easy to document. It was simple to photograph black schools, dilapidated shacks, and compare them with white schools' new brick buildings. With equal ease, the NAACP could obtain statistics from state officials that showed the differences in per capita spending between black children and white children, as well as the disparity in salaries paid to black and white teachers. It required no great detective work to demonstrate the almost complete absence of opportunities for blacks to pursue graduate and professional training. Attacking inequalities in public education, Houston believed, would prove to be a popular cause, and would help NAACP branches to drum up support, especially from teachers.

Houston calculated that it would be easier to find plaintiffs, and to secure favorable decisions, in the upper South and border states. Then, having won important precedents, suits could be filed in the more oppressive and recalcitrant Deep South states. Although the NAACP's immediate aim was to improve black schools and colleges within the existing framework of racial segregation, it did not regard equalization as an endorsement of the "separate but equal" concept of *Plessy* v. *Ferguson*. "Our ultimate goal," stated Walter White, "is the abolition of segregation in education because it is economically unsound in practice and . . . works against the development of mutual respect and understanding in the field where separation does more harm than in any other."[30]

Houston developed his strategy despite deep skepticism on the part of black intellectuals that the courts would provide any relief against racial discrimination. He also pressed ahead in the teeth of many problems and setbacks, including hostile judges, opposition from teachers, plaintiffs who proved weak and unreliable, and, in at least one case, a black college president who deliberately sabotaged a promising lawsuit. This was a new field of law: should the NAACP sue in state courts or federal courts? Should it target the state officials or local school boards? Houston was learning through trial-and-error; every case lost provided a valuable lesson.

His skill and persistence paid off. The result was a series of courtroom victories which, while rather modest in scope, actually undermined the legal basis of racial discrimination in the South. In 1938 the Supreme Court decided a lawsuit brought by Lloyd Gaines, who had sued for admission to the University of Missouri law school. The Court declined to order integration. But it did state that if Missouri provided a legal education for white students, it had a duty to provide a "substantially equal" opportunity for blacks. Giving black students tuition scholarships to attend out-of-state law schools amounted to discrimination. The state must either provide a law school for blacks within the state or allow Gaines to attend the University of Missouri.[31]

The *Gaines* decision reverberated throughout the South. For the first time, the Southern states were on notice that they must drastically improve educational opportunities for black people. Missouri quickly established a law school at Lincoln University; during the 1940s state after state added graduate and professional programs to their black state colleges. Although *Plessy* still stood, writes historian Mark Tushnet, "the NAACP had secured its first Supreme Court decision eroding the principle of 'separate but equal.'"[32]

A second victory followed in 1939, after a black teacher in Anne Arundel County, Maryland, sued the local school board. In the first decision of its kind, a federal judge ruled that the lower salaries received by black teachers bore no relation to qualifications or competence: they stemmed from illegal racial discrimination. A string of lawsuits ensued over the next six years, as teachers in every Southern state except North Carolina and Mississippi sued for equal salaries. School boards retaliated by firing plaintiffs, a tactic that created fear and division among teachers. A more subtle and effective ploy was to disguise salary discrimination by devising pay scales ostensibly based on "merit." Yet the cumulative effect of teachers' victories in the federal courts wore down official resistance. Many school boards settled out of court. By the end of World War II the NAACP had virtually closed the salaries gap.

By then another black lawyer, Thurgood Marshall, had assumed the role of principal legal strategist. A native of Baltimore and a graduate of Lincoln University and Howard University Law School, Marshall joined the NAACP as Houston's assistant in 1936, succeeding him as special counsel four years later. Marshall was thoroughly in accord with Houston's approach to the law, and believed just as strongly as his mentor did that lawsuits should be used to build the NAACP as a mass organization rooted in local communities. Tall, handsome, convivial, and forceful, Marshall was an effective public speaker and a legendary private raconteur—not only the NAACP's top lawyer but also one of its most effective spokesmen. With apparently inexhaustible energy, he racked up tens of thousands of miles each year, travelling throughout the country, especially the South, consulting lawyers and plaintiffs, addressing NAACP branches, and speaking at public meetings.

In 1944, under Marshall's direction, the NAACP won the third, and arguably the most important, of its precedent-setting legal decisions. Four years earlier, the Supreme Court had ruled, in a Louisiana case involving vote-stealing, that the Democratic primary was an integral part of the state's electoral machinery, and therefore subject to relevant federal safeguards. The decision opened the door to a lawsuit against the Democratic primary as a disfranchising device. Blacks in Texas, who had already taken the white primary to the Supreme Court three times, mobilized for a knock-out blow. Backed by the NAACP, Houston dentist Lonnie Smith sued a state election official who refused to let him vote in the Democratic primary. In April 1944, in *Smith* v. *Allwright*, the Supreme Court ruled that the "white primary" constituted illegal racial discrimination.[33]

Hailing the decision as a "Second Emancipation," black civic leagues stepped up their voter registration efforts. New leagues came into being, stronger and more broadly based. Statewide organizations gave an additional push, and a National Progressive Voters League aimed to supply strategy and direction.

When Thurgood Marshall visited Houston a week after the *Smith* decision, he encountered surging optimism and political energy:

Mass meeting on the night of the 11th was the largest meeting I have seen in Texas. Church was packed at seven for an eight o'clock meeting. They had loud speakers outside and the crowd outside was as large as the crowd inside. The only way the plaintiff could get in the church was by climbing through the window at the back of the church. White people driving by including policemen stopped their cars to hear the "nigger lawyer from New York." Traffic was thereby blocked. . . . Don't know about other states but bet even money that the Negroes in Texas are going to vote.

Throughout the South, in fact, blacks visited the registration offices in greater numbers than any time since disfranchisement. In hundreds of counties, registrars enrolled black voters for the first time in forty or fifty years.[34]

Knocking out the "white primary," however, was merely a first step. Fear of white violence restrained many people from even attempting to register; those who did apply encountered blatantly unfair registration procedures. White politicians still controlled the registration process itself, and although some were ready to tolerate a small black electorate, many were still determined to keep blacks disfranchised. None were prepared to register blacks on the same basis as whites. The struggle by black Southerners to secure the right to vote continued for twenty more years.

As World War II drew to an end, blacks were well aware that America's political future was up for grabs. They had chalked up gains, but had achieved no great breakthrough. The basic pattern of race relations remained intact. Southern whites seemed bent on maintaining racial segregation. At a conference in Chicago, Mordecai Johnson, the president of Howard University, warned that far from the South being democratized and liberalized by the North, the North was in danger of succumbing to the South's "diseased suggestions" on race. Johnson wondered "whether in the next few months Fascism will crystallize in this country."

Charles Houston was more sanguine. The black soldiers who returned from fighting, he predicted, would introduce a new element into the equation. "For the first time in the history of the United States, you will have a generation of young Negroes with a world point of view." Yet the question remained: would the democratic idealism of the Second World War carry over into peacetime? Or would history repeat itself and 1946, like 1919, bring the destruction of black hopes?[35]

A. Philip Randolph, on left, leading a picket line at the Democratic
National Convention, Philadelphia, 1948

Bettmann/CORBIS

10

Two Steps Forward and
One Step Back, 1946–55

On October 8, 1946, four hundred schoolchildren in the town of Lumberton, North Carolina, walked out of their classes to protest against the dilapidated, insanitary, unsafe buildings that housed the two black high schools of Robeson County. Instigated by members of the NAACP Youth Council, the "strike" lasted for nine days. The students conducted it with discipline, and their elders supported them. One morning, waving flags and placards bearing slogans such as "How Can I Learn When I Am Cold" and "It Rains on Me," the children paraded down Lumberton's main street, accompanied by about twenty-five cars. When the parade ended, the children were treated to a showing of the film *Jesse James* by the Robeson Theater.

State officials were surprisingly sympathetic to the children's protest. "It would be difficult for the most gifted writer to picture the actual conditions as being worse than they really are," reported Nathan C. Newbold, North Carolina's veteran director of Negro education. "The Negro schools of North Carolina are a disgrace," admitted state health officer Carl Reynolds. Photographs of black schools "make you weep just to look at them." The *Raleigh News and Observer,* North Carolina's most influential newspaper, called for "immediate and adequate action" to provide "equal educational opportunity to every boy and girl in the state."[1]

To say that states like North Carolina "poured money" into black schools after World War II might convey the wrong impression. Expenditure on black education was so niggardly compared to spending on white schools that any increase looked statistically impressive. Yet the Southern states did, finally, begin to take seriously the problem of educational inequality. In the 1940s, governors appointed commissions to study the situation and make recommendations. With an assist from the tax revenues generated by the postwar economic boom, state legislatures appropriated substantial sums to replace wooden schools with brick buildings, build black high schools where none had existed before, and expand black state colleges. In Louisiana, for example, the per capita sum allocated to black children increased from $16 to $116 between 1940 and 1955, from 24 percent of the amount spent on white children to 72 percent. South Carolina earmarked a $75 million bond issue, and a 3 percent sales tax, for equalizing black schools. In 1950 even Mississippi, where white opposition to black education had always been strongest, started an ambitious school-building program.[2]

Viewed from one angle, the years after World War II were a time of steady advance for black Southerners. They not only enjoyed improvements in educational opportunities, but also made substantial political gains. Black voter registration campaigns continued apace, and now spread to previously untouched rural counties. Registering was still an infuriating obstacle course that ended, more often than not, in rejection. Yet blacks sometimes found redress from the federal courts when district judges, taking their cue from the Supreme Court's ruling in *Smith* v. *Allwright,* ordered recalcitrant registrars to stop discriminating against black applicants.

By 1952 the black electorate in the South had grown from a few thousand to about one million. For the first time since disfranchisement fifty years earlier, black candidates won elections. In Winston-Salem the Reverend Kenneth Williams defeated a white candidate to gain a seat on the city's board of aldermen. In Greensboro, North Carolina, Dr. William Hampton, a physician, was elected to the city school board. Rufus C. Clement, a black college president, became the first black person to sit on Atlanta's board of education. In the small Louisiana town of Crowley, deep in Cajun country, two blacks were elected to the city council.

The number of black elected officials did not exceed single figures; they were a drop in the ocean. Yet although white people still all but monopolized political power in the South, they recognized the importance of the black electorate. In a tight race, black votes could be decisive. Sheriffs like D. J. Doucet of St. Landry Parish, mayors like William B. Hartsfield of Atlanta, and governors like James Folsom of Alabama courted black voters and encouraged further black registration. A modicum of political influence enabled blacks to secure a greater share of public spending. They gained parks and playgrounds, sewers and street lights, libraries and hospitals. Many Southern cities appointed black policemen.

The rise of black voting seemed to indicate that many white Southerners were no longer committed to an all-out defense of white supremacy. Indeed, an optimistic observer might have concluded that the South's *ancien régime* was crumbling; certainly, it was far less secure in 1950 than it had been in 1930. Economic, political, and ideological changes, wide-ranging and profound, were reordering Southern society and eroding the foundations of racial domination.

The most obvious outward change was the transformation of the South's economy. Headlong urbanization went hand-in-hand with the precipitous decline of agriculture. The continuing reduction of acreage devoted to cotton, and the introduction of the mechanical cotton picker, hastened the displacement of black agricultural workers that had begun during the 1930s. The number of black farmers declined from 680,000 in 1940 to 104,000 twenty years later. In 1940, blacks had comprised 22 percent of the South's farm operators; by 1969 that figure had dwindled to 6.8 percent. The proportion of black people that lived on farms plummeted from 35 percent to 2 percent. "Sharecropping . . . had passed into insignificance," writes economic historian Jay Mandle, "and so too had the Southern plantation economy."[3]

The South's black population was swiftly transformed from a rural peasantry into an urban proletariat. The proportion of blacks living in rural areas had already fallen from 73 percent in 1910 to 51 percent in 1940. By 1950 it had dipped to 38 percent, and in 1960 it reached 27 percent. Whereas 347,000 blacks left the South during the 1930s, net migration climbed to 1.6 million in the 1940s, with almost as many leaving in the 1950s. Yet so great was the flight from the countryside that the South's cities also absorbed large numbers of black migrants.

The streets of the cities were hardly paved with gold—blacks were still largely excluded from manufacturing jobs and confined to low-paying laboring, portering, and domestic work. Segregation was ubiquitous, police brutality commonplace. Yet the cities freed blacks from the tyranny of sharecropping. They were freer and safer than the rural areas: sheer numbers, segregated black areas, and the general anonymity of urban life provided a kind of security. Black institutions—churches, businesses, unions, social clubs—were stronger in the cities. Many cities had a black-owned newspaper; all of them had an NAACP branch.

A more subtle, but no less profound, change was in the realm of thought. The ideology of white supremacy had become an anachronism. Anthropologists and social scientists had undermined the intellectual case for racial hierarchy. The discovery of the Nazi death camps in 1945, and the subsequent war crimes trials, stamped racism with the crime of genocide. The rise of anticolonial movements in India and elsewhere made racism an international political issue—one that put the United States on the defensive, and one that the

Soviet Union was quick to exploit. The Cold War compelled America to begin putting its own house in order. No longer could the federal government endorse systematic and legalized racial discrimination. For the first time since Reconstruction, it had to confront racism as a serious national issue.

Congress, still subject to the veto of Southern legislators, failed dismally to offer any redress for racial discrimination. But President Truman, and the Supreme Court, gradually set in place a new national policy. The postwar decade began with the appointment of a President's Committee on Civil Rights. It ended with the Supreme Court ruling, in *Brown* v. *Board of Education,* that segregated public schools were unconstitutional and must be phased out. The stage was thus set for the Civil Rights Movement, a nonviolent rebellion by black Southerners that rendered white supremacy unworkable.

POSTWAR RACIAL VIOLENCE AND
THE TRUMAN CIVIL RIGHTS COMMITTEE

In 1945 many blacks in the South anticipated a repetition of the "Red Summer" of 1919. The restoration of peace, they worried, would prompt whites to forcibly reassert their domination, cracking down on any blacks—especially returning veterans—who challenged the status quo. A string of violent racial incidents seemed to bear out these fears.

In February 1946 Isaac Woodward, a black uniformed veteran, lost his sight when a policeman hauled him off a bus—Woodward had argued with the driver—and bludgeoned him across the face with a blackjack. Another black veteran, John Jones, was beaten to death by a group of white men near Minden, Louisiana, after being released from jail. A third veteran—together with his wife and another couple, four victims in all—were ambushed and shot dead outside Monroe, Georgia. In Taylor County, also in Georgia, a black veteran who attempted to vote paid with his life.

The most extensive violence occurred in Columbia, Tennessee, on February 25–26, 1946. The trouble began when a dispute over a radio in a radio repair shop led to a fight between Billy Flemming, a white army veteran, and James Stephenson, a black navy veteran. After Flemming got the worst of it, Stephenson and his mother were arrested. As whites gathered in the town square with lynching in mind, Sheriff James Underwood decided to release the Stephensons to the safekeeping of several well-respected black businessmen, who arranged for James Stephenson to be spirited away to Chicago. As the white mob grew more belligerent, however, blacks with guns prepared to defend the area of town known to blacks as the "Bottom," to whites as "Mink Slide." As four policemen walked into the neighborhood, blacks opened fire on them. All four were hit by shotgun pellets, and one was seriously wounded.

Declaring the incident an armed insurrection, the governor of Tennessee mobilized the National Guard, five hundred of whom repaired to Columbia under the command of General Jacob M. Dickinson. Throughout the night there was spasmodic firing from Mink Slide. At the same time, armed whites gathered around the area. The following morning, shortly after six, police and highway patrolmen cleared the area by force, ransacking stores and wrecking buildings. One hundred and six blacks were arrested. Two black prisoners were shot dead inside the town jail. After whites had regained control, twenty-eight blacks were indicted for attempted murder.[4]

To the NAACP, which organized the defense of the accused men, the prosecutions had greater potential for injustice than the riot itself. Walter White's fears of a "legal lynching" grew as the trials of twenty-five men got under way in the small community of Lawrenceburg. "Open threats were made by the unshaven, overall-clad spectators that the lawyers who dared defend Negroes would wind up in Duck River," recalled White. The chief prosecutor, Paul Bumpus, indulged in demagogic invective extreme even for Southern district prosecutors, lashing out at "lousy pinks and pimps and punks," "long-nosed men and short-chinned women," "filthy, loathsome birds of prey," "Reds, Yellows, Communists," "subversive vermin and rodents"—all of whom were viciously maligning the state of Tennessee.[5]

Yet as historian Gail O'Brien notes, the Columbia riot and its aftermath betrayed subtle but profound changes in race relations. Columbia had witnessed lynchings in the past; in 1946, however, Sheriff James Underwood averted the lynching of James Stephenson by arranging for his release. Moreover, unlike race riots of earlier times, when white mobs had rampaged at will, blacks in Columbia had kept the white mob at bay by defending their streets and homes. Thirdly, the all-white jury at the state court in Lawrenceburg rendered what O'Brien called "a most extraordinary decision," acquitting all but two of the first twenty-five defendants to be tried. The assistant district attorney, Bud Harwell, even shook hands with the defense lawyers, congratulating them on their victory and pronouncing his happiness with the verdict.[6]

Many white Southerners, truth be told, no longer had the stomach for harshly repressing the black population. They feared, and were sometimes ashamed of, mob violence. In Columbia, for example, one company commander of the Tennessee National Guard prevented a crowd of civilians from breaking open the arsenal and seizing weapons. The subsequent assault on Mink Slide by police and highway patrolmen disgusted many of the guardsmen. The police had been guilty of looting, vandalism, and shooting at unarmed men, reported one soldier. "Two wrongs do not make a right," he wrote General Dickinson. "Justice goes right down the middle of the road." Dickinson concurred: in a confidential report, he complained that the police in Columbia had run amok. "It is of the greatest importance to the future of Tennessee and its citizens and for the improvement of race relations that there be no pitched battles even though the officers of the law are victorious." Once a disturbance has been suppressed, the authorities should protect "the lives and property of all of our citizens, regardless of race, creed or color."[7]

Bad as it was, then, the racial violence of 1946 did not nearly approach the levels of 1919. Preventive action by governors and sheriffs (taken in part to head off federal legislation) had already reduced the number of lynchings to single figures. The decline was especially noticeable after 1935: the time when the NAACP's antilynching campaign peaked, and when the Roosevelt administration created a Civil Rights Section (CRS) within the Justice Department. In 1940 the CRS had brought the federal government's first police brutality prosecution; two years later it instituted the first federal investigation of a lynching. Thurgood Marshall, among others, was bitterly critical of the FBI's performance in such cases. Yet the Justice Department's failure to secure convictions should not obscure the significance of federal intervention. Even without a federal lynching law—which Congress still refused to pass— FBI probes and federal prosecutions had their effect. Between 1937 and 1946 lynch mobs killed 44 people but the authorities rescued 226 people. Six died in 1946; twenty-two were rescued.

The Justice Department failed to convict the police chief who beat Isaac Woodward; it failed even to win indictments in the Minden and Monroe lynching cases. Nevertheless, the incidents of 1946 led to an event of great significance. On September 19 Walter White, representing the National Emergency Committee Against Mob Violence, met with President Harry Truman to discuss the situation. "My God! I had no idea it was as terrible as that!" Truman exclaimed. "We've got to do something!" On December 5, he appointed a President's Committee on Civil Rights (PCCR), asking it to recommend "more adequate and effective means and procedures for the protection of the civil rights of the American people."[8]

Chaired by the head of the General Electric Corporation, Charles E. Wilson, the fifteen-member committee included union leaders, white Southerners, clergymen from the three main faiths, two blacks (Channing H. Tobias and Sadie T. Alexander), and Franklin D. Roosevelt, Jr. The PCCR's report, *To Secure These Rights,* called for federal laws against lynching and police brutality, abolition of the poll tax, federal protection of voting rights, a federal fair employment law, the establishment of a permanent Civil Rights Commission, and more vigorous action by the FBI in civil rights violations. It also advocated the "elimination of segregation, based on color, creed, or national origin" from the armed services, public transportation, housing, health care, and education—from every area of American life.[9]

To Secure These Rights was a milestone. Truman's commitment to the cause of "civil rights"—a phrase that sounded more innocuous, and less inflammatory, than "racial equality"—marked a historic shift in the policy of the federal government. The Roosevelt administration had enunciated a general principle of nondiscrimination, but it had condoned racial segregation. The Truman administration not only withdrew its support from segregation but also proposed a comprehensive program to integrate blacks into the mainstream of American life. It took twenty years, and relentless pressure from the Civil Rights Movement, to induce Congress to enact that program. Nevertheless, *To Secure These Rights* had set the agenda.

It is not cynical, merely realistic, to suggest that Truman's espousal of civil rights coincided with his own political interests as well as the broader interests of the Democratic Party. Truman had made his political career in a border state, Missouri, where blacks freely voted; he was accustomed to cultivating black support. Truman became president, moreover, at a time when black migration from South to North—a flow that continued after 1945—made black voters increasingly important to the Democratic Party. Black leaders had long awaited the day when black votes would constitute a "balance of power" in national politics. That day had now arrived. As the NAACP's Henry Lee Moon pointed out, in the 1944 presidential election there were 28 states where a shift of 5 percent of the popular votes would have reversed the result; "In twelve of these . . . the potential Negro vote exceeds the number required to shift the states from one column to the other." Black voters had grown to a critical mass, sufficient in size to provide the margin of victory or defeat in a close election.[10]

In 1948 the issues of communism and civil rights threatened to tear apart the Democratic Party and destroy Truman's presidency. From the left came the threat of the Progressive Party. Led by former vice president Henry Wallace—whom Truman had recently fired as secretary of commerce—the Progressives opposed Truman's aggressive anti-Communism, which had exacerbated the Cold War abroad and, at home, threatened civil liberties and signalled a retreat from New Deal reform. Campaigning for the presidency, Wallace expected to garner support from liberals, union members, and blacks. The Democratic Party also faced rumblings of dissension from its Southern wing, which detested Truman's overtures to the growing black vote, and sensed that the party was drifting away from the white South's position on racial segregation.

Truman, heeding the counsel of adviser Clark Clifford, endeavored to strengthen his appeal to traditional Democratic voters outside the South, including blacks. In 1947 he became the first president to address the

NAACP's annual meeting. In February 1948 he addressed a joint session of Congress on the subject of civil rights. Six months later, the Democratic Party adopted a civil rights plank that precipitated a "bolt" by many Southern delegates. Meeting in Birmingham, Alabama, six thousand disaffected white Southerners formed the States Rights Party and nominated Senator Strom Thurmond of South Carolina as their candidate for president.

Truman responded by redoubling his efforts to attract support from blacks and white liberals. He called Congress into special session to consider civil rights legislation, including a bill to prohibit the poll tax as a requirement for voting in federal elections. He also issued Executive Order 9981, which, despite strong opposition from the military, led to the abolition of racial segregation within the armed services. At a time when, according to one opinion poll, most white people thought that blacks were already being treated fairly, Truman's civil rights stand entailed some political risk.

Yet Truman's investment in civil rights paid dividends. Despite losing four Southern states to "Dixiecrat" candidate Strom Thurmond, he narrowly beat the Republican candidate, Thomas E. Dewey of New York. Confounding predictions that blacks would support Henry Wallace, Truman won two-thirds of the black vote. Without strong black support, Truman would have lost California, Ohio, and Illinois. Wallace failed to carry a single state.

The struggle for black equality, however, has never been a straight line, still less a line of uninterrupted progress. Defeats, disappointments, and setbacks have dogged every plan, strategy, and effort. Between Reconstruction and the Second World War, blacks usually took one step forward only to find themselves two steps back.

The ten years between the end of World War II and the start of the Civil Rights Movement resembled this depressingly familiar pattern. In spite of favorable court decisions and encouraging presidential statements, black Americans remained locked into second-class citizenship. In the South, whites still vehemently defended racial segregation. Moreover, whites in the rural Black Belt—who were grossly overrepresented in the state legislatures—adamantly opposed black voting. Even in the cities, white politicians imposed ceilings on black registration to prevent the black vote from posing a serious threat. In the North, despite exercising the franchise more or less freely, blacks encountered pervasive job discrimination and, in housing, patterns of segregation more rigid than anything found in the South.

The basic problem was the absence of strong action by the federal government to end segregation and discrimination. In Congress the conservative coalition of Southern Democrats and Northern Republicans stymied all efforts to promote racial equality. A campaign to abolish the poll tax failed. The FEPC was abolished. Truman proved incapable of translating his civil rights proposals into legislation. Heavy Democratic losses in the 1946 midterm elections produced a Congress firmly in the hands of conservative Republicans and segregationist Southern Democrats. Truman's surprise victory in 1948 did not change that situation. The most radical government program for racial equality since Reconstruction, *To Secure These Rights* sank like a stone.

In the eyes of many historians, the postwar years destroyed the tentative gains that blacks had made between 1941 and 1945. The 400,000 black veterans who returned South confronted the same conditions they had left in 1941. To make matters worse, the Cold War, and the anti-Communist purge known as McCarthyism, split the New Deal coalition, crippled Southern liberalism, and destroyed many civil rights organizations. By 1950 communism had become a national obsession. "The postwar liberal tide was now receding," wrote William Berman, "carrying with it the frustrated hopes of millions of American Negroes."[11]

ANTICOMMUNISM AND CIVIL RIGHTS

Hysterical anticommunism came to bear the name of Republican Senator Joseph McCarthy, who seized upon the issue in 1950. But the Truman administration let the anti-Communist genie out of the lamp. By instituting a federal loyalty program in 1947, by prosecuting and jailing the leaders of the Communist Party in 1948, and by adopting tough rhetoric in order to "scare hell out of the American people," the federal government made it clear that communism was beyond the political pale. Communists were denied the constitutional protections normally accorded to American citizens. The Communist Party was not a legitimate political group, but a conspiracy to overthrow the government by teaching revolution. Truman's intervention in Korea, which embroiled America in a war with China between 1950 and 1953, made communism tantamount to treason.

The principal victims of government repression were Communists themselves: the Communist Party, Communist-controlled unions, and Communist "front" organizations like the Civil Rights Congress. Congressional and state committees also "exposed" Communists in the schools, universities, ports, industry, and Hollywood. Individuals who refused to denounce communism and "name names" faced personal ruin. An indeterminate number of people were fired, blacklisted, prosecuted, and deported. The Cold War did not merely sideline the issue of racial discrimination; it inflicted direct damage on the cause of civil rights by silencing some of the most consistent and vocal supporters of racial equality.

The fact that Communists were active in virtually every liberal, labor, and civil rights organization amplified the destructive impact of anti-Communist policies. The Cold War placed every organization under intense pressure to support American foreign policy and to purge its ranks of Communists. Organizations that refused to toe the Cold War line faced FBI surveillance and damaging investigations by hostile congressional committees. They were also liable to be placed on the attorney general's list of "subversive organizations"—the kiss of death. State investigating committees added to the harassment.

The fate of the Southern Conference for Human Welfare (SCHW) illustrated the lethal effect of anticommunism on a liberal organization that refused to compromise its principles by excluding Communists. The SCHW never recovered from a report by the House Un-American Activities Committee (HUAC) labelling it a Communist front. The ecumenical SCHW had been a beacon of hope for Southerners, white and black, who wished to combat poverty, racism, and one-party rule. Its demise was a grievous loss. Its tax-exempt arm, the Southern Conference Education Fund, managed to survive, but a Senate investigation in 1954—chaired by Mississippi segregationist James O. Eastland—recycled the old allegations of communism.

The issue of communism divided and weakened the labor movement. The Taft-Hartley Act, passed by Congress in 1947 over Truman's veto, required unions to file affidavits testifying that no Communists held office; if they refused to do so, they could not participate in representation elections supervised by the National Labor Relations Board (NLRB). Initially loath to comply with such an antilabor measure, the leaders of the CIO decided to use Taft-Hartley to isolate and destroy the Communist-led unions—which, for obvious reasons, refused to file the affidavits. In 1949 the CIO expelled from its ranks eleven noncomplying unions. Out in the cold, and subject to "raids" on their membership by the CIO, which chartered rival organizations, most of the eleven expelled unions withered away and died. Whether these Communist-led unions were more racially egalitarian than the rest, as some historians claim, is open to debate. Still, they did have many black members and generally represented them well. They had also been an important source of backing for the NAACP, the SCHW, and other civil rights organizations.

Blacks were suspicious of anticommunism. "Politicians seeking Negro support need more than the Red bogey to garner this vote," wrote Henry Lee Moon of the NAACP in 1948. "Communism is not regarded as the enemy." Blacks respected the Communists' record in "sharpening the Negro's fight for equal rights." They distrusted the motives of the anti-Communists, who included the worst racists and reactionaries. And they feared that if the rights of Communists were abridged, their own rights would be further curtailed. "There is every reason," Moon concluded, "why Negroes should oppose any attempt to purge the Communists from American life." Other NAACP leaders, including Clarence Mitchell, Charles Houston, and Thurgood Marshall, agreed.[12]

Between 1948 and 1950, however, domestic and foreign events combined to accelerate the anti-Communist purge: the government prosecuted the leaders of the Communist Party, the CIO expelled Communist-led unions, the Soviet Union blockaded Berlin, Communist forces won the Chinese civil war, the Soviet Union exploded an atomic bomb, half a dozen spies were unmasked, and in June 1950 the United States went to war to halt Communist forces in Korea. In a climate in which communism was tantamount to treason, the vehemently anti-Communist Walter White succeeded in persuading the NAACP's 1950 convention to adopt an anti-Communist resolution. It empowered national officials to expel individuals and dissolve branches in the event of infiltration or domination by Communists.

Anti-Communist purges, however, were almost as damaging to the purger as to the purged. The NAACP's policy of excluding Communists, although perhaps the price of survival, exacted a heavy toll. Walter White warned members not to make "hysterical and wild accusations"; he did not want a "witch hunt." Yet the impossibility of identifying Communists, Thurgood Marshall warned, made a witch hunt inevitable. "I can conceive of some well-known Democrats, Republicans as well as Catholics who will be called Communists," he predicted. Certainly, by the early 1950s the NAACP was smaller, weaker, and more conservative. So was the labor movement. Bitter internal faction fights almost paralyzed the United Auto Workers union, the National Maritime Union, and the Transport Workers Union. The expulsion of Communist officials resolved internal conflicts but weakened internal democracy. As Brenda Gayle Plummer argues, "Purges limited the scope and capped the resources of many mass organizations that had been militant during the war years."[13]

The anti-Communist purge also weakened the efforts of black Americans to link their struggle for equal rights with the cause of anticolonial movements abroad. Indeed, the Cold War discouraged any opposition to the basic tenets of American foreign policy. The government's treatment of W. E. B. Du Bois and Paul Robeson, two of the most distinguished black Americans, provided a stark warning of the consequences of violating the anti-Communist orthodoxy.

In 1951 Du Bois, America's greatest black intellectual, was arrested under a federal warrant because, as director of the Peace Information Center, the State Department considered him the "agent of a foreign power." The eighty-two-year-old man was taken to jail in handcuffs. A federal court dismissed the charge. Nevertheless, the government confiscated his passport, preventing him from travelling abroad until 1958, when the Supreme Court ruled that tactic illegal. Du Bois joined the Communist Party and moved to Ghana. The State Department refused to renew his passport; Du Bois became a Ghanaian citizen. When he died in 1963, he had been marginalized, exiled, and virtually forgotten.

Paul Robeson was at the pinnacle of his international career as a singer and actor in the 1940s. However, he fell afoul of the Truman administration because he praised the Soviet Union, and criticized the United States, when speaking overseas. The State Department confiscated his passport, and announced that he would not be allowed to leave the United States to enter Canada—a journey that did not even require a passport. When he sang at Peekskill, New York, rock-throwing, stick-wielding vigilantes wrecked the concert. Denied the use of concert halls, his singing career ended. The government intimated that Robeson's problems would disappear if he abandoned his outspoken stand against racism and colonialism. Robeson, a friend of the Communist Party although never a member, refused. "Following prolonged isolation, harassment, and exclusion from work and travel," writes Penny Von Eschen, "he suffered a series of emotional and physical breakdowns and spent his last years virtually forgotten."[14]

Inevitably, white defenders of segregation exploited the issue of communism. Indeed, conservatives and racists had long attacked anyone supporting racial equality as "Communist." But the Cold War made such attacks much more damaging. Moreover, however far-fetched and irresponsible they seemed—and such unlikely people as Benjamin Mays and Mary McLeod Bethune suffered from charges of communism—the crude smear tactics associated with "McCarthyism" found encouragement from the very heart of the federal establishment.

Even such an innocuous and apolitical figure as Josephine Baker, a cabaret artist long resident in France, became a government target. When in the early 1950s Baker began criticizing American racism during her performing tours of Latin America, the State Department attempted to undercut her influence. In Cuba, prompted by the American embassy, theater owners in Havana cancelled her engagements, and the Cuban military police, alerted by the FBI that Baker might be an "active Communist," arrested the artist and interrogated her for three hours. When Baker flew into New York in 1955, immigration officials detained her and she left without entering the country.[15]

The government relied upon the FBI to ascertain the exact extent of the "Communist threat." To the archconservative director of the bureau, J. Edgar Hoover, the millions of Americans who supported radical or liberal causes were all suspect. And to the average FBI agent, even the staunchly anti-Communist NAACP was tainted. In fact, the FBI harbored suspicions about virtually every black American organization and leader, whatever their political complexion. After reviewing many of the files, Brenda Gayle Plummer concluded that the FBI was less interested in deterring subversion than in discrediting blacks "deemed too independent, unconventional, or influential."[16]

The FBI didn't target only black leaders; it also opened files on ordinary workers. In the late 1940s, for example, dozens of black postal workers found themselves being suspended and fired. Ironically, workers who had been protected by federal civil service rules during the worst days of Jim Crow were now hauled before loyalty boards if there were "reasonable grounds"—later amended to "reasonable doubt"—to suspect their loyalty. The people who fell afoul of these "security" measures were invariably those who were most active in the NAACP and NAPE. Even the staunchly anti-Communist Walter White complained that the FBI equated civil rights militancy with communism. "Investigating agencies of the federal government have been asking white persons whether they associate with colored people," he complained to Truman. "Colored people have been asked whether they entertained white people in their homes." NAPE official William C. Jason warned that opposing racial discrimination was being construed as disloyalty. "All pro-Negro, pro–civil rights, anti–white supremacy utterances, if more dynamic than . . . platitudes, become the 'you sees' that destroy." Forced out of NAPE in 1955, Jason later reflected that "the loyalty program was the last open, overt effort to discount the breakdown of racial policies within the Post Office."[17]

It is easy to conclude that the Cold War was a disaster for black Americans. In the late 1940s, many historians believe, a progressive coalition, rooted in the New Deal and operating within the Democratic Party, was evolving into a strong force for racial equality. An alliance of civil rights organizations, the CIO, Southern white radicals, and the Communist Party, this coalition was attempting to unionize Southern industry, enfranchise Southern blacks, and dislodge the segregationists who monopolized Southern politics. A tremendous opportunity existed to democratize the South and, in so doing, to make liberalism—even social democracy—the dominant voice of the Democratic Party. Anticommunism, however, fractured the center-left coalition and aborted a nascent civil rights movement. The Cold War gave white supremacy a new lease on life, delaying the Civil Rights Movement for at least ten years.[18]

This historical critique of anticommunism is persuasive, but it represents only a partial truth. That the Cold War was a disaster for American radicalism, and hardly less so for American liberalism, is incontestable. Yet it is difficult to see how the Communist Party, even in the absence of government repression, could have avoided isolation and decline. In some ways, the Communist Party was its own worst enemy. The party's secrecy, tactical inconsistency, and ideological rigidity alienated most of its supporters and many of its members. At a time when Stalin was erecting police states in Eastern Europe, blockading West Berlin, and intensifying repression inside the Soviet Union, the CPUSA's steadfast allegiance to Moscow made the party a moral leper.

Many of the liberals who gladly worked with the Party during the halcyon days of the Popular Front could no longer stomach associating with Communists. Postwar anticommunism was not merely a right-wing plot to discredit the Left: it was also a genuine defense of democratic ideals. We must not oversimplify the moral dilemmas posed by the Cold War.

Whether a black-labor-liberal coalition might have, in the absence of the Cold War, gained ascendancy within the Democratic Party and pushed through a civil rights program is unknowable. Yet it seems unlikely. Anticommunism was a useful, but not essential, weapon to the South's ruling elite. White employers and politicians already possessed the means to defeat "Operation Dixie," the CIO's plan to unionize Southern industry. They also, with ease, limited the growth of the black electorate, ensuring that black voters remained powerless. Unions in the South were too small, white liberals too few, and black voters too scarce to seriously threaten white supremacy. Nationally, a conservative reaction against the New Deal was inevitable; it had been growing since 1938. The Republicans gained control of Congress in 1946, before the Cold War was fully under way. The power of the conservative coalition in Congress made a civil rights breakthrough unlikely, an attack on organized labor inevitable.

More fundamentally, the Cold War in some ways *assisted* the cause of racial equality. Most black leaders harbored no illusions that the government's high-sounding declarations about democracy and human rights had much substance. America had condemned Nazi racialism but, as Charles S. Johnson pointed out, "our racial theories and practices were not very different from those of Germany." Yet Johnson believed that the Cold War, which exposed America to "terrific and infuriating pressure" from the Soviet Union, would compel the government to repudiate white supremacy and take action against racial discrimination. "We are learning the awful truth that our exhibitions of undemocratic behavior have made a large part of the world vulnerable to the Soviet doctrine that supports the sovereignty of the common man." In Africa, Asia, and the Far East nonwhite peoples were struggling against colonial rule, and emerging nations were wavering between the United States and the Soviet Union. The Cold War had turned America's "race problem" into an international issue.[19]

Black leaders were accustomed to tailoring their tactics to political circumstances. To the leaders of the NAACP, and to Socialists like A. Philip Randolph, the Cold War represented a golden opportunity to influence the federal government. By critically supporting American foreign policy, they could argue that action against discrimination would enable the United States to wage the Cold War more effectively. As George M. Johnson, the dean of Howard University Law School, told a meeting of black unionists, "The colonial policies of the so-called democracies, and the ineffectiveness of our own government in dealing with mob violence against Negroes, has caused minority groups throughout the world to question the sincerity of the champions of Democracy who so violently criticize Russia." American racism accounted for about half the total content of the Soviet Union's anti-American propaganda. In the United Nations, Soviet delegates played up every lynching and every race riot.[20]

Soviet propaganda, in fact, was a godsend to the civil rights cause. After a Florida sheriff killed a black prisoner, Walter Irvin, during an alleged escape attempt in 1951, NAACP official Harry T. Moore called Governor Fuller Warren's attention to a speech by Soviet ambassador Andrei Vishinsky:

No doubt Vishinsky was delighted to be able to announce this case in the U.N. General Assembly . . . and to brand this shooting as "the American way of life." No doubt [secretary of state] Mr. Acheson and other American delegates were terribly embarrassed when they could not truthfully rebut Vishinsky's charges that "some people should look after their own business, before sticking their noses into other people's houses." . . . Florida and America are on trial in the World Court of public opinion.

Letters from men and women across America echoed Moore's argument. The slaying of Irvin "must gladden the hearts of our domestic and external enemies who will not fail to exploit it to the hilt," complained a Detroit businessman. "When Russian and Oriental Communists murder unarmed prisoners in cold blood, we call it an atrocity," wrote a woman from Washington, D.C. "Yet, in America, the Walter Irvin case revolts even conservative southern members of my family."[21]

The Truman administration was both sensitive to Soviet propaganda and concerned about the loyalty of black citizens. At the same time that it silenced left-wing critics, therefore, it also cultivated anti-Communist black leaders and tried to impress upon the world that America took racial discrimination seriously. As the government gradually moved in the direction of racial equality, it clothed each step in the language of the Cold War. "I think it is quite obvious," Dean Acheson stated in 1946, "that the existence of discriminations against minority groups in the United States is a handicap in our relations with other countries." Truman repeated the point when he created the Fahey Committee, charged with ending racial discrimination in the armed forces. The Korean War hastened integration—partly by exposing the depth of racial friction, and black bitterness, inside the army. As a semiliterate black GI wrote to a Southern politician: "No killing Negro in Russia. No killing Negro in Red China. Negro dont want your women but he want be free."[22]

While Congress stonewalled on civil rights, the executive and the judicial branches began to chip away at legalized segregation. In *Shelley* v. *Kraemer* (1948), the Justice Department filed an *amicus curiae* (friend of the court) brief in support of the NAACP's successful challenge to "restrictive covenants" in housing. In 1950 the solicitor general told the Supreme Court that segregation on railway dining cars branded black passengers as inferiors, and that the "separate but equal" doctrine was unconstitutional. The following year the government supported a legal challenge to segregation in Washington, D.C., arguing that Jim Crow in the nation's capital had a disproportionate impact upon foreign diplomats, conveying a "misleading impression of American life." Campaigning for the White House in 1952, Dwight D. Eisenhower promised to abolish segregation in Washington, a pledge he fulfilled as president by working quietly to desegregate restaurants, theaters, and hotels.[23]

Foreign policy played a part, too, in persuading the government to back the NAACP in the most important case of them all: the challenge to school segregation that led to *Brown* v. *Board of Education*. "Racial discrimination furnishes grist for the Communist propaganda mills," stated the government's *amicus curiae* brief, filed in 1952, "and it raises doubts even among friendly nations as to the intensity of our devotion to the democratic faith."[24]

SIGNIFICANCE OF THE *BROWN* DECISION

The NAACP's decision to launch a direct legal attack upon racial segregation represented an enormous gamble. If the Supreme Court failed to sustain such a challenge, then *Plessy* v. *Ferguson* might survive for another fifty years. Yet in three decisions handed down on the same day in 1950—the year that McCarthy hit the headlines and the Korean War erupted—the Supreme Court knocked large holes in *Plessy*. In *Sweatt* v. *Painter*, the most important, the Court ordered the University of Texas to admit a black applicant, Heman Sweatt, to its law school. A hastily improvised black law school in Houston, it ruled, could not possibly provide Sweatt with a legal education "substantially equal" to that available to white students at UT. In *McLaurin* v. *Oklahoma State Regents*, the Court ruled that the University of Oklahoma had been wrong to admit George McLaurin as a graduate student but then require him to sit apart from the white students. In the third case, *Henderson* v. *United States*, the Court ruled that segregated railway dining cars were unconstitutional.[25]

These decisions were "replete with road markings," Thurgood Marshall believed, "telling us where to go next." At a lawyers' conference in June 1950, the NAACP endorsed the strategy of challenging segregation head-on. The NAACP filed lawsuits on behalf of black parents in Virginia, South Carolina,

Louisiana, Kansas, Delaware, and Washington, D.C., seeking the admittance of black children to white schools. In 1952 five of the cases reached the Supreme Court, consolidated under the title of *Brown* v. *Board of Education,* the title of the case from Topeka, Kansas.[26]

Knowledgeable observers warned the NAACP that even if the Supreme Court reversed *Plessy,* its strategy might not work. All too often, noted Yale law professor John P. Frank, Supreme Court decisions "were stones dropped in the water, forgotten as soon as the ripples disappeared." Abolition of the restrictive covenant had hardly dented housing segregation; rulings against Jim Crow aboard interstate buses and trains had failed, in fact, to end segregation. Will Maslow of the American Jewish Congress highlighted the danger of a Supreme Court ruling being "publicly and contemptuously disregarded" in the South. If a state "throws down the gauntlet," the Court had no means of enforcing its mandates.[27]

Black parents and teachers in the South harbored another set of doubts. Integration was uncharted territory: how would it work, what would it mean? If it entailed black children applying to attend white schools, then the pressures, dangers, and uncertainties would be immense; few parents would be happy volunteering their children as guinea pigs. And what would happen to the small number of children who might gain admission to white schools? Evidence from the North suggested they lagged behind the white children, becoming frustrated and demoralized, often dropping out. NAACP officials had a hard time convincing their members that integration would be more effective than equalization in obtaining a better education for their children. For black teachers, integration posed an obvious threat to their jobs. If the Southern states really did merge the inefficient and wasteful dual school system, there would be fewer schools, fewer principals, and fewer teachers. Some feared that up to 75,000 jobs might be jeopardized. "We cannot expect a wave of enthusiasm for integration" among black teachers, warned Fred Patterson of Tuskegee Institute.[28]

The NAACP was prepared to accept all of these risks. Equalization suits had reached the point of diminishing returns, explained Thurgood Marshall; they were not yielding "results in keeping with time, effort and money expended." A direct attack on segregation would affect the entire South and promised to be far more effective in producing tangible change. As for the fears of parents and teachers, the NAACP made light of them. If the first black children in integrated schools dropped out, said NAACP lawyer William Ming, so be it: "There are fatalities in all social change." The NAACP doubted that many black teachers would lose their jobs, but even if they did that was a price worth paying. And the NAACP was unconcerned about the fate of the black state colleges. As Walter White put it: blacks must be prepared to "give up the little kingdoms" that segregation had created.[29]

On May 17, 1954, speaking for a unanimous court, Chief Justice Earl War-ren, recently appointed by President Eisenhower, handed down the decision. "In the field of public education," he read, "the doctrine of separate but equal has no place. Separate educational facilities are inherently unequal." *Brown* de-stroyed the legal basis for Jim Crow. It was the capstone of liberal anticommu-nism, a personal triumph for Thurgood Marshall, and the NAACP's greatest victory.

Marshall was realistic enough to know that *Brown* merely set a precedent. Implementation would require many more lawsuits. "We will have to go from state to state and county to county even after we get it." Yet the NAACP downplayed the likelihood of strong white resistance to desegregation. Mis-sissippi would obviously hold out, yet Marshall noted that some white schools in Arkansas had already admitted black children—"and Arkansas is just barely, by the skin of its teeth, above Mississippi." At a meeting in Atlanta a week after *Brown,* Southern NAACP officials were cautiously opti-mistic. They predicted that the border states would quickly comply, and that some integration would soon come about in Arkansas, Louisiana, Texas, North Carolina, Tennessee, and Virginia. White resistance, they believed, would be limited mainly to Mississippi, and to the Black Belt counties of other states. In many areas, the NAACP advised its branches, "legal action may not be necessary."[30]

In light of the ferocious white backlash against *Brown* that within two years all but overwhelmed the NAACP, such optimism seems absurdly misplaced. Yet things need not have turned out as badly as they did: initial white reac-tions to the decision were by no means uniformly hostile. Indeed, many Southern newspapers urged calm compliance. In the opinion of the *Knoxville Journal,* "No citizen, fitted by character and intelligence to sit as a justice of the Supreme Court . . . could have decided this question other than the way it was decided." "Segregation has been ruled out," stated the *Greensboro Daily News,* "and the responsibility now is to readjust to that reality." Even in the Deep South, editors counselled acceptance of *Brown.* "Wisdom calls for calmness and moderation," preached the *New Orleans States-Item,* "for re-flection and discussion of the best ways to live with the decision." The *Baton Rouge Morning Advocate* told its readers that segregation was "doomed."[31]

But if a swift phasing out of segregated schools was ever a possibility, the psychological moment for it quickly passed. Instead of issuing a deadline for compliance, the Court offered the South a year of grace, delaying its imple-mentation ruling until May 31, 1955. Even then, in the decision known as *Brown II,* the Court declined to impose a deadline, merely urging "all delib-erate speed" in complying with *Brown.* Moreover, the Court failed to define what a "racially nondiscriminatory" school system would look like, charging the federal district courts with fashioning an appropriate remedy. To further muddy the water, the Court provided a list of complicating factors—administrative problems and the like—that district judges might consider in allowing school boards "additional time." The ruling disappointed the NAACP, delighted die-hard segregationists.

Delayed, vague, and half-hearted, *Brown II* proved disastrous to the cause of integration. Rather than using their year of grace constructively, planning for desegregation, the South's political leaders had done nothing to prepare whites for the inevitable. To be sure, there were "moderate" segregationists in the South, liberal governors like Earl Long of Louisiana and James Folsom of Alabama, who deplored vicious racism and privately wished that segregation would somehow go away. But while they did nothing actively to thwart *Brown*, they were not prepared to campaign openly for integration. As historian Tony Badger has argued, the inaction of Southern liberals played into the hands of the die-hard segregationists who, in an atmosphere of political drift, seized the initiative. The South's liberals "never attempted to campaign for, or build up support for, gradual racial change. Southern conservatives, by contrast, mounted a righteous crusade to convince [white] southerners that they need not tolerate any racial change, no matter how gradual." From their strong base in the Black Belt—where whites, often outnumbered, had the most to lose if blacks ever gained equality—the ultrasegregationists organized a campaign of "massive resistance" to render *Brown* a dead letter.[32]

The "Citizens Councils" spearheaded the offensive. Inspired by Judge Tom P Brady's virulent condemnation of *Brown*—a speech, then pamphlet, titled "Black Monday"—a plantation manager in Sunflower County, Mississippi, Robert P. Patterson, organized the first Citizens Council in July 1954. The movement spread like wildfire. Local chapters sprang up throughout Mississippi, Alabama, South Carolina, and Louisiana. Similar organizations, with different names, appeared in other states.

At their peak, in 1956, the Citizens Councils boasted perhaps 250,000 members. Many were doctors, lawyers, farmers, businessmen, politicians, and school superintendents. Banding together in state associations, and cooperating closely across the region, the Citizens Councils implemented a multifaceted strategy designed to stop the emerging Civil Rights Movement in its tracks. They flooded the South with racist propaganda, subjected civil rights activists to threats and economic pressure, erected new barriers to black voting, tried to suppress the NAACP, condemned white liberals as traitors, and made segregation, and how to defend it, the central issue in Southern politics.

The NAACP soon felt the Citizens Councils' presence. The NAACP's tactic of having local branches petition school boards for integration quickly backfired when the Citizens Councils retaliated against the signatories. Historian James C. Cobb provides a typical example from Yazoo City, Mississippi, where fifty-three people had lent their names to such a petition. "One by one those who signed . . . began to lose their jobs or whatever 'business' or 'trade' they had with whites." All but two people removed their names, and those two had both left town. "We expected pressure," admitted one NAACP official, "but not this much."[33]

The Citizens Councils denied any connection whatever with the lower-class Ku Klux Klan, which had a well-earned reputation for sadistic violence. They presented themselves as God-fearing, hardworking, and peaceable middle-class folk; they abjured violence and claimed to respect the law. Yet in practice, writes Numan V. Bartley, "they more closely resembled vigilante committees." Certainly, the NAACP drew little distinction between the Citizens Councils and the Ku Klux Klan. Thanks in part to the Councils, writes Bartley, "The Deep South sank deeper into hysterical reaction." Such a climate was bound to encourage acts of racial violence, including murder. "Make no mistake about it," reported NAACP official Daniel Byrd from Louisiana, "the Citizens Councils are following the pattern instituted by the White South during Reconstruction."[34]

Much of the defiant posturing indulged in by Southern legislators—censuring the Supreme Court, declaring *Brown* "null and void," asserting the right of "interposition" against the federal government—consisted of bombast and hot air. Even the weightier "Southern Manifesto" of 1956, a condemnation of *Brown* signed by nineteen U.S. senators and eighty-two U.S. representatives, meant little in practical terms. Although deeply discouraged by the "Southern Manifesto," the NAACP could live with it.

Yet the volleys of anti-integration laws fired off by the South's state legislatures left the NAACP's litigation strategy in tatters. One battery of laws sought to avert integration by providing for the outright abolition of public education. They forbade the expenditure of public monies on integrated schools, they authorized school closing as a local option, and they allowed governors to close integrated schools. They also provided tuition grants, allowed school boards to sell or lease public schools, and generally encouraged whites to set up private, all-white schools. Every state suspended its compulsory attendance law to allow parents to boycott integrated schools. Faced with court-ordered integration, a few cities, including Norfolk and Little Rock, closed their schools for a time. One Virginia county, Prince Edward, kept its schools shut for eight years. Louisiana tried and failed to close the public schools of New Orleans, attempted to throttle them financially, and induced whites to boycott the schools that integrated.

Closing the schools, however, was not the worst threat to *Brown*'s implementation. Indeed, school closure was rather like the nuclear bomb: useful only as a deterrent, its actual employment indicated that deterrence had failed. With one or two exceptions, abolishing public schools proved deeply unpopular with the mass of white voters; it could not be sustained for any length of time at the local, let alone the state or regional, level. As a form of "brinkmanship" designed to intimidate the courts, the threat of school closing proved ineffective. Starting in 1959, when the Supreme Court declared that a state had to close all its schools or none, defiant governors beat as hasty a retreat as their dignity permitted them.

"Pupil placement" acts proved a much more subtle, insidious, and effective method of resisting integration. Pioneered by Alabama and copied by more "moderate" states like Florida and North Carolina, these laws complied with the letter of *Brown* while flouting its spirit. In theory, they allowed children to transfer to a school other than the one to which the school board had assigned them. Thus whites could apply to transfer to black schools, blacks to white schools. Although bitter-end segregationists regarded them as the thin end of the wedge—for they at least admitted the possibility of integration—pupil placement laws ensured that applications for transfers had to satisfy so many criteria, and go through such labyrinthine administrative procedures, that hardly any survived the obstacle course.

The result: schools remained segregated. No whites applied for reassignment; black applications were routinely rejected. The Supreme Court's 1958 decision to uphold Alabama's pupil placement law on the grounds that it did not discriminate on its face represented a retreat even from the mild terms of *Brown II*. It meant that virtually anything short of outright defiance would pass muster with the federal courts. As Judge John J. Parker of North Carolina put it, *Brown* did not require integration, only the abolition of enforced segregation by law. The very best that blacks could now hope for in the short term was "tokenism"—that, after years of persistence, a handful of black children might be admitted to one or two white schools.

The most shocking attack on *Brown* was the attack upon the NAACP itself. In the spring of 1956 the Southern states launched a coordinated legal offensive, planned with care and stealth, to cripple the association. They prohibited state employees from advocating integration, forcing black teachers—one of the mainstays of the NAACP—to resign from the NAACP or face dismissal. In South Carolina, twenty-four teachers at Elloree Training School in Orangeburg County quit their jobs rather than renounce their membership. Columbia schoolteacher Septima P. Clark also chose dismissal (a great gain for the Civil Rights Movement, because the Highlander Folk School hired her to teach "citizenship education" classes). Such instances of defiance, however, were comparatively rare. Teachers resigned from the NAACP in droves, often dropping out of all conspicuous civil rights activity.

Few NAACP members, however, could breathe easy. Resurrecting long-forgotten and obscure laws, state prosecutors hauled the NAACP into court for neglecting to file its membership lists with the state authorities. The association found itself between the devil and the deep blue sea. If they complied with the law and handed over the lists, as the NAACP in Louisiana chose to do, they lost most of their members—for the Citizens Councils immediately published the lists, inviting whites to fire, boycott, and intimidate those whose names appeared. After surrendering its lists, the NAACP's membership fell from 13,190 to 1,698; of sixty-five branches operating in 1955, only seven survived the following year. Yet refusal to hand over the membership lists, the line taken by the NAACP in Alabama, proved even more costly. Ruling the NAACP to be in contempt of court, state judge Walter B. Jones enjoined it from operating anywhere in Alabama. His ban stood for eight years.

The NAACP's local lawyers also found themselves under fire, charged with violating professional ethics by soliciting clients and inciting litigation. "The 'p' in NAACP means 'Pick the Place, Prepare the setting, Procure the Plaintiffs, and Push them forward like Pawns,'" thundered the attorney general of Texas. A few lawyers were disbarred. Most survived, but they were virtually paralyzed by the costly, time-consuming necessity of defending themselves in court.[35]

The attacks of the ultrasegregationists never stopped. Seven states appointed committees to investigate and harass the NAACP. Faculty members at Florida A&M, including university president George W. Gore, were grilled about their civil rights activities. An investigation of the NAACP at South Carolina State College provoked a student strike that caused five teachers to be fired and twenty-six students to be dismissed. Investigating committees routinely levelled baseless charges of communism. One even tried to link the NAACP with homosexuals.

By 1958 the NAACP was stymied throughout the South. Even its most famous victory, the admission of nine black children into Little Rock Central High School over the opposition of Governor Orval Faubus, proved to be more symbol than substance. The blatant defiance of Faubus, who had used the National Guard to prevent integration, and then encouraged mobs to physically harass the children, compelled President Dwight D. Eisenhower to dispatch troops in order to enforce the court's order. Yet this massive display of force—the troops remained in Little Rock for the duration of the school year—did not settle the issue. Little Rock closed its schools in 1958–59. Moreover, Orval Faubus, far from suffering a loss of public support, coasted to victory in his 1958 reelection campaign. The result stunned the NAACP: Faubus had been a political moderate, even a liberal; few had expected strong opposition to integration in Arkansas. Roy Wilkins, who became head of the

NAACP upon Walter White's death in 1955, warned members to brace themselves for worse. "We must recognize that the Faubus victory will have an effect far beyond the borders of Arkansas."[36]

Brown is one of the most written-about and analyzed Supreme Court decisions in the history of the United States. Some historians have disparaged the ruling, arguing that it had little substance and little effect. Without support from the president and the Congress, the decision meant little; moreover, it placed the entire burden of securing implementation upon the shoulders of vulnerable black plaintiffs. *Brown* "resembled nothing more than an order for the infantry to assault segregation without prospect of air and artillery support," writes J. Harvie Wilkinson III. Small wonder it took at least ten years before even token integration occurred in the South, and at least fifteen until Mississippi and other states in the Deep South took the decision seriously.[37]

Perhaps the Court should have heeded Justices Black and Douglas and ordered immediate integration. Violent resistance would occur in the Deep South anyway, they predicted, and appeasing the ultrasegregationists would only encourage the opposition, not diminish it. That is indeed what happened. Yet faced with white intransigence, the Court backed away from even the weak pronouncements of *Brown II*. Between 1955 and 1968, writes Wilkinson, "the Court abandoned the field of public school desegregation. Its pronouncements were few . . . and its leadership was almost nonexistent."[38]

To left-wing skeptics, *Brown* illustrated the destructiveness of anticommunism, as well as the folly of the NAACP's reliance upon the courts. True, the association's vigorous anticommunism enabled it to curry favor with the federal government. But the federal government proved to be a most unreliable ally. Eisenhower privately disapproved of *Brown*; Congress did absolutely nothing to enforce it. Moreover, when the white South attacked the NAACP, the federal government, with the laudable exception of a few federal judges, declined to defend it. Without the kind of mass action pioneered by the Communist Party and developed by the CIO, litigation alone was bound to fail.

All these criticisms have weight. Yet for all its messy and disappointing consequences, the *Brown* decision still turned out to be a turning point in the struggle for black equality. It destroyed the legal basis for racial segregation. It inspired blacks with the knowledge that the Supreme Court was on their side. And it compelled a reluctant Eisenhower to use federal power to overrule state power. Like a Newtonian law of politics, the NAACP's campaign against segregation was bound to precipitate an equal and opposite white reaction. That reaction did not indicate failure: it showed that the Civil Rights Movement needed new tactics, broader support, and deeper commitment in order to push the struggle forward.

Rosa Parks being fingerprinted, Montgomery, Alabama, December 1, 1955

AP/Wide World Photos

11

The Nonviolent Rebellion, 1955–60

THE MONTGOMERY BUS BOYCOTT, 1955–56

At the beginning of the twentieth century, blacks in Southern cities, including Montgomery, had refused to ride in newly segregated streetcars. Those long-forgotten protests petered out in failure. The Montgomery bus boycott, which began on December 5, 1955, lasted for 381 days and ended in a resounding victory.

Initiated in response to the arrest of Mrs. Rosa Parks, who refused a bus driver's peremptory order to give up her seat, the Montgomery bus boycott mobilized the entire black population of Alabama's capital city. About 50,000 men, women, and children walked to work, gave each other lifts, and even on the coldest, wettest days refused to ride the buses. Prosecuted with a degree of unity that had never been seen before, the boycott astounded the world, and even surprised the black people of Montgomery. For Martin Luther King, Jr., "It was the most amazing thing I've ever seen in my life."[1]

In some ways it was the obstinacy of the whites in Montgomery, not the deliberate planning of the blacks, that turned the boycott into an international *cause célèbre*. After all, blacks in Montgomery asked only for a fairer application of "separate but equal," not an end to segregation itself. There had been a bus boycott in Baton Rouge, Louisiana, two years beforehand, which had ended after a week because both sides agreed to a compromise within segregation. But the refusal of Montgomery's white leaders to yield even modest concessions not only prolonged the boycott beyond anyone's expectations, but also prompted blacks to demand complete integration. In a similar way, Martin Luther King, Jr., only emerged as the symbol of the protest when whites began to persecute him. Whites calculated that by breaking King they could break the boycott; instead, they made King a martyr, a hero, and the outstanding symbol of black resistance.

To conclude that blacks in Montgomery merely reacted to white intransigence, however, is to profoundly misunderstand the significance of the bus boycott. The place may have been fortuitous, the leader accidental, and the event "unplanned," but the Montgomery bus boycott was both a logical extension of the developing black freedom struggle and a historical breakthrough.

The Montgomery bus boycott could have happened virtually anywhere in the South. Black resentment of bus segregation was intense and widespread; scarcely a week went by without a black passenger being arrested. And although few people noticed at the time, black protests about bus segregation were increasingly common. On May 18, 1953, for example, about a thousand blacks in Richmond, Virginia, held a public meeting to protest against a string of bus-related arrests: seven people had been recently jailed for refusing to move back. On May 21, 1954—five days after the *Brown* decision—the mayor of Montgomery received a letter from Jo Ann Robinson, president of the Women's Political Council (WPC), seeking better treatment for black passengers. "Even now," Robinson warned, "plans are being made to ride less, or not at all, on our busses."[2]

If the Montgomery bus boycott was an event waiting to happen, the people who instigated it acted from well-founded convictions. Rosa Parks never went beyond eighth grade, but her years at Montgomery Industrial School for Girls, an elementary school started in 1886 by two New England women, profoundly influenced her. Housed in an antebellum mansion, the school enrolled over three hundred girls and employed ten teachers, all of them white women. "What I learned best," Rosa Parks remembered, "was that I was a person with dignity and self-respect, and I should not set my sights lower than anybody else just because I was black." In 1943 Parks joined the NAACP and served for many years as secretary of the Montgomery branch. Only a few months before her arrest, she attended a school desegregation "workshop" at the Highlander Folk School in Monteagle, Tennessee, at the suggestion of Virginia Durr, a white veteran of the Southern Conference for Human Welfare. Highlander was founded in 1932 as a labor school; in the 1950s it focused on racial equality.[3]

Edgar Daniel Nixon, one of the primary organizers of the boycott, was probably the most prominent black activist in Montgomery. A fifty-six-year-old Pullman car porter, Nixon was a stalwart of the Brotherhood of Sleeping Car Porters who idolized A. Philip Randolph. He served as president of the

Montgomery NAACP between 1946 and 1950 and had also headed the state organization. In addition to founding the Montgomery Voters League, he was the perennial head of the Progressive Democratic Association, a black political organization. A bluff, plain-spoken man, Nixon was the person to whom many blacks turned when they were harshly treated by white authority.[4]

Jo Ann Robinson, another prime mover, was a professor of English at Alabama State College. Having experienced humiliating treatment at the hands of a bus driver, she had long awaited a propitious opportunity to strike a blow against bus segregation. The moment she learned of Parks's arrest, she enlisted the Women's Political Council to spread the word. Working throughout the night over a mimeograph machine at Alabama State College, Robinson and a few helpers printed thousands of flyers announcing a boycott. The women of the WPC—about three hundred people—distributed them throughout Montgomery.[5]

The speed and enthusiasm with which the black community mobilized in support of the boycott underlines the point: blacks were initiating, not simply reacting. On Friday, December 2, E. D. Nixon called a meeting to involve black ministers and to plan a mass meeting for the evening of the boycott. On Sunday, ministers announced these plans from their pulpits. The following afternoon a committee was formed, resolutions drafted, and officers elected. The Montgomery Improvement Association (MIA), the boycott organization, scheduled a mass meeting on Monday evening in order to test popular support for the boycott. Black leaders from Birmingham, Tuscaloosa, and Mobile were contacted; they promised their support.

When white newspaper reporter Joe Azbell arrived at Holt Street Baptist Church for the December 5 mass meeting, he had to fight his way through thousands of people—the building was jammed, and as many people stood outside as inside. Writing in the *Montgomery Advertiser*, Azbell described, almost in awe, the fervent prayers, soaring hymns, and rousing speeches that "thundered through the church." The combination of emotional religion and "almost a military discipline," he thought, demonstrated that blacks possessed a capacity for united action that few whites had suspected. In fact, white ignorance of the black community ran deep. Azbell failed to identify any of the speakers—not even the pastor of Dexter Avenue Baptist Church, a modest but distinguished looking red-brick building that stood in plain view of, and only a hundred yards from, the Alabama Capitol.[6]

The selection of Martin Luther King, Jr., as president of the Montgomery Improvement Association owed little to personal ambition or community influence. Only twenty-six years old, a native of Atlanta who had moved to Montgomery in 1954, King was still something of an unknown quantity. Because of the swiftness with which he was nominated and elected—without opposition—we shall never know who else besides King might have emerged as leader. E. D. Nixon was an obvious contender. Yet although widely respected, Nixon possessed little formal education and spoke in a gnarled dialect which, some believed, disqualified him from the position. The man who nominated King, Rufus Lewis, happened to be a rival of Nixon, as well as a member of King's church. Whatever Lewis's motive, it seems that longer-established ministers and leaders accepted King as a "neutral" figure who could bridge the factions. Besides, he was an articulate and well-educated man—he held a Ph.D. from Boston University—and Dexter Avenue Baptist Church, with its largely middle-class congregation, placed him at the heart of the black community.

King's hurriedly prepared speech at Holt Street Baptist Church was perfectly attuned to the excited mass meeting. Already an accomplished preacher, he precisely calibrated his words to sustain the emotion of the moment while instilling a sense of discipline, historical mission, and high moral purpose. "My friends," he began, "we are certainly happy to see each of you out this evening":

> We are here this evening for serious business. We are here in a general sense because first and foremost, we are American citizens, and we are determined to acquire our citizenship to the fullness of its meaning. We are here also because of our deep-seated belief that democracy transformed from thin paper to thick action is the greatest form of government on earth. But we are here in a specific sense because of the bus situation in Montgomery.

Negroes had been repeatedly humiliated, he reminded the audience, because of the mere fact that they were Negroes. Mrs. Rosa Parks, "one of the finest citizens in Montgomery," white or Negro, had been arrested and taken to jail for refusing to give up her seat to a white man. People were "tired of being trampled over by the iron feet of oppression . . . tired of being plunged into the abyss of humiliation." It was time to protest.

Astutely, King clothed the boycott in patriotism. In a Communist dictatorship, he averred, "we couldn't do this." But the right to protest was "the great glory of American democracy"; it was embedded in the Constitution. More fundamentally, he rooted the protest in the soil of Christianity. "We must keep God in the forefront. Let us be Christian in all of our actions." Yet talking about Christian love was not enough, he reminded the audience, for love had to be accompanied by justice. "And justice is really love in calculation. Justice is love correcting that which revolts against love." From the first, therefore, the ministers sought out the moral high ground, clearly distinguishing their protest from the coercive tactics of the white Citizens Councils and the violent actions of the Ku Klux Klan.

There was a harder edge to King's speech, however. King was not merely preaching from a black folk tradition: he also drew upon the education and training he had received at the university. Making a nod to Protestant theologian Reinhold Niebuhr, who dismissed moral suasion as ineffective unless undergirded by pressure, King warned that asking whites for justice would not be enough. "Not only are we using the tools of persuasion, but . . . we've got to use the tools of coercion. Not only is this thing a process of education, but it is also a process of legislation." Aware, perhaps, that he was addressing a predominantly working-class audience, King also invoked the struggle of labor unions to resist being "trampled over by capitalistic power." There had been "nothing wrong with labor getting together and organizing and protesting for its rights."[7]

The mass meeting voted to continue the boycott until such time as the MIA could "work out a solution" to their grievances. In fact, the MIA's demands could have been speedily adjusted. Blacks sought courteous treatment by bus drivers; the seating of black passengers from rear to front, and white passengers from front to rear, on a "first-come, first-served" basis, with no seats reserved for the exclusive use of either race; and the employment of black bus drivers on routes that went mainly through black neighborhoods. The first demand could be easily obtained, at least as a written commitment. The third demand was a "discard" that the MIA was prepared to sacrifice in order to secure the first two. The most contentious item was number two. Yet the "first-come, first-served" seating arrangement already operated in the Alabama city of Mobile, and it did not entail the scrapping of racial segregation.

Negotiations with bus company officials and members of the city council, however, proved fruitless. The whites insisted that they could not yield to the crucial "first-come, first-served" demand without violating state and city segregation laws. Moreover, in the wake of the *Brown* decision, white attitudes were hardening. Whites believed that abolishing the "reserved" seats for white people would erode the principle of racial segregation and encourage blacks to up their demands; concession would be tantamount to humiliating defeat. From their own perspective the whites were correct. If segregation *truly* embodied "separate but equal," it lost its point, which was to underline white supremacy. Rebuffed in the negotiations, the MIA learned what they already half-knew: that "separate but equal" was a myth.[8]

After the last round of negotiations sputtered out, the city tried to trick blacks into ending the boycott by falsely announcing that the issues had been "settled." The ruse failed. The three city commissioners then determined to break up the protest. They joined the white Citizens Council. The police began to harass, and sometimes arrest, the drivers who operated the "car pool," the MIA's efficiently organized transportation system that used private cars to ferry people to and from work. On January 26 King was arrested for speeding. Four day later, dynamite exploded on the porch of King's home and on the lawn of E. D. Nixon's—not the work of the city commissioners, to be sure, but certainly a consequence of their "get tough" policy.

All this backfired spectacularly. King's arrest incensed black people. "I'm so mad I don't know what to do," a store maid told a researcher from Fisk University. "Do you know those bastards put Rev. King in jail last night, and this morning they all parked on the corners asking folks how come they don't ride the bus?" Vowed another domestic: "I'll crawl on my face 'fo I get back on dem buses." The vehemence of such sentiments, and their universality, convinced the leadership of the MIA (an executive committee of about forty people) that they could not call off the boycott even if they wished to. Even when it poured with rain, one member pointed out, the people still walked. "If they don't want to go back, I don't see why we should decide otherwise." E. D. Nixon warned of the popular outrage that would ensue if they cancelled the protest—"I don't want to be here when you tell the people." King agreed. "If we went tonight and asked the people to get back on the bus, we would be ostracized. They wouldn't get back."[9]

The MIA then took a fateful decision that transformed the character of the boycott. The MIA's demand for "separate but equal" had failed to garner the support of the NAACP, which six years earlier had adopted a policy of across-the-board opposition to segregation. With the backing of Thurgood Marshall and the NAACP, however, the MIA agreed to challenge the segregation laws in federal court. The protest was no longer a local affair seeking minor adjustments within segregation: it now became the cutting edge of the struggle for integration across the South. The MIA knew full well that this direct challenge to segregation would entail danger, sacrifice, hardship, and further months of protest. Yet the mass meetings were generating such emotional power—not to mention about $2,000 a week—that leaders felt absolutely confident that the protest would endure.

Traditionally, Southern whites had defeated black protests through intimidation, economic pressure, violence, prosecution, and trickery. Whites in Montgomery employed all of these tactics. Yet the dynamic of Southern race relations was now miraculously reversed: instead of undermining the boycott, white harassment strengthened it. This effect was so marked, in fact, that blacks learned a basic lesson that they applied over and again during the next ten years: white repression could be turned to their advantage. In responding to harassment, arrests, bombings, and indictments, the MIA demonstrated a sure-footed ability to retain both the tactical initiative and the moral advantage. For example, when a grand jury indicted 115 people, including two dozen ministers, the black community put on a show of solidarity that utterly defeated the intended effect of the prosecution. After deputies started making arrests, those under indictment decided to turn themselves in. Instead of cowering in their homes or fleeing the city, the MIA leaders boldly marched up, one by one, to the police station. "You are looking for me?" E. D. Nixon asked a startled officer. "Here I am." As others presented themselves, a crowd of black supporters, dressed in their Sunday finest, applauded, cheered, and laughed. "The most disappointed people in Montgomery were Negro leaders who were not indicted," recalled Rev. Robert Graetz.[10]

Blacks marvelled at the stupidity of the indictments. Nothing could have been better calculated to arouse the ire of ordinary people than the prosecution of their ministers. At a mass meeting on February 23, more than 2,000 blacks answered the indictments with resounding support for the boycott. "They chanted and sang," wrote one reporter, "they shouted and prayed. . . . They pledged themselves again and again to 'passive resistance.'" In due course King was tried and convicted, but the city, recognizing the self-defeating nature of its tactics, suspended the other trials while King appealed his verdict.[11]

White persecution failed for another reason: it helped turn the Montgomery bus boycott into an international story. Not since the Scottsboro trials of the early 1930s had so many reporters gathered in one place in the South to cover a racial story. Dozens of reporters from across the country, and some from Europe, converged on Montgomery. The boycott made the front page of the *New York Times* and the cover of *Time* magazine. With publicity, nearly all of it favorable, came moral and financial support. The MIA was deluged with telegrams and letters of support, many of them containing donations. Black churches held collections and forwarded the proceeds. Union branches did the same. Checks arrived from abroad, including one from Canon John Collins of St. Paul's Cathedral, who helped to mobilize support from Britain's anti-apartheid movement. The week after the indictments, $12,000 poured in from outside.

The Montgomery bus boycott continued for nine more months, and whites fought integration every step of the way. But the unity of the black population, although severely tested, was never again in doubt. In June 1956 a three-judge federal court ruled in *Browder* v. *Gayle* that city and state bus segregation laws were unconstitutional. In November the Supreme Court affirmed the decision. On December 20, when the order finally became effective, the MIA ended the boycott. Returning to the buses, black passengers sat wherever they pleased.

It seemed like a small gain for such a mammoth effort; then and now, people have questioned the significance of the bus boycott. The NAACP, which deeply resented the fact that the MIA refused to accept its leadership, flatly maintained that the lawsuit, not economic pressure or mass popular protest, brought about integration. Several historians have echoed this view, arguing that the Supreme Court was about to rule against bus segregation anyway, and that the bus boycott was incidental to its decision. Moreover, the boycott did not end bus segregation throughout the South: many other cities ignored the Supreme Court and continued to enforce it, in some cases until the 1960s. Even in Montgomery, a feeling of letdown ensued, and the MIA became bogged down in factionalism, achieving little else of substance.[12]

Yet although there had been dozens of legal challenges to segregated trains and buses in the previous decades, segregation had persisted. As the NAACP's Roy Wilkins had admitted in 1946, even favorable court rulings often had little effect: "Decisions on paper mean nothing unless the people act to enforce them." The Montgomery bus boycott showed how black people could circumvent the legal impasse of massive resistance through mass action.[13]

If *Brown* was the legal turning point in the struggle for black equality, the Montgomery bus boycott was the psychological turning-point. Ten years earlier, Thurgood Marshall had predicted that nonviolent protests in the South would lead to "wholesale slaughter." Yet one of the striking features of the bus boycott had been the relative absence of violent retaliation on the part of the whites. Unity really had brought strength; the paralyzing fear of white persecution lifted. "Strange," one visitor noted. "Whites are scared stiff and Negroes are cool as cucumbers." The spiritual and institutional strength of the black church proved to be a powerful force. For the first time since Reconstruction, the fight for equality became a true "movement"—a people's affair that directly engaged the masses of everyday, ordinary folk. Montgomery truly was the birthplace of the Civil Rights Movement.[14]

MARTIN LUTHER KING, JR., AND THE SOUTHERN CHRISTIAN LEADERSHIP CONFERENCE

The Southern Christian Leadership Conference (SCLC), founded in January 1957, attempted to capitalize on the momentum of the Montgomery bus boycott. Composed mainly of black ministers, it cemented the new union between the black church and the civil rights struggle. Based entirely in the South, it harnessed the pride that black Southerners felt when they organized and controlled their own efforts. Wedded to nonviolence, it melded black Christianity with the Gandhian concept of mass direct action, aiming to replicate the Montgomery example throughout the region. Led by Martin Luther

King, Jr., it utilized the fame and talent of a young leader who had become the symbol of the Montgomery bus boycott.

The SCLC attempted to fill the void left by the repression of the NAACP; Alabama, where the NAACP had to cease all operations, became the SCLC's principal base. By not soliciting dues-paying members, however, the SCLC also went some way toward mollifying the NAACP's hostility toward a rival organization.

Yet the SCLC was not simply a substitute for the NAACP; it represented something new and different. For one thing, it was an indigenous Southern movement—a deliberate effort to cultivate strength and assertiveness among black Southerners, as well as to parry charges that the Southern struggle was controlled by Northerners. In the second place, SCLC was based upon the black church. The emphasis upon Christianity situated the organization "above" politics and appealed to the most cherished of American values. It made the organization far less vulnerable to the kind of state repression that had crippled the NAACP—as one group of black ministers put it, "No earthly authority has any right to interfere with the minister in the discharge of his duties." The SCLC's loose structure afforded another layer of protection: it had no individual members, hence no membership lists.[15]

Apart from these shrewd tactics, the choice of name also accurately described the organization's basic personality. Baptist ministers, "Southern Christian leadership," comprised the SCLC's heart, soul, and backbone. In addition to King, they included C. K. Steele, leader of the Tallahassee, Florida, bus boycott; Fred L. Shuttlesworth, head of the Birmingham-based Alabama Christian Movement for Human Rights; Joseph L. Lowery, who led a similar group in Mobile; and Ralph D. Abernathy, King's close friend and a leading figure in the MIA. These men were not representative of the black church in the sense of being typical: the great majority of black ministers steered clear of political activism. Yet because they were in some respects the "best and the brightest" among the clergy, they exercised an influence disproportionate to their small numbers.

Although the SCLC was a homegrown Southern movement, King came to rely upon a small group of Northern advisers to help him breathe life into the organization. Early in the Montgomery bus boycott, King had demonstrated his openness to outside expertise. "King runs out of ideas quickly," noted Glenn Smiley, an official of the Fellowship of Reconciliation. "He wants help, and we can give it to him without attempting to run the movement or pretend we know it all." In the early months of the Montgomery bus boycott, Smiley, a white man, helped persuade King to get rid of his armed guards and to embrace nonviolence. Another pacifist who came to Montgomery armed with advice, Bayard

Rustin, a black man, reinforced King's commitment to nonviolence and developed a close and important relationship with him. Rustin, the executive director of the War Resisters League, was seventeen years King's senior, and had a wealth of experience in pacifist and civil rights organizations. King and Rustin quickly forged a partnership that lasted, with ups and downs, until King's assassination in 1968.[16]

A chain-smoking Quaker who liked to sing folk songs and play the guitar, Bayard Rustin was an unusual combination of the practical and the idealistic. After a youthful spell in the Communist Party, he had worked with A. Philip Randolph in the March on Washington Movement, and after the war in Randolph's League for Nonviolent Civil Disobedience Against Military Segregation. In each case he denounced Randolph for ending the campaign too soon but somehow managed to remain in his mentor's good graces. Rustin's pacifism earned him two years in a federal prison during World War II. After the war he visited India and became known in America as a leading expert on Gandhi. In 1947 he took part in a protest against segregation on interstate buses, the "Journey of Reconciliation." It landed him on a North Carolina chain gang. His individual stands against discrimination—in restaurants, on buses, in jail—cost him innumerable beatings. A garrulous intellectual, Rustin was also an indefatigable organizer who gave King very practical assistance. He raised money, drafted speeches, "ghosted" articles, wrote leaflets, suggested slogans, devised tactics, and put King in touch with a wide array of Northern supporters. And with two of his political associates from New York, Ella J. Baker and Stanley D. Levison, Rustin helped King sketch out the basic structure of the SCLC.

The basic idea was simple. The SCLC would promote mass action throughout the South—not only encouraging bus boycotts but also attacking segregation and disfranchisement across a broad front. While it disclaimed any desire to compete with the NAACP, the architects of the SCLC were highly critical, in private, of the NAACP's failure to utilize its large membership, and believed that the NAACP's litigation strategy was narrow, unimaginative, and ineffective. Veterans of the New York left, they recalled the effectiveness of the Communist Party's Scottsboro campaign, the élan of the CIO's sit-down strikes, and the brilliance of the March on Washington Movement of 1941. Baker, a black woman who had served as the NAACP's director of branches for five years, envisaged the SCLC as a counterweight to the increasingly conservative NAACP. Levison, a Jewish businessman and attorney, shared that perspective. When Roy Wilkins dismissed demonstrations as "blowing off steam," Levison retorted that "the steam propels a piston which drives the train forward."[17]

The role of Rustin, Baker, and Levison in founding the SCLC provided the origin of a canard that King was manipulated by Communists—or was even a

Communist himself. Like most activists of their generation, the trio of New Yorkers had been influenced by the Communist Party. Baker had rubbed shoulders with Communists, as New York intellectuals did in the 1930s, but she was also a friend of the archconservative journalist George Schuyler. In the early 1950s she cooperated with the NAACP's policy of *excluding* Communists. Very much a free spirit, she was more interested in promoting grassroots activism, in whatever form that took, than in serving an organization or political party. Rustin had indeed joined the Communist Party in the late 1930s, but he resigned in 1941 when the party demanded all-out support for the war—pacifism was his strongest allegiance. The politics of Stanley Levison, a self-effacing man who shunned publicity, were more mysterious. He had been close to the Communist Party, and may have been a secret supporter in the early 1950s. Yet by 1957 he regarded the party, by then a decaying shell, as an irrelevant nuisance. King himself had never so much as flirted with communism.

In a broader sense, however, conservative critics were correct to sense a strain of left-wing radicalism in King. Although only a child during the Great Depression, that economic catastrophe made an impression upon him; the mass poverty of the era starkly exposed the weaknesses of private enterprise and imbued King with what he described as "anticapitalistic feelings." As a seminary student, he was profoundly influenced by the theologian Walter Rauschenbusch, proponent of the Social Gospel and a harsh critic of industrial capitalism. In *Stride Toward Freedom,* his first book, King condemned Marx's "metaphysical materialism," "ethical relativism," and "strangulating totalitarianism." But in the same sentence he praised Marx for having exposed the weaknesses of capitalism, stimulated class consciousness among the masses, and challenged the conscience of the Christian churches. "[C]apitalism can lead to a practical materialism," King wrote, "that is as pernicious as the materialism taught by communism." His editor was alarmed by King's treatment of Marxism and argued that the evils of communism far outweighed the faults of capitalism. King agreed to revise the passage; nevertheless, the favorable references to Marx stayed in.[18]

If a person can be judged by the company he keeps, then it was surely no coincidence that King was drawn to a trio of New York radicals—people who were accustomed to thinking in Marxist categories and who regarded themselves, in the broad sense of the term, socialists. King's New York helpers provided a generational link between the Old Left of the 1930s and the Civil Rights Movement of the 1950s.

Yet King was nobody's puppet. It was a mark of his open-mindedness that King accepted Rustin's help despite both his Communist past and his publicly known homosexuality (arrested for having sex with two men in the back of a car, Rustin had been fired from the Fellowship of Reconciliation for his indiscretions). But King was sensible enough to realize that nothing would be more damaging to the Civil Rights Movement than the perception that it was controlled by Northern radicals. He insisted that the flamboyant Rustin remain in the background, and in 1960, when threatened with a red-baiting attack by the unscrupulous black politician Adam Clayton Powell, Jr., King banished Rustin from his inner circle. Three years later King dropped Levison, too, when the Kennedy administration, convinced that Levison was a Communist, pressured him to do so. King was an astute manager of people. "It was not so much we *directing* him," Levison recalled, "as we *working with* him and giving expression to ideals we knew he had."[19]

From the very start, in fact, King dominated the SCLC. While he lived, he was the SCLC's only president. The SCLC's thirty-three person board of directors functioned largely as a rubber stamp. A smaller executive committee wielded some influence, but King always—almost—had the last word. Not only was the SCLC synonymous with King, but also the organization promoted a personality cult that grew to excessive proportions.

Ella Baker, who agreed to set up an office in Atlanta and to serve as the SCLC's acting executive director, soon became highly critical of the organization's dependence upon King and failure to encourage a democratic mass movement. The SCLC's history consisted largely of King's comings and goings: King meeting Vice President Nixon, King meeting President Eisenhower, King attending Ghana's independence ceremonies, King addressing a "Prayer Pilgrimage" at the Lincoln Memorial, King receiving awards and honors. King's willingness to occupy center stage suggested, to Baker, a reprehensible degree of egotism and self-importance. Baker also found it difficult to work with black ministers, many of whom she regarded as pompous, arrogant, and sexist—qualities which, she believed, King himself personified. Certainly, the SCLC was the most male-dominated of all the civil rights organizations. Only one woman sat on its board of directors; apart from Baker herself, only a couple of women ever served in senior staff positions.

It is impossible to understand King's role in the SCLC, however, without reference to religious faith. The son and grandson of prominent Atlanta ministers, King entered the Baptist church almost as a matter of course. "Called to the pulpit" at eighteen, formally trained at Crozer Theological Seminary, and the recipient of a Ph.D. in systematic theology, King assumed the pastorate of Dexter Avenue Baptist Church without ever having experienced the kind of conversion experience that characterized the American evangelical tradition. Seven weeks into the Montgomery bus boycott, however, when threatening phone calls kept him from sleeping, King prayed over his kitchen table and sought God's help with a directness and earnestness born from despair.

At that moment I experienced the presence of the Divine as I had never experienced Him before. It seemed as though I could hear the quiet assurance of an inner voice saying: "Stand up for righteousness; stand up for truth and God will be at your side forever." Almost at once my fears began to go. My uncertainty disappeared. I was ready to face anything.

For the next twelve years King drew spiritual strength from that revelation. And while he often doubted his own worthiness for the role, he always returned to the belief that his leadership was providential.[20]

The concept of Christ-like leadership fit naturally within the culture of the black church. Indeed, messianic faith enabled many ministers who assumed leadership in the civil rights struggle to confront situations of extreme danger. Birmingham's Fred L. Shuttlesworth, for example, was just as convinced as King—perhaps more so—that he was an instrument of God's will. Only providential intervention, he believed, could account for how on Christmas Eve in 1956 he survived a bomb planted by the Ku Klux Klan, an explosion that wrecked his home but left Shuttlesworth virtually unscathed. "I know it was the hand of God," Shuttlesworth told reporters. "I know I was preserved for a purpose." Black churchgoers, too, found nothing strange in the idea of providential leadership: by suffering persecution in a just cause, their ministers followed the example of Jesus. King exploited his role as persecuted Christian to the hilt: every time he was bombed, attacked, and jailed, his reputation soared. There was nothing insincere about this stance: redemption through self-sacrifice lay at the heart of Christian theology.[21]

The SCLC's lack of internal democracy also reflected the structure of the black church. A Baptist preacher answered to no bishop or archbishop; although selected by the church deacons (and occasionally, like King's predecessor Vernon Johns, ousted by them) the minister's authority was seldom questioned. "The pastor's authority is not merely humanly conferred, but divinely sanctioned," King told his flock as soon as he arrived at Dexter. "Leadership never ascends from the pew to the pulpit, but . . . descends from the pulpit to the pew." To the pious women who filled most of the pews in black churches, the minister was a Jesus-like figure, to be obeyed and adored. The SCLC transferred the religious fervor of black Christians, and the prestige of the black minister, from the church to the Civil Rights Movement.[22]

The Montgomery bus boycott reinforced what King already sensed as a minister. "As I became involved," he explained, "and as people began to derive inspiration from their involvement, I realized that the choice leaves your own hands. The people expect you to give them leadership." Although often uncomfortable with the honors and adulation that he received, King recognized the symbolic value of his leadership: people needed to rally around a unifying figure. He knew, too, how much the SCLC's fortunes depended upon his own prestige.[23]

Sometimes cited as its Achilles' heel, the SCLC's dependence upon King was also its greatest strength. King's great eloquence enabled him to express the hopes and fears of black Southerners, as well as communicate those sentiments to white Americans, better than any other black leader. Wedded to the respect he commanded for his skillful leadership of the Montgomery bus boycott, his oratory evoked adulation and enthusiasm that translated into practical support for the Civil Rights Movement. When crisis situations demanded swift decisions, King could make them. Yet he consulted widely, patiently listened to different points of view, and set an example of commitment that unified rather than divided. Although perceived by whites as an emotional, even rabble-rousing, orator, King was actually a reserved, introspective man who, in Bayard Rustin's words, "was always struggling to make sure that he was trying to do the right thing in the right way."[24]

Between 1957 and 1960, however, the SCLC was more a hope than a reality. Lacking funds, it had no full-time staff except for Ella Baker and some clerical assistants. Coordinating the church-based "affiliates" in a common action program proved well-nigh impossible. A wave of bus boycotts failed to materialize—partly because, ironically, the Montgomery victory enabled blacks in Atlanta, New Orleans, and elsewhere to achieve integration through lawsuits alone. When Congress passed the 1957 Civil Rights Act, which empowered the Justice Department to sue biased voter registrars, and which created a Commission on Civil Rights to investigate complaints of discrimination, the SCLC shifted its emphasis to voting. However, its ambitious plan to mount a regional voter registration drive, a "Crusade for Citizenship," evoked only patchy local activity. "We are losing the initiative in the civil rights struggle," Ella Baker complained, because the SCLC was failing to "develop and use our major weapon—mass resistance."[25]

During these frustrating years of drift, however, King spread the gospel of nonviolence. Montgomery had shown that nonviolent direct action could unite blacks and disarm whites, he argued; litigation alone could not reform the South. In fact, despite an impression of apparent inactivity, the South witnessed several instances of nonviolent protest in the late 1950s—boycotts of downtown merchants in Tuskegee, Alabama, and Orangeburg, South Carolina; a full-blown bus boycott in Tallahassee, Florida, and a smaller-scale bus protest in Shreveport, Louisiana. And in 1958–59, albeit on the fringes of the South, members of NAACP Youth Councils in Wichita and Oklahoma City demanded to be served at department store lunch counters that customarily excluded blacks. Their "sit-ins" succeeded. Typically, however, the national leadership of the NAACP failed to capitalize on this initiative, having little faith in the efficacy of nonviolent direct action.

None of these scattered protests added up to a regional movement. Nevertheless, they furnished additional evidence that open defiance of white supremacy did not necessarily provoke a violent white retaliation. The extent to which King and the SCLC influenced the explosion of nonviolent direct action that occurred in 1960 is impossible to precisely measure. It is enough to state that they helped to popularize and legitimate what soon became the dominant strategy of the Civil Rights Movement.

The Student Sit-ins and the Formation of SNCC

As with Rosa Parks's refusal to yield her bus seat, early accounts of the protest that sparked off the student sit-in movement stressed the spontaneity of the act, and its lack of any connection with existing organizations. In the sense that this interpretation underlines the indigenous, "grassroots" character of the sit-ins, the emphasis on spontaneity and independence is accurate. Yet it should not be overstated. The sit-ins were the products of thought as well as feeling, of communities as well as individuals. The decision of four black college students to order cups of coffee at a Woolworth's counter in downtown Greensboro, North Carolina, was not only a carefully considered action, but was also, in the words of historian William Chafe, "a dramatic extension of, rather than a departure from, traditional patterns of black activism in Greensboro."[26]

The students—Joseph McNeill, Ezell Blair, Jr., Franklin McCain, and David Richmond did not decide upon the precise format of their protest until shortly before their sit-in. Yet the quartet had long talked of taking *some* direct, dramatic stand against segregation. They drew upon many influences, including their religious beliefs, their study of black history, their activity in the NAACP, their impressions of Gandhi, King, and the Montgomery bus boycott, and, of course, their personal experiences of racial discrimination. They were encouraged, too, by the advice and support of several older people. By the time they took the plunge on February 1, 1960, seating themselves on vacant stools at the white-only lunch counter, they knew precisely what they were doing. "The scenario had been well rehearsed," writes Chafe. The foursome made sure to arrange for a newspaper reporter to be on hand. Refused service by a black waitress ("Fellows like you make our race look bad"), the four refused to budge. A photographer from the *Greensboro Record* pictured the four young men sitting there, looking grimly determined.[27]

The sit-in evoked an immediate response from fellow students at North

Carolina A&T University. The following day, twenty-nine students sat-in. On day three, students occupied all but two of the sixty-five available seats. By Friday, day five, the protest involved more than three hundred students, and the sit-ins had spread to a nearby S. H. Kress store. On Saturday, as yet more students flocked downtown, both Woolworth and Kress closed their doors. The Greensboro sit-in quickly became a national news item, and the topic of the hour on black college campuses. Within days, sit-ins were happening in Raleigh, Durham, Winston-Salem, and High Point. They quickly spread to adjacent states: Virginia, South Carolina, and Tennessee. In March and April, students in the Deep South joined the act, staging sit-ins in Tallahassee, Montgomery, and Baton Rouge. Every Southern state, including Mississippi, witnessed these extraordinary acts of defiance. According to one tally, during 1960 about 70,000 students participated in the sit-ins in one way or another. The speed with which black students emulated the example of Greensboro transformed a local protest into a regional movement.

"This is a new stage in the struggle," Stanley Levison wrote King. "It begins at the higher point where the Montgomery bus boycott left off." Not only was the sit-in movement regional in scope, but the character of the individual protests involved a much more direct confrontation with segregation. If boycotts were passive, sit-ins were assertive. Students physically challenged segregation, placing their bodies directly in the way of Jim Crow. They did so, moreover, with no reassurance that the federal courts would back them up: stores were privately owned institutions and, unlike public transportation, it was not at all clear that the *Brown* principle applied to them. Basing their actions on morality, not legality, the students challenged one of America's most sacred cows: the sanctity of private property.[28]

The sit-ins also entailed a struggle over public space. Black students backed up sit-ins by picketing stores and by staging marches and rallies. Such actions boldly challenged the unwritten rule that the South's streets, squares, and sidewalks belonged to white people, not blacks. Public demonstrations by black people were virtually unheard-of—only ten years earlier, civil rights groups had dismissed them as suicidal. Yet black students now braved the threat of police brutality and mob violence to assert the right of peaceful assembly. As with the sit-ins themselves, however, the legal basis of their actions was far from solid. As interpreted by the courts, the First Amendment provided far less protection to public demonstrations, including peaceful picketing, than it did to free speech and freedom of the press.

The willingness to brave white mobs and to defy the police distinguished the sit-ins from the Montgomery bus boycott. The students placed themselves in a vulnerable position that required considerable courage. In many places hostile whites, undeterred and even encouraged by the police, shoved, kicked, and punched demonstrators, poured ketchup on their heads, and thrust lighted cigarettes against their bodies. In the cities of the Deep South, including Montgomery, police forcibly broke up public protests, sometimes using tear gas, and automatically arrested all sit-in demonstrators. All told, about 3,600 students were arrested during 1960 for offenses such as criminal trespass, breach of the peace, and disorderly conduct.

The sit-ins did not, at first, evoke wholehearted support from older blacks. "A lot of our people don't seem to understand what the young people are doing," confessed Rev. Solomon S. Seay, an MIA stalwart. Indeed, many parents chided their children for imperiling their hard-earned chance to acquire a college education. His parents were "shocked and ashamed" when he was jailed, recalled John Lewis, a young man from Alabama then in Nashville studying for the ministry. "My mother made no distinction between being jailed for drunkenness and being jailed for demonstrating for civil rights." It took years for parents and son to be reconciled. In Baton Rouge, a student boycott of Southern University divided the black community, many of whom, fearing the destruction of a revered black institution, withdrew their support from the protests. Some black college presidents, including Felton Clark of Southern and II. C. Trenholm of Alabama State, expelled student leaders at the behest of white politicians.[29]

Yet the generational divide soon narrowed. Older blacks, for the most part, rallied behind the students' cause, setting aside doubts about their tactics. Adults raised bail money, and backed the sit-ins by supporting boycotts of downtown stores. Moreover, many black college presidents, including heads of state-funded institutions, *did* support the students. For example, the president of North Carolina A&T, Warmoth T. Gibbs, refused to take any disciplinary action against the students who staged the Greensboro sit-in. To youngsters who regarded him as an aging Uncle Tom, his stand defied expectations. Yet Gibbs, a World War I veteran and an authority on the history of Reconstruction—he was named after Henry C. Warmoth, a Republican governor of Louisiana—was acting upon deeply held beliefs.

Even the NAACP, which on one level viewed the sit-in movement as another unwelcome challenge to its organizational hegemony, supported the student protests. Reluctant to employ the sit-in tactic itself, the association nevertheless urged its members to support the sit-ins through picketing and boycotts. Thurgood Marshall's endorsement was especially significant. Despite strong reservations about direct action—he once said that a lawyer's job was to get clients out of jail, not get them in—Marshall praised the students, condemned college presidents like Felton Clark, and committed the services of the NAACP Legal Defense and Educational Fund (popularly known as the "Inc. Fund") to the defense of arrested students.

Like the Montgomery bus boycott, the sit-ins also evoked warm sympathy from many white people in the North. Northern press reports of the sit-ins were overwhelmingly positive. An NBC documentary, "The Nashville Sit-in Story," portrayed the black protesters as committed, earnest, and religious. "It was a powerful piece of television," recalled John Lewis, "broadcast nationally in prime time." The students' nonviolent discipline, dignified demeanor, middle-class values, and commitment to Christianity as well as democracy impressed conservatives and liberals alike. Eleanor Roosevelt lauded the students as champions of democracy. *Time* magazine hailed the sit-ins as a "non-violent protest the likes of which the U.S. had never seen." President Eisenhower said that the students were standing up for American values. On the campuses of Northern universities, students were thrilled by the bravery and initiative of the South's black collegians; they collected money, picketed Northern branches of Woolworth, and drummed up moral support. Harry Truman condemned the sit-ins as Communist agitation, but his opinion was widely dismissed in the North as the eccentric musings of a crusty old man.[30]

Perhaps the most striking fact about the moral effect of the sit-ins was that it reached some white Southerners. Arch-segregationist James J. Kilpatrick, editor of the *Richmond News-Leader,* conceded nothing to the demonstrators' goals, but contrasted their smart dress and impeccable behavior with the white youths—"a ragtail rabble, slack-jawed, black-jacketed, grinning fit to kill"—who taunted and harassed them. In New Orleans, television news editor Bill Monroe praised the students' sincerity and urged whites not to be alarmed by them or try to suppress them. "The feeling among Southern Negroes against segregation," he added, in a powerful understatement, "is more widespread than some officials like to admit." In Florida, in a televised speech, Governor LeRoy Collins insisted that the sit-ins were raising basic moral issues. "We can never stop Americans struggling to be free," he told Floridians. A white store owner might have the legal right to refuse service to black people, "but I still don't think he can square that right with moral, simple justice." The speech effectively ended Collins's career as an elected politician.[31]

Some white Southerners even took the radical step of joining the Civil Rights Movement. In Greensboro, Tallahassee, New Orleans, and elsewhere, white students sat-in, walked on picket lines, and went to jail. Whites joined CORE chapters, which multiplied dramatically in the wake of the sit-ins. They also joined SNCC—the Student Nonviolent Coordinating Committee—a new organization (see page 245). Most of these white students, moreover, were Southern-born-and-bred: people like Hugh Murray, from a working-class family in New Orleans; Robert Zellner, son of an Alabama minister; Joan Browning, raised on a farm in south Georgia; and Connie Curry, who grew up in Greensboro, the daughter of an Irish-born businessman. They were few in number, to be sure. Yet in the context of the Jim Crow South, this incipient interracialism represented a revolutionary challenge to white supremacy.

The sit-in movement made a massive dent in the structure of segregation. In the Deep South, crushed by violence and arrests, they failed to integrate lunch counters. But in the upper South, and in the "rim South" states of Florida and Texas, they proved effective. The disruption caused by the sit-ins themselves, and the economic impact of consumer boycotts, hurt the dime stores: the profits of Woolworth, the main target, plummeted. Downtown merchants as a group also suffered. The cash-register logic of the sit-ins proved hard to resist: on March 19, 1960, San Antonio, Texas, became the first city in the South to desegregate its lunch counters; Nashville did so in May; by the end of the year store owners in at least eighty other towns and cities had agreed to serve blacks. In 1961 the sit-in movement gained a beach-head in the Deep South when Atlanta merchants agreed to integrate. In 1962, after a tenacious boycott of Canal Street, store owners in New Orleans agreed to open eating facilities to black customers.

On April 15–17, 1960, about two hundred people, most of them black stu dents from the South, met at Shaw University, in Raleigh, North Carolina, to discuss the significance of the sit-ins and decide how best to capitalize on the breakthrough. The conference was organized by Ella Baker, the SCLC provided funding, and King was one of the principal speakers. There was some expectation, therefore, that if the students formed a new organization, they would affiliate it with the SCLC. Baker, however, deeply disillusioned with King—"the prophetic leader [who] turns out to have heavy feet of clay"—believed that any attempt to subject the students to older leadership would stifle the energy and enthusiasm of the sit-in movement. She urged the students to go it alone and, in a not-so-veiled dig at King, advised them to develop "group-centered leadership" rather than a "leader-centered group." The students wanted it that way anyhow. Veterans of the sit-ins, many of them "jail-birds," they were proud of what they had initiated, confident of their own abilities, and somewhat skeptical of older black leaders. Refusing to surrender their independence, they established the Student Nonviolent Coordinating Committee (SNCC).[32]

SNCC quickly outgrew its origins. It acquired a permanent staff of full-time workers and began to initiate actions of its own. Yet its beginnings in the student sit-in movement molded its character. It was Southern and it was largely (although not wholly) black. It prided itself on informality, lack of hierarchy, looseness of structure, and commitment to internal democracy. It liked to arrive at decisions through discussion and consensus, not by voting. It abhorred factionalism and politicking. It deplored the SCLC's "cult of leadership," and consciously developed a kind of *anti*leadership principle. SNCC attracted some strong personalities, but it did not permit any one leader, or even group of leaders, to dominate the organization. Although it recruited several older staff members ("older" in this context meaning anyone over the age of twenty-five) SNCC remained youth-oriented. Only Ella Baker, who served as an "adult adviser" and played a key role in getting SNCC off the ground, represented a different generation altogether—indeed, she was two generations older than many of the students.

The fact that Baker enjoyed a respect in SNCC that she had been denied in the SCLC symbolized another difference between the two organizations: SNCC was far less male-dominated. From the start, women held positions of responsibility. Connie Curry served as an adult adviser. Jane Stembridge became SNCC's first administrator. Diane Nash and Ruby Doris Smith took part in the demonstrations, went to jail, and enjoyed more authority and respect than most of the male staff members. In these years before the Women's Movement, conservative ideas about gender roles were bound to influence the way young men and women behaved. Even so, SNCC proved remarkably receptive to the participation of women on something approaching equality.

SNCC included many young blacks who were devout Christians and committed Gandhians. A group of students from Nashville, in particular, had been profoundly influenced by James M. Lawson, Jr., a black Methodist minister, the same age as King, who had lived in India, served jail time as a conscientious objector during the Korean War, and in 1960 worked as a field secretary of the Fellowship of Reconciliation. Idealistic and religious, admirers of Lawson such as John Lewis, James Bevel, and Diane Nash made sure that SNCC adopted nonviolence as both a method and a philosophy. Other students had a more pragmatic and secular attitude to nonviolence. Some lacked religious faith, saw no need to "love" their oppressor, and did not share the Christian belief in the redemptive nature of unmerited suffering. Most viewed nonviolence as a practical necessity and a useful tool of protest, yet were unwilling to abjure self-defense under any and all circumstances. Debates about nonviolence and self-defense soon became a routine feature of SNCC staff meetings, their passion fueled by beatings suffered and murders witnessed.

Like the SCLC, SNCC believed that confrontation and direct action, not litigation, was the best way forward for the Civil Rights Movement. Unlike the SCLC, however, SNCC did little to disguise its disdain for the NAACP's methods. Indeed, relations between SNCC and the NAACP never really recovered from James Lawson's keynote address at the Raleigh conference in which he criticized "overreliance on the courts" and the "futile middle-class technique of sending letters to the centers of power." Yet SNCC's establishment, three years after the organization of the SCLC, clearly ended the NAACP's dominance over strategy. King had become the most influential black leader in the South. SNCC now established itself as the cutting-edge of the Civil Rights Movement.[33]

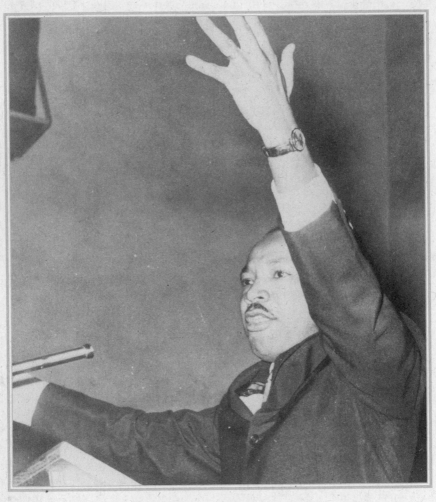

**Martin Luther King, Jr., preaching at a freedom rally,
Washington Temple Church, 1962**

Library of Congress, Prints and Photographs Division, NYWT&S Collection

12

The Civil Rights Movement, 1960–63

White supremacy, as a formal system, collapsed with such suddenness between 1963 and 1965 that one is tempted to conclude in hindsight that Jim Crow was a social, economic, and political anachronism, and that the Civil Rights Movement was pushing against an open door. Only extraordinary factors, one might think, delayed the movement's triumph: but for the Cold War, the South might have been liberalized nearly a generation earlier; but for the "checks and balances" of a rigid Constitution, the South's lack of democracy might never have endured for so long. In retrospect, it seems almost incredible that the United States should have tolerated a regional version of apartheid as late as the 1960s.

Yet before 1963 the triumph of the Civil Rights Movement did not look at all inevitable. It was far from obvious that nonviolent protests had the capability of transforming the South. Despite the formation of the SCLC and SNCC, and the revival of CORE, it proved immensely difficult to translate the energy of a local protest like the Montgomery bus boycott—or even a regional one like the student sit-ins—into a sustained, effective, South-wide movement. When nonviolent direct action was sporadic and localized, whites could usually contain it. In the Deep South, especially, whites appeared willing to go to great lengths—and to employ violence—in order to suppress it. The Civil Rights Movement suffered repeated reverses and appeared at times to be on the verge of collapse. Thus although court decisions and nonviolent direct action nibbled away at the Jim Crow edifice, the structure of segregation remained substantially intact until 1963. The Civil Rights Movement wielded moral power, but it possessed little political power. White manipulation of the registration procedures ensured that fewer than a third of the adult black population could vote in 1960—an impressive improvement on the 1940 figure of 3 percent, to be sure, but still too few to elect more than a score of black politicians. With their near-monopoly of political power, whites retained control of the police and the courts, which they used to buttress white supremacy and throttle black protests. White Southern voters, moreover, remained an integral part of the Democratic Party and, after flirting with the Dixiecrats in 1948 and the Republicans in 1952 and 1956, a sufficient number returned to the fold in 1960 to help elect a Democratic president, John F. Kennedy of Massachusetts.

The Civil Rights Movement believed that the moral rightness of its cause would sway Northern whites, and the federal government, to support it. It gradually became clear, however, that the Kennedy administration regarded a certain level of racist repression as politically acceptable. Only when the Civil Rights Movement learned how to solve that political predicament did it achieve a decisive breakthrough.

John F. Kennedy and the Politics of Civil Rights

Despite his obvious courting of Southern white voters, Kennedy's election imbued many black people with a sense of optimism. Part of this feeling was simply the "Kennedy effect." Americans of all backgrounds were charmed by Kennedy's wit, boyish good looks, and beautiful wife. They also found themselves stirred by Kennedy's forward-looking, idealistic-sounding rhetoric, and rather naively assumed that the youthful president understood what needed to be done and possessed the energy and wisdom to do it.

Black Americans had more substantial reasons for expecting good things of the Kennedy administration. Eisenhower had declined to exercise strong leadership in the cause of civil rights, and his lack of enthusiasm for the *Brown* decision, although expressed privately, was obvious to all. Kennedy publicly endorsed *Brown* and accepted the strong civil rights plank adopted by his party at the Democratic National Convention in 1960. Unlike its Republican counterpart, the Kennedy campaign team undertook a major effort to increase black voter registration and to maximize black turnout on Election Day.

Barely a week before the election, Kennedy boosted his popularity among black voters by intervening in the sit-in movement to help secure Martin

Luther King's release from jail. King had been arrested, along with fifty-one others, at Rich's department store in downtown Atlanta on October 1. Yet when the students left jail five days later—a settlement having been brokered by Mayor William B. Hartsfield—King remained incarcerated. It transpired that a few months earlier, Judge Oscar Mitchell had imposed a twelve-month suspended sentence on King for driving in Georgia on Alabama license plates. Mitchell now sentenced King to four months' hard labor for violating his probation.

A bewildered and frightened King, wearing shackles on his arms and legs, found himself being transported in the early hours of the morning to Reidsville state prison. In a plaintive letter to his wife, Coretta, he reported that he was "asking God hourly to give me the power of endurance." And he shared with Coretta his hope that "this excessive suffering that is now coming to our family will in some way serve to make . . . America a better country. Just how I do not yet know, but I have faith to believe it will." King's friends and supporters wired the two presidential candidates, Kennedy and Nixon, and demanded a response.[1]

Richard Nixon, the Republican candidate, had a good record on civil rights—better than Kennedy's. Moreover, he had met King on several occasions, and the two men respected each other. Nixon calculated, however, that any pro-King statement would alienate Southern whites, so he said nothing. The Democratic strategists, on the other hand, turned King's incarceration to their candidate's advantage. Kennedy placed a telephone call to Mrs. King expressing his personal concern about her husband's continuing detention. And his brother Robert called Judge Mitchell to ask that King be released on bail. "It made me so damn angry," Robert Kennedy recalled, "to think of that bastard sentencing a citizen to four months of hard labor for a minor traffic offense and screwing up my brother's campaign and making our country ridiculous before the world." His intercession, added to that of Governor Ernest Vandiver, did the trick; King left jail. King's father, a staunch Republican who had believed that Kennedy's Catholicism disqualified him from the presidency, told the press that he had a "suitcase of votes" and intended to "dump them in his lap." Milking the incident for all it was worth, the Democrats printed a leaflet entitled *"No Comment" Nixon versus a Candidate with a Heart, President Kennedy,* distributing about two million copies in black neighborhoods.[2]

Obviously, Kennedy's intervention in the King affair did not account for all of the 7 percent increase in Democratic support among black voters—from 61 percent in 1956 to 68 percent in 1960. But it certainly helped. As historian Steven F. Lawson notes, Nixon actually won 52 percent of the white votes;

without the black vote Kennedy would undoubtedly have lost the election, for fewer than 120,000 popular votes separated the two candidates.[3]

Yet Kennedy took pains to dampen black expectations. From the first, the new president made it clear that winning the Cold War remained his most urgent mission. When it came to depicting America's struggle against godless communism, Kennedy used overblown, moralistic, apocalyptic rhetoric—this was a cause for which Americans should "bear any burden, pay any price." When it came to racial injustice, however, Kennedy spoke dispassionately, as if analyzing a technical problem.

Kennedy's refusal to dramatize race as a moral issue was partly a matter of temperament, reflecting his cerebral, almost cynical, approach to politics. It also indicated a lack of imagination and empathy. The cultural and class distance between black Southerners and the fabulously wealthy, Harvard-educated, Boston-bred Kennedys could hardly be greater. As Robert Kennedy later drolly recalled, he and his brother had not "lied awake at night" worrying about the problems of blacks. John Kennedy knew that the problem of racial discrimination was serious, would not go away, and needed constant attention. But he treated it as a minor irritant rather than a major priority, and he delegated day-to-day responsibility for civil rights questions to his brother, whom he appointed attorney general.[4]

Kennedy knew very well, of course, that the civil rights issue had the potential to split the Democratic Party down the middle. It had divided the party in 1948 and had been an open sore throughout the 1950s. Convinced that civil rights presented political dangers without holding out the prospect of political rewards, Kennedy ruled out the passage of major civil rights legislation. In the Congress, especially the Senate, white Southerners controlled key committees and had the power to sidetrack bills and black appointments. If he pushed for strong action over public accommodations, employment, or voting rights, Kennedy would find the rest of his legislative program derailed, and to no effect. A canny, cautious politician, Kennedy had no inclination to mount a strong challenge to Jim Crow. Kennedy's civil rights program was therefore modest in scope. It relied upon executive action to combat racial discrimination within the federal government, strong backing for federal court decisions, and litigation by the Justice Department to advance black voting in the South. These steps held out no hope for an early end to segregation and disfranchisement.

THE FREEDOM RIDES

In a classic comment on the dynamics of Gandhian nonviolence, Bayard Rustin noted that "protest becomes effective to the extent that it elicits brutality and oppression from the power structure." That lesson was very hard for the Civil Rights Movement to swallow, and still harder to act upon. In 1960 it was not at all evident that white brutality could be turned to the movement's advantage. The Montgomery bus boycott had benefitted from the crass errors of the segregationist opposition, but it had seen all forms of violence as a threat. White violence had often defeated the student sit-in movement.[5]

The Freedom Rides of 1961, however, gave the clearest possible demonstration that the Civil Rights Movement could, in certain circumstances, reap huge dividends by deliberately evoking—critics said "provoking"—white violence. Launched by the Congress of Racial Equality on May 4, 1961, the Freedom Rides challenged segregation in interstate travel, which most Southern states continued to enforce despite a Supreme Court ruling of 1960 holding it to be unconstitutional.

The concept of the Freedom Rides was deceptively simple: an interracial group of thirteen volunteers would board two buses, a Greyhound and a Trailways, in Washington, D.C., having purchased tickets to New Orleans. Blacks and whites would sit together, and when the buses stopped, the group would use all the terminal facilities (waiting rooms, toilets, cafeterias) regardless of any racial restrictions. The catch, of course, was that CORE anticipated serious violence once the passengers entered the Deep South. The Freedom Riders were consciously placing their lives at risk in the hope that their suffering would arrest the nation's attention and force the Kennedy administration to intervene.

That is precisely what happened. Assaulted in Rock Hill, South Carolina, the Riders encountered mobs intent on murder when they entered Alabama. They were barely across the state line when a dozen white thugs boarded the Trailways bus, beat the Freedom Riders, and forced the blacks to sit in the back. The Greyhound bus reached Anniston only to be surrounded by enraged white men. The riders refused to disembark. Pursued by about fifty cars and pickup trucks and its tires slashed, the bus halted about six miles west of town. The driver fled. The pursuing vehicles disgorged white thugs, who threw a firebomb into the bus by smashing a window. With the bus in flames, the choking riders stumbled out. Only the presence of a plainclothes Alabama policeman, who waved his pistol at the attackers, saved the riders from being beaten and possibly killed. Fred Shuttlesworth organized a fifteen-car convoy to extricate them. The Trailways bus managed to reach Birmingham, but a crowd organized by the Ku Klux Klan awaited them at the terminal. The man in charge of the Birmingham Police Department, the ironically titled commissioner of public safety, Eugene "Bull" Connor, ensured that the mob had a good fifteen minutes to beat the riders before any police arrived to intervene.

The Freedom Rides ground to a halt, and not even Robert Kennedy, with all the power of the federal government at his command, could get the buses rolling again. "Somebody better get in the damn bus and get it going and get these people on their way," he barked at the Greyhound manager in Birmingham. But every bus driver adamantly refused to carry the battered passengers any further. "I have only one life to give," one driver told them, "and I'm not going to give it to the NAACP or CORE!" To Kennedy, the Freedom Riders were irresponsible incendiaries; moreover, he was incensed by the fact that the crisis in Alabama threatened to overshadow his brother's meeting in Vienna with Soviet leader Nikita Khrushchev. "Tell them to call it off!" he barked at Harris Wofford, his civil rights adviser. "Stop them!"[6]

The Civil Rights Movement, however, decided that the Freedom Rides should continue. Overcoming the misgivings of James Farmer, CORE's executive director—who regarded further protests as tantamount to suicide—Nashville student and SNCC founder Diane Nash insisted that the Freedom Rides would be a pointless failure if white violence went unchallenged. A second group of Freedom Riders set out from Nashville only to be arrested outside Birmingham, held overnight, and dumped by the police at the Tennessee state line. Undeterred, they quickly made their way back to Birmingham and purchased tickets to Montgomery. After Robert Kennedy personally negotiated with Greyhound officials to furnish transportation and interceded with Governor John Patterson to secure police protection, a bus took them out of Birmingham. When the bus arrived in Montgomery, however, the local police made no effort to prevent a waiting mob from assaulting the riders, three of whom sustained serious injuries. A Justice Department official, John Siegenthaler, was knocked unconscious in the melee.

The government had to intervene in spite of itself. For one thing, the refusal of Alabama governor John Patterson to curb mob violence exposed the impotence of the federal government in a highly embarrassing manner. Interstate travel fell clearly within the federal sphere of responsibility, and the government, faced with a similar challenge to that thrown out by Governor Orval Faubus in Little Rock, could scarcely back down. In addition, if the government failed to act, Freedom Riders stood to lose their lives in a highly public fashion. Although some Alabama law enforcement officers, notably Floyd Mann, director of the state highway patrol, did their best to keep the mobs in check, their efforts were nullified by politicians in Birmingham and Montgomery, who, egged on by Patterson, were determined to give the "bunch of rabble-outsiders" a bloody nose.[7]

On the evening of Sunday, May 21, the situation became critical. Several thousand hostile whites surrounded the First Street Baptist Church, where fifteen hundred blacks gathered to honor the Freedom Riders and hear speeches by Fred Shuttlesworth, Ralph Abernathy, and Martin Luther King. Faced with the prospect of wholesale mayhem, Robert Kennedy acted. While a small contingent of federal marshals kept the mob at bay, the attorney general pressured Governor Patterson to deploy the Alabama National Guard. With surly ill-grace, Patterson reluctantly agreed; shortly before dawn guardsmen escorted the weary and frightened people out of the church.

The Nashville contingent of Freedom Riders eventually left Montgomery with six National Guardsmen on the bus, dozens of highway patrol cars in front and behind, helicopters hovering overhead, and U.S. spotter planes surveying the convoy from on high. Yet if the Kennedy administration and the state authorities had hoped to say "goodbye and good riddance" to the Freedom Rides, they were soon disappointed. From Nashville, from Atlanta, from colleges across the South, students travelled to Alabama to keep the Freedom Rides going. Then came students from the North, professors from Ivy League universities, Jewish rabbis, and a group of Episcopalian ministers that included a son-in-law of Nelson Rockefeller, the governor of New York. The Freedom Riders, moreover, not only pledged to court arrest in Mississippi but also to stay in jail. Over the following months, 328 Freedom Riders were arrested for challenging segregation at the Jackson, Mississippi, bus terminal. Incarcerated at Parchman Farm, a state facility with a notorious record of prisoners beaten, tortured, and killed, a good number of the Freedom Riders served all, or a substantial part, of their two-month sentences.

The refusal of the Civil Rights Movement to accede to his request for a "cooling-off period" incensed the attorney general. So did the Freedom Riders' "jail-no-bail" tactic. "The fact that they stay in jail is not going to have the slightest effect on me," he lectured King. When King responded by warning that students might become Freedom Riders "by the hundreds and thousands," Kennedy frostily retorted: "Don't make statements that sound like a threat." Later, speaking to reporters, Kennedy derided the Freedom Riders as "the safest people on earth" and criticized them for providing "good propaganda for America's enemies." [8]

Yet if Kennedy remained icily unimpressed by the moral example of the Freedom Riders, he responded to the political pressure generated by their actions. He instructed the Justice Department to prod the Interstate Commerce Commission (ICC)—a lumbering bureaucracy with a lamentable record on civil rights—to ban segregation and discrimination in interstate travel. The ICC devised the ban in record time, and it became effective on November 1, 1961. The Freedom Rides had forced the Kennedy administration to act against its will. And they rescued CORE from insignificance, transforming it into a major civil rights organization that acquired the resources and personnel to establish a solid presence in half a dozen Southern states.

A signal victory for the Civil Rights Movement, the Freedom Rides bestowed heroic stature upon their participants. Far from breaking the Freedom Riders, Parchman Farm served as a veritable college for civil rights activists: people emerged stronger and more determined. "They were no longer the idealistic, inexperienced college students they had been at the beginning of the lunch counter sit-ins," writes historian Cynthia Griggs Fleming. "They were now experienced freedom fighters whose idealism had been tempered by experience." Many of the Freedom Riders who passed through Parchman Farm bristled with confidence that they could now take on Mississippi, the worst state in the South.[9]

The government's dealings with the white authorities in Mississippi, however, hinted at the limits of federal support for civil rights. The Justice Department did nothing to stop the arrests in Jackson. Indeed, assured by Governor Ross Barnett that the Freedom Riders would not be exposed to the kind of mob violence that had disgraced Alabama, Kennedy agreed to turn a blind eye. As the Civil Rights Movement escalated its attack on white supremacy, it encountered ever tougher and ever more violent opposition. But when it turned to the Kennedy administration for support and protection, it found, to its horror, that the federal government refused to act. Mississippi, a major focus of the Civil Rights Movement between 1961 and 1964, symbolized both the shallowness of the Kennedy civil rights policy and the vulnerability of activists to white brutality.

SNCC's Work in Mississippi, 1961–63

Widely regarded as the most oppressive state in its treatment of black people, Mississippi had the lowest rate of black voter registration in the South, only 5 percent. It also had the largest proportion of blacks to whites, and the greatest potential for black political power. Mississippi, therefore, became the obvious testing ground for the Kennedys' commitment to black voting rights; it ought to have been the centerpiece of their civil rights policy. Time and again, however, the administration found excuses for refusing to stay the hand of the white segregationists who harassed, beat, jailed, and even murdered in the cause of white supremacy. By the time of John Kennedy's assassination in November 1963, black voter registration stood at only 6 percent, and a large number of young civil rights workers despised the federal government.

In July 1961, Robert Parris Moses, a SNCC staff member then in his midtwenties, journeyed to McComb, Mississippi, to help a local NAACP leader, C. C. Bryant, begin a voter registration project. Voter registration was a new undertaking for SNCC, and some SNCC members opposed it. After all, voter registration had been a staple of black activism for almost twenty years: if SNCC merely replicated the work of other civil rights groups, it would lose its distinctive identity, which was above all associated with nonviolent direct action. Some also feared that SNCC would be drawn into the orbit of the Kennedy administration, which, for obvious political reasons, was anxious to divert the energies of the Civil Rights Movement from direct action to voter registration.

Moses, however, had learned that seasoned activists like C. C. Bryant and the NAACP's Amzie Moore were skeptical about direct action. In the harsh climate of Mississippi, they told him, sit-ins and demonstrations would fail, causing further repression for no gain. Besides, they added, integrated public accommodations held little relevance to rural blacks, most of whom were too poor, in any case, to eat in restaurants or stay in motels. What black Mississippians needed above all, they argued, was a share of political power. White supremacy rested upon black disfranchisement; it would fall when blacks won the franchise. In absorbing that advice, Moses recalled, SNCC "stumbled on the key—the right to vote and the political action that ensued."[10]

On the surface, voter registration lacked the drama, excitement, and immediacy of nonviolent direct action. In the context of Mississippi, however, voter registration possessed all those attributes. It represented as direct a challenge to white power as could be imagined, short of violent revolt. And the white response that it evoked soon put paid to the idea that voter registration was tame, nonconfrontational, and safe. Escorting black applicants to the courthouse in Liberty, which housed the office of the registrar of voters for Amite County, Moses was arrested, and a few days later beaten up. Fellow SNCC worker John Hardy entered the office of the Walthall County registrar only to have the official open a desk drawer, take out a pistol, and hit him on the head with it. A sheriff then arrested Hardy for disorderly conduct. In separate incidents, two other SNCC workers, Travis Britt and Bob Zellner, also received severe beatings—Zellner almost lost an eye when an attacker gouged an eyeball from its socket. The full danger of SNCC's position became apparent when a member of the state legislature, E. H. Hurst, shot and killed a black farmer, Herbert Lee, on September 25, 1961. The killing—and the fact that a coroner's jury accepted Hurst's claim that he had acted in self-defense—so frightened local blacks that SNCC felt compelled to quit the area and abandon its project.

Yet SNCC's first foray into voter registration work provided a political education that transformed the organization's outlook. The very severity of the white resistance that it encountered served to validate Moses's project. SNCC workers continued to engage in tactical debates about the appropriateness of nonviolent direct action, as opposed to voter registration, in specific situations. But nobody could any longer doubt that voter registration spoke directly to the question of black powerlessness. Opposition to voter registration *in principle* evaporated. Reginald Robinson summed up the realization that voter registration and direct action were two sides of the same coin. "[I]f you went into Mississippi and talked about voter registration, they [were] going to hit you on the side of the head and that's as direct as you can get."[11]

The McComb experience also brought SNCC workers face-to-face with death. Some had already confronted that possibility during the Freedom Rides. They now had to consider the reality that their actions might lead to the deaths of others. Robert Moses, a sensitive, reflective man, was torn by anguish over the murder of Herbert Lee, and realized that SNCC, by asking ordinary people to stand up for their rights, would be sending some people to their doom. As SNCC chairman Chuck McDew put it, "It's okay to put our own lives in jeopardy, but when you can cause somebody else to get killed, then that's a different question. . . . [W]e did have thoughts that if we had never come here, this would never have happened." That sobering realization gave SNCC workers a deeper level of commitment, a closer bond with the ordinary people of Mississippi, and a more intense conviction that they represented a moral cause that deserved—*demanded*—the support of the federal government.[12]

Over the next four years, Mississippi became the most important focus of SNCC's work and the most sustained, intensive project of the entire Civil Rights Movement. The repressive conditions of the Magnolia State forced SNCC to develop new kinds of organizing techniques. SNCC workers had to buckle down for the long haul, spending long months, stretching into years, "in the field." Winning the confidence of local people, breaking down barriers of fear and apathy, required infinite patience and tact. They had to convince local people that they were not fair-weather friends, that they would stick with them through thick and thin. They prided themselves on being part of the community and worked hard to win the community's trust. They tried not to offend the moral and religious sensibilities of the local people: SNCC forbade cohabitation between men and women, frowned upon alcohol, and encouraged even nonbelievers to attend church.

SNCC workers lived with a high level of tension. "It was always there," recalled Cleveland Sellers, a South Carolina native who joined SNCC from Howard University, "always stretched like a tight steel wire between the pit of the stomach and the center of the brain." Continually harassed, often arrested, sometimes beaten, and occasionally shot at, SNCC workers developed survival tactics that included unconventional driving techniques (including the execution of U-turns at high speeds), a sophisticated communications system, and constant vigilance. "When the strain became unbearable," Sellers remembered, "when sanity was stretched to the breaking point—and then a little beyond—they would pile into mud-spattered cars and head for Atlanta."[13]

Yet SNCC workers could not afford to betray fear or act "humble": their influence in the black community depended upon their ability to face down threats and intimidation. Many became renowned for their coolness and bravado. When stopped by the police while driving, for example, some indignantly recited the Bill of Rights and threatened to bring in the Justice Department, the FBI, and the federal government. When the sheriff of LeFlore County told Sam Block to pack his bags and leave town because "I don't want to see you anymore," Block replied, "Well, sheriff, if you don't want to see me here, I think the best thing for you to do is pack *your* clothes and leave, get out of town, 'cause I'm going to stay."[14]

Such audacity endowed SNCC organizers with prestige and charisma. Indeed, although SNCC's work was dangerous and poorly paid, it offered the compensations of being challenging, exciting, and rewarding. SNCC workers knew that they were on the leading edge of historical change; there was no more important place to be. The pressures of their situation, moreover, encouraged an emotional closeness among SNCC workers, a special bond of trust, friendship, and shared commitment that contributed to the SNCC "mystique."

If SNCC workers knew that they were doing work of extraordinary importance, they regarded the interests of ordinary black Mississippians as paramount. Although SNCC did work with middle-class NAACP activists like Amzie Moore of Cleveland and Aaron Henry of Clarksdale, it regarded the black middle class as unreliable. Often spurned by teachers, ministers, and businessmen, SNCC attempted to identify and nurture leaders from sections of the black population that had hitherto been voiceless, especially the poor and the young. They lived on irregular wages of $15 a week and boarded in rude shacks, their own poverty heightening their sympathies for the black working class. Many abandoned jackets and ties for denim work overalls, the traditional garb of black farmers and laborers.

In Mississippi, as elsewhere in the South, more black women supported the Civil Rights Movement than black men. The reason for this disparity is not entirely clear. Sociologist Charles Payne suggests that women were more religious, more concerned with kinship networks, and more active in community organizations—all of which, like the movement, involved them in social activities outside the home. Women may also have been somewhat better educated than men. What is certain, according to Payne, is that women were more ready to offer food and shelter to SNCC workers, "canvassed more often than men, showed up more often at mass meetings and demonstrations, and more frequently attempted to register to vote."[15]

Yet the Civil Rights Movement was very much a male-dominated movement. Dorothy Height, president of the National Council of Negro Women, recalled that at a typical mass meeting, "you had predominantly women and children in the audience and predominantly male leadership on the platform." Indeed, Stokely Carmichael, a native of Trinidad who joined SNCC via Howard University, once quipped that "the only position for women in SNCC is prone." This lighthearted remark has been endlessly quoted as evidence of the male chauvinism within SNCC.[16]

Still, historians of the Mississippi movement agree that SNCC, of all the different organizations, was the most open to women's participation. As Charles Payne puts it, SNCC's "antibureaucratic and antihierarchal" structure disposed the group to work with "anyone who was willing to have them, traditional considerations of status notwithstanding." Moreover, SNCC saw its principal role as that of helping local people to help themselves. "Part of our strategy in each local community," Ella Baker emphasized, "should be to shift as much of the responsibility as soon as possible to local handling, looking to the day when the Movement would be on its own in a local community and SNCC staff could leave." Taking to heart Baker's notion of "group-centered leadership," SNCC recruited local Mississippians into the Civil Rights Movement, giving positions of responsibility to young people, poor people, and women. And SNCC recognized that women, in Payne's words, "represented an enormous pool of untapped leadership potential."[17]

Fannie Lou Hamer was the best-known example of how SNCC harnessed the courage and dedication of black women. The youngest of twenty children, Hamer had lived all her life on a white man's plantation, where she and her husband, Perry, worked as sharecroppers. A civil rights meeting in Ruleville addressed by SNCC staffers James Bevel and James Forman inspired her to seek the vote; in August 1962, with seventeen others, she travelled to the Sunflower County courthouse to take the voter registration "test." The Hamers were promptly evicted from the plantation. Their niece's house, where they found temporary shelter, was shot up by white men from a passing car.

Thus drawn into the Civil Rights Movement, in June 1963 Hamer attended the SCLC's "citizenship school" in Georgia; on the return bus journey she and five others were arrested, taken to jail, and beaten. The vicious assault merely reinforced her commitment. She joined the SNCC staff, helped to organize the Mississippi Freedom Democratic Party, and devoted the rest of her life to the cause of racial equality and economic justice. Deeply religious, Hamer possessed a marvelous singing voice, and had the ability to express the ideals of the Civil Rights Movement simply but effectively. She and other black women—Winson Hudson, Annelle Ponder, Victoria Gray Adams, Annie Devine, June Johnson, Unita Blackwell—became stalwarts of the Mississippi movement.

Although SNCC had to surrender its initial beachhead in McComb, its sphere of influence slowly widened. In Jackson, the state capital, veterans of the Nashville sit-in movement and the Freedom Rides, including James Bevel, Diane Nash, Lester McKinnie, and Bernard Lafayette, worked with black students from Tougaloo College to stage nonviolent protests against Jim Crow. Arrests, jail sentences, and lack of support from older blacks soon snuffed it out, but the Jackson movement revived in 1962–63 to mount a boy-cott of downtown stores, backed up with picketing, sit-ins, and mass demon-strations.

Voter registration, however, became SNCC's forte, and it concentrated its efforts on the Mississippi Delta, a ten-county area stretching from Vicksburg in the south to Memphis in the north. Famed for its rich alluvial soil, the Delta was the center of the state's cotton production. The Delta also symbolized systematic racism, for nowhere in America were inequalities between whites and blacks more stark.

A small number of wealthy white planters dominated the Delta's economy. About 5 percent of the farmers owned about three-quarters of the land, and they received generous subsidies from the Department of Agriculture to boost their incomes. In 1967, for example, the government paid out $60 mil-lion to Delta planters who, according to the historian James C. Cobb, com-prised about 0.3 percent of the population. Senator James O. Eastland, for example, who owned 2,000 acres in Sunflower County, received $168,000 in taxpayers' money.

Blacks comprised the majority of the Delta's people, and between half and two-thirds of them lived below the official poverty line. Yet their share of gov-ernment largesse consisted mainly of "food stamps," the value of which amounted to scarcely one-sixth of the subsidies received by white planters. In Tunica County, 80 percent of the dwellings had neither bathrooms nor toi-lets. A majority of black children were anemic and malnourished. The rate of infant mortality among blacks was more than double the rate among whites. Many blacks never saw a doctor. Black farm laborers received $3.50 for a twelve-hour day. Yet many blacks could not find work at even those low wages: weedkillers, mechanical cotton pickers, and reduced cotton acreage were displacing black labor and accentuated black poverty. According to Cobb, only 5 percent of the Delta's cotton was picked by hand in 1967, and black sharecroppers, who in 1959 numbered 17,563 people, had virtually disappeared.[18]

The Delta was also the bastion of white political power in Mississippi. Precisely because they were so heavily outnumbered, whites enforced black disfranchisement rigorously and thoroughly. With the exception of Coahoma County, where a determined NAACP branch in Clarksdale, led by druggist Aaron Henry, had pushed black registration to 13 percent, black voting was insignificant. Sunflower County, birthplace of the Citizens Councils and home of Senator Eastland, had no black voters at all. Nowhere in the South did the ballot have such potential to bring about social and political change. Black voting would challenge an entire social order, weakening the grip of diehard white supremacists on the politics of Mississippi, the South and the nation.

Sam Block, a twenty-three-year-old native of Cleveland, Mississippi, initiated SNCC's work in the Delta by starting a voter registration campaign in Greenwood, LeFlore County. Working alone at first, and without pay, Block patiently made contact with black residents. "Each morning," writes historian John Dittmer, "the tall, gaunt young visitor . . . went into the community, hanging out in the laundromats, grocery stores, pool halls, and juke joints—wherever local people congregated—listening to people's problems and subtly introducing the topic of voter registration." Eventually Block felt sufficiently confident to call a "mass meeting," where he enlivened proceedings by teaching the dozen or so participants "freedom songs." After more meetings, Block took three women and one man to the registrar's office, where the four applicants took the "test." At that time only 1.97 percent of LeFlore County's adult black population could vote. In the summer of 1962 SNCC sent other workers to Greenwood and started up similar projects in Ruleville, Greenville, and Clarksdale.[19]

White opposition quickly turned nasty. Block received threatening telephone calls. Police harassment—threats, curses, arrests—became routine. Block's landlady, a schoolteacher, evicted him under pain of losing her job. Whites broke into the SNCC office and trashed it. The county commission then retaliated against the black community as a whole, ending its participation in a federal "surplus commodities" program and cutting off a vital source of food to the poorest black families. When SNCC organized shipments of food and clothing from the North, whites attempted to burn the supplies, torching a four-building block in the black business district. After his seventh arrest in eight months, Block was sentenced to six months in jail for "public utterances designed to incite breach of the peace." Block spurned the alternative of leaving town and receiving a suspended sentence. On February 28, 1963, whites drove alongside a SNCC vehicle and shot at the occupants. Robert Moses and Randolph Blackwell escaped injury, but the driver, Jimmy Travis, was wounded in the neck and shoulder.[20]

The white campaign of intimidation confronted SNCC with a crucial test of strength. If it bowed to threats and violence, its ability to organize among local blacks would be fatally compromised; its entire strategy would suffer. SNCC had to demonstrate staying power, matching escalating white pressure with increased resources, personnel, and determination. After the shooting of Travis, SNCC concentrated its entire Mississippi staff, twenty-four people, in Greenwood. With support from CORE, the SCLC and the NAACP, all of which cooperated with SNCC under the banner of the Council of Federated Organizations (COFO), the Greenwood project mustered forty full-time civil rights workers. They held weekly mass meetings, distributed food and clothes, and launched an intensified voter registration campaign. In March 1963 SNCC organized marches to city hall and sent local people to the courthouse in large groups. SNCC knew, however, that in the absence of intervention by the federal government, whites could always muster superior force to crush black protests. Civil rights groups peppered the Justice Department with letters, phone calls, and telegrams—backed up with personal meetings with government officials—demanding decisive action to halt the repression.

SNCC believed that the Kennedy administration had a moral obligation to take such action because the government had played an active role in setting up the Voter Education Project. The VEP, created in 1962, encouraged voter registration work by distributing money from several philanthropic foundations among the various civil rights groups. The federal government enthusiastically backed the VEP and made sure that it received tax-exempt status. Initially skeptical, SNCC was persuaded to support the initiative with the understanding that the Justice Department would take strong action in the event of harassment and violence.

The Kennedy administration, however, failed to provide the assistance that SNCC demanded and expected. Justice Department officials and FBI agents were constantly on the scene at Mississippi trouble spots. Yet apart from filing a few lawsuits against the most recalcitrant voter registrars—litigation that proved slow and ineffective—the government took virtually no action to help the Civil Rights Movement.

The government's most conspicuous sin of omission was its refusal to offer any kind of protection against intimidation, violence, and arrests. The head of the Civil Rights Division of the Justice Department, Yale-educated lawyer

Burke Marshall, contended that the Constitution prescribed a system of federalism that made law enforcement a state and local responsibility. Most criminal acts were state crimes, and it was up to state police and prosecutors to bring offenders to account. The federal government possessed neither the authority nor the means to furnish the kind of physical protection that civil rights workers desired. Only under the most extraordinary circumstances could, or should, the government employ direct coercion. The use of troops—such as Eisenhower's deployment of paratroopers in Little Rock—tended to do more harm than good, and threatened to destroy the delicate balance between federal and state power upon which domestic tranquility depended. Such intervention should be avoided if at all possible.

Underlying such arguments was the dread memory of Reconstruction—or, rather, a white-tinged version of that memory that reflected the writings of white supremacist historians like William A. Dunning. That highly selective account stressed the futility of attempting to enforce racial equality on the points of federal bayonets. Military force during Reconstruction had merely embittered Southern whites, summoned up armed resistance in the form of the Ku Klux Klan, and poisoned race relations for several generations. The lesson, Marshall believed, was that "having the military run a civil rights movement is a terrible step to take if it can be avoided."[21]

Marshall's theory of federalism embodied a certain practical wisdom. Use of the military in domestic situations was a drastic and dangerous step. The political consequences were incalculable, but it was certain to generate bitter resentment and possibly violent resistance. Moreover, military force put the government on a slippery slope: if it deployed troops in one area, why not another? It did not overtax the imagination to envisage a military occupation of the entire state of Mississippi, or the entire Deep South. In addition, if the government committed troops, it might prove extremely difficult to extricate them. The example of Northern Ireland, where troops were deployed in 1969 to protect the Catholic population, but which are still in the province thirty years later—hated by the Catholic minority—suggests that the Kennedys' horror of military coercion may have been sound. Ultimately, the Kennedy administration argued, the Southern states themselves had to take responsibility for curbing racist violence and enforcing the law impartially. Persuading them to do so was a slow and difficult task, and many civil rights workers and ordinary black people were likely to suffer in the meantime.

The Civil Rights Movement, however, scoffed at the Justice Department's line of reasoning. For one thing, the theory of federalism failed to address the basic reality of Mississippi: the very people who were supposed to enforce the law, the police, abused it. The police aided and abetted the most violently racist elements in the state; in many areas, the police and the Ku Klux Klan were one and the same. In the second place, SNCC disputed the notion that the federal government lacked the constitutional authority to protect civil rights: it had all the authority it needed under the Fourteenth and Fifteenth Amendments. SNCC also rebutted the argument that federal protection had to involve troops. The federal government already possessed an agency that had the means and the manpower to combat racist violence and terror: the Federal Bureau of Investigation. Yet FBI agents frequently stood by and merely took notes when black people and civil rights workers were publicly threatened, harassed, beaten, and arrested on trumped-up charges. SNCC accused the FBI of sympathizing with the white racists.

The government's failure to order the FBI to protect civil rights became a bitter source of controversy. The truth was, however, that the bureau was a rogue agency, and its boss, J. Edgar Hoover, a law unto himself. Hoover had run the FBI for more than forty years, turning it into a personal fiefdom that he ruled with a rod of iron. Moreover, through skillful lobbying of politicians and journalists and astute public relations, he enjoyed a formidable reputation as an intrepid gangbuster and dedicated foe of communism. He was one of the most respected men in America—and one of the most feared. The FBI held files on millions of Americans, including top-level politicians, and their contents detailed drinking habits, financial irregularities, sexual indiscretions, and miscellaneous scuttlebutt. With all this dirt at his disposal, Hoover was politically impregnable. Robert Kennedy, his nominal superior, insisted on installing a direct telephone line on Hoover's desk. He also tried to persuade the FBI to pursue civil rights cases more vigorously. But Hoover, a thinly disguised racist, scornfully rejected suggestions that the FBI "furnish protection" to civil rights workers.

Nevertheless, the government possessed other means of influencing the behavior of Southern whites. It could, for example, request federal courts to enjoin violence and harassment, and it did take some steps in this direction. Thus in 1961 the Justice Department filed a successful suit that blocked the state prosecution of SNCC worker John Hardy. However, as John Dittmer points out, on the only other occasion when it employed this tactic, the government backed down. In March 1963 the Justice Department sought an injunction against the City of Greenwood to stop interference with voter registration and to allow blacks to hold peaceful demonstrations without being arrested or harassed. Yet four days later the Justice Department abandoned its lawsuit in exchange for the release of eight imprisoned SNCC workers. The white authorities gave no undertaking to cease their repressive actions. The government's climbdown knocked the stuffing out of the Greenwood campaign. It was a bitter defeat for the Civil Rights Movement. By the summer of 1963, most SNCC workers were thoroughly disillusioned with the federal government.[22]

The refusal of the Kennedy administration to aid blacks in Mississippi illustrated the stark realities of political power. "Until his death," writes Dittmer, "John Kennedy tried to maintain good relations with Mississippi's congressional delegation. The president went out of his way to avoid conflict." Kennedy simply did not wish to alienate men like Senator Eastland, who, as chairman of the Senate Judiciary Committee, had the capacity to block any nomination to the federal bench that Kennedy put forward. As long as the white authorities in Mississippi avoided a complete breakdown of law and order—one that might attract unfavorable international publicity and embarrass the government—the administration refused to intervene.[23]

In the case of the court-ordered integration of "Ole Miss" (the University of Mississippi) in September 1962, that reluctance had disastrous consequences. Engaging in marathon negotiations to persuade Governor Ross Barnett to protect the black applicant, James Meredith, from violence, the Kennedys allowed the situation to drift out of control. While Robert Kennedy tried to shift responsibility for guaranteeing law and order onto Barnett—at the same time going to absurd lengths to gratify Barnett's desire to save political face—a mob gathered and a full-scale riot erupted. By the time the president had decided to commit troops, two people were dead and the campus of Ole Miss resembled a battlefield. Despite the debacle, the Kennedys refused to allow the U.S. Civil Rights Commission to hold hearings in the state.

LEARNING FROM FAILURE: THE ALBANY MOVEMENT

While the SNCC workers in Mississippi pressed on with voter registration and patient community organizing, elsewhere in the South civil rights organizations, including SNCC, developed new techniques of nonviolent direct action. Learning by trial and error, with little sense of overall strategy at first, they encouraged local communities to challenge Jim Crow through sit-ins, boycotts, and marches. In Albany, Georgia, for example, SNCC and the SCLC led a broad attack on every facet of racial discrimination, demanding fair employment, an end to police brutality, and the desegregation of buses, bus and train terminals, parks, playgrounds, the public library, and all public accommodations.

Its broad membership, militant tactics, comprehensive goals, and alliance of local and "outside" leadership made the Albany Movement the first of its kind; it profoundly influenced the subsequent development of the Civil Rights Movement. A wide coalition of local organizations, the Albany Movement drew in ministers, businessmen, professionals, college students, and working people. Its inclusiveness recalled the Montgomery Improvement Association. In Albany, however, blacks were asked to make greater personal sacrifices: sit-ins and demonstrations entailed direct confrontations with the police and the probability of arrest. Moreover, while the Albany Movement was locally based, SNCC and the SCLC—especially King—provided much of the leadership. For those "outside" civil rights groups, Albany provided an invaluable learning experience. It taught them how to mobilize an entire community for a prolonged campaign of nonviolent protest.

Albany witnessed the flowering of "freedom songs" as an integral part of the Civil Rights Movement. Initially rather embarrassed by the Old Leftish hymns and union anthems that had been taught them by Guy Carawan at the Highlander Folk School, SNCC workers soon realized the marvellous potential of community singing as an organizing tool. Albany was the first singing movement. People sang in the mass meetings, during marches, and in jail. They put new words to old hymns such as "This Little Light of Mine" and "Over My Head I See Trouble (Freedom) in the Air." They also sang new songs like "Ain't Gonna Let Nobody Turn Me Around" and "If You Miss Me at the Back of the Bus."

Freedom songs lent themselves to creative improvisation. For example, after the first verse:

> *Ain't gonna let nobody turn me 'round, turn me 'round, turn me 'round*
> *Ain't gonna let nobody turn me 'round, turn me 'round, turn me 'round*
> *I'm gonna keep on a-walking, keep on a-talking*
> > *Marching up the freedom land*

singers could then express their defiance of other opponents and obstacles:

> *Ain't gonna let Chief Pritchett etc.*
> *Ain't gonna let segregation etc.*
> *Ain't gonna let no jail house etc.*

Such songs were simple, accessible, and infinitely adaptable.

The Albany Movement made "We Shall Overcome," an old union song from the 1940s, the most beloved anthem of the Civil Rights Movement, a song that became so popular that protest movements all over the world adopted it. Like the Baptist hymn from which it originally derived, "We Shall

Overcome" was easy to sing and had a majestic melody that endowed the
verses with nobility. Sung slowly with swelling harmonies, it beautifully exemplified the idealism and optimism of the Civil Rights Movement:

We shall overcome
We shall overcome
We shall overcome someday.
Oh, deep in my heart
I do believe
We shall overcome someday.

We are not afraid etc.
The truth shall make us free etc.
God is on our side etc.

Freedom songs melded naturally with the tradition of church singing. They
encouraged the active participation of ordinary people, and made the audience, rather than the speakers, the center of attention. They made the mass
meetings in Albany some of the most enthusiastic and inspirational occasions
of the entire Civil Rights Movement.

The Albany Movement inspired a large cross-section of the black population to participate in nonviolent direct action. For the first time in the history
of the Civil Rights Movement, large numbers of adults went to jail. At one
point, during the height of the protests in December 1961, more than 700 of
Albany's 23,000 black people were incarcerated. "These were common, ordinary, everyday people," recalled Dr. W. G. Anderson, president of the Albany
Movement, "housewives, cooks, maids, laborers, children out of school." The
Rev. Wyatt T. Walker, the SCLC's executive director, hailed the Albany Movement as a "milepost in the early stage of the nonviolent movement."[24]

Yet the Albany Movement was also a crushing disappointment. Judged in
terms of its stated goals, it failed. After a period of intensive protests, which
lasted from December 1961 to August 1962, Albany remained as segregated,
as white-dominated, and as unyieldingly racist as ever. Far from softening up
the segregationists and inducing them to make concessions, nonviolent direct
action made white businessmen and politicians even more intransigent. They
simply refused to negotiate, branding the civil rights activists "law violators."
And they went to unexpected extremes in their determination to break the Albany Movement. When blacks organized a bus boycott, the city commission
let the bus company shut down rather than concede integration. Faced with a
federal court order to integrate parks and playgrounds, the city closed them.
When a similar order compelled it to integrate the public library, the city kept

it open but removed the tables and chairs. The city repealed all its segregation ordinances, but continued to enforce Jim Crow in stores, hotels, movie theaters, and restaurants by arresting blacks for breach of the peace.[25]

The Albany Movement asked King for help, calculating that King's participation would bolster the protests, generate national media attention, and exert political pressure on white leaders. King certainly achieved the first two goals. He went to jail three times in nine months, and each time he did so the mass meetings became packed, optimism surged, and Albany became international news. "[King] can cause more hell to be raised by being in jail one night than anyone else could if they bombed city hall," noted SNCC worker Bill Hansen. "The good town of Albany is taking on the aspect of a newspaper reporter convention." Yet King failed to intimidate the city commission, which denounced him as a "recognized agitator" and refused to negotiate "under duress."[26]

The wily tactics of Chief of Police Laurie G. Pritchett added to the Albany Movement's discomfiture. Pritchett was a thoroughly professional law enforcement officer who had the acumen to realize that police brutality, or violence from white mobs, would draw newspaper reporters to Albany and create sympathy for the movement. Pritchett trained his men to employ a "nonviolent approach" toward demonstrators. Off-camera, beatings took place—Bill Hansen, for example, was assaulted inside the Dougherty County jail and had his jaw broken. Yet out-of-sight violence was far less newsworthy. The burly police chief also knew, having read King's book, *Stride Toward Freedom,* that the Civil Rights Movement would attempt to fill the jails in an effort to frustrate the city's policy of mass arrests. He therefore arranged in advance to use jails in neighboring counties. As Hansen ruefully recalled, "We ran out of people before he ran out of jails." Finally, Pritchett understood that it was better to have King outside jail than inside jail. At one point he secretly arranged to have his bond paid, compelling King—to his acute embarrassment and loss of face—to leave prison against his will.[27]

In the face of white intransigence and cunning, the Albany Movement could ill afford the luxury of disunity. Yet it was beset with divisions over tactics, organizational rivalries, and petty jealousies. The NAACP shunned the Albany Movement on the grounds that it was created by two SNCC workers, Charles Sherrod and Cordell Reagon, and SNCC was anathema to the NAACP. SNCC sought to exploit King's prestige, yet at the same time it both envied him and resented his presence. SNCC workers mocked King as "De Lawd," criticized him for being insufficiently militant, and bristled at the SCLC's tendency to "take over." The SCLC was happy to work with SNCC, but found it difficult to treat the latter as an equal partner. The Albany Movement, ostensibly independent, was caught in the middle. SNCC adhered to the fiction that it merely advised the Albany Movement, but in practice it subtly manipulated it. The SCLC, on the other hand, made decisions for the Albany Movement with barely a pretense at consultation. Torn between SNCC, the SCLC, and its own desire for autonomy, the Albany Movement eventually disintegrated.

Lack of planning compounded all these problems. When King first arrived in Albany he had only a sketchy idea of what the situation was; he did not intend going to jail. The Albany Movement embarked upon mass demonstrations with little thought of the consequences and with no contingency plans. It did not even have a bail fund. Pritchett, on the other hand, anticipated the demonstrations, prepared for mass arrests, and insisted that prisoners pay cash bonds—$200 a person—before being released. Throughout the protests, the Albany Movement stumbled; every time it tried to regain the initiative, Pritchett and the city commission outfoxed it. At times, the Albany Movement even lost control of its own supporters. On July 22, 1962, for example, a crowd of about 1,500 blacks booed and cursed as the police arrested two small groups of demonstrators. Two days later, onlookers pelted the police with bricks and bottles. "See them nonviolent rocks?" gloated Pritchett. These unruly spectators, who had emptied the taverns and pool halls, were not "part" of the Albany Movement, but their behavior nevertheless tarnished it. An embarrassed King declared a "day of penance."[28]

Albany disabused the Civil Rights Movement of its more romantic notions about nonviolence. If nonviolent direct action were reduced to a raw trial of strength between black protesters and white elites, the Civil Rights Movement could not possibly win. Without help from the federal government—the kind of action the Justice Department took in Alabama during the Freedom Rides—demonstrations were likely to fail.

Yet the Kennedy administration declined to intervene in the Albany situation. The Justice Department, ignoring broader constitutional issues raised by the city's violation of the First and Fourteenth Amendments, contended that the arrests in Albany violated no federal laws, that the government had no authority to intervene. The administration's studied neutrality, of course, reflected its close political ties with Georgia segregationists like Ernest S. Vandiver, the governor, and James H. Gray, chairman of the Democratic State Committee and editor of the *Albany Herald*. The fact that Kennedy had appointed segregationist Robert Elliott to the federal bench underlined these political realities: Elliott granted the City of Albany an injunction against demonstrations.

By the beginning of 1963 the Civil Rights Movement had reached a crossroads. Without some change in the political equation, it confronted frustration, demoralization, and imminent collapse. After licking its wounds, the SCLC took stock of the situation and decided to seize the initiative. The unpalatable truth of the Freedom Rides, and of Albany, stared it in the face. Only "tension and crisis," Wyatt Walker said in a speech on March 26, "forces a resolution of the dilemma." A week later, the SCLC precipitated the biggest crisis in the history of the Civil Rights Movement.[29]

Members and supporters of the Student Nonviolent Coordinating
Committee, and Alabama state troopers, Montgomery, 1965

Alabama Department of Archives and History

13

Birmingham, the Freedom Summer, and Selma

THE IMPACT OF BIRMINGHAM

Between April 3 and May 8, 1963, Martin Luther King and Fred L. Shuttlesworth led blacks in a determined campaign to attack segregation in Birmingham, Alabama, the South's most segregated city. The protests included enthusiastic mass meetings, a tight boycott of downtown stores, persistent lunch counter sit-ins, and repeated attempts to march to City Hall. Defying a state court injunction banning parades, King went to jail, as did 3,300 others. When the SCLC called off the protests on May 10, it had secured a written agreement from the city's business leaders that desegregated store facilities, pledged the hiring of black sales clerks, and promised continuing biracial negotiations to upgrade black employment opportunities across the board.

It was hardly the millennium, and the businessmen were slow to honor even these small commitments. Fred Shuttlesworth believed that the SCLC should have held out for much more. As founder and leader of the Alabama Christian Movement for Human Rights, Shuttlesworth had almost single-handedly kept black protest alive in Birmingham since the banning of the NAACP in 1956. His invitation, moreover, had brought the SCLC to the city in the first place. He had a right to feel disappointed.

Nevertheless, in the context of Birmingham itself, where whites had previously yielded nothing, and where police repression had long kept the Civil Rights Movement in check, the agreement amounted to a breakthrough. Furthermore, the SCLC compelled the Kennedy administration to intervene in the crisis—something it had signally failed to do in Albany—and to side with the Civil Rights Movement. During King's incarceration, President Kennedy phoned Coretta King to reassure her about the government's concern for her husband's safety. When the crisis intensified, the attorney general sent Burke Marshall to Birmingham to mediate between the two sides. And when the Klan tried to wreck the resulting agreement by exploding several bombs, Kennedy mobilized federal troops in readiness to intervene. "The Birmingham agreement was and is a fair accord," the president stated. "The federal government will not permit it to be sabotaged."[1]

The Birmingham protests also transformed the Civil Rights Movement. As the SCLC had calculated, its demonstrations achieved much more than a local victory. Birmingham, recalled Wyatt T. Walker, was the most notorious symbol of inflexible Southern racism. "We decided on Birmingham with the attitude that we may not win it, we may lose everything. But we knew that as Birmingham went, so went the South." The SCLC's protests electrified black Southerners. They were thrilled when hundreds of schoolchildren marched out of the Sixteenth Street Baptist Church and into lines of waiting policemen, taunting them and singing as police vans hauled them off to jail. They were incensed when blacks were chased by police dogs, then drenched and pounded by high-pressure fire hoses. Above all they were inspired by the sheer audacity of it all—and moved to action.[2]

The weeks and months after Birmingham saw an explosion of black protest on a scale never seen before. Across the South, in what *Time* described as a "feverish, fragmented, almost uncontrollable revolution," black Southerners poured into the streets. They boldly asserted their right to use "whites only" parks, playgrounds, beaches, libraries, theaters, restaurants, and hotels. They boycotted and sat-in. Above all, they marched to the twin bastions of white power that graced the center of every Southern town, the courthouse and the city hall, in challenges to white domination that were both symbolic and physically real.[3]

In its regional breadth, the uprising resembled the sit-in movement of 1960. But the 1963 demonstrations were more widespread, involved much larger numbers, and drew in people of all ages and backgrounds. To list the places where black people engaged in nonviolent protests would be to name virtually every town and city in the South: about 115 communities experienced 930 demonstrations of one kind or another. The number of people arrested topped 20,000, four times as many as in 1960.

The 1963 surge of nonviolent direct action made the maintenance of segregation in public accommodations untenable. Black people knew that if segregation could be cracked in Birmingham, it could be cracked anywhere. Birmingham exposed the vulnerability of the South's political regime, and black people seized the opportunity to attack it. In city after city, under the relentless pressure of demonstrations, whites sat down to negotiate. During a single three-week period after Birmingham, the Justice Department noted that 143 cities had acceded to some degree of integration. By year's end the number exceeded three hundred. Many cities set up biracial committees that enabled blacks to press for further desegregation.

Often, as in Birmingham, businessmen made the concessions. Not beholden to white voters, they had more freedom of action than the politicians; once they took the decision, it was a relatively straightforward matter to desegregate restaurants, movie theaters, and store facilities. Getting *all* merchants to act in concert proved more difficult, but it could be done; retailers were extremely vulnerable to black pressure. Boycotts deprived white-owned stores of black customers; demonstrations frightened away white ones. Racial tension and disruption hampered economic growth generally. As journalist Reese Cleghorn noted, Birmingham's economic decline—"payrolls slipping, prospective new industry frightened away by racial turmoil, downtown business stagnating"—furnished a grim warning that repression in the defense of Jim Crow exacted an increasingly heavy cost.[4]

Why did the SCLC succeed in Birmingham when it had failed so miserably in Albany? Having a strong base in Shuttlesworth and the Alabama Christian Movement for Human Rights was crucial: there were none of the debilitating organizational rivalries that had afflicted the Albany protests. The SCLC also shrewdly targeted the business community, not the elected politicians, and put forward modest, achievable demands. In addition, thanks to James Bevel's initiative in recruiting children from the black high schools, the SCLC actually succeeded in filling the jails.

Many outside observers credited the violence of the Birmingham police force with tipping the balance in the SCLC's favor. The rough police tactics had an extraordinary impact on public opinion: photographs of dogs and fire hoses were flashed around the world, evoking near universal condemnation. It is tempting, therefore, to believe that the SCLC deliberately targeted Birmingham because of its reputation for violence, and, specifically, that it intended all along to provoke "Bull" Connor into a violent reaction.

Circumstantial evidence for the provocation thesis is not hard to find. Everyone knew that Birmingham was a powder keg. A Klan stronghold, it had experienced so many explosions—about fifty since 1947—that local blacks dubbed it "Bombingham." Targets included the homes of black people who had moved into white neighborhoods, the homes of civil rights activists, and Bethel Baptist Church, Fred Shuttlesworth's church. The police seemed incapable of apprehending the perpetrators: many policemen sympathized with the Klan and some belonged to it. *New York Times* reporter Harrison Salisbury described Birmingham as a racist dictatorship in the grip of terror. "Every reasoned approach, every inch of middle ground has been fragmented by the emotional dynamite of racism, reinforced by the whip, the razor, the gun, the bomb, the torch, the club, the knife, the mob, the police and many branches of the state's apparatus."[5]

No individual had done more to encourage this state of affairs than "Bull" Connor, whose position as commissioner of public safety put him in charge of both the police force and the fire department. In temperament and style, Connor was the antithesis of the calm, professional Laurie Pritchett. He was a vain, short-tempered, publicity-seeking bully, with a notorious reputation for racial extremism. First elected in 1938 after a stint as union-busting head of security for the Tennessee Coal and Iron Company, he revelled in outrageous behavior in defense of segregation. In 1938 he forcibly segregated the inaugural meeting of the Southern Conference for Human Welfare, despite the presence of First Lady Eleanor Roosevelt. Ten years later he arrested a U.S. senator. Connor turned a blind eye to police brutality, harassed and spied on civil rights leaders, and connived in Klan violence. "Racial prejudices are incredibly tense in Birmingham," the U.S. Civil Rights Commission warned; the least provocation "can be expected to unleash acts of violence."[6]

Responding to the alarm of Birmingham's white moderates, who were trying to abolish Connor's office (in 1962 they succeeded, although Connor stayed in power until 1963), the Kennedy administration begged the SCLC to stay out. When King refused, the government condemned the protests as ill-timed. The SCLC's demonstrations were also opposed by many blacks, who agreed with the white moderates that street protests were dangerous, provocative, and likely to make the racial situation, which was finally beginning to improve, much worse. A. G. Gaston, the city's wealthiest black businessman, deplored the protests. So did the Masons, the Baptist Ministers Conference, the bulk of the middle class, and the local black newspaper.

In "Letter from Birmingham City Jail," which became the best-known defense of civil disobedience to come out of the Civil Rights Movement, King eloquently defended the SCLC's motives and methods. "Nonviolent direct action," he explained, "seeks to create such a crisis and establish such creative tension that a community that has constantly refused to negotiate is forced to confront the issue." King was vague about the exact nature of the "crisis" the SCLC sought. Yet, clearly, the SCLC went into Birmingham with its eyes open; it knew precisely what it was up against. It launched demonstrations knowing full well that they might lead to violence. Indeed, King solemnly warned his staff that, in his own judgment, not all of them would come out of Birmingham alive.[7]

Still, the SCLC adamantly denied that it went to Birmingham with the intention of provoking a violent response from Connor. Many years later, more-over, two of King's closest friends and colleagues repeated the denial. "We never wanted racists to retaliate," attests Andrew Young. "That was not an SCLC plan. What we did say was that we would put so many people in jail that we would bring the system to a halt. . . . [O]ur emphasis was on non-cooperation and economic withdrawal." According to Ralph Abernathy, the SCLC considered Birmingham's violent reputation to be a "serious draw-back," and regarded Connor—a "shrewd and bold adversary"—as a negative factor. "We were also concerned about our own hides. . . . [W]e would cer-tainly be happy with a new police chief."[8]

Such disclaimers might seem disingenuous. Of course the SCLC denied harboring provocative intentions, argues historian David Garrow: it would have been folly to do otherwise. Most whites, North as well as South, disap-proved of demonstrations in the first place. Many already regarded the SCLC's tactics as irresponsible and manipulative, and were especially shocked by the SCLC's decision to send schoolchildren to confront Connor's police. "An in-jured, maimed, or dead child is a price that none of us can afford to pay," Robert Kennedy scolded King. Even sympathetic whites often argued that demonstrations that provoked violence negated the meaning of nonviolence. To have openly admitted to provocation, therefore, would have compromised the SCLC's moral standing and undermined its support. Garrow concluded that the SCLC's strategy hinged upon eliciting and publicizing a violent white response; it "bordered on nonviolent provocation."[9]

Yet in the most thorough study of the campaign yet published, historian Glenn Eskew has endorsed the SCLC's denials. Eskew points out that the SCLC twice delayed its campaign so as not to give Connor political ammuni-tion in his race for mayor: it wanted Connor out of office. The fact that the SCLC *did*, in fact, end up confronting Connor—the commissioner, having lost the election for mayor, refused to leave office—was a bizarre turn of events that nobody could have predicted. Eskew notes, too, that there is practically no evidence of provocative intentions on the SCLC's part during the plan-ning stage of the campaign. Moreover, the SCLC's own analysis of why the campaign succeeded did not emphasize the police violence. Walker thought that economic pressure had been the decisive factor: the "*boycott was it.*"[10]

The murky truth of the matter lies somewhere between these two interpre-tations. The SCLC could scarcely have been ignorant of the fact that segrega-tionists discredited themselves when they resorted to violence—the practice of staging nonviolent protests in the hope that the oppressor would react vio-lently was fundamental to the Gandhian concept of *satyagraha,* or civil dis-obedience. It hardly seems credible, therefore, that the SCLC chose the most violent city in the South by chance; Connor or no Connor, they were virtually guaranteed a rough reception. Then again, some of the people on King's staff, including the hard-boiled Walker, may have been more calculating in their attitude toward provoking Connor than others. Yet it would be a mistake to assume that the SCLC went into Birmingham with a cut-and-dried strategy. It did a certain amount of planning, to be sure, but when its plans came unstuck—and they came unstuck almost immediately—the SCLC had to improvise. "[W]e allowed our problems to dictate our decisions for us," recalled Abernathy, "as they frequently did during these years of struggle."[11]

The secret of the SCLC's success in Birmingham was not that its demonstrations provoked white violence, but that they brought about a visually dramatic confrontation. Violence—serious bloodshed and fatalities—was the last thing the SCLC wanted. The deaths of demonstrators, the SCLC feared, would so anger blacks that support for nonviolence would evaporate, and the situation would degenerate into a violent free-for-all that blacks would certainly lose. The SCLC therefore counted on the strict order of its own supporters, who were thoroughly trained in nonviolent discipline, and the presence of the news media, to deter the police from responding violently. There were, in fact, few serious casualties during the demonstrations themselves. The only fatalities occurred four months later, when the Klan bombed the Sixteenth Street Baptist Church, killing four young girls, and in the ensuing disorders two other blacks died at the hands of white people.

The power of nonviolence lay in its ability to *symbolize* the violence of segregation. "We wanted the world to know what was going on in the South," Andrew Young explained. "We had to craft a concise and dramatic message that could be explained in just sixty seconds. That was our media strategy." The demonstrations were, to use a popular phrase of the late 1960s, "street theater." The SCLC sought vivid images that would attract the news media—especially the cameras—and evoke sympathy for the protesters. Blatant provocation, if it led to bloodshed, would have destroyed that sympathy. Obviously, the SCLC sought to capitalize on Connor's blunders: his use of police dogs and fire hoses evoked a chorus of condemnation. Yet his crowd-control tactics, while unpleasant, were dramatic rather than deadly. The resulting pictures chimed perfectly with the news values of television journalism; they had an immediacy and impact that text could not rival. Despite the lack of serious casualties, congressmen, newspaper editors, religious leaders, and private citizens lined up to denounce Connor's tactics. And the president himself denounced the "shameful scenes," which were "so much more eloquently reported by the news camera than by any number of explanatory words."[12]

In many cities—Shreveport; Louisiana; Gadsden, Alabama; Jackson, Mississippi—the white authorities suppressed black protests with great brutality. The scale and persistence of the 1963 demonstrations, however, rendered such tactics ineffective. Segregation depended upon its everyday acceptance by blacks, as well as upon a perception by the nation at large that racial separation was too deeply embedded in Southern "folkways" to be quickly or easily uprooted. Birmingham and its shock waves shattered that sense of normality. They banished the illusion that Southern blacks were so docile and apathetic that they would put up with segregation indefinitely.

THE KENNEDY ADMINISTRATION AND THE CIVIL RIGHTS BILL

The force of the 1963 demonstrations so surprised and disturbed white Americans that the Kennedy administration decided to fundamentally revise its approach to the civil rights question. The nonviolent revolt had riveted the attention of the nation onto the South, revealing the underlying ugliness of the Jim Crow system. The federal government realized that segregation was destabilizing the South and embarrassing the United States in the eyes of the world. The government also worried that racial conflict and violence might engulf the entire nation. "It is obvious that this country is undergoing one of its most serious internal clashes since the Civil War," one aide warned Robert Kennedy. "It is obvious that this turmoil will not go away if we shut our eyes."[13]

The government was just as apprehensive about black violence as about white. As the Civil Rights Movement became less middle class, and more proletarian, the difficulties of maintaining nonviolence increased. In Birmingham, the SCLC had almost lost control on one occasion when bystanders battled police; on another occasion it did lose control when Klan bombings sparked a riot. Some mainstream black leaders seemed almost to welcome such developments. "My basic strength," stated Cecil Moore, the president of Philadelphia's NAACP branch, "is those 300,000 lower-class guys who are ready to mob, rob, steal, and kill." King himself made a similar argument, albeit phrased more diplomatically. Unless whites supported the Civil Rights Movement, he warned, "millions of Negroes . . . will seek solace and security in black nationalist ideologies, a development that will lead inevitably to a frightening racial nightmare." Demagogic threat or calm statement of fact, such predictions could not be dismissed. Nation of Islam spokesman Malcolm X was increasingly popular among black people: his chilling denunciations of nonviolence and talk of "white devils" obviously struck a chord. The

Kennedy administration feared that the "responsible" leadership of King and Roy Wilkins might soon be eclipsed by radical, extreme, violence-prone elements. The Civil Rights Movement seemed to be spinning out of control.[14]

Robert Kennedy knew what needed to be done. Only a thorough commitment to eradicating racial discrimination would enable the government to damp down the crisis, persuade black people to quit demonstrating, and shore up the responsible leaders. The situation demanded both strong legislation and determined moral leadership. "The Negroes are going to be satisfied with nothing less than a convincing demonstration that the president is on their side."[15]

On June 11—the day that Governor George Wallace of Alabama went through the charade of attempting to "block" the admission of two black students to the University of Alabama, and the day that a white supremacist shot and killed Mississippi NAACP leader Medgar Evers—President Kennedy made a television address to the nation. "We are confronted primarily with a moral issue," he stated. "It is as old as the scriptures and as clear as the American Constitution. The heart of the question is whether all Americans are to be afforded equal rights and equal opportunities, whether we are going to treat our fellow Americans as we want to be treated." The president asked Congress to pass a sweeping Civil Rights Bill. And during the following weeks he called a series of meetings in the White House to persuade businessmen, educators, religious groups, lawyers, union leaders, and Southern governors to oppose racial discrimination and support his bill. Despite plummeting popularity among white voters in the South, the president, backed to the hilt by Robert Kennedy, did not waver in his new commitment.[16]

Sensing a historic opportunity to influence the federal government, King and civil rights leaders took up A. Philip Randolph's proposal for a "March on Washington." For Randolph, it was the fulfilment of a lifetime ambition, and he appointed his old protégé Bayard Rustin—who had helped him with the 1941 March on Washington Movement—to organize it. With a staff of fifty helpers, Rustin planned the event with meticulous attention to detail. Three instruction pamphlets told participants what to wear, where to assemble, what signs to carry, what slogans to chant, and even what sandwiches to bring. They liaised with the Washington police force and held weekly meetings with federal officials. They ensured that on the day of the march people had access to 120 portable toilets, 33 drinking fountains, 6 water trucks, 19 first-aid posts, and 64 ambulances. In a movement that normally prided itself on spontaneity, nothing was left to chance.[17]

About 250,000 people turned up on August 28, 1963, to hear the songs and speeches at what was—to SNCC's disappointment—a peaceful rally rather than a militant protest. Although the March on Washington did little to spur the passage of the Civil Rights Bill, it did give the Civil Rights Movement a national platform, an opportunity to present itself as strong, united, determined, and responsible. Moreover, the presence of many white people, including prominent religious leaders, made it a visible expression of racial integration. The high moral tone of King's speech, "I Have a Dream," memorably expressed the optimism, idealism, and determination of the Civil Rights Movement. Best known for its moving vision of reconciliation and racial harmony, "I Have a Dream" also warned America that the "whirlwinds of revolt" would "continue to shake the foundations of our nation."[18]

Ironically, the march also confirmed J. Edgar Hoover's assessment of King as not only the "strongest" of the black leaders but also the most "dangerous from the standpoint of communism." Driven by Hoover's warped perception, the FBI hatched plans to discredit him. Hoover told Robert Kennedy that King's close adviser, Stanley Levison, was a Communist, and obtained permission to place wiretaps on King's telephones (it was already tapping Levison's telephones). Unbeknownst to the attorney general, the FBI also undertook a covert campaign of "dirty tricks" to undermine King's support and impede the SCLC's activities. Perhaps the most deplorable aspect of Hoover's efforts to, in his own words, "destroy the burrhead," was the bugging of hotel rooms in a search for salacious evidence of King's extramarital affairs. The FBI played the resulting tape recordings to journalists and newspaper editors, and even blackmailed King directly by sending him an audiotape with an accompanying note that invited him to commit suicide. To Hoover's frustration, however, the news media refused to cooperate and King's adultery never became public knowledge.[19]

When John Kennedy died from an assassin's bullets on November 22, 1963, the Civil Rights Bill was bogged down in Congress, and the administration appeared ready to weaken it drastically in order to buy off opposition. Lyndon Johnson, however, made passage of the bill one of his top priorities when he assumed the duties of the presidency. He urged Congress to pass the bill as a tribute to John Kennedy's memory. He not only refused to water the bill down, but he also strengthened it.

Johnson was well-equipped for this legislative task. When in the Senate, he had carefully positioned himself between the Northern liberals and the Southern segregationists—a difficult balancing act, but one that his background as a Texan enabled him to pull off. Johnson cannily refused to sign the Southern Manifesto of 1956, and played a key role in passing (and watering down) the Civil Rights Bill of 1957. While cultivating Northern liberals like Hubert H. Humphrey, he retained close friendships with Southern conservatives like Senator Richard B. Russell of Georgia. In order to obtain Senate approval for the bill, therefore, Johnson could draw upon a large reservoir of political goodwill. Johnson's political skill, continued pressure from the Civil Rights Movement, and a highly effective lobbying effort by religious groups spurred the bill's passage.

The 1964 Civil Rights Act, which Johnson signed on July 2, 1964, went further than anyone would have thought possible eighteen months earlier. It banned discrimination in employment, federally assisted programs, public facilities, and public accommodations. The Act empowered the government to initiate lawsuits to desegregate Southern school districts, and to withhold federal funds from recalcitrant school boards. It set up an Equal Employment Opportunities Commission, and created a Community Relations Service to mediate racial problems. The Act not only prohibited discrimination on the grounds of race and color, but also on the grounds of religion and national origin. In the case of employment, it included discrimination on the grounds of sex—a conservative wrecking amendment that backfired on its sponsor.

The most immediate and obvious effect of the Act was the integration of public accommodations. Title II applied to hotels, motels, restaurants, lunch counters, movie theaters, concert halls, and sports stadiums. There was some doubt as to whether the Act covered bars and taverns, but in due course the courts ruled that it did. Only private clubs were excluded. Almost overnight, the South's elaborate structure of racial segregation collapsed. Jim Crow had finally expired. To most people's surprise, white Southerners accepted integration with relatively little resistance.

Although it could justly celebrate getting rid of the most egregious and humiliating forms of racial discrimination, the Civil Rights Movement quickly realized that the 1964 Civil Rights Act was merely another milestone in a long and difficult journey. The abolition of segregated public accommodations was gratifying, but swift white adjustment to the change provided an ironic indication of its superficial nature. The more substantive sections of the Act, those dealing with schools and employment, were statements of intent that demanded an enormous effort of enforcement. Whites continued to fight school integration, and showed little willingness to surrender the economic benefits of job discrimination. Finally, the voting section of the Civil Rights Act was so inadequate that it left the problem of black disfranchisement virtually untouched. The Civil Rights Movement had to campaign all over again, and more people had to suffer and die, in order to remedy that defect.

SNCC AND THE FREEDOM SUMMER

For black people in Mississippi, the Civil Rights Act changed little. A few brave and determined souls, like Mrs. Mae Bertha Carter of Drew, Mississippi, managed to enroll their children in "white" schools, but they encountered violence, harassment, and isolation. The vast majority of schools stayed segregated. A trickle of blacks succeeded in registering to vote, but not enough to make any political difference. Herein lay the fundamental weaknesses of the Act: it not only failed to guarantee that most basic of rights, the right to vote, but it also failed to protect people from racist violence.

The Civil Rights Movement in Mississippi, spearheaded by SNCC, had demonstrated resilience and staying power. By 1963, however, it had reached a stalemate that threatened to sap its vitality. "Collusion between the police and vigilantes was still the major problem facing civil rights workers," writes John Dittmer, "who after two years of intense activity had not yet won the right to organize black communities." In the winter of 1963–64, moreover, the problem of white violence increased geometrically when a new incarnation of the Ku Klux Klan unleashed a campaign of terror. Cross-burnings, church-burnings, beatings, shootings, and murders followed. The victims included Louis Allen, who had witnessed the shooting of Herbert Lee in 1961, and Clinton Walker, a paperworker and union activist from Natchez.[20]

In pondering how to overcome this bloody impasse, Robert Moses suggested a massive campaign of community organization and political education in 1964, a "Mississippi Freedom Summer." The heart of his plan was to recruit Northern white students to assist in the campaign. In 1963 eighty students from Yale and Stanford had visited Mississippi for about two weeks to assist in the organization of a mock "Freedom Vote." Moses now proposed to import up to *one thousand* white students, and ask them to stay for two months. "Previous projects have gotten little or no national publicity . . . and hence little national support either from public opinion or from the federal government," he explained. "A large number of students from the North making the necessary sacrifices to go South would make it abundantly clear that this is not a situation which can be ignored any longer."[21]

The plan to import Northern white students received strong support from Fannie Lou Hamer and other local activists. They wanted all the help that they could get. It was also consistent with SNCC's strong ideological commitment to integration—the organization's symbol was a black hand clasping a white hand.

Many SNCC staff members, however, expressed outright opposition. The reasons for their misgivings were complex. In 1964 SNCC was still a small, tightly knit group of about 120 full-time staff members, four-fifths of whom were blacks. All but a handful of the forty-one Mississippi staff were blacks. Most of those black staffers feared the consequences of so many Northern whites descending upon Mississippi. They believed that the students, only in the state for seventy days, would disrupt the relationships with local communities that SNCC staff members had patiently built over many months and years. They worried that local black people would be awed by the students, placing their trust in Northern white people rather than relying on themselves. They feared that Ivy League students would upstage poorly educated SNCC workers and "take over."

Finally, as former SNCC chairman John Lewis recalled, some black staff members were developing "anger and rage about whites in general, and white people in the room naturally became targets." Many frankly resented the idea that the Civil Rights Movement could be "saved" by white people—especially students who viewed spending a summer in Mississippi as a way of injecting some spice, adventure, and "meaning" into their otherwise safe, bourgeois lives. The comments of SNCC worker Ralph Allen typified this resentment. Too many white staff members, he reported, were "insensitive oafs." It was embarrassing "when you see them trying to wring some kind of tortuous rhythm out of their pale souls in a mass meeting."[22]

The issue of white participation became intertwined with a debate over nonviolence and self-defense. Many SNCC workers rebutted the notion that blacks in Mississippi were defenseless and that the situation required the intervention of a thousand white students. Most black families already owned shotguns for shooting game; confronted with a wave of Klan violence, they used them to defend themselves, their families, and civil rights workers. "In rural areas particularly," writes Charles Payne, "self-defense was just not an issue among Blacks. If attacked, people were going to shoot back." Veteran SNCC workers like Charles MacLaurin, Sam Block, and Hollis Watkins applauded this move toward armed self-defense, and welcomed the protection of local blacks. SNCC itself began to flirt with guns. Willie Peacock arranged to have weapons brought into SNCC's Freedom House in Greenwood. Charles Cobb and others carried guns in their cars.[23]

By 1964 few SNCC workers clung to a pure ideal of nonviolence: they knew very well that their unmerited suffering did little to soften the racist attitudes of white Mississippians. Yet Moses and others were profoundly skeptical that armed self-defense offered a way forward. As one staff member put it, "There is no protection against Mississippi. That's what we're fighting for. Only the federal government can protect us. . . . If we concentrate only on staying alive, people will be too frightened to cross the street." Underlying such arguments was the assumption that out of a thousand white students, some were bound to get hurt, even killed; indeed, that was the principal reason for inviting them to Mississippi. The death of a white college student, recalled Dave Dennis of CORE, was bound to attract national attention, whereas the death of a black person would go unnoticed. SNCC was loath to state this intention openly, for it smacked of the very manipulation that it condemned in the SCLC. Yet everyone understood. "We know that the summer project was conceived with the idea of bloodshed," Ruby Doris Smith told a staff meeting in June 1964. As Prathia Hall put it, "We must bring the reality of our situation to the nation. Bring our blood to the White House door."[24]

Moses's plan carried the day. Things could not go on as they were, he insisted; something drastic needed to be done. Only a massive effort of unprecedented size could achieve a breakthrough. Up to now, the federal government had largely ignored the situation in Mississippi. The presence of so many white students from the North would focus national attention on Mississippi and create irresistible pressure for the Johnson administration to furnish protection. The students would be coming from America's leading universities; they were the sons and daughters of wealthy, influential, and politically connected parents, including congressmen and governors. "We wanted to break Mississippi open," recalled SNCC staff member Casey Hayden. "So many people were getting picked off one by one, the local leaders were getting murdered, people were being evicted, and the white power structure was so strong that . . . we needed an enormous amount of outside support to punch a hole in the whole system of segregation."[25]

That violence would greet the students was a certainty. At the beginning of June, Robert Kennedy warned President Johnson that acts of terrorism were on the rise, and that the situation in Mississippi presented "new and quite unprecedented problems of law enforcement." Put simply, the Klan had the support of police, politicians, "and a substantial segment of the white population." Many police were themselves Klansmen. The outgoing attorney general suggested that the FBI pursue white terrorists with the same vigor that it hounded Communists, sending in "specially trained" agents to infiltrate the Klan. SNCC bombarded Washington with demands for federal marshals to protect civil rights workers.[26]

On June 21, barely two weeks after Johnson received Kennedy's report, and as the first group of 250 volunteers attended a training school in Ohio, three civil rights workers visited Neshoba County, Mississippi, to investigate the burning of a black church. They never returned. James Chaney, a black Mississippian, Michael Schwerner, a white CORE staff member from New York, and Andrew Goodman, one of the student volunteers, were arrested by deputy sheriff Cecil Price, murdered by the Ku Klux Klan, and then buried in a dam. "I don't believe there's three missing," Senator Eastland assured President Johnson. "I believe it's a publicity stunt."[27]

The disappearance of Chaney, Schwerner, and Goodman created a national sensation. Bombarded by demands that he protect the civil rights work-

ers, Johnson was just as reluctant to commit troops as Eisenhower and
Kennedy had been. But he told FBI director J. Edgar Hoover in no uncertain
terms that he wanted the murder case solved and the Klan hounded:

> How many people you bring in there? . . . I think you ought to put fifty,
> a hundred people after this Klan. . . . Their very presence may save us a
> division of soldiers. . . . You ought to have the best intelligence system—
> better than you've got on the Communists. I read a dozen of your re-
> ports here last night—here till one o'clock—on Communists, and they
> can't open [their] mouths without your knowing what they're saying.
> [Hoover: "Very true."] Now I don't want these Klansmen to open their
> mouths without your knowing what they're saying.

To reinforce the message, Johnson dispatched former CIA director Allen
Dulles to Mississippi. Hoover promptly opened a new FBI office in Jackson
and increased the number of agents working in the state to 153. He also
added the Ku Klux Klan and other "white hate groups" to the list of targets
included in the Bureau's no-holds-barred "counterintelligence program"
(COINTELPRO). The FBI's pursuit of the Klan was a victory, albeit a bitter
one, for the Freedom Summer.[28]

The fact that 1964 was a presidential election year gave the Freedom Summer additional political impact. In parallel with its efforts at voter registration—an effort unlikely to produce many new voters—the Freedom Summer
mounted a statewide campaign of political mobilization leading to the establishment of a "shadow" political party. Working under the auspices of the
Council of Federated Organizations (COFO), which brought in the other
civil rights groups, SNCC organized a "freedom registration," arranged the
election of delegates to district and state conventions, and then set up the
Mississippi Freedom Democratic Party.

Although overwhelmingly black, the Mississippi Freedom Democratic
Party (MFDP) was open to all and included some white people. By sending
a delegation to the 1964 Democratic National Convention it intended to
expose the racist, undemocratic character of the official Democrats and to
challenge their right to represent the Democratic Party in Mississippi. The
discovery of the bodies of the three murdered civil rights workers on August 5
gave the MFDP challenge a particular poignancy. SNCC believed that the
MFDP's moral case was unassailable, and it had high hopes that, with the
sympathy and support of Northern liberals, the MFDP would gain official
recognition from the national Democratic Party.

President Johnson reacted to the MFDP challenge with consternation and
anger. Anxiously awaiting his party's nomination, he saw the 1964 conven-

tion, which met in Atlantic City, as the fulfillment of his lifelong ambition. He was furious that the occasion might be marred by a bitter public quarrel over the credentials of the Mississippi delegation. He worried, as well, that the dispute might ruin his prospects for winning the election. He knew full well that Mississippi itself, and probably Alabama as well, were lost causes: white voters there were all but certain to support the anti–civil rights Republican, Barry Goldwater, in the election. But if Mississippi's delegation were ejected from the convention, Johnson confided to a friend, "we're gonna lose every southern state, including Kentucky and Oklahoma and Missouri." He fretted, too, that the whites in the North were also unhappy about the party's identification with the civil rights cause. "Your labor people are upset," he told Senator Hubert Humphrey. "Think that nigra's going to get his job. They think a nigra's going to move next door to him." Johnson simply could not comprehend how the Civil Rights Movement could push the MFDP challenge to the point of endangering a Democratic victory.[29]

Summoning up all the powers at his command, but masking his moves, Johnson worked to stymie the MFDP challenge. He instructed the FBI to spy on the MFDP delegates and report their every move to him. He told Hubert Humphrey to settle the dispute if he wanted to be vice president. He enlisted Walter Reuther, president of the United Auto Workers union, to apply pressure to the civil rights leaders, including King. He ordered other political heavyweights to undermine support for the MFDP among the convention delegates. "The heat was on to a terrific degree," recalled Joseph L. Rauh, an eminent lawyer who represented the MFDP. "There were so many hatchetmen that you had to stand with your back to the wall." Johnson even commandeered the national news networks in order to interrupt television coverage of Fannie Lou Hamer, who was describing to a hushed convention committee how she had been "beat until I was exhausted" for her effort to vote.

To his credit, Johnson also approved a four-point compromise that offered something to the MFDP. The convention proposed to seat two of the MFDP leaders as delegates "at-large," welcome the rest of the delegates as "honored guests," require the Mississippi regulars to sign an oath of loyalty to the party ticket, and revise the party's rules to eliminate racial discrimination in the selection of delegates. "If I were the Negro," Johnson told Roy Wilkins, "I'd just let Mississippi sit up on the platform . . . and I'd stand to attention and salute the son of a bitch. Then I'd nominate Johnson for President. . . . And the next four years, I'd see the promised land."

The MFDP delegation rejected the compromise, dubbing it a "back of the bus" deal that betrayed the interests of black Mississippians. "We didn't come all this way for no two seats!" declared Fannie Lou Hamer. The SNCC workers, already deeply suspicious of the Democratic Party, felt especially angry. They had worked within the political system, played by the rules, and built up an unanswerable moral case, only to find their liberal allies melt away when President Johnson cracked the whip. Coming on top of the Freedom Summer—a thousand people arrested, eighty people beaten, thirty-five churches burned to the ground, six people murdered—the failure to gain recognition at Atlantic City was the last straw. Politically inexperienced, when the SNCC workers saw party politics up close—the blatant careerism, the naked power displays, the seemingly unprincipled dealmaking—they felt betrayed. SNCC lost faith in the Democratic Party, in white liberals, in King. It lost faith in America. "We are a country of racists," concluded Charles Sherrod.[30]

Yet the compromise, which the convention adopted, did represent an important victory for the Civil Rights Movement. The white Mississippians balked at the loyalty oath, and walked out of the convention. The party did, indeed, ensure that future delegations were selected fairly: the 1968 Democratic National Convention barred the white regulars, and seated the civil rights–based challengers. Moreover, the MFDP had highlighted the suffering of black Mississippians and the political oppression that underpinned it.

Having defeated the MFDP in an exercise of raw power, Johnson could now indulge his warmer, more benevolent instincts. The Democratic Party existed for "the poor and the downtrodden and the bended," he told Hubert Humphrey and Walter Reuther. "That's why it was born. And that's why it survives." For all his irritation over the MFDP's intrusion, Johnson recognized the validity of its cause. Mississippi "oughtn't to be seated," he confessed to one Southern friend, referring to the official delegation. "She wouldn't let those nigras vote. And that's not right." The disfranchisement of black people had become a running political sore, and Johnson knew that it would continue to bedevil the Democratic Party.[31]

After his crushing defeat of Barry Goldwater in the presidential election, Johnson, now president in his own right, decided to act. Against the advice of some aides—who argued that it would be impossible to pass another civil rights bill so soon after the last one—he told Congress that he intended to "eliminate every remaining obstacle to the right and the opportunity to vote." He asked his new attorney general, Nicholas Katzenbach, "to write the goddamnedest toughest voting rights act that you can devise." Johnson warned King, however, not to expect miracles: it would be a tough job getting such a bill through Congress. King told Johnson that the SCLC planned a campaign of nonviolent direct action in Selma, Alabama, to dramatize the need for such legislation and mobilize support for it. Johnson made no effort to discourage him.[32]

SELMA AND THE VOTING RIGHTS ACT

Selma epitomized the scandal of black disfranchisement. Dallas County, of which the city of Selma was a part, contained 15,000 black people of voting age; only 335 had managed to become registered voters. Whites, who were slightly outnumbered in the overall population, made up 99 percent of the electorate.

Whites retained their monopoly of political power through the tried-and-tested methods of trickery and discrimination that were common to much of the South. The details varied from place to place and constantly changed, but they were broadly similar. Complicated and deliberately misleading application forms invited error; requirements to establish "good character" disbarred black people in common-law marriages or with illegitimate children; the need to furnish identification and proof of residence proved maddeningly difficult to fulfill; above all, "constitutional interpretation tests" demanded answers to difficult and often nonsensical questions. The registrars—minor functionaries who took orders from the local politicians—enjoyed complete discretion to decide what constituted a "mistake." They routinely failed blacks but let whites sail through.

Wherever few or no blacks voted, it was safe to assume that white repression undergirded disfranchisement. Selma was no exception. Stronghold of the white Citizens Councils, it boasted a sheriff, Jim Clark, who, in the words of Ralph Abernathy, "had grown up believing that in dealing with blacks you could only use billy clubs and guns, since that is all we understood." Standing foursquare behind Clark was state judge James A. Hare, a man of extreme racist views who, in July 1964, had responded to a SNCC voter registration drive by banning public gatherings of more than three people, and enjoining fifteen organizations and nearly fifty individuals. Standing behind both men was Governor George Corley Wallace, a combative racist who was cementing his domination of Alabama politics and furthering his national political ambitions by opposing the Civil Rights Movement in no uncertain terms: "Segregation today. Segregation tomorrow. Segregation forever."

The SCLC was attracted to Selma partly because it had a strong local movement, the Dallas County Voters League, led by Rev. Frederick D. Reese and Mrs. Amelia P. Boynton, that eagerly sought its help. Boynton was a former NAACP stalwart (the organization was still banned in Alabama) from a family of civil rights activists. Andrew Young remembered her as "determined and persistent" behind her "deceptively ladylike" manner. "The local black leadership was really responsible for the Selma movement," Young insists.

"Selma was not a place that we picked out. We did not choose them. They chose us."[33]

Still, the prospect of confronting Jim Clark strongly appealed to the SCLC. A vain man with an explosive temper, he could be counted on, the SCLC believed, to abuse, bully, and jail any organized groups of black people who went to the courthouse to apply to register. With a posse of "special deputies"—local roughnecks nicknamed "squirrel shooters"—Clark seemed the perfect foil for the SCLC's tactics. But if Clark failed to oblige with arrests and outrageous behavior, the SCLC stood ready to mount demonstrations in other, even less hospitable, locations. Precisely where the white reaction occurred did not really matter: as long as it kept pushing and probing, the SCLC believed, it could precipitate a confrontation somewhere in Alabama that would seize the nation's attention. Indeed, SCLC worker James Bevel had long argued that Governor George Wallace's political ambitions, which led him to contemptuously defy the federal government, made Alabama the perfect setting for such a confrontation. For more than a year—since the Birmingham church bombing of September 15, 1963—Bevel and his wife, Diane Nash, had been preparing the groundwork for a direct and dramatic showdown between the Civil Rights Movement and Wallace. They called their scenario G.R.O.W. (Get Rid of Wallace).

An element of provocation, therefore, was apparent from the start in the Selma campaign. "With any luck we would be visibly abused without being maimed or killed," recalled Abernathy. "The line we walked was increasingly thin in these matters." King's instructions to Andrew Young, written from a Selma jail cell in early February, were cryptic but revealing. "Have a night march to the city jail protesting my arrest," wrote King. "Have another night march to court house to let Clark show his true collors [sic]." King then urged his staff to expand the campaign into the neighboring counties of Perry and Lowndes, where no blacks voted, and where demonstrations were even more likely to arouse white opposition. Simultaneous demonstrations in different parts of the state would be the next step. "Please don't be too soft," he told Young. "It was a mistake not to march today. In a crisis we must have a sense of drama."[34]

The white response to the SCLC's protests gave the Selma campaign a dynamic momentum, producing a series of escalating and increasingly violent confrontations. "Sheriff Clark's temper," recalled SNCC's John Lewis, "play[ed] right into our hands." He not only arrested demonstrators but also shoved, prodded, and thumped them; news reporters and cameramen lapped it up. However, neither Clark's brutal antics, nor the jailing of 3,500 people, commanded the journalists' attention for long. As President Johnson procrastinated over whether to propose voting legislation, and as the news media lost interest in the Selma campaign, the SCLC felt impelled to embark on bolder, more dangerous tactics—what King called "broader forms of civil disobedience."[35]

On February 18, during a night march in the small town of Marion, 400 marchers were attacked by state troopers, Jim Clark's posse, local police, and assorted toughs. A young black man, Jimmie Lee Jackson, was shot by a trooper and mortally wounded. He died eight days later. Jackson's lingering death prompted the SCLC to initiate the direct confrontation with Governor Wallace that had been part of its game plan all along. It proposed a fifty-four-mile march from Selma to Montgomery, with the aim of placing the responsibility for Jackson's death at Wallace's door. The governor obligingly banned the march and ordered the state police to stop it. On Sunday, March 7, 1965, about six hundred people, walking two abreast, set out from Selma. After they crossed Edmund Pettus Bridge, which spanned the Alabama River, they encountered a phalanx of state troopers, backed by Sheriff Clark and his posse, some of them on horseback. After the marchers halted, and refused to disperse, the white lawmen attacked. They clubbed, teargassed, trampled, rode down, and chased the marchers. *Time* described it as "an orgy of police brutality."[36]

What became known as "Bloody Sunday" unfolded in full view of the world's press. Everyone who bought a newspaper read about it. Everyone who owned a television set saw it. Rarely has an event aroused public opinion so quickly and decisively. Politicians, editors, religious leaders, and private citizens joined the Civil Rights Movement in denouncing the violence—and, significantly, the chorus of condemnation included some white Southerners. "What the public felt," one aide wrote Johnson, "was the deepest sense of outrage it has ever felt on the civil rights question." "The horses, the whips, and the tear gas was what shocked and aroused the public," echoed another. "It was the television films of these tactics which circulated around the world to our nation's detriment."[37]

Many people acted as well as spoke. Protest marches took place in New York, Detroit, Toronto, Chicago, Boston, Los Angeles, Philadelphia, St. Louis, and elsewhere. People picketed the White House and sat-in at the Justice Department. Responding to the SCLC's call for help, more than 400 clergymen, including nuns, ministers, rabbis, and an Orthodox archbishop, travelled to Selma to participate in further marches. One of them, James Reeb, a Unitarian minister from Boston, died from a blow to the head when a group of white men assaulted him. His death prompted further denunciations and sympathetic actions, especially from the churches. Religious delegations lobbied President Johnson and the National Council of Churches sponsored a rally in Washington, D.C.'s, Lafayette Square that attracted 15,000 people.

Deluged by calls for federal action from both within the government and without, President Johnson seized the political moment to propose the legislation he had been quietly considering for months. On March 15 he addressed a joint session of Congress to propose the enactment of a Voting Rights Bill. Comparing Selma to Lexington, Concord, and Appomattox, Johnson called Selma a "turning point in man's unending search for freedom." In a remarkable tribute to the Civil Rights Movement, he praised the heroism of "the American Negro," whose "actions and protests—his courage to risk safety, and even to risk his life—have awakened the conscience of this Nation." Outlining the details of the bill, he vowed to "protect the right of every American citizen to vote." He challenged Congress to act swiftly and decisively. "This time, on this issue, there must be no delay, or no hesitation, or no compromise." Urging the nation to overcome "the crippling legacy of bigotry and injustice," Johnson astonished his listeners by invoking the anthem of the Civil Rights Movement: "We Shall Overcome."[38]

As the Selma campaign wound down, white racists claimed another victim, Viola Liuzzo, a white sympathizer from Detroit, shot dead by Klansmen. The SCLC adamantly denied that it sought to create politically useful martyrs by provoking white violence. "When you give witness to an evil," King explained, "you do not cause that evil but you expose it so that it can be cured." Andrew Young put the same point in more worldly terms. "The movement did not 'cause' problems in Selma," he insisted. "Sheriff Clark has been beating black heads in the back of the jail for years, and we're only saying to him that if he still wants to beat heads, he'll have to do it on Main Street, at noon, in front of CBS, NBC, and ABC television cameras."[39]

The tragedy of Selma, and of the three people who died, was not that the SCLC's provocative tactics led to violence; but, rather, that the cynicism of the news media, and the indifference of the nation's political leaders, made that violence inevitable. As *Time* commented when a demonstration led by King came off peacefully, if nonviolent direct action met a nonviolent response, it was "like driving a tack into a marshmallow." Without conflict, the press got bored. The SCLC would have been delighted to stop its protests once the president introduced voting legislation. But Johnson bided his time. As Attorney General Katzenbach advised him on March 1, the administration needed "to mobilize as much of a consensus as possible" in order to put forward legislation. It took "Bloody Sunday" to produce such a consensus.[40]

Christian faith helped the SCLC, and many other black Southerners, accept such grim realities. As King put it, "There can be no remission of sin without the shedding of blood." Yet, despite the jailings, the beatings, and the deaths, the Civil Rights Movement succeeded in transforming Southern race relations with remarkably few casualties. The genius of nonviolence was its ability to expose and discredit the South's racism while inhibiting the white propensity to violence. As Stanley Levison put it, "We would be at fault if we believed our own propaganda that Selma was a terrible expression of brutality and terrorism. Considerable restraint was shown by the authorities. The degree of violence was shocking and startling, but not extensive."[41]

"We are on the move now, and no wave of racism can stop us," King assured 25,000 people at the conclusion of the march from Selma to Montgomery—a march finally sanctioned by a federal judge and protected by federal troops. As King addressed a victory rally from the steps of the state capitol, the seat of political power in Alabama, King could not help but see his old church. The distance from the Dexter Avenue Baptist Church to the Alabama state capitol measured a hundred yards or so. It had taken ten years to travel that hundred yards.[42]

Five months later, the Voting Rights Act became law. It disallowed literacy tests, "constitutional interpretation tests," and "good character" requirements in any state or county where less than half the voting-age population were registered voters, or actually voted, in the 1964 presidential election. The formula covered Louisiana, Mississippi, Alabama, Georgia, South Carolina, North Carolina, and Virginia. The Act also empowered the attorney general to appoint federal registrars in those states without having to gain the permission of a federal court. The crowning achievement of the Civil Rights Movement, the Voting Rights Act reenfranchised black Southerners and democratized the South. It ended the era of Jim Crow.

Black Panthers demonstrating their support for Huey Newton, circa 1970

Bettmann/CORBIS

14

The Rise and Fall of Black Power

RIOTING AND THE GHETTO REVOLT

On the evening of August 11, 1965, as Los Angeles sweltered in a smog-laden summer heat wave, a California Highway Patrol officer, Lee Minikus, pulled over a Buick at Avalon Avenue and 122nd Street. In the driver's seat was Marquette Frye, a twenty-one-year-old black man; beside him sat his younger brother, Ronald. Marquette had never graduated from high school, possessed a juvenile record, and was currently unemployed. Having recently downed several "screwdrivers," his driving was noticeably erratic, and when Minikus administered a sobriety test, Frye failed it. A crowd gathered as more police arrived, and Frye's mother, Rena Frye, joined the scene. Shamed or emboldened by his mother's presence, Marquette became loud, uncooperative, and unruly. He cursed the policemen. Tension mounted as the altercation unfolded.

Who first hit whom was later disputed, but it seems that a police officer either struck, or roughly handled, Mrs.Frye. People in the crowd—which now exceeded a hundred and was still growing—yelled their disapproval. "Leave the lady alone!" "It's just like Selma!" "They'd never treat a white woman like that!" "Motherfuckers!"[1]

As officers moved to disperse the onlookers, what began as the routine arrest of a drunk driver turned into a riot. "Rocks began flying," reported the *Los Angeles Times,* "then wine and whiskey bottles, chunks of concrete, pieces of wood—anything that could be thrown." Six consecutive days of ur-

ban violence followed, with rioters looting and burning stores, attacking firemen, battling the police, and assaulting white people. Labelled the "Watts
riot," after the black section of south Los Angeles in which it erupted, the violence ranged over forty-five square miles, destroyed an estimated $200 mil-
lion of property, led to 4,000 people being arrested, and left thirty-four
people dead.[2]

The bloodiest race riot since the Detroit outbreak of 1943, Watts dwarfed
the 1964 disturbances in New York, Philadelphia, and Rochester. Although
black leaders had been ritualistically warning that the Northern ghettos were
combustible, the destructiveness of the Watts riot, and the fact that it occurred amid the palm trees of Los Angeles—not the popular image of a typical
ghetto—shocked everyone.

The McCone Commission, however, appointed by Governor Pat Brown to
investigate the riot, tried to downplay the significance of the outbreak by calling
it "senseless." This was criminal vandalism, it argued, not purposeful protest.
The commission's report made light of racial discrimination, virtually exoner-
ated the Los Angeles Police Department, and criticized the Civil Rights Movement for having weakened black respect for law and order. The commission
blamed the violence on a small, unrepresentative minority of unemployed
young men, many of them recent migrants from the South, who were on the
criminal fringes of society. Only 10,000 people, it argued, had engaged in rioting—at the very most, 5 percent of the area's black population. Watts had been
an "insensate rage of destruction . . . engaged in by a few but bringing distress
to all."[3]

The McCone Report's "riffraff" theory, however, badly misstated the riot's
significance. If the figure of 10,000 was accurate, critics pointed out, then 40
percent of all the rioters had been arrested—a claim that was plainly absurd.
On the basis of postriot interviews, social scientists more plausibly estimated
that 15 percent of the population—80,000 people—had rioted, and reckoned
that a further 34 percent had approved of the riot as they watched it unfold.
Critics of the report also disputed the contention that the riot had been pur-
poseless: most blacks defined it as a protest which, they believed, would draw
attention to their grievances. Bayard Rustin pointed out that the rioters acted
with a degree of deliberation and rationality: they attacked property rather
than people, singling out white-owned stores that they regarded as exploita-
tive. Sociologist Robert Blauner likened the outbreak to a "mass rebellion
against colonial status."

Perhaps the most striking aspect of the riot, apart from its sheer destructiveness, was the lack of remorse felt by the local black population. Despite
the fact that all but a handful of the dead were black people, most blacks in

Los Angeles did not conclude that the riot had been a tragic mistake. Even those who disapproved of the riot felt sympathy for the rioters, placed most of the blame upon the police, and believed that the riot had drawn attention to black grievances. Many blacks felt a positive pride in having seized control of the streets and given the police—universally loathed for their racism and brutality—a bloody nose. "The mood of Watts last week smacked less of defeat than of victory and power," noted *Newsweek*.[4]

This celebratory, unrepentant attitude boded ill for the Civil Rights Movement. Ever since the much smaller riots of 1964, King had been weighing the possibility of taking the SCLC North, applying the methods of nonviolence to the problems of the ghetto. In moving North, however, the SCLC had to contend with apathy, skepticism, and outright hostility. When Andrew Young and James Bevel tried to explain nonviolence to black youths in Rochester, New York, after a riot there in 1964, they got nowhere. "What is all this Jesus crap?" asked one nonconvert. Now, visiting Watts, King evoked the same cynical response. Gerald Horne describes a typical encounter. "With his rolling cadences King began, 'All over America . . . the Negroes must join hands . . .' 'And burn,' added a heckler." Shouted another: "Go back where you came from."[5]

The rioters' cries of "Burn, baby, burn!" and "Get whitey!" seemed to express a visceral hatred of white people. Sensational reporting by the news media may well, in fact, have exaggerated the depth of that hatred: some whites were beaten up during the Watts riot, but not a single white person died through the direct action of rioters. The rioters directed their wrath against the police, not white people in general. Nevertheless, Watts brought into the open a widespread hostility toward whites that had been festering beneath the surface in the Northern ghettos—a gut resentment of white people that seemed far more intense in the North than in the South.

Only a few months earlier, *Newsweek* had reported that "Far from being an explosively frustrated mass," blacks were "caught up by an exhilarating sense of progress" and were "more deeply committed than ever to the strategy of nonviolence." Judged by the gains of the Civil Rights Movement and the beneficence of the Johnson administration, they had every reason to be. But appearances were deceptive. The civil rights reforms had been designed with the South in mind; the legislation of Johnson's "Great Society," especially the much-ballyhooed "War on Poverty," raised black expectations but offered no route out of the ghetto. The situation for many blacks in the North had not improved at all, and in some respects it was deteriorating.[6]

SEGREGATION AND DISCRIMINATION IN THE NORTH

Some urban experts believed that the difficulties faced by blacks in the North were akin to those experienced by European immigrants half a century earlier: in both cases, the arrival of large numbers of impoverished rural folk created overcrowded slums and caused political tension. Certainly, the scale of the continuing black migration was bound to strain the urban fabric: about 4 million blacks left the South for the North between 1940 and 1965. The black population of New York increased from 6 percent of the total population to 16 percent; that of Chicago, from 8 percent to 27 percent; that of Los Angeles, from 4 percent to 18 percent; that of Detroit, from 9 percent to 29 percent; that of Washington, D.C., from 28 percent to 63 percent. Sheer numbers, argued Professor Philip M. Hauser, "made the Negro in-migratory stream relatively unassimilable—economically, socially and politically." Like the immigrants, blacks *would* eventually climb up America's economic ladder, but "it requires time—time measured in human generations rather than years."[7]

Time, however, was not operating in a benign manner. The latest and largest wave of black migrants had started during the Second World War, when an enormous increase in industrial production eliminated mass unemployment and created new opportunities for black people to enter the blue-collar workforce. These were the kind of factory jobs that had provided generations of European immigrants—Poles, Czechs, Slovaks, Hungarians, Italians, Greeks, and others—with stable employment and decent livelihoods. But the black migrants gained a toehold in the industrial economy at precisely the time when advances in technology were eliminating blue-collar jobs, and when changes in the organization of industry shifted employment away from central cities and towards suburbs, small towns, and green fields. Moreover, many employers imposed skills tests on job applicants that previous generations of immigrants had never had to face—a considerable handicap to Southern migrants who had been educated in some of the worst schools in America.

Many migrants did, to be sure, achieve a degree of economic security, and the proportion of black workers classified as "white-collar" increased from 10 percent in 1940 to 18 percent in 1960. For a large segment of the black working class, however, wartime employment gains did not last. In 1948 black unemployment stood at a low of 5.9 percent, a ratio of 1.7 compared to white unemployment. By 1954, however, almost 10 percent of black workers were jobless, double the rate among whites. Black unemployment stayed at twice the white level for the rest of the decade and throughout the 1960s. Equally discouraging was a sharp decline in black participation in the workforce, especially among men: from 87 percent in 1948 to 77 percent twenty years later. A growing number of young black males between the ages of sixteen and twenty-four dropped out of legal employment. Many of them joined gangs and engaged in criminal activities.[8]

The problems faced by blacks in the North were undoubtedly complex. Still, white prejudice, which often derived from the clannishness and conservatism of recently arrived ethnic groups, helped to isolate blacks and retard their progress. Racial discrimination in employment, for example, was commonplace, despite fair employment laws in most Northern states. The unions were often to blame. In the construction industry, for example, it was virtually impossible for blacks to obtain a union card. Limiting the size of their membership, the craft unions accepted new apprentices on a friends-and-relatives basis, thereby perpetuating a white monopoly. The apprenticeship itself could last up to five years, giving union officials ample opportunity to discourage black interlopers. Such practices ensured that the plumbers union was 99.8 percent white; electrical workers 99.4 percent white; and carpenters 98.4 percent white. Even in unions with substantial black memberships, like the UAW, blacks found themselves concentrated in lower-paid, "unskilled" jobs, and underrepresented at the leadership level.[9]

Housing was perhaps the strongest and most visible expression of racial discrimination in the North. Despite the Supreme Court's invalidation of "restrictive covenants" in 1948, residential segregation persisted in every city. Supported by the vast majority of white homeowners, who viewed the proximity of black people as a threat, the real estate industry covertly operated a dual housing market, with the object of maintaining separation of the races. In practice, this involved preventing blacks from buying or renting in areas occupied by whites. When the pressure of numbers became too great, neighborhoods on the edge of the ghetto shifted from white to black—and real estate agents often made large profits by exploiting the panic selling of white homeowners. However, the black population was not permitted to disperse throughout the city, large sections of which remained off-limits to black people.

White politicians quietly reinforced segregation. They ensured that public housing projects were either all-black (those located in the ghetto) or all-white (those situated in white areas). Sporadic attempts to integrate public housing evoked vehement white resistance and were soon abandoned. Politicians also used urban redevelopment—the routing of expressways, for example—to create physical barriers between white and black areas. Until 1948 the federal government had actively encouraged segregation; until 1962 it had silently acquiesced in it. Segregation became even more solidly entrenched as whites moved to new suburbs. White-only developments like Levittown on Long Island, the model for postwar suburban housing, were built with the support of the Federal Housing Authority. Even after President Kennedy banned discrimination in federal housing programs—which the 1964 Civil Rights Act reinforced—the government did little to oppose segregation. As a result, the races lived apart and the ghettos grew; residential segregation was more rigid in the North than in the South. Segregated housing patterns produced "de facto" segregated public schools. School boards further discouraged integration by gerrymandering school attendance zones and permitting whites to transfer out of predominantly black schools.

Whites in the North expressed their opposition to integration in no uncertain terms. In 1964, only months before the Watts riot, California voters passed Proposition 14, a referendum that repealed a recently enacted fair housing law. Voters in other states also rejected antidiscrimination laws. White determination to exclude blacks sometimes turned violent: in Chicago, black families who settled in white neighborhoods met with harassment, arson attacks, physical assaults, and at least a dozen riots between 1945 and 1964. In 1952 Illinois governor Adlai Stevenson called out the National Guard when the arrival of blacks in the satellite town of Cicero triggered rioting. The blacks departed and Cicero remained an all-white enclave of 70,000 people. Where housing was concerned, racial discrimination in the North lost its subtlety; it was raw and open.

THE SCLC'S CHICAGO CAMPAIGN AND THE WHITE BACKLASH

This is what the SCLC discovered in Chicago, where King led his first campaign in the North. After floundering for the first half of 1966, the SCLC focused its attack upon housing segregation, organizing marches in the city's all-white neighborhoods. It was a brilliantly effective tactic. By evoking the same kind of violent opposition it had encountered in the South—white mobs burned cars, hurled bricks, and bodily assaulted the marchers—the SCLC exposed the depth of Chicago's racial division and exerted intense political pressure upon Mayor Richard J. Daley. Forced to the negotiating table, Daley accepted a "Summit Agreement" that consisted of promises by the city of Chicago, and by local real estate agents, to promote housing integration. Having defused the immediate crisis, however, Mayor Daley quietly shelved the Summit Agreement. King was bitterly disappointed by the betrayal.

On one level, Daley simply outfoxed King. Yet the SCLC's failure in

Chicago had deeper causes. A Southern organization accustomed to mobilizing small communities, the SCLC lacked the know-how and the resources to reach a massive black population of one and a half million people. Used to dealing with one-dimensional villains like "Bull" Connor and Jim Clark, the SCLC found Mayor Richard J. Daley a subtle, skillful politician, who opposed the Civil Rights Movement with kind words and smart gestures rather than fire hoses and billy clubs. Supporting Daley, and opposing the SCLC, were Chicago's black politicians—elected officials, like Congressman William L. Dawson, who not only enjoyed a certain legitimacy but also, because they were part of the Democratic "machine," possessed patronage and favors to dispense or withhold.

The SCLC also found it difficult to adapt to the hard-edged, more secular, urban culture of the North. The black church lacked the prestige and influence that it commanded in the South. In the North, many blacks seemed cynical, alienated, and impervious to the SCLC's idealism. "We were particularly disturbed by the youth gangs," recalled Ralph Abernathy; they looted, robbed, and raped; terrorized whole neighborhoods; fought with each other. "[T]hose hard-eyed black boys had no respect for anything or anybody. To them a preacher was the next worse thing to a policeman, and religion was for old folks and suckers, both of whom they regarded with a fine contempt." A serious riot that erupted in the West Side ghetto in July 1966 sharply illuminated the SCLC's inability to influence these gangs. King, stranded in the middle of the riot area, tried to stop the spreading violence. People refused to listen, heckling and cursing him.[10]

The more profound reasons for the SCLC's failure, however, had to do with white people, not blacks. Southern brutality had aroused the conscience of the nation, causing whites in the North, from presidents down, to assist the cause of the Civil Rights Movement. The SCLC's marches in Chicago evoked similar violence, but they did not gain white sympathy. Indeed, the liberals who had lauded King a year earlier—and even marched beside him at Selma—now condemned his tactics as irresponsible and provocative. Sympathy for the Civil Rights Movement seemed to evaporate when it crossed the Mason-Dixon line.

Northern politicians attributed this lack of sympathy to a "white backlash" that had been caused by black lawlessness and violence. According to this theory, the outbreak of riots and the spread of antiwhite rhetoric alarmed basically well-meaning whites. Most whites believed that demonstrations encouraged riots and should stop. By 1966, according to an opinion poll, 85 percent of all whites had come to the conclusion that demonstrations were "hurting the Negro cause." The number of white people in the North who believed that the Johnson administration was pushing integration "too fast" grew from 28 percent in April 1965 to 36 percent in August 1965 (after Watts), and to 52 percent in September 1966. "White people are scared and sore and the consensus behind improvement of the Negro's condition is running out—has run out," White House aide Harry McPherson wrote Johnson. The 1966 Civil Rights Bill, which proposed to ban housing discrimination, failed to pass. Shortly afterwards, in the midterm elections, the Democrats lost forty-nine seats in the House and four in the Senate.[11]

Bayard Rustin contended that the Civil Rights Movement had to shift "from protest to politics," investing its energies in building support for a progressive agenda within the Democratic Party. Yet race was splitting apart the traditional New Deal coalition. In state after state, wrote pollsters William Brink and Louis Harris, elections showed "the defections from the Democratic party of the late-arriving Catholic minorities."[12]

Few sensible people—and certainly not King—denied that rioting had set back the cause of racial equality. Yet while riots might have intensified the "white backlash," they did not cause it. In 1963, before any serious rioting had occurred, opinion polls documented the fact that "anti-Negro prejudice is widespread and deeply rooted in the U.S., extending to the vast majority of ordinary, well-meaning Americans." North and South, most whites shunned social contact with black people, did not want integrated housing, and thought blacks were moving ahead "too fast." In 1964, when Alabama governor George Wallace, the symbol of Southern racism, campaigned in the Democratic presidential primaries, he won a third of the vote in Indiana and Wisconsin, drawing most of his support from working-class ethnic Catholics. Yet middle-class whites were just as loath to associate with black people, constituting what Louis Harris described as "the strong silent partner to overt anti-black sentiment"—people who felt that "Negroes should be kept in their place."[13]

None of this should have come as a surprise. Yet since World War II, politicians in the North had avoided the issues of white prejudice and racial segregation, fully aware of the fact that any effort to confront them would drive away white voters. They denied that racial prejudice in the North was comparable to racism in the South. In 1963 Mayor Daley even denied the very existence of ghettos in Chicago, asserting that different ethnic and racial groups naturally preferred to live among their own kind. This massive exercise in denial had been possible because the Cold War, and the general prosperity of the postwar era, had muted the voices of protest. As long as blacks in the North remained politically quiescent, racial divisions could be ignored. In 1963, however, when Birmingham sparked off demonstrations in the North as well as the South, politicians suddenly took note of a rising "white backlash." As historian Thomas J. Sugrue insists, that backlash "had deep roots in a simmering politics of race and neighborhood defensiveness that divided northern cities well before . . . the long, hot summers of Watts, Harlem, Chicago, Newark, and Detroit."[14]

Police brutality brought Northern racism into sharp focus. Studies of the police indicated that almost three-quarters of all officers harbored "extreme" or "considerable" prejudice against black people. Many belonged to right-wing extremist groups such as the John Birch Society; attributing society's ills to "Jews, niggers and Communists," and openly supporting George Wallace. Many, perhaps most, treated black people with contempt, failed to distinguish between criminals and law-abiding citizens, and resorted to violence with or without provocation. "It's the police really make people mad," three Washington teenagers explained to White House aide Harry McPherson. "They get you in a station house and really bounce you around."[15]

When a police officer shot a black person in the line of duty, he rarely incurred any adverse consequences. In Los Angeles, for example, the police shot and killed sixty-five people during the two and a half years preceding the Watts riot. Of the victims, writes Gerald Horne, "twenty-seven . . . were shot in the back, twenty-five were unarmed, twenty-three were suspected of theft or other nonviolent crimes, and four had committed no crime at the time of the shooting." In all but one case, the verdict of the coroner's inquest was "justifiable homicide." The riots, moreover, prompted the police to assert their power even more forcefully. During the riots themselves, they abandoned all restraint, treating the outbreaks as race wars and inflicting fearsome casualties. After the riots, enjoying overwhelming support from the white population, police forces built up exotic arsenals and contemptuously defied the efforts of liberal politicians to rein them in. A statement by LAPD chief William Parker during the Watts riot unconsciously betrayed the attitude of the police toward black people: "We're on top and they are on the bottom." No wonder most blacks feared and distrusted the police.[16]

Chicago was the first and only real attempt by the Civil Rights Movement to mount a major campaign of nonviolent direct action in the North. Its failure confirmed what most blacks in the North already knew: white racism was too deep, and too violent, to be susceptible to the moral appeal of nonviolent protest. For King, however, Chicago was a revelation, convincing him that the Civil Rights Movement had badly underestimated the depth and tenacity of racism. He also learned that a substantial minority of black people vocally advocated violence, and that a smaller but still significant minority were ready to engage in it. The problem was not so much King's lack of support in the North—he commanded widespread respect—as the ability of a violent minority to render his leadership ineffective. Nonviolent protest could only be sustained by hope and optimism. In the North, bitterness and disillusionment seemed to rule. As a Harlem high school student told a group of visiting high schoolers from Mississippi, "Turning the other cheek is a load of trash. Up here we understand what snake is biting us." This was the language of Malcolm X, not Martin Luther King.[17]

MALCOLM X AND HIS LEGACY

Malcolm X had been murdered six months before the Watts riot—gunned down by members of the Nation of Islam—at the age of thirty-nine. However, he had already established a formidable reputation as the leading black critic of nonviolence, the foremost black advocate of armed self-defense, and the black man who most effectively articulated antiwhite anger. In the early 1960s Malcolm X had represented an ideological counterforce to the Civil Rights Movement—one that was often invoked by civil rights leaders themselves for the purpose of frightening white elites. After his death, Malcolm became a heroic symbol both to advocates of violence and proponents of black nationalism. In the Northern ghettos, Malcolm, dead, often seemed more influential than King, alive.

Given his longtime attachment to the small, cultist Nation of Islam (NOI), Malcolm's influence seemed remarkable. Founded in 1930 by Wallace D. Fard, and led since 1934 by Elijah Muhammad, the NOI's strange theology, strict discipline, financial demands upon members, and uncompromising rejection of American society kept its support small—smaller than all but the most esoteric Christian denominations. Yet the NOI commanded respect and influence out of proportion to its numbers, largely because it sought, with considerable success, to combat the destructive influences of the ghetto by inculcating values of racial pride, sobriety, hard work, and self-respect into its members. It specialized in recruiting criminals, drug addicts, and prostitutes and transforming them into models of piety and puritanism—Malcolm X himself had been converted while in prison for burglary. Urging blacks to practice self-help and to build a separate economy, the NOI developed successful business enterprises by pooling the resources and efforts of its members. By 1959 the NOI boasted 30 temples in 28 cities.

Left to Elijah Muhammad, the Nation of Islam would never have become a political force in black America. Characterizing white people as "blue-eyed devils," the NOI believed that black people should separate from American society to form their own black nation—an unrealistic and unconvincing message. The Nation of Islam abstained from politics and refused to have anything to do with the Civil Rights Movement, regarding its quest for integration as thoroughly misguided. Thus the NOI was nonpolitical and nonrevolutionary. "Like other successful messianic or revolutionary movements," writes historian George Fredrickson, "[it] created a separate world for its converts that isolated and prevented them from the pain of confronting the world outside."[18]

Malcolm X had recoiled from that world while shut away from it, serving a prison sentence for burglary, between 1946 and 1952. Born in 1925 in Omaha, Nebraska, Malcolm Little's early life made a striking contrast to that of Martin Luther King, Jr. King was raised in a tight-knit family in which parents and children had clearly defined roles, and where strict discipline, exerted by a stern father, had been balanced by love and security. King's family, moreover, was rooted in a strong institution, the church, and a stable community, Auburn Avenue, the heart of black Atlanta. By any standard, King's family was a model of success and achievement. Malcolm's childhood, by contrast, was scarred by instability, extreme poverty, and absence of familial affection. His father, Earl Little, a devoted follower of Marcus Garvey, came from a family "riddled with criminality" and plagued by "self-destructive violence." A jackleg preacher, occasional laborer, and would-be businessman, Earl died in a streetcar accident in 1931 when Malcolm was six years old. Eight years later his mother, Louise, an immigrant from the British West Indies, was committed to a mental institution. The eight children separated; Malcolm was placed in a juvenile home run by a white couple, then with black foster parents. But he never settled down, and in 1941, at age fifteen, he went to live with his halfsister, Ella, in Boston, only to drift into a life of drugs and crime.[19]

Strangely, but with a certain logic, King's background in the segregated black community of the South gave him the confidence to seek racial integration as a partnership of equals. He accepted the strain of white blood in his ancestry with equanimity, and there is little evidence that he suffered from self-hatred or felt conflicted over his racial identity. The Michigan towns where Malcolm grew up, however, failed to provide Malcolm with a cultural anchor, for the black population was both too small and too diffuse. Moreover, Malcolm's close contact with white society—he was the only black child in his class, for example—exacerbated feelings of emotional insecurity and cultural confusion. Having experienced integration under the most distressing circumstances, he spent his adult life denouncing whites as evil and seeking to build the secure black community that he never knew as a child.

Prison, ironically, proved Malcolm's salvation. First, he became an avid reader and succeeded in being transferred to an institution that boasted the best prison library in the state. "I only just finished the eighth grade," he wrote his sister Ella, "but I've always been all eyes and ears (even all nose) on the side." Now he deepened his quick-witted intelligence with serious study, especially in history, philosophy, and religion. Second, Malcolm learned to practice self-discipline: restraint of emotions, a refusal to be goaded, was both a necessary survival tactic and a means of developing inner strength. "One good thing you learn how to do when you're in here, and that is how to use a little self-control." Malcolm soon came to equate self-control with an almost Hegelian belief in the omnipotence of willpower:

> If we could only most fully realize the importance and power of thought and thinking. It is the most inspiring Force in the universe. . . . Words that we speak cause vibrations that traverse the entire universe. . . . For one to control one's thoughts and feelings, means one can actually control one's atmosphere and all who walk into its sphere of influence.

Such single-mindedness and self-confidence endowed Malcolm with extraordinary charisma. It also, however, caused him to exaggerate the power of the spoken word. In terms of racial leadership, Malcolm Little became a talker rather than a doer, a rhetorician, not a tactician.[20]

The third crucial event of Malcolm's prison years, his conversion to the Nation of Islam in 1948–49, not only gave him a new purpose in life but also enabled him to review his past so that the family tragedies and personal failures of his youth were caused by the deliberate actions of racist whites. His father had not accidentally stumbled under the wheels of a streetcar but had been pushed onto the track by members of the Klan-like Black Legion. His grandmother had been raped by his white grandfather on the island of Grenada. His mother had been committed so as to stop her teaching Islam. Both his parents, Malcolm convinced himself, had been Muslims. "We children were too young to fully ever know what was going down . . . but, Brother, these devils were even *then* stamping out Islam." A strong element of fantasy, even paranoia, buttressed his new faith.[21]

After his release from prison in 1952 Malcolm X—the X stood for the African name he never knew—became the most dynamic and successful minister in the Nation of Islam. He organized temples, raised funds, recruited new members, and acted as Muhammad's principal spokesman and representative. A 1959 television documentary, "The Hate That Hate Produced," projected Malcolm to a wider public audience: whites, for the first time, were exposed to the NOI's bloodcurdling rhetoric, and they came away both appalled and fascinated. Malcolm's debating skills and taste for publicity soon made him a familiar figure on the university speaking circuit, a regular guest on radio, and a man who could always be relied upon to provide newspaper reporters with good copy.

Malcolm presented himself as the authentic spokesman of the poor, oppressed black masses; a fearless truth teller who exposed the timidity and hypocrisy of civil rights leaders like King; an uncompromising prophet whose jeremiads described the historic crimes of the white race in all their infamy. Few blacks failed to relish Malcolm's quick repartee, gift for phrasemaking, and ability to best his opponents in debate. "He was a mesmerizing speaker," recalled Roy Wilkins, "the toughest man in debate that I've ever seen."[22]

Although whites usually viewed him as a racist, Malcolm's wholesale denunciation of white people as "snakes" and "devils" failed to offend blacks. Malcolm openly expressed the bitterness and anger, albeit in an extreme manner, that virtually every black person shared. "Deep in the heart of every black adult," James Farmer believed, "lives some of Malcolm and some of King, side by side." Malcolm "helped us enormously," thought Roy Wilkins, by "cataloguing the wrongs done Negroes in such powerful language." Just as black people could respect King without necessarily accepting the philosophy of nonviolence, so they could applaud Malcolm X without believing in the Nation of Islam's theology. "When Malcolm spoke," writes George Fredrickson, "listeners . . . did not need to accept the literal truth of his fantastic account of human history but could appreciate it instead as . . . symbolic rendering of the black experience."[23]

Four aspects of Malcolm X's message proved particularly influential. The first was his strong emphasis on racial pride. This was nothing new, of course, having been central to Marcus Garvey's popularity in the 1920s. In the 1950s and early 1960s, however, it represented a striking contrast to the integration-minded Civil Rights Movement. Malcolm insisted that black Americans had to purge themselves of the false consciousness that, through slavery and racism, had distorted their personalities, hidden their true identity, and divided them among themselves. Light-complexioned himself, Malcolm condemned color consciousness within the group, praising the beauty of all black people, including—especially—those with the darkest skins and most African features. "In some ways," wrote Farmer, "his appeal to the black consciousness was as strong as King's; in other ways, stronger." Malcolm's appeal to racial pride had a particularly strong appeal to lower-class blacks who resented the integrationist ambitions of middle-class, and often lighter-skinned, blacks.[24]

Malcolm also, like Garvey, stressed the African dimension of the black American identity. He was hardly unique in looking to Africa: in the 1950s and 1960s, as states like Ghana, Kenya, and Nigeria emerged from British colonialism, and as blacks in South Africa struggled against apartheid, the Civil Rights Movement drew inspiration from African nationalism. Medgar

Evers named a son after Mau Mau leader Jomo Kenyatta; Ralph Abernathy named a son after Kwame Nkrumah, who led Ghana to independence, and Albert Luthuli, president of the African National Congress. To Malcolm, however, the rise of black Africa was part of a much wider revolt of dark-skinned peoples against racism and colonialism—a worldwide revolution of such inexorable force that the dominance of the "white world" would be shattered by the power and numbers of "black, brown, red, and yellow." Malcolm drew inspiration from black Africa, yes, but also from the Chinese revolution, the Algerian revolution, and the Cuban revolution. "The black revolution is sweeping Asia, is sweeping Africa, is rearing its head in Latin America."[25]

Malcolm's third contribution was his outspoken advocacy of violence. Malcolm condemned nonviolence as cowardly and ineffective, insisting that black people had both a right and a duty to defend themselves and their families. "We believe in a fair exchange. An eye for an eye. A tooth for a tooth. A head for a head and a life for a life. If this is the price of freedom, we won't hesitate to pay the price." This was hardly an extreme view. Many blacks in the South believed in, and practiced, armed self-defense, sometimes on an organized basis. The NAACP endorsed self-defense as a constitutional right. The Old Testament *lex talionis* was thoroughly in accord with American tradition.[26]

Malcolm's position, however, went beyond self-defense. Despite his mock-innocent denials, Malcolm often insisted that violence had to be central to black liberation. Repeatedly, he predicted racial warfare, mass bloodshed, and a "day of slaughter . . . for this sinful white world." In one of his more chilling rhetorical flights, he argued that blacks needed their own "Mau Mau" in order to eliminate "Uncle Toms." In Kenya, the Mau Mau "started getting them one by one, all those Toms. One after another, they'd find those Uncle Tom Africans by the roadside. Today they're free. . . . That's the same thing that will happen here. We've got too many of our own people who stand in the way. They're too squeamish." In railing against black ministers, he urged that "Churches should be bombed and preachers killed." Seemingly endorsing indiscriminate retaliatory violence, he explained that "If I go home and my child has blood running down her leg and someone tells me a snake bit her, I'm going out and kill snakes, and when I find a snake I'm not going to look and see if he has blood on his jaws."[27]

The fourth ingredient in Malcolm's popularity was his appeal to black manhood. Historically, black men had found it difficult to establish a secure position as head of the family. Slavery, discrimination, poverty, unemployment, and the disorganizing impact of migration had all contributed to family instability, and made the mother, in many cases, the main breadwinner and principal fount of authority in the family. Women, more often than men, held black families together. The sociological literature of the 1950s and 1960s attributed many of the difficulties experienced by blacks in the Northern cities to the allegedly "matriarchal" character of the black family and the black man's lack of status. Whatever the truth of the matter—and the notion of black society as matriarchal aroused fierce controversy—it was undeniably true that many blacks, men and women, yearned for the restoration of a "traditional" family structure, with fathers clearly at the head. The Nation of Islam practiced a division of the sexes that represented an exaggerated version of the "traditional" family: women obeying men, men protecting women—and guarding them against the sexual predations of white men.

As the Civil Rights Movement challenged Jim Crow, however, Malcolm X became dissatisfied with the apolitical stance of the NOI. Elijah Muhammad's only proposed solution to America's race problem was the resettlement of America's black population inside a separate state. How that state would be created, who would furnish the land, and how blacks might be persuaded to move there remained unanswered questions. Malcolm dutifully parroted the separatist line, but with increasing lack of conviction. Elijah Muhammad's secret dealings with white supremacist groups heightened Malcolm's unease: like Garvey in the 1920s, Muhammad entered into secret negotiations with the Ku Klux Klan—talks to which Malcolm himself was a party. While attacking King and other civil rights leaders as "Uncle Toms," and while preaching the need to retaliate against white racists, the Nation of Islam was trying to reach an accord with people who were bombing black churches and killing black children. Malcolm was ashamed and frustrated. The Nation of Islam, he believed, should be "engaged in more *action*. . . . [W]herever black people committed themselves, in the Little Rocks and Birminghams and other places, militant Muslims should also be there."[28]

Taciturn, camera-shy, and devoid of obvious charisma, Muhammad concluded that Malcolm's popularity and ambition threatened his own control of the NOI. Malcolm, for his part, lost all respect for Muhammad when he discovered the extent of the latter's extramarital affairs. The final break came in the winter of 1963–64. Muhammad tried to bring Malcolm to heel. When Kennedy was assassinated, Malcolm commented: "Being an old farm boy myself, chickens coming home to roost never did make me sad; they've always made me glad." Muhammad suspended Malcolm for ninety days and ordered him to cease all public comment. On March 8, after it became abundantly clear that Muhammad was determined to break him, Malcolm X quit the NOI.[29]

Founding his own church, Muslim Mosque, Inc., and his own political group, the Organization of Afro-American Unity, Malcolm X cast about for a new leadership role. Shedding the far-fetched dogmas of the NOI, he renounced the idea that all whites were "devils," embraced orthodox Islam, and modified his views on violence—although he called upon blacks to form "rifle clubs," he made it clear that he advocated self-defense only, and that he knew full well that a violent uprising would be suicidal. He edged toward a rapprochement with the Civil Rights Movement; shortly before his death he visited Selma while King was in jail there. Elijah Muhammad, however, was intent on silencing him. If Muhammad did not directly order Malcolm's assassination, concludes historian Claude Andrew Clegg, "he had made it quite clear . . . that the slaying of his former minister had his implicit support."[30]

During his year of independence from the Nation of Islam, Malcolm failed to build either an organizational base or a plausible strategy for black liberation. Nevertheless, according to historian Clayborne Carson, Malcolm X was "the key individual in the transformation of African-American political thought" between 1964 and 1966. Every element in "Black Power," the slogan popularized by SNCC in 1966, was anticipated in Malcolm's speeches.[31]

Yet, ironically, Black Power repudiated the very qualities of the Civil Rights Movement—interracialism and nonviolent direct action—that Malcolm X had been struggling to accept shortly before his death. Apart from its celebration of racial pride, Black Power invoked the most destructive and unrealistic aspects of Malcolm's pre-1964 position: his bitter critique of nonviolence, his call for black separatism, and his denunciation of white people. Above all, Black Power adopted Malcolm's rhetoric of violence. To be sure, Malcolm's best-known phrases—"the ballot or the bullet" and "by any means necessary"—implied the possibility of peaceful liberation. But Malcolm made it clear that if blacks resorted to violence, whites would be responsible. Most important of all, Malcolm's rhetoric suggested that violence, or threatening violence, was a realistic strategy for black Americans.

SNCC AND "BLACK POWER"

SNCC's embrace of Black Nationalism was rooted in its experiences in Mississippi. By 1966, SNCC's bruising and prolonged encounter with racism in that state had left many staff members physically attenuated, mentally exhausted, and emotionally drained. A condition called "battle fatigue," or simply "burnout," now merged with bitter disillusionment. The failure of the MFDP challenge in 1964 represented, for many, the last straw, demonstrating the bankruptcy of SNCC's political strategy.

In addition, SNCC had become wracked by internal tensions, the most serious of which was a division between blacks and whites. The Freedom Summer had seen about 900 white students descend upon Mississippi. Many blacks resented the volunteers for their middle-class backgrounds, missionary attitudes, superior education, as well as for the media interest they attracted. "White workers," complained one volunteer, "are often subject to severe racial abuse and even violence from Negro workers." Sexual relationships between white and black staff members complicated and exacerbated interracial tensions. White female volunteers received persistent and aggressive sexual attentions from some black staff members. If they refused such attentions, they might be abused as racists. "I always dreaded Saturday nights," recalled one white woman, "because we'd all meet in our apartment, and drink wine and then when the black guys got a little drunk, they'd pour out all their hatred—racial hatred—at . . . us 'white bitches.'" The addition of so many white staff members after the Freedom Summer compounded the problem, and made some blacks feel that SNCC had lost its basic identity.[32]

By 1966, SNCC was an exhausted, demoralized, and divided organization. Some simply withdrew from the struggle: Bob Moses changed his name, ceased speaking to white people, and emigrated to Tanzania. Others, like chairman John Lewis, clung to their faith in nonviolence and still believed in the possibilities of liberal reform. But a growing number concluded that nonviolence had failed, that whites could not be trusted, and that the political system was rotten to the core.

As SNCC floundered, some activists attempted to devise a new political strategy. In Alabama, Stokely Carmichael organized the Lowndes County Freedom Organization (LCFO), a third party that sported a growling black panther as its symbol. The LCFO embodied Carmichael's belief that neither the Democrats nor the Republicans could represent black interests. "You don't imitate white politics," he explained, "because white politics are corrupt. . . . Negroes have to view themselves as colonies, and right now is time for them to quit being white men's colonies and become independent." Meanwhile, in Atlanta, a group of SNCC staff members led by Bill Ware argued that SNCC ought to become "Black staffed, Black-controlled, and Black-financed." White people no longer had any useful role in the Civil Rights Movement; in fact, their continuing presence was positively harmful because it perpetuated the myth of white superiority. "If we are to proceed toward true liberation," stated the Atlanta Project, "we must cut ourselves off from white people. . . . We must form our own institutions . . . [and] write our own histories."[33]

In May 1966, in a chaotic election that highlighted SNCC's internal decay, a rump of staff members displaced John Lewis and elected Stokely Carmichael as chairman. The election did not indicate a wholehearted acceptance of the

Atlanta Project's black separatism, which even Carmichael and his supporters viewed as extreme. It did, however, signal a repudiation of the principles that had guided SNCC since its inception in 1960. SNCC no longer had any interest, in the short term at least, in seeking common ground with white liberals, or in interracial coalitions of any kind. "Coalition's no good," Carmichael explained. " 'Cause what happens when a couple of Negroes join in with a bunch of whites? They get absorbed, that's what." Only when blacks could negotiate from a position of strength should they enter into coalitions with whites. SNCC also rejected integration, dismissing it as a middle-class concern that had no relevance to the vast majority of black people. Integration was tokenism, Carmichael explained, "a subterfuge for white supremacy." Given its new stress on black consciousness, SNCC expected white staff members to organize inside the white, not the black, community; it soon voted to expel them altogether. The new-look SNCC abandoned its commitment to nonviolence.[34]

The "Meredith March" of June 1966—a protest march through Mississippi initiated by James Meredith, and then taken up, when Meredith was shot, by SNCC, CORE, and the SCLC—gave SNCC a means of publicizing its new stance. SNCC bowed to King's insistence that white people be allowed to take part in the march, because only King—who said he would quit if whites were excluded—could guarantee the media interest that SNCC planned to exploit. SNCC gained a point, however, when King accepted, albeit reluctantly, the participation of the Deacons for Defense, a group of armed men from Bogalusa, Louisiana. Then, when the march arrived at the SNCC stronghold of Greenwood, SNCC publicly and directly challenged King's leadership. After being arrested, Carmichael told a crowd that "Every courthouse in Mississippi ought to be burned tomorrow to get rid of the dirt." "What do you want?" he shouted. "Black power!" the audience replied. "What do you want?" he repeated. "Black power," they roared back again. Aghast, King tried to persuade Carmichael to abandon the aggressive-sounding slogan. Carmichael refused.[35]

Although SNCC did not really explain what it meant, the slogan "Black Power" spread like wildfire, in some way capturing the mood of a large segment of black America. The conjunction of the two words, and the assertive, defiant manner in which they were hurled forth, transcended their literal meaning. The term "black" had a particular resonance. "Colored" and "Negro" had always struck some blacks as weaselly circumlocutions that sought to deny the racial identity of African Americans. Moreover, white Southerners, even polite ones, tended to mangle the word "Negro," pronouncing it "nigro" or even "nigra." More important, "Black" embraced, rather than evaded, racial identity. It seemed bolder and stronger than "Negro"; it stressed the dark features of the majority rather than the light physiognomy of the elite. By promoting racial pride, Black Power represented, in King's words, "a psychological call to manhood" that performed the valuable function of overcoming deeply rooted feelings of insecurity and inferiority. Blackness was something to celebrate, not be ashamed of. Indeed, the most obvious and enduring effect of the slogan was to consign the word Negro to semantic oblivion.[36]

Whatever SNCC meant it to signify, the term "Black Power" appealed to a growing sense of confidence among many black people. The Civil Rights Movement had rarely discussed the matter of how black Southerners should use the vote once they had gained it. King's talk of creating a "beloved community" neglected the fact that blacks needed to develop a coherent political strategy for obtaining power—or at least a share of power—as a group. Simply voting for the Democratic Party was not enough. Like Italian-Americans, Irish-Americans, and Jewish Americans, blacks needed to exercise a degree of political solidarity.

The movement's stress on integration, moreover, might be relevant to the issues of public accommodations and schools, but segregation still defined much of the everyday lives of black people, both North and South. The Civil Rights Movement had given virtually no thought to the future of black churches, colleges, businesses, clubs, and neighborhoods—to the survival of blacks as a distinctive *community*. Facing the reality of the ghetto, groups like CORE had already implemented local "community organizing" projects that sought short-term improvements in the living conditions of poor people.

In some respects, therefore, Black Power flowed from the success of the Civil Rights Movement, and was a logical extension of it. Having achieved legal equality, blacks needed to unite, and to organize effectively, in order to maximize their political and economic power. Defined in terms of racial pride, group solidarity, and the strengthening of black businesses, Black Power was an unexceptionable concept. Indeed, part of the explanation for the slogan's broad appeal was its vagueness and elasticity. Conservatives could define Black Power as black capitalism. Moderates could define it as electoral politics. Nationalists could define it as the cultivation of a separate black culture. Churchmen could define it as liberation theology.

Its vagueness, however, was also its weakness; by failing to explain what Black Power meant, SNCC allowed critics to define it in the most negative terms. As soon as SNCC coined the slogan, whites rushed to condemn it. *Time* called it a "new racism" that was "almost indistinguishable from the wild-eyed doctrines of the Black Muslims." Black Power pointed toward separatism and even "black Jacobinism." Even the *New Republic,* usually sympathetic to black militancy, considered it "dangerously counterproductive." President Johnson, Vice President Humphrey, and Senator Robert Kennedy all criticized the slogan. "Racism is racism," intoned Humphrey, "and there is no room in America for racism of any color."[37]

As well as alienating white liberals, Black Power split the Civil Rights Movement, shattering the fragile coalition that had proved so effective between 1960 and 1965. Roy Wilkins did not mince words:

No matter how endlessly they try to explain it, the term "black power" means anti-white power. . . . It is a reverse Mississippi, a reverse Hitler, a reverse Ku Klux Klan. . . . We of the NAACP will have none of this. We have fought it too long. It is the ranging of race against race on the irrelevant basis of skin color. It is the father of hatred and the mother of violence. It is the wicked fanaticism which has swelled our tears, broken our bodies, squeezed our hearts, and taken the blood of our black and white loved ones. It shall not poison our forward march.

A. Philip Randolph, Bayard Rustin, and Whitney Young, head of the National Urban League, also denounced the slogan, although less stridently. Of the major civil rights organizations, only CORE, now led by Floyd McKissick, supported SNCC. King, who considered Black Power to be fundamentally unsound, tried to keep the discussion within the realms of rational debate, and struggled to retain his position as a unifying force at the center of the Civil Rights Movement. He failed in both respects, as each side attacked the other in what Clayborne Carson has aptly called "more a clash of emotions than of ideas."[38]

President Johnson's continuing escalation of the war in Vietnam, beginning in the summer of 1965 and showing no sign of abatement in 1966, added to the fragmentation of the Civil Rights Movement. SNCC was bitterly opposed to the war, and in 1966 took a strong position against it. When former SNCC staff member Julian Bond, who had just been elected to a seat in the Georgia state legislature, endorsed SNCC's stand, the Georgia House of Representatives barred him. It required two Supreme Court decisions to remedy this egregious violation of the democratic process and allow Bond to take his seat. The NAACP and the Urban League, on the other hand, not only refused to condemn the war, but criticized those who did. By stressing their loyalty, Roy Wilkins and Whitney Young tried to ingratiate themselves with President Johnson and boost their political influence.

King was appalled by the war, but for many months he kept his views largely to himself. When he found himself cold-shouldered by the White House in 1966, however, it became evident that even his rare and relatively mild criticisms of U.S. policy infuriated President Johnson. In April 1967, when King finally condemned the war in forthright terms and aligned himself with the peace movement—"breaking the betrayal of my own silence"—the

Johnson administration branded him an ingrate, a political enemy, a naive and gullible man who, according to presidential aide John P. Roche, was manipulated by "the Communist-oriented 'peace' types." From then until King's death a year later, aides and advisers egged on Johnson's anger over King's apostasy. Many blacks also condemned King's stand, variously calling him a traitor, a fool, and a man who was hurting the Civil Rights Movement.[39]

More generally, the carnage in Vietnam fostered a climate of violence that made belief in peaceful reform—especially reform through nonviolent protest—hard to sustain. Blacks were dying in Vietnam in disproportionate numbers; civil rights workers were being drafted to fight in a war they found repugnant; the government that condemned the violence of Watts, Newark, and Detroit was visiting death and destruction on a faraway country inhabited by people of a different race. When the United States had become, in King's words, "the greatest purveyor of violence in the world," the Civil Rights Movement could no longer sustain an ethic of nonviolence.

THE APOTHEOSIS OF VIOLENCE

Uninterested in making Black Power acceptable to its critics, SNCC refused to go on the defensive. It relished the notoriety of Black Power, revelled in the publicity it generated, and gladly exploited the news media's obsession with violence. Instead of refuting charges that Black Power meant antiwhite violence, SNCC's fiery rhetoric fanned the flames of the controversy. Carmichael's speeches brimmed with what Clayborne Carson described as "purposeful ambiguity"—no specific threats of violence, but plenty of "vague implications of future racial retribution." What was a statement like "Move on over, or we'll move on over you" actually supposed to mean?[40]

Soon, however, Carmichael's calls for violence became explicit. "When you talk of Black Power," he told one audience, "you talk about bringing this country to its knees. When you talk of Black Power, you talk of building a movement that will smash everything Western civilization has created." SNCC workers discovered the writings of Martinique-born psychiatrist Frantz Fanon, who witnessed and supported Algeria's struggle for independence from France. In his most famous book, *The Wretched of the Earth,* Fanon argued that violence, for a colonized people, was a "cleansing force" that "frees the native from his inferiority complex." By the time that H. Rap Brown replaced Carmichael as chairman of SNCC in 1967, SNCC's rhetoric lost all restraint.[41]

SNCC's rapid decline, mirrored by CORE, showed how difficult it was to translate Black Power into a practical program that could win popular support. In the South, blacks gladly invoked Black Power, but grassroots activism remained firmly within the tradition of the Civil Rights Movement: boycotts, demonstrations, voter registration drives, political campaigns, cooperative business ventures, and government-funded "community action" programs. Most blacks recognized that the South was changing for the better; they knew that talk of revolution was absurd. Separatism, too, held out little appeal: when blacks constituted a minority in every state, and a majority in only 83 counties, Carmichael's proposal that blacks form independent political parties seemed impractical. Even in SNCC's former stronghold of Mississippi, writes John Dittmer, SNCC's "strident black nationalism, . . . with its underlying theme that whites no longer had a role to play in a black movement, did not attract a large following among local people." Many churchgoing blacks were offended by antiwhite rhetoric.[42]

In the North, where urban rioting was an annual occurrence between 1965 and 1968, Black Power seemed perfectly attuned to the mood of the ghettos. Even so, writes Clayborne Carson, SNCC proved "unable to transform racial anger into local movements that could be sustained." This was partly because SNCC mistook the riots for rebellions and falsely concluded that a revolutionary situation was at hand. But the riots did not necessarily indicate that most blacks were alienated from the political system: they were explosions of anger against police brutality that evoked brutal overreactions by the police and National Guard. Insofar as they had a political purpose, it was to draw attention to racial discrimination and to extract concessions from government.[43]

As its income evaporated—it had depended on white contributors, most of whom stopped giving—SNCC withered away; by 1967 its presence in the South had virtually disappeared. FBI infiltration and dirty tricks helped to dig SNCC's grave, but the root cause of its demise came from within SNCC itself. As the historian Richard H. King has written, "[T]he tragedy of SNCC was exemplified in its trajectory from non-violence to violence, from indigenous community organizing to affirmations of solidarity with the Third World. It was stranded in a no man's land of the revolutionary consciousness without a revolutionary situation, a decolonized psyche outside a colonial setting." By 1968 SNCC was moribund.[44]

The ghetto riots, however, inadvertently encouraged what was, perhaps, the most self-defeating aspect of Black Power: a cult of the gun. Ironically, for all its bloodcurdling rhetoric, SNCC itself never resorted to violence in a serious or systematic way. Although Stokely Carmichael brandished a submachine gun on the cover of one of his books, it was a dramatic pose only.

Neither he nor others in SNCC were prepared to use guns in the service of the revolution they advocated. But other groups were.

US (United Slaves) and the Black Panther Party for Self-Defense (BPP) were founded in the same year, 1966, and in the same state, California. Both were inspired by Malcolm X, and represented competing visions of black nationalism. Both not only amassed weapons but also used them. The surprise bestseller of 1967, *Quotations of Chairman Mao Tse-tung,* put the phrase "Power grows out of the barrel of a gun" on everybody's lips. But these new Black Power groups were more likely to use their guns against each other than against whites.

The Black Panther Party, founded in Oakland, California, by Huey P. Newton and Bobby Seale, espoused an eclectic mixture of black nationalism and Marxism. It recruited the same kind of people as the Nation of Islam: in Seale's words, "brothers off the block—brothers who had been out there robbing banks, brothers who had been pimping, brothers who had been peddling dope, brothers who ain't gonna take no shit, brothers who had been fighting pigs [police]." Consciously departing from orthodox Marxism, the Panthers considered this "lumpen proletariat" to be the natural base of a revolutionary movement. Vehemently contemptuous of groups that made racial identity the center of their consciousness—it derided US's emphasis on African culture as "pork chop nationalism"—the Panthers denied that they were anti-white, and stressed their willingness to ally with white radicals. The BPP's ten-point program combined reformist, revolutionary, and nationalist demands; it included the exemption of black men from military service, the release from jail of all black prisoners, an end to police brutality, a United Nations–supervised plebiscite to decide the future of the "black colony," and "land, bread, housing, education, clothing, justice, and peace."[45]

Wearing a stylish uniform of black leather jacket, black beret, and dark sunglasses, the Panthers exuded charisma and were immensely photogenic. Sprinkling their talk with expletives and insults, they turned profanity into a form of political rhetoric. They personified the cool, streetwise, hard-edged, image to which many young men in the ghettos aspired. The Panthers attracted youths from the street gangs and politicized them. They also attracted wider support in the black community by patrolling ghetto neighborhoods to deter police harassment, providing free breakfasts for needy children, recruiting doctors and medical students to staff free health clinics, conducting voter registration programs, and setting up "Liberation Schools" for black children.

The Panthers made guns, however, the focus of their identity and appeal. They collected a veritable arsenal of pistols, shotguns, and rifles and, invoking the Second Amendment, carried them around in public, sometimes sporting bandoliers filled with shotgun cartridges. On May 2, 1967, in a display of bravado that made national news, thirty armed Panthers strode into the state capitol in Sacramento to protest against a bill that proposed to restrict the public display of guns. "Huey understood a revolutionary culture," explained Seale, "and Huey understood how arms and guns become a part of the culture of a people in the revolutionary struggle."[46]

Ostensibly committed to violence in self-defense only, the Panthers attempted to "police" the Oakland police, whom they accused of harassment, brutality, and racism, by shadowing their patrols. If the occasion called for it, the Panthers confronted the police by brandishing their weapons. Inevitably, such clashes sparked gun battles between police and Panthers—in one, Huey Newton killed policeman John Frey. The Panthers' slogan "Off the Pig!" (kill the police) was hardly calculated to ease friction between the two groups.

But the Panthers usually got the worst of it. Encouraged by the Nixon administration—"The Panthers are nothing but hoodlums," said one Justice Department official, "we've got to get them"—law enforcement authorities targeted the Panthers and cracked down hard. Between October 1967 and December 1969, writes historian Kenneth O'Reilly, "party members engaged police officers in more than a dozen firefights . . . and at least two policemen and as many as ten Panthers died." Over 300 Panthers were arrested in 1969 alone, "on murder, armed robbery, rape, bank robbery, drug trafficking, burglary, and dozens of other charges." On December 4, 1969, at 4 A.M., fourteen Chicago police officers burst into an apartment and shot dead Panther leaders Fred Hampton and Mark Clark. Hampton was asleep in bed; Clark fired a single round before being felled by a hail of bullets. Four others in the apartment were seriously wounded.[47]

The FBI also played a major role in destroying the Black Panthers. FBI agents tapped telephones, recruited spies and informers, and utilized a panoply of "covert action" techniques—the kind it had used against the Communist Party and the Ku Klux Klan—in order to disrupt the Black Panthers. One ploy was to embitter personal relationships inside the organization by spreading rumors of sexual infidelities. Another was the use of *agents provocateurs* and "black propaganda" in order to incite violence between the Panthers and rival organizations. For example, a bitter feud between the Panthers and US, surreptitiously urged on by the FBI, left several people dead. Given the FBI's efforts to discredit the moderate, nonviolent King, it was hardly surprising that the Bureau targeted the Panthers. Still, in Kenneth O'Reilly's words, "Hoover's pursuit of the Black Panthers was unique . . . in its total disregard for human rights and life itself."[48]

The repression of the Black Panthers was a classic case of "overkill." The Panthers' talk of revolution was largely bombast, the kind of angry braggadocio that was typical of Black Power rhetoric at the end of the 1960s. The Panthers' violent language and fearsome slogans were not meant to be taken literally. The notion that the Panthers presented a revolutionary threat to America was absurd.

Nevertheless, the Panthers were not wholly innocent victims. Although amateurishly inept as revolutionaries, they took their political doctrines seriously. They amassed weapons and, for a time, went out of their way to provoke the police. They also found it difficult to throw off earlier criminal habits: the Panthers engaged in extortion, robbery, prostitution, drug trafficking, and other illegal activity. They enforced internal discipline through beatings. They did not hesitate to inflict violence on, and even kill, informers, undercover agents, and other opponents. Huey Newton, the Panthers' handsome, intense, charismatic leader, became a cocaine-addicted autocrat who committed acts of brutal and sadistic violence, including murder. He died in 1989, shot by a drug dealer.[49]

The fate of the Black Panthers illustrated the dangers of organizing a political movement around guns. With no semblance of internal democracy, the Panthers depended upon the dictatorial authority, violently enforced, of an individual leader. Challenges to that authority invariably led to violent feuds and schisms that sometimes resulted in death. The Panthers' commitment to violence also made them especially vulnerable to the destabilizing tactics of the FBI. Adopting the conspiratorial methods of revolutionaries, but lacking the fanaticism of true revolutionaries, the Panthers developed a siege mentality. That feeling of vulnerability was easily exploited by FBI agents, who were past masters at infiltrating secretive organizations, and who had unlimited supplies of cash to buy informers. When internal discipline came to be viewed as a matter of life and death, the fear of spies and traitors tipped over into a destructive paranoia that fed upon itself. Finally, the Panthers fatally erred in believing that a revolutionary situation existed.

In the view of historian William Van Deburg, Black Power was by no means a failure. It fuelled an upsurge of black consciousness that had profound and constructive psychological benefits. "By decolonizing their minds, cultivating feelings of racial solidarity, and contrasting their world with that of the oppressor, black Americans came to understand themselves better." Black Power also educated blacks politically, fostering grassroots activism as well as national political caucuses. Its greatest impact, perhaps, was in the realm of culture: Black Power embodied a new aesthetic that stimulated an outburst of creativity in music, art, literature, and fashion. "Black Power's unconquerable spirit and its message of self-definition are visible to all who take the time to familiarize themselves with contemporary Afro-American culture," writes Van Deburg.[50]

Others are far less positive, regretting Black Power as a tragic wrong turn. "Black Power was a dead end," movement veteran Andrew Young believes. "It provided emotional release and the illusion of manhood, without the content. . . . The advocates of Black Power had failed to master their own fears. With their posturing, they could trigger polarization but not genuine social change." To the historian Gerald Horne, Black Power promoted a cult of black masculinity that was anti-intellectual, misogynic, and violent; its "potent antiwhite character" further isolated blacks, rendering them even more vulnerable to repression and exploitation. Clayborne Carson made a similar assessment: "While failing to produce greater power to black people, black power militancy actually led to a decline in the ability of African-Americans to affect the course of American politics." Ultimately, Carson concludes, "the black power movement . . . promised more than the civil rights movement but delivered less."[51]

THE ASSASSINATION OF MARTIN LUTHER KING

In 1967–68, King had contended against the divisiveness and irrationality of Black Power by trying to forge an interracial coalition around the issue of poverty. Racial inequalities, he argued, were rooted in the structure of American capitalism; they could never be eliminated without a thoroughgoing reform of the economic system. King never explained how the white majority might be induced to support a radical redistribution of wealth and power in favor of the poor. Yet he believed that the issue of stark poverty, if skillfully dramatized through nonviolent protest, had the capacity to arouse the conscience of the nation and create the kind of broad consensus that President Johnson had tried, but failed, to mobilize for his own War on Poverty.

The SCLC's Poor People's Campaign recruited representatives of the poor—blacks, whites from Appalachia, Chicanos, Indians—in an effort to exert political pressure upon the federal government. King proposed to take the poor to Washington, to house them in a shantytown, and to stay there, engaging in nonviolent demonstrations, until the government acted. Before he could put his plan into operation, however, he was shot and killed in Memphis, Tennessee, by James Earl Ray, a career criminal and convinced racist. King was not yet forty years old. His death triggered rioting in Washington, Chicago, Baltimore, Kansas City, and half a dozen other cities.

King's staff and close advisers had always doubted the feasibility of the

Poor People's Campaign. Nevertheless, buoyed by an inpouring of money and sympathy in the wake of King's death, the SCLC's new president, Ralph David Abernathy, decided to proceed with the protests. Without King's guiding hand and moral authority, however, the SCLC stumbled and fell. Dogged by incessant rain, inept leadership, and lack of clear purpose, the Poor People's Campaign was a shambles. Instead of being a shining symbol of the dignity of the poor, the SCLC's shantytown, "Resurrection City," became a gang-infested jungle—an eyesore and an embarrassment. The campaign sputtered to a dispiriting conclusion, having achieved virtually nothing. The SCLC never recovered from the fiasco. Whether King's presence would have made a difference is unknowable. Nevertheless, his death removed the one person who had the capacity to unify the black population, command broad respect from whites, and bridge the racial divide. It was an incalculable loss.

Jimmy Carter and Rosalynn Carter sing with Martin Luther
King, Sr., Andrew Young, Coretta Scott King, and other civil rights
leaders, Ebenezer Baptist Church, Atlanta, January 14, 1979

Jimmy Carter Library

The Continuing Struggle

The Momentum of the Civil Rights Revolution

Following King's death, a sense of pessimism engulfed African Americans. The collapse of the Civil Rights Movement as a national force, followed by the failure of Black Power as a political strategy, dashed hopes that either racial integration or black self-determination would become realities. The election of Richard Nixon in 1968, and his overwhelming reelection four years later, seemed to show that whites were setting firm limits to black progress. According to a 1970 opinion poll, most blacks felt "profound cynicism about the American political system."[1]

Richard Nixon eschewed the visceral racism of George Wallace, whose third-party presidential campaigns in 1968 and 1972—the latter prematurely aborted by Arthur Bremer's assassination attempt, which left Wallace a wheelchair-bound cripple—evoked widespread enthusiasm among many whites. Nevertheless, Nixon shrewdly exploited the racial fears and resentments that Wallace had whipped up. Promising "law and order," courting Senator Strom Thurmond of South Carolina, vowing to appoint a Southern conservative to the Supreme Court, and vociferously denouncing the busing of children to promote school integration, Nixon neither expected nor received much black support. Blacks, for their part, expected little from Nixon. In the words of Daniel Patrick Moynihan, one of Nixon's advisers, the best policy toward the race problem was "a period of 'benign neglect.'" For black people, of course, government neglect was anything but benign—most of them still attended segregated schools, suffered from unemployment and poverty, and experienced racial discrimination of varying severity.[2]

Yet political appearances were deceptive. Codified in law, institutionalized in the federal bureaucracy, and enforced by the federal judiciary, the changes unleashed by the Civil Rights Movement were too profound to be reversed. Moreover, despite having little direct influence over the Nixon administration, black voters were becoming increasingly important in local, state, and congressional elections. By 1969, the Voting Rights Act had added 900,000 black voters in the covered states; by 1976, black voter registration in the South stood at 63 percent—only five percentage points below the white level. Congress renewed the Voting Rights Act in 1970 and again in 1975.[3]

Even under Nixon, therefore, the dismantling of Jim Crow proceeded apace. Indeed, according to historian Hugh D. Graham, "Nixon presided with quiet firmness and surprising success over a sustained effort to ease the path of school desegregation throughout the South." Between 1968 and 1971 the proportion of black children attending all-black schools in the South plummeted from 68 percent to 18 percent. By 1974, when Nixon was forced from office over the Watergate scandal, nearly half of the South's black children attended majority-white schools. By then, in fact, schools in the *North* were far more racially segregated than those in the South.[4]

The Nixon administration could lay claim to other civil rights achievements. In 1969 the Justice Department filed suit to desegregate the South's system of segregated state colleges. In the same year the Department of Labor devised the "Philadelphia Plan," which required federal contractors to submit targets for minority recruitment. Embodying the principle of "affirmative action" but eschewing hard-and-fast "quotas," the plan represented a major step forward in enforcing the 1964 Civil Rights Act by extending equal employment opportunity. Nixon's "Family Assistance Plan" was a bold attempt to help the poor—including married couples, then excluded from welfare—by establishing a guaranteed annual income. (Democratic opposition in Congress, however, derailed the plan.) Finally, Nixon promoted "black capitalism," creating an Office of Minority Business Enterprise (MBE).[5]

The federal judiciary, however, probably played a greater role in consolidating and sometimes extending the victories of the Civil Rights Movement. Although Nixon wished for a more conservative Supreme Court, the Senate rebuffed his first two nominations—both of them white Southerners—forcing him to put forward moderate candidates who did not radically alter the Court's political balance. Under Chief Justice Warren Burger, therefore, the Court's civil rights decisions followed, rather than repudiated, the precedents set by the Warren Court.

The federal courts, moreover, were finally running out of patience with the shameless foot-dragging of Southern school boards. In *Alexander* v. *Holmes County Board of Education* (1969) the Supreme Court ordered 33 school districts in Mississippi to desegregate their schools "now"—ending once and for all the subterfuges and delays that the vague wording of *Brown* ("all deliberate speed") had encouraged. *Alexander* finally made school integration a reality throughout much of the South; it gave the Nixon administration little choice but to smooth its path. Two years later, in *Swann* v. *Charlotte-Mecklenberg Board of Education*, the Supreme Court approved a court-ordered program of citywide busing in Charlotte, North Carolina, designed to achieve racially integrated schools.

In fact, the federal courts were now treating civil rights cases with an increasingly bold "judicial activism," expanding black rights in ways that sometimes went beyond the narrow letter of the law. It approved busing to achieve integrated schools despite the fact that desegregation, according to the 1964 Civil Rights Act, should *not* require the busing of pupils from one school to another "in order to overcome racial imbalance." It upheld affirmative action plans that embodied the idea of racial quotas, although the sponsors of the Civil Rights Bill had assured Congress that employers would *not* be required to achieve any kind of "racial balance" in their workforce. Federal courts struck down various employment aptitude tests because they had a "disparate impact" upon poorly educated black applicants, rather than because they intentionally discriminated against them. Congress had designed the 1964 Civil Rights Act, explained Chief Justice Burger, to outlaw employment practices that had discriminatory consequences, not merely discriminatory intent. This was another highly questionable interpretation of the Civil Rights Act.[6]

The Supreme Court also greatly widened the scope of the Voting Rights Act, barring racial discrimination in electoral arrangements, as well as the discrimination that hampered or prevented blacks from registering and voting. The Department of Justice, writes historian Steven Lawson, became adept at detecting "sophisticated practices designed to diminish the influence of the black electorate," routinely disallowing electoral reforms that had the intent or effect of "diluting" the black vote. Thus encouraged, blacks increasingly took the initiative in challenging electoral arrangements—for example, multimember districts where candidates were elected "at large"—that put blacks at a disadvantage. The courts never endorsed the principle of racial proportional representation. Nevertheless, guided by the premise that whites still tended to vote en masse to defeat black candidates, the courts became increasingly sympathetic to the idea that in areas where blacks constituted a substantial portion of the electorate, districts should be drawn up so as to maximize, or at least enhance, the chances of black candidates gaining election.[7]

The Voting Rights Act, and the Justice Department's rigorous policing of the South's electoral system, yielded a political bonanza. In 1964 there were perhaps 500 black elected officials, of whom about twenty-five resided in the South. By 1980 the number of black elected officials had soared to nearly 4,000, and most of them—2,458—were elected in the South. After extensive reapportionment and redistricting following the 1990 census, the number of black elected officials surpassed 8,000, the majority in the South. Fittingly, the old bastions of disfranchisement—Mississippi, Alabama, Louisiana, and Georgia—boasted the largest number of BEOs. In some states, and at some levels of government, black voters were achieving or at least approaching representation proportionate to their numbers. In Louisiana, for example, where blacks made up about 30 percent of the population, blacks held 21 percent of the seats in the legislature, two of the state's seven congressional seats, and 12.8 percent of all the elective offices. Across the nation, the thirty-seven black congressmen elected in 1994 made up 8.5 percent of the House of Representatives—a figure not far from 11.3, the percentage of blacks in the voting-age population.[8]

In both the North and the South, black migration to cities and white movement to suburbs created a demography that transformed urban politics. Following the election of Carl Stokes as mayor of Cleveland in 1967, black candidates triumphed in one city after another. They included Marion Barry in Washington, D.C., Maynard Jackson in Atlanta, Ernest Morial in New Orleans, Richard Arrington in Birmingham, Kurt Schmoke in Baltimore, Coleman Young in Detroit, and Willie Herenton in Memphis. Even when black voters were in the minority, moreover, substantial white support helped to elect Wilson Goode in Philadelphia, Tom Bradley in Los Angeles, Harold Washington in Chicago, and David Dinkins in New York. In the South, whites remained reluctant to vote across the color line. Yet the election of black mayors in Charlotte, Roanoke, Tallahassee, and Dallas—Southern cities where whites made up a substantial majority of the population—indicated that tribal prejudices were breaking down. In 1989 Virginia, with a population less than one-fifth black, elected Douglas Wilder to the governorship— the first black governor of a Southern state since Reconstruction.[9]

Partly because of the Civil Rights Movement, many black Americans substantially improved their economic position. As discrimination in the labor market diminished, the number of blacks in the more highly paid occupations increased dramatically. Black employment in the textile industry, for example, grew to a quarter of the entire workforce—before the 1960s the mills had been virtually all-white. In 1960 blacks accounted for only 2.5 percent of the nation's firefighters; by 1990 they made up 11.5 percent. The number of black police officers more than tripled between 1964 and 1990; 41 percent of all the new positions went to black applicants. The proportion of black workers who held jobs loosely described as "white collar" or "middle class" increased from 12.1 percent in 1960 to 30.4 percent three decades later. During the same period the black share of aggregate family income grew from 5.4 percent to 7.2 percent. Taking a longer perspective, the economic improvements were even more striking: in 1948 a black man who worked earned, on average, about 54 percent of a white man's wage; by 1995 he earned 67 percent of the white level. The earnings of black women relative to white women soared from 43 percent to 89 percent.[10]

THE PERSISTENCE OF INEQUALITY

The gains of the 1970s, however, left black Americans far short of equality. For one thing, large numbers of African Americans—perhaps the majority—experienced little improvement when it came to jobs and income, especially when they compared their own position with that of white people. In fact, the situation of many blacks actually deteriorated after 1975: the income gap between blacks and whites, having narrowed considerably, began to widen. Younger blacks, in particular, fell farther behind. That high school dropouts fared especially badly suggests that lack of skills, rather than racial discrimination, accounted for this deterioration. Yet better-educated blacks also lost ground. In the 1970s, for example, black college graduates were as likely to find managerial and professional jobs as white graduates. But by the late 1980s, writes Ronald F. Ferguson, "they were 13 percent less likely than young whites to be in these occupations." Between 1970 and 1990 the income gap between black and white families widened: in 1970 the median income for black families had reached 61 percent of the white level; twenty years later it had declined to 58 percent. Only in 1995 did blacks regain their 1970 position.[11]

If averages disguised the affluence of the growing black middle class, they also hid the desperate poverty of an even larger "underclass." In 1970 about a third of all black families earned less than $15,000 a year; by 1990 that figure had grown to 37 percent. Even by the miserly definition of the federal government, 32 percent of the black population lived in "poverty" in 1990, compared with 8.8 percent of the white population. Worse still, the number of black children living in poverty climbed to the staggering figure of 44 percent, about three times the rate among whites. Throughout the 1970s and 1980s, blacks were at least twice as likely to be unemployed as white people. Moreover, unemployment figures masked the fact that a growing number of blacks had given up seeking regular employment. Gangs proliferated at an alarming rate, fostering a criminal subculture that prized guns, drugs, and hustling.[12]

By the 1980s it had become painfully apparent that some of the hard-won victories of the Civil Rights Movement entailed costs as well as benefits. For example, the integration of lunch counters and other public accommodations, and the construction of out-of-town shopping malls, doomed Southern black business districts to economic decline. Whether it was St. Augustine's Lincolnville, Albany's Harlem, New Orleans' Dryades Street, or Houston's Fifth Ward, these once vibrant areas became depressing ghost towns of boarded-up stores and derelict buildings. More generally, the whole ethos of integration encouraged middle-class blacks—teachers, doctors, social workers, businessmen—to depart the older neighborhoods for new subdivisions. In 1992 poet Tom Dent, the son of a black college president who grew up in New Orleans, lamented the resulting damage to social cohesion:

> The ability to move out became proof of economic means. Once the black middle class moved elsewhere, the old communities began to collapse. . . . And because the black middle class was smaller than the number of those who fell below the poverty line and those who suffered from fractured families, the removal of key support has become all the more disastrous for black neighborhoods.

The barbed wire that surrounded the dormitories of Bethune-Cookman College in Daytona, Florida, symbolized, for Dent, the social fragmentation that was an unanticipated by-product of the Civil Rights Movement. Instead of embracing the surrounding black community, the private black college now shunned it.[13]

School integration, for which the NAACP fought so hard and so long, turned out to be a massive disappointment. Most whites were never reconciled to it. When legal resistance could no longer stave off integrated schools, most whites either moved to lily-white suburbs, where the public schools were overwhelmingly white, or placed their children in all-white private schools. As the white population of urban public school systems shrunk, the NAACP proposed extensive intracity busing in an increasingly desperate attempt to achieve a modicum of racial mixing. Busing, however, merely spurred "white flight," and Southern cities like Memphis and Richmond found that their newly integrated school systems had, virtually overnight, "resegregated." In the North, too, busing, where it was attempted, usually backfired: in Boston, white enrollment fell from 60 percent of the total in 1973 to 26 percent in 1987. Yet cities that avoided drastic busing schemes also experienced resegregation. In New Orleans, for example, white enrollment plummeted from 33 percent to 8 percent (1968–93); in Atlanta, from 55 percent to 18 percent (1961-73); in Houston from 50 percent to 17 percent (1970-85).[14]

Even when blacks and whites attended the same schools, integration rarely brought the anticipated benefits. Racial segregation often persisted *inside* the school, as tracking concentrated black children in classes for the educationally retarded. White teachers often felt uncomfortable teaching black children; black teachers frequently stopped pushing black children as hard. Tensions between white and black children were never far below the surface, and from time to time they erupted in verbal rows and physical violence. In many schools classroom discipline suffered, truancy increased, and large numbers of black students were suspended. "Black students are dropping out, copping out, rebelling and being driven out of school," complained J. K. Haynes, the executive secretary of the Louisiana Education Association, in 1974.[15]

When the educational payoff of mixed classes failed to materialize, many blacks began to question the wisdom of insisting upon integration at any cost. "I don't believe it is necessary for a black child to sit next to a white child to get a good education," stated Benjamin Mays, president of Morehouse College and head of Atlanta's school board. Blacks also lamented the palpable loss of community that followed upon the closure of a Booker T. Washington High School so that blacks could attend a Robert E. Lee High School. Today, there is a growing nostalgia for the black high schools of the pre-civil rights era. Although segregated, these black-run institutions had maintained discipline, instilled ambition, provided black leadership, and encouraged neighborhood cohesion. "Maybe we ought to go back to 'neighborhood choice,'" suggested SNCC veteran Charles Sherrod, now a resident of Albany, Georgia. "This would lead to resegregation, but . . . maybe black kids would do better."[16]

The public school system remains riddled with inequality. For one thing, it is not a "system" at all—rather a balkanized patchwork of local systems, each with its own school board, each one jealously guarding its independence. Without centralization of funding and control, it is impossible to achieve uniform standards. Moreover, the Supreme Court, by underlining the political autonomy of school districts in a crucial 1973 decision, *San Antonio School District* v. *Rodriguez,* has made it impossible to remedy the enormous disparities in per capita spending between one school system and another. A year later, in *Milliken* v. *Bradley,* the Court decreed that integration could not be furthered by busing students between school districts. These rulings, writes Numan V. Bartley, "assured that the schools most likely to be integrated— those in the southern countryside and those within the cities—would be the

most inadequately financed, while the schools least likely to experience anything beyond token desegregation would also be the most generously supported." No wonder so many whites relocated to the suburbs.[17]

THE POLITICAL VULNERABILITY OF AFRICAN AMERICANS

In the years since 1968, black leadership has become increasingly fragmented
and uncertain. No one person has ever rivaled the prestige and influence of
Martin Luther King, Jr. In the 1970s and 1980s, former SCLC staffer Jesse
Jackson aspired to a similar position of moral authority. Establishing himself
as a ubiquitous commentator on racial matters, making highly publicized in-
terventions in international disputes, and running for the Democratic presidential nomination in 1984 and 1988, the media-savvy Jackson acquired an
enormous popular following. However, although not without influence, Jackson failed to carve out a clear role for himself and never established a real
power base—his "Rainbow Coalition" existed largely on paper. Although his
son is now a congressman from Chicago, Jackson's own influence in the Democratic Party has been negligible. The disappointing trajectory of Jackson's
career showed that the traditional "civil rights" approach to black problems
had limited value in the post-King era. The decline of the older civil rights organizations—including the SCLC and the NAACP—reinforced the point.

Black politicians, in fact, were the new black leadership class. Indeed,
throughout the South many former civil rights activists hung up their march-
ing shoes and ran for public office. Veterans of SNCC, the SCLC, and the
NAACP became sheriffs, mayors, judges, city councilmen, and congressmen.
Following Bayard Rustin's injunction to move "from protest to politics,"
they hoped to translate the black vote into better schools, better jobs, and better communities. To some extent, they succeeded. Charles Sherrod, who
served on the Albany city council for twelve years, pointed to some of the
concrete benefits that black politicians could deliver: "Paved streets and gut-
ters in black neighborhoods, increased black homeownership, better salaries,
running water in homes where none existed, upward mobility in terms of
hiring and promotions of black policemen, firemen, and heads of city departments."[18]

Yet the election of black politicians also led to great disappointments.
Some turned out to be all too human, pursuing their own self-interest to the
point of corruption. Others performed poorly because they lacked experience
or were incompetent. But even the most dedicated and talented politicians
found it difficult to get things done, and their capacity to bring about radical
social change was virtually nil. Big-city mayors, for example, found them-

selves beset by industrial decline, falling revenues, spiraling crime rates, and racist policemen who doggedly resisted political control. The vicious beating of Rodney King by members of the Los Angeles Police Department in 1991, which received worldwide publicity because a member of the public video-taped it, starkly exposed the inability of a black mayor—and a former police officer at that—to curb police brutality and racism. The acquittal of the officers charged with King's beating sparked the worst rioting since the 1960s. The Los Angeles riot of 1992, which left 44 people dead, 1,800 injured, and 6,345 arrested, represented a massive failure of the political system.

At the national level, black calls for a revival of New Deal/Great Society–type federal spending programs fell upon deaf ears. In pursuing the goal of economic equality, blacks continually confronted the stumbling block of white political power. Despite the growth of the black electorate, black politicians lacked the political influence commensurate with the size of the black population. In addition, for much of the past thirty years, blacks have been politically isolated.

Political isolation is a relative term, of course; blacks have wielded *some* political influence at every level of government. In the 1976 and 1992 presidential elections, for example, black voters supplied the margin of victory for Democratic candidates and reaped some political rewards. President Carter appointed thirty-seven black federal judges, more than the total appointed by all previous presidents. President Clinton appointed four blacks to his cabinet, more than any of his predecessors; within two years he had increased the proportion of black federal judges from 5.4 percent to 7.8 percent. Even under Republican administrations, Democratic strength in Congress has enabled blacks to win occasional legislative victories. In 1982, for example, Congress not only renewed the Voting Rights Act but also strengthened it. The following year President Reagan signed a bill making the birthday of Martin Luther King, Jr., a federal holiday. In 1991 President Bush approved a Civil Rights Bill that made it easier to challenge job discrimination.[19]

Yet the most striking political fact of the period between 1968 and 1992 was the dominance of the Republican Party, a political ascendancy that owed much to the defection of *white* voters from the Democratic Party. In the South, especially, whites flocked to the Republicans, transforming a region that had long been a Democratic bastion into a stronghold of the GOP. White Southerners had once made up a third of the Democratic Party; by 1988, writes historian Dewey Grantham, they "constituted barely a fifth of all Democrats." From 1968 until 1992, in every presidential election, most whites voted Republican, while a large majority of blacks cast Democratic ballots. As a consequence, blacks found themselves on the losing side in 1968, 1972, 1980, 1984, 1988, and 2000.[20]

If the momentum of the Civil Rights Movement continued through the Nixon years, the election of Ronald Reagan in 1980 brought it to a standstill. Launching his campaign in Philadelphia, Mississippi, Reagan ardently courted white Southerners and made barely a nod to black voters. Once elected, the new administration set out to weaken the kind of group-based challenges to racial discrimination that lay at the heart of civil rights enforcement. In the name of antistatism and "color-blindness," the government weakened its commitment to equal employment opportunity. Reagan forced the resignation of liberal members of the U.S. Civil Rights Commission, appointing as chair a black conservative who opposed affirmative action. Reagan and his successor, George Bush, regularly denounced "racial quotas."

The rightward drift of the Supreme Court was even more potentially damaging to black interests. William H. Rehnquist, a Nixon appointee who succeeded Warren Burger as Chief Justice in 1986, had had no sympathy for the Civil Rights Movement. As law clerk to Justice Robert H. Jackson, he had argued that "*Plessy* v. *Ferguson* was right and should be reaffirmed." In the long run, he added, "it is the majority who will determine what the constitutional rights of the minority are." Together with three Reagan appointees, Rehnquist was often able to form a conservative majority on civil rights cases. The Rehnquist court narrowed the scope of affirmative action and made it more difficult for blacks to challenge employment discrimination. Bush's appointment of black conservative Clarence Thomas—who replaced civil rights pioneer Thurgood Marshall—shifted the balance still farther to the right. In *Shaw* v. *Reno* (1993), a decision that stunned blacks, the Court rejected a majority-black congressional district in North Carolina because its "extremely irregular" shape betrayed an attempt to "segregate the races for the purposes of voting." This precedent threatened to reduce black congressional representation.[21]

The election of Bill Clinton in 1992 and his decisive reelection in 1996 ended the period of Republican hegemony. Yet the revival of the Democratic Party's national fortunes can be attributed, at least in part, to a shift in party leadership from liberals to conservatives. The two terms of Ronald Reagan represented a forthright repudiation of New Deal–Great Society liberalism. The Reagan-Bush administrations cut welfare programs, attacked organized labor, declared a "War on Drugs," endorsed the death penalty, and encouraged a steep rise in the prison population. When it came to race, Clinton sought to conciliate rather than divide. However, he made no real attempt to turn back the clock: aside from his failed effort to reform the health care system, he eschewed liberal policies and swam with the conservative tide. Promising to "end welfare as we know it," he signed a Republican-sponsored bill that ended Aid to Families with Dependent Children, turned welfare over to the states, and cut people from welfare rolls after two years. Making a point of demonstrating his lack of squeamishness in signing death warrants, Clinton supported "three strikes and you're out" laws that further swelled the burgeoning prison population.

Prison statistics starkly expose the nation's repudiation of liberal reform. Between 1945 and the early 1970s the rate of incarceration remained relatively constant, fluctuating between 93 and 119 prisoners per 100,000 people. By 1996 the national average had skyrocketed to 427; in Louisiana it stood at 615. In 1971 the state and federal prison population stood at about 200,000; by 1996 it had climbed to 1.2 million, and another half a million prisoners were housed in local jails. Some comparisons made by Elliott Currie underline the staggering magnitude of America's prison explosion. In Texas, for example, the *increase* in the state's prison population between 1991 and 1996 was greater than the *entire* population of Britain's jails. In West Germany, the prison population actually decreased between 1968 and 1987; in the United States it more than tripled. As the United States entered the third millennium, its prison population passed 2 million—a quarter of all the world's prisoners.[22]

Black people made up the bulk of this enormous increase. In 1970 about 35 percent of America's prison population was black (only about 6 percent higher than the figure for 1950). By 1998, blacks comprised over half of all prisoners. Today, there are twice as many black men in jail than there were *all* men in jail in 1978. Black men are seven times as likely to wind up in jail than white men. More black men are in prison than are enrolled in college—in California the ratio is four prisoners for every student.[23]

White politicians and tough-minded prosecutors are unapologetic about the expansion of the prison population. Society, they point out, faced an unprecedented increase in violent crime: it soared by about 450 percent between 1960 and 1990. And they argue that the disproportionate number of blacks in prison and on Death Row—48 percent of those awaiting execution in 1992—simply reflected the fact that blacks were far more likely to commit the most serious crimes: in 1990, for example, they comprised 54 percent of all arrested murderers, 61 percent of arrested robbers, and 43 percent of all those apprehended for rape. It seems that this crime explosion was so sudden and massive that a panicked society, including many law-abiding blacks, supported calls for draconian punishments, including the death penalty. Defenders of tough sentencing flatly rebut charges that the criminal justice system is biased against poor people and racial minorities.[24]

Crime and punishment, however, are inseparable from questions of social and economic inequality. There is no need to excuse criminals of their violent

actions in order to note society's responsibility for the crime wave of 1984–
91. The ravaging of black communities by "crack" cocaine and murderous
gang warfare reflected poverty, social isolation, continuing police brutality,
and spiritual hopelessness. And these in turn were exacerbated by government decisions that encouraged the decline of inner cities, the decay of public
schools, and the growth of an alienated and increasingly desperate "underclass." Instead of launching another War on Poverty, or trying to curb the
ownership of guns, the government initiated an ill-conceived "War on Drugs"
that continued to increase the prison population even as violent crime declined after 1992. By 2000 about a quarter of all prison inmates—half a million people—are serving sentences for nonviolent drug violations. An ever
harsher criminal justice system merely papers over the deep fissures in American society.

THE CURRENT CRISIS

As Jesse Jackson's star faded in the 1990s, Nation of Islam leader Louis Farrakhan rose to national prominence. On the face of it, his sudden popularity
was remarkable. It reflected, in part, a wave of nostalgia for Malcolm X of
which Farrakhan—even though he had been Malcolm's deadly foe—was a
beneficiary. It also mirrored a profound crisis of confidence within the black
community that meshed, in a strange way, with the political conservatism of
the times. Farrakhan's message, shorn of its anti-Semitism, was perfectly attuned to the conservatism of the Reagan-Bush-Clinton era. Instead of looking
to white people or the government to solve their problems, blacks needed to
help themselves by building black-owned businesses, strengthening male-
headed families, and banishing alcohol, drugs, and sexual immorality.

Although Farrakhan's nostrums might be dismissed as wishful thinking,
similar calls for self-help issued from the pens of respected black intellectuals
such as Thomas Sowell, an economist at Stanford University. Sowell pointed
to the breakdown of the black family as one of the major sources of black
poverty, and argued that the welfare system, by denying benefits to mothers if
they had a partner, "subsidized both male desertion and teenage pregnancy."
The figures spoke for themselves; they indicated a social tragedy of colossal
proportions. Between 1960 and 1991 the proportion of black households
headed by women increased from 24 percent to 58 percent; three-quarters of
those women were divorced, separated, or had never married. In 1991 two-
thirds of all black children were born to unmarried mothers; 40 percent of all
black girls had become pregnant by the age of eighteen. True, the traditional
two-parent family was in decline among whites as well. The lack of a male in-

come, however, hit black families especially hard. Whereas 38 percent of white female-headed families lived in poverty, 56 percent of black female-headed families were poor.[25]

Sowell urged blacks to cease viewing themselves as victims of white racism, an attitude that merely promoted apathy, defeatism, and antisocial behavior. Instead, black people should accept responsibility for their own fortunes, cultivating individual, family, and group reliance. Rather than place their hope in politics and government, they should emulate other ethnic groups—including West Indian immigrants—who achieved success through their own strengths. The jobs were there for the asking, Sowell argued, if blacks were prepared to begin at the minimum wage. Adequate education was also freely available, if only children were prepared to study, parents to participate. Self-help—study, hard work, frugality, and group cooperation—was the surest path to equality.[26]

Although many other scholars dispute the notion that racism is a factor of declining importance, there is little likelihood that the nation will embark upon a "Third Reconstruction"—a massive government effort to rebuild decaying cities and eliminate poverty—to finish the work of the "Second Reconstruction," the Civil Rights Movement. Moreover, the spread of "rights consciousness" among other groups, although sparked by the Civil Rights Movement, has ironically made it more difficult for blacks to press their case for compensatory treatment. The growth of other minorities, especially Hispanic Americans; the massive influx of immigrants (a million a year in the 1990s); the politicization of homosexuals; and the efforts of women to combat gender discrimination have tended to crowd out the claims of black Americans. As a consequence, the division between the black middle class and the black underclass remains a gulf; the alienation of the black poor from the mainstream of society shows little sign of abating. "The victories of the civil rights movement," claims historian Glenn Eskew, "failed to solve the problems experienced by many black people. The movement had gained access for a few while never challenging the structure of the system"[27]

Movement veterans express quiet satisfaction at what they have achieved, mixed with deep unease about continuing inequality and confusion over what should be done about it. Charles Sherrod believes that Albany, Georgia, is "just as racist as it has always been." Others, however, note that racism often appears in a subtle guise, making it hard for the black community—itself differentiated by class—to mobilize against it. "Everything is more complex now," stresses Bill Saunders, a black leader in Charleston, South Carolina. "Almost any issue you bring up, blacks are on both sides. Race is always a factor, but not so simply as was the case in the sixties and before." Twenty years ago, the Reverend L. Francis Griffin, longtime NAACP leader in Prince Edward County, Virginia, acknowledged the post-civil rights era for what it was.

"In essence, there's a new status quo here. There is still a battleground, the lines of separation still exist—but the pressures are not such that there will be . . . all-out fighting. It's a cold war now, and I look for it to go on." North and South, East and West, a path to freedom had petered out. More than thirty years after the death of King, the next road—the right road—is hard to discern.[28]

NOTES

PREFACE

1. John W. Cell, *The Highest Stage of White Supremacy: The Origins of Segregation in South Africa and the American South* (Cambridge: Cambridge University Press, 1982), pp. 257–62.

CHAPTER ONE

1. Herbert Aptheker, ed., *A Documentary History of the Negro People in the United States*, 7 vols. (New York: Citadel Press, 1992), vol. 2, p. 546.

2. Leon Litwack, *Been in the Storm So Long: The Aftermath of Slavery* (New York: Vintage Books, 1980), pp. 244–45, 399–420, 462–71.

3. Eric Foner, *Reconstruction: America's Unfinished Revolution, 1863–1877* (New York: Harper and Row, 1988), pp. 199–201, 208–09; John Hope Franklin, *From Slavery to Freedom: A History of Negro Americans* (New York: Alfred A. Knopf, 1974), pp. 241–42.

4. Foner, *Reconstruction,* pp. 158–64; U.S. Department of Commerce, *The Social and Economic Status of the Black Population in the United States: An Historical View, 1790–1978* (Washington, D.C.: U.S. Government Printing Office, 1978), p. 81.

5. Ibid., pp. 88, 91.

6. Foner, *Reconstruction,* pp. 454–59, 558–63, 575–83.

7. J. Morgan Kousser, *The Shaping of Southern Politics: Suffrage Restrictions and the Establishment of the One-Party South, 1880–1910* (New Haven: Yale University Press, 1974), pp. 83–138; C. Vann Woodward, *Origins of the New South, 1877–1913* (Baton Rouge: Louisiana State University Press, 1951, 1971), pp. 55–56.

8. Kousser, *Shaping of Southern Politics,* pp. 12–44.

9. Vernon Lane Wharton, *The Negro in Mississippi, 1865–1890* (New York: Harper and Row, 1965), pp. 203–15.

10. Woodward, *Origins of the New South,* pp. 256–58.

11. H. Leon Prather, *Resurgent Politics and Educational Progressivism in the New South: North Carolina, 1890–1913* (Cranbury, N.J.: Associated University Presses, 1979), pp. 98–100; Eric Anderson, *Race and Politics in North Carolina, 1872–1901: The Black Second* (Baton Rouge: Louisiana State University Press, 1981), p. 227; Oliver H. Orr, *Charles Brantley Aycock* (Chapel Hill: University of North Carolina Press, 1961), p. 106.

12. C. Vann Woodward, *The Strange Career of Jim Crow* (New York: Oxford University Press, 1966), pp. 31–65.

13. William Ivy Hair, *Bourbonism and Agrarian Protest: Louisiana Politics, 1877–1900* (Baton Rouge: Louisiana State University Press, 1969), pp. 234–67; Kousser, *Shaping of Southern Politics,* pp. 46–47, 131–32, 153–54; Edward L. Ayers, *The Promise of the New South: Life After Reconstruction* (New York: Oxford University Press, 1992), pp. 275–76.

14. Prather, *Resurgent Politics and Educational Progressivism in the New South,* pp. 141, 151; Henry L. West, "The Race War in North Carolina," *Forum* 26 (1898–99), p. 588; Glenda E. Gilmore, *Gender and Jim Crow: Women and the Politics of White Supremacy in North Carolina, 1896–1920* (Chapel Hill: University of North Carolina Press, 1996), pp. 83–88.

15. John E. Talmadge, *Rebecca Latimer Felton: Nine Stormy Decades* (Athens, Ga.: University of Georgia Press, 1960), pp. 113–14.

16. Orr, *Charles B. Aycock,* p. 124; H. Leon Prather, *We Have Taken a City: Wilmington Racial Massacre and Coup of 1898* (Cranbury, N.J.: Associated Universities Press, 1984), passim; Prather, *Resurgent Politics and Educational Progressivism in the New South,* pp. 151–66; Anderson, *Race and Politics in North Carolina,* pp. 252–79; Ayers, *Promise of the New South,* pp. 301–04; Gilmore, *Gender and Jim Crow,* pp. 105–14; James B. Dudley to Booker T. Washington, August 28, 1903, in Louis R. Harlan, ed., *The Booker T. Washington Papers,* 13 vols. (Urbana: University of Illinois Press, 1972–84), vol. 7, pp. 271–72.

17. Orr, *Charles B. Aycock,* p. 150.

18. Ayers, *Promise of the New South,* pp. 269–74.

19. Kousser, *Shaping of Southern Politics,* pp. 246–47; Gilmore, *Gender and Jim Crow,* p. 267, n. 35.

20. Linda Gordon, *Women's Body, Women's Right: Birth Control in America* (New York: Penguin, 1977), pp. 136–56.

21. Janette T. Greenwood, *Bittersweet Legacy: The Black and White "Better Classes" in Charlotte, 1850–1910* (Chapel Hill: University of North Carolina Press, 1994), pp. 209, 216; Thomas Nelson Page, *The Negro: The Southerner's Problem* (1904; reprint, New York: Johnson Reprint Co., 1970), p. 64.

22. James M. McPherson, *The Abolitionist Legacy: From Reconstruction to the NAACP* (Princeton: Princeton University Press, 1975), pp. 333–34.

23. Francis Butler Simkins, *Pitchfork Ben Tillman: South Carolinian* (Baton Rouge: Louisiana State University Press, 1967), p. 355; S. C. Chiles, "The South and the School," in *Proceedings of the Eighth Conference for Education in the South, Columbia, South Carolina, April 26–28, 1905* (New York: Committee on Publication, 1905), pp. 150–51; Oscar Underwood, "The Negro Problem in the South," *Forum* (1904), p. 217.

24. Seth Low, "Some Phases of Educational History in New York City," in *Proceedings of the Eighth Conference for Education in the South,* p. 89; David L. Lewis, *W. E. B. Du Bois: Biography of a Race, 1868–1919* (New York: Henry Holt, 1993), p. 276.

25. *Plessy v. Ferguson,* 163 U.S. 537 (1896), in Leslie H. Fishel and Benjamin

Quarles, *The Negro American: A Documentary History* (Glenview, Ill.: Scott, Foresman, 1967), pp. 339–42; C. Vann Woodward, *American Counterpoint: Slavery and Race in the North-South Dialogue* (Boston: Little, Brown, 1971), pp. 227–31; Ayers, *Promise of the New South,* p. 327.

26. Woodward, *Origins of the New South,* pp. 329–40; Kousser, *Shaping of Southern Politics,* pp. 139–69. Only the blatantly discriminatory "grandfather clause," which exempted men from suffrage restrictions if they, their fathers, or their grandfathers had been entitled to vote on January 1, 1867—before Radical Reconstruction had enfranchised black men—fell afoul of the Court.

27. Ayers, *Promise of the New South,* pp. 304–09; Kousser, *Shaping of Southern Politics,* p. 224.

28. Kousser, *Shaping of Southern Politics,* pp. 232–33; Ayers, *Promise of the New South,* p. 411.

29. Ray Stannard Baker, *Following the Color Line: An Account of Negro Citizenship in the American Democracy* (1908; reprint, New York: Harper and Row, 1964), p. 263.

30. Ayers, *Promise of the New South,* pp. 136–46, 432–33; Howard N. Rabinowitz, "From Exclusion to Segregation: Southern Race Relations, 1865–1890," *Journal of American History* 58 (Sept. 1976), pp. 325–50; "Segregation and Reconstruction," in *The Facts of Reconstruction: Essays in Honor of John Hope Franklin,* Eric Anderson and Alfred A. Moss, Jr., eds. (Baton Rouge: Louisiana State University Press, 1991), pp. 91–92; Cell, *Highest Stage of White Supremacy,* pp. 89–93, 132–35, 175–80; Elizabeth Grace Hale, *Making Whiteness: The Culture of Segregation in the South, 1890–1940* (New York: Vintage, 1999), p. 93.

31. John H. Haley, *Charles N. Hunter and Race Relations in North Carolina* (Chapel Hill: University of North Carolina Press, 1987), pp. 126, 135; Gilmore, *Gender and Jim Crow,* p. 117.

32. Charles W. Chesnutt, *The Journals of Charles W. Chesnutt,* ed. Richard Brodhead (Durham, N.C.: Duke University Press, 1993), p. 172; August Meier, *Negro Thought in America, 1880–1915* (Ann Arbor: University of Michigan Press, 1988), pp. 146–49.

33. William H. Councill, "The Future of the Negro," *Forum* 27 (1899), p. 575; Aptheker, ed., *Documentary History of the Negro People,* vol. 2, p. 757; Clarence A. Bacote, "Negro Proscriptions, Protests, and Proposed Solutions in Georgia, 1880–1908," in *The Negro in the South Since 1865,* ed. Charles E. Wynes (New York: Harper Colophon, 1968), pp. 168–76.

34. T. Thomas Fortune to Booker T. Washington, May 9, 1900, in Harlan, ed., *Washington Papers,* vol. 5, pp. 505–06.

35. Greenwood, *Bittersweet Legacy,* p. 85.

36. John H. Haley, *Charles N. Hunter and Race Relations in North Carolina* (Chapel Hill: University of North Carolina Press, 1987), pp. 80–81; Edward L. Blackshear, *The Future of the Negro: The Race Problem Discussed* (1898 pamphlet), Barker Center for Texas History, University of Texas, Austin, Texas.

37. Edward L. Wheeler, *Uplifting the Race: The Black Minister in the New South, 1865–1902* (Lanham, Md.: University Presses of America, 1986), pp. 23–30, 65, 75, 110–11; David M. Tucker, *Black Pastors and Leaders: Memphis, 1819–1972* (Memphis: Memphis State University Press, 1975), p. 52; Gilmore, *Gender and Jim Crow,* pp. 116–17.

38. Cell, *Highest Stage of White Supremacy,* p. 262; Meier, *Negro Thought in America,* p. 169.

CHAPTER TWO

1. W. Fitzhugh Brundage, *Lynching in the New South: Georgia and Virginia, 1880–1930* (Urbana: University of Illinois Press, 1993), pp. 7–8. These figures represent an estimate, not an accurate record.

2. Robert R. Moton to James H. Dillard, January 16, 1922, folder 577, box 77, Robert R. Moton Papers (Hollis Burke Frissell Library, Tuskegee University, Tuskegee, Alabama).

3. Stuart Grayson Noble, *Forty Years of the Public Schools in Mississippi: With Special Reference to the Education of the Negro* (1918; reprint, New York: Negro Universities Press, 1969), pp. 110, 122–25; Simkins, *Pitchfork Ben Tillman,* p. 394; *Proceedings of the Twelfth Conference for Education in the South, Atlanta, April 14–16, 1909* (Nashville: Executive Committee of the Conference, 1909), n.p; Fishel and Quarles, *The Negro American,* p. 379.

4. George C. Wright, *Racial Violence in Kentucky, 1865–1940: Lynchings, Mob Rule, and "Legal Lynchings"* (Baton Rouge: Louisiana State University Press, 1990), pp. 61–63; Simkins, *Pitchfork Ben Tillman,* p. 224.

5. Brundage, *Lynching in the New South,* pp. 68–70; Simkins, *Pitchfork Ben Tillman,* pp. 397–98.

6. W. J. Cash, *The Mind of the South* (1941; reprint, London: Penguin, 1973), pp. 103–06, 132–34; Jacquelyn Dowd Hall, "'The Mind That Burns in Each Body': Women, Rape, and Racial Violence," in *Powers of Desire: The Politics of Sexuality,* Ann Snitow, Christine Stansell, and Sharon Thompson, eds. (London: Virago, 1983), pp. 343–47; Joel Williamson, *New People: Miscegenation and Mulattoes in the United States* (New York: Free Press, 1980), pp. 91–95; Charles H. Smith, "Have American Negroes Too Much Liberty?" *Forum* 16 (1893–94), p. 181.

7. Arthur W. Calhoun, *A Social History of the American Family,* 3 vols. (1918; reprint, New York: Barnes and Noble, 1960), vol. 3, p. 43; Gunnar Myrdal, *An American Dilemma: The Negro Problem and Modern Democracy,* 2 vols. (New York: Harper & Brothers, 1944), vol. 2, p. 1194, n. 44; David L. Cohn, *Where I Was Born and Raised* (Boston: Houghton Mifflin, 1935), p. 79.

8. Stewart E. Tolnay and E. M. Beck, *A Festival of Violence: An Analysis of Southern Lynchings, 1880–1930* (Urbana: University of Illinois Press, 1995), pp. 76–77; Cash, *Mind of the South,* p. 134.

9. Booker T. Washington, "Education Will Solve the Race Problem: A Reply," August 1900, in *Washington Papers,* Harlan, ed., vol. 5: p. 616; Councill, "The Future of the Negro," p. 574; William E. Benson, "The Prevention of Crime Among Colored Children," *Proceedings of the National Conference of Charities and Corrections* (1904), pp. 260–61.

10. Brundage, *Lynching in the New South,* p. 58; Smith, "Have American Negroes Too Much Liberty?," p. 182; Atticus G. Haygood, "The Black Shadow in the South," *Forum* 16 (1893–94), pp. 167–75.

11. Haygood, "The Black Shadow in the South," p. 171; Washington, "Education Will Solve the Race Problem," p. 617.

12. C. Eric Lincoln and Lawrence H. Mamiya, *The Black Church in the African-American Experience* (Durham: Duke University Press, 1990), pp. 276–77; Wright, *Racial Violence in Kentucky,* pp. 78–79.

13. Ida B. Wells, *Crusade for Justice: The Autobiography of Ida B. Wells,* ed. Alfreda M. Duster (Chicago: University of Chicago Press, 1970), pp. 7–9.

14. Linda O. McMurry, *To Keep the Waters Troubled: The Life of Ida B. Wells* (New York: Oxford University Press, 1998), pp. 13–14; Ida B. Wells, *The Memphis Diary of Ida B. Wells: An Intimate Portrait of the Activist As a Young Woman,* ed. Miriam De-Costa-Willis (Boston: Beacon Press, 1995), pp. 77–78.

15. Wells, *Autobiography,* pp. 18–20; McMurry, *To Keep the Waters Troubled,* pp. 25–30. The judge who decided in favor of Wells, James Pierce, was a Union veteran from Minnesota.

16. McMurry, *To Keep the Waters Troubled,* pp. 128–29; Wright, *Racial Violence in Kentucky,* pp. 163, 169.

17. Wells, *Autobiography,* pp. 47–65; McMurry, *To Keep the Waters Troubled,* pp. 123–48.

18. Wells, *Autobiography,* pp. 69–71; Ida B. Wells, *Southern Horrors and Other Writings: The Anti-Lynching Campaign of Ida B. Wells, 1892–1900,* ed. Jacqueline Jones Royster (Boston: Bedford Books, 1997), pp. 53–57, 64, 120. Fortune employed Wells as a writer, and gave her a quarter share in the newspaper in exchange for the subscription list of the *Free Speech.*

19. Wells, *Autobiography,* pp. 85–223; McMurry, *To Keep the Waters Troubled,* pp. 186–99, 211–22; Gail Bederman, "'Civilization,' the Decline of Middle-Class Manliness, and Ida B. Wells's Antilynching Campaign (1892–94)," in *"We Specialize in the Wholly Impossible": A Reader in Black Women's History,* Darlene Clarke Hine, Wilma King, and Linda Reed, eds. (Brooklyn, N.Y.: Carlson Publishing, 1995), pp. 407–32.

20. Fannie Barrier Williams, "The Club Movement Among Colored Women in America," in *A New Negro for a New Century,* John E. McBrady, ed. (1900; reprint, Miami: Mnemosyne Publishing, 1969), pp. 382, 428; Ann Firor Scott, "Most Invisible of All: Black Women's Voluntary Associations," *Journal of Southern History* 56 (Feb. 1990), p. 12; Paula Giddings, *When and Where I Enter: The Impact of Black Women on Race and Sex in America* (New York: William Morrow, 1984), pp. 96–98; Deborah Gray White, *Too Heavy a Load: Black Women in Defense of Themselves, 1894–1994* (New York: Norton, 1999), pp. 27–39.

21. McMurry, *To Keep the Waters Troubled,* pp. 245–48; Williams, "The Club Movement Among Colored Women in America," pp. 396–400, 417.

22. Meier, *Negro Thought in America,* pp. 136–37; Stephanie J. Shaw, "Black Club Women and the Creation of the National Association of Colored Women," in *"We Specialize in the Wholly Impossible,"* Hine, ed., pp. 436–42; Kathleen C. Berkeley, "'Colored Ladies Also Contributed': Black Women's Activities from Benevolence to Social Welfare, 1866–1896," in *The Web of Southern Social Relations: Women, Family, and Education,* Walter J. Fraser, Jr., R. Frank Saunders, Jr., and Jon C. Wakelyn, eds. (Athens: University of Georgia Press, 1985), pp. 181–96; White, *Too Heavy a Load,* p. 16. According to Meier, there was "no sharp dividing line" between the benevolent societies and the secret societies.

23. Wells, *Autobiography,* pp. 40–41; White, *Too Heavy a Load,* pp. 59, 73.

24. White, *Too Heavy a Load,* pp. 27–33; Shaw, "Black Club Women and the Creation of the National Association of Colored Women," pp. 438–41; Linda Gordon, "Black and White Visions of Welfare: Women's Welfare Activism, 1890–1945," *Journal of American History* 78 (Sept. 1991), pp. 560–66; Lillian S. Williams, "And Still I Rise: Black Women and Reform, Buffalo, New York, 1900–1940," in *"We Specialize in the Wholly Impossible,"* Hine, ed., pp. 526–28.

25. Gilmore, *Gender and Jim Crow,* pp. 147–48.

26. Scott, "Most Invisible of All," p. 13; Jacqueline Anne Rouse, *Lugenia Burns Hope: Black Southern Reformer* (Athens: University of Georgia Press, 1989), p. 70; White, *Too Heavy a Load*, pp. 70–76.

27. White, *Too Heavy a Load*, pp. 76–77, 106–9.

28. Wells, *Autobiography*, pp. 252–55; McMurry, *To Keep the Waters Troubled*, pp. 236–43.

29. McMurry, *To Keep the Waters Troubled*, pp. 156–75.

30. Vincent Vinikas, "Specters in the Past: The Saint Charles, Arkansas, Lynching of 1904 and the Limits of Historical Inquiry," *Journal of Southern History* 65 (Aug. 1999), p. 549.

31. Bederman, "'Civilization,' the Decline of Middle-Class Manliness, and Ida B. Wells's Antilynching Campaign (1892–94)," in *"We Specialize in the Wholly Impossible,"* Hine, ed., pp. 422–23.

32. Brundage, *Lynching in the New South*, pp. 169–78, 238–42; Wright, *Racial Violence in Kentucky*, pp. 177–83, 190–98; Tolnay and Beck, *Festival of Violence*, pp. 213–33; David M. Tucker, *Memphis Since Crump: Bossism, Blacks, and Civic Reformers, 1948–1968* (Knoxville: University of Tennessee Press, 1980), pp. 6, 13–14.

Chapter Three

1. Booker T. Washington, *Up from Slavery*, ed. William L. Andrews (1901; reprint, New York: W. W. Norton, 1996), pp. 99–102.

2. Elizabeth L. Wheeler, "Isaac Fisher: The Frustrations of a Negro Educator at Branch Normal College, 1902–1911," *Arkansas Historical Quarterly* 41 (Spring 1982), p. 43; Stephen Kantrowitz, *Ben Tillman and the Reconstruction of White Supremacy* (Chapel Hill: University of North Carolina Press, 2000), p. 259.

3. Booker T. Washington, "A Speech Before the Philosophical Lyceum of Lincoln University," April 26, 1888, in *The Booker T. Washington Papers*, Harlan, ed., vol. 2, p. 442; Washington, "An Abraham Lincoln Memorial Address in Philadelphia," February 14, 1899, ibid., vol. 5, pp. 32–38; Washington, *Up from Slavery*, pp. 23–24.

4. Washington, *Up from Slavery*, p. 68; Roscoe Conkling Bruce, "Tuskegee Institute," in *From Servitude to Service* (1905; reprint, New York: Negro Universities Press, 1969), p. 113.

5. Washington, "A Speech before the New York Congregational Club," January 16, 1890, in *The Booker T. Washington Papers*, Harlan, ed., vol. 3, p. 286.

6. Robert Francis Engs, *Educating the Disfranchised and Disinherited: Samuel Chapman Armstrong and Hampton Institute, 1839–1893* (Knoxville: University of Tennessee Press, 1999), pp. 79–81; Washington, *Up from Slavery*, p. 69.

7. Buell G. Gallagher, *American Caste and the Negro College* (New York: Columbia University Press, 1938), p. 211; Timothy Thomas Fortune, *Black and White: Land, Labor and Politics in the South* (1884; reprint, New York: Arno Press, 1968), pp. 80–90.

8. Basil Matthews, *Booker T. Washington: Educator and Inter-Racial Interpreter* (London: SCM Press, 1949), p. 284; James D. Anderson, "Education As a Vehicle for the Manipulation of Black Workers," in *Work, Technology and Education: Dissenting Essays in the Intellectual Foundations of American Education*, Walter Feinberg and Henry Rosemont, eds. (Urbana: University of Illinois Press, 1975), p. 38; idem, *The Education of Blacks in the South, 1860–1935* (Chapel Hill: University of North Carolina Press, 1988), p. 44; Donald S. Spivey, *Schooling for the New Slavery: Black Industrial Education, 1868–1915* (Westport, Conn.: Greenwood Press, 1978), p. 66.

9. Kelly Miller, "The Education of the Negro," in *Education Report, 1900–1901*,

U.S. Commissioner of Education (Washington, D.C.: Government Printing Office, 1901), p. 816; idem, *Out of the House of Bondage* (1914; reprint, New York: Schocken, 1971), p. 152; W. E. B. Du Bois, *The Souls of Black Folk* (1903; reprint, New York: Dover, 1994), p. 62.

10. John Dittmer, *Black Georgia in the Progressive Era, 1900–1920* (Urbana: University of Illinois Press, 1977), p. 142; Anderson, *Education of Blacks in the South*, pp. 115–34.

11. Robert G. Sherer, *Subordination or Liberation: The Development of Conflicting Theories of Education in Nineteenth-Century Alabama* (University, Ala.: University of Alabama Press, 1977), p. 53.

12. Woodward, *Origins of the New South*, pp. 61–64; Anderson, *Education of Blacks in the South*, p. 248.

13. Josephus Daniels, "The Progress of Southern Education," *Annals of the American Academy of Political and Social Science* 22 (1903), pp. 310–11; *Biennial Report of the State Superintendent of Public Education, 1896–97* (Baton Rouge, La.: The Advocate, 1898), pp. 81–82.

14. Stuart Grayson Noble, *Forty Years of Public Schools in Mississippi: With Special Reference to the Education of the Negro* (New York: Negro Universities Press, 1969), p. 111; Simkins, *Pitchfork Ben Tillman*, p. 461; *Proceedings of the Twelfth Conference for Education in the South, Atlanta, April 14–16, 1909* (Nashville, Tenn.: Committee on Publications, 1909).

15. Booker T. Washington, "Industrial Education and Public Schools," *Annals of the American Academy of Political and Social Sciences* 49 (Sept. 1913), p. 227; idem, "A Speech Before the National Educational Association," July 16, 1884, in *Washington Papers*, Harlan, ed., vol. 2, pp. 259–60; idem, *Up from Slavery*, p. 57.

16. Richard D. Ralston, "American Episodes in the Making of an African Leader: A Case Study of Alfred B. Xuma," *International Journal of African Historical Studies* 6 (1973), pp. 76–77; Louis R. Harlan, *Booker T. Washington: The Wizard of Tuskegee, 1901–1915* (New York: Oxford University Press, 1983), pp. 142, 144, 172.

17. Kelly Miller, *Radicals and Conservatives, and Other Essays on the Negro in America* (1908; reprint, New York: Schocken Books, 1968), p. 30; Washington, "Speech Before the National Education Association," pp. 259–60.

18. J. H. Phillips, "The Essential Requirements of Negro Education," *Southern Education Association: Journal of Proceedings and Addresses, 19th Annual Session, Atlanta, Georgia, December 29–31, 1908* (1908), pp. 121–29; Marshall Fred Phillips, "A History of the Public Schools in Birmingham, Alabama" (M.A. thesis, University of Alabama, 1939); Arthur Harold Parker, *"A Dream That Came True": Autobiography of Arthur Harold Parker* (Birmingham: Industrial High School, 1932).

19. In 1893 Washington persuaded the Alabama legislature to make Tuskegee's Board of Trustees "independent and self-perpetuating"; Robert G. Sherer, *Subordination or Liberation: The Development and Conflicting Theories of Education in Nineteenth-Century Alabama* (University, Ala.: University of Alabama Press, 1977), pp. 61–62.

20. Anderson, *Education of Blacks in the South*, pp. 79–103; Louis R. Harlan, *Separate and Unequal: Public School Campaigns and Racism in the Southern Seaboard States, 1901–1915* (Chapel Hill: University of North Carolina Press, 1958), pp. 75–80.

21. William H. Baldwin, "The Present Problem of Negro Education, Industrial Education," in *Proceedings of the First, Second, and Third Conferences for Christian Education in the South, 1898–1900* (Washington, D.C., 1900), pp. 72, 74.

22. Harlan, *Booker T. Washington: The Making of a Black Leader*, p. 324.

23. Harlan, *Separate and Unequal,* pp. 131, 204–5; Noble, *Forty Years of the Public Schools in Mississippi,* pp. 73–75, 90–96, 110, 142; J. Morgan Kousser, "Progressivism—For Middle-Class Whites Only: North Carolina Education, 1880–1910," *Journal of Southern History* 46 (May 1980), pp. 169–92; Lester C. Lamon, "Black Public Education in the South: 1861–1920; By Whom, For Whom and Under Whose Control?" *Journal of Thought* 18:3 (Fall 1983), pp. 76–89.

24. Charles W. Dabney, *Universal Education in the South, Vol. 2: The Southern Education Movement* (Chapel Hill: University of North Carolina Press, 1936), pp. 50–53; Woodward, *Origins of the New South,* p. 403; Harlan, *Separate and Unequal,* pp. 92–97; Harlan, *Booker T. Washington: The Wizard of Tuskegee,* p. 130; Ullin W. Leavell, *Philanthropy in Negro Education* (1930; reprint, Westport, Conn.: Negro Universities Press, 1970), pp. 97–103, 175.

25. Harlan, *Wizard of Tuskegee,* pp. 186–94; Washington to William H. Baldwin, September 9, 1903; Baldwin to Washington, September 11, 1903; Washington to Baldwin, January 22, 1904, all in *Washington Papers,* Harlan, ed., vol. 7, pp. 278, 409–10.

26. Harlan, *Wizard of Tuskegee,* pp. 131–38.

27. Harlan, *Wizard of Tuskegee,* pp. 140–42, 197–99.

28. Fortune to Washington, October 13, 1899, in *Washington Papers,* Harlan, ed., vol. 5, p. 233.

29. Washington, "A Statement in the *Philadelphia North American,*" June 7, 1903, in *Washington Papers,* Harlan, ed., vol. 7, p. 173; Washington, "A Statement on Lynching," *Birmingham Age-Herald,* April 25, 1899, in *Washington Papers,* Harlan, ed., vol. 5, pp. 90–91; Harlan, *Making of a Black Leader,* pp. 262–63.

30. Edward H. Clement to Washington, February 2, 1899, in *Washington Papers,* Harlan, ed., vol. 5, p. 5; Samuel Laing Williams to Washington, April 14, 1899, ibid., vol. 5, p. 81; Louis G. Gregory, January 15, 1904, ibid., vol. 7, pp. 384–87.

31. John H. Milholland to Washington, February 12, 1903, in *Washington Papers,* Harlan, ed., vol. 7, p. 73; *Boston Globe,* July 31, 1903, ibid., vol. 7, pp. 229–39; Harlan, *Wizard of Tuskegee,* pp. 44–46; Stephen R. Fox, *The Guardian of Boston: William Monroe Trotter* (New York: Atheneum, 1970), pp. 31–58.

32. Ibid., pp. 43, 89–92; Lewis, *Du Bois,* pp. 315–17.

33. Du Bois to black leaders, June 13, 1905; "Declaration of Principles"; *Voice of the Negro,* September 1905; all in *Documentary History of the Negro People,* Aptheker, ed., vol. 2, pp. 900–07.

34. James Weldon Johnson, *Along This Way: The Autobiography of James Weldon Johnson* (1933; reprint, New York: Penguin, 1990), p. 313.

35. Washington to James H. Hayes, February 9, 1903, in *Washington Papers,* Harlan, ed., vol. 7, p. 61; Washington to Oswald Garrison Villard, May 28, 1909, ibid., vol. 10, pp. 118–19.

36. Theodore W. Jones to Washington, January 28, 1904, ibid., vol. 7, pp. 417–19.

37. Washington to Charles Fleischer, February 17, 1903, ibid., vol. 7, p. 82; Washington to Theodore Roosevelt, September 15, 1903, ibid., vol. 3, pp. 284–85; Washington to Ray Stannard Baker, May 24, 1910, ibid., vol. 10, pp. 333–34; Washington to Robert R. Moton, October 24, 1910, ibid., vol. 10, pp. 416–17; Washington to Charles Lee Coon, November 11, 1910, ibid., vol. 10, p. 454; Washington to Travers Buxton, November 19, 1910, ibid., vol. 10, pp. 478–79.

38. Thomas Sowell, *Educational Assumptions Versus History: Collected Papers* (Stanford, Calif.: Hoover Institution Press, 1986), pp. 197–99.

39. Bernard A. Weisberger, *Booker T. Washington* (New York: Mentor, 1972), p. 113.

40. Washington, "A Memorandum for Theodore Roosevelt," c. November 1904, in *Washington Papers,* Harlan, ed., vol. 8, pp. 150–51; Washington to Roosevelt, December 26, 1904, ibid., vol. 5, pp. 162–63.

41. Washington to Kelly Miller, November 19, 1906, ibid., vol. 9, pp. 129–31; Washington to Samuel W. Bacote, May 5, 1908, ibid., vol. 9, p. 527; U.S. Congress, U.S. Senate, *Summary Discharge or Mustering Out of Regiments or Companies: Message from the President of the United States,* 59th Congress, 2d sess., 1906, Document No. 155, p. 9; Lewis L. Gould, *The Presidency of Theodore Roosevelt* (Lawrence: University Press of Kansas, 1991), pp. 236–44; Harlan, *Booker T. Washington: The Wizard of Tuskegee,* pp. 309–22; Ann J. Lane, *The Brownsville Affair: National Crisis and Black Reaction* (Port Washington, N.Y.: Kennikat Press, 1971), pp. 91–107.

42. Washington to Chesnutt, December 6, 1907, in *Washington Papers,* Harlan, ed., vol. 9, pp. 414–15; Chesnutt to Washington, January 1, 1908, ibid., vol. 9, pp. 428–29; Washington to Ray Stannard Baker, July 7, 1910, ibid., vol. 10, p. 353.

43. Virginia L. Denton, *Booker T. Washington and the Adult Education Movement* (Gainesville: University of Florida Press, 1992), pp. 167–68.

44. Gunnar Myrdal, *An American Dilemma: The Negro Problem and Modern Democracy,* 2 vols. (New York: Harper and Brothers, 1944), vol. 1, p. 237.

45. U.S. Department of Commerce, Bureau of the Census, *Social and Economic Status of the Black Population in the United States: An Historical Overview, 1790–1978* (Washington, D.C.: U.S. Government Printing Office, 1978), p. 81.

46. Washington, *Up from Slavery,* p. 38; Washington to George A. Gates, January 13, 1910, in *Washington Papers,* Harlan, ed., vol. 10, p. 196.

47. Washington, "An Interview by Frank G. Carpenter in the Memphis Commercial-Appeal," December 2, 1899, ibid., vol. 5, pp. 279–82; Washington, "An Address before the White House Conference on the Care of Children," ibid., vol. 10, pp. 19–20; Washington to William P. Blake, December 12, 1911, ibid., vol. 11, p. 413.

48. Du Bois, *Souls of Black Folk,* p. 31; Miller, *Radicals and Conservatives,* p. 37.

49. Washington, "A Speech Delivered before the Women's New England Club," January 27, 1889, in *Washington Papers,* Harlan, ed., vol. 3, pp. 25–32; Harlan, *Making of a Black Leader,* pp. 236–37; Donald J. Calista, "Booker T. Washington: Another Look," *Journal of Negro History* 49 (Oct. 1964), p. 250; Meier, *Negro Thought in America,* pp. 110–13.

50. Washington to Oswald Garrison Villard, November 16, 1904, in *Washington Papers,* Harlan, ed., vol. 8, p. 132.

51. Sherer, *Subordination or Liberation,* pp. 23–40; idem, "William Burns Paterson: 'Pioneer As Well As Apostle of Negro Education in Alabama,'" *Alabama Historical Quarterly* 36 (1974), pp. 137–42.

52. Chesnutt to Washington, August 11, 1903, in *Washington Papers,* Harlan, ed., vol. 7, p. 265; Fortune to Washington, March 2, 1899, ibid., vol. 5, p. 49.

53. Aptheker, ed., *Documentary History of the Negro People,* vol. 2, p. 758; Lawrence J. Friedman, "Life 'In the Lion's Mouth': Another Look at Booker T. Washington," *Journal of Negro History* 59 (Oct. 1974), p. 344.

54. Washington to T. Thomas Fortune, January 31, 1907, in *Washington Papers,* Harlan, ed., vol. 9, pp. 206–08; Washington to Portia Washington, November 15, 1906, ibid., vol. 9, p. 112; Meier, *Negro Thought in America,* p. 118.

55. Horace Mann Bond to J. J. Coss, February 15, 1937, Horace Mann Bond Papers, series 1, reel 5.

56. Washington to Theodore Roosevelt, September 15, 1903, in *Washington Papers*, Harlan, ed., vol. 7. p. 285.

CHAPTER FOUR

1. William English Walling, "The Race War in the North," *Independent* 65 (September 3, 1908); "Call for a National Negro Conference," February 12, 1909; both in *The Negro American: A Documentary History*, Leslie H. Fishel and Benjamin Quarles, eds. (Glenview, Ill.: Scott, Foresman and Company, 1967), pp. 377–78, 383–85.

2. Charles Flint Kellogg, *A History of the National Association for the Advancement of Colored People, 1909–1920* (Baltimore: Johns Hopkins University Press, 1967), pp. 9–18; Mary White Ovington, "How the National Association for the Advancement of Colored People Began," in *The Negro in Twentieth Century America*, John Hope Franklin and Isadore Starr, eds. (New York: Vintage, 1967), pp. 95–101; Mary White Ovington, *The Walls Came Tumbling Down* (1947; reprint, New York: Schocken Books, 1970), pp. xiii–11; *Proceedings of the National Negro Conference, 1909* (New York: *New York Times* and the Arno Press, 1969), pp. 79–85, 222–24.

3. *Proceedings of the National Negro Conference*, pp. 79–83.

4. James M. McPherson, *The Abolitionist Legacy: From Reconstruction to the NAACP* (Princeton, N.J.: Princeton University Press, 1975), pp. 386–88; Lewis, *W. E. B. Du Bois*, pp. 386–88; Robert L. Zangrando, "The 'Organized Negro': The National Association for the Advancement of Colored People and Civil Rights," in *The Black Experience in America: Selected Essays*, James C. Curtis and Lewis L. Gould, eds. (Austin: University of Texas Press, 1970), pp. 153–54; Ovington, *Walls Came Tumbling Down*, p. 106; *Proceedings of the National Negro Conference*, pp. 14–40, 67–73, 197–206, 222–24.

5. Ovington, *Walls Came Tumbling Down*, p. 106; Kellogg, *History of the National Association for the Advancement of Colored People*, pp. 21–22; Stephen R. Fox, *The Guardian of Boston: William Monroe Trotter* (New York: Atheneum, 1970), pp. 103–14, 127–30; McMurry, *To Keep the Waters Troubled*, pp. 281–82.

6. McPherson, *Abolitionist Legacy*, p. 389; B. Joyce Ross, *J. E. Spingarn and the Rise of the NAACP, 1911–1939* (New York: Atheneum, 1972), pp. 3–4, 26–30, 50–62.

7. Lewis, *W. E. B. Du Bois*, p. 428.

8. Ibid., p. 135.

9. Du Bois, *Souls of Black Folk*, p. 2.

10. Washington, *Up from Slavery*, p. 42; Du Bois, *Souls of Black Folk*, pp. 9–28.

11. Ibid., p. 67.

12. J. R. Oldfield, ed., *Civilization and Black Progress: Selected Writings of Alexander Crummell on the South* (Charlottesville: University Press of Virginia, 1995), pp. 195–99.

13. Lewis, *W. E. B. Du Bois*, p. 317.

14. August Meier and Elliott Rudwick, "The Boycott Movement against Jim Crow Streetcars in the South, 1900–1906," *Journal of American History* 55 (March 1969), pp. 756–75.

15. Dominic J. Capeci and Jack C. Knight, "Reckoning with Violence: W. E. B. Du Bois and the 1906 Atlanta Race Riot," *Journal of Southern History* 62 (November 1996), pp. 727–66.

16. Elliott Rudwick, "The Niagara Movement," in *The Making of Black America, Vol.*

2: *The Black Community in Modern America,* August Meier and Elliott Rudwick, eds. (New York: Atheneum, 1969), pp. 131–48.

17. W. E. B. Du Bois, *The Autobiography of W. E. B. Du Bois: A Soliloquy on Viewing My Life from the Last Decade of Its First Century* (1968; reprint, New York: International Publishers, 1980), p. 260.

18. Kellogg, *History of the NAACP,* pp. 94–101; Lewis, *W. E. B. Du Bois,* pp. 468–500.

19. "The Philosophy of Mr. Dole," *Crisis,* May 1914, in *Selected Writings of W. E. B. Du Bois,* Walter Wilson, ed. (New York: Mentor, 1970), pp. 110–12.

20. Arnold Rampersad, *The Art and Imagination of W. E. B. Du Bois* (New York: Schocken Books, 1976, 1990), p. 140; Broderick quoted in *The Selected Writings of W. E. B. Du Bois,* Walter Wilson, ed., p. 103; Lewis, *W. E. B. Du Bois,* p. 478.

21. Robert L. Zangrando, *The NAACP Crusade Against Lynching 1909–1950* (Philadelphia: Temple University Press, 1980), pp. 29–30, 42–43.

22. "Triumph," *Crisis,* September 1911; "Divine Right," March 1912; "The Fruit of the Tree," September 1913; "Cowardice," October 1916; "A University Course in Lynching," June 1923; all in *The Seventh Son: The Thought and Writings of W. E. B. Du Bois, vol. 2,* Julius Lester, ed. (New York: Random House, 1971), pp. 4–17.

23. Washington to Fred Moore, June 8 and July 15, 1911, *Washington Papers,* Harlan, ed., vol. 11, pp. 196–97, 268–69.

24. Kellogg, *History of the NAACP,* pp. 184–86, 205–06.

25. Kenneth Wogemuth, "Woodrow Wilson and Federal Segregation," in *Understanding Negro History,* Dwight W. Hoover, ed. (Chicago: Quadrangle, 1968), pp. 369–82; Desmond King, *Separate and Unequal: Black Americans and the Federal Government* (Oxford: Oxford University Press, 1995), pp. 48–49; *Chicago Defender,* November 21, 1914, in Quarles, *The Negro American,* pp. 392–93.

26. Everett Carter, "Cultural History Written with Lightning: The Significance of *The Birth of a Nation,*" in Hoover, *Understanding Negro History,* pp. 177–86; Thomas R. Cripps, "The Reaction of the Negro to the Motion Picture *Birth of a Nation,*" in Hoover, *Understanding Negro History,* pp. 224–38; John Hope Franklin, "*The Birth of a Nation*: Propaganda as History," in *Race and History: Selected Essays, 1938–1988* (Baton Rouge: Louisiana State University Press, 1988), pp. 10–23.

27. Kellogg, *History of the NAACP,* pp. 120–32; Lewis, *W. E. B. Du Bois,* p. 507.

28. Johnson, *Along This Way.*

29. Ibid., pp. 314–17; Walter White, *A Man Called White: The Autobiography of Walter White* (London: Victor Gollancz, 1949), pp. 34–35.

CHAPTER FIVE

1. "The Present," *Crisis,* 14 (August 1917), p. 165.

2. Mark Karson and Ronald Radosh, "The American Federation of Labor and the Negro Worker, 1894–1910," in *The Negro and the American Labor Movement,* Julius Jacobson, ed. (Garden City, N.Y.: Doubleday, 1968), pp. 155–59; William H. Harris, *The Harder We Run: Black Workers Since the Civil War* (New York: Oxford University Press, 1982), pp. 36–45, 52.

3. Benjamin Brawley, *A Social History of the American Negro* (1921; reprint, New York: Macmillan, 1970), p. 346.

4. August Meier and Elliott Rudwick, *Black Detroit and the Rise of the UAW* (New York: Oxford University Press, 1979), pp. 5–6; Jacqueline Jones, *Labor of Love, Labor*

of Sorrow: Black Women, Work and the Family, From Slavery to the Present (New York: Vintage, 1985), pp. 163–66.

5. Elliott Rudwick, *Race Riot at East St. Louis, July 2, 1917* (New York: Atheneum, 1972), pp. 12–14; Alex D. Pitts to Samuel J. Graham, October 27, 1916; Raymond G. Lincoln to Attorney General, November 2, 1916, in reel 20, *Black Workers in the Era of the Great Migration, 1916–1929*, edited by James Grossman (25 reels, University Microfilms International).

6. Fishel and Quarles, eds., *The Negro American*, p. 397; William M. Tuttle, Jr., *Race Riot: Chicago in the Red Summer of 1919* (New York: Atheneum, 1974), p. 79.

7. *Crisis* 16 (August 1918), pp. 172–74.

8. Judith Stein, *The World of Marcus Garvey: Race and Class in Modern Society* (Baton Rouge: Louisiana State University Press, 1986), p. 38.

9. *Crisis* 14 (July 1917), p. 138; *Crisis* 16 (August 1918), pp. 163–64.

10. Arthur E. Barbeau and Florette Henri, *The Unknown Soldiers: African-American Troops in World War I* (1974; reprint, New York: Da Capo Press, 1996), pp. 14–17; *Crisis* 16 (July 1917).

11. Kellogg, *History of the NAACP*, pp. 250–56; Ross, *J. E. Spingarn*, pp. 88–94; Lewis, *W. E. B. Du Bois*, p. 531; *Crisis* 15 (December 1917), p. 78.

12. *Crisis* 15 (July 1917), p. 77; "Close Ranks," *Crisis* 16 (July 1918), p. 111.

13. U.S. Congress, House of Representatives, *Report of the Special Committee Authorized by Congress to Investigate the East St. Louis Riots,* 65 Cong., 2nd sess., July 15, 1918, pp. 1–24; Martha Gruening and W. E. B. Du Bois, "The Massacre of East St. Louis," *Crisis* 14 (September 1917), pp. 219–38; Rudwick, *Race Riot at East St. Louis,* pp. 27–57.

14. Martha Gruening, "Houston," *Crisis* 5 (November 1917), pp. 14–19; Barbeau and Henri, *Unknown Soldiers,* pp. 26–31.

15. Ibid., pp. 138, 154, 161.

16. Ibid., pp. 66–68; "Negro Officers," *Crisis* 18 (June 1919).

17. Barbeau and Henri, *Unknown Soldiers,* pp. 89–91.

18. "Documents of the War," *Crisis* 18 (May 1919), pp. 16–18; Barbeau and Henri, *Unknown Soldiers,* pp. 114–15.

19. Ibid., pp. 44–48.

20. Robert R. Moton [report to the War Department, 1919], "General Summary," box 35, folder 234, Moton Papers; Albon L. Holsey, "A Man of Courage," in *Robert Russa Moton of Hampton and Tuskegee,* William Hardin Hughes and Frederick D. Patterson, eds. (Chapel Hill: University of North Carolina Press, 1956), pp. 123–27.

21. Mark Ellis, "'Closing Ranks' and 'Seeking Honors': W. E. B. Du Bois in World War I," *Journal of American History* 79 (June 1992), pp. 96–124; "Robert Moton," *Crisis* 18 (May 1919), pp. 9–10.

22. Leila B. Michael to Moton, May 5, 1919; letter to Moton (name of author illegible), March 24, 1919, both from box 58, folder 417, Moton Papers; Du Bois, "History of the Black Man in the Great War," *Crisis* 18 (June 1919), p. 87.

23. *Crisis* 18 (May 1919), pp. 13–14; Major J. E. Cutler to Brig. Gen. Marlborough Churchill, in "The Negro Situation," August 15, 1919, in *The Marcus Garvey and UNIA Papers,* 12 vols., ed. Robert A. Hill et al. (Berkeley: University of California Press, 1983), vol. 1, p. 491.

24. "The Failure of Our Negro Leaders," *Messenger,* January 1918; "The Negro in Politics," "Who's Who: Du Bois," *Messenger,* July 1918; "Who's Who: Theodore Roosevelt," *Messenger,* March 1919; "Who's Who: Woodrow Wilson," "The March of So-

viet Government," *Messenger,* May–June 1919; "The Failure of the Negro Church," *Messenger,* October 1919.

25. "Future of Africa," *Crisis* 15 (January 1918), p. 114; "Addresses Denouncing W. E. B. Du Bois," April 5, 1919, in *Garvey Papers,* Hill, ed., "Madison Square Garden Meeting," August 3, 1920, *Garvey Papers,* vol. 1, p. 501.

26. *Ninth Meeting, University Commission on Southern Race Questions, Nashville, Tennessee, April 25 and 26, 1919,* Phelps-Stokes Fund Papers, Manuscripts, Archives and Rare Books Division, Schomburg Center for Research in Black Culture, New York, N.Y.

27. Ovington, *Walls Came Tumbling Down,* p. 124.

28. Ibid., p. 177; "Mary Morris Talbert," in *Black Women in America: An Historical Encyclopedia,* 2 vols., ed. Darlene Clark Hine (Brooklyn, N.Y.: Carlson Publishing, 1993); Steven A. Reich, "Soldiers of Democracy: Black Texans and the Fight for Citizenship, 1917–1921," *Journal of American History* 82 (March 1996), pp. 1490–93.

29. Ibid., p. 1499; Benjamin E. Mays, *Born to Rebel: An Autobiography* (Athens, Ga.: University of Georgia Press, 1987), p. 68; "Race War," *Crisis* 18 (September 1919), pp. 247–49.

30. *Selected Poems of Claude McKay* (New York: Harvest, 1953), p. 36; "Let Us Reason Together," *Crisis* 18 (September 1919), p. 231.

31. Walter White, *A Man Called White,* pp. 45–46.

32. Ibid., pp. 47–48; Monroe N. Work, "A Report on the Elaine Riot," letter, March 29, 1920, pp. 5–6, box 22, Local Correspondence, Moton Papers.

33. "The Real Causes of Two Race Riots," *Crisis* 19 (December 1919), pp. 56–62; Richard C. Cortner, *A Mob Intent on Death: The NAACP and the Arkansas Riot Cases* (Middletown, Conn.: Wesleyan University Press, 1988), p. 8; Major Eugene F. Barton, "Race Riot at Elaine, Ark.," October 9, 1919, reel 20, *Black Workers in the Age of the Great Migration.*

34. Work, "Report on the Elaine Riot," p. 3; Captain John B. Campbell, "Race Riot at Elaine, Arkansas," October 2, 1919; reel 20, *Black Workers in the Era of the Great Migration.*

35. Cortner, *Mob Intent on Death,* pp. 10–18; Captain Edward P. Passailaigue, "Report," October 13, 1919; Robert A. Poague, "Report," October 14, 1919; both in reel 20, *Black Workers in the Era of the Great Migration.*

36. Johnson, *Along This Way,* pp. 320–21, 361–73; White, *A Man Called White,* pp. 52–53; *Crisis* 18 (June 1919), p. 92.

37. "The Case of Mr. Shillady," *Crisis* 18 (October 1919), pp. 300–01; Johnson, *Along This Way,* pp. 343–44, 356; White, *A Man Called White,* pp. 46–47.

38. *Crisis* 18 (October 1919), p. 301; Reich, "Soldiers of Democracy," pp. 1500–04.

39. Wilma Dykeman and James Stokely, *Seeds of Southern Change: The Life of Will Alexander* (New York: W. W. Norton, 1962), pp. 52–81; Thomas J. Woofter, *The Basis of Racial Adjustment* (Boston: Ginn & Co., 1925), pp. 166–67.

40. Allan H. Spear, *Black Chicago: The Making of a Negro Ghetto* (Chicago: University of Chicago Press, 1967), p. 221.

41. Judy J. Mohraz, *The Separate Problem: Case Studies of Black Education in the North, 1900–1930* (Westport, Conn.: Greenwood Press, 1979), pp. 93–137; Vincent P. Franklin, *The Education of Black Philadelphians: The Social and Educational History of a Minority Community, 1900–1950* (Philadelphia: University of Pennsylvania Press, 1979), pp. 37–75.

42. George K. Hunton, *All of Which I Saw, Part of Which I Was* (New York: Doubleday, 1967), p. 140.

43. Ovington, *Walls Came Tumbling Down,* p. 175.

CHAPTER SIX

1. "Report of the UNIA Parade," *Negro World,* August 3, 1920, in *Garvey Papers,* Hill, ed., vol. 2, pp. 490–94; Roi Ottley, *Inside Black America* (London: Eyre and Spottiswoode, 1948), p. 60.

2. "Addresses Denouncing W. E. B. Du Bois," *Negro World,* April 5, 1919, in *Garvey Papers,* Hill, ed., vol. 1, pp. 394–99; "UNIA Meeting at Carnegie Hall," August 25, 1919, in ibid., vol. 1, pp. 500–09.

3. Amy Jacques Garvey, *Garvey and Garveyism* (1963; reprint, New York: Octagon Books, 1978), pp. 31–33. .

4. Winston James, *Holding Aloft the Banner of Ethiopia: Caribbean Radicalism in Early Twentieth-Century America* (London: Verso Press, 1998), pp. 110–11.

5. Garvey to Robert R. Moton, February 29, 1916, in *Garvey Papers,* Hill, ed., vol. 1, p. 179.

6. Garvey, "The Negro's Greatest Enemy," *Current History,* September 1923, in *Garvey Papers,* Hill, ed., vol. 1, pp. 4–12; "Pamphlet by Marcus Garvey," ca. July-August 1914, in ibid., vol. 1, p. 56; Marcus Garvey to Moton, February 29, 1916, in ibid., vol. 1, p. 180.

7. Marcus Garvey, speech at Liberty Hall, New York City, March 13, 1920, in *Garvey Papers,* Hill, ed., vol. 2, p. 252.

8. "UNIA Meeting at Carnegie Hall," August 25, 1919, in *Garvey Papers,* Hill, ed., vol. 1, p. 500.

9. Amy Jacques Garvey, *Garvey and Garveyism,* pp. 5–9; Tony Martin, *Race First: The Ideological and Organizational Struggles of Marcus Garvey and the Universal Negro Improvement Association* (Westport, Conn.: Greenwood Press, 1976), pp. 4–7; Theodore G. Vincent, *Black Power and the Garvey Movement* (Berkeley: Ramparts Press, 1971), pp. 93–94; Lawrence W. Levine, "Marcus Garvey and the Politics of Revitalization," in *Black Leaders of the Twentieth Century,* ed. John Hope Franklin and August Meier (Urbana: University of Illinois Press, 1982), pp. 105–111; Amy Jacques Garvey, ed., *Philosophy and Opinions of Marcus Garvey* (1923; reprint, New York: Atheneum, 1968), pp. 126–27.

10. Ottley, *Inside Black America,* p. 54; Martin, *Race First,* pp. 7–11.

11. Vincent, *Black Power and the Garvey Movement,* p. 99; David Levering Lewis, ed., *W. E. B. Du Bois: A Reader* (New York: Henry Holt, 1995), p. 333; Bureau of Investigation Report, October 14, 1919, in *Garvey Papers,* Hill, ed., vol. 2, p. 72.

12. Martin. *Race First,* p. 9; Lewis, ed., *W. E. B. Du Bois: A Reader,* p. 335; J. Edgar Hoover to Special Agent Ridgely, October 11, 1919, in *Garvey Papers,* Hill, ed., vol. 2, p. 72. Sound recordings of Garvey can be accessed on the Marcus Garvey Papers Project Web site, http://www.isop.ucla.edu/mgpp.

13. "Pamphlet by Marcus Garvey," ca. July-August 1914, in *Garvey Papers,* Hill, ed., vol. 1, pp. 57–61; "Universal Negro Catechism," March 1921, in ibid., vol. 3, pp. 302–19.

14. Marcus Garvey, speech at Mt. Carmel Baptist Church, Washington, D.C., July 24, 1920, in *Garvey Papers,* Hill, ed., vol. 2, p. 457; "UNIA Meeting at Carnegie Hall," August 25, 1919, in ibid., vol. 1, p. 505.

15. "Universal Negro Catechism," in *Garvey Papers,* Hill, ed., vol. 3, pp. 302–03.

16. Amy Jacques Garvey, *Garvey and Garveyism,* p. 27.

17. Ottley, *Inside Black America*, p. 55.

18. Madison Square Garden meeting, August 8, 1920, in *Garvey Papers*, Hill, ed., vol. 2, p. 559.

19. Speech, Washington, D.C., September 24, 1920, in *Garvey Papers*, Hill, ed., vol. 3, p. 16.

20. *Garvey Papers*, Hill, ed., vol. 2, p. 303, note 2; James, *Holding Aloft the Banner of Ethiopia*, pp. 62–66.

21. Speech at Liberty Hall, New York City, March 13, 1920, in *Garvey Papers*, Hill, ed., vol. 2, p. 257.

22. Madison Square Garden meeting, in *Garvey Papers*, vol. 2, p. 501.

23. Stein, *World of Marcus Garvey*, p. 64.

24. Bureau of Investigation Report, November 1, 1919, in *Garvey Papers*, Hill, ed., vol. 2, pp. 144–45; *Garvey Papers*, Hill, ed., vol. 2, p. xxxxiii.

25. Stein, *World of Marcus Garvey*, p. 89.

26. Ibid., pp. 115–16.

27. *Garvey Papers*, Hill, ed., vol. 3, p. xxxiii; ibid., vol. 1, p. 515, note 2; "Speech, New Orleans," July 14, 1921, in ibid., vol. 3, p. 529; Stein, *World of Marcus Garvey*, pp. 76–80; Levine, "Marcus Garvey," pp. 125–26; James, *Holding Aloft the Banner of Ethiopia*, p. 134.

28. Stein, *World of Marcus Garvey*, pp. 76–80; Saunders Redding, *On Being Negro in America* (1951; reprint, New York: Bantam, 1964), p. 25. Tony Martin, on the other hand, argues that the South was "the most thoroughly UNIA organized area in the world," and that the UNIA "was not only the organization of newly urbanized Afro-Americans . . . [but also] the organization of black peasants all over the South, Southwest and elsewhere." However, Martin bases this argument on the distribution of UNIA branches, rather than members, gathered from records dating from 1925–28, when the UNIA was in steep decline. See Martin, *Race First*, pp. 15–17.

29. James, *Holding Aloft the Banner of Ethiopia*, pp. 137–55; White, *Too Heavy a Load*, pp. 120–24, 135–40.

30. William Pickens to Claude Hudson, June 4, 1922, reel 1, William Pickens Papers, Schomburg Library; Marcus Garvey, editorial letter, September 7, 1920, in *Garvey Papers*, Hill, ed., vol. 3, p. 9.

31. Garvey, *Garvey and Garveyism*, pp. 147–55; Stein, *World of Marcus Garvey*, pp. 120–24; Cyril Henry to O. M. Thompson, July 1, 1921, in *Garvey Papers*, Hill, ed., vol. 3, pp. 502–03; Vincent, *Black Power and the Garvey Movement*, pp. 183–84.

32. Stein, *World of Marcus Garvey*, pp. 192–93.

33. *Garvey Papers*, Hill, ed., vol. 4, pp. xxxii–xxxiii; Levine, "Marcus Garvey," p. 132.

34. Speech by Marcus Garvey, October 21, 1919, in *Garvey Papers*, Hill, ed., vol. 2, p. 92.

35. Meeting at Mt. Carmel Baptist Church, Washington, D.C., July 24, 1920, in *Garvey Papers*, Hill, ed., vol. 2, p. 450.

36. Vincent, *Black Power and the Garvey Movement*, p. 168; Martin, *Race First*, pp. 276–77; Garvey, speech in New Orleans, July 14, 1921, in *Garvey Papers*, Hill, ed., vol. 3, p. 529; Garvey speech reported in *Negro World*, February 10, 1923, in ibid., vol. 5, p. 216; Levine, "Marcus Garvey," pp. 131–32.

37. W. E. B. Du Bois to James Burghardt, August 27, 1919, in *Garvey Papers*, Hill, ed., vol. 2, p. 3.

38. Theodore Kornweibel, Jr., *No Crystal Stair: Black Life and the "Messenger,"*

1917–1928 (Westport, Conn.: Greenwood Press, 1975), pp. 136–45; Chandler Owen, et al., to Harry M. Daugherty, January 15, 1923, in *Garvey Papers*, Hill, ed., vol. 5, pp. 182–87; Lewis, ed., *W. E. B. Du Bois: A Reader*, p. 342.

39. Garvey to Harry M. Daugherty, February 4, 1923, in *Garvey Papers*, Hill, ed., vol. 5, p. 217; editorial letter by Garvey, February 6, 1923, in ibid., pp. 220–28; editorial letter by Garvey, February 13, 1923, in ibid., pp. 232–41.

40. J. Max Barber to William Pickens, June 18, 1930, reel 1, Pickens Papers.

41. Williamson, *New People*, pp. 111–28.

42. Kornweibel, *No Crystal Stair*, pp. 149–51.

43. Martin, *Race First*, p. 324.

44. Levine, "Marcus Garvey," p. 133; *Garvey Papers*, Hill, ed., vol. 6, pp. xxxiii–xxxiv; Kenneth O'Reilly, *"Racial Matters": The FBI's Secret File on Black America, 1960–1972* (New York: Free Press, 1989), pp. 12–14; Stein, *World of Marcus Garvey*, pp. 186–208.

45. Stein, *World of Marcus Garvey*, p. 86; report by the British Cabinet Office, November 10, 1919, in *Garvey Papers*, Hill, ed., vol. 2, p. 153; John Sargent to Calvin Coolidge, January 27, 1926, in ibid., vol. 6, p. 314.

46. Stein, *World of Marcus Garvey*, p. 192; interview with Chandler Owen and A. Philip Randolph by Charles Mowbray White, August 20, 1920, in *Garvey Papers*, Hill, ed., vol. 2, p. 609.

47. Levine, "Marcus Garvey," p. 121.

CHAPTER SEVEN

1. Haywood Patterson and Earl Conrad, *Scottsboro Boy* (London: Victor Gollancz, 1951), pp. 13–17.

2. Stephen Roddy to "Friends of the Nine Negro Boys," April 11, 1931, in *NAACP Papers*, August Meier, Sharon Harley, and John H. Bracey, eds. (microfilm, University Publications of America), part 6, reel 2.

3. Dan Carter, *Scottsboro: A Tragedy of the American South* (1969; reprint, New York: Oxford University Press, 1971), pp. 3–48.

4. Excerpt from a Confidential Report on the Scottsboro Cases, May 7, 1931, *NAACP Papers*, reel 2, part 6.

5. Walter White to Bob and Herbert, May 5, 1931; White, handwritten notes, May 5, 1931, both in *NAACP Papers*, reel 2, part 6.

6. Patterson and Conrad, *Scottsboro Boy*, p. 29.

7. White to Bob and Herbert, May 5, 1931; White to William Pickens, May 12, 1931; White to Roy Wilkins, May 13, 1931, all in *NAACP Papers*, reel 2, part 6. Clarence Norris and Sybil D. Washington, *The Last of the Scottsboro Boys: An Autobiography* (New York: G. P. Putnam's Sons, 1979), p. 58.

8. Carter, *Scottsboro*, pp. 141–42; Hugh T. Murray, Jr., "Aspects of the Scottsboro Campaign," *Science and Society* (Summer 1971), pp. 179–80.

9. James Goodman, *Stories of Scottsboro: The Rape Case That Shocked 1930s America and Revived the Struggle for Equality* (New York: Pantheon Books, 1994), p. 48.

10. Harvard Sitkoff, *A New Deal for Blacks: The Emergence of Civil Rights As a National Issue* (New York: Oxford University Press, 1978), p. 142; Murray, "Aspects of the Scottsboro Campaign," p. 179.

11. *Powell v. Alabama*, 287 U.S. 45 (1932); Carter, *Scottsboro*, pp. 160–65; Hugh T. Murray, Jr., "The NAACP versus the Communist Party: The Scottsboro Rape Cases,

1931–1932," in *The Negro in Depression and War: Prelude to Revolution, 1930–1945*, Bernard Sternsher, ed. (Chicago: Quadrangle Books, 1969), pp. 276–79.

12. Carter, *Scottsboro*, pp. 235–36.

13. Ibid., pp. 265–69; Patterson, *Scottsboro Boy*, appendix 5, pp. 271–88.

14. Norris and Washington, *The Last of the Scottsboro Boys*, p. 79; Patterson and Conrad, *Scottsboro Boy*, p. 289; Carter, *Scottsboro*, pp. 274–302.

15. *Norris v. Alabama*, 294 U.S. 587 (1935).

16. Carter, *Scottsboro*, pp. 308–09; Goodman, *Tales of Scottsboro*, pp. 278–328. The ILD participated in the Scottsboro Defense Committee, but the group was dominated by liberals.

17. Carter, *Scottsboro*, pp. 163, 263; Lewis, ed., *W. E. B. Du Bois: A Reader*, p. 586; Hugh T. Murray, Jr., "Changing America and the Changing Image of Scottsboro," *Phylon* (March 1977), pp. 88–90; Dykeman and Stokely, *Seeds of Southern Change*, pp. 154–55.

18. Murray, "NAACP versus the Communist Party," pp. 277–79; Patricia L. Sullivan, *Days of Hope: Race and Democracy in the New Deal Era* (Chapel Hill: University of North Carolina Press, 1996), p. 88.

19. Irving Howe and Lewis Coser, *The American Communist Party: A Critical History, 1919–1952* (Boston: Beacon, 1957); Wilson Record, *Race and Radicalism* (Ithaca, N.Y.: Cornell University Press, 1964); Harvey Klehr, *The Heyday of American Communism: The Depression Decade* (New York: Basic Books, 1984); Redding, *On Being Negro in America*, pp. 36–39.

20. Sitkoff, *A New Deal for Blacks*, pp. 140–68; Fraser Ottanelli, *The Communist Party of the United States: From the Depression to World War II* (New Brunswick, N.J.: Rutgers University Press, 1991); Robin D. G. Kelley, *Hammer and Hoe: Alabama Communists during the Great Depression* (Chapel Hill: University of North Carolina Press, 1990).

21. Harvey Klehr and William Tompson, "Self-Determination in the Black Belt: Origin of a Communist Policy," *Labor History* 30 (Summer 1989), pp. 354–66; James, *Holding Aloft the Banner of Ethiopia*, pp. 177–82; Ottanelli, *The Communist Party of the United States*, pp. 36–38; Roy Wilkins, *Standing Fast: The Autobiography of Roy Wilkins* (New York: Penguin, 1984), p. 158; Mark Naison, *Communists in Harlem during the Great Depression* (Urbana: University of Illinois Press, 1983), pp. 17–18.

22. Mark Naison, "Remaking America: Communists and Liberals in the Popular Front," in *New Studies in the Politics and Culture of U.S. Communism*, Michael E. Brown, Randy Martin, Frank Rosengarten et al., eds. (New York: Monthly Review, 1993), p. 60; Junius I. Scales, *Cause at Heart: A Former Communist Remembers* (Athens, Ga.: University of Georgia Press, 1987), p. 320.

23. Ottley, *Inside Black America*, p. 189.

24. Ellen Schrecker, *The Age of McCarthyism: A Brief History with Documents* (Boston: Bedford Books, 1994), p. 5.

25. Francis L. Broderick and August Meier, ed., *Negro Protest Thought in the Twentieth Century* (Indianapolis: Bobbs-Merrill Educational Publishing, 1965), p. 34; Roy Wilkins to Walter White, May 7, 1931, *NAACP Papers*, reel 2, part 6; Redding, *On Being Negro in America*, p. 10.

26. Nell Irvin Painter, *The Narrative of Hosea Hudson: The Life and Times of a Black Radical* (New York: W. W. Norton, 1994), p. 120; George Fredrickson, *Black Liberation: A Comparative History of Black Ideologies in the United States and South Africa* (New York: Oxford University Press, 1995), p. 204.

27. Naison, "Remaking America: Communists and Liberals in the Popular Front," pp. 67–70.

28. Naison, *Communists in Harlem during the Great Depression*, pp. 313–14.

29. Sitkoff, *New Deal for Blacks*, pp. 250–57; John B. Kirby, *Black Americans in the Roosevelt Era: Liberalism and Race* (Knoxville: University of Tennessee Press, 1980), pp. 104–05; Sullivan, *Days of Hope*, pp. 88–90.

30. Lewis, ed., *W. E. B. Du Bois: A Reader*, pp. 543–44, 589; Du Bois, "Segregation," in *Documentary History of the Negro People in the United States*, Aptheker, ed., vol. 4, pp. 63–65; Du Bois, "A Free Forum: The NAACP and Race Segregation," in ibid., vol. 4, pp. 65–70; Du Bois, *Dusk of Dawn: An Essay Toward an Autobiography of a Race Concept* (New York: Harcourt, Brace and Co., 1940), p. 201, 205; Du Bois, "A Philosophy of Race Segregation," *Quarterly Review of Higher Education for Negroes 3* (1936), pp. 190–92.

31. Unless otherwise noted, this account of Randolph and the BSCP is based on William H. Harris, *Keeping the Faith: A. Philip Randolph, Milton P. Webster, and the Brotherhood of Sleeping Car Porters, 1925–37* (1977; reprint, Urbana: University of Illinois Press, 1991); Harris, *The Harder We Run*, pp. 77–94; Brailsford R. Brazeal, *The Brotherhood of Sleeping Car Porters: Its Origins and Development* (New York: Harper & Brothers, 1946); Benjamin Quarles, "A. Philip Randolph: Labor Leader at Large," in *Black Leaders of the Twentieth Century*, John Hope Franklin and August Meier, eds. (Urbana: University of Illinois Press, 1982), pp. 139–65; Jack Santino, *Miles of Smiles, Years of Struggle: Stories of Black Pullman Porters* (Urbana: University of Illinois Press, 1989).

32. Saunders Redding, *No Lonesome Road: The Story of the Negro's Part in America* (Garden City, N.J.: Doubleday, 1958), p. 260.

33. Harris, *Keeping the Faith*, p. 216; Santino, *Miles of Smiles*, pp. 61–66.

34. Harris, *Keeping the Faith*, p. 218.

35. Redding, *The Lonesome Road*, pp. 264–65.

36. Brenda Gayle Plummer, *Rising Wind: Black Americans and U.S. Foreign Policy, 1935–1960* (Chapel Hill: University of North Carolina Press, 1996), pp. 36–56; Ottley, *Inside Black America*, p. 87.

37. A. Philip Randolph, "Keynote Address," in *Documentary History of the Negro People*, Aptheker, ed., vol. 4, pp. 212–30.

38. Roger Keeran, "The Communist Influence on American Labor," in *New Studies in the Politics and Culture of U.S. Communism*, Brown, Martin, and Rosengarten, eds., p. 182.

39. Broderick and Meier, eds., *Negro Protest Thought*, pp. 196–201; Jervis Anderson, *A. Philip Randolph: A Biographical Portrait* (New York: Harcourt, Brace, Jovanovich, 1972), pp. 235–40.

40. Fredrickson, *Black Liberation*, pp. 203–05.

41. Arna Bontemps, *100 Years of Negro Freedom* (New York: Dodd, Mead, 1961), p. 243.

42. Broderick and Meier, eds., *Negro Protest Thought*, pp. 201–10; Michael W. Fitzgerald, "'We Have Found a Moses': Theodore Bilbo, Black Nationalism, and the Greater Liberia Bill of 1939," *Journal of Southern History* 63 (May 1997), pp. 293–320.

43. Quarles, "A. Philip Randolph," p. 154; Herbert Garfinkel, *When Negroes March* (1959; reprint, New York: Atheneum, 1968), pp. 49–50.

44. Ottley, *Inside Black America*, pp. 226–27.

45. Bontemps, *100 Years of Negro Freedom*, p. 244.

46. A. Philip Randolph, "Why Should We March?" in *Documentary History of the Negro People*, Aptheker, ed., vol. 4, pp. 4:418–21; Fredrickson, *Black Liberation*, pp. 232–33; Garfinkel, *When Negroes March*, pp. 118–19.

CHAPTER EIGHT

1. Gunnar Myrdal, *An American Dilemma: The Negro Problem and Modern Democracy*, 2 vols. (New York: Harper and Brothers, 1944), vol. 2, p. 777.

2. Mamie Garvin Fields with Karen Fields, *Lemon Swamp and Other Places: A Carolina Memoir* (New York: Free Press, 1983), p. xvi.

3. Ibid., p. 192; Susan L. Smith, *Sick and Tired of Being Sick and Tired: Black Women's Health Activism in America, 1890–1950* (Philadelphia: University of Pennsylvania Press, 1995), pp. 33–57.

4. Gilmore, *Gender and Jim Crow*, pp. 195–202; Jacquelyn Dowd Hall, *Revolt Against Chivalry: Jesse Daniel Ames and the Women's Campaign Against Lynching* (New York: Columbia University Press, 1993), pp. 87–95.

5. Hall, *Revolt Against Chivalry*, pp. 102–03.

6. Ibid., p. 106.

7. Ibid., pp. 227–28.

8. Chas. P. Manship to Ames, December 19, 1941, folder 165, box 7, Commission on Interracial Cooperation Papers (microfilm), Alderman Library, University of Virginia; Edwin C. Morgenroth, "Race Relations, Heritage, Arkansas." [1934], folder 1, box 334, Julius Rosenwald Fund Papers, Fisk University. A photograph of the "good darky" statue can be found in William Ivy Hair, *The Kingfish and His Realm: The Life and Times of Huey P. Long* (Baton Rouge: Louisiana State University Press, 1991).

9. Hall, *Revolt Against Chivalry*, pp. 42–47.

10. Thomas Jesse Jones to James H. Dillard, March 28, 1928, folder 10, box 17, Phelps-Stokes Fund Papers; Anson Phelps Stokes to Lawrence W. Ricky, January 22, 1930, folder 1, box 17, ibid.; Edgar B. Stern to Thomas F. Holgate, July 30, 1930, January 8, 1931; Stern to Fred L. Brownlee, March 16, 1931; Stern to Edwin R. Embree, January 8, 1931, all in folder 7, box 191, Rosenwald Fund Papers.

11. Sullivan, *Days of Hope*, p. 23.

12. Ibid., pp. 53–55.

13. Sitkoff, *New Deal for Blacks*, pp. 77–81; John B. Kirby, *Black Americans in the Roosevelt Era: Liberalism and Race* (Knoxville: University of Tennessee Press, 1980), pp. 110–21.

14. Hortense Powdermaker, *After Freedom: A Cultural Study in the Deep South* (1933; reprint, New York: Atheneum, 1969), p. 299. On the determination of black parents to seek secondary education for their children, see also Ambrose Caliver, *A Background Study of Negro College Students* (1933; reprint, Westport, Conn.: Negro Universities Press, 1970), pp. 68–75.

15. Howard N. Rabinowitz, "Half a Loaf: The Shift from White to Black Teachers in the Urban South, 1865–1890," *Journal of Southern History* 40 (Nov. 1974), pp. 565–94; Edmund L. Drago, *Initiative, Paternalism, and Race Relations: Charleston's Avery Normal Institute* (Athens, Ga.: University of Georgia Press, 1990), pp. 174–76, 183.

16. John J. Coss, "Some Notes on Education in Southeast Georgia, June 15–19, 1936, with John Curtis Dixon," folder 2, box 333, Rosenwald Fund Papers.

17. Alferdteen B. Harrison, *Piney Woods School: An Oral History* (Jackson: University of Mississippi Press, 1982), pp. 109, 116.

18. Myrdal, *American Dilemma*, p. 880.

19. Drago, *Initiative, Paternalism, and Race Relations*, p. 177; Horace Mann Bond and Julia W. Bond, *The Star Creek Papers: Washington Parish and the Lynching of Jerome Wilson*, ed. Adam Fairclough (Athens, Ga.: University of Georgia Press, 1997), pp. 43–45.

20. Myrdal, *American Dilemma*, p. 774.

21. J. Saunders Redding, *Stranger and Alone* (New York: Harcourt, Brace and Co., 1950).

22. Lewis K. McMillan, "Negro Higher Education As I Have Known It," *Journal of Negro Education* 8 (January 1939), pp. 14–15; Saunders Redding, *On Being Negro in America* (New York: Bobbs-Merrill, 1951; Bantam, 1964), pp. 66–67.

23. Myrdal, *American Dilemma*, p. 776; Powdermaker, *Stranger and Friend*, pp. 144, 148–49.

24. Lance G. E. Jones, *The Jeanes Teacher in the United States, 1909–1933* (Chapel Hill: University of North Carolina Press, 1937); James L. Leloudis, *Schooling the New South: Pedagogy, Self, and Society in North Carolina, 1880–1920* (Chapel Hill: University of North Carolina Press, 1996), pp. 187–89.

25. Horace Mann Bond, *Education of the Negro in the American Social Order* (New York: Prentice-Hall, 1934), pp. 12–13, 171.

26. Clark Foreman, *Environmental Factors in Negro Elementary Education* (New York: W. W. Norton, 1932), p. 40.

27. Arthur F. Raper, *Preface to Peasantry: a Tale of Two Black Belt Counties* (1936; reprint, New York: Atheneum, 1968), p. 334; Myrdal, *American Dilemma*, pp. 902–03.

28. Charles S. Johnson, *Growing Up in the Black Belt: Negro Youth in the Rural South* (1941; reprint, New York: Schocken Books, 1967), pp. 128–34; Charles S. Johnson, *The Negro Public Schools: A Social and Educational Survey* (Baton Rouge: Louisiana Educational Survey Commission, 1942), pp. 42–58, 89–90, 107–09.

29. Idus A. Newby, *Black Carolinians: A History of Blacks in South Carolina from 1865 to 1968* (Columbia: University of South Carolina Press, 1973), pp. 82–94, 102–111, 258–73. In 1940 about one-fifth of the South's black children went on to attend public high schools, nearly all of them located in cities.

30. Anderson, *Education of Blacks in the South*, p. 276; Bond, *Education of the Negro in the American Social Order*, pp. 148–49.

31. Ivan E. Taylor, "An Appraisal of the Symposium," *Negro College Quarterly* 2 (June 1944), p. 103; Harold F. Lee, "The Educational and Social Implications of the Negro College," ibid., p. 94.

32. Diane Ravitch, *The Revisionists Revised: A Critique of the Radical Attack on the Schools* (New York: Free Press, 1978), p. 67; Myrdal, *An American Dilemma*, p. 881.

33. Andrew Young, *An Easy Burden: The Civil Rights Movement and the Transformation of America* (New York: HarperCollins, 1996), pp. 18–19.

34. George Longe, "The Study of the Negro," *Crisis* 43 (October 1936), pp. 304, 309. On Woodson and the Negro history movement in general, see August Meier and Elliott Rudwick, *Black History and the Historical Profession, 1915–1980* (Urbana: University of Illinois Press, 1986), pp. 7–62.

35. Aaron Brown, "An Evaluation of the Accredited Secondary Schools for Negroes in the South," Ph.D. diss., University of Chicago, 1944, p. 64.

36. "General Discussion," *Quarterly Review of Higher Education for Negroes* 6 (October 1938), p. 254; Wendell Grant Morgan, "A Survey of the Social Science Offerings in Negro Colleges, 1935–1936," *Quarterly Review of Higher Education Among Negroes* 2 (1936), pp. 169–79.

37. Christopher Jencks and David Riesman, *The Academic Revolution* (Garden City, N.Y.: Doubleday, 1968), pp. 421–22. On student strikes and protests, see Maxine D. Jones, "Student Unrest at Talladega College, 1877–1914," *Journal of Negro History* 70 (Summer-Fall 1985), pp. 73–81; Raymond Wolters, *The New Negro on Campus: Black College Rebellions of the 1920s* (Princeton: Princeton University Press, 1975).

38. Johnetta Richards, "The Southern Negro Youth Congress: A History," Ph.D. diss., University of Cincinnati, 1987, pp. 17–32, 40–41, 49–56, 95–107, 137–47.

39. William H. Chafe, *Civilities and Civil Rights: Greensboro, North Carolina, and the Black Struggle for Freedom* (New York: Oxford University Press, 1981), pp. 20–21.

40. Benjamin E. Mays, *Born to Rebel: An Autobiography* (Athens, Ga.: University of Georgia Press, 1971, 1987), pp. 213–20; Raymond S. Gavins, *The Perils and Prospects of Southern Black Leadership: Gordon Blaine Hancock, 1884–1970* (Durham, N.C.: Duke University Press, 1977), pp. 104–27.

41. Leloudis, *Schooling the New South*, p. 228.

CHAPTER NINE

1. W. C. Knight to Ralph Handlin, July 12, 1935, February 20, 1936, August 18, 1936, January 20, 1937; W. W. Kerr to A. Daste, March 26, 1936; Kerr to Joseph Ferguson, January 26, 1937; Kerr to Handlin, January 26, 1937; Kerr to Ferguson, March 5, 1937; all in *NAACP Papers*, Meier, Harley, and Bracey, eds., part 10, reel 6.

2. Linda Przybyszewski, *The Republic According to John Marshall Harlan* (Chapel Hill: University of North Carolina Press, 1999), p. 98.

3. Ralph J. Bunche, "The Programs, Ideologies, Tactics, and Achievements of Negro Betterment and Interracial Organizations," pp. 142–55, Carnegie-Myrdal Papers, microfilm, Alderman Library, University of Virginia.

4. A. L. Glenn, Sr., *History of the National Alliance of Postal Employees, 1913–1955* (Washington, D.C.: National Alliance of Postal Employees, 1955).

5. Bunche, "Programs, Ideologies, Tactics, and Achievements of Negro Betterment and Interracial Organizations," p. 135; August Meier and Elliott Rudwick, *Black Detroit and the Rise of the UAW* (New York: Oxford University Press, 1979), pp. 20–21; Ottley, *Inside Black America*, p. 219; Adam Fairclough, *Race and Democracy: The Civil Rights Struggle in Louisiana, 1915–72* (Athens, Ga.: University of Georgia Press, 1995), pp. 54–55.

6. Fairclough, *Race and Democracy*, pp. 76–77.

7. John H. Overton, "Radio Address," August 28, 1942, box 1819, Allen J. Ellender Papers, Nicholls State University, Thibodaux, Louisiana.

8. Merl E. Reed, "The FEPC, the Black Worker, and the Southern Shipyards," *South Atlantic Quarterly* 74 (Autumn 1975), pp. 451–55; Ottley, *Inside Black America*, p. 235; Sullivan, *Days of Hope*, p. 158; Jerry Purvis Sanson, *Louisiana During World War II: Politics and Society, 1939–1945* (Baton Rouge: Louisiana State University Press, 1999), pp. 266–67.

9. Sullivan, *Days of Hope*, p. 157; Virgil Williams to Carlos Castenada, "Training and Utilization of Negro Workers in the New Orleans Area," December 18, 1943, Weekly Reports, Region 10, *FEPC Papers* (microfilm), reel 52; Joy P. Davis to John A. Davis, "New Orleans, Louisiana: Delta Shipbuilding Company," March 31, 1944, Tension File, Headquarters Files, ibid., reel 75; John Beecher to Lawrence W. Cramer, "Field Report on New Orleans, Louisiana," March 7, 1942, Office Files of John Beecher, Headquarters Files, ibid., reel 78.

10. Ottley, *Inside Black America*, p. 235; Sullivan, *Days of Hope*, p. 157.

11. Fairclough, *Race and Democracy*, pp. 87–98.

12. Minutes of Group Superintendents Meetings in Winston-Salem and Carthage, June 5, 1940, box 11, Special Subject Files, Division of Negro Education, Department of Public Instruction, North Carolina State Archives.

13. Thomas Doherty, *Projections of War: Hollywood, American Culture, and World War II* (New York: Columbia University Press, 1993), p. 139.

14. Sherie Mershon and Steven Schlossman, *Foxholes and Color Lines: Desegregating the U.S. Armed Forces* (Baltimore: Johns Hopkins University Press, 1998), p. 22.

15. Ibid., pp. 26–27, 40–44.

16. Ibid., pp. 14–16.

17. Ibid., pp. 47–50.

18. White, *A Man Called White*, p. 223.

19. Robin D. G. Kelley, "'We Are Not What We Seem:' Rethinking Black Working-Class Opposition in the Jim Crow South," *Journal of American History* 80 (June 1993), pp. 102–09.

20. Ruth Gambrell-Theorgood to Tampa Transit Lines, Inc., July 31, 1944; W. S. Diuguid to Edward R. Dudley, January 15, 1945; both in *NAACP Papers,* Meier, Harley, and Bracey, eds., part 15, series A, reel 10; Earl Lewis, *In Their Own Interests: Race, Class, and Power in Twentieth-Century Norfolk, Virginia* (Berkeley: University of California Press, 1991), p. 190.

21. Kenneth R. Janken, "African-American Intellectuals Confront the 'Silent South': The *What the Negro Wants* Controversy," *North Carolina Historical Review* 70 (April 1993), pp. 153–79; Sullivan, *Days of Hope,* p. 164; John Egerton, *Speak Now Against the Day: The Generation Before the Civil Rights Movement in the South* (New York: Alfred A. Knopf, 1994), pp. 248–61, 273–74; Cyrus M. Johnson, "Statement from the Director" (1949?), box 4, Special Subject Files, Division of Negro Education, Department of Public Instruction, North Carolina State Archives.

22. Sullivan, *Days of Hope,* p. 132.

23. "Conference on Race Relations, Sherman Hotel, Chicago, March 21–22, 1944," p. 73, folder 3, box 549, Rosenwald Fund Papers.

24. Meier and Rudwick, *Black Detroit and the Rise of the UAW,* pp. 197–205.

25. Edward F. Haas, "Huey Long and the Communists," *Louisiana History* 32 (Winter 1991), pp. 33–34.

26. Sullivan, *Days of Hope,* pp. 143–44; Kelley, *Hammer and Hoe,* pp. 182–84.

27. *Trudeau v. Barnes,* 65 F.2d 563 (1933); *Grovey v. Townsend,* 295 U.S. 45 (1935).

28. Mark V. Tushnet, *The NAACP's Legal Strategy against Segregated Education, 1925–1950* (Chapel Hill: University of North Carolina Press, 1987), pp. 25–28.

29. Genna Rae McNeil, "Charles Hamilton Houston: Social Engineer for Civil Rights," in *Black Leaders of the Twentieth Century,* Franklin and Meier, eds., p. 224; Tushnet, *NAACP's Legal Strategy against Segregated Education,* p. 35.

30. Walter White to Anson Phelps Stokes, November 2, 1936, folder 2, box 27, Phelps-Stokes Fund Papers.

31. *Missouri ex rel. Gaines v. Canada,* 305 U.S. 337 (1938).

32. Tushnet, *NAACP's Legal Strategy against Segregated Education,* p. 75.

33. *Smith v. Allwright,* 321 U.S. 649 (1944).

34. Thurgood Marshall, "Memorandum to the Office," April 15, 1944, in *NAACP Papers,* Meier, Harley, and Bracey, eds., part 3, series B.

35. "Conference on Race Relations, Sherman Hotel, Chicago, March 21–22, 1944," pp. 94, 113.

CHAPTER TEN

1. N. C. Newbold, "Lumberton Negro School Strike," October 21, 1946, folder 16, General Correspondence, Division of Negro Education, Department of Public Instruction, North Carolina State Archives; "Schools for Negroes Hit by Reynolds," *Charlotte Observer,* October 11, 1946; "Must Be Remedied," *Raleigh News and Observer,* October 9, 1946.

2. Fairclough, *Race and Democracy,* pp. 108–09; Truman M. Pierce, James B. Kincheloe, R. Edgar Moore et al., *White and Negro Schools in the South: An Analysis of Biracial Education* (Englewood Cliffs, N.J., 1955), pp. 164–78; Numan V. Bartley, *The New South, 1945–1980* (Baton Rouge: Louisiana State University Press, 1995), pp. 148–51.

3. Jay R. Mandle, *The Roots of Black Poverty: The Southern Plantation Economy after the Civil War* (Durham, N.C.: Duke University Press, 1978), p. 95.

4. Dorothy Beeler, "Race Riot in Columbia, Tennessee, February 25–27, 1946," *Tennessee Historical Quarterly,* 39 (1980), pp. 50–54; Gail Williams O'Brien, *The Color of the Law: Race, Violence, and Justice in the Post–World War II South* (Chapel Hill: University of North Carolina Press, 1999), pp. 7–33; "Journal of Second Infantry Brigade Task Force—'Mink Slide Operation,'" February 25–March 1, 1946, in folder 1, box 62, Jacob McGavock Dickinson Papers, Tennessee State Archives, Nashville.

5. White, *A Man Called White,* pp. 313–14; O'Brien, *Color of the Law,* pp. 49–50.

6. O'Brien, *Color of the Law,* pp. 44, 52, 88–90, 149–57.

7. J. W. Barker to Commanding General, 2nd Infantry Brigade, "Report of Armory Incident, Columbia, Tennessee," April 15, 1946; W. W. Hogan to Dickinson, April 21, 1946; General Jacob M. Dickinson to Attorney General of Tennessee, "Recommendations Relative to the Tennessee National Guard," March 12, 1946, all in Dickinson Papers.

8. White, *A Man Called White,* pp. 330–31.

9. *To Secure These Rights: The Report of the President's Committee on Civil Rights* (Washington, D.C.: U.S. Government Printing Office, 1947), pp. 151–73.

10. Henry Lee Moon, *Balance of Power: The Negro Vote* (Garden City, N.Y.: Doubleday, 1948), p. 198.

11. William C. Berman, *The Politics of Civil Rights in the Truman Administration* (Columbus: Ohio State University Press, 1970), p. 179.

12. Moon, *Balance of Power,* pp. 120–21, 131.

13. Walter White to Branches, August 29, 1950, folder 8, box 10, A. P. Tureaud Papers, Amistad Research Center, Tulane University; "Memorandum to Mr. Current from Mr. Marshall," May 4, 1951; Marshall to Alfred Baker Lewis, May 18, 1951; Marshall to Lewis, June 5, 1951, box 328, part 2, series C, NAACP Papers, Library of Congress; Plummer, *Rising Wind,* p. 214.

14. Penny M. Von Eschen, *Race Against Empire: Black Americans and Anticolonialism, 1937–1957* (Ithaca, N.Y.: Cornell University Press, 1997), p. 184.

15. Mary L. Dudziak, "Josephine Baker, Racial Protest, and the Cold War," *Journal of American History* 81 (September 1994), pp. 543–65.

16. Plummer, *Rising Wind,* p. 195.

17. Berman, *Politics of Civil Rights in the Truman Administration,* pp. 134–35; *Proceedings of the National Alliance of Postal Employees, Twentieth National Convention, Houston, Texas, August 21–24, 1951* (Washington, D.C.: NAPE, 1951), p. 79; "Oral Histories of the National Alliance of Postal Employees" (Washington, D.C.: National Alliance of Postal Employees, c. 1979), pp. 47–48.

18. See, for example, Anthony P. Dunbar, *Against the Grain: Southern Radicals and Prophets, 1929–1959* (Charlottesville: University Press of Virginia, 1981), pp. 225–58; Robert Korstad and Nelson Lichtenstein, "Opportunities Found and Lost: Labor, Radicals, and the Early Civil Rights Movement," *Journal of American History* 75 (December 1988), pp. 786–811; Gerald Horne, *Communist Front? The Civil Rights Congress, 1946–1956* (Cranbury, N.J.: Associated University Presses, 1988); Joshua B. Freeman, *In Transit: The Transport Workers Union, 1933–1966* (New York: Oxford University Press, 1989); Steve Rosswurm, "Introduction," *The CIO's Left-Led Unions* (New Brunswick, N.J.: Rutgers University Press, 1992), p. 13; Horace Huntley, "The Red Scare and Black Workers in Alabama: The International Union of Mine, Mill, and Smelter Workers, 1945–1953," in *Labor Divided: Race and Ethnicity in United States Labor Struggles, 1835–1960,* Robert Asher and Charles Stephenson, eds. (Albany: State University of New York, 1990), pp. 143–44; Sullivan, *Days of Hope,* pp. 3–9, 220–74.

19. Charles S. Johnson, "Opening of the [Race Relations] Institute," speech at Fisk University, July 2, 1951, folder 16, box 160, Charles S. Johnson Papers, Fisk University.

20. *Proceedings of the Thirteenth Biennial Convention of the National Alliance of Postal Employees, Cleveland, Ohio, 1947* (Washington, D.C.: NAPE, 1947).

21. Harry T. Moore to Fuller Warren, November 15, 1951; Harold K. Daniels to Warren, November 26, 1951; Virginia Lee Grimes to Warren; all in box 53, Fuller Warren Papers, Department of Archives and History, Tallahassee, Florida.

22. Mary L. Dudziak, "Desegregation As a Cold War Imperative," *Stanford Law Review* 41 (November 1988), pp. 61–120; Dudziak, "Josephine Baker and the Cold War," pp. 545–55; "G.I. in U.S. Army" to Fuller Warren, November 22, 1951, box 53, Warren Papers.

23. Plummer, *Rising Wind,* p. 199.

24. Mark V. Tushnet, *Making Civil Rights Law: Thurgood Marshall and the Supreme Court, 1936–1961* (New York: Oxford University Press, 1994), p. 173.

25. *Sweatt* v. *Painter,* 339 U.S. 634 (1950); *McLaurin* v. *Oklahoma State Regents,* 339 U.S. 641 (1950); *Henderson* v. *United States,* 339 U.S. 816 (1950).

26. Tushnet, *NAACP's Legal Strategy against Segregated Education,* p. 135.

27. John P. Frank, "Can Courts Erase the Color Line?" *Journal of Negro Education* 21 (Winter 1952), pp. 312–13; "Discussion," ibid., p. 328.

28. F. D. Patterson, "The Private Negro College in a Racially Integrated System of Higher Education," *Journal of Negro Education,* 21 (Winter 1952), p. 376.

29. Thurgood Marshall, "An Evaluation of Recent Efforts to Achieve Racial Integration in Education through Resort to the Courts," *Journal of Negro Education* 21 (Winter 1952), pp. 318–23; "Discussion," ibid., p. 302; Walter White, "Some Tactics Which Should Supplement Resort to the Courts in Achieving Racial Integration in Education," ibid., pp. 340–41.

30. "Discussion," ibid., p. 335; "Suggested Program for Southern Branches, 1954–1955," folder 7, box 4, Daniel E. Byrd Papers, Amistad Research Center, Tulane University.

31. Franklin, *From Slavery to Freedom,* p. 422; William H. Chafe, *Civilities and Civil Rights: Greensboro, North Carolina, and the Black Struggle for Freedom* (New York: Oxford University Press, 1981), p. 42; Fairclough, *Race and Democracy,* p. 167.

32. Tony Badger, "The Crisis of Southern Liberalism," in *The Making of Martin Luther King and the Civil Rights Movement,* Brian Ward and Tony Badger, eds. (London: Macmillan, 1996), p. 88.

33. James C. Cobb, *The Most Southern Place on Earth: The Mississippi Delta and the Roots of Regional Identity* (New York: Oxford University Press, 1992), p. 215.

34. Numan V. Bartley, *The Rise of Massive Resistance* (Baton Rouge: Louisiana State University Press, 1969), pp. 81, 193; Daniel E. Byrd, "Activity Report," April 1956, folder 3, box 4, Byrd Papers.

35. Tushnet, *Making Civil Rights Law,* pp. 272–73.

36. Roy Wilkins to Branch Presidents, August 1, 1958, folder 67, box 28, New Orleans Branch, NAACP Papers, Earl K. Long Library, University of New Orleans.

37. J. Harvie Wilkinson III, *From Brown to Bakke: The Supreme Court and School Integration, 1954–1978* (New York: Oxford University Press, 1979), p. 81.

38. Ibid., pp. 61–62.

CHAPTER ELEVEN

1. Martin Luther King, Jr., recorded speech, Chicago, September 1966, on *In Search of Freedom* (Polygram Records, 1995).

2. Jo Ann Gibson Robinson, *The Montgomery Bus Boycott and the Women Who Started It,* ed. David J. Garrow (Knoxville: University of Tennessee Press, 1987), p. viii.

3. Rosa Parks with Jim Haskins, *Rosa Parks: My Story* (New York: Scholastic Inc., 1992), p. 49.

4. John White, "Nixon *Was* the One: Edgar Daniel Nixon, the MIA and the Montgomery Bus Boycott," in *The Making of Martin Luther King and the Civil Rights Movement,* Ward and Badger, eds., pp. 46–49.

5. Robinson, *Montgomery Bus Boycott and the Women Who Started It,* pp. 43–47.

6. Clayborne Carson, David J. Garrow, Gerald Gill, et al., eds., *The Eyes on the Prize Civil Rights Reader* (New York: Penguin, 1991), p. 51.

7. Clayborne Carson, Stewart Burns, Susan Carson, et al., eds., *The Papers of Martin Luther King, Jr., Vol. 3: Birth of a New Age, December 1955–December 1956* (Berkeley: University of California Press, 1997), pp. 71–78.

8. J. Mills Thornton III, "Challenge and Response in the Montgomery Bus Boycott of 1955–1956," *Alabama Review* 33 (July 1980), pp. 200–04, 233–34.

9. Stewart Burns, ed., *Daybreak of Freedom: The Montgomery Bus Boycott* (Chapel Hill: University of North Carolina Press, 1997), pp. 125–27; "Executive Board 'Call' Meeting," January 30, 1956, Preston Valien Papers, Amistad Research Center, Tulane University.

10. Taylor Branch, *Parting the Waters: America in the King Years, 1954–1963* (New York: Simon and Schuster, 1988), p. 70; Robert S. Gractz, *Montgomery: A White Preacher's Memoir* (Minneapolis: Fortress Press, 1991), p. 78.

11. Wayne Phillips, "Negroes Pledge to Keep Boycott," *New York Times,* February 24, 1956, pp. 1, 8.

12. Thornton, "Challenge and Response," pp. 163–235; Catherine A. Barnes, *Journey from Jim Crow: The Desegregation of Southern Transit* (New York: Columbia University Press, 1983), pp. 124–28; Robert Jerome Glennon, "The Role of Law in the Civil Rights Movement: The Montgomery Bus Boycott, 1955–1957," *Law and History Review* 9 (Spring 1991), pp. 59–112.

13. Roy Wilkins to Wilson A. Head, October 11, 1946, in *NAACP Papers,* Meier, Harley, and Bracey, eds., part 15, series A, reel 12.

14. Jervis Anderson, *Bayard Rustin: Troubles I've Seen: A Biography* (New York: HarperCollins, 1997), p. 114; Glenn Smiley to John M. Swomley, March 2, 1956, in

The Bayard Rustin Papers, John H. Bracey, Jr., and August Meier, eds. (microfilm, 22 reels, University Publications of America), reel 4.

15. Andrew M. Manis, *A Fire You Can't Put Out: The Civil Rights Life of Birmingham's Reverend Fred Shuttlesworth* (Tuscaloosa: University of Alabama Press, 1999), p. 193.

16. Smiley to Swomley, March 2, 1956, in *Bayard Rustin Papers,* Bracey and Meier, eds., reel 4.

17. Stanley D. Levison to Roy Wilkins, [1958], in *Rustin Papers,* Bracey and Meier, eds., reel 9.

18. Martin Luther King, Jr., *Stride Toward Freedom: The Montgomery Story* (1958; reprint, London: Victor Gollancz, 1959), pp. 86–89; Melvin Arnold to King, May 5, 1958, in *The Papers of Martin Luther King, Jr.: Vol. 4: Symbol of the Movement, January 1957–December 1958,* Clayborne Carson, Susan Carson, Adrienne Clay, et al., eds. (Berkeley: University of California Press, 2000), pp. 404–05.

19. Stanley Levison and Bayard Rustin, telephone conversation, July 21, 1968, from Stanley D. Levison Federal Bureau of Investigation file, copy in Library and Archive, Martin Luther King, Jr., Center for Nonviolent Social Change, Atlanta, Georgia.

20. King, Jr., recorded speech, Chicago, September 1966.

21. Manis, *A Fire You Can't Put Out,* pp. 108–09.

22. Carson et al., eds., *Papers of Martin Luther King, Jr.,* vol. 2, p. 287.

23. King quoted by Stanley D. Levison, interview by James Mosby, February 14, 1970, p. 9, Ralph J. Bunche Oral History Collection, Moorland-Spingarn Library, Howard University.

24. Bayard Rustin, interviewed by Herbert Allen, July 27, 1983, in *Rustin Papers,* Bracey and Meier, eds., reel 4.

25. Ella J. Baker to King, "Re: Meeting in Norfolk, Virginia, October 1–2, 1958," July 16, 1958; Baker to Bayard Rustin and Stanley D. Levison, July 16, 1958; both in *Rustin Papers,* Bracey and Meier, eds., reel 3.

26. William H. Chafe, *Civilities and Civil Rights: Greensboro, North Carolina, and the Black Struggle for Freedom* (New York: Oxford University Press, 1981), p. 98.

27. Ibid., p. 83.

28. Levison to King, [March 1960], folder 29, file drawer 1, Martin Luther King, Jr. Papers, Mugar Library, Boston University.

29. Adam Fairclough, *To Redeem the Soul of America: The Southern Christian Leadership Conference and Martin Luther King, Jr.* (Athens, Ga.: University of Georgia Press, 1987), p. 61; John Lewis with Michael D'Orso, *Walking with the Wind: A Memoir of the Civil Rights Movement* (New York: Simon and Schuster, 1998), p. 121.

30. Lewis, *Walking with the Wind,* p. 68; *Time,* May 2, 1960, p. 14.

31. Clayborne Carson, *In Struggle: SNCC and the Black Awakening of the 1960s* (Cambridge, Mass.: Harvard University Press, 1981), p. 14; WDSU editorial, April 6, 1960, folder 70, box, 28, New Orleans Branch, NAACP Papers; Tom R. Wagy, *Governor LeRoy Collins of Florida: Spokesman of the New South* (University, Ala.: University of Alabama Press, 1985), p. 135.

32. Carson, *In Struggle,* pp. 20–24.

33. James Lawson, "Non-violent Way," *Southern Patriot,* April 1960.

CHAPTER TWELVE

1. King to Coretta King, October 26, 1960, King Papers, King Center, Atlanta.

2. Harris Wofford, *Of Kennedys and Kings: Making Sense of the Sixties* (New York:

Farrar, Straus and Giroux, 1980), pp. 11–25; Herbert S. Parmet, *JFK: The Presidency of John F. Kennedy* (New York: Penguin, 1984), p. 55.

3. Steven F. Lawson, *Running for Freedom: Civil Rights and Black Politics in America Since 1941* (New York: McGraw-Hill, 1991), pp. 78–79.

4. Edwin O. Guthman and Jeffrey Shulman, eds., *Robert Kennedy: In His Own Words* (New York: Bantam, 1988), p. 66.

5. Bayard Rustin, *Strategies for Freedom: The Changing Patterns of Black Protest* (New York: Columbia University Press, 1976), pp. 23–24.

6. Telephone conversation between George E. Cruit and Robert Kennedy, May 15, 1961, State Archives, Montgomery, Alabama; Henry Hampton and Steve Fayer, *Voices of Freedom: An Oral History of the Civil Rights Movement from the 1950s through the 1980s* (New York: Vintage, 1990), p. 84; Wofford, *Of Kennedys and Kings,* p. 153.

7. Branch, *Parting the Waters,* p. 427.

8. Edwin Guthman, *We Band of Brothers: A Memoir of Robert Kennedy* (New York: Harper and Row, 1971), pp. 154–55; Branch, *Parting the Waters,* p. 476.

9. Cynthia Griggs Fleming, *Soon We Will Not Cry: The Liberation of Ruby Doris Smith Robinson* (Lanham, Md.: Rowman and Littlefield, 1998), p. 88.

10. Hampton and Fayer, *Voices of Freedom,* p. 140.

11. Carson, *In Struggle,* p. 50.

12. John Dittmer, *Local People: The Struggle for Civil Rights in Mississippi* (Urbana: University of Illinois Press, 1994), p. 109.

13. Cleveland Sellers with Robert Terrell, *The River of No Return: The Autobiography of a Black Militant and the Life and Death of SNCC* (New York: William Morrow, 1973), pp. 51–52.

14. Dittmer, *Local People,* p. 134.

15. Charles Payne, *I've Got the Light of Freedom: The Organizing Tradition and the Mississippi Freedom Struggle* (Berkeley: University of California Press, 1995), p. 200.

16. White, *Too Heavy a Load,* p. 178; Sara Evans, *Personal Politics: The Roots of Women's Liberation in the Civil Rights Movement and the New Left* (New York: Vintage, 1980), p. 87.

17. Payne, *I've Got the Light of Freedom,* p. 268; minutes of SNCC staff meeting, March 6, 1962, Student Nonviolent Coordinating Committee Papers, King Library, Atlanta.

18. Cobb, *Most Southern Place on Earth,* pp. 255–64.

19. Dittmer, *Local People,* p. 129.

20. Ibid., p. 147.

21. Hampton and Fayer, *Voices of Freedom,* pp. 175–76.

22. Dittmer, *Local People,* pp. 153–57.

23. Ibid., p. 197.

24. Hampton and Fayer, *Voices of Freedom,* p. 103; Wyatt T. Walker, "The American Dilemma in Miniature: Albany, Georgia," text of speech, March 26, 1963, folder 8, box 37, Southern Christian Leadership Conference Papers, King Library, Atlanta.

25. "Statement from City Commission, Albany, Georgia," July 16, 1962, City Archives, Albany, Georgia.

26. William W. Hansen, "Field Report, July 7–22, 1962," Hansen Papers, King Library; "Statement from the City Commission, Albany, Georgia," August 11, 1962, Albany City Archives.

27. Laurie Pritchett to Mayor Asa Kelley, "Albany Movement," October 19, 1962, Albany City Archives; Pat Watters, *Down to Now: Reflections on the Southern Civil Rights Movement* (New York: Random House, 1971), p. 206.

28. Branch, *Parting the Waters,* p. 618.

29. Walker, "American Dilemma in Miniature."

CHAPTER THIRTEEN

1. Branch, *Parting the Waters,* p. 800.

2. Wyatt T. Walker, interview by John H. Britton, October 11, 1967, pp. 52–53, Bunche Oral History Collection, Moorland-Spingarn Library, Howard University.

3. "Civil Rights: The Moral Crisis," *Time* (June 21, 1963), p. 14.

4. Reese Cleghorn, "'Bustling' Birmingham," *New Republic* (April 20, 1963), p. 9.

5. Harrison Salisbury, "Fear and Hatred Grip Birmingham," *New York Times* (April 12, 1960), p. 28.

6. U.S. Commission on Civil Rights, *1961 Report: Justice* (Washington, D.C.: U.S. Government Printing Office, 1961), pp. 29–36.

7. Martin Luther King, Jr., *Letter from Birmingham City Jail* (Philadelphia: American Friends Service Committee, May 1963), p. 5.

8. Hampton and Fayer, *Voices of Freedom,* p. 215; Ralph David Abernathy, *And the Walls Came Tumbling Down: An Autobiography* (New York: Harper and Row, 1989), pp. 233–35.

9. David J. Garrow, *Protest at Selma: Martin Luther King, Jr., and the Voting Rights Act of 1965* (New Haven, Conn.: Yale University Press, 1978), pp. 4, 224–27; *Washington Post,* May 3, 1963, p. 4.

10. Glenn Eskew, *But for Birmingham: The Local and National Movements in the Civil Rights Struggle* (Chapel Hill: University of North Carolina, 1997), pp. 213–216; "Minutes of Staff Conference Held at Dorchester," September 5–7, 1963, p. 2, folder 21, box 153, SCLC Papers. After the campaign, a belief arose that Wyatt Walker had devised a campaign blueprint called "Operation C" (C for Confrontation) that envisaged more or less what happened. In fact, Walker had dubbed the plan "Operation X," only changing it to "C" when Connor's deployment of police dogs against onlookers rather than demonstrators alerted him to the propaganda value of police brutality.

11. Judith Brown, *Gandhi: Prisoner of Hope* (New Haven, Conn.: Yale University Press, 1989), pp. 240–41; Abernathy, *And the Walls Come Tumbling Down,* p. 245.

12. Andrew Young, *An Easy Burden: The Civil Rights Movement and the Transformation of America* (New York: HarperCollins, 1996), p. 208; John F. Kennedy, speech of June 11, 1963, draft, box 9, General Correspondence, Robert F. Kennedy Papers, John F. Kennedy Presidential Library.

13. "Confidential Memorandum," May 24, 1963, in Carl M. Brauer, ed., *Civil Rights Under the Kennedy Administration* (microfilm, 39 reels, University Publications of America).

14. "Civil Rights: The Awful Roar," *Time,* August 30, 1963, p. 9; King, *Letter from Birmingham City Jail,* p. 10.

15. "Confidential Memorandum," May 24, 1963.

16. John F. Kennedy, "Radio and Television Report to the American People on Civil Rights," June 11, 1963, in *The Negro in the Twentieth Century,* ed. John Hope Franklin and Isidore Starr (New York: Vintage, 1967), p. 218.

17. March on Washington Committee Meeting, August 17, 1963, reel 8, Rustin Papers.

18. King, "I Have a Dream," speech, August 28, 1963, King Papers.

19. David J. Garrow, *The FBI and Martin Luther King, Jr.: From "Solo" to Memphis* (New York: W. W. Norton, 1981). Ironically, Hoover became so obsessed with King's

sex life that the FBI overlooked something in his past that might well have discredited him: large portions of his Ph.D. dissertation were plagiarized.

20. Dittmer, *Local People*, p. 193.

21. "Prospectus for the Mississippi Freedom Summer," 1964, SNCC Papers.

22. Lewis, *Walking with the Wind*, p. 244; Ralph Allen, "Field Report," [1963], box 96, SNCC Papers.

23. Payne, *I've Got the Light of Freedom*, p. 204.

24. "SNCC Executive Staff Meeting Minutes," June 10, 1964, pp. 12–15, box 7, SNCC Papers; Howell Raines, *My Soul Is Rested: Movement Days in the Deep South Remembered* (New York: Bantam, 1978), p. 301.

25. Hampton and Fayer, *Voices of Freedom*, pp. 192–93.

26. Robert F. Kennedy to Lyndon B. Johnson, "Memorandum for the President," June 5, 1964, box 2, Legislative Background, Voting Rights Act of 1965, Lyndon B. Johnson Presidential Library, Austin, Texas.

27. Michael R. Beschloss, ed., *Taking Charge: The Johnson White House Tapes, 1963–1964* (New York: Simon and Schuster, 1997), p. 432.

28. Ibid., p. 450; Kenneth O'Reilly, *Racial Matters: The FBI's Secret File on Black America, 1960–1972* (New York: Free Press, 1989), pp. 161–68.

29. Beschloss, ed., *Taking Charge*, pp. 470, 515.

30. Ann C. Romaine, "The Mississippi Freedom Democratic Party through August 1964," M.A. thesis, University of Virginia, 1969, pp. 311–18; Dittmer, *Local People*, pp. 288–302; Beschloss, ed., *Taking Charge*, p. 517; Carson, ed., *Eyes on the Prize*, p. 189.

31. Beschloss, ed., *Taking Charge*, pp. 534–35.

32. Raines, *My Soul Is Rested*, p. 371; Garrow, *Protest at Selma*, pp. 36–40; Lee C. White to Bill Moyers, December 30, 1964; Ramsey Clark, "Civil Rights," February 5, 1965, box 2, Legislative Background, Voting Rights Act of 1965, Johnson Library.

33. Abernathy, *Walls Came Tumbling Down*, p. 303; Young, *An Easy Burden*, p. 338.

34. Abernathy, *Walls Came Tumbling Down*, p. 308; Martin Luther King, Jr., to Andrew Young, notes from Selma jail, February 2–4, 1965, King Papers.

35. Lewis, *Walking with the Wind*, p. 311; *New York Times*, February 18, 1965.

36. "The Central Point," *Time*, March 19, 1965, p. 15.

37. Harry McPherson to Lyndon B. Johnson, March 12, 1965, box 2, Legislative Background, Voting Rights Act, Johnson Library; Gene Rostow to Bill D. Moyers, to Lyndon B. Johnson; Lee C. White to Johnson, March 13, 1965, box 1, ibid.

38. Lyndon B. Johnson, "Message to Congress," March 15, 1965, box 2, Legislative Background, Voting Rights Act of 1965, Johnson Library.

39. King, handwritten notes, [March 1965], King Papers; James H. Laue, "Power, Conflict, and Social Change," in *Riots and Rebellion: Civil Violence in the Urban Community*, ed. Don R. Bowen and Louis H. Masotti (Beverly Hills, Calif.: Sage Publications, 1968), p. 90.

40. "Difference of Impact," *Time*, February 19, 1965, p. 17; Nicholas DeB. Katzenbach to Lyndon B. Johnson, March 1, 1965, box 1, Legislative Background, Voting Rights Act of 1965, Johnson Library.

41. King, handwritten notes, [March 1965], King Papers; Levison to King, April 7, 1965, King Papers.

42. Martin Luther King, Jr., "Address at Conclusion of Selma March," March 25, 1965, King Papers.

CHAPTER FOURTEEN

1. Robert Conot, *Rivers of Blood, Years of Darkness* (New York: Bantam, 1967), pp. 6–21.

2. Gerald Horne, *Fire This Time: The Watts Uprising and the 1960s* (New York: Da Capo, 1997), p. 56.

3. David J. Olson, "Black Violence As Political Protest," in *Black Politics: The Inevitability of Conflict,* Edward S. Greenberg, Neal Milner, and David J. Olson, eds. (New York: Holt, Rinehart and Winston, 1971), pp. 280–82.

4. Paul Jacobs, *Prelude to Riot: A View of Urban America from the Bottom* (New York: Random House, 1967), pp. 237–62; Anthony Oberschall, "The Los Angeles Riot of August 1965," in *Cities Under Siege,* T. Boesel and P. H. Rossi, eds. (New York: Basic Books, 1971), pp. 84–100; T. M. Tomlinson, "Riot Ideology Among Urban Negroes," in *Riots and Rebellion,* Bowen and Masotti, eds., pp. 418–420; Nathan Cohen, ed., *The Los Angeles Riots: A Socio-Psychological Study* (New York: Praeger, 1970); Robert M. Fogelson, *Violence As Protest* (Garden City, N.Y.: Doubleday, 1971), pp. 192–216; Bayard Rustin, "The Watts Manifesto and the McCone Report," *Commentary* 41 (March 1966), pp. 29–35; Robert Blauner, *Racial Oppression in America* (New York: Harper and Row, 1972), p. 89; "Why Watts," *Time,* August 27, 1965, p. 11.

5. James Ridgeway, "Saul Alinsky in 'Smugtown,'" *New Republic* (June 26, 1965), p. 16; Horne, *Fire This Time,* p. 183.

6. "The Negro in America—1965," *Newsweek* (February 15, 1965), p. 18.

7. *U.S. News and World Report* (March 6, 1967), pp. 59–60.

8. U.S. Department of Commerce, *Social and Economic Status of the Black Population,* pp. 67, 69.

9. Herbert Hill, "The Racial Practices of Organized Labor: The Contemporary Record," in *The Negro and the American Labor Movement,* Julius Jacobson, ed. (Garden City, N.Y.: Anchor Books, 1968), pp. 293–320; Herbert Hill, "Black Workers, Organized Labor, and Title VII of the 1964 Civil Rights Act," in *Race in America: The Struggle for Equality,* Herbert Hill and James E. Jones, eds. (Madison: University of Wisconsin Press, 1993), pp. 263–341.

10. Abernathy, *Walls Came Tumbling Down,* pp. 376–77.

11. William Brink and Louis Harris, *Black and White: A Study of U.S. Racial Attitudes Today* (New York: Simon and Schuster, 1967), pp. 120–24; Harry McPherson to Lyndon B. Johnson, September 12, 1966, box 22, McPherson Papers, Johnson Library.

12. Bayard Rustin, "From Protest to Politics: The Future of the Civil Rights Movement," *Commentary* 39 (February 1965), pp. 25–31; Brink and Harris, *Black and White,* p. 108.

13. "Prejudice: Widespread and Deep," *Newsweek* (October 21, 1963), p. 26. For further opinion poll evidence of white racial attitudes, see also William Brink and Louis Harris, *The Negro Revolution in America* (New York: Simon and Schuster, 1964), pp. 138–53.

14. Thomas J. Sugrue, "Crabgrass-Roots Politics: Race, Rights, and the Reaction Against Liberalism in the Urban North, 1940–1964," *Journal of American History* 82 (September 1995), p. 578. See also Arnold R. Hirsch, "Massive Resistance in the Urban North: Trumbull Park, Chicago, 1953–1966," ibid., pp. 522–50.

15. Horne, *Fire This Time,* pp. 134–39; Harry McPherson to Lyndon B. Johnson, August 8, 1967, box 6, Ex HU2, Johnson Library.

16. Horne, *Fire This Time*, p. 68; Don Moser, "There's No Easy Place to Pin the Blame," *Life* (August 27, 1965), p. 33.

17. Jonathan Steele, "Mississippi Comes to Harlem," *New Republic* (January 30, 1965), pp. 10–11.

18. Fredrickson, *Black Liberation*, p. 288.

19. Bruce Perry, *Malcolm: The Life of a Man Who Changed Black America* (Barrytown, N.Y.: Station Hill Press, 1992), pp. xiii, 11.

20. Malcolm Little to Ella Little Collins, December 12, 1946; Malcolm Little to Raymond, March 18, 1950; both box 1, Malcolm X Collection, Robert W. Woodruff Library, Emory University.

21. Malcolm Little to Raymond, March 18, 1950, Malcolm X Collection; Perry, *Malcolm*, pp. 12–13, 202.

22. Perry, *Malcolm*, pp. 174–79; Roy Wilkins with Tom Matthews, *Standing Fast: The Autobiography of Roy Wilkins* (New York: Penguin, 1984), p. 317.

23. Ibid., p. 318; James Farmer, *Lay Bare the Heart: An Autobiography of the Civil Rights Movement* (Fort Worth: Texas Christian University Press, 1985), p. 224; Fredrickson, *Black Liberation*, p. 289.

24. Farmer, *Lay Bare the Heart*, p. 223.

25. Malcolm X, "Message to the Grassroots," in *Eyes on the Prize*, Carson, ed., p. 253.

26. Bruce Perry, ed., *Malcolm X: The Last Speeches* (New York: Pathfinder, 1989), p. 68.

27. Malcolm X, "Message to the Grassroots," pp. 252–53; James H. Cone, *Martin and Malcolm and America* (London: Fount, 1991), pp. 176, 182; Peter Goldman, *The Death and Life of Malcolm X* (Urbana: University of Illinois Press, 1979), p. 186.

28. Bruce Perry, ed., *Malcolm X: The Last Speeches* pp. 123–24; Cone, *Martin and Malcolm and America*, p. 187.

29. Claude Andrew Gregg III, *An Original Man: The Life and Times of Elijah Muhammad* (New York: St. Martin's Press, 1998), pp. 200–216.

30. Ibid., p. 228.

31. Clayborne Carson, "Rethinking African-American Political Thought in the Post-Revolutionary Era," in *The Making of Martin Luther King and the Civil Rights Movement*, Ward and Badger, eds., p. 119.

32. Mary Aiken Rothschild, *A Case of Black and White: Northern Volunteers and the Southern Freedom Summers, 1964–1965* (Westport, Conn.: Greenwood Press, 1982), pp. 73, 137–44.

33. "Growl of the Panther," *Newsweek*, May 30, 1966, pp. 23–24; Members of the Atlanta Project, "A Position Paper on Race," in *Black Protest: History, Documents, and Analyses*, Joanne Grant, ed. (New York: Fawcett, 1968), pp. 452–56.

34. "Growl of the Panther," pp. 23–24; Stokely Carmichael, "What We Want," in *Civil Rights and the Black American: A Documentary History*, Albert P. Blaustein and Robert L. Zangrando, eds. (New York: Washington Square Press, 1970), p. 602.

35. *Washington Post* (June 18, 1966), p. A1; Martin Luther King, Jr., *Where Do We Go from Here: Chaos or Community?* (Boston: Beacon, 1968), pp. 29–31.

36. King, *Where Do We Go from Here*, pp. 33–36.

37. "The New Racism," *Time* (July 1, 1966), pp. 9–10; *New Republic* (June 18, 1966), pp. 5–6; *Washington Post* (July 7, 1966), p. A1.

38. Roy Wilkins, "Steady As She Goes," in *Black Viewpoints*, A. C. Littleton and M. W. Burger, eds. (New York: Mentor, 1971), pp. 295–96; Carson, *In Struggle*, p. 218.

39. King, "Beyond Vietnam," April 4, 1967, King Papers; John P. Roche to Lyndon B. Johnson, April 5, 1967, box 56, HU2 ST1 (CF), Johnson Library.

40. Carson, *In Struggle,* p. 218.

41. Ibid., p. 221.

42. Dittmer, *Local People,* p. 411.

43. Carson, *In Struggle,* p. 235.

44. Richard H. King, *Civil Rights and the Idea of Freedom* (New York: Oxford University Press, 1991), p. 200.

45. Bobby Seale, *Seize the Time: The Story of the Black Panther Party* (London: Arrow Books, 1970), pp. 47, 84–90.

46. Seale, *Seize the Time,* p. 178.

47. O'Reilly, *Racial Matters,* pp. 297–98, 311–15. In 1982 the federal government agreed to pay $1.85 million in compensation to the four survivors and to the families of the dead men.

48. Ibid., p. 294.

49. Hugh Pearson, *Shadow of the Panther: Huey Newton and the Price of Black Power in America* (Reading, Mass.: Addison-Wesley, 1994), pp. 314–15.

50. William Van Deburg, *New Day in Babylon: The Black Power Movement and American Culture* (Chicago: University of Chicago Press, 1992), pp. 306–07.

51. Young, *An Easy Burden,* p. 404; Horne, *Fire This Time,* pp. 12–16, 186–87; Carson, "Rethinking African-American Political Thought," p. 122.

CHAPTER FIFTEEN

1. *Time* (April 6, 1970), pp. 18–28.

2. Steven F. Lawson, *Running for Freedom: Civil Rights and Black Politics in America Since 1941* (New York: McGraw-Hill, 1991), pp. 139–40.

3. Ibid., p. 228; *Time* (September 27, 1976), pp. 40–41.

4. Hugh Davis Graham, *Civil Rights and the Presidency: Race and Gender in American Politics, 1960–1972* (New York: Oxford University Press, 1992), p. 139.

5. Ibid., pp. 150–69; Tom Wicker, *One of Us: Richard Nixon and the American Dream* (New York: Random House, 1991), pp. 529–38.

6. Graham, *Civil Rights and the Presidency,* pp. 120–21, 179–86.

7. Steven F. Lawson, *In Pursuit of Power: Southern Blacks and Electoral Politics, 1965–1982* (New York: Columbia University Press, 1985), pp. 189–90.

8. Lawson, *Running for Freedom,* p. 260; Stephan Thernstrom and Abigail Thernstrom, *America in Black and White: One Nation Indivisible* (New York: Simon and Schuster, 1997), p. 289; Fairclough, *Race and Democracy,* p. 466.

9. Thernstrom and Thernstrom, *America in Black and White,* pp. 286–97; Andrew Hacker, *Two Nations: Black and White, Separate, Hostile, Unequal* (New York: Ballantine, 1992), p. 208.

10. Hacker, *Two Nations,* pp. 113, 130, 233; U.S. Department of Commerce, *Social and Economic Characteristics of the Black Population,* p. 46; Thernstrom and Thernstrom, *America in Black and White,* p. 195.

11. Lawson, *Running for Freedom,* p. 262; Ronald F. Ferguson, "Shifting Challenges: Fifty Years of Economic Change Toward Black-White Earnings Equality," *Daedalus* 124 (Winter 1995), p. 55; Hacker, *Two Nations,* p. 94; Thernstrom and Thernstrom, *America in Black and White,* p. 197.

12. Hacker, *Two Nations,* pp. 98–100.

13. Tom Dent, *Southern Journey: A Return to the Civil Rights Movement* (New York: William Morrow, 1997), p. 194.

14. Fairclough, *Race and Democracy,* pp. 453–461; Robert A. Pratt, "A Promise Unfulfilled: School Desegregation in Richmond, Virginia, 1956–1986," *Virginia Magazine of History and Biography* 99 (October 1991), pp. 415–48; Roger Biles, "A Bittersweet Victory: Public School Desegregation in Memphis," *Journal of Negro Education* 55 (Fall 1986), pp. 470–83; Ronald P. Formisano, *Boston Against Busing: Race, Class, and Ethnicity in the 1960s and 1970s* (Chapel Hill: University of North Carolina Press, 1991), pp. 210–11; Ronald H. Bayor, *Race and the Shaping of Twentieth-Century Atlanta* (Chapel Hill: University of North Carolina Press, 1996), pp. 226, 249; William Henry Kellar, *Make Haste Slowly: Moderates, Conservatives, and School Desegregation in Houston* (College Station: Texas A & M Press, 1999), pp. 161–67.

15. J. K. Haynes to Daniel E. Byrd, April 26, 1974, folder 10, box 3, Daniel E. Byrd Papers, Amistad Research Center, Tulane University, New Orleans. The LEA was the association of black teachers in Louisiana.

16. Alton L. Hornsby, Jr., "Black Public Education in Atlanta, Georgia, 1954–1973," *Journal of Negro History* 86 (1991), p. 40; Dent, *Southern Journey,* p. 218.

17. Numan V. Bartley, *The New South 1945–1980* (Baton Rouge: Louisiana State University Press, 1995), pp. 421–22.

18. Dent, *Southern Journey,* p. 217.

19. Huey L. Perry, "A Theoretical Analysis of National Black Politics in the United States," in *Blacks and the American Political System,* Huey L. Perry and Wayne Parent, eds. (Gainesville: University of Florida Press, 1995), pp. 29–30; Henry B. Sirgo, "Blacks and Presidential Politics," in ibid., p. 94.

20. Dewey W. Grantham, *The South in Modern America: A Region at Odds* (New York: HarperCollins, 1994), p. 303.

21. Tushnet, *Making Civil Rights Law,* p. 190; *Voting Rights Review* (Fall 1993), pp. 1–11.

22. Elliott Currie, *Crime and Punishment in America* (New York: Henry Holt, 1998), pp. 11–16, 25; Duncan Campbell, "Anger Grows as the US Jails Its Two Millionth Inmate," *Guardian,* February 15, 2000, p. 3.

23. Hacker, *Two Nations,* p. 197; Earl Shinholster, "Criminal Disfranchisement Laws," *Southern Changes* 20 (Fall 1998), p. 26; Currie, *Crime and Punishment in America,* p. 13.

24. Hacker, *Two Nations,* p. 181; Thernstrom and Thernstrom, *America in Black and White,* pp. 259–79. The argument for racial bias in the criminal justice system is set forth in Coramae Richey Mann, *Unequal Justice: A Question of Color* (Bloomington: Indiana University Press, 1993).

25. Joseph G. Conti and Brad Stetson, *Challenging the Civil Rights Establishment: Profiles of a New Black Vanguard* (Westport, Conn.: Praeger, 1993), p. 50; Hacker, *Two Nations,* pp. 68–74; Donna L. Franklin, *Ensuring Equality: The Structural Transformation of the African-American Family* (New York: Oxford University Press, 1997), pp. 202–93.

26. Ibid., pp. 90–106; Thomas Sowell, *Assumption Versus History: Collected Papers* (Stanford, Calif.: Hoover Institution Press, 1986).

27. Eskew, *But for Birmingham,* p. 331.

28. Dent, *Southern Journey,* pp. 166, 216; John Egerton, *Shades of Grey: Dispatches from the Modern South* (Baton Rouge: Louisiana State University Press), p. 127.

I N D E X

Page numbers in *italics* refer to photographs.

Abernathy, Ralph D., 235, 255, 277, 278, 289, 290, 301, 308, 321
accommodationism, xiv, xv, 19–20, 21, 39, 41–42, 64
  teachers and, 173
  of Washington, 62, 63–64, 65
Acheson, Dean, 217
Adams, Lewis, 50
affirmative action, 324, 325, 332
AFL (American Federation of Labor), 89, 101, 102, 144, 150, 152
Africa, 18, 99, 156
  image of, 117
  Malcolm X and, 307–8
  UNIA and, 111, 112–13, 117, 119–22, 123, 124, 130
Afro-American Council, 38
Afro-American League, 18–19, 38, 152
agitation and protest, xiv, 20, 39, 42, 59, 64, 78, 161
  Garvey and, 112
  Roosevelt's view of, 193
  Washington and, 57, 64, 77
agriculture, 61, 88, 104, 188, 261
  decline of, 205
  sharecropping, 104, 162, 205, 262
Alabama Dry Dock Company, 187–88
Albany Movement, 266–71, 275
Alexander, Will, 169
Alexander v. Holmes County Board of Education, 325
Ali, Duse Mohammed, 115
Allen, Louis, 283
Allen, Ralph, 284

Along This Way (Johnson), 84–85
Amenia Conference, 85, 146, 147, 152
American Citizens Equal Rights Association, 19
Ames, Jesse Daniel, 166
Amsterdam Star-News, 184
Anderson, Eric, 7
Anderson, James D., 47
Anderson, W. G., 268
Armstrong, Samuel Chapman, 44, 45
Ashwood, Amy, 116, 122
ASWPL (Association of Southern Women for the Prevention of Lynching), 166
Atlanta Compromise, 39, 41–42, 48, 76, 77, 125
Atlanta Project, 311–12
Aycock, Charles B., 9, 10
Ayers, Edward, 15
Azbell, Joe, 229

Badger, Tony, 221
Bagnall, Robert, 126, 127
Baker, Ella J., 184, 236–37, 238, 240, 245, 246, 260
Baker, Frazier, 37
Baker, Josephine, 214
Baker, Newton D., 97
Baldwin, William H., 50–51
Baltimore, Charles W., 95
Barber, J. Max, 78, 128
Barnett, Ferdinand L., 37
Barnett, Ross, 256, 266
Barrett, Thomas H., 31
Barringer, Paul, 12
Bartley, Numan V., 222, 329–30
Bass, Charlotta, 122

Bates, Ruby, 134, 135
Bederman, Gail, 38
Beecher, John, 187
Bennett, Belle, 165
Bentley, Charles E., 55, 69
Berman, William, 211
Bethune, Mary McLeod, 165, 169, 178, 193, 214
Bevel, James, 260, 261, 275, 290, 297
Biddle, Francis, 193–94
Bilbo, Theodore G., 156
Birmingham, 273–79
Birth of a Nation, The, 83, 84
"black," use of term, 312–13
Black Codes, 3–4
black nationalism, 112, 113, 129, 156, 279, 310, 317
    Garvey and, 112, 117–18, 129
Black Panther Party for Self-Defense (BPP), *294,* 317–19
Black Power, 310, 312–14, 315–16, 319–20, 323
    guns and, 316–18, 319
black separatism, xiv, xv, 309, 310, 311, 312, 316
Blackshear, Edward L., 20
Black Star Line (BSL) Steamship Corporation, 113, 115, 121, 123, 126
Blackwell, Randolph, 263
Blair, Ezell, Jr., 241
Blair Bill, 47
Blauner, Robert, 296
Block, Sam, 259, 262–63, 284
Bloody Sunday, 291, 292
Blyden, Edward Wilmot, 115
Boas, Franz, 70
Bolshevik Revolution, 99, 102–3, 108
Bond, Horace Mann, 64–65, 172, 173, 174, 175
Bond, Julian, 314
Bontemps, Arna, 157
Bowen, John, 78
boycotts, 240, 242, 243, 245, 261, 266, 273, 275, 277
    of buses, 227–34, 235, 238, 239, 240, 242, 249, 253, 268
    of streetcars, 77–78, 227
Boynton, Amelia P., 289
Brady, Tom P., 221
Branch, Mary, 178
Brawley, Benjamin, 89
Bremer, Arthur, 323
Briggs, Cyril, 142
Brink, William, 302
Britain, 130, 191, 233
    colonialism of, 120
    Garveyism and, 112
    Ireland and, 120
    lynch law criticized by, 33, 34, 38
Britt, Travis, 257
Broderick, Francis, 80
Brodsky, Joseph, 138
Brooks, Arthur L., 50
Brooks, J. G., 125

Browder v. *Gayle,* 233
Brown, Charlotte Hawkins, 164, 165
Brown, Henry, 14
Brown, H. Rap, 315
Brown, Pat, 296
Brown, Roscoe D., 163
Browning, Joan, 244
Brownsville Affair, 58–59, 92
Brown v. *Board of Education,* 206, 218–25, 231, 234, 242, 250, 325
    Brown II, 220, 221, 223, 225
Bruce, John E., 116, 122
Bruce, Roscoe Conkling, 44
Brumfield, Thomas M., 100
BSCP (Brotherhood of Sleeping Car Porters), 149, 150–52, 228
Buchanan v. *Warley,* 82
Buffalo Soldiers, 58, 92
Bulkley, William L., 69
Bullard, Robert, 96
Bumpus, Paul, 207
Bunche, Ralph J., 136, 182–83
Burger, Warren, 324, 325, 332
Burleson, Albert, 82–83
buses:
    boycotts of, 227–34, 235, 238, 239, 240, 242, 249, 253, 268
    Freedom Rides and, 253–56, 271
    segregation on, 228, 229, 233, 234, 236, 266
Bush, George, 331, 332
Byrd, Daniel, 222

Calhoun, Arthur W., 27
Calista, Donald J., 62
Callahan, William Washington, 139
Calvert, Gertrude, 35
Campbell, John B., 104–5
Camp Des Moines, 92, 96, 148
Candler, Allan D., 46
Carmichael, Stokely, 260, 311–12, 315, 316–17
Carnegie, Andrew, 51, 53
Carson, Clayborne, 310, 314, 315, 316, 320
Carter, Jimmy, *322,* 331
Carter, Mae Bertha, 282–83
Carter, Rosalynn, *322*
Cash, Wilbur J., 26
Catholic Church, 108
Cell, John W., xiv, xv
Chafe, William, 241
Chalmers, Allan Knight, 139
Chambliss, Rollin, 26–27
Chaney, James, 285–86
Chesnutt, Charles W., 17–18, 57, 59–60, 63
Chicago, 107–8, 194, 195, 298, 300, 302
    SCLC in, 300–301, 303
Chicago Defender, 93, 194
Chivers, Walter, 177
Church, Catholic, 108
churches, black, 20, 35, 47, 99, 233, 234, 237, 239, 246, 308

ministers of, 20–21, 35–36, 62, 122, 151, 229,
230–31, 233, 234, 235, 238, 239, 308
in the North, 301
SCLC and, 234, 235, 238, 239, 240
UNIA and, 117–18
CIC (Commission on Interracial Cooperation),
106–7, 163, 164, 165–66, 167–68, 169, 170,
178
CIO (Congress of Industrial Organizations), xv,
144, 147–48, 183, 184, 215, 216, 236
communism and, 212, 213
Citizens Councils, 221–22, 224, 231, 289
Civil Rights Act (1957), 240
Civil Rights Act (1964), 282–83, 300, 324, 325
Civil Rights Bill (1957), 281
Civil Rights Bill (1963), 280–82
Civil Rights Bill (1966), 302
Civil Rights Bill (1991), 331
Civil Rights Commission, U.S., 208, 266, 276,
332
Civil Rights Movement, xiv–xv, 23, 131, 133, 162,
178, 206, 209, 225, 234, 249–71
Albany Movement in, 266–71, 275
antiwhite hostility and, 297, 304
Birmingham and, 274
Black Power and, 310, 313, 314, 320
Citizens Councils and, 221–22
collapse of, 323
communism and, 209, 211–17, 218
costs of, 328
Freedom Rides, 253–56, 271
imprisonments in, 268, 269, 275
Kennedy administration and, 250–52, 255, 256,
257, 263 66, 270, 273 74, 276, 278, 279 81
as male-dominated, 260
momentum of, 323–27, 332
Nation of Islam and, 304–5
nonviolence in, see nonviolent direct action
in the North, 301, 303–4
SNCC's work in Mississippi, 256–66, 283, 310,
311
Vietnam War and, 314–15
white backlash and, 301–3
white Southerners in, 244–45
women's support for, 259–60
Clark, Jim, 289, 290, 291, 292
Clark, Mark, 318
Clark, Septima P., 223
Clarke, Edward, 126
class consciousness, 101, 146
Clegg, Claude Andrew, 310
Cleghorn, Reese, 275
Clement, Rufus C., 204
Clifford, Clark, 209
Clinton, Bill, 331, 332–33
Cobb, Charles, 284
Cobb, James C., 222, 261, 262
COFO (Council of Federated Organizations), 263,
286
Cohn, David, 27

Cold War, 142, 159, 185, 206, 209, 211, 212, 213,
214, 215–17, 249, 252, 302
Cole, Bob, 84
Cole, Nathaniel, 94
Collins, John, 233
Collins, LeRoy, 244
colonialism, 88, 120, 205, 213, 216–17, 308
color differences among blacks, 113–14, 127–28,
307
Colored University, 63
color line, 17
Color Line, The (Smith), 27
Columbia riot, 206–8
Commission on Civil Rights, 240
communism, Communist Party, xv, 99, 102–3, 133,
141–46, 147, 148, 154–55, 158–59, 183, 209,
230
anticommunism and, 211–17, 218, 220, 225
Cold War and, 142, 159
decline of, 215–16
Kennedy and, 252
King and, 236–38, 281
March on Washington and, 156
NAACP and, 184
Nazis and, 137, 153
NNC and, 154–55
racial discrimination and, 142–44
Scottsboro affair and, 136–38, 139, 140, 141,
145, 146, 198, 236
Communist International (Comintern), 142–43,
144, 145
community organizing, 313
Connor, Eugene "Bull," 253, 275, 276, 277, 278
Constitution, U.S., 71, 174, 182, 230, 249, 264
segregation and, 197–98, 206, 218
convict-lease system, 27–28, 36
Coolidge, Calvin, 129
CORE (Congress of Racial Equality), 158, 244,
249, 253, 254, 255–56, 313, 314, 315
Meredith March and, 312
SNCC and, 263
Coss, John J., 171
Councill, William H., 18, 63
CPUSA, see communism, Communist Party
crime, 25, 27, 58, 333–34
see also prisoners
Crisis, 73, 78, 79–82, 84, 88, 93, 95, 97, 127, 149,
186
Crummell, Alexander, 76
Cuba, 214
Currie, Elliott, 333
Curry, Connie, 244–45, 246

Dabney, Charles W., 52
Daley, Richard J., 300–301, 302
Daniels, Jonathan, 194
Daniels, Josephus, 8, 9, 48
Daugherty, Harry M., 126
Davies, Henrietta Vinton, 122
Davis, Benjamin O., 189

Davis, Jeff, 39
Davis, John P., 152
Davis, John W., 82
Davis, Sarah Morris, 192
Dawson, William, 301
Deacons for Defense, 312
democracy, 185, 188, 216–17, 230, 249
    education and, 176
Democratic Party, 15, 16, 19, 21, 47, 50, 146, 154,
    168, 194, 209, 210, 211, 216, 250, 251, 252,
    288, 302, 311, 331, 332
    anticommunism and, 215
    in 1800s, 5, 6, 7
    Fusion and, 7–8, 10
    National Conventions of, 202, 286–87, 288
    primary elections of, 197, 200
    white supremacy and, 2, 5, 6, 7, 8–10, 15
demonstrations, 156, 157–58, 242, 261, 267,
    274–79, 290, 292
    Albany Movement and, 269, 270
    white backlash and, 301–3
Dennis, Dave, 284
Dent, Tom, 328
Denton, Virginia, 60
Depression, Great, 133–34, 141, 146, 148, 155,
    166, 169, 173
Deshotels, John, 196
Detroit, 298
De Valera, Eamon, 120
Dewey, John, 70
Dewey, Thomas E., 210
Dickerson, Earl, 187
Dickinson, Jacob M., 207–8
Dittmer, John, 262, 265, 266, 283, 316
Dixon, Frank, 186
Dobbs, John Wesley, 196
Doherty, Thomas, 189
Douglass, Frederick, 18, 39, 128
Drago, Edmund, 172
Du Bois, W.E.B., 55–58, 62, 66, 68, 70–81, 83, 84,
    97, 99, 103, 117, 120, 128, 140, 148, 168,
    175, 177
    arrest of, 213
    background of, 73–74
    black soldiers and, 92–93, 97–98
    Crisis and, 73, 78, 79–82, 88, 93, 97, 127, 149
    exile of, 213–14
    Garvey and, 112, 116, 126, 127, 129
    Johnson and, 85
    on lynching, 81
    NAACP and, 70–71, 73, 78, 79–82, 149
    Niagara Movement and, 77–78
    segregation and, 148–49
    The Souls of Black Folk, 75, 76, 77
    "Talented Tenth" idea of, 76, 77, 79, 175
    Washington and, 70, 73, 74, 75–76, 80, 85
    Washington compared with, 73–74
Dudley, James B., 10, 31
Dulles, Allen, 286
Dunbar-Nelson, Alice, 145

Dunning, William A., 264
Durham Manifesto, 178
Durr, Virginia, 228
Dyer, Leonidas C., 83

Eason, James Walker Hood, 122, 124, 129
Eastland, James O., 212, 261, 266, 285
East St. Louis riot, 93–94, 99, 105
education and schools, 4, 7–8, 13, 20, 69, 71, 76,
    175–79, 190, 209, 282, 283
    better schools campaign, 169–75
    black, nostalgia for, 329
    black principals in, 172
    black teachers in, 170–71, 172, 173, 175, 176,
        177, 178, 185, 199, 219, 223
    Brown v. Board of Education and, 206, 218–25,
        325
    Brown II and, 220, 221, 223, 225
    closing of, 222–23
    college presidents, 172–73, 177, 178, 243
    colleges and universities, 45, 46, 47, 175,
        176–77, 178–79, 324
    democracy and, 176
    disparity between black and white schools, 52,
        54
    Du Bois and, 76
    increased expenditure on, 203–4
    industrial, 44–47, 49, 50, 51, 54, 58
    integration of, 323, 324, 325, 328–30
    Lumberton protest and, 203
    NAACP and, 198–99
    private, 171
    pupil placement in, 223
    rural, 173, 174
    segregation in, 12, 13, 108, 148, 198–99, 206,
        218–25, 300
    textbooks in, 175
    Washington and, 43–47, 48–49, 50–53, 54
    white attitudes toward, 46–50
Egypt, 115, 117, 118, 120
Eisenhower, Dwight D., 218, 220, 224, 225, 244,
    250, 264
Elaine riot, 104–5
elected officials, black, 4, 6, 204, 250, 326, 330–31
Elliott, Robert, 270
employment and labor, 2, 39, 169, 185–88, 208,
    210, 266, 298–99, 325, 326–27, 331, 332
    affirmative action in, 324, 325, 332
    agricultural, see farm workers
    Civil Rights Act and, 282
    convict-lease system and, 27–28, 36
    in defense industries, 155, 157
    education and, 44–47, 48, 49, 50, 51
    FEPC and, 157, 186–88, 210
    industrial, 85, 88, 89–90, 93–94, 298
    NAACP and, 182–85
    segregation in government jobs, 82–83
    sexuality and, 27
    World War I and, 89–90
England, see Britain

Eskew, Glenn, 277, 335
Ethiopia, 112, 115, 117, 118, 121
    Italy and, 152–53
Ethiopia Peace Movement, 156
Ethridge, Mark, 187
Evers, Medgar, 280, 307–8

Fahey Committee, 217
Fanon, Frantz, 315
Fard, Wallace D., 304
Farmer, James, 158, 307
farm workers, 61, 88, 104, 188, 261
    sharecroppers, 104, 162, 205, 262
Farrakhan, Louis, 334
Farrand, Livingston, 70
fascism, 152, 185, 186, 188, 201
    Popular Front against, 145, 153, 154, 216
Faubus, Orval, 224–25, 254
FBI (Federal Bureau of Investigation), 121, 129–30,
    188, 194, 208, 212, 285, 286, 287, 316
    anticommunism and, 214–15
    Black Panthers and, 318, 319
    civil rights and, 265
    King and, 281
Felton, Rebecca Latimer, 8–9
FEPC (Fair Employment Practices Committee),
    157, 186–88, 210
Ferdinand, Franz, 87
Ferguson, Ronald F., 327
Ferris, William H., 122
Fields, Mamie Garvin, 163
Fifteenth Amendment, 4, 14, 71, 265
First Amendment, 242, 270
First World War, see World War I
Fisher, Isaac, 100
Fisk University, 100, 178
Fleming, Cynthia Griggs, 256
Flemming, Billy, 206
Folsom, James, 221
Ford, James W., 143
Ford Motor Company, 185, 187
Foreman, Clark, 169, 174
Fortune, T. Thomas, 17, 18–19, 32, 38, 45, 54, 63,
    122, 152
"forty acres and a mule," 2, 4
Foster, Wilbur F., 50
Fourteenth Amendment, 3–4, 14, 71, 138, 197,
    265, 270
Frank, John P., 219
Franklin, John Hope, 3, 68
Fredrickson, George, 145, 305, 307
freedmen, 1–3
Freedmen's Bureau, 4
Freedom Rides, 253–56, 271
freedom songs, 267–68
Freedom Summer, 283–88, 311
Freeman, Elizabeth, 81
free Negroes, 127–28
Frey, John, 318
Friedman, Lawrence J., 64

Frye, Marquette, 295
Frye, Rena, 295

Gaines, Lloyd, 199
Gandy, John M., 177
Garrow, David, 277
Garvey, Amy Ashwood, 116, 122
Garvey, Amy Jacques, 118–19, 122
Garvey, Marcus Mosiah, xv, 99, 101, 110, 111–31,
    142, 156, 305, 307
    Black Star Line of, 113, 115, 121, 123, 126
    and color differences among blacks, 127–28
    deportation of, 129–30
    influence of, 130
    Ku Klux Klan and, 126, 127, 130
    mail fraud conviction of, 123, 126, 129
    movement against, 126–27, 128–31
    nationalism of, 112, 117–18, 129
    rise and popularity of, 116–17, 118–19
    segregation and, 124–26, 129, 130
    as speaker, 116
    West Indian background of, 113–14, 128–29
Gaston, A. G., 276
GEB (General Education Board), 52, 53, 172,
    173
Germany, 120, 137, 154
    Nazi, 137, 146, 153, 159, 205, 216
ghettos, 12, 149, 296, 297, 298, 299, 302, 304,
    316
Gibbs, Warmoth T., 243
Gilmore, Glenda, 8, 10–11, 36, 172
Glass, Carter, 14
Goldwater, Barry, 287, 288
Goodman, Alexander, 285–86
Goodman, James, 137
Gordon, Mittie Maud Lena, 156
Gore, George W., 224
Gorst, John, 33
Graetz, Robert, 233
Graham, Hugh D., 324
grandfather clause, 82, 197
Granger, Lester, 154
Grant, Ulysses S., 5–6
Grantham, Dewey, 331
Graves, Bibb, 139–40
Gray, James H., 270
Great Britain, see Britain
Great Depression, 133–34, 141, 146, 148, 155,
    166, 169, 173
Great Migration, 17–18, 88–90, 93–94, 102, 105,
    107, 109, 125, 194, 209, 298
Green, Edward, 193
Greensboro sit-in, 241–42, 243
Greer, Allen J., 96
Griffin, L. Francis, 335–36
Grimké, Archibald, 59
Grovey v. Townsend, 197
Gruening, Martha, 95
Guinn v. United States, 82
guns, Black Power and, 316–18, 319

Haas, Francis J., 187
Hale, Elizabeth Grace, 16
Hall, Jacqueline, 166
Hall, Prathia, 285
Hamer, Fannie Lou, 260–61, 283, 287
Hampton, Fred, 318
Hampton, William, 204
Hampton Institute, 44, 45, 50
Handlin, Ralph, 181, 182
Hansen, Bill, 269
Harding, Warren, 124
Hardy, John, 257, 265
Hare, James A., 289
Harlan, John M., 14, 182
Harlan, Louis, 49, 52, 53, 60
Harris, Abram, 146, 147
Harris, Louis, 302
Harris, William H., 151
Harris Committee, 147
Harwell, Bud, 207
Haskin, Sara Estelle, 164
Hastie, William, 189
Hauser, Philip M., 298
Hawkins, Alfred E., 135
Hayden, Casey, 285
Hayes, Rutherford B., 74
Haygood, Atticus G., 28
Haynes, Elizabeth Ross, 165
Haynes, J. K., 329
Haywood, Harry, 142
health, public, 61, 163–64
Height, Dorothy, 260
Henderson v. *United States,* 218
Henry, Aaron, 259, 262
Henry, Cyril, 124
Herndon, Alonzo F., 55
Hill, Robert, 122
Holcomb, Thomas, 190
Hood, John Walker, 21
Hooper, W. W., 29
Hoover, Herbert, 156
Hoover, J. Edgar, 116, 130, 214, 265, 281, 286, 318
Hope, John, 64
Horne, Gerald, 297, 303, 320
Horton, James E., 138–39, 140
Hose, Sam, 54–55
housing, 163
    discrimination in, 82, 107–8, 149, 194, 209, 210,
        218, 219, 299–300, 302
Houston, Charles Hamilton, 140, 147, 197–98,
        200, 201, 213
Houston riot, 94–95
Howard College, 63
HUAC (House Un-American Activities Commit-
    tee), 212
Hubbard, W. H., 171
Huddleston, George, 135–36
Hudson, Hosea, 144, 145
Hughes, Charles Evans, 105
Hughes, Langston, 144, 177

Humphrey, Hubert H., 281, 287, 288, 313
Hunter, Charles N., 20
Huntington, Collis P., 50
Hurst, E. H., 257

Ickes, Harold, 158, 168–69
"If We Must Die" (McKay), 103
ILD (International Labor Defense), 136–40, 143
Illinois State Journal, 67
immigrants, 119, 335
    European, 11–12, 89, 119, 298
    West Indian, 113, 122, 124, 128
Impey, Catherine, 33
income gap, 327
Indians, 12, 13
interracial cooperation, 164–68, 178, 245
Ireland, 119, 120, 264
Irvin, Walter, 217
Italy, 119
    Ethiopia and, 152–53
I.W.W. (Industrial Workers of the World), 103,
    105

Jacks, John W., 34–35
Jackson, Jesse, 330, 334
Jackson, Jimmie Lee, 291
Jackson, Robert H., 332
Jacques, Amy, 118–19, 122
Jamaica, 113–14, 115, 116, 117, 120, 128, 129
James, Winston, 113
Japan, 120
Japanese, 12, 119
Jason, William C., 215
Jeffries, Edward J., 195
Jencks, Christopher, 177
Jim Crow, *see* segregation
Johnson, Andrew, 3
Johnson, Carrie Parks, 164, 165, 168
Johnson, Charles S., 174, 178, 216
Johnson, George M., 216–17
Johnson, James Weldon, 56, 84–85, 102, 128, 177
    Du Bois and, 85
Johnson, Lyndon, 281–82, 285–88, 290, 291–92,
        297, 302, 313, 314–15, 320
    Voting Rights Bill and, 288, 292
Johnson, Mordecai, 201
Johnson, Rosamond, 84
Jones, David, 178
Jones, John, 206
Jones, Laurence C., 171
Jones, Theodore W., 56
Jones, Thomas Jesse, 168
Jones, Walter B., 224
Justice Department, U.S., 208, 218, 240, 255, 256,
        265, 270, 291, 324, 325–26

Katzenbach, Nicholas, 288, 292
Kennedy, John F., 250–53, 255–57, 263–66, 270,
        273–74, 276, 278–81, 300, 309
    Civil Rights Bill and, 280–81

Kennedy, Robert, 251, 252, 265, 266, 277, 279, 280, 281, 285, 313
    Freedom Rides and, 254, 255
Kerr, W. W., 181–82, 183
Kilpatrick, James J., 244
King, C.D.B., 124
King, Coretta Scott, 274, 322
King, Martin Luther, Jr., 65, 133, 177, 229–30, 235–36, 242, 245, 247, 248, 255, 267, 279, 280, 287, 288, 290, 291, 292, 293, 302, 304, 307, 310, 313, 318, 330, 331
    Albany Movement and, 269, 270
    assassination of, 320–21, 323
    in Birmingham, 273, 274, 276
    Black Power and, 312–13, 314, 320
    communism and, 236–38, 281
    Freedom Rides and, 255
    "I Have a Dream" speech of, 281
    imprisonment of, 250–51, 276
    "Letter from Birmingham Jail," 276
    Malcolm X's background compared with, 305
    Meredith March and, 312
    Montgomery bus boycott and, 227, 228, 229–31, 232, 233, 235, 238, 239, 240
    in the North, 297, 300 301, 303–4
    poverty and, 320–21
    religious faith of, 238–39
    Rustin and, 235–36
    SCLC and, 234–41
    SNCC and, 269
    Stride Toward Freedom, 237, 269
    Vietnam War and, 314–15
King, Martin Luther, Sr., 322
King, Richard H., 316
King, Rodney, 331
Köusser, J. Morgan, 10, 15
Kruttschnitt, E. B., 14
Ku Klux Klan, xv, xviii, 5, 83, 106, 119, 125, 222, 231, 239, 253, 264, 265, 274, 275, 276, 278, 279, 283, 284, 285, 286, 292
    Garvey and, 126, 127, 130
    Muhammad and, 309

labor, see employment and labor
labor unions, xv, 12, 89, 93–94, 101, 102, 103, 108, 119, 125, 133, 144, 185, 216, 231, 233
    as cause of racial discrimination, 299
    communism and, 212, 213
    growth of, 101
    labor movement in 1930s, 146–52
    NAACP and, 183, 184, 185
LaGuardia, Fiorello, 156
land, 4, 54, 61
Latham, Charlie, 134
Lawson, James M., Jr., 246
Lawson, Steven F., 251, 325
Lee, Harold, 175
Lee, Herbert, 257, 258, 283
left-wing thinking, xv, 102, 103, 108, 133, 183, 194
    see also communism, Communist Party

Leloudis, James, 173, 179
"Letter from Birmingham Jail" (King), 276
Levison, Stanley D., 236–37, 238, 242, 281, 293
Lewis, Barbara, 192
Lewis, David Levering, 13–14, 73, 77, 80, 81, 84
Lewis, John, 243, 244, 246, 284, 290, 311
Lewis, John L., 154
Lewis, Rufus, 230
Liberia, 117, 121–22, 123, 124, 152–53
Liebowitz, Samuel L., 138, 139
"Lift Every Voice and Sing" (Johnson and Johnson), 84–85
Lincoln, Abraham, 2–3
Little, Earl, 305
Little Rock Central High School, 224, 264
Liuzzo, Viola, 292
Logan, Rayford W., 193
Long, Earl, 221
Long, Huey, 141, 196
Longe, George S., 176
longshoremen, 149, 183
Los Angeles, 298
    1992 riot in, 331
    police brutality in, 303
    Watts riot in, 295–97, 300, 302, 303, 304
Los Angeles Times, 295
L'Ouverture, Toussaint, 96
Low, Seth, 13
Lowndes County Freedom Organization (LCFO), 311
lunch counters, 241–42, 243, 245, 273, 328
lynching, 7, 23–33, 36, 55, 83, 91, 94, 103, 119, 125, 136, 140, 166, 168, 196, 207, 217
    black veterans and, 109
    British criticism of, 33, 34, 38
    CIC and, 106
    Crisis and, 80, 81
    decline of, 38–39, 166, 208
    Du Bois's editorials on, 81
    federal intervention in, 208
    Garvey on, 126
    of Italians, 119
    NAACP campaign against, 23, 24, 105, 126, 166, 208
    and President's Committee on Civil Rights, 208–9
    rape and, 9, 25–26, 28, 31–32, 34, 38, 58, 67, 134–35, 166
    rise of, 24–28
    Scottsboro affair and, 134–35
    Stephenson and, 206, 207
    Washington and, 54, 55
    Wells's campaign against, 23, 29, 31–33, 34, 37–39
    West Indians and, 113
Lyons, Maritcha, 34

McCain, Franklin, 241
McCarthy, Joseph, 211
McCone Commission, 296

McDew, Chuck, 258
McDowell, Calvin, 31, 32
McGhee, Frederick, 55
McGill, Ralph, 193
McGuire, George Alexander, 118, 122
McKay, Claude, 103, 144
McKinley, William, 11, 13, 37, 38, 60
McKissick, Floyd, 314
McLaurin, George, 218
McLaurin v. Oklahoma State Regents, 218
McMillan, Lewis K., 173
McMurry, Linda, 38
McNeill, Joseph, 241
McNutt, Paul, 187
McPherson, Harry, 302, 303
McPherson, James M., 72
Malcolm X, 279, 304–10, 317, 334
   King's background compared with, 305
Mandle, Jay, 205
Manley, Alexander L., 8, 9, 10
Manley, Charles, 9
Mann, Floyd, 254
March on Washington (1963), 280–81
March on Washington, proposal for, 155–57, 185, 186, 280
March on Washington Movement, 157–58, 159, 236, 280
Margold, Nathan, 197
marriage and sex, interracial (miscegenation), 26, 27, 32, 34, 42, 113, 126, 129, 191
Marshall, Burke, 264, 274
Marshall, Thurgood, *180,* 200–201, 208, 213, 218, 232, 234, 332
   Brown decision and, 219, 220
   student protests and, 243
Martin, Tony, 129
Maslow, Will, 219
Matthews, Victoria Earle, 34
Mayo, Isabelle Fyvie, 33
Mays, Benjamin, 102, 214, 329
Memphis Free Speech, 30, 31, 32, 35–36
Meredith, James, 266, 312
Meredith March, 312
Merrill, J. N., 96
Messenger, 98–99, 125, 126, 127, 150
MFDP (Mississippi Freedom Democratic Party), 286–88, 310
MIA (Montgomery Improvement Association), 229–30, 231–34, 235, 267
middle class, black, 20, 29, 34, 35, 37, 61, 64, 127, 182, 183, 259, 327, 328, 335
Milholland, John, 55, 59
militancy, xiv–xv, 63, 99–100, 101, 103
   Roosevelt and, 194
   World War I and, 97, 98, 99, 101
military, 92–93, 94, 95, 96–97, 189–91, 209, 210, 217
   see also soldiers, black
Miller, Benjamin M., 134
Miller, Kelly, 46, 49, 62, 177

Milliken v. Bradley, 329
Mimms, Henry L., 183
Mind of the South, The (Cash), 26
Ming, William, 219
Minikus, Lee, 295
ministers, 20–21, 35–36, 62, 122, 151, 229, 230–31, 233, 238, 239, 308
   in SCLC, 234, 235, 238
miscegenation (interracial sex), 26, 27, 32, 34, 42, 113, 126, 129, 191
Mississippi, 256, 283
   constitution of, 6
   Freedom Summer in, 283–88, 311
   Meredith March in, 312
   SNCC's work in, 256–66, 283, 310, 311
Mississippi, University of, 266
Mississippi Freedom Democratic Party (MFDP), 286–88, 310
Mitchell, Clarence, 213
Mitchell, Oscar, 251
Mitchell, Samuel Chiles, 13
Monroe, Bill, 244
Montgomery bus boycott, 227–34, 235, 238, 239, 240, 242, 249, 253
Montgomery Improvement Association (MIA), 229–30, 231–34, 235, 267
Moody, Dwight L., 38
Moon, Henry Lee, 209, 212
Moore, Amzie, 257, 259
Moore, Cecil, 279
Moore, Harry T., 217
Moore v. Dempsey, 105
Morgan, Clement, 55
Morgenroth, Edwin, 167
Morris, Elias Camp, 28
Moses, Robert Parris, 256–57, 258, 263, 283, 284, 285, 311
Moss, Thomas, 31, 32
Moton, Jenny B., 165
Moton, Robert R., 24–25, 97–98, 163, 168, 195
Moynihan, Daniel Patrick, 323
Muhammad, Elijah, xv, 304, 305, 309, 310
mulattoes, 26, 32, 113, 127, 128
Murphy, Carl, 145
Murray, Hugh, 137, 140, 244
Myrdal, Gunnar, 161, 172, 173, 174, 175

NAACP (National Association for the Advancement of Colored People), xiv, 38, 65, 78, 95, 99, 102, 103, 105, 109, 125, 141, 142, 145, 147, 149, 151–54, 156, 159, 161, 174, 176, 178, 182–83, 187, 188, 191, 192, 196, 197, 210, 216, 218, 228, 229, 232, 241, 273, 289, 308, 314, 328, 330
   Albany Movement and, 269
   anticommunism and, 212–13, 214, 215, 225, 237
   Black Power and, 314
   black teachers and, 170
   black workers and, 182–85

and *Brown* v. *Board of Education,* 218–25
bus boycott and, 233–34
character of, 69–73
CIC and, 107
Citizens Councils and, 221–22, 224
collapse of, 106
Columbia riot and, 207
Committee of Forty in, 71–72
Crisis magazine of, 73, 78, 79–82, 84, 88, 93, 95,
    97, 127, 149, 186
criticism of, 147
Du Bois and, 70–71, 73, 78, 79–82, 149
early campaigns of, 82–84
founding of, 67–70, 71
growth of, 84, 91, 100–101, 106, 182, 184, 196
as interracial organization, 71, 72, 73, 130–31
Johnson as field secretary of, 84, 85
labor unions and, 183, 184, 185
legal attacks on, 223–24
legal strategies of, 82, 140, 147, 197–200,
    218–19, 225
lynching and, 23, 24, 105, 126, 166, 208
NAPE and, 184
SCLC and, 235, 236
Scottsboro affair and, 136, 139, 140
segregation and, 92, 148, 197–99, 225
Shillady and, 105–6
SNCC and, 246–47, 263, 269
student protests and, 243
UNIA and, 112, 117, 118, 122, 123, 130–31
women's role in, 100–101
Youth Councils of, 203, 240
NACW (National Association of Colored Women),
    33, 34, 35, 36, 37, 38
Naison, Mark, 143, 145, 146
NAPE (National Alliance of Postal Employees),
    149, 182, 183–84, 215
Nash, Diane, 246, 254, 261, 290
National Association of Colored Women, 164
National Conference on the Negro, 68–71
nationalism, 129
    black, *see* black nationalism
    European, 119, 120
National Urban League, 68, 118, 151, 154, 314
Nation of Islam (NOI), xv, 304–5, 306, 307, 309,
    310, 317, 334
Native Son (Wright), 144
Nazi Germany, 137, 146, 153, 159, 205, 216
NCNW (National Council of Negro Women), 178
NCRA (National Citizens Rights Association), 19
"Negro," use of term, 312, 313
Negro History movement, 176
Negro National Anthem, 85
Negro World, 116, 122, 123, 130
Nerney, May Childs, 72
Newbold, Nathan C., 203
Newby, Idus A., 175
New Deal, 146, 149, 151, 152, 154, 155, 157, 159,
    168–69, 176, 193, 194, 196, 209, 211, 215
New Republic, 313

newspapers, black, 185, 186
Newsweek, 297
Newton, Huey P., *294,* 317, 318, 319
New York Age, 17, 32, 34, 42
New York City, 98, 195, 298
New York Times, 103, 105, 233
Niagara Movement, 55–56, 57, 59, 72, 77–78, 85
Niebuhr, Reinhold, 231
Nineteenth Amendment, 195
Nixon, Edgar Daniel, 228–29, 230, 232, 233
Nixon, Richard, 251–52, 318, 323, 324, 325, 332
NNC (National Negro Congress), 152–55, 178
NNC (National Negro Council), 143, 144
NOI (Nation of Islam), xv, 304–5, 306, 307, 309,
    310, 317, 334
nonviolent direct action, 240–41, 246, 249, 252,
    257, 266, 268, 274, 276–79, 284, 292,
    320
    Black Power and, 310
    Malcolm X and, 34, 308, 310
    Vietnam War and, 315
Norris, Clarence, 137, 139–40
Norris v. *Alabama,* 139
North, xiii, xiv
    black migration to, 17–18, 88–90, 93–94, 102,
        105, 107, 109, 125, 194, 209, 298
    Black Power in, 316
    Civil Rights Movement in, 301, 303–4
    industries in, 88, 89–90, 93–94
    SCLC in, 297, 300–301, 303
    segregation and discrimination in, 298–300,
        302–4
North Carolina, 11
    elections in, 7, 8
    Wilmington riot in, 8–10, 11, 165

O'Brien, Gail, 207
O'Neal, Emmett, 105
"one-drop rule," 128
O'Reilly, Kenneth, 129–30, 318
Orr, Oliver, 7
Ottley, Roi, 116, 119, 144, 153, 157, 184
Overton, John, 186
Ovington, Mary White, 68, 69, 71, 72, 79, 100
Owen, Chandler, 98–99, 125, 126, 127

Page, Thomas Nelson, 12–13
Palmer, A. Mitchell, 102–3
Pan-African Congress, 99
Parker, Arthur Harold, 50
Parker, John J., 147, 223
Parker, William, 303
Parks, Rosa, *226,* 227, 228, 229, 230
Paterson, William B., 63
Patterson, Fred L., 178, 219
Patterson, Haywood, 134, 136, 138, 139, 140
Patterson, John, 254, 255
Patterson, Robert P., 221
Patterson, William L., 143
Payne, Charles, 259–60, 284

PCCR (President's Committee on Civil Rights), 208–9
Peacock, Willie, 284
Philippines, 13, 92
Phillips, John Herbert, 49–50
Phillips, U. B., 162
Pickens, William, 123, 126, 136
Pittsburgh Courier, 185, 194
Plessy v. *Ferguson,* 14, 77, 182, 197–98, 199, 218, 219, 332
Plummer, Brenda Gayle, 213, 214
Poe, Clarence, 26
police brutality, 208, 291, 303, 316, 318
political power, 36, 41, 50, 60, 186, 195, 196, 204, 250, 257, 289, 311, 313, 330–34
    see also voters, black; voting rights; *specific parties*
Popular Front, 145, 153, 154, 216
Populist Party (People's Party), 7, 8, 10–11, 15, 19, 146
    Republican coalition with, 7–8, 10
postal workers, 149, 181–82, 183–84, 215
poverty, 320–21, 327, 328, 335
Powdermaker, Hortense, 170, 173
Powell, Adam Clayton, 91
Powell, Adam Clayton, Jr., 238
Powell, Ozzie, 139
Powell v. *Alabama,* 138, 140
PPMPA (Pullman Porters and Maids Protective Association), 151
Pratt, Charles W., 104
Price, Cecil, 285
Price, Joseph C., 19
Price, Victoria, 134, 135, 138–39
prisoners, *333–34*
    convict-lease system and, 27–28, 36
Pritchett, Laurie G., 269, 270, 276
Progressive Era, 36, 67, 69, 70
Progressive Farmers and Household Union of America, 104
Progressive Party, 209
Pullman, George, 149
Pullman porters, 149–50, 151, 157, 183

Rabinowitz, Howard, 16
racial uplift, 162, 163, 166, 169
Radical Reconstruction, *see* Reconstruction
Raleigh News and Observer, 8, 203
Ralston, Richard, 49
Rampersad, Arnold, 80
Randolph, A. Philip, 97, 98–99, 125, 126, 130, 150–52, *202,* 216, 228, 236, 314
    and March on Washington, 155–57, 185, 186, 280
    and March on Washington Movement, 157–58, 159
    as NNC president, 152, 153–54
rape, 8–9, 25, 27, 28, 78, 135–36, 138, 191
    black soldiers and, 97
    lynching and, 9, 25–26, 28, 31–32, 34, 38, 58, 67, 134–35, 166
    Scottsboro affair and, 134–36, 138–39

Raper, Arthur, 174
Rauh, Joseph L., 287
Rauschenbusch, Walter, 237
Ravitch, Diane, 176
Ray, James Earl, 320
Reagan, Ronald, 331, 332
Reagon, Cordell, 269
Reconstruction, xiii, 3–5, 7, 11, 12, 13, 17, 21, 41, 47, 48, 51, 83, 170, 175
    Du Bois's defense of, 75–76
    military force used in, 264
Redding, J. Saunders, 122, 145, 150, 152, 172, 173
Red Scare, 102, 108
Red Summer, 102, 103, 105, 107, 206
Reeb, James, 291
Reed, Merl, 186
Reese, Frederick D., 289
Rehnquist, William H., 332
Reich, Steve, 101
Republican Party, 10, 11–12, 15, 18, 19, 21, 47, 58, 60, 71, 83, 194, 195–96, 211, 216, 250, 311, 331, 332
    disfranchisement and, 11, 13
    in 1800s, 2–3, 5, 6
    Populist coalition with, 7–8, 10
    Reconstruction program of, 3–5; *see also* Reconstruction
    white supremacy and, 11
restrictive covenants, 194, 218, 219, 299
Reuther, Walter, 287, 288
Rex Theatre for Colored People, *160*
Reynolds, Carl, 203
Richmond, David, 241
Riesman, David, 177
rights consciousness, 335
riots, 102, 103–4, 119, 125, 156, 194–95, 217, 266, 279, 300, 301, 303, 316
    in Atlanta, 78
    in Chicago, 107
    in Columbia, 206–8
    in East St. Louis, 93–94, 99, 105
    in Elaine, 104–5
    in Houston, 94–95
    in Los Angeles, 331
    in Springfield, 67
    in Watts, 295–97, 300, 302, 303, 304
    white backlash and, 301–3
    in Wilmington, 8–10, 11, 165
Rives, Hallie Erminie, 25
Robeson, Paul, 144–45, 177, 213, 214
Robinson, James H., 131
Robinson, Jo Ann, 228, 229
Robinson, Reginald, 258
Roche, John P., 315
Rockefeller, John D., 46, 52
Roddy, Stephen, 135
Rogers, Henry H., 51, 53
Roosevelt, Eleanor, 156, 169, 193, 244, 276

Roosevelt, Franklin D., 141, 146, 151, 154, 155,
    166, 168, 178, 185, 193, 194, 195, 196, 208,
    209
  black soldiers and, 189, 190
  FEPC and, 186, 187
  March on Washington and, 156, 157
Roosevelt, Franklin D., Jr., 208
Roosevelt, Theodore, 13, 42–43, 58, 60, 61, 70, 84,
    92, 99
  Brownsville Affair and, 58–59
Rosenwald, Julius, 53, 168
Rosenwald Fund, 169, 171–72, 174
Rudwick, Elliott, 77
Russell, Richard B., 281
Rustin, Bayard, 158, 235–38, 240, 252–53, 280,
    296, 302, 314, 330

Salisbury, Harrison, 275–76
San Antonio School District v. Rodriguez, 329
Sargent, John S., 130
Saunders, Bill, 335
Scales, Junius, 143
Scarborough, William, 69
schools, see education and schools
Schrecker, Ellen, 144
Schuyler, George, 158, 237
SCHW (Southern Conference for Human Welfare),
    144, 212
Schwerner, Michael, 285–86
SCLC (Southern Christian Leadership Confer-
    ence), 234–41, 249, 260, 271, 281, 285, 300,
    330
  in Albany Movement, 260–71, 275
  in Birmingham, 273–74, 275, 276–79
  in Chicago, 300–301, 303
  founding of, 236–37
  Meredith March and, 312
  in the North, 297, 300–301, 303
  Poor People's Campaign of, 320–21
  in Selma, 288, 289–93
  SNCC and, 245–46, 263, 269
Scottsboro affair, 133–36
  Communist Party and, 136–38, 139, 140, 141,
    145, 146, 198, 236
  ILD and, 136–40
  protesters in, 132
Scottsboro Defense Committee, 139–40
Seale, Bobby, 317, 318
Seay, Solomon S., 243
SEB (Southern Education Board), 52, 53
Second World War, see World War II
segregation (Jim Crow), 7, 13, 16–17, 25, 42, 51,
    54, 60, 62, 77, 100, 119, 138, 148–49,
    161–62, 193–94, 201, 210, 225, 231, 274–75,
    279, 313
  Albany Movement and, 266, 268–69
  Birmingham and, 273–79
  Catholic Church and, 108
  CIC and, 107
  Civil Rights Act and, 282

Civil Rights Movement and, 249–50; see also
    Civil Rights Movement
  communism and, 214
  constitutionality of, 197–98, 206, 218
  Du Bois and, 148–49
  education reform efforts and, 169–75
  federal policies on, 209, 210, 211, 218
  FEPC and, 187
  Garvey and, 124–26, 129, 130
  in government jobs, 82–83, 183
  in housing, 82, 107–8, 149, 194, 209, 210, 218,
    219, 299–300, 302
  interracial cooperation movement and, 167, 178
  Kerr and, 181–82
  in military, 92–93, 94, 95, 96–97, 190–91, 209,
    210, 217
  miscegenation and, 26
  NAACP and, 92, 148, 197–99, 225
  in the North, 298–300, 302–4
  origins of, 16
  Plessy v. Ferguson and, 14, 77, 182, 197–98, 199,
    218, 219
  and President's Committee on Civil Rights,
    208–9
  progressivism and, 70
  in public transportation, see transportation, pub-
    lic, segregation in
  racial uplift and, 162, 163, 166
  Rex Theatre for Colored People, 160
  in schools, 12, 13, 108, 148, 206, 218–25, 300
  "separate but equal" doctrine in, 198, 199, 218,
    220, 227, 231, 232
  sexuality and, 27
  sit-ins and, 245, 249
  Wallace and, 289
  Washington and, 58, 63
  West Indians and, 113
  World War II and, 186, 188–89
Seligman, Edwin R. A., 70
Sellers, Cleveland, 258, 259
Selma, 288, 289–93
"separate but equal" doctrine, 198, 199, 218, 220,
    227, 231, 232
separatism, xiv, xv, 309, 310, 311, 312, 316
sex and sexuality, 26–27
  interracial (miscegenation), 26, 27, 32, 34, 42,
    113, 126, 129, 191
  rape, see rape
shade prejudice, among blacks, 113–14, 127–28,
    307
sharecroppers, 104, 162, 205, 262
Shaw v. Reno, 332
Shelley v. Kraemer, 218
Sherer, Robert, 47
Sherrod, Charles, 269, 288, 329, 330, 335
Shillady, John R., 105–6, 109
Shuttlesworth, Fred L., 235, 239, 253, 255, 273,
    275
Simmons, W. J., 21
Sinclair, William, 69

sit-ins, 240, 241–45, 249, 250–51, 253, 261, 266,
    267, 273, 274, 291
Sitkoff, Harvard, 138, 142
slaves, 1, 2, 12, 25, 27, 162, 175
    former (freedmen), 1–3
    free Negroes and, 127, 128
    West Indians and, 113
Smiley, Glenn, 235
Smith, Charles H., 26
Smith, Harry C., 56
Smith, Hoke, 48, 126
Smith, Ruby Doris, 246, 285
Smith, Susan L., 163
Smith, William Benjamin, 27
Smith, William C., 20
Smith v. Allwright, 200, 204
SNCC (Student Nonviolent Coordinating Commit-
    tee), 244, 245–47, 249, 260, 272, 280, 283,
    289, 330
    in Albany Movement, 266–71
    Black Power and, 310, 312–14, 315–16
    black/white division in, 310–12
    decline of, 315–16
    freedom songs and, 267
    Freedom Summer and, 283–88, 311
    King and, 269
    Meredith March and, 312
    in Mississippi, 256–66, 283, 310, 311
    NAACP and, 246–47, 263, 269
    SCLC and, 245–46, 263, 269
SNYC (Southern Negro Youth Congress), 143,
    144, 177–78
social equality, 41–42, 124, 186
    CIC and, 107
    Washington on, 58
soldiers, black, 148, 189–91
    in Houston riot, 94–95
    public transportation and, 192–93
    veterans, 98, 102, 201, 206, 211
    in World War I, 86, 92–93, 95–98, 119
Souls of Black Folk, The (Du Bois), 75, 76, 77
South, xiii, xiv–xv, 161–62
    black business districts in, 328
    black migration to North from, 17–18, 88–90,
        93–94, 102, 105, 107, 109, 125, 194, 209,
        298
    Black Power in, 316
    industries in, 88–89
    population in, 1, 89, 205
    urbanization in, 205
Southern Manifesto, 222, 281
Southern University, 243
Soviet Union, 141, 142, 146, 153, 154, 158–59,
    206, 213, 214, 215, 216, 217
    Bolshevik Revolution, 99, 102–3, 108
    propaganda of, 217, 218
Sowell, Thomas, 57–58, 334, 335
Spear, Allan H., 38, 107
Spingarn, Joel Elias, 72–73, 79, 85, 92, 146
Spivey, Donald, 45–46

Springfield riot, 67
SRC (Southern Regional Council), 178, 193
Stalin, Joseph, 141, 154, 215
State Normal and Industrial School, 63
Stein, Judith, 91, 121, 122, 130
Stephenson, James, 206, 207
Stern, Edgar B., 168
Stevens, Thaddeus, 2
Stevenson, Adlai, 300
Steward, Theophilus G., 21
Stewart, Will, 31, 32
Stimson, Henry L., 190
Stokes, Carl, 326
Storey, Moorfield, 72, 82
Stranger and Alone (Redding), 172
Stride Toward Freedom (King), 237, 269
student protests, 177, 178, 203
    see also sit-ins
Sugrue, Thomas J., 303
Sullivan, Patricia, 168, 194
Sumner, Charles, 2
Supreme Court, U.S., 107, 147, 199, 206, 218,
    219, 253, 299, 324–25
    Brown v. Board of Education, 206, 218–25, 231,
        234, 242, 250, 325
    Brown II, 220, 221, 223, 225
    Buchanan v. Warley, 82
    bus segregation and, 233, 234
    Guinn v. United States, 82
    Moore v. Dempsey, 105
    NAACP and, 71
    Norris v. Alabama, 139
    Plessy v. Ferguson, 14, 77, 182, 197–98, 199,
        218, 219, 332
    Powell v. Alabama, 138, 140
    rightward drift in, 332
    school districts and, 329
    Scottsboro affair and, 138, 139, 140
    voting rights and, 197, 200, 204
    Swann v. Charlotte-Mecklenburg Board of Educa-
        tion, 325
Sweatt, Heman, 218
Sweatt v. Painter, 218

Taft, William Howard, 60
Taft-Hartley Act, 212
Talbert, Mary Burnett, 100
Terrell, Mary Church, 37, 59, 70
Thirteenth Amendment, 1
Thomas, Clarence, 332
Thurmond, Strom, 210, 323
Tillman, Ben, 9, 13, 15, 16, 25–26, 42–43, 126
Time, 233, 244, 274, 291, 292, 313
To Secure These Rights, 208–9
Tourgee, Albion W., 19
transportation, public, segregation in, 16, 62,
    77, 191–93, 209, 219
    on buses, 228, 229, 233, 234, 236, 266,
        268
    Freedom Rides and, 253–56

Montgomery bus boycott and, 227–34, 235, 238, 239, 240, 242, 249, 253
streetcar boycotts and, 77–78, 227
Travis, Jimmy, 263
Trotter, William Monroe, 55, 56, 78, 83
NAACP and, 70, 71–72, 73
Trudeau v. Barnes, 197
Truman, Harry S., 195, 206, 208–10, 212, 214, 217, 244
black vote and, 209–10
communism and, 211, 215, 217
Tucker, David M., 39
Turner, Henry M., 18
Tushner, Mark, 199
Tuskegee Idea, 44, 69
Tuskegee Institute, 41, 43–47, 49, 50–51, 53, 61, 63, 68, 80, 97, 102, 115, 164, 178

UAW (United Auto Workers), 185, 187, 213, 299
Underwood, James, 206, 207
Underwood, Oscar, 13
UNIA (Universal Negro Improvement Association), 99, 101, 111–13, 115–26, 128
Africa and, 111, 112–13, 117, 119–22, 123, 124, 130
Black Star Line of, 113, 115, 121, 123, 126
decline of, 129–31
founding of, 116
growth of, 116
leadership of, 122
members of, 122
NAACP and, 112, 117, 118, 122, 123, 130–31
potential of, 130
thuggishness in, 129
unions, see labor unions
United Mine Workers of America, 71, 89, 101
United Nations, 185, 217
United Negro Improvement Association, xv
University Commission on Southern Race Questions, 100
Up from Slavery (Washington), 41, 43, 75
US (United Slaves), 317

Van Deburg, William, 319, 320
Vandiver, Ernest S., 251, 270
Vardaman, James K., 15, 16, 25, 48
Vass, S. N., 21
VEP (Voter Education Project), 263
Vietnam War, 142, 314–15
Villard, Oswald Garrison, 59, 68, 69, 71–72, 73, 79, 80, 82, 83
Vinikas, Vincent, 38
violence, 105, 106, 191, 206–8, 217, 222, 279, 283, 285, 291, 292–93
Malcolm X and, 308, 310
police brutality, 208, 291, 303, 316, 318
and President's Committee on Civil Rights, 208–9
Southern change of attitude toward, 207–8
Vietnam War and, 315

voting and, 5, 206
white backlash and, 301–3
see also lynching; rape; riots
Vishinsky, Andrei, 217
Von Eschen, Penny, 214
voters, black, 5, 6, 10, 12, 15–16, 200–201, 204–5, 206, 209, 210, 216, 221, 262, 290, 313, 324, 331, 332
CIC and, 107
migration and, 90
in 1930s, 196
registration of, 196, 200, 201, 204, 210, 240, 250, 256, 257–58, 261, 262–63, 265–66, 283, 286, 289, 324
see also political power
voting rights, 2, 6, 8, 9, 27, 194, 195–97, 208, 256
Chesnutt on, 59–60
disfranchisement, 10, 11, 13–15, 21, 36, 48, 51, 52, 54, 55, 62, 63, 70–71, 78, 82, 147, 165, 194, 195–97, 200, 201, 257, 262, 282, 288, 289
Fifteenth Amendment and, 4, 14
Populist-Republican alliance and, 7, 8
tests and other requirements for, 14, 48, 54, 82, 195, 197, 208, 210, 293
Voting Rights Act and, 288, 292, 293, 324, 325–26, 331
Washington's view of, 59, 60
see also political power

Waddell, Alfred M., 9, 165
Walden, A. T., 196
Walker, Clinton, 283
Walker, Wyatt T., 268, 271, 274, 277, 278
Wallace, George, 280, 289, 290, 291, 302, 303, 323
Wallace, Henry, 195, 209, 210
Walling, William English, 67–68
Walters, Alexander, 69
Ware, Bill, 311
Warren, Earl, 220
Warren, Fuller, 217
Washington, Booker T., xv, 21, 27, 40, 41–43, 53–54, 68, 72, 78, 82, 84, 85, 97, 99, 100, 108–9, 117, 118, 128, 133, 163, 174, 175
accommodationism of, 62, 63–64, 65
achievements of, 60–65
agitation and, 57, 64, 77
Atlanta Compromise of, 39, 41–42, 48, 76, 77, 125
criticisms of, 53–60, 63–64, 65, 78
Du Bois and, 70, 73, 74, 75–76, 80, 85
Du Bois compared with, 73–74
education and, 43–47, 48–49, 50–53, 54
Garvey's admiration of, 115
and National Conference on the Negro, 70
philanthropists and, 50–53, 60–61, 79
political involvement of, 58, 59, 60
Up from Slavery, 41, 43, 75
Washington, D.C., 298
Washington, Jesse, 81

Washington, Margaret Murray, 164, 165
Watson, Tom, 7, 10
Watts riot, 295–97, 300, 302, 303, 304
Weaver, Robert C., 169
Weems, Charlie, 139, 140
welfare, 332–33, 334
Wells, Elizabeth Warrenton, 29–30
Wells, James, 29–30
Wells-Barnett, Ida B., 21, 22, 29–31, 35–36, 62, 128
    antilynching campaign of, 23, 29, 31–33, 34,
        37–39
    clubwomen and, 34
    marriage of, 37, 39
    NAACP and, 70, 71–72
"We Shall Overcome," 267–68, 292
West Indies, 130
    Garvey's background in, 113–14, 128–29
    immigrants from, 113, 122, 124, 128
What the Negro Wants (Logan, ed.), 193
White, Debra Gray, 36, 37
White, George H., 17
White, Walter, 85, 103–4, 106, 135, 136–37, 140,
        149, 154, 180, 185, 198–99, 207, 208, 219,
        225
    anticommunism and, 213, 215
"white devils," 118, 279, 304, 310
white primaries, 200, 201
white supremacy, xiii–xv
    black education and, 48, 170, 171, 172, 175, 177
    black soldiers and, 95, 96–97
    CIC and, 107, 167–68
    Cold War and, 215
    collapse of, 205–6, 249
    Democratic Party and, 2, 5, 6, 7, 8–10, 15
    Garvey and, 112, 117, 125, 126, 129
    interracial cooperation and, 167, 245
    left-wing thinking and, 103, 108
    lynching and, 23, 25; see also lynching
    progressivism and, 70
    rape and, 26
    Republican Party and, 11
    segregation laws and, 17; see also segregation
    Southern heyday of, 161–62
    strategies and responses to, 17–21, 39
    Washington and, 42, 51–52, 62
    and women's role in community, 164
    World War I and, 88, 91, 92
    see also segregation
Wilder, Burt G., 70
Wilkins, Roy, 143, 145, 180, 224–25, 234, 236,
        280, 287, 307, 314
    Black Power and, 314
Wilkinson, J. Harvie, III, 225
Willard, Frances, 38
Williams, Addie Hunton, 35
Williams, Aubrey, 156, 169

Williams, Elbert, 196
Williams, Fannie Barrier, 33–34
Williams, Fannie C., 176
Williams, Henry, 193
Williams, Kenneth, 204
Williams, Samuel Laing, 55
Williamson, Joel, 128
Wilmington Record, 8, 10
Wilmington riot, 8–10, 11, 165
Wilson, Charles E., 208
Wilson, Woodrow, 60, 83, 87, 88, 90, 91, 95, 97,
        99, 101, 102–3, 183
WMC (War Manpower Commission), 187
Wofford, Harris, 254
women, 35, 164–66, 259–60, 335
    matriarchal families and, 309
    Memphis meeting of, 164–66, 167–68
    rape and, see rape
    in SNCC, 246, 260
    UNIA and, 122, 124
    white, 33, 36, 164–65
women's clubs, black, 23, 33–37, 105, 163, 164,
        169, 195
    NAACP and, 100–101
    Wells and, 34
women's clubs, white, 33, 36, 165
Women's Missionary Council, 164
Woodson, Carter G., 176
Woodward, C. Vann, 6, 7, 16
Woodward, Isaac, 206, 208
Woofter, Thomas J., 107
Woolworth's, 241–42, 243, 244, 245
World War I, 85, 87–88, 100, 102, 108, 115, 119,
        120, 189
    black soldiers in, 86, 92–93, 95–98, 119
    black support for, 88, 91, 93
    Great Migration and, 88, 89
World War II, 97, 158–59, 185–86, 188–89, 193,
        201, 298
Wretched of the Earth, The (Fanon), 315
Wright, Andy, 139, 140
Wright, Richard R., 144, 171
Wright, Robert R., Jr., 69–70
Wright, Roy, 135

Xuma, Alfred B., 49

Yokinen, August, 143
Young, Andrew, 176, 277, 278, 289–90, 292, 297,
        320, 322
Young, Charles H., 96
Young, James H., 8
Young, Nathan B., 170–71
Young, Whitney, 314

Zellner, Robert, 244, 257